AF681867

MUSIC BORROWING AND COPYRIGHT LAW

This ground-breaking book examines the multifaceted dynamics between copyright law and music borrowing within a rich diversity of music genres from across the world. It evaluates how copyright laws under different generic conventions may influence, or are influenced by, time-honoured creative borrowing practices.

Leading experts from around the world scrutinise a carefully selected range of musical genres, including pop, hip-hop, jazz, blues, electronic and dance music, as well as a diversity of region-specific genres, such as Jamaican music, River Plate Tango, Irish folk music, Hungarian folk music, Flamenco, Australian indigenous music, Maori music and many others.

This genre-conscious analysis builds on a theoretical section in which musicologists and lawyers offer their insights into fundamental issues concerning music genre categorisation, the typology of music borrowing and copyright law's ontological struggle with musical borrowing in theory and practice. The chapters are threaded together by a central theme, ie, that the cumulative nature of music creativity is the result of collective bargaining processes among many 'musicking' parties that have socially constructed creative music authorship under a rich mix of generic conventions.

Music Borrowing and Copyright Law

A Genre-by-Genre Analysis

Edited by
Enrico Bonadio
and
Chen Wei Zhu

•HART•
OXFORD • LONDON • NEW YORK • NEW DELHI • SYDNEY

HART PUBLISHING

Bloomsbury Publishing Plc

Kemp House, Chawley Park, Cumnor Hill, Oxford, OX2 9PH, UK

1385 Broadway, New York, NY 10018, USA

29 Earlsfort Terrace, Dublin 2, Ireland

HART PUBLISHING, the Hart/Stag logo, BLOOMSBURY and the Diana logo are trademarks of Bloomsbury Publishing Plc

First published in Great Britain 2023

Copyright © The editors and contributors severally 2023

The editors and contributors have asserted their right under the Copyright, Designs and Patents Act 1988 to be identified as Authors of this work.

All rights reserved. No part of this publication may be reproduced or transmitted in any form or by any means, electronic or mechanical, including photocopying, recording, or any information storage or retrieval system, without prior permission in writing from the publishers.

While every care has been taken to ensure the accuracy of this work, no responsibility for loss or damage occasioned to any person acting or refraining from action as a result of any statement in it can be accepted by the authors, editors or publishers.

All UK Government legislation and other public sector information used in the work is Crown Copyright ©. All House of Lords and House of Commons information used in the work is Parliamentary Copyright ©. This information is reused under the terms of the Open Government Licence v3.0 (http://www.nationalarchives.gov.uk/doc/open-government-licence/version/3) except where otherwise stated.

All Eur-lex material used in the work is © European Union, http://eur-lex.europa.eu/, 1998–2023.

A catalogue record for this book is available from the British Library.

A catalogue record for this book is available from the Library of Congress.

Library of Congress Control Number: 2023940304

ISBN: HB: 978-1-50994-938-0
ePDF: 978-1-50994-940-3
ePub: 978-1-50994-939-7

Typeset by Compuscript Ltd, Shannon
Printed and bound in Great Britain

To find out more about our authors and books visit www.hartpublishing.co.uk. Here you will find extracts, author information, details of forthcoming events and the option to sign up for our newsletters.

FOREWORD

Alongside Aplin and Bently's *Global Mandatory Fair Use: The Nature and Scope of the Right to Quote Copyright Works* (Cambridge University Press, 2020), this volume offers a solution to the most vexing problem confronting musicians and music copyright lawyers today: how can the law better align the expectations of musicians with the strictures of copyright? As Burkholder puts it in this volume, 'current legal frameworks do not adequately address a musical world where not everything that is borrowed is a melody and not every form of borrowing is either quotation or plagiarism'. Put more starkly, numerous headlines in the USA after the infamous *Blurred Lines* case queried whether its interpretation of copyright law would 'stifle creativity'.

Aplin and Bently provide one half of a much-needed response and this volume provides the other half in the music context. Aplin and Bently make an extended argument based on Article 10(a) of the Berne Convention: 'It shall be permissible to make quotations from a work which has already been lawfully made available to the public, provided that their making is compatible with fair practice'. Thoughtfully canvassing history and legislative materials, they conclude that Article 10(a) means precisely what it says: every member of the Berne Convention is obligated to allow quotations, including musical borrowing, as long as the borrowing is consistent with the norms observed by the relevant community.

The central inquiry in the typical case involving the copyright in a musical work should be: was the borrowing consistent with the norms and practices of working musicians?

Aplin and Bentley's argument expands far beyond music, but it has special traction for composers, arrangers and performers of musical works. As Burkholder again explains in this book:

> In the history of Western music, using existing music to make new music is not an anomaly: it is a central thread … from long before the emergence of copyright law up to the present day, musicians have freely and frequently borrowed from each other, in many different ways.

As a historical matter, not all borrowing has been tolerated, but much borrowing is permissible and even celebrated. Where musical practice tolerates or encourages a particular sort of borrowing, copyright law has no business forbidding it.

But where do borrowing norms come from? What do they look like? And, importantly, do they very significantly from genre to genre?

Professors Enrico Bonadio and Chen Zhu have put together here a volume that goes a long way to answering these critical questions. The chapters focusing on music history, written by prominent musicologists, lay the groundwork and explain the ubiquitous nature of borrowing. Not surprisingly, learning and making music is a social activity, and pro-copying and anti-copying norms have been developing from the very beginning, long before copyright law was formulated.

Subsequent chapters explore in depth different musical genres from a wide variety of international jurisdictions (as Anthony Kakooza demonstrates, culture matters). Given the social nature of musical practices, we are not surprised to learn that musicians working within classical, pop, hip-hop, reggae, jazz, electronic dance, tango, calypso, Irish/Hungarian/Greek/Israeli folk and various African and Asian traditional genres have tended to develop different borrowing norms. All these important genres merit their own chapter that dives deep into local practices, demonstrating that is quite possible to realise the promise of Article 10(a) by collecting evidence of what is 'fair practice'.

Professor Leo's chapter on jazz is typical. She notes that 'For over one hundred years, collaborative, cumulative creative practices in jazz have been misaligned with US copyright law … Penalties for violating these norms rarely align with formal legal relief'. She eloquently describes the professional distortions that result from a copyright law that tells musicians how to behave instead of asking them what they consider to be acceptable and unacceptable behaviour. Not surprisingly, attribution plays an important role in jazz norms but no role in the formal determination of copyright infringement.

To conclude, this is a very important contribution to copyright law, one that provides the raw material necessary for a rational law of music copyright – a law that could, and should, defer much more to musicians themselves. And, as the book illustrates beautifully, that deference should emerge in a genre-specific manner.

Paul J Heald

ACKNOWLEDGEMENTS

This volume is partially based on ideas initially developed from a cross-disciplinary workshop entitled 'Law and Norms of Music Borrowing', co-organised by Professor Paul Heald and one of the editors (Chen Zhu) in 2015 at the Birmingham Law School. Quite a few contributors attended that workshop. We thank Paul for his continuous guidance and support throughout this journey.

We wish to express our sincere thanks to Hart Publishing's wonderful editors Roberta Bassi and Verity Stuart for their trust in and patience for the book project, which seemed nearly impossible at its embryonic stage. Seven anonymous reviewers (from a variety of academic backgrounds, including law, musicology and media studies) have provided invaluable feedback for the book proposal and we are indebted to their constructive comments, which were essential to the further development of this project. We are also grateful to Tiffany Sillanpää for her careful proofreading before the final submission of the whole manuscript.

Enrico wishes to thank his whole family (including his wife, children, mother and brother), who were so supportive during the COVID pandemic period. We should never take for granted this kind of support, especially during challenging times. And Chen wants to give thanks to Xiaomin for her unwavering support during the process of preparing this volume. He is grateful to his mother Meili for all the care and love throughout his career. Chen's father Jianzhong Zhu (1951–2020) sadly passed away when the book was being prepared in the middle of the global pandemic. May you rest in peace, dad. Finally, Chen also wants to thank Dr Jean Harrison for her tremendous support and warm friendship for many years, where our common interest in music has played a pleasantly large role.

TABLE OF CONTENTS

Section D: Africa and Middle East

Section E: Asia and Oceania

LIST OF CONTRIBUTORS

Ann van Allen-Russell is the BMus Programme Coordinator at the Royal College of Music, UK. Her principal publications and research interests are on music and culture of the eighteenth century, including the music publishing industry in England and its legal and economic facets, and the development of intellectual property and copyright and its impact on creativity, with a specific focus on Johann Christian Bach, his works and orchestration, and the legal proceedings between Bach and the publishers Longman and Lukey. She has presented papers at conferences in the UK, the USA and Europe. Her current project explores cultural economics and music business practices relating to the Bach–Abel concerts.

Olufunmilayo B Arewa is the Shusterman Professor of Business and Transactional Law, Temple University Beasley School of Law, USA. Her scholarship focuses on music, entrepreneurship, business law, technology, accounting and Africana studies. Her book *Disrupting Africa: Technology, Law and Development* received the 2022 ISA STAIR best book award.

Jonathan Barrett is Associate Professor at the Wellington School of Business and Government, Victoria University of Wellington Te Herenga Waka, New Zealand. Jonathan has a particular research interest in the intersection between art law and human rights. His most recent publications include: 'Copyright in Artistic Works as a Divisible Asset on Divorce' (*European Intellectual Property Review*); 'On the Right to Enjoy the Arts' (*Columbia Journal of Law & the Arts*); 'Proportionate Engagement with the Artworks of Immoral Artists' (*Texas Review of Entertainment and Sports Law*); and 'Engaging with Outlaw Art' (*Chicago-Kent Journal of Intellectual Property*).

Gergely Békés is an attorney-at-law, specialising in copyright law in Budapest, Hungary. He has been a member of the Hungarian Council of Copyright Experts since 2004, carrying out expert witness activity during judicial and extrajudicial procedures. He is an author of numerous articles that deal with legal questions of copyright and neighbouring rights. He is also Chairman of the Supervisory Board of ProArt Alliance for Copyright and a board member of the Árpád Tóth Foundation.

Jose Bellido teaches law at the University of Kent, UK. He is particularly interested in the history of intellectual property law and has additional research interests in legal theory, evidence and legal history. His latest publications are *Landmark Cases in Intellectual Property Law* (Hart Publishing, 2017) and *Adventures in Childhood: Intellectual Property, Imagination and the Business of Play* (Cambridge University Press, 2022) (coauthored with Kathy Bowrey).

Joe Bennett is a musicologist, writer and researcher, specialising in popular music and song writing at Berklee College of Music, USA. As a professor, he teaches artist development, song writing, music copyright and song analysis. He has written more than 30 tuition books, and his music education compositions are performed by students all over the world. As an expert witness forensic musicologist, Joe advises lawyers, publishers, artists and songwriters on matters of musical similarity. He holds a PhD in Music from the University of Surrey and a National Teaching

Fellowship from the Higher Education Academy. Joe blogs about song-writing copyright at joebennett.net.

Michael Blakeney is Winthrop Professor at the University of Western Australia and holds visiting professorships in intellectual property at the University of Ferrara and Zhongnan University of Economics and Law, Wuhan. He formerly worked in the Asia Pacific Bureau of the World Intellectual Property Organization (WIPO). He has directed a number of EC projects concerned with the establishment of an intellectual property infrastructure in a number of new EU Member States and EU Applicant States. He has also directed a number of projects to assist developing countries to become members of the World Trade Organization.

Enrico Bonadio is Reader in Intellectual Property (IP) Law at City, University of London, UK. A frequent visitor to many universities and research centres around the world, Enrico has research interests in several IP areas, including the protection of non-conventional forms of creativity. He has attracted funds from a variety of institutions, including the European Commission, the Australian Research Council, UK Research and Innovation, the UK Economic and Social Research Council and the UK Higher Education Innovation Funding. He frequently appears in the media as an IP expert and regularly joins training and technical assistance missions organised by the World Intellectual Property Organization. Enrico is also an avid collector of Jamaican music vinyls and regularly spins records at events in London and other cities.

J Peter Burkholder is Distinguished Professor Emeritus of Musicology at the Indiana University Jacobs School of Music, USA. He founded and edits *Musical Borrowing and Reworking: An Annotated Bibliography* (https://chmtl.indiana.edu/borrowing/) and has written numerous works on borrowing, including *All Made of Tunes: Charles Ives and the Uses of Musical Borrowing* and the groundbreaking article 'Borrowing' in *Grove Music Online*. His research on topics from Renaissance masses to modern music has won awards from the American Musicological Society, the Society for American Music, ASCAP and the Association of Recorded Sound Collections, and has been translated into Japanese, Chinese, Arabic, Italian, German and Spanish.

Franco Fabbri teaches popular music history at the State University of Milan, Italy, and is course coordinator at the Civica Scuola di Musica Claudio Abbado, Milan. He is among the founders and served as chairman of the International Association for the Study of Popular Music. He is co-founder and co-editor, with Goffredo Plastino, of the Routledge Global Popular Music series. Fabbri has also worked as a musician, recording eight studio albums and two live albums with his band and two solo albums of electronic music. In 2019, he was awarded the Tenco Prize for cultural operator. In 2021, he received an IASPM honorary membership.

Tianxiang He is Assistant Professor at the School of Law, City University of Hong Kong. Dr He received a PhD degree in IP Law at Maastricht University, the Netherlands (2016), and another PhD degree in Criminal Law at Renmin University of China (2017). His articles have appeared in top journals, such as the *American Journal of Comparative Law*. He is the author of the book *Copyright and Fan Productivity in China: A Cross-jurisdictional Perspective* (Springer). He is currently on the editorial board of the *Chinese Journal of Comparative Law*.

Paul Heald, the Albert J Harno and Edward W Cleary Chair in Law, joined the University of Illinois faculty in 2011 after 22 years at the University of Georgia School of Law, USA. He is also a Fellow and Associated Researcher at CREATe, the RCUK Centre for Copyright and New Business Models in the Creative Economy, based at the University of Glasgow. He spent 2018 as an Erskine Fellow in the Economics Department of the University of Canterbury, Christchurch,

New Zealand and as a Research Fellow at the Stellenbosch Institute for Advanced Study in South Africa. He lectures on patent, copyright and international intellectual property law around the world and has previously held visiting positions at universities in Helsinki, Buenos Aires, Bournemouth, London, Lyon and Regensburg, as well as at the University of Chicago, University of Texas and Vanderbilt University. He ran the UGA/OSU programme at St Anne's College, Oxford University, during the spring of 2009. He was Herbert Smith Visitor at Cambridge University in 2012.

Anthony CK Kakooza is a Partner in the law firm of Byenkya, Kihika & Co Advocates in Kampala, Uganda. He also holds academic positions at Makerere University and Uganda Christian University, and Visiting Professorships at Cornell Law School and University of Illinois in the USA as well as Masaryk University in the Czech Republic, where he teaches a specialised course on intellectual property in traditional knowledge and folklore. Furthermore, he undertakes IP consultancies for the World Intellectual Property Organization on matters related to traditional knowledge, genetic resources and folklore.

Stavroula Karapapa is Professor of Law at the School of Law of the University of Essex, UK. She is the author of *Defences to Copyright Infringement* (Oxford University Press, 2020) and publishes regularly on aspects of intellectual property law.

Bryan Khan is an economist and intellectual property scholar based between Italy and Trinidad and Tobago. He lectures with the WIPO Joint LLM in Intellectual Property co-organised with the University of Turin, and also the Economics Department at the University of the West Indies (St Augustine, Trinidad). His research interests focus on intellectual property, economic development theory, the creative industries and postcolonial cultural studies. Bryan is also a music industry professional, with experience as a music producer, composer, performer and consultant.

Ryu Kojima is a Professor at Kyushu University Faculty of Law, Japan. He specialises in intellectual property law, cultural policy, and science, technology and innovation policy. He received an LLB from the University of Tokyo Faculty of Law in 2000 and an LLM from Harvard Law School in 2003. Between 2000 and 2005, he served as a Research Fellow at the University of Tokyo Faculty of Law. He has taught in the Kyushu University Faculty of Law since 2005. He has published several articles in English, including 'The Role of "Author's Right" in Landscape Design' in *AIDA (Italian Annals of Copyright, Culture and Entertainment)* and 'Free and Open Source Software (FOSS) and other Alternative License Models in Japan' in A Metzger (ed), *Free and Open Source Software (FOSS) and other Alternative License Models: Comparative Analysis* (Springer, 2015).

Joyce Lee is a Media Counsel at NASCAR Media Ventures, LLC in Charlotte, North Carolina, USA. She graduated with BA degrees in Film Studies and Economics from Wesleyan University in Middletown, Connecticut in 2010. She earned her JD degree from University of Connecticut School of Law in Hartford, Connecticut in 2018. She worked as a student intern at Cantor Colburn LLP in the summer of 2017. Her interests include copyright law, media law, privacy law and how they are evolving in the era of the metaverse. She participated in the 11th WIPO Advanced Intellectual Property Research Forum with a presentation on copyright registration of unpublished film scripts using blockchain technology.

Katherine M Leo, PhD, JD, is Associate Professor of Music at Millikin University, USA and author of *Forensic Musicology and the Blurred Lines of Federal Copyright History* (Lexington, 2021). Serving as both an academic and a forensic musicologist, Dr Leo's research investigates the intersection of music and legal histories in the USA, with emphases on matters of authorship and originality, as well as musical style and similarity analysis in federal copyright litigation. As a specialist in early-twentieth-century US commercial musics, Dr Leo has published on the player piano industry, Duke Ellington, the Original Dixieland Jazz Band and Paul Whiteman.

Jing Li holds an LLM degree in International Commercial Law from the University of Birmingham, UK. She earned a PhD in Law and Post-doctoral Fellowship of Applied Economics (Financing) at Jinan University, China. She was promoted to Associate Professor of Law in 2010 at Jinan University, China. Her main research interest is intellectual property law. In 2008, she translated and published the book titled *In the Public Interest: The Future of Canadian Copyright Law*, edited by Michael Geist. She also previously co-published an academic article on Australian copyright law with Andrew Christie in Australia.

Nicola Lucchi is Serra Hunter Professor of Comparative Law at the University Pompeu Frabra of Barcelona, Spain. He holds law degrees from the University of Padua (PhD) and the University of Ferrara (LLB). Nicola's research interests focus on comparative business law and policy and the interaction between law and innovation.

Maximiliano Marzetti is Professor of Law and the Head of the Law Track at IÉSEG School of Management in Paris, France. He is also adjunct faculty at ESCP-Paris, Cergy Paris University, Turin University and the Latin American School of Social Sciences. He is a Teaching Fellow of Harvard University Law School's Copyright X and Coordinator of the World Intellectual Property Organization's Distance Learning Courses. Before becoming a full-time academic, Maximiliano was a trial lawyer and industrial property consultant in Buenos Aires, Argentina.

Luke McDonagh joined LSE Law School, UK, as an Assistant Professor in 2020. He undertakes research in the areas of intellectual property law and constitutional law. Prior to taking up his position at LSE, he was a Senior Lecturer at City, University of London (2015–20), a Lecturer at Cardiff University (2013–15) and an LSE Fellow (2011–13). Luke holds a PhD from Queen Mary, University of London (2011), an LLM from the London School of Economics (LSE) (2006–07) and a BCL degree from NUI, Galway (2002–05). He is a Fellow of the Higher Education Academy (FHEA). Luke has published widely in respected journals, including *Modern Law Review*, *Journal of Law and Society*, *Intellectual Property Quarterly* and *Civil Justice Quarterly*. He is the author of *Performing Copyright: Law, Theatre and Authorship* (Hart Publishing, 2021).

Péter Mezei is a Professor of Law at the University of Szeged, Hungary. He was awarded an honorary adjunct professorship (dosentti) at the Faculty of Law, University of Turku (Finland) in December 2014. He is a professor invité of the Université Jean Moulin Lyon III (France). He coordinates the joint intellectual property LLM programme of the Technical University of Dresden and University of Szeged on the Szeged side. His courses and research focus on comparative law, as well as comparative, digital, international and European copyright law. He is a member of the European Copyright Society and the Hungarian Copyright Expert Board.

Marc Mimler is a Senior Lecturer in Law at City, University of London, UK. Marc's research interests cover intellectual property law in general with its interfaces with human rights and international trade law, information technology law and competition law. He was involved in research projects for the EU Commission, the EU Intellectual Property Office and the UK Intellectual Property Office, and has presented widely on IP topics on four continents. His work was also cited by the Advocate General of the Court of Justice of the European Union. He currently acts as Editorial Advisor for the bimonthly Japanese IP journal *Patents &Licensing*.

Marisella Ouma is one of the leading intellectual property law experts in Africa, specialising in copyright and related rights, enforcement, intellectual property and trade, and traditional knowledge. She also has a wealth of knowledge in entertainment law. Dr Ouma has made a significant contribution to the development of copyright and related rights in Kenya and within the African region. She was the founding Executive Director of the Kenya Copyright Board (KECOBO), has taught copyright and related rights at the tertiary level, and has several publications on the subject matter.

Guy Protheroe was a chorister at Canterbury Cathedral, UK, and in 1966 won a foundation scholarship to Magdalen College, Oxford to read music. Since 1970, he has been a freelance professional musician: conductor, musical director, composer, arranger, lyricist, singer, writer and musicologist. He has always been involved in classical music, from medieval to avant-garde. With his contemporary music ensemble Spectrum, he worked with many of the world's leading composers, and for some years was guest conductor of the Xenakis Ensemble in Holland. For 50 years he has been conductor of the English Chamber Choir. He has also been involved throughout with popular music and film. He was musical director and arranger to Vangelis for 17 years, has been with Rick Wakeman for 50 years, with concerts around the world, and for 30 years has filled the same roles in French new age music and film. He has directed major festivals of Greek music and culture in London, Byzantine culture in London, Athens and Bulgaria, and is a guest conductor of the Eastern Orthodox choir Cappella Romana, based in Portland, Oregon. For seven years (1978–85) he was also Music Presentation Editor for the BBC, based in London. He has been active as a forensic musicologist since 1987, when he appeared as an expert in the Chariots of Fire court case.

Omri Rachum-Twaig is an Adjunct Professor of Law at the Faculty of Law, Tel Aviv University, Israel and a partner at FISCHER. He teaches, practices and writes in the fields of copyright, cyber and information law, artificial intelligence and emerging technologies. He has published on all these matters in leading law reviews and journals, has won several academic awards and prizes, and his work is frequently cited in scholarly work and courts, including the Supreme Court of Israel. As a percussionist, he also played in leading orchestras such as the Israeli Philharmonic Orchestra and the West-Eastern Divan Orchestra, under the baton of Daniel Barenboim, Gustavo Dudamel, Zubin Mehta, Pierre Boulez and others.

Giovanni Maria Riccio is Professor of Comparative Law at the University of Salerno, Italy, where he teaches comparative art law and cultural heritage law. He has a PhD in Civil and Comparative Law. An attorney at law, he is founder and managing partner of E-Lex Law Firm, Rome. A former consultant of the EU Commission, he has taught and researched in several European universities, including Birkbeck College, University of London, Oxford Intellectual Property Research Centre and University of Grenoble.

Antoni Rubí-Puig is Associate Professor of Civil Law at Universitat Pompeu Fabra, Spain. His main areas of expertise lie in copyright law and policy and the intersections between art and the law. Dr Rubí-Puig is the current director of the postgraduate programme in data protection law and information security at UPF-BSM. In the past, he has been a visiting researcher at the Max Planck Institute for Comparative and International Private Law in Hamburg and in the law schools of Yale University and the University of California, Berkeley.

Tobias Schonwetter is Associate Professor at the University of Cape Town, South Africa. He directs both the IP Unit and the iNtaka Centre for Law & Technology. He has led several development and innovation-oriented research projects. Tobias is an Associate Member of the Centre of Law, Technology and Society at the University of Ottawa, Canada, and serves on Open Science Advisory Board for South Africa's Department of Science and Innovation. He is also a board member of UCT Press. Previously, Tobias was a Senior Manager at PwC South Africa, Regional Coordinator Legal Lead (South Africa) for Creative Commons and a guest editor for the *African Journal of Information and Communication*. Tobias specialises in IP law and cyberlaw.

Matt Stahl is Associate Professor of Information and Media Studies at the University of Western Ontario, Canada. His research examines historical legal contests over the commodification of musical labour and its products. His book *Unfree Masters: Recording Artists and the Politics of Work* won the 2013 IASPM book prize.

Bram Van Wiele is a Senior Lecturer at the University of Auckland Business School, New Zealand and a research associate at the Intellectual Property Unit at the University of Cape Town, South Africa. He holds law degrees from the University of Cape Town and the University of Antwerp. His current research focuses on industrial copyright in the digital age, and copyright and architecture.

Chen Wei Zhu is Associate Professor of Law at the University of Birmingham, UK, teaching intellectual property law. He has an abiding research interest in the changing socio-material conditions where subject matters of IP law are constructed and regulated. His published works cover areas such as software licensing, music copyright and the regulation of sports sponsorship. Chen is also an advocate of free and open-source software for sustainable legal pedagogy and research. He uses *Emacs*, which is a programmable text editor equipped with a LISP dialect, for doing his everyday academic work and for fun.

LIST OF FIGURES

LIST OF FIGURES

Chapter 1

Chapter 3

Chapter [illegible]

Chapter [illegible]

Chapter [illegible]

Introduction: Music Borrowing and Copyright Law

ENRICO BONADIO AND CHEN ZHU

I. Introduction

What is music borrowing? How may age-old music borrowing activities be understood or misunderstood by copyright law? What are the legal and musicological challenges posed by a rich diversity of music borrowing practice to copyright jurisprudence in different music genres?[1] This volume attempts to address these questions by forging a forum where international experts in music and law share their views on how the theory and practice of music copyright may be recalibrated in the fascinating field of music borrowing. The collective efforts by contributors to this volume examine the multifaceted dynamics between copyright law and music borrowing situated in a rich diversity of music genres in both Western and non-Western music traditions. It evaluates how copyright law under different generic conventions may influence, or be influenced by, time-honoured creative borrowing practice. The assessment is based on a carefully conducted analysis of the balance between creators' proprietary rights and the need to safeguard the expressive freedom that permits downstream musicians to use and reuse music building blocks within different generic conventions.

The book is structured around a central theme that explores copyright's struggle with the almost amorphous shape of music creativity related to borrowing activities. This theme has many variations that are illustrated by what we call a genre-specific analysis of music borrowing associated with different music genres. Based on this dyadic 'theme-and-variations' structure, the book is divided into two major parts.

Part I includes chapters querying some foundational issues of music borrowing in relation to genre formation, historical typology, copyright jurisprudence, forensic musicology and music as traditional cultural expressions. The first three chapters offer a high-level overview that problematises three different aspects of music borrowing and copyright law. Franco Fabbri, in chapter one, employs a semiotic approach to music genres, whose formation needs to be treated dynamically for a nuanced understanding of cultural units of music creation. Peter Burkholder, in chapter two, carefully delineates a historical typology of music borrowing and reworking, whose complexity

[1] These questions have become increasingly relevant in many contemporary music copyright legal disputes. For example, famous song writers such as Ed Sheeran have constantly faced legal allegations for 'borrowing' more than is legally permissible. Drawing a fine balance between permissible borrowing and illegal appropriation becomes a fundamental task for courts in adjudicating these disputes. For Sheeran's most recent court case at the time the book is being produced, see E Millman, '"A Sigh of Relief": What Ed Sheeran's Victory Means for the Future of Music Copyright Claims' (*Rolling Stone*, 5 April 2023) www.rollingstone.com/music/music-news/what-ed-sheeran-thinking-out-loud-trial-means-1234729350/.

goes well beyond a binary division between permitted copying and illegal appropriation understood by conventional music copyright law. Then Chen Zhu, in chapter three, tackles copyright law long's ontological struggle with music borrowing. He argues that music copyright is driven by a nominalist impulse to individuate ever-smaller units of creation for protection when dealing with substantiality in music borrowing copyright litigations. This triad of chapters build the theoretical foundation for a better recalibration of copyright law for music borrowing practice discussed further in this book.

The following two chapters within Part I are written by two forensic musicologists, who examine the toolbox of music experts for preparing testimonies to music copyright courts. Guy Protheroe, who has served as a leading forensic expert for over 30 years both in the UK and beyond, reflects on his first-hand experience of helping courts to adjudicate on various hard issues, including music borrowing. Joe Bennett critiques the prevalent methodology that underpins forensic practice, where the *Anstein* test formulated by Jerome Frank continues to play a large role in contemporary music borrowing cases. Both musicologists' insights corroborate Zhu's assertion that legal objects contested in music borrowing cases tend to be ontologically unstable and, as a result, music copyright law has to appraise probative copying and substantial appropriation on a case-by-case basis. Chapter six, by Anthony Kakooza, widens the discussion by treating music borrowing in a broader framework of traditional cultural expressions from an African perspective. This non-Western perspective allows traditional music to be seen as part of cultural heritage, the borrowing from which inserts new dynamics into the problem regarding the legal ownership (as opposed to custodianship) of traditional music. Kakooza's analysis sets the scene for some of the later chapters in the book that deal specifically with traditional music genres.

Part II of the book is composed of contributions that delve further into genre-specific analyses of music borrowing. Music genres in this context can be both fascinating and bewildering. As a matter with considerable social and aesthetic significance, genres have been poorly understood by, if not entirely invisible to, the global copyright legal system. Inspired by Fabbri's insightful exposition of the dynamic and malleable nature of music genres in the opening chapter of the book, these genre-focused chapters evaluate how copyright law influences, or is influenced by, those established and still-evolving music conventions situated in relevant jurisdictions. In short, this genre-by-genre analysis seeks to find possible genre-specific parameters that may otherwise be neglected through conventional legal analysis. It is also worth noting that the selected genres for analysis are by no means comprehensive and there is no intention for them to be so. Given an almost unlimited number of music genres in the music world, it is hoped that the book will serve as a first step to stimulating further discussion of the relation between music genres and the kind of creativity regulated under copyright law.

Under this scenario, Part II of the book is divided into five sub-sections, where music genres are grouped roughly according to their geographical affiliation or lack thereof. We are conscious that this categorisation of genres can be ontologically problematic and theoretically unsatisfactory,[2] but this grouping is purely for the purposes of organisation, in an attempt to help readers to locate a music genre relatively quickly through geographical cues.

Section A groups together the 'general' genres that are geographically diffuse and thus may appear in any part of the globe. Chapter seven (by Jose Bellido) re-examines what is meant by 'popular' in the pop music genre by focusing on the less-well-known aspect of the former

[2] For an excellent reflection on music genres and geographical locations see I Biddle and V Knights (eds), *Music, National Identity and the Politics of Location: Between the Global and the Local* (Routledge, 2007).

Beatle George Harrison's music borrowing copyright case. It reveals the subtle relation between cryptomnesia and music borrowing that is prevalent in the pop genre. Chapter eight (by Joyce Lee and Marc Mimler) dissects the hip-hop genre, where music sampling as a type of borrowing plays an indispensable role. It shows that sampling as a creative art form needs to be more fully recognised by copyright law. Chapter nine (by Nicola Lucchi) analyses the electronic and dance music (EDM) genre, which also heavily relies on sampling techniques employed by disc jockeys. EDM is interesting in the sense that the kind of borrowing activities involved in this genre blurs the line between compositional copyright and recording copyright, both of which need to be reformed to allow more room for secondary creation. Chapter ten (by Katherine Leo) tackles the multifaceted jazz genre, where Leo skilfully weaves the music and legal threads together by showing how jazz borrowing activities persist at the periphery of music copyright. Chapter eleven (by Olufunmilayo Arewa and Matt Stahl) provides a unique and refreshing lens through which the 'racialised' music genres (such as 'blues' and 'R&B') are examined. Arewa and Stahl eloquently expose the dark side of music borrowing, which tends to extract creative outputs from ethnically 'black' musicians without fair compensation. Chapter twelve (by Ann van Allen-Russell) traces what later became today's 'classical music' genre in its original eighteenth-century context. Allen-Russell insightfully shows that copyright disputes regarding classic music in this period were caused by unauthorised printing more than music borrowing per se, which actually served as a source of music innovation.

The rest of Part II (sections B–E) covers music genres with a relatively strong regional association. Section B travels to the American continent. Chapter thirteen (by Enrico Bonadio and Bryan Khan) traces the borrowing-based development of Jamaican music that includes ska, rocksteady and reggae. Chapters fourteen and fifteen (both by Bryan Khan) respectively deal with calypso music and Indo-Caribbean chutney music. Chapter sixteen (by Max Marzetti) tells a legal tale of 'River Plate tango' concerning the cultural appropriation and music borrowing of tango music. Section C delves into some European music genres, specifically Irish folk music in chapter seventeen (by Luke McDonagh), Hungarian folk music in chapter eighteen (by Peter Mezei and Gergely Békés), flamenco in chapter nineteen (by Antoni Rubí Puig), Neapolitan music in chapter twenty (by Giovanni Maria Riccio) and Greek traditional music in chapter twenty-one (by Stavroula Karapapa). Section D analyses music genres coming from Africa and Middle East. It covers Israeli music in chapter twenty-two (by Omri Rachum-Twaig), Kenyan benga music in chapter twenty-three (by Marisella Ouma) and South African music in chapter twenty-four (by Tobias Schonwetter and Bram Van Wiele). Last but not least, section E ends the book's journey in Asia and Oceania, where Chinese traditional music is scrutinised in chapter twenty-five (by Tianxiang He and Jing Li), Japanese music in chapter twenty-six (by Ryu Kojima), Australian indigenous music in chapter twenty-seven (by Michael Blakeney) and Māori music in chapter twenty-eight (by Jonathan Barrett). In short, it is hoped that these region-based music genres will help to illustrate the dynamic relation between music borrowing and copyright law in rich, socio-culturally embedded, generic conventions.

Again, the scope of music genres covered by these chapters is far from comprehensive, but they need to be read as an invitation to further scholarly discussion. In other words, they merely represent the beginning of a much longer musico-legal journey that we hope many more interested people will join beyond this book in the future.

PART I

Music Genres, Borrowing and Copyright

1

Defining Music Genres: Critical Issues with Music Taxonomies

FRANCO FABBRI

I. Introduction: Genre as a Type of Work

In the arts, literature and communication, a *genre* is a type of work, text[1] and/or performance.[2] Epic poem, sonnet, biography, essay, novel; portrait, fresco, sketch; bust, equestrian statue, bas-relief; comedy, tragedy, cabaret, *commedia dell'arte*; ballet, dance theatre, *bharatanatyam*, contact improvisation; toccata, opera, *qasa'id*, *Singspiel*, symphony, *raga*, Kraut rock, be-bop; documentary, spaghetti western, thriller, sci-fi film; editorial column, *causerie*, *elzeviro*; radio drama, news, soap opera, sports report; quiz, talent show, talk show, sitcom; shooter, brawler, survival horror. The list is clearly not homogeneous: it includes types and sub-types, types mainly related to a work's (or text's) technique or form, and others to its content or its context. However, such a lack of homogeneity can be found in the whole diachronic development of the genre concept, as well as in its synchronic aspects, even within one discipline. Genre quite often deals with the interrelation between form and content or between text and context, or both. Other taxonomic concepts focus on just one of the above aspects: *style* is mainly focused on form or text; *scene* (or *school*) is mainly focused on context. A common trait of the genre concept across disciplines is that it appears to be useful to ask questions, or give answers, about a multiplicity of works, texts or performances. More generally, it is useful to talk or write about several such objects, rather than about just one.[3]

Concepts like 'genre', 'style', 'form' and 'mode' – and their equivalents – have been used for centuries in many cultures to classify music, by creating 'types of music' characterised by recurrences and similarities. One of the purposes of such taxonomies, according to a tradition originating from Aristotelian philosophy and developed throughout European music history,[4]

[1] 'From a semiotic perspective, a text is any portion of reality: a) which is endowed with a meaning for someone; b) whose limits can be clearly defined, so that text can be distinguished from everything that is out of it; c) which can be separated into discrete units, according to many hierarchical analytic levels, going from the most concrete and superficial to the most abstract and profound; d) such that the above separation follow objective criteria.' G Cosenza, *Introduzione alla semiotica dei nuovi media* (Laterza, 2014, my translation).

[2] All terms in this sentence are meant in their broadest meaning. It is not at all implied that they be universal; but they can be found in many different cultures and languages.

[3] Parts of the following paragraphs are drawn from F Fabbri, 'Music Taxonomies: An Overview', keynote paper presented at the conference 'Musique Savante/Musiques Actuelles: Articulations. JAM 2014: Journées d'analyse musicale 2014 de la Sfam', Ircam, Paris, 15–16 December 2014; F Fabbri, 'Rebetiko as a Testing Device for Genre Theories and Musical Categorizing Processes' (2012) 21 *Journal of Mediterranean Studies* 321.

[4] See F Fabbri, 'I generi musicali. Una questione da riaprire' (1981) 4 *Musica/Realtà* 43; F Fabbri, 'A Theory of Musical Genres. Two Applications' in D Horn and P Tagg (eds), *Popular Music Perspectives* (IASPM, 1982) 52–81; F Fabbri,

as well as in other music traditions, has been to devise norms connecting the way music events are made with their meaning and social function; another fundamental purpose has been to facilitate discourse about music, by making it easier to recognise music events, describe and 'point at' them.

Such musical taxonomic concepts have a great impact on everyday music life. People choose a certain radio station (or listen to a certain Internet radio, or to playlists offered by streaming platforms) because they like the selection of genres or styles available there; concert venues and clubs are specialised according to genre (their location in the urban space, the profile of their customers, the way in which the space is designed and the acoustics of the halls are genre-oriented); record shops have shelves where similar music is assembled together (by genre), and record companies have created genre-specific labels since their inception in the late nineteenth/early twentieth century: their organisation as corporate companies is genre-oriented.[5] All musical taxonomic concepts play a central role in music making (see how 'form' and 'mode' are articulated in many different music cultures around the world), in music theory and criticism, and in any kind of verbal communication about music. Music categorisation contributes substantially to give music events a socially recognised meaning.[6]

II. Genre as a Cultural Unit: A Semiotic Theory

Genre facilitates communication. On the one hand, people talking (or writing) about music genres use the concept as shorthand for music practices, techniques, social, economic and historical contexts, ideologies, etc, which would otherwise require lengthy and often contradictory descriptions. On the other hand, definitions are usually given in the form of a *dictionary entry*, that is, a statement presenting a compact representation of the relevant aspects of a genre, allowing it to be distinguished from other genres. Other definitions are in the form of an *encyclopaedic entry*, that is, a more articulated representation of the concept, including references to various social, economic and historical contexts, which leave room to changes and contradictions.

Umberto Eco introduced the distinction between dictionary and encyclopaedia in his *A Theory of Semiotics*,[7] while describing his 'Revised Semantic Model'. In his critique of Katz and Fodor's 'The Structure of a Semantic Theory',[8] Eco comments on an article by NL Wilson,[9] which is in turn criticised by Katz:[10]

> [A] semantic theory ought to concern not the ideal competence of an ideal speaker, but the factual beliefs that people share about things. Meanings are common social beliefs, sometimes mutually contradictory and historically rooted, rather than undated and theoretically fixed constructs.[11]

'Browsing Music Spaces: Categories and the Musical Mind' in A Moore (ed), *Critical Essays in Popular Musicology* (Ashgate, 2007) 49–62; F Fabbri, 'Tipi, categorie, generi musicali. Serve una teoria?' (2007) 82 *Musica/Realtà* 71.

[5] See K Negus, *Music Genres and Corporate Cultures* (Routledge, 1997); TD Taylor, 'Fields, Genres, Brands' (2014) 55, *Culture, Theory and Critique* 159.

[6] Fabbri, 'Browsing Music Spaces' (n 4); D Brackett, *Interpreting Popular Music* (Cambridge University Press, 1995); David Brackett, *(In Search of) Musical Meaning: Genres, Categories and Crossover* (Arnold, 2002); D Brackett, *Categorizing Sound: Genre and Twentieth-Century Popular Music* (University of California Press, 2016); P Tagg, *Music's Meanings. A Modern Musicology for Non-Musos* (The Mass Media Music Scholars' Press, 2013).

[7] U Eco, *A Theory of Semiotics* (Indiana University Press, 1976).

[8] JL Katz and JA Fodor, 'The Structure of a Semantic Theory' in JL Katz and JA Fodor (eds), *The Structure of Language* (Prentice Hall, 1964).

[9] NL Wilson, 'Linguistic Butter and Philosophical Parsnips' [1967] *Journal of Philosophy* 64.

[10] JJ Katz, *Semantic Theory* (Harper & Row, 1972).

[11] Eco, *A Theory of Semiotics* (n 7) 99.

Eco adds:

> Katz is rightly preoccupied with the fact that the notion of factual belief does not introduce into semantic theory all the modifications introduced by the speakers' day-to-day factual experience. But it will suffice to reformulate Wilson's requirements as follows: factual beliefs, even if widespread, *must be coded*, or in some way conventionally recognized by a society. Katz asks on what basis they might be recognized. The reply is: on the same basis that allows the KF [Katz-Fodor] Model to assume that a/bachelor/is an unmarried man and not a toothpaste; on the basis which allows not only an encyclopaedia but also a dictionary that a given entry means one thing in a certain context or for given uses, and in other cases means another.[12]

In a section titled 'The Sememe as Encyclopaedia', Eco comments on the various meanings of the expression 'whale' to a zoologist, to the medieval author of a bestiary, to a modern layman and to a writer like Herman Melville, who interpreted the state of knowledge of the mariners of Nantucket. Accordingly:

> [W]e can now imagine a certain cultural level at which/whale/gives rise to a contradictory sememe considering both the medieval, the scientific and the popular system of units. This exactly represents the sort of competence as 'encyclopaedia' (instead of 'dictionary') that was outlined ... The fact that, in the above example, the encyclopaedia seems closer to a medieval 'speculum mundi' than to the *Encyclopaedia Britannica* suggests that the universe of natural languages is a rather unformalized and 'primitive' one, and thus far from being scientific or highly formalized.[13]

The sememe, or semantic unit, is described by Eco in a preceding chapter (quoting Schneider) as a *cultural unit*:

> What, then, is the meaning of a term? From a semiotic point of view, it can only be a *cultural unit*. In every culture 'a unit ... is simply anything that is culturally defined and distinguished as an entity. It may be a person, place, thing, feeling, situation, sense of foreboding, fantasy, hallucination, hope or idea. In American culture such units as uncle, town, blue (depressed), a mess, a hunch, the idea of progress, hope and art are cultural units'.[14] We shall see later how a cultural unit can be defined semiotically as a semantic unit inserted into a system.[15]

From Eco's comment on the Katz–Wilson debate, and from the full description of his 'Revised Semantic Model', we gather that the process of cultural definition and distinction suggested by Schneider is translated into Eco's semiotic theory as *coding*. Meaning is defined by a community through the acceptance and sharing of codes. Codes are layered, include circumstantial and context information, and can be hierarchically ordered. The hierarchy or hypercode that controls the relative value of individual codes is referred to by Eco as ideology. Cultural units, or units of meaning (sememes), are based on (or, we might extrapolate, consist of) networks of codes established within a community, modelled by the context, by circumstances, by ideology. Music genres are cultural units, or, at least, can be considered and studied as such. I will use this statement as a first approach. (I will comment on other approaches soon.)

If genre is a cultural unit, all individual genres are cultural units as well, 'anything that is culturally defined and distinguished as an entity'. If we focus on music genres, rap is a cultural unit, tango is a cultural unit, jazz-rock, *raï*, *chanson à texte*, are cultural units, and so on. How are they 'culturally defined and distinguished'?

[12] ibid.
[13] ibid 113.
[14] DM Schneider, *American Kinship: A Cultural Account* (Prentice Hall, 1968) 2.
[15] Eco, *A Theory of Semiotics* (n 7) 67.

III. Social Acceptance versus Essentialism

One of the most common pitfalls encountered by musicians, scholars, journalists, people in the music business in search of a definition of genre, or of any individual genre, is that what distinguishes a genre is somehow embedded in the text (for music genres, in the music and associated lyrics, if any). Such an essentialist approach is typical of historical genre theories, like the one that was hegemonic in Europe from Greek and Roman antiquity until the late eighteenth century and was accepted as a regulating principle in rhetoric and in various arts: that is, that the form of a text shall be adequate to its content, ie the so-called 'theory of the three styles'. While a genre was defined by a work of art's content and/or social function (epic poem or lyric poetry, sacred music or music for feasts, or dance, tragedy or comedy), the work's style had to be adequate to the genre (*gravis stylus, mediocris stylus, humilis stylus*). Such connection is the historical foundation of the equivalence between genre and style, of which there are still traces in everyday language or in some currents of musicology. But style (from the Latin word *stilus*, ie the stick used to write on a tablet covered with wax) is literally 'a way of writing', and does not imply any reference to functions, contexts or circumstances, which are contrarily included in all encyclopaedic definitions of genre and are the object of social conventions. The development of the aesthetic of 'absolute music' in nineteenth-century musicology, with its dismissal of functions, contexts, circumstances and anything that is not embedded in a printed score, is the main reason for the essentialist perspective, which is still hegemonic in conventional musicology and exerts an influence over music journalism. (This is also true for other genres such as jazz, pop and rock.) A few genres are strongly defined by stylistic traits, but many others are not.

IV. Convention

Cognitive scientists and neurologists have offered empirical results and theories that were quickly included in approaches to categorisation by other disciplines (like musicology and computer science), with concepts like prototypes and schemas,[16] and other concepts, such as mirror neurons,[17] which are not directly related to categorisation but have left their mark on many music studies in the past 15 years.[18]

This research now seems to be in a phase where cognitive scientists are more eager to give than to receive suggestions, probably due to the complex nature of their experiments, the cost and bulkiness of the equipment involved (eg MRI scanners), and the fact that they are more often dealing with fundamental aspects of categorisation than with the very specific details of music categories.

Communities are a crucial concept in all disciplines involved in this research. It has been noted that although communities are included in the definition of other fundamental concepts,

[16] See G Lakoff, *Women, Fire, and Dangerous Things. What Categories Reveal about the Mind* (University of Chicago Press, 1987); G Lakoff and M Johnson, *Metaphors We Live By* (first published 1980, University of Chicago Press, 2003); U Eco, *Kant and the Platypus: Essays on Language and Cognition* (first published in Italian 1997, Secker & Warburg, 1999).

[17] See G Rizzolatti, 'The Mirror Neuron System and Imitation' in S Hurley and N Chater (eds), *Perspectives on Imitation. From Neuroscience to Social Science*, vol 1 (MIT Press, 2005) 55–76.

[18] I Molnar-Szakacs, and K Overy, 'Music and Mirror Neurons: From Motion to "E'motion"' (2006) 1 *Social Cognitive and Affective Neuroscience* 235.

from 'meaning' and 'cultural unit'[19] to 'genre'[20] and even 'nation',[21] little has been done to provide a detailed description of what is meant by the term whenever the concept is extended beyond its original formulation in sociology or anthropology.[22] What kind of community is a 'virtual community'? Can the idea of an 'imagined community' be applied to the fans of a certain artist or genre? Do communities overlap?

It is a matter of fact that musical genres exist in many cultures. Nineteenth-century positivist musicologists even treated genres (or what was conceived as them at the time) as living entities. Such biological metaphors – implying concepts of birth, infancy, growth, maturity and death – were soon abandoned in the wake of the hegemony of formalist musicology, and its devaluation of any concept related to function, context or community. Genres, however, continued to survive and are still flourishing: their existence today is attested in the domains of culture – that is, of shared opinions in the semiosphere – in the discourses and practices of musicians, critics, fans, concert promoters, record industry executives, salespeople, web designers and so on. One of the main challenges for scholars is to relate such existences to an understanding of the meaning and working of music taxonomies: ethnographies are useful, but without theory they are blind.[23]

As cultural units (and not metaphysical categories), genres are rooted in history: this implies that for each genre that comes to mind, there must have been a time when it did not yet exist. This might be an obvious observation, but it is one that does not seem to have troubled many of the scholars who have dealt with the subject. On the contrary, I believe that no genre theory – be it a 'strong' theory or a simple description of how the concept is used in contemporary communities – can be valid if it does not take genre formation and diachronic processes into consideration.

According to several theoretical approaches, which in my view should be seen as overlapping and/or complementing (rather than contradicting and opposing) each other, the 'birth' of a genre can be located in the establishment of conventions within a community, in the 'semiotic act' of naming, as well as in the acknowledgement of 'family resemblances', in the acceptance of prototypes. Such processes do not take place in a void, but within a system or network of existing genres: this also implies that some or all of them can be activated, catalysed or polarised by existing genres to which the new genre is opposed, or put at their side as a variant. For example: is popular music a genre? According to colloquial usage and to some definitions, yes, but when referring to it as a superordinate category, which includes many genres, one may prefer to call it a type of music. Also, in discourses where distinctions between genre and style are not relevant, type may be a useful synonym for both.

I must admit that, to date, my suggestion of a kind of 'complementarity principle' among theories (or between two main theoretical categories) is little more than wishful thinking. Proponents of general or music-specific taxonomic theories, in fact, seem to be convinced that theories based on conventions (on the one side) and theories based on prototypes, family resemblances and schemata (on the other side) do oppose and exclude one another. There seems to be something in common between such diverse theories as George Lakoff's (and other

[19] Eco, *A Theory of Semiotics* (n 7).

[20] See my own early articles on the subject.

[21] B Anderson, *Imagined Communities* (Verso, 1983).

[22] K Khelemay, 'Musical Communities: Rethinking the Collective in Music' (2011) 64 *Journal of the American Musicological Society* 349.

[23] This is my basic critique of otherwise excellent works, such as F Holt, *Genre in Popular Music* (University of Chicago Press, 2007). For a review, see F Fabbri, 'Genre in Popular Music, by Fabian Holt' (2008) 27 *Popular Music* 490.

cognitive scientists') theory on prototypes and 'basic level recognition',[24] Pierre Bourdieu's *habitus*[25] and Daniel Levitin's neo-Kantian 'schemas' (or *schemata*):[26] they all strongly oppose rules and property-based definitions (to the point, in Levitin's case, of ridiculing them),[27] and are in favour of explanations based ultimately on neural phenomena, on the formation of cognitive and behavioural habits hardwired in human bodies. In terms that those authors would probably not accept or have accepted, this means bringing such phenomena well below the domain of semiosis. At least in Bourdieu's case, the dismissal of rules was part of an anti-structuralist stance (aimed especially at French structuralist anthropology, as developed by Claude Lévi-Strauss);[28] and in Levitin's case, with his grotesque description of property-based definitions, I would claim a misunderstanding of the basic principles of semiotics (such as coding). In Lakoff's case, moreover, a thorough commentary, as well as a revision of semiotic theories, has been provided by Umberto Eco in his *Kant and the Platypus*.[29] In all cases, even in Eco's theory of 'cognitive types', a kind of black box is invoked: all we seem to be allowed to know is that there is something functioning at the interface between perception and cognition, and that it influences our behaviour. It is suggested that our neural system, with specific associations of neurons 'firing', is at the physical base of such a black box. It is also implied that we 'learn' how to recognise and behave (Bourdieu worked the most on this issue, though he admitted that it was a very complex matter), but it is unclear what learning processes are involved, and whether cognition plays any part in it.

Most of these explanations (whose authors have been particularly keen in reproaching other theories for the same reason) tend to be 'static' in one way or another. It is clear that we are not born with a schema to recognise heavy metal (Levitin's example), and that at some point we can form one, based on family resemblances or prototypes. But how does it happen? Is it possible to improve our schemata so that we recognise heavy metal more promptly? Is it possible to forget them? And how was heavy metal first recognised (as there must have been someone who had this experience before any other)? Moreover, does the expression 'heavy metal' exist only to allow a listener to recognise specific pieces of music? What about guitarists who want to learn to play like one of the prototypical heavy metal guitarists: must they develop specific schemata? Will they be similar to or different from those of an average listener? What about the manager of a stadium where a heavy metal gig is planned: will their considerations about seat placement, security and so on be part of a distinctive *schema*? Or of a *habitus*? Or are such considerations in the domain of cognition, of 'conscious aiming at ends'?

How we recognise things is very important, as is how we make sense of such recognition. Unfortunately, albeit even more interestingly, concepts (cultural units) such as genre extend over both domains. Humans use genre – genre names, especially – to talk about music. For many, this is one or maybe the only way to verbalise their own experience of music. Some people are able to talk about a genre without even being able to recognise a piece of music that 'belongs' to it. Genres are also about beliefs and lies. As such, they can be an object of semiotic study. But can semiotics make sense of the diachronic aspects of genre? Is a semiotic approach to genre (as a cultural unit, or 'a semantic unit inserted into a system')[30] really 'static', as a few scholars maintain?[31]

[24] Lakoff (n 16).

[25] 'Principles which generate and organize practices and representations that can be objectively adapted to their outcomes without presupposing conscious aiming at ends or an express mastery of the operations necessary in order to attain them', P Bourdieu, *The Logic of Practice* (first published in French 1980, Stanford University Press, 1992) 53.

[26] D Levitin, *This Is Your Brain on Music* (Atlantic Books, 2008).

[27] ibid 142–43.

[28] See R Jenkins, *Bourdieu* (Routledge, 2002).

[29] Eco, *Kant and the Platypus* (n 16).

[30] See Eco, *A Theory of Semiotics* (n 7) 67.

[31] See M Santoro, *Effetto Tenco. Genealogia della canzone d'autore* (Il Mulino, 2010) 27–28.

Often what emerges from such criticism is a distorted image of semiotic concepts: not distorted enough to make the destructive rhetoric clear even to those who are not familiar with the discipline, but just right to accommodate common sense prejudices against a field of study that has not been fashionable in the past decades. Semiotic codes – according to that rhetoric – are like commandments; they are agreed upon deliberately by fixed communities and are there for good. Codes (or norms or conventions) are binding, they are not negotiable and no conflicts about their meaning are possible. It is implied by such criticisms that semioticians (and their associates: linguists and language philosophers) do not know how to handle collective processes: only sociologists know what a socially shared norm is and how it works. I would argue that this is not so.

Another advantage of semio-linguistic approaches to genre, opening new, interesting perspectives to the otherwise 'mysterious' act of initial codification, is highlighted by the philosophical study of convention made by David K Lewis (1941–2001) in 1969.[32] Aimed at a rigorous definition of one of the fundamental processes that make language possible, the study is based on a class of games (coordination games) that were overlooked by game theorists at the time. With examples of growing complexity, Lewis shows how conventions can be established without ever stipulating them explicitly. Therefore, the conventional nature of language, and of any code (or set of norms) established conventionally, does not imply that at any point there is a clear agreement, or that the involved parties (or community) shall declare their acceptance of the convention(s). Of course, the existence of a convention can be recognised and even officially acknowledged, but recognition happens when the convention is already in place and is based on the actual functioning of the convention itself. There is no black box, though. Here is the first rough definition of convention given by Lewis:

> A regularity R in the behaviour of members of a population P when they are agents in a recurrent situation S is a convention if and only if, in any instance of S among members of P,
>
> (1) everyone conforms to R;
> (2) everyone expects everyone else to conform to R;
> (3) everyone prefers to conform to R on the condition that the others do, since S is a coordination problem and uniformity to R is a proper coordination equilibrium in S.[33]

Given the other, more refined definitions in the book, Lewis himself warns against the risk of hiding 'the concept beneath its refinements'.[34] The rough definition is enough for our purpose, especially if we complement it with an extract from the book's Foreword, by Willard Van Orman Quine:

> We have before us a study, both lucid and imaginative, both amusing and meticulous, in which Lewis undertakes to render the notion of convention independent of any fact or fiction of convening … in the course of the book the reader comes to appreciate convention, not analyticity, as a key concept in the philosophy of language.[35]

The final comment, made by the quintessential analytical philosopher Quine about one of his pupils, is meaningful. But are we allowed to extrapolate Lewis's ideas from the philosophy of language to genre theory? Yes, without any doubt, I would say. In fact, Lewis does the opposite: he attaches to the philosophy of language a theory based on the observation of ordinary recurrent

[32] DK Lewis, *Convention, a Philosophical Study* (first published 1969, Blackwell, 2002).
[33] ibid 42.
[34] ibid.
[35] W Van Orman Quine, 'Foreword' in Lewis (n 32) xi–xii.

situations, such as: who should recall first if a telephone call is unexpectedly cut off? Such coordination problems are essential in music practice. Although Lewis's examples do not cover music activities, one of the earliest examples in the book could easily be translated into musical terms:

> An example from Hume's *Treatise of Human Nature*: Suppose you and I are rowing a boat together. If we row in rhythm, the boat goes smoothly forward; otherwise, the boat goes slowly and erratically, we waste effort, and we risk hitting things. We are always choosing whether to row faster or slower; it matters little to either of us at what rate we row, provided we row in rhythm. So, each is constantly adjusting his rate to match the rate he expects the other to maintain.[36]

In a recurring music event, maximising the pleasure of each of the participants, ensuring everyone has the best understanding of what's going on or minimising the amount of information that must be processed to obtain pleasure and understanding may be perceived as coordination problems; conforming to genre conventions, to use Lewis's words, is 'a proper coordination equilibrium' in that recurring event.

What is especially fascinating in Lewis's theory is that it makes sense of the 'subconscious' aspects of categorisation and behaviour (see Bourdieu's 'practices and representations that can be objectively adapted to their outcomes without presupposing conscious aiming at ends'), but without making use of black boxes – or, instead, looking into them.

To make a comparison, I must return to some other theories. According to prototype-based theories, genres are defined by resemblance; in my opinion, it may well be that crucial resemblances are established by convention. Moreover, I would argue that although prototypes and family resemblances are fundamental in the recognition of stylistic features by individuals, what makes them meaningful in collective music practice is that they are conventionally formalised; that is, a community socialises such recognition and takes full advantage of it. Of course, an individual can learn a schema to distinguish 'heavy metal' as the genre where music resembles pieces by Led Zeppelin, the 'quintessential heavy metal band'.[37]

But which piece(s)? Who developed that schema first? How is it transmitted to a whole community? And is that resemblance enough to define all aspects of the genre? Levitin himself acknowledges that prototypes and family resemblances are not satisfactory explanations for the many nuances of music competence, though he does not seem worried by the circularity of arguments such as 'we say that something is heavy metal if it resembles heavy metal'. Looking for diachronicity based on a theory that is exemplified by such statements can be a hopeless task.

On the other hand, convention (as described by Lewis) is a process situated in time: there is a time before a convention takes place and a time after; it is also possible to describe the process by which a convention ceases to exist (when, for example, it is recognised that a certain regularity in the behaviour of the population is not a coordination equilibrium anymore, and members of the population stop conforming to it). Looking for a theory that helps to explain how genres are born, we also need a theory that accounts for 'dead' genres.

V. Naming Genres

Of all the conventions that define a musical genre – that is, of all the regularities in the behaviour related to music events to which members of a community conform – naming conventions

[36] Lewis (n 32) 5.

[37] Levitin (n 26) 142. Incidentally, Led Zeppelin were initially dubbed a 'heavy rock' band and 'heavy metal' later became a name for the genre, or maybe another genre.

deserve special attention. In many historical cases I can think of, it seems that the naming of a genre is a kind of sanction, a kind of ratification that other conventions exist and have been acknowledged. In such cases, practice anticipates naming: that is, a general acceptance of styles, social practices, functions, etc under a specific name follows years, decades, maybe even centuries of similar music activities, as with fado, flamenco, tango, the blues, jazz and rebetiko up to rock 'n' roll. Often, music historians wonder if a certain genre existed before any reference to its name could be found. I would suggest that in many cases some of the most relevant conventions defining a genre tend to operate before a name for the genre is agreed upon, but that the act of naming makes other conventions more visible and helps to create new ones. Though apparently pointing in the opposite direction, the way film historian Rick Altman describes the early development of cinema could also be interpreted in the light of the above-mentioned theoretical scheme:

> During the last years of the nineteenth century and the first of the twentieth, it simply cannot be said that there was such a thing as 'cinema', clearly separate from other phenomena. On the contrary, what we now retrospectively think of as cinema was at the time recognized as several quite different phenomena, each overlapping with an already existing medium. This multiple identity is made manifest by contemporary terminology, which applied to moving picture projection such shared terms as 'views', 'pictures', 'electric theatre', 'living photographs', and 'advanced pictorial vaudeville', each self-evidently identifying the new technology with an already existing medium.[38]

In the case of cinema, names based on existing media polarised practices around each of a few established conventions and prevented the main common element (moving picture projection, ie 'cinematography') to emerge both as a name and as the activity around which new conventions could be formed. From this example we may concede that rather than identifying previously unnamed practices (and conventions), a new naming convention can, so to speak, rearrange the whole field by deleting previous names. That is how 'cinema' worked (and maybe 'jazz'). Names are crucial.[39]

However, while I would insist that a name may be a sufficient condition to define a genre (though a named genre that keeps together any kind of music events, without any kind of codified regularity among them, is hard to imagine), it is not a necessary one. A genre with no name may exist: that is, a set of music events that conform to some conventions established within a community, while the community itself has not given it (and/or does not want to give it) a name at all; unless we decide that 'music that does not belong to any genre' is actually a genre name, such a genre exists (a few festivals celebrate it every year in some European countries).[40] And, of course, many genres with a name probably existed without one (for a short or long period) before getting one.

VI. Music Genre: A Definition

To sum up some of the issues discussed so far, and to investigate the diachronic processes by which genres are created, changed and deleted, we need to consider the definition of a musical genre as 'a set of music events regulated by conventions accepted by a community'. This is a

[38] R Altman, *Silent Film Sound* (Columbia University Press, 2004) 19.

[39] See G Marino, '"What Kind of Genre Do You Think We Are?". From Technique to Lyrics, "Genre Definers" within Music Intermedial Ecology', paper delivered at the 12th International Congress on Musical Signification (ICMS12), Université catholique de Louvain, Louvain-la-Neuve, 4 April 2013.

[40] I am thinking of the Angelica festival in Bologna, for example.

compact form of a definition that has circulated for 30 years,[41] which benefits from the refinements I suggested above, namely that, first, 'convention' must be intended within the framework of David K Lewis's study; second, prototypical effects and family resemblances can be intended as socially acknowledged by convention, so they do not need to be referred to specifically; third, norms or rules can also be omitted in the definition, because although laws and regulations act as regulatory principles and may help in defining genres, they perform this function within or among genres only if they are made relevant by convention (for example, a juridical norm can exist on paper, while being ignored by a community); and fourth, 'community', in the strictest sense, is the 'population' where a convention is established. Usually, the community accepting genre conventions is the union or stratification of many diverse communities. Can such a short definition be of any use for the study of music(s)? Can it shed some light on the work of scholars? We will now see.

What does it mean for a music historian to study the birth of a genre? It means, first, to examine any kind of document (manuscripts, scores, newspapers and magazines, letters, marketing material, recordings if available, etc), with the help, where possible, of direct witnesses, for the earliest traces of the genre's name; second, to investigate, similarly, the genre's community, and evaluate recurring behaviours, norms, codes and prototypes (within the framework of other existing genres, so evaluating oppositional functions); and third, to confront the chronologies of naming and other conventions, and to formulate hypotheses on a possible prehistory of the genre. Of course, this is what historians usually do.

But there is a strong tradition in musicology that favours notated music above all other sources (not just because scores are more easily found)[42] and, in the end, what scholars often come up with is an evolutionary description of styles, rather than a history of genres. There is much to learn from the methods of the École des Annales, as suggested by Rick Altman in his study of silent film sound:

> Just as the French 'new' historians of the Annales school found the texture of history in the daily fabric of common lives, rather than in the exceptional existence of the ruling class, so I find the most important lessons in the most common uses of sound located in the most banal practices. Who plays the piano? Where is it located? Is it used just for the film or for other parts of the program as well? And what kind of music is selected?[43]

The 'daily fabric of common lives' is made with conventions and, as Altman suggests when discussing methodology, it is essential that historians look at past practices as they were, without being influenced by their subsequent evolution.[44]

Musical historical investigation, I would add, requires a continuously shifting perspective, an uninterrupted comparison among conventionally accepted practices before and after a genre is born.

Investigating the present, which is what music sociologists, music anthropologists and/or cultural scholars do, demands a similar approach. To be more than snapshots of passing instants,

[41] It was first formulated in F Fabbri, 'Musica tra le musiche' (1980) 42(Luglio–Agosto) *Laboratorio musica* 14.

[42] An example: scholars of the Italian language and popular music were informed by a record producer that the neologism *cantautore* was first used in the summer of 1960, in the press material of the Italian subsidiary of RCA, to promote singer-songwriter Gianni Meccia; the word – according to interviews – was also included in the liner notes of one of Meccia's singles. None of the documents were ever found. Just imagine how difficult it could be to find similar documents for earlier genres. See G Cartago, 'Cantautore, canzone d'autore e le voci della popular music nella lessicografia non specializzata' in *Lingua letteraria, delle arti e degli artisti* (Franco Cesati Editore, 2005) 317–28; J Tomatis, 'Ideology, Neologisms, Neo-realistic Aesthetics: Definition of a Musical Genre. The Case of Italian Cantautori', paper presented at the International Conference on Popular Music Studies, Liverpool, 2009.

[43] Altman (n 38) 6.

[44] ibid 17.

demographic studies and ethnographies must give historical sense to their specific context and circumstances, in particular to their time and place. And this means, at least, to provide links, hooks to the past and the future, and to other places and cultures. There is a kind of study of the present (whatever that is: I know that 'present' is not an easily definable concept!) that I would like to see: a real-time monitoring of new genre names and new conventions. For many contemporary genres, this might be performed on the Internet: a chronological listing of the number of web pages containing a certain genre's name (obtained from a search engine) is a very rough approximation to what I intend as a web-based research method, but software engineers could develop ways to trace new genre names before they become commonplace.[45]

New conventions are a tougher matter, of course, but a large enough team could successfully create the proper mesh to collect 'early warnings' for practices that seem to emerge as new. To some extent, this is what already happens sometimes in scholars' blogs and mailing lists, like those set up by the International Association for the Study of Popular Music (IASPM). However, a far quicker method needs to be found. When a scholar writes to a mailing list or posts on social media asking for more information on some new music practices, a new genre has existed long enough to make the request outdated.

Perceiving genres as sets of music events regulated by conventions accepted by a community is not an obstacle to understanding diachronic processes, like those that can be metaphorically described as the birth, change or death of a genre.[46] Rather, such a definition can help by describing more accurately than others (or, at least, better than no definition) diachronic processes and, thereby, may suggest methods for music historians, sociologists, anthropologists and other scholars, be they interested in music(s) of the past or in current music practices. Here, 'community' and 'convention' are the key concepts: an interdisciplinary approach to their understanding is fundamental for the study of genre.

As I have discussed above, categories in music are in constant evolution. Many musical genres emerge every year (for example, in so-called 'electronic music'), others die. As has occurred since early times, music's evolution has been directly related to technological development. So, in a given historical period, a number of contemporary music categories evolve on parallel paths. Even the creation of music genres can be related to specific technology, so specific music descriptors derived from that may not represent a musical category but a musical period.

The goal is to connect diachronic development in music categorisation to music histories, to build a model of how genres work through time. How do changes in music practices and technologies, as well as in the media landscape, affect categorising processes? How can categorisation be understood in its wider cultural and historical context?

To answer these questions, further investigations into past categorisation are needed. Sources can include music publications from the past, such as magazines, music press, popular press, newspapers; TV and radio broadcasts; critical essays and music books; advertisements and press releases; etc. Enquiries must encompass different music cultures and their specific practices, to challenge any simplistic Anglo-American-centric perspective. Also, 'folksonomies' and labelling practices, which have developed strongly over the past 20 years thanks to the Internet, must be addressed from the point of view of their diachronic and diatopic developments.[47]

[45] See the impressive results of Every Noise at Once, a research project initiated in 2013 by The Echo Nest principal engineer Glenn McDonald, where a listing of genres from all over the world, 'found' on the Internet, is displayed, https://everynoise.com/everynoise1d.cgi?scope=all.

[46] See F Fabbri, 'How Genres Are Born, Change, Die: Conventions, Communities and Diachronic Processes' in S Hawkins (ed), *Critical Musicological Reflections* (Ashgate, 2012) 179–91.

[47] P Lamere, 'Social Tagging and Music Information Retrieval' (2008) 37(2) *Journal of New Music Research* 101.

VII. Genre, Music Information Retrieval and Digital Platforms

As files with audiovisual content started circulating over the Internet, the need arose to attach digital 'tags' to them, to indicate their content and make it easier for users to find them. Soon, researchers in computer science started working on algorithms enabling the automatic recognition of music properties by the scansion of audio data, as one of the most challenging tasks in the music information retrieval (MIR) research field;[48] with the expansion of interactive features in the so-called Web 2.0 and the huge success of social media, MIR researchers started considering 'social tagging', 'folksonomies' and other user-generated sources of information as a complement to the analysis of audio content.[49] Genre, style and other taxonomic concepts are now largely used in Internet, and big enterprises like Amazon, iTunes, Spotify and Last.fm improve their business by suggesting that customers and listeners ('users', in Internet jargon) should buy or listen to music similar to previous purchases or listenings, by means of music recommender systems.[50]

VIII. Recurring Traits and Copyright

Music pieces are classified as 'belonging' to genres according to the presence of recurring traits. These traits may be related to sound (music as a phenomenon perceived through our ears) or to 'paramusical' practices (who sings/plays, where the music event take place, how the audience – if any – is located, which conventions regulate the economy of a music event, which ideological or religious meanings are involved, etc). Inevitably, music pieces belonging to the same genre may present similarities, or family resemblances. Often, music experts and lawyers dealing with supposed cases of plagiarism seem to be encouraged to use the genre concept to strengthen their positions: 'this piece is similar to that other piece, and moreover they belong to the same genre'; on the contrary, 'these pieces look similar just because they belong to the same genre'; or, again, 'this piece sounds similar to that other piece, but it belongs to a completely different genre', and so on. In plagiarism cases I have dealt with as a consultant, the genre issue was raised often and unsuccessfully, with just one exception: when the author of one piece (a disco-dance number) appropriated exactly the music of a piece belonging to a different genre (a film soundtrack, from an Academy Award-winning film). But appropriation (or borrowing) and genre are related in more complex ways. First, it appears that sensitivity to plagiarism varies across genres and is regulated by social conventions. In mainstream Western pop, the ears of songwriters, producers, publishers, record companies' executives and fans (on Facebook, Twitter and other social media) are sharply focused on possible appropriations, especially during big festivals. The issue of appropriation is raised more rarely in other genres, but conflicts may take place in cross-genre contexts: for example, a plagiarism case was raised by the authors and the publisher of an Italian song, 'Zingara', which won the Sanremo Festival in 1969, whose initial line ('Prendi questa mano,

[48] Among the earliest works, see F Pachet and D Cazaly, 'A Taxonomy of Musical Genre' (2000) 2 *RIAO* 1238; G Tzanetakis and P Cook, 'Musical Genre Classification of Audio Signals' (2002) 10(5) *IEEE Transactions on Speech and Audio Processing* 293.

[49] M Sordo, Ó Celma, M Blech and E Guaus, 'The Quest for Musical Genres. Do the Experts and the Wisdom of the Crowds Agree?' [2008] *ISMIR* 255.

[50] Ó Celma, *Music Recommendation and Discovery. The Long Tail, Long Fail, and Long Play in the Digital Music Space* (Springer Verlag, 2010).

zingara')[51] was used – lyrics and melody – as the first line of Francesco De Gregori's 'Prendi questa mano zingara' (1996). De Gregori, a singer-songwriter, maintained that it was clearly a quotation from a 'classic' song, but it took a long time before a court acknowledged De Gregori's right – in fact, not until he had lost the case twice.[52]

Second, musicologists and philosophers are confronted with the issue of a musical work's identity. Conventional musicologists maintain that a musical work must be identified with the score. This is what is usually taught in universities and conservatories. But what about music that is not notated? Some popular musicologists opt for recordings, pointing out the fact that from the 1950s songs are created in the form that will be listened to by an audience, in a recording studio, and scores are mere transcriptions, made for legal or commercial purposes.[53] Others have attenuated this view, arguing that a popular music piece, as a work, is (i) an abstract or notated musical structure (the song), (ii) its arrangement and (iii) the track.[54] Years ago, I proposed Umberto Eco's concept of *cognitive type*[55] to address the multiplicity of sound events and types that are usually referred to with a unique title, implying that they are different aspects of the same work: 'we can say that they are occurrences of a cognitive type, intending by this term a private instruction set located in the obscure, pre-semiotic zone between perception and recognition'.[56]

According to this view, then, genres (as sets of music events) may be seen as sets of sets (musical works, identified as collections of different aspects of the same item).

IX. Conclusions

The term 'genre' (and its equivalents in many languages, eg *gênero*, *género*, *gènere*, *genre*, *genws*, *ghéineas*, *genere*, *Gattung*, *γενος*)[57] is used in everyday speech to refer to a type of text or work of art. It belongs to many people's basic linguistic competence: even those who lack any analytical competence of individual art forms (music, literature, cinema, etc) know that different types of works are classified as belonging to different genres. It can be said that genre is often the most used term in conversations about art, or even the only one. Genre is rooted in language and in culture. As such, it invites study from various perspectives, among which I have favoured semiotics. To understand genre, we need to connect the individual to the social, expression to meaning, text to context, abstract to concrete: I maintain that semiotics is the best analytical tool to help making those connections. Some of the key concepts I used in this chapter are drawn from semiotics or related disciplines: semantics, sociolinguistics, analytical philosophy. Of course, other approaches are useful (sociology, anthropology, cognitive sciences), although none of them in my opinion has proved able to fully explain the multifaceted, mobile nature of genre: it is not by

[51] 'Take this hand, gipsy woman.'

[52] See G Casaburi, 'Novità sul plagio: la soluzione del caso Zingara (tra estetica marxista e un po' di Borges) (Osservaz a Cass, 19 febbraio 2015, n 3340)' (2015) 140(6) *Il Foro Italiano*.

[53] T Gracyk, *Rhythm and Noise: An Aesthetics of Rock* (Duke University Press, 1996).

[54] A Zak, *The Poetics of Rock: Cutting Tracks, Making Records* (University of California Press, 2001).

[55] Eco, *Kant and the Platypus* (n 16).

[56] 'possiamo dire che si tratta di occorrenze di un tipo cognitivo, intendendo con questo termine quell'insieme privato di istruzioni che si colloca nella zona oscura, pre-semiotica, tra percezione e riconoscimento', F Fabbri, 'La musica: un falso molto autentico, veramente fasullo' (2006) 31 *Rivista di Estetica* 161.

[57] Plus many others, derived from different roots, in Nordic or Slavic languages, to limit ourselves to Europe and the Americas.

chance, I believe, that descriptions of genre as a 'static' concept come from researchers who base their theories on those 'other' disciplines. Studies in the MIR branch of computer science have offered a new approach in the past 20 years, based mainly on data mining. Some of the results are astonishing, while others leave us perplexed: it is clear that the urgency of analysing billions of data and the pressure of major corporations has the effect of putting theory aside, but when researchers do so, actually they are not avoiding theory but are simply accepting old, outdated musicological or sociological assumptions on the nature of music and genre.

2

A Brief History and Typology of Musical Borrowing and Reworking

J PETER BURKHOLDER

I. Introduction

In the history of Western music, using existing music to make new music is not an anomaly: it is a central thread. In repertoires from early music to jazz and pop, performers add new twists to standard tunes; arrangers transcribe pieces for new media or craft new accompaniments; creators use melodies, bass lines and other materials from existing pieces to make new ones; and composers and improvisers draw on conventional gestures, formulas, styles and types from their musical tradition or from others.[1] In every case, the interplay of old and new elements, the familiar and the fresh, engages listeners on many levels, capturing our attention, keeping our interest, playing with our expectations, embodying feelings and conveying meanings.

The law is clearest at either end of this spectrum. Performance and arranging rights are well established, and widely shared gestures and styles are generally understood to be common property. Anyone performing, recording or arranging a copyrighted piece is expected to pay the owner, but no one can claim ownership of sonata form, the meter and style of the waltz or the chord progression for the 12-bar blues. It is the middle category, taking something from a specific piece of music and reworking it as part of a new piece, that presents a challenge to notions of intellectual property. Composer or improviser, individual or group, the creator of a new piece of music is rightly regarded as its author, with the rights of ownership. But what if that work contains material that originated in another piece of music, and therefore 'belongs' to someone else? Musicologists and music theorists call this 'musical borrowing', a metaphor that acknowledges the origin of the material in someone else's work. As composer and writer Johann Mattheson wrote in 1739, 'Borrowing is permissible; but one must return the thing borrowed with interest, i.e., one must so construct and develop imitations that they are prettier and better than the pieces from which they are derived'.[2] Yet such repayment and interest exist only metaphorically, in the realm of art. In a legal sense, such borrowing, if done without recompense or permission, may be judged theft or misappropriation.

[1] JP Burkholder, 'Making Old Music New: Performance, Arranging, Borrowing, Schemas, Topics, Intertextuality' in V Kostka, PF DeCastro, and W Everett (eds), *Intertextuality in Music: Dialogic Composition* (Routledge, 2021) 68–84.

[2] J Mattheson, *Der vollkommene Kappellmeister* (trans EC Harriss, UMI Research Press, 1981) 298. For literature on borrowing and reworking in music, see *Musical Borrowing and Reworking: An Annotated Bibliography*, https://chmtl.indiana.edu/borrowing/.

Or it would be if ownership were understood as a concept in music. But throughout music history, from long before the emergence of copyright law up to the present day, musicians have freely and frequently borrowed from each other, in many ways. Time and again, they have adapted existing music for new uses. In many repertoires, creators have treated the material they borrow as collectively owned, such as the melodies of a religious tradition, the popular music of their time or the folk music of a nation. Some have borrowed to pay homage to or compete with a peer or predecessor, implicitly acknowledging a sense of intellectual ownership.[3] More often, material is borrowed not to allude to its author, but for some other purpose, from spinning new variations on a theme to conveying meanings through the associations the borrowed music carries. Over the centuries, musicians have developed a remarkable variety of procedures for borrowing and reworking the music of others. The motivations, methods and results differ so greatly that all these ways of using existing music cannot be treated alike, and their differences should be recognised in some way by the law.

Being aware of the numerous ways musicians have borrowed from and reworked existing pieces in new ones and the many reasons for doing so, and recognising both how these types differ from each other and how they relate to each other historically, is crucial for understanding each new case of borrowing we encounter. The following brief overview illustrates the wide variety of ways in which musicians have borrowed and reworked existing music by highlighting some of the most common types and briefly tracing the history of each from its early appearances to the present. Most are still in use, while others were practised in past eras then fell out of fashion; some of the latter were revived or reinvented in a later time. Like other classifications of human behaviour, these types are not entirely separate categories. Rather, each type is defined by shared procedures and motivations, some of which may overlap with other types, and individual pieces may encompass more than one type. By discussing these types roughly in order of origin, while grouping together types that share common roots and histories, the following offers both a typology and a historical sketch, a tapestry of many interweaving threads.

II. Oldest Types

Too little music survives from antiquity to trace patterns of borrowing. The oldest large body of music to be preserved is the liturgical chant of the Catholic Church, sung in public services by celebrants, soloists and choirs, in monasteries by monks and in convents by nuns. After centuries of developing chant as an oral tradition, church musicians began in the late eighth or ninth century to devise means of writing down chant melodies in order to preserve and standardise them. Because for centuries only those trained as church musicians could read and write musical notation, it is in music for the church that we find the earliest known examples of musical borrowing and reworking, using chant melodies to create new chants or polyphonic (multi-voiced) music based on chant. Although some chants had known authors – typically chants created for local use, such as those composed by Hildegard of Bingen (1098–1179) and sung at the convent where she was abbess – the core repertoire was collectively owned by the Church and all her servants; it was the music of daily, weekly and annual services, widely familiar and readily adapted to new uses. Most types of borrowing first seen in music based on chant continued into later centuries in other repertoires as well.

[3] HM Brown, 'Emulation, Competition, and Homage: Imitation and Theories of Imitation in the Renaissance' (1982) 35 *Journal of the American Musicological Society* 1.

A. Contrafactum

One type is *contrafactum*, setting an existing melody with new text to create a new song.[4] When creating a liturgy for a new feast day or saint's day, church musicians often wrote suitable words to an existing melody or adjusted existing words to suit the new occasion. There are numerous introits (entrance chants) beginning *Gaudeamus omnes* (Let us all rejoice), all with the same melody and mostly the same words, each celebrating a different saint or Marian feast and changing the text to fit. Many hymns were set to the same melody; for example, the hymns 'Aurora solis nuntia', 'Caelestis aulae nuntius', 'O gloriosa Virginum', 'O prima Virgo prodita' and 'Te gestientem gaudiis' all use the same tune, and each is sung in a different religious service.

Contrafacta have been created ever since, in many repertoires. Medieval troubadours, trouvères and Minnesingers wrote new poems to be sung to existing melodies. Renaissance poets created spiritual madrigals, laude, chorales and other religious music by writing sacred texts for secular songs. Familiar tunes have been used for topical songs from sixteenth-century broadside ballads and seventeenth-century vaudevilles to the current YouTube parodies of Randy Rainbow, and many patriotic songs have used existing tunes, including 'The Star-Spangled Banner' (on 'The Anacreontic Song'), 'America' (to the tune of 'God Save the King') and 'America, the Beautiful' (set to the hymn tune 'Materna'). Stage plays with music have often used popular songs with new texts, as in the English ballad opera, French *comédie en vaudevilles* and German *Singspiel*.

In reusing well-known melodies for new words, songwriters rely on a shared musical heritage. Popular tunes are useful for adaptations because almost everyone in a given cultural community is likely to be familiar with them, and they are often regarded as common property, especially when the original composer is unknown, as is true of folk songs. When the original authors (or performers) and texts are known, as are the sources for pop song parodies by Weird Al Yankovic or Bob Rivers, the relation of old and new can become part of the meaning; in Rivers's parody of a famous Andy Williams holiday song as 'It's the Most Fattening Time of the Year', the echoes of words and rhymes from the original help to create the humour, heightened by a dead-on imitation of Williams's singing and backup arrangement.[5]

On the other hand, many composers have reused their own music with new texts simply to give the music an opportunity to be heard again, without assuming that listeners would know the earlier work (and perhaps hoping they would not). Johann Sebastian Bach (1685–1750) adapted several secular cantatas as sacred ones and used portions of others in his *Christmas Oratorio* and *Mass in B Minor*, and Gioachino Rossini (1792–1868) occasionally recycled an aria from one opera in a new one destined for a different city. The term often used for Bach's practice of reusing his own music with new texts is *parody*: not in the sense of the comic parodies of Yankovic and Rivers, but in the literal sense of a song alongside another, from the Greek *para-* (beside) and *ode* (song). In some cases, such parodies go beyond contrafactum (simply replacing the text) to include more substantial *recomposition*, discussed below.

[4] Some chant melodies were adjustable for use with many different texts – for instance, each of the reciting formulas called *psalm tones* could be used for all 150 psalms in the Bible – but these were not considered new songs.

[5] Compare Bob Rivers's song, www.youtube.com/watch?v=rPxCssN9KW8, to Andy Williams's recording of 'It's the Most Wonderful Time of the Year' by Edward Pola and George Wyle, www.youtube.com/watch?v=AN_R4pR1hck.

B. Melodic Paraphrase

While contrafactum involves reusing a melody with little change beyond what adjustments may be needed to fit a new text, church musicians also created new melodies through *melodic paraphrase*: taking some elements from an existing tune, altering or omitting some and adding new material. For example, the melody for the sequence *Christus hunc diem* by Notker (d 912) was adapted from the chant 'Alleluia Dominus in Sina', using its first phrase almost exactly, then following its general contour, omitting some notes and adding others. The adaptation through paraphrase was at least partly prompted by the change of genre, style and form. An Alleluia is a highly elaborate chant featuring several melismas (many notes sung to one syllable). The text is short, consisting of the word 'Alleluia', a psalm verse and 'Alleluia' again, and the music takes the form ABA, repeating the melody for 'Alleluia' after different music for the verse. A sequence, by contrast, is syllabic, with one note for each syllable, and has a much longer text and more complex form. In *Christus hunc diem*, as in many early sequences, the first and last versicles stand alone while the middle ones are paired, with each pair sung to the same music, for a musical form of A BB CC DD EE F. In effect, the older style of the Alleluia, developed through centuries of elaboration by soloists, was brought up to date in Notker's sequence, as the basic melodic contour was reshaped for a new use.

Similar uses of paraphrase to create a melody of a different style or type can be found in many later repertoires. In the early fifteenth century, English composers Leonel Power (d 1444) and John Dunstable (*c*1390–1453) and French composer Guillaume Du Fay (*c*1397–1474) recast hymns and other chants in a style akin to polyphonic songs of the time, with the chant melody paraphrased in the top voice supported by two or more vocal lines below; in place of the even, unmetered flow of chant, here the melody is typically in triple meter, lightly syncopated, with its rhythm constantly varied from one measure to the next and with notes interpolated to give it a pleasing and up-to-date style. In the late fifteenth and sixteenth centuries, composers such as Josquin Desprez (*c*1450–1521), Nicolas Gombert (*c*1495–*c*1560) and Giovanni Pierluigi da Palestrina (1525–94) paraphrased chant melodies as subjects suitable for imitative polyphony (in which one or more voices echo a melody first stated by another) in motets and masses. In the early years of the Reformation, Martin Luther and his associates paraphrased chant melodies and tunes of the Meistersingers to create a new repertoire of chorale melodies, hymns for the Lutheran Church, in a style akin to the popular songs of their time and region. In turn, Bach paraphrased chorales in the style of aria melodies in several of his cantatas, such as *Christ lag in Todesbanden* BWV 4. In the nineteenth century, hymn composers often paraphrased themes from classical works as hymn tunes, while composers of instrumental works paraphrased folk tunes and popular songs as themes, as did Amy Beach (1867–1944) with Irish tunes in her *Gaelic* Symphony in E Minor and Charles Ives (1874–1954) with American popular songs, fiddle tunes, patriotic songs, and hymns in his Symphony No 2.[6]

In all these cases, a composer reshapes a melody of one type and style into another type or style of melody through paraphrase, absorbing most or all of the source melody into the new one along with added notes and features typical of the new type and style, while preserving many of the associations and meanings (and often the text) of the original. Whether there is a continuous history of paraphrase in which each composer is aware of earlier practices or paraphrase procedures were invented anew in different generations by composers adapting old melodies to new uses has yet to be established.

[6] JP Burkholder, *All Made of Tunes: Charles Ives and the Uses of Musical Borrowing* (Yale University Press, 1995) 102–36.

C. Setting or Arranging a Melody

Other types of borrowing grew from practices of performing and arranging chant. Treatises describe methods of adding one or more melodies to a chant following rules to ensure consonance between voices: in the ninth century, parallel organum at the fifth or fourth below; in the 11th and twelfth, adding a voice above the chant in freer note-against-note or florid organum; in the twelfth and thirteenth, the expansive and majestic style of polyphony associated with Notre Dame in Paris; in the fourteenth and fifteenth, parallel triads in faburden and fauxbourdon. All of these were ways of performing a chant, enriching the melody with accompanying lines of music that – depending on the method – were generated by strict rules, were improvised or were worked out in rehearsal and retained in memory. The result was a *setting* of the chant, placing it in a musical context that deepened its beauty, akin to setting a gemstone in a ring. Essentially, these were *arrangements* of the chant, new performing versions that served the same liturgical role. Some examples were preserved in musical notation that was developed for the purpose.

These polyphonic settings of chant melodies inaugurated the written tradition of arrangements that continues to the present day and includes both sacred and secular music. The chant paraphrases of Power, Dunstable and Du Fay are part of this tradition, as are countless later settings of chorales and hymns, the common songs of Protestant churches. There are hundreds of polyphonic settings of secular monophonic songs in the fifteenth and sixteenth centuries. Later centuries have seen countless settings of folk songs for voices, voice and piano, voice and chamber group (including dozens by Joseph Haydn and Ludwig van Beethoven) and instruments alone. Chant, chorales and folk songs were all originally sung unaccompanied, but even songs whose accompaniments were part of their composers' conception have been given new settings; the songs of Stephen Foster, of the British music hall, of Broadway and of Tin Pan Alley from Irving Berlin through to George Gershwin and Cole Porter are more often heard in new settings and arrangements than as originally written.

Strictly speaking, settings and other kinds of arrangements are not instances of musical borrowing when regarded as new versions of the same piece. However, in some cases, the arranger may be seen as a kind of coauthor, or the setting may be so different in style and function that it can be considered a new piece rather than a new way of performing an older one. For example, Bach's chorale preludes for organ – elaborate settings of chorale tunes – are seen as new pieces, performed in church as a prelude to singing the chorale or separately as an interlude or in an organ recital. Moreover, the procedures of reworking given material that are first developed in settings and arrangements are often later used in creating new works, and thus become fundamental techniques of borrowing.

III. Types Originating in the Late Middle Ages and Renaissance

Several types of borrowing emerged in the twelfth to sixteenth centuries in both sacred and secular music. As with the older types, some of these may have been practised earlier in music that was not written down or does not survive.

A. Medieval Motet and Structural Cantus Firmus

One offshoot of chant settings was the *medieval motet*, in which a segment of melody, usually a melisma borrowed from a chant and set into a regularly recurring rhythmic pattern, serves as the structural foundation (called the *tenor*), with one to three more quickly moving voices above it, each with its own text. In the early thirteenth century, motets were often created through a kind of contrafactum, by adding words to the upper voice or voices of a setting in the Notre Dame style of a melisma from chant, and others were newly composed in a similar style (sometimes borrowing the tenor from an existing chant setting or motet), showing that the new genre grew directly from Notre Dame polyphony. Some motets may have been used in church, but most were apparently sung as entertainment in gatherings of the clerical and educated elite. From the mid-thirteenth to the early fifteenth century, hundreds of motets in various styles were composed in Latin or French on both sacred and secular subjects, all based on borrowed melodies from chant or other sources in the lowest voice. Often the borrowed melody was chosen because its original words, although not sung in the motet, reflected or enhanced the meaning of the texts of the upper voices. For example, Philippe de Vitry's motet *Cum statua/Hugo, Hugo/Magister invidie* (*c*1320), a bitter attack on hypocrisy in the church and on someone who, because of envy, unfairly criticised Vitry, is built on a segment of chant whose original text was 'magister invidie saevit in illum' (the master of envy rages in the [stone]).[7] For the meaning to come across, performers and listeners must recognise the melody, recall its text and comprehend its import.

The use of a melodic segment borrowed from chant as the lowest voice for a motet led directly to the tradition of presenting a borrowed melody as a *structural cantus firmus*, stated in relatively long durations as other voices weave counterpoint above, below or around it.[8] In the fifteenth and sixteenth centuries, in addition to motets based on cantus firmi, composers often wrote cyclic masses (polyphonic settings of the five main texts of the Catholic Mass Ordinary) using a structural cantus firmus drawn from chant or a secular song. Masses that use the same borrowed melody as a cantus firmus in each movement, known as *cantus firmus masses*, are typically named after that melody. The first such masses, from the 1430s, are *Missa Rex seculorum*, attributed to both Power and Dunstable, and Power's *Missa Alma Redemptoris mater*. Later examples include over 40 masses on the French song *L'homme armé*, with later composers often emulating and trying to outdo earlier masses on the same cantus firmus. As in a motet, the melody chosen as a cantus firmus may convey meanings to those hearing or singing the mass through the source melody's original text or associations.[9] In some cases, the cantus firmus is paraphrased from the source, blending the techniques of cantus firmus and melodic paraphrase in a single work.

Protestant composers likewise used chorale and hymn tunes as structural cantus firmi in both vocal and instrumental sacred music. The technique occurs in secular and instrumental music as well. In sixteenth- and seventeenth-century England, a tradition developed of consort music based on a cantus firmus, stemming from performances by instrumental ensembles of the *In nomine* section of John Taverner's *Missa Gloria tibi trinitas*, as dozens of other composers wrote instrumental pieces using the same cantus firmus – a tradition of emulation and competition akin to the *L'homme armé* masses on the Continent. In music from the seventeenth century on, cantus firmus texture has been used especially when composers draw on its associations with sacred music and older styles to convey an effect of the religious, elevated, dignified, learned or ancient.

[7] A Zayaruznaya, *The Monstrous New Art: Divided Forms in the Late Medieval Motet* (Cambridge University Press, 2015) 106–41.

[8] Some writers use *cantus firmus* (Latin for 'fixed song') for all uses of borrowed melodies in the Renaissance, including settings and melodic paraphrase, as in EH Sparks, *Cantus Firmus in Mass and Motet, 1420–1520* (University of California Press, 1963).

[9] See, eg AW Robertson, 'The Savior, the Woman, and the Head of the Dragon in the *Caput* Masses and Motet' (2006) 59 *Journal of the American Musicological Society* 537.

B. Quotation

A type of borrowing whose earliest traces are found in secular song rather than in religious music is *quotation*. Although writers have sometimes used the term 'quotation' for a wide range of borrowing practices, rightly understood quotation in music is a close parallel to quotation in literature: incorporating a phrase or brief passage of one text in another, usually to convey or create meaning through the juxtaposition of texts or associations carried by the source text. Indeed, the apparently earliest musical quotations were linked to poetic quotations, typically quoting secular songs in the vernacular rather than Latin chant. For example, the motet *De ma dame vient/Dieus, comment porroie/Omnes* by Adam de la Halle (*c*1240–*c*1288) borrows a chant melody in the lowest voice as usual but also begins the middle voice by quoting the music and words of a refrain from a French secular song by Adam, ends that voice with another quoted refrain and quotes lines from other poems in the text for the top voice. Such combined quoting of a song's text and melody can also be found in monophonic (one-voice) French secular songs from the mid-twelfth to the mid-fourteenth century; in fourteenth-century polyphonic songs; and in many later repertoires, including recent pop songs that weave in fragments of pop songs from earlier generations.

As we saw in Vitry's motet, quoting a melody without its text can recall its words, and that is often the reason for the quotation. According to Carl Czerny, Beethoven quoted 'Notte e giorno faticar' (Toiling night and day) from Wolfgang Amadeus Mozart's opera *Don Giovanni* and the waltz tune 'Keine Ruh bei Tag und Nacht' (No rest by day or night) in his *Diabelli Variations* (1819–23) as a humorous response to his publisher's pressing him to finish the piece.[10] Purely musical quotations have many uses: to depict the act of performing music, as when in *Battalia* (1673) Heinrich Biber quotes a melange of folksong tunes to represent soldiers singing on the eve of battle; to evoke people associated with a piece, as when Pyotr Ilyich Tchaikovsky represents the French and Russian armies in his *1812 Overture* (1880) through their national anthems and band music; to allude to or honour a fellow musician, as when one jazz improviser quotes another; to invoke ideas or feelings, as when Alban Berg quotes the yearning opening of Richard Wagner's *Tristan und Isolde* in his *Lyric Suite* (1925–26), whose secret programme, like the plot of the opera, centres on forbidden love between a man and the wife of a close friend; to create humour, as Erik Satie does in citing (and altering) Fryderyk Chopin's funeral march at a weepy moment in *Embryons desséchés* (1913); and to highlight the distance between present and past, as when George Crumb quotes Chopin's *Fantaisie-Impromptu* amid much more modern sounds in his *Makrokosmos I* for amplified piano (1972).

In all these cases, a creator who quotes implies a listener who will recognise the quotation and catch the associations it carries. Unlike contrafactum and other adaptations of material viewed as common property, the act of quotation strongly implies a recognition of the individuality of the source and – when its creator is known – of authorship.

C. Patchwork

Although rarer than quoting from a single melody, a closely related practice appeared soon after quotation itself: *patchwork*, stitching a melody together from fragments of multiple melodies, often interspersed with new material. Some thirteenth-century motets include a voice that strings

[10] W Zoor, 'Correspondence' (1983) 61 *Gramophone* 416.

together a series of quoted refrains. From the fifteenth to the early nineteenth century, patchwork voices appeared in some quodlibets (see below). Some popular songs use patchwork, including several by Tin Pan Alley songwriters from the early twentieth century; the verse of George M Cohan's 'The Yankee Doodle Dandy' (1904) weaves original melodic ideas together with excerpts from 'Yankee Doodle', 'Dixie', 'The Girl I Left Behind Me' and 'The Star Spangled Banner', evoking their words and associations.[11] Whether patchwork has a continuous history or emerges at times from the more general practice of quotation is unclear.

D. Allusion

Closely related to quotation is *allusion*: a deliberate reference to another work through a resemblance that creates meaning for those who perceive it. An allusion may take the form of similarity in melody (including inexact quotation) or in any other parameter where what is shared is distinctive enough to recognise, such as a striking timbre, sonority or procedure. Melodic allusions can be found in music of the fourteenth and fifteenth centuries alongside more precise quotations, but most studies have focused on the nineteenth and twentieth centuries, when composers such as Robert Schumann, Johannes Brahms, Gustav Mahler and George Crumb used allusions as a kind of intellectual play, creating symbols, engaging in dialogue with earlier pieces and composers, and leaving clues for listeners to create their own interpretations.[12] Ultimately, allusion is not so much a technique of borrowing, since most cases can be assimilated under other types, as it is a motive for borrowing, adding levels of meaning that only discerning listeners – perhaps even only the composer's close associates – are likely to catch.

E. Intabulation and Transcription

We saw above that setting – enriching a melody with an accompaniment – is one kind of arrangement, creating a new version of a piece. Another is *transcription*: taking a piece of music conceived for one medium and arranging it for another. The earliest type of written transcription is *intabulation*, notating a vocal piece for a keyboard or plucked-string instrument using *tablature*, any of several systems for indicating keyboard pitches by letter or number (rather than noteheads on a staff) or showing where to put one's fingers on the strings of a lute or vihuela and when to pluck each string (rather than what notes would result). The first intabulations, preserved in the manuscripts Robertsbridge Codex (*c*1360) and Faenza Codex (*c*1400), are keyboard versions of motets or secular songs, reproducing all the voices and adding sometimes spectacular embellishments, especially in the upper voices. With the rise of music publishing after 1501 came many intabulations for lute, vihuela or guitar, most aimed at amateur performers but some representing the skilful elaborations of virtuoso players, such as the lutenists Francesco da Milano (1497–1543)

[11] Burkholder, *All Made of Tunes* (n 6) 322–26.

[12] Y Plumley, 'Intertextuality in the Fourteenth-Century Chanson' (2003) 84 *Music and Letters* 355; CA Reynolds, 'The Counterpoint of Allusion in Fifteenth-Century Masses' (1992) 45 *Journal of the American Musicological Society* 228; R Knapp, 'Utopian Agendas: Variation, Allusion, and Referential Meaning in Brahms's Symphonies' (2001) 3 *Brahms Studies* 129; CA Reynolds, *Motives for Allusion: Context and Content in Nineteenth-Century Music* (Harvard University Press, 2003); AL Ringer, '"Lieder eines fahrenden Gesellen": Allusion und Zitat in der musikalischen Erzählung Gustav Mahlers' in H Danuser et al (eds), *Das musikalische Kunstwerk: Geschichte, Ästhetik, Theorie: Festschrift Carl Dahlhaus zum 60. Guburtstag* (Laaber-Verlag, 1988) 589–602; SM Bruns, '"In stilo Mahleriano": Quotation and Allusion in the Music of George Crumb' (1993) 3 *American Music Research Center Journal* 9.

and Valentin Bakfark (*c*1526–76). The growing market for music for amateurs also led to the production of many alternate versions of vocal pieces that added a line of counterpoint, substituted a new one, changed the number of voices or adapted the music to instrumental ensembles as well as soloists. The remarkable variety of ways the same pieces were arranged and sold for different media shows the freedom with which musicians treated music as common property in an era when copyright laws still lay in the future.

Intabulations ceased in the seventeenth century with the decline in tablature notation, but transcriptions have remained a mainstay of music publishing, including piano-vocal scores of operas (reducing the instrumental parts to keyboard); the nineteenth-century vogue for piano or piano-four-hands versions of symphonic and chamber music; transcriptions of orchestral and operatic music for bands; and modern arrangements of film scores for keyboard. Like settings, these are arrangements rather than instances of borrowing, except in cases when the adaptation results in a new piece, as in the recompositions by Liszt, Stravinsky and others discussed below.

F. Imitation of a Model

As with quotation, recognition of individuality and often of authorship is typical when musicians *imitate a model*: using an existing piece as a starting point for composing a new one. Students learning how to compose a type of piece or to use a new procedure or style have often imitated exemplary models of that type, procedure or style. Among the earliest surviving examples of this, written into the final pages of a manuscript songbook in the early sixteenth century, is a chanson for three voices, *En contemplant la beauté de m'amye*, whose infelicities and on-the-page corrections strongly suggest that it is the work of someone learning how to compose. Several features link it closely to another three-voice chanson copied earlier in the same manuscript, *Vivent en payx*, which must have served as the student's model: both chansons begin with virtually the same music; they share a similar pattern of musical phrases, text divisions and cadences, including repeating the first phrase at the end; and there are frequent parallels of melody and counterpoint. At the same time, the later work often seems deliberately to introduce something new, such as a more extended ending to the first phrase, so that the new song is not too much like its model.[13] This combination of echoing some aspects of the model while changing others is characteristic of learning to master a skill through emulating the exemplary works of experts.

The practice of using an existing piece as a model is not limited to students, however. Both young composers and well-established ones have emulated models, in genres and periods from motets, masses and madrigals of the fourteenth to sixteenth centuries to string quartets, concertos, symphonies and film scores from the eighteenth century to the present.[14] Such emulation often involves borrowing aspects of the model's rhythm, texture, form or sound in addition to or instead of a melody. The relationship between new work and source can be subtle, as when a composer adopts some aspects of the model while departing from or reversing others. For instance, Charles Ives's song 'Feldeinsamkeit' (1898), modelled on the setting of the same poem by Johannes Brahms, uses a similar pattern of text repetition and features momentary parallels

[13] Brown (n 3) 1–10.

[14] See, eg D Leech-Wilkinson, 'Related Motets from Fourteenth-Century France' (1982–83) 109 *Proceedings of the Royal Musical Association* 1; J Cohen, 'Thomas Weelkes's Borrowings from Salamone Rossi' (1985) 66 *Music and Letters* 110; ME Bonds, 'The Sincerest Form of Flattery?: Mozart's "Haydn" Quartets and the Question of Influence' (1993) 22 *Studi musicali* 365; J Yudkin, 'Beethoven's Mozart Quartet' (1992) 45 *Journal of the American Musicological Society* 30; C Rosen, 'Influence: Plagiarism and Inspiration' (1980) 4 *19th-Century Music* 87; Burkholder, *All Made of Tunes* (n 6) 89–102.

in rhythm, contour, climax and chromaticism, but it is faster than Brahms's song, rhythmically more active and different in mood, form and harmonic plan; despite their common features, the two songs sound entirely different, and likely no court would rule that Ives borrowed Brahms's melody. In an even more distant instance of modelling, Mel Powell derived the structure of his string quartet *Beethoven Analogs* (1948) from Beethoven's String Quartet in F Major, Op 18, No 1, through a process of 'formal analogs', creating parallels for phrasing, cadences, form, syntax and rhetoric of his tonal model in an atonal context through techniques such as double stops, octave doubling and changes in dynamics, tempo or texture.[15] More overt use of familiar models can convey meanings to an audience, as in John Williams's scores for the *Star Wars* films, which echo distinctive textures and effects from Gustav Holst's *The Planets* to suggest action in space.

G. Recomposition and Parody

Closely related to imitation of a model is *recomposition*, sometimes called *parody*: taking the main substance of a piece and reworking it to make a new piece. Fourteenth-century composers reshaped existing mass movements into new ones by reworking or omitting passages or by interpolating new material. Around 1430, Hugo de Lantins (or perhaps another composer) recomposed his motet *Christus vincit* as the motet *O lux et decus Hispanie*, changing the opening two sections considerably to suit the new text while treating the remainder primarily as a contrafactum. Johannes Martini (*c*1440–97) recomposed his own instrumental piece *La Martinella* in shortened form as *La Martinella pittzulo* (The Little Martinella), and two other composers reworked it in still other ways, recasting some of the melodic material, expanding points of imitation from two voices to three and adding new material, often echoing textures from Martini's original.[16] As these examples suggest, recomposition may overlap with other types of borrowing, such as contrafactum and imitation of a model, or may exist alongside them in a single piece; composers' imaginations are not limited by our retrospective catalogues of ideal types.

Recomposition is basic to the sixteenth-century tradition of the *imitation mass* (also called *parody mass*), a cyclic polyphonic mass that borrows from and reworks all voices from a polyphonic model. The practice developed from fifteenth-century *cantus firmus-imitation masses*, in which composers used one voice (usually the tenor) from a polyphonic piece as a cantus firmus and borrowed at times from the other voices of the model; as in a cantus-firmus mass, meanings and associations from the source often carry over to the mass. Du Fay's *Missa Se la face ay pale* (*c*1453), based on his own ballade, may be the first such mass, and like many of its type the borrowing from other voices is occasional, reserved for marking prominent places such as the end of a movement.[17] But later composers wrote masses that take over and recompose the entire texture of the model in each movement, as Johannes Martini did in *Missa Ma bouche rit*, *Missa Coda di Pavon* and *Missa La Martinella* (on his own instrumental work).[18] In mature imitation masses,

[15] Burkholder, *All Made of Tunes* (n 6) 31–34; J Perry, 'Constructing a Relevant Past: Mel Powell's *Beethoven Analogs*' (2011) 29 *American Music* 491.

[16] R Jackson, 'Musical Interrelations between Fourteenth Century Mass Movements (A Preliminary Study)' (1957) 29 *Acta Musicologica* 54; JM Allsen, 'Intertextuality and Compositional Process in Two Cantilena Motets by Hugo de Lantins' (1993) 11 *Journal of Musicology* 174; Brown (n 3) 29–35.

[17] For its meanings, see AW Robertson, 'The Man with the Pale Face, the Shroud, and Du Fay's *Missa Se la face ay pale*' (2010) 27 *Journal of Musicology* 377.

[18] M Steib, 'A Composer Looks at His Model: Polyphonic Borrowing in Masses from the Late Fifteenth Century' (1996) 46 *Tijdschrift van de Koninklijke Vereniging voor Nederlandse Muziekgeschiedenis* 5; JP Burkholder, 'Johannes Martini and the Imitation Mass of the Late Fifteenth Century' (1985) 38 *Journal of the American Musicological Society* 470.

from *Missa Ave Maria* by Antoine de Févin (*c*1470–1511/12) through the dozens composed by Giovanni Pierluigi da Palestrina (1525/26–1594), Orlando di Lasso (*c*1532–94) and Tomás Luis de Victoria (1548–1611), no voice is a cantus firmus, and each of the five movements is a different recomposition of all or parts of the model, changing rhythms, realigning the voices, creating new points of imitation on motives from the model, reworking passages in other ways and adding new material.

Although the imitation mass as a genre had a limited lifespan of just over a century, recomposition as a procedure has continued. In later eras, recomposition is often present when composers recycle their own music with new words, as in Bach's *Mass in B Minor* and *Christmas Oratorio*, or in new formats, such as John Corigliano's arrangements of music from his film score for *The Red Violin* (1997) as *The Red Violin: Chaconne for Violin and Orchestra* and *The Red Violin Caprices* for solo violin. George Frideric Handel (1685–1759) recomposed both his own music and that of others, from his own Italian duos that he recycled in *Messiah* (1741) to multiple passages from Antonio Francesco Urio's *Te Deum* that he reworked in his oratorio *Saul* (1738). Mozart created his first four piano concertos in 1767 by recomposing piano sonata movements by several older contemporaries.

With the rise of originality as a criterion for judging music, beginning in eighteenth-century England and becoming foundational for nineteenth-century critics, such remaking of music by others – including recomposition, imitation of models and even quotation – came to be regarded as plagiarism, a complete turnaround from earlier centuries' belief that composers and performers demonstrated their excellence by how they worked with their material rather than whether they invented it. Handel was particularly criticised.[19]

In response to the changes, composers since the nineteenth century who have used recomposition have typically announced their sources and made the relationship of new music to old part of the purpose and meaning of the music. In his piano works *Reminiscences de Don Juan*, *Reminiscences de Norma* and *Reminiscences de Robert le Diable*, Franz Liszt (1811–86) recomposed and reordered material from famous operas (by Mozart, Vincenzo Bellini and Giacomo Meyerbeer, respectively) to create a new, subjective interpretation of each opera, focusing on just a few characters and even suggesting changes in the plot through the sequence of musical events.[20] Some orchestral arrangements of older music, such as Tchaikovsky's suite *Mozartiana* (1887, on piano pieces by Mozart) and Ottorino Respighi's three suites of *Ancient Airs and Dances* (1917–31, on Italian and French songs and lute pieces from the sixteenth and seventeenth centuries), convey a wistful nostalgia for the past by recasting old, intimate music for one or two performers as works for an orchestra, the largest and most public of ensembles. More drastic recompositions, like Igor Stravinsky's *Pulcinella* (1920, on music from the early eighteenth century), Arnold Schoenberg's Concerto for String Quartet and Orchestra (1933, on Handel's Concerto Grosso in B-flat Major, Op 6, No 7) and Maurizio Kagel's *Variationen ohne Fuge* (1972, on Brahms's *Variations and Fugue on a Theme by Handel*), emphasise the distance between past and present by overlaying the style,

[19] GJ Buelow, 'Originality, Genius, Plagiarism in English Criticism of the Eighteenth Century' in C-H Mahling (ed), *Florilegium Musicologicum: Festschrift Hellmut Federhofer zum 75. Geburtstag* (Hans Schneider, 1988) 57–66; GJ Buelow, 'The Case for Handel's Borrowings: The Judgment of Three Centuries' in S Sadie and A Hicks (eds), *Handel Tercentenary Collection* (Macmillan, 1987) 61–82; FW Horncastle, 'Plagiarism' (1822) 4 *Quarterly Musical Magazine and Review* 141; S Taylor, *The Indebtedness of Handel to Works by Other Composers: A Presentation of Evidence* (first published 1906, Da Capo Press, 1979).

[20] S Döhring, 'Reminiscences: Liszts Konzeption der Klavierparaphrase' in J Schläder and R Quandt (eds), *Festschrift Heinz Becker zum 60. Geburtstag am 26. Juni 1982* (Laaber-Verlag, 1982) 131–51; A Riethmüller, 'Franz Liszts Reminiscences de Don Juan' in W Breig, R Brinkmann and E Budde (eds), *Analysen: Beiträge zu einer Problemgeschichte des Komponierens: Festschrift für Hans Heinrich Eggebrecht zum 65. Geburtstag* (F Steiner Verlag, 1984) 276–91.

tonality and themes of the original with modernist elements and post-tonal motivic relationships, creating a struggle of new versus old within the piece itself.[21] By presenting 'Silent Night' as if performed by a loud punk band, Bob Rivers's 'Not So Silent Night' subverts the tone, mood and meaning of the famous Christmas carol.[22] What makes all of these recompositions rather than arrangements is that what results is a new piece, even if most or all of the notes are the same as the source.

H. Quodlibet and Medley

Borrowing is featured in the *quodlibet* (Latin for 'what you please'), which combines segments from several melodies, either in succession or simultaneously (or both), usually to humorous effect. The genre emerged in the fifteenth and sixteenth centuries, especially in German-speaking lands, as a musical parallel to comic poems and extemporised speeches featuring lists of often absurdly juxtaposed items. Similar pieces from the sixteenth century are called *fricassée* in France, *ensalada* in Spain and *misticanza* in Italy. Successive quodlibets string together a series of short excerpts; examples span from *Wer ich eyn Falck* (late fifteenth century), with fragments from several German songs in the tenor accompanied by free counterpoint in three other voices, through 11 by Melchior Franck (1579–1639) to the quodlibet movement in a symphony by Paul Wranitzky (1756–1808) that borrows from 11 melodies and the quodlibet songs in Viennese comedies in the early nineteenth century. Simultaneous quodlibets include three types: a polyphonic combination of two or more voices that each feature successive fragments of borrowed melodies; a combination of one such voice with a cantus firmus, as in three pieces from the Glogauer Liederbuch (*c*1480); or a combination of two or more existing melodies, as in the closing variation in Bach's *Goldberg Variations* that overlays two German popular songs.[23]

With occasional exceptions such as Peter Schickele's *Quodlibet* (1959, revised 1965), which whimsically combines familiar tunes from classical and popular music, the quodlibet as a genre virtually disappeared after the mid-nineteenth century. But as a type of borrowing, it endures: the tradition of juxtaposing or superimposing music borrowed from two or more sources for comic purposes has continued in *coups de théâtre* such as *Fly Me Off the Handel* by the Ukelele Orchestra of Great Britain, with a Handel theme underpinning the popular songs 'Fly Me to the Moon', 'Love Story', 'Autumn Leaves', 'Killing Me Softly', 'Hotel California' and 'I Will Survive', first one by one and then all at once.

A related genre that continues from the late sixteenth century to the present is the *medley* (or *potpourri* in French), comprising a series of tunes in succession, usually complete melodies rather than the fragments often used in quodlibets. Medleys aim for pleasure rather than humour, presenting a string of pleasing tunes that typically have something in common, as in a medley of folk songs or of Christmas carols, or an opera overture that presents a medley of melodies featured in the opera to follow.

[21] JN Straus, *Remaking the Past: Musical Modernism and the Influence of the Tonal Tradition* (Harvard University Press, 1990) 44–73.

[22] Burkholder, 'Making' (n 1) 72–73 and 78.

[23] W Rogge, *Das Quodlibet in Deutschland bis Melchior Franck* (Möseler, 1965); J LaRue, 'A "Hail and Farewell" Quodlibet Symphony' (1956) 37 *Music and Letters* 250.

I. Variations

Another genre that foregrounds borrowing is the *variation set*, which presents a theme and a series of variations that each preserve some elements of the theme and alter others, customarily introducing new figuration for each variation. The theme may be a melody, bass line or harmonic progression, or a combination of them, either borrowed or newly composed; variations may add new material while the melody, bass or harmony repeats essentially unchanged, or may vary or decorate it as well. Whereas paraphrases and recompositions can greatly alter the length, phrasing and structure of the source and often introduce sections with new material, variations normally keep the phrasing and structure strictly parallel with that of the theme.

The idea of adding variations each time a tune or bass line recurs surely goes back centuries as a performance practice for strophic songs and dance melodies. The first notated sets of variations were published in the 1538 collection of pieces for vihuela by Luis de Narváez, *Los seys libros del delphín*, including variations on the hymn tune 'O gloriosa Domina' and on the secular song 'Guárdame las vacas'. The latter consisted of a melodic outline over a bass line that became known in Italy as the Romanesca, one of several bass patterns used for variations by countless composers and improvisers. One of the most popular, borrowed in at least 128 surviving pieces, including numerous variation sets, was the *Ballo del Gran Duca* by Emilio de' Cavalieri (*c*1550–1602), taken from the opening chorus for the final dance in a 1589 festive stage spectacle in Florence celebrating the wedding of Ferdinando I de' Medici, Grand Duke of Tuscany, to Christine of Lorraine.[24]

The sheer number of times Cavalieri's piece was used as a source, without any complaint from its composer, shows that at the time musical ideas – melodies, bass lines, harmonic progressions and turns of phrase – were regarded as common property, so much so that over time the most popular became standard formulas, akin to the 12-bar blues, no longer considered borrowed material. In contrast, ideas *about* music, such as a new musical style, were regarded by their creators as their own intellectual property (in a moral rather than legal sense); in 1600, Cavalieri insisted on his right to be acknowledged as the inventor of recitative, a new style that others also said they had pioneered, and soon after Claudio Monteverdi (1567–1643) staked his claim to having devised the *seconda pratica* (second practice), which allowed breaking the rules of counterpoint when necessary to better convey the meaning and emotions of a text, and the *concitato genere* (agitated style), a new means for depicting anger and agitation.

English keyboard composers in the late sixteenth and early seventeenth century wrote numerous variations on popular tunes, such as those on *John Come Kiss Me Now* by William Byrd (*c*1540–1623). Variation sets remained a mainstay of music publication through the nineteenth century, providing both amateur and professional players of keyboard, guitar, violin, flute and other instruments with a variety of textures and figurations to challenge their abilities and to show off their skill. Most free-standing variation sets are based on borrowed themes, while others – including most variation movements in larger works, like sonatas, string quartets and symphonies – are on newly composed themes. Variations were never treated as plagiarism, since the borrowed material was duly acknowledged, usually in the title; for that reason, variations on borrowed themes continued to be popular even after the growing insistence on originality in the nineteenth century.

In some cases, multiple composers wrote variations on the same theme, showing off what they could do with the same material and creating traditions of homage and competition akin to the

[24] W Kirkendale, *L'Aria di Fiorenza, id est Il ballo del Gran Duca* (LS Olschki, 1972).

L'homme armé masses of the Renaissance. Among the most famous are variations on the theme from Nicolò Paganini's Caprice No 24 in A Minor (*c*1807), itself a theme with 11 variations (plus a final section that spins ideas from the theme while departing from its regular phrasing); more than three dozen composers have written their own sets of variations on this theme, including Johannes Brahms (piano, 1863), Sergei Rachmaninoff (*Rhapsody on a Theme of Paganini*, piano and orchestra, 1934), Witold Lutoslawski (two pianos, 1941), Boris Blacher (orchestra, 1947), George Rochberg (solo violin, 1970), Andrew Lloyd Webber (*Variations*, cello and rock band, 1977), David Baker (*Ethnic Variations on a Theme of Paganini*, violin and piano, 1982) and James Barnes (*Fantasy Variations*, wind band, 1988, with variations for every instrument and section). In these and other variation sets, the old idea lives that originality lies in what one does with the material, not whether one invented it.

IV. Types Originating Since the Seventeenth Century

Since the seventeenth century, most older types of borrowing and reworking have continued to be practised, while several newer types have emerged, each suited to a particular purpose.

A. Pastiche

Somewhere between borrowing and arrangement lies the category of *pastiche*: piecing together the music for a stage show, film or other large entertainment from borrowed material. In the late seventeenth and eighteenth centuries, opera productions known as *pasticcios* were created by selecting arias from different composers' settings of the same libretto or by writing a new libretto to suit the music (and often the original texts) of arias from multiple operas. The English ballad opera and French *comédie en vaudevilles* likewise were musical pastiches, with texts altered by contrafactum, and the tradition continued into the nineteenth century throughout Europe and the Americas. Ballet scores have also been compiled from existing music, as in Alexander Glazunov's score for *Les Sylphides* orchestrated from piano pieces by Chopin. Silent films were often accompanied by excerpts from classical or popular music that fit each scene, assembled by the accompanist or on cue sheets issued by film studios. Some sound films continued the practice, from *The Jazz Singer* (1927) through compilation scores like Stanley Kubrick's for his *2001: A Space Odyssey* (1968) and countless films that draw on pop music, using the style and associations of each familiar excerpt to set the scene, comment on the action or provide a musical interlude between moments of dialogue.

B. Borrowed Melody as Theme

Using a borrowed melody as a theme is less common outside variation form, yet there are examples from the late eighteenth century to the present. In one movement in each of his three Razumovsky String Quartets, Op 59 (1806) – respectively a sonata-form finale, a scherzo and a slow movement – Beethoven used a Russian folk song as a theme in honour of his Russian patron.[25] Later composers also adopted folk tunes as themes, as in Vincent d'Indy's *Symphony on*

[25] M Ferraguto, 'Beethoven *à la moujik*: Russianness and Learned Style in the "Razumovsky" String Quartets' (2014) 67 *Journal of the American Musicological Society* 77.

a French Mountain Air (1886) for piano and orchestra, which opens with a French folk song in the English horn, then paraphrases the song in the main themes of all three movements, sometimes placing different versions in counterpoint with each other. A few composers have used hymn tunes as themes, as Ralph Vaughan Williams did in his *Fantasia on a Theme by Thomas Tallis* (1910) and Ives did in his Third Symphony (*c*1908–1911) and violin sonatas, where he turned the tables by fragmenting, developing and paraphrasing each hymn tune theme before presenting it in full near the end of the movement, a procedure called *cumulative form*.[26]

C. Collage

Several twentieth-century composers created works that juxtapose multiple borrowed fragments in a *collage*. Unlike quodlibet, in collage, borrowed tunes do not fit together in good counterpoint; rather, they sound like simultaneous but conflicting events, giving the impression of something outside the mainstream of the music, like clippings of paper or other materials pasted on a surface in a visual collage. Ives may have been the first to create such textures, using them in the barn dance episode of *Washington's Birthday* (*c*1915–17) and at the climax of *The Fourth of July* (*c*1914–18) to suggest the swirl of memory as he recalls the events and sounds of holidays of his youth, one remembered tune triggering another.[27] Interest in collage peaked in the 1960s as composers used it to reconnect current music to the traditions, styles and composers of the past; to express the multivalence of modern life; or to convey other kinds of meaning. The most famous collage is the third movement of Luciano Berio's *Sinfonia* (1968), which takes the third movement scherzo of Mahler's Symphony No 2 ('Resurrection') as its canvas, silences some sections or elements in the texture as if whiting out parts of a painting and overlays fragments from about 100 other pieces of classical music (plus texts from Samuel Beckett's *The Unnamable* and others) in a stream of consciousness encompassing memories of the modern repertoire from Bach and Beethoven to Pierre Boulez and Berio himself.[28]

D. Jazz Contrafact

Jazz improvisers sometimes quote or allude to other pieces, from familiar tunes to snatches from other artists' improvisations. But the most fundamental form of borrowing in jazz is the *contrafact*: a new tune composed to fit the chord changes borrowed from another song.[29]

A typical jazz performance consists of the *head* – a tune with its harmonisation – followed by a series of *choruses*, in which players take turns improvising over the same chord progression as the tune, ending with a reprise of the head. To a listener more familiar with classical music, this

[26] Burkholder, *All Made of Tunes* (n 6) 137–266.

[27] ibid 376–85.

[28] D Metzer, *Quotation and Cultural Meaning in Twentieth-Century Music* (Cambridge University Press, 2003) 108–59; M Hicks, 'Text, Music, and Meaning in the Third Movement of Luciano Berio's *Sinfonia*' (1981–82) 20 *Perspectives of New Music* 199; D Osmond-Smith, *Playing on Words: A Guide to Luciano Berio's 'Sinfonia'* (Royal Musical Association, 1985). The chain of borrowing starts even earlier; Mahler adapted his scherzo from his orchestral song 'Des Antonius von Padua Fischpredigt' from *Des Knaben Wunderhorn*.

[29] The term *melodic contrafact*, adapted from *contrafactum*, was coined by J Patrick, 'Charlie Parker and Harmonic Sources of Bebop Composition: Thoughts on the Repertory of New Jazz in the 1940s' (1975) 2 *Journal of Jazz Studies* 3, the first serious study of the phenomenon. The shortened form *contrafact* was popularised by D Baker, 'The Contrafact' in *How to Play Bebop* (Alfred Publishing, 1987) 3:1–4.

description may sound like a set of variations, but in jazz it is regarded as a performance of the tune, and each such performance is expected to be different from the last. By the 1930s, certain songs were so familiar to jazz musicians that a composer could borrow the chord progression from one and invent a new tune to fit it, creating a new piece on whose chord changes players could immediately improvise. The practice became even more common in 1940s bebop. Because copyright applied to the melody and not the chord progression, the new piece could be performed, recorded and published without paying fees to the earlier song's creator, and indeed could itself be copyrighted. The most widely borrowed set of chord changes is from the chorus of 'I Got Rhythm' (1930) by George Gershwin, known as 'rhythm changes', used (sometimes in varied form) in Sidney Bechet's 'Shag' (1932), Lester Young's 'Lester Leaps In' (1939), Duke Ellington's 'Cotton Tail' (1940), Dizzy Gillespie's 'Salt Peanuts' (1942), Charlie Parker's 'Anthropology' (1945) and 'Moose the Mooche' (1946), Sonny Rollins's 'Oleo' (1954), Thelonious Monk's 'Rhythm-A-Ning' (1957) and countless others. The use of such borrowed chord progressions is reminiscent of the vogue for variations on the Romanesca and *Il Ballo del Gran Duca* in the sixteenth and seventeenth centuries, although there is apparently no historical connection.

E. Avant-Garde Borrowings

Despite the long history and varied types of borrowing outlined above, art music composers in the mid-twentieth century were so inculcated in the ethos of originality that some came to view explicit borrowing as an avant-garde gesture, a deliberate violation of ownership. Collage was one route, as in Berio's *Sinfonia*; another was to seek to renew music of the present by interweaving elements of the past, including borrowed material, with current sounds and techniques, as Peter Maxwell Davies (1934–2016) did in numerous works based on Gregorian chant, on Taverner's *Missa Gloria tibi trinitas* and on other medieval and Renaissance music.[30]

Perhaps most radical in undermining the authority of past works and composers was a kind of recomposition that might better be called *decomposition*, in which crucial elements of the source are effaced. In a piece that is more takedown than tribute, Maurizio Kagel marked Beethoven's bicentennial with *Ludwig van* for chamber ensemble (1970), remaking Beethoven's *Archduke* Trio and other works by disrupting the relationship between the players, each of whom proceeds at their own pace without regard to a common tempo, thereby eviscerating any drama or meaning in the music.[31] Refused permission to perform his two-piano transcription of Satie's *Socrate* to accompany choreography by Merce Cunningham, John Cage created *Cheap Imitation* (1970) by subjecting the main melody at each point in *Socrate* to segmentation, transposition and modal substitution through chance operations, creating a melodic line whose length, rhythm and phrasing preserved that of *Socrate* (and thus fit the choreography) but whose notes were new, making it usable for the performance without permission. His subsequent pieces *Some of 'The Harmony of Maine'* (1978) and *Hymns and Variations* (1979) were created from sacred choral works by New England composers Supply Belcher (1751–1836) and William Billings (1746–1800) using chance methods to remove random notes from the texture, as if erasing part of the music. In these works, not a note is by Cage, yet the pieces reflect his ideas and aesthetic rather than those of the composer of the source material.

[30] P Griffiths, *Modern Music: The Avant-Garde since 1945* (JM Dent & Sons, 1981) 189–95.

[31] This particularly describes the recorded version: M Kagel, *Ludwig van* (Deutsche Grammophon 2530 014, 1970). That Kagel leaves Beethoven's last name out of his title emphasises his desire to efface rather than celebrate his predecessor.

F. Reworking Recorded Music

All the techniques described above were invented for music that was improvised or notated and performed live, but most can also be created by manipulating music that was recorded, whether on record, film, tape, compact disc, DVD, digital sampler or other media. Contrafactum can be achieved through visual means, as in the YouTube classic 'O Fortuna Misheard Lyrics' (2012), which plays a recording of 'O Fortuna' from Carl Orff's *Carmina Burana* while showing comic words ('Gopher Tuna! Bring more tuna!') that closely track the sound of the original text; close your eyes and you hear the Latin words in the score, but watch the video and you cannot help but hear the words on the screen.[32] Splicing together fragments of a melody on tape or digital recording can be used to create a paraphrase of a familiar tune, as Karlheinz Stockhausen does with the German national anthem at one point in his tape piece *Hymnen* (1966–67).[33] Modern production techniques allow one to separate a melodic line from a source recording and give it a new setting, as in Natalie Cole's 1991 recording of 'Unforgettable', which alternates her voice with her father Nat King Cole's from his 1952 recording. Quotation by sampling is common today, pioneered decades ago in works like Simon and Garfunkel's 'Save the Life of My Child' (1968), a song about a suicidal teen which quotes the opening lines from their recording of 'The Sound of Silence' ('Hello darkness, my old friend, I've come to talk with you again'), emerging like a moment of revelation amid a dense musical texture. Samples are basic to hip-hop, which often features rapping over a repeating groove borrowed from older recordings, akin to a medieval motet tenor or a cantus firmus. Some music based on samples resembles patchwork or collage, assembling recorded material from multiple sources to create something new, as in Public Enemy's 'Fight the Power' or the 'Plunderphonics' of John Oswald. The smooth combination of disparate sources in the quodlibet tradition continues in the *mashup*, combining simultaneous layers from different recordings as in *The Grey Album* by Danger Mouse (Brian Burton), which mixes the vocal track of Jay-Z's *The Black Album* with segments of instrumental tracks from The Beatles' *White Album* reconfigured to fit, or stitching song fragments together both simultaneously and successively as in DJ Earworm's 'United State of Pop', an annual mashup of the year's 25 top pop songs in the USA (along with segments of their associated music videos).[34]

Given these historical echoes, there are also new possibilities and issues in borrowing recorded music itself rather than a melody or theme. The new possibilities lie in the technologies of recording and reproducing sound; cutting recorded pieces into segments, from long, recognisable excerpts to brief blips or pops whose sources can hardly be traced; and manipulating timbre, pitch, speed, volume and other parameters to produce sounds far from the original source. These have been explored using records, from Cage's use of recorded classical music as noise in his percussion piece *Credo in Us* (1942) to scratching LPs and 45s for rhythmic effects in early hip-hop; wire and tape recordings in Pierre Schaeffer's *musique concrète* and tape pieces by Cage, Stockhausen and others; and, since the 1970s and 1980s, digital sampling technology, which makes it possible (among other things) to fit the elements of a mashup smoothly together

[32] 'O Fortuna Misheard Lyrics', www.youtube.com/watch?v=nIwrgAnx6Q8.

[33] Griffiths (n 30) 211–12.

[34] JA Williams, *Rhymin' and Stealin': Musical Borrowing in Hip-Hop* (University of Michigan Press, 2013); R Walser, 'Rhythm, Rhyme, and Rhetoric in the Music of Public Enemy' (1995) 39 *Ethnomusicology* 193; K Holm-Hudson, 'Quotation and Context: Sampling and John Oswald's Plunderphonics' (1997) 7 *Leonardo Music Journal: Journal of the International Society for the Arts, Sciences, and Technology* 17; K Adams, 'What Did Danger Mouse Do?: *The Grey Album* and Musical Composition in Configurable Culture' (2015) 37 *Music Theory Spectrum* 7; DJ Earworm, *United State of Pop 2021–2007* (playlist) www.youtube.com/playlist?list=PLezvkLNQcE8q4Y9K3t3h6XG0N8qy_5ZvF.

by electronically changing them all into the same key and tempo or to drop a single note or sound into the texture.

The issues are not only aesthetic – how to use these new possibilities to create new and convincing music – but also legal, since recorded sound is usually under copyright and permissions can be hard to get, expensive or whimsically denied. As both musical and legal scholars have argued, current copyright law regards sampling as theft, ignoring the long and rich history of musical borrowing in the Western tradition and the creativity involved in reworking borrowed material. What needs to emerge is a legal framework that grants to creators the rights to their recorded music but also grants to others the right to borrow from it and rework it, perhaps through a mechanism for securing automatic permission from and paying appropriate fees to the originators of borrowed material.[35]

V. Conclusions

Borrowing has been a continuous thread in both art and popular music, manifested in a variety of ways. The centrality of borrowing throughout the history of Western music and the diversity of methods musicians have used to remake existing pieces as new ones suggest that the law must be flexible: making accommodations for borrowing, so that the tradition may continue, while recognising that current legal frameworks do not adequately address a musical world where not everything that is borrowed is a melody and not every form of borrowing is either quotation or plagiarism.

There are reasons for optimism. The essays in this book address numerous cases and types of borrowing and offer insight into how each can best be treated. More generally, along with the changes to the treatment of recorded sound suggested in the previous section, it may be possible to construct a comprehensive framework for how musicians may use copyrighted material by using the types of borrowing and reworking discussed here as guides. Arrangements and transcriptions are already covered by law and precedent, which can easily apply to contrafactum (treating the new work as an arrangement of the music but with new words) and instances of melodic paraphrase that change the melody relatively little, as well as to medley and pastiche (regarding the new work as a series of arrangements). Some forms of borrowing, such as parody (in the Rivers and Yankovic sense) and jazz contrafact, are already permitted under fair use (as is pastiche in the UK). Tanya Aplin and Lionel Bently have recently argued that there is a global fair use right to quote copyrighted works under Article 10(1) of the Berne Convention, if the material is attributed and is used in line with proportionality and fair practice.[36] Applied to music, this could cover most cases of quotation, patchwork, quodlibet, cantus firmus, using a borrowed melody as a theme and collage. Allusion, imitation of a model and decomposition are presumably permissible when the result is sufficiently distant from the source, and instances that involve direct borrowing may be covered by the right to quote unless extensive. Melodic paraphrase, recomposition, parody (in the Bach sense) and variations present more difficult cases, since the

[35] H Davies, 'A History of Sampling' (1996) 1 *Organised Sound: An International Journal of Music Technology* 3; Metzer (n 28) 160–87; C Cutler, 'Plunderphonia' in C Cox and D Warner (eds), *Audio Culture: Readings in Modern Music* (Continuum International, 2004) 138–56; OB Arewa, 'From J C Bach to Hip Hop: Musical Borrowing, Copyright, and Cultural Context' (2006) 84 *North Carolina Law Review* 547; J Boyle, J Jenkins and K Aoki, *Theft: A History of Music* (Duke Center for the Study of the Public Domain 2017) https://law.duke.edu/musiccomic.

[36] T Aplin and L Bently, *Global Mandatory Fair Use: The Nature and Scope of the Right to Quote Copyright Works* (Cambridge University Press, 2020).

amount of material used from the source is typically too extensive to be covered by the right to quote; perhaps, remembering Mattheson's comment that 'borrowing is permissible' if you 'return the thing borrowed with interest', these could be treated as types that require some permission (akin to arrangements) while also being recognised as works of art in themselves that deserve copyright protection in turn (as would a work that quotes), or even as examples of the 'transformative use' of copyrighted works allowed as fair use under copyright law in the USA. Whatever approaches are taken, the need is urgent to clarify the law and clear the way for continued creativity through musical borrowing in all its forms.

3

Litigating Musical Universals and Particulars: Copyright Law's Ontological Struggle with Music Borrowing

CHEN WEI ZHU

I. Introduction

This chapter explores copyright law's ongoing ontological struggle with the time-honoured practice of music borrowing. This struggle is torn between two competing metaphysical schools of thoughts – Platonism and nominalism – which have led to unresolved tensions in music copyright jurisprudence. The first school, also known as Platonic realism, treats music as *universals* that are abstract by nature with no spatio-temporal bound. The second school – whose music variant known as 'music nominalism' – holds that music exists only as concrete *particulars*, which are individually localised and embodied in written scores or performances. One of the main thrusts of this chapter is that there has been an increasing pressure from the previously under-examined nominalist ontological impulse in modern music copyright law, whereever smaller units of creations become localised as copyrightable materials. A nuanced understanding of this nominalist tendency would help to explain the metaphysical background for some doctrinal difficulties (especially the one on substantial taking) in legal disputes regarding music borrowing. The rest of the chapter is divided into three sections. Section II introduces the ontological struggle between music Platonism and musical nominalism, which respectively offer two competing visions about the existence (or non-existence) of musical works in philosophy and law. Section III traces contemporary Anglo-American copyright law's nominalist struggle with music borrowing back to the landmark case of *Arnstein v Porter* (1946), which established the controversial 'lay listener' test in the USA. The majority opinion, written by the fact-sceptical realist Judge Jerome Frank, is ontologically underpinned by an under-scrutinised nominalist commitment to copyrightable objects. I try to reveal that a nominalist music copyright regime can be pressured to individuate music objects for property protection, and these objects are nonetheless ontologically unstable and unpredictable in the realm of music borrowing. Furthermore, the attempt to distinguish permissible borrowing from illicit appropriation will be examined in a broader ontological context that deals with the age-old sorites paradox that tries to futilely tell a sand 'heap' apart from a 'non-heap'. Section IV concludes with a call for a departure from 'music borrowing' to 'music returning', whose concept needs to be reified for a balanced copyright ecosystem for nurturing and enriching interconnected music creativity.

II. Platonism versus Nominalism: Music as Universals and Particulars

Music copyright law's struggle with music borrowing is essentially an ontological one. It begs a set of fundamental metaphysical questions that have long bewildered philosophers since time immemorial: what is music? Is music 'discovered' or 'created' by human agencies? Do so-called 'musical works' exist as abstract universals or concrete particulars? Translating into something slightly more familiar to copyright lawyers, these questions can be reframed as follows: what is meant by music under copyright law? What can be qualified as 'musical works' that deserve copyright protection? What constitutes the smallest meaningful unit of music creations where copyright can subsist? What can be legitimately borrowed from pre-existing musical works without permission? How can a line be drawn between acceptable music borrowing and actionable copyright infringement?[1]

To tackle the above questions, it is useful to begin with a brief delineation of the two schools of metaphysics – Platonism and nominalism – that have offered competing views regarding the existence (or non-existence) of musical works either as abstract or concrete objects. The difference between these two schools would have many implications for the jurisprudence of music borrowing understood or misunderstood by copyright law, whose ontological struggle could adjust parameters for deciding protectable and non-protectable elements in given musical works. The following discussion attempts to show how Platonism fails to be an ontological fit for music copyright and how nominalism rises to dominate in contemporary aesthetics and copyright jurisprudence.

A. Platonism and Compositional Discovery

A critical examination of the *nominalist* impulse in modern music copyright would be impossible without exploring the plausibility of nominalism's opposite – ie the Platonic view of music – to explain the metaphysics of music copyright. The Platonic school believes that a 'real' thing can exist only as an abstract universal that has no spatio-temporal bound. This view is also often known as 'Platonic realism', which counterintuitively situates 'reality' in a transcendental abstract domain that is not empirically derived. For example, a Platonically perfect circle is a non-physical ideal form that exists transcendentally beyond space and time regardless of being made aware to people. In this mundane world, there can be a plethora of imperfect circles, which are merely inferior instantiations from, and approximations towards, the Platonically ideal circle. These instantiations, for instance, may be hand-drawn or computer-made circular graphs consisting of a finite (however large) number of dots, each of which strives to fit onto the curve of a Platonically perfect circle. They would result in many different imperfect physical renditions of an ideal circle. In other words, these scattered mundane-world dots arranged in a circular fashion constitute merely imperfect particulars that approximate to a Platonically perfect circle.

[1] These questions echo what Peter Burkholder calls the 'middle category' problem in music borrowing. This 'middle category' represents a big grey area sitting uncomfortably between clearly acceptable borrowing and clearly illegal plagiarism, and it makes copyright's struggle with music borrowing particularly difficult. 'It is the middle category, taking something from a specific piece of music and reworking it as part of a new piece, that presents a challenge to notions of intellectual property': JP Burkholder, 'A Brief History and Typology of Musical Borrowing and Reworking', ch 2 of this volume.

An important corollary from Platonic realism is the denial of the *creatability* or *inventability* of abstract objects, including music by humans: abstract objects are pre-existing universals and can only be *discovered* rather than created or invented, and can never be the product of individuals' intellectual creation. To illustrate, one may only discover a circle in its abstract form rather than create it. Similarly, music Platonism holds that musical works are pre-existing abstract Platonic objects that can only be discovered but not created or invented. Think about the vertical juxtaposition of the four musical notes F, B, D♯ and G♯ played together as a chord, which is immortalised in Richard Wagner's opera *Tristan und Isolyde*. These four notes form the longing and yearning leitmotif associated with the opera's protagonist Tristan, which gives it the name 'Tristan chord'.[2] According to the music Platonist Peter Kivy, the Tristan chord was merely 'discovered' rather than 'invented' by Wagner, and was the result of Wagner's 'compositional discovery':

> It seems to me quite plausible to regard [the Tristan chord] as a discovery of Wagner's rather his invention, although, of course, the discovery of that chord required the labor of more than one lifetime. Nor does it stagger the metaphysical imagination to picture the *Tristan* chord – that particular relationship of four pitches – as pre-existing its discovery, in the manner of a Platonic object. But, after all, the *Tristan* chord is part of a larger relationship of pitches called *Tristan under Isolde*.[3]

It is important to note that, from the Platonic viewpoint, an abstract object like the Tristan chord does not only pre-exist its compositional discovery, but also post-exists the demise of any of its concrete instantiations embodied in performances or score copies, whose existence is regarded as ephemeral. This means an abstract music object is not only uncreatable but also indestructible. According to Kivy, the Tristan chord is immortal and immutable in the sense that it cannot be destroyed even after its physical instantiations are gone. Its Platonic existence is independent from and unaffected by people's awareness (or the lack) of this music object.[4] In short, music Platonism is committed to the belief that music exists eternally as abstract universals rather than ephemeral concreta in a spatio-temporally bounded format.

It is not difficult to see that music Platonism is ontologically incompatible with the normal regulatory mode of copyright law that gives protection to *individually created* works. Modern copyright law seems to commit itself to an ontological presumption that all copyright works are capable of being *created* and *owned* by their human creators. Around the world, a foundational doctrine of copyright is to protect creatorship rather than discovership. For example, under the UK's copyright act, an 'author' 'means the person who *creates*' (emphasis added) a work.[5] Similarly, the European Union's copyright law is based on a form of what I call *intellectual creationism*, which overtly requires protectable subject matters to be based on authors' 'intellectual creation'.[6] Clearly copyright law's underlying ontology regarding protectable subject matters does not tally well with the Platonic metaphysics. In a Platonic world, where works are merely

[2] The Tristan chord is also known as the F half-diminished chord and is notable for its discomforting dissonance and tonal ambiguity. It is one of the most studied chords in music history. See, eg J Rothgeb, 'The Tristan Chord: Identity and Origin' (1995) 1 *Music Theory Online*, https://mtosmt.org/issues/mto.95.1.1/mto.95.1.1.rothgeb.html; E Reiman, 'The "Tristan Chord" as Music-Historical Metaphor' (1998) 67 *University of Toronto Quarterly* 768; J Kennedy, M Kennedy and T Rutherford-Johnson (eds), 'Tristan Chord' in *The Oxford Dictionary of Music* (Oxford University Press, 2013) www.oxfordreference.com/view/10.1093/acref/9780199578108.001.0001/acref-9780199578108-e-10383.

[3] P Kivy, 'Platonism in Music: A Kind of Defense' (1983) 19 *Grazer Philosophische Studien* 109, 118.

[4] 'But if the *Tristan* chord existed before it was thought of or notated, why should it cease to be when all notations, performances, and memories of it pass away? If it existed before anyone ever was aware of it, why should its existence be influenced by our ceasing to be aware of it?' ibid 119.

[5] Copyright, Designs and Patents Act (CDPA) 1988, s 9(1).

[6] See, eg Case C-5/08 *Infopaq v Danske* [2009] ECR I-6569; Case C-145/10 *Painer v Standard Verlags GmbH* [2012] E.CDR. 6.

'discovered' from pre-existing universals, there would be no place for intellectual creationism. This is because no individual 'creations' would be confidently credited to, let alone owned by, any human 'discovers'. No Platonic music discoverers would be regarded as fully autonomous agents who can carve out 'works' that have individuated identities. In fact, these 'works' in question are no more than imperfect and ephemeral instantiations of pre-existing Platonic ideals. In short, it would be ontologically absurd for any compositional discoveries to be subject to copyright protection as there could be no ownership right in Platonic music ideals. This misfit between music Platonism and copyright law naturally leads me to an exploration of Platonism's archenemy, which is the nominalist approach to music.

B. Music Nominalism and Copyright Law

In contrast to Platonic realism, the school of nominalism offers a devastatingly revolutionary view about the reality (or, more precisely, the *unreality*) of abstract universals. Nominalism is said to be 'parsimonious' in the ontological sense[7] as it avoids bringing in abstract universal entities, which are deemed unnecessary for understanding the world around us. This is precisely what Ockham's nominalist razor intends to do: avoid multiplying needless universals.[8] Historically, nominalism served as a theological reaction against Platonic scholasticism. Unsurprisingly, one of the most prominent nominalist revolutionaries was the Franciscan friar William of Ockham from England, who, apart from inventing the eponymous Ockham's razor, also set in motion a nominalist revolution towards a radically individualised modern world for better or worse.[9]

Nominalism arguably liberates *individual* things from those totalitarian and absolutist Platonic universals, which are perceived to be non-existent ontologically. It holds the belief that Platonic universals are no more than replaceable linguistic terms and they do not deserve a *real* existential status. Instead, what is deemed to exist are those individuated concrete *particulars* situated in a given spatio-temporal framework. Universal abstract objects are thus dismissed as merely figments of Platonists' wishful imagination. For example, the nominalist school would see a purportedly perfect circle in a different way than Platonism. From a nominalist point of view, the Platonic ideal of a perfect circle beyond time and space can be imaginary and delusional. Only individual circles, however imperfect they may be, exist as concrete things in this mundane world. Similarly, a nominalist musical work, not unlike those connected dots making up individual circles, would only exist through concrete individual performances (live or recorded), score copies or other physical forms made up of music notes, however ephemeral these instantiations may exist in a given time and space.

In the following two sub-sections, I will explore the nominalist individuation of musical works and its consequence for copyright law through the ontological lens offered by Nelson Goodman, whose sharp analysis on music nominalism has proven to be both influential and controversial for contemporary philosophy of art.

[7] 'The chief arguments in nominalism's favor are that it does not traffic in anything except seen, concrete entities, that it is ontologically parsimonious, and that all forms of realism are saddled with grievous problems': M Wreen, 'The Ontology of Intellectual Property' (2010) 93 *The Monist* 433, 441.

[8] Gillespie observes that 'the guiding principle of nominalist logic for Ockham was his famous razor: do not multiply universals needlessly. While we cannot, as finite beings, make sense of the world without universals, every generalization takes us one more step away from the real. Hence, the fewer we employ the closer we remain to the truth': MA Gillespie, *The Theological Origins of Modernity* (University of Chicago Press, 2008) 23.

[9] ibid.

C. Goodman's Music Nominalism: A Score-Centric View

Nelson Goodman (1906–98) was an American analytical philosopher who left an indelible intellectual legacy on, among many other things, contemporary philosophy of art and aesthetics.[10] As a committed philosophical nominalist, Goodman did not see music as transcendental Platonic objects[11] that exist outside time and space. A musical work, from a Goodmanian viewpoint, only exists when it is realised through a notational system – ie a music score[12] – and corresponding performances. These performances would together form a compliance class of the given score. A Goodmanian musical work is different from a Platonic one because it is individualised and particularised through a work-defining score, which symbolically represents music. This view is in line with Goodman's nominalistic *Weltanschauung* in general. Goodman declared: 'For me, as a nominalist, the world is a world of individuals.'[13] Goodman further commented that his nominalist commitment 'demands only that all entities admitted, no matter what they are, be treated as individuals'.[14]

Following Goodman's individualistic ontology, a musical work cannot be a universal abstractum, but needs to be separated as a self-contained individual entity existing in a spatio-temporal framework. A music notation system, according to Goodman, is argued to be a primary, if not the only, vehicle for such nominalistic individuation. In this sense, it is those individuated music concreta (including individual music scores and those scores' compliance classes consisting of individual performances) that constitute a musical work rather than the other way round. Cohnitz and Rossberg correctly point out that Goodmanian musical works cannot be self-standing abstract objects, but are constituted by concreta embodied in scores and performances:

> Scores are symbols in the notation system. They have performances as their compliance-classes. There is nothing more to a work of music than the various physical objects that are notations of a correct performance, and the correct performance of physical sound waves, which accord to the notations. The performances are performances of the score, and the scores are notations of the performances; they together constitute the work. There is not in addition a third thing that they are performances and notations of.[15]

In a Goodmanian music universe, instances of musical performances are not seen as hierarchically subordinate to the musical 'work' concept. There is no vertical relation between a 'work' and its performing instances as in a Platonic hierarchy between an abstractum and its concrete instantiations. In the same way, Goehr points out that a music nominalist considers, instead, 'the *horizontal* relations obtaining between performances and score-copies'.[16]

D. Goodmanism in Copyright History: *Bach v Longman* (1777)

In music copyright history, Goodman's score-centric model of musical-work-making – ie the nominalistic mode of music individuation through written scores – can be stretched back at least

[10] D Cohnitz and M Rossberg, *Nelson Goodman* (Acumen, 2006); D Cohnitz and M Rossberg, 'Nelson Goodman' in EN Zalta (ed), *The Stanford Encyclopedia of Philosophy* (Summer edn, 2019) https://plato.stanford.edu/archives/sum2019/entries/goodman/.

[11] N Goodman, *Languages of Art: An Approach to a Theory of Symbols* (Hackett Publishing, 1968); N Goodman, *Problems and Projects* (Bobbs-Merrill, 1972) ch IV.

[12] 'A score is a character in a notational system': Goodman, *Languages of Art* (n 11) 177.

[13] Goodman, *Problems and Projects* (n 11) 155.

[14] ibid 157.

[15] Cohnitz and Rossberg (n 10) 180.

[16] L Goehr, *The Imaginary Museum of Musical Works: An Essay in the Philosophy of Music* (Oxford University Press, 1992) 17.

to the late eighteenth century. In 1777, Lord Mansfield handed down the landmark ruling in *Bach v Longman*, where he explicitly recognised JC Bach's private ownership of his music compositions as notated 'signs and marks'.[17]

Conventionally, *Bach v Longman* is seen as an early landmark ruling where a major legal system formally gave copyright protection to some musical works.[18] However, the significance of the *Bach* ruling should go well beyond the invention of a new copyrightable subject matter, ie music. I argue that this ruling is not just doctrinally significant, but it also has a revolutionary ontological significance, which tends to be overlooked by lawyers and philosophers alike. The 1777 ruling by Mansfield should be seen as the first one of its kind that explicitly embraced the score-centric music nominalism into copyright law. Anachronistically speaking, Mansfield's judicial conception of music falls neatly under Goodman's ontological model that treats music as a notational system made of symbols. According to Mansfield, symbolically represented music should be protected by copyright law, because it was made of textual objects that represent a form of 'writings' recognised by the Statute of Anne:

> The words of the Act of Parliament are very large: 'books and other writings'. It is not confined to language or letters. Music is a science; it may be written; and the mode of conveying the ideas, is by *signs and marks* … If the narrow interpretation contended for in the argument were to hold, it would equally apply to algebra, mathematics, arithmetic, hieroglyphics. All these are conveyed by *signs and figures* … a musical composition is a *writing* within the Statute of the 8th of Queen Anne. (emphasis added)[19]

The above reasoning was significant not merely because it firmly established for the first time music as an eligible subject matter for copyright protection; more importantly, it also posits a *nominalistic* principle whereby protectable musical works were required to have individuated identity through written scores. This nominalistic jurisprudence makes copyright characteristically different from the earlier royal privileges – also known as 'warrants' or 'patents'[20] – given to artists by the Crown. These royal privileges were not modern in the sense that they were not issued to protect clearly individuated works. Instead, their blanket coverage could cover a range of specified and unspecified works. Royal privileges were not guided by any nominalistic doctrines because their subject matters were often insufficiently individuated and lacked clearly demarcated boundaries required by the kind of individualistic private ownership rights more familiar to the modern copyright system. It is interesting to note that, only one year after the plaintiff JC Bach arrived in England in 1762, he also managed to secured a non-nominalistic Royal Warrant (dated 15 December 1763) issued by the then monarch, who forbade his subjects

> to reprint, abridge, copy out in writing for sale, or publish the same, either in the like or in any other size or manner whatsoever, or to import, buy, vend, utter or distribute any copy or copies thereof, reprinted or written, for sale beyond the seas.

The whole Warrant reads:

> Whereas our trusty and well-beloved John Christian Bach, gent., has by his petition humbly represented unto Us that he hath, with great study, labour and expense composed *divers works* consisting

[17] *Bach v Longman* 2 Cowper 623 (1777) 98 Eng rep.

[18] In the UK, the 1709 Statute of Anne did not explicitly cover music; it only covered literary works. Mansfield's ruling extended copyright protection to music for the first time in the UK. See J Small, 'JC Bach Goes to Law' (1985) 126 *The Musical Times* 526; A van Allen-Russell, '"For Instruments Not Intended": The Second JC Bach Lawsuit' (2002) 83 *Music & Letters* 3.

[19] *Bach v Longman* (n 17).

[20] These terms were used interchangeably. S Rogers, 'The Use of Royal Licences for Printing in England, 1695–1760: A Bibliography' (2000) 1 *The Library* 133, 136.

> of Vocal and Instrumental Music, and being desirous to print the same, and apprehending, unless he can obtain our Royal Licence and Privilege, other persons may be induced to print and publish the said works, and so invade his property therein, he hath therefore most humbly prayed Us to grant him our Royal Licence and Privilege for the sole printing and publishing of the above mentioned Works for the term of fourteen years agreeable to the Statute in that case made and provided. We, being willing to give all due encouragement to this his undertaking, are graciously pleased to condescend to his request, and We do therefore, by these Presents, so far as may be agreable to the Statute in that behalf made and provided, grant unto him, the said John Christian Bach, his Executors, Administrators … (emphasis added)[21]

It is worth noting that Bach's Royal Warrant used similar boilerplate terms to those appearing in the royal music privilege granted to George Frideric Handel over four decades before, in 1720.[22] Bach's music partner Abel secured a similar royal patent in 1760 (three years earlier than Bach).[23] These royal licences were pre-modern in the sense that they were not nominalistic devices protecting musical works with clearly individuated legal identities. The terms in these licences were deliberately vague and often failed to specify which individual works were to be protected. Unlike the later copyright system, they tended to cover a collection of unindividuated works vaguely called 'divers works' or 'several pieces of musick', some of which might not even have been produced by a given composer at the time when the licence was granted.

Under any modern nominalistic copyright system, it would be much more difficult to give legal protection to something not yet fully completed or 'works' in question that have not yet gained individuated identities. In contrast, during JC Bach's time (when the music copyright system did not yet operate under a fully nominalistic mode), it was not unusual for a composer to have their unfinished or yet-to-be-composed works retrospectively protected by such pre-nominalist royal privileges. For example, George Frideric Handel managed to use his 1720 music warrant to prospectively protect his three-act opera seria *Rodelinda*, which was only finished in 1725 (ie five years after the grant).[24] This means *Rodelinda* was not a completed individual work firmly fixed onto a tangible medium (as 'writings') when the privilege was first granted to Handel. John Small rightly points out the 'divers works' wording enabled a royal grantee to gain more extended and flexible protection because such privilege 'could be printed together with music composed years later, perhaps giving potential pirate the impression that the new publication was protected or partly protected by that privilege'.[25]

The *Bach* ruling was by no means the first judicial authority that employed the nominalist principle to afford private ownership to individuated written works made up of marks and signs. Ironically, eight years before *Bach*, a thoughtfully nominalist account of individuated 'intellectual

[21] This Royal Warrant was reproduced in CS Terry, *John Christian Bach* (Oxford University Press, 1929) 78–79; Terry observes that JC Bach's 'popularity as a composer, and the necessity to protect himself against the piracy of unlicensed printers, are evident' from this Royal Warrant (78). The same licence was also reprinted in H Gärtner, *John Christian Bach: Mozart's Friend and Mentor* (RG Pauly trans, Amadeus Press, 1994) 187, where Gartner argues that the 'document is impressive evidence of the interest and care the young royal couple, aged twenty-five and nineteen bestowed on the twenty-eight-year-old Christian'.

[22] J Small, 'The Development of Musical Copyright' in M Kassler (ed), *The Music Trade in Georgian England* (Ashgate, 2011) 284.

[23] Kassler believes that the royal music licence could be a main reason why Bach himself never registered his works at the Stationers' Company for statutory copyright protection. M Kassler, *Music Entries at Stationers' Hall, 1710–1818* (Ashgate, 2004). In 1774, the House of Lord's ruling in *Donaldson vs Beckett* extinguished common law copyright in published works in favour of statutory copyright. This legal development might give enough worry to Bach, who believed that his music would be deprived of common law protection. Small, 'JC Bach Goes to Law' (n 18) 528.

[24] Small, 'The Development of Musical Copyright' (n 22) 284.

[25] ibid.

property' was already present in Justice Yates's dissenting opinion against Mansfield's majority opinion in *Millar v Taylor* in 1769. Yates felt deeply uncomfortable with the idea of giving property rights to unindividuated creations that were not fixed with reasonably clear-cut boundaries:

> But the property here claimed is all *ideal*; a set of ideas which *have no bounds or marks whatsoever, nothing that is capable of visible possession, nothing that can sustain any one of the qualities or incidents of property*. Their whole existence is in the mind alone; incapable of any other modes of acquisition or enjoyment than by mental possession or apprehension; safe and invulnerable, from their own immateriality: no trespass can reach them; no tort affect them; no fraud or violence diminish or damage them. Yet these are the phantoms which the author would grasp and confine to himself: and these are what the defendant is charged with having robbed the plaintiff of. (emphasis added)[26]

Yates's dissenting opinion in *Millar* implies an inchoate nominalist principle negatively formulated for eighteenth-century copyright law: unindividuated human creations that lacked clearly defined *physical* boundaries should not be protected. Barron rightly points out that Yates's concern reveals the 'physicalist' obsession of the common law of property, 'which had initially developed to deal with competing claims to *tangible* things, primarily land':

> The questions that plagued the participants in the literary property debate were accordingly the following: how can those aspects of a text that are uniquely attributable to its author (and so amenable to the author's exclusive control) be reliably distinguished from those that result from the effects on the author of the works of others (and so are someone else's private property), or his/her general education (and so form part of the 'public domain' of ideas)? And relatedly, where does a text begin and end? Where are the boundaries or fence posts of this *res* and what would constitute a trespass upon it?[27]

It is not often noticed, but Yates's argument against literary property in non-individuated 'ideal' creations is actually a nominalistic one from the metaphysical point of view: an abstract textual object in its airy-fairy 'ideal' form does not deserve private property protection because it is not sufficiently individuated or particularised as a self-contained protectable thing.

Going beyond Yates's nominalist questioning, later developments of copyright law further interestingly show that the emerging 'intellectual' property (literary, musical or otherwise in individuated creations) becomes less concerned about its subject matters' *physical* or *immaterial* status.[28] Instead, copyright law becomes so forcefully driven by its nominalist obsession with *particularisation* that even some immaterial creations may get protection if they can be made particularistic enough.[29] In music borrowing copyright litigations, selective uses of forensic musicological methods are partially responsible for individuating or particularising new and sometimes exotic music objects (eg music grooves and feels) for copyright protection. Forensic musicologists, in an increasingly adversarial litigation environment, can be incentivised to invent 'constellations' of music similarities as new protectable copyright subject matters.[30] The following section will focus on some of the ontological challenges posed by music borrowing to copyright law in particularising music objects.

[26] *Millar v Taylor* (1769) 4 Burr 2361.

[27] A Barron, 'Copyright Law's Musical Work' (2006) 15 *Social & Legal Studies* 101, 112.

[28] For the intellectualiation or immaterialisation of IP in Britain, see B Sherman and L Bently, *The Making of Modern Intellectual Property Law: The British Experience, 1760–1911* (Cambridge University Press, 1999).

[29] See, eg Griffith's critique of the dematerialiatioin of European copyright subject matters. J Griffiths, 'Dematerialization, Pragmatism and the European Copyright Revolution' (2013) 33 *OJLS* 767.

[30] See, eg Madison and Lombardi's critique of forensic methodologies used in the 'Blurred Line' case. A Madison and P Lombardi, 'Blurred Justice' (2019) 39 *Loyola of Los Angeles Entertainment Law Review* 145. See also Bennett's critique of 'hired gun' musicology in this volume.

III. Nominalism Recalibrated: Music Borrowing and Copyright Law

The metaphysics of music borrowing hinges on a similar ontological question to that concerning the individuality of musical works, as discussed before. In the copyright context, this question needs to be only slightly reformulated for the purpose of our query: what can be counted as individuated units of music creation, the *borrowing* of which may constitute copyright infringement? By way of comparison, the ontology of musical works (as discussed above) concerns *copyright subsistence* by asking what can be regarded as individual protectable musical 'works'. In contrast, the ontology of music borrowing is more directly linked to *copyright infringement* parameters by asking how much music creation can legitimately be 'borrowed' without infringing copyright. Conversely, when will music borrowing amount to illegitimate appropriation that leads to copyright infringement?

A. Music Nominalism and Music Borrowing

It is first worth finding out which of the two aforementioned ontological approaches to music – ie Platonism and nominalism – would be a better fit for music borrowing related to copyright infringement. First, according to the Platonist position, there would be no music 'creations' but only compositional 'discoveries' in the first place. Since music as Platonic universals cannot be *created*, it is not *ownable* by any individual human musicians.[31] Logically, then, it would be impossible and unnecessary to 'borrow' from a party who does not create and own their Platonically 'discovered' music. This is simply because music discoveries only give rise to mere instantiations (rather than partial or full reproduction) of those non-ownable Platonic music universals. Ontologically, music borrowing would not happen in this Platonic context as nothing is created or owned in the first place.

In contrast, nominalism seems to provide a more plausible ontological scaffolding for understanding music borrowing and related infringement issues. There are at least two reasons for this. First, music nominalism acknowledges that music can be created and owned so long as a piece of music creation is sufficiently individuated by one or more human authors. Second, nominalism can also explain why protection should be given to a *borrowed* portion from an existing work if this portion forms a *substantial* part of the borrowed source work.[32]

The nominalist approach, though useful for understanding copyright law's ontological struggle with music borrowing, is not entirely unproblematic. I will try to show, in the following two sub-sections, a nominalist legal object is inherently indeterminate and unstable as it is *particularisable* by human creators in an almost unlimited number of ways. This is especially true when a court needs to assess the degree of borrowing, ranging from *de minimis* to substantial taking, for establishing copyright infringement. In short, unlike Platonic music universals – which are by nature immutable and immune from human interventions – nominalist objects from a borrowed work are ontologically malleable and mutable, which is why there can be even more legal uncertainty surrounding music borrowing disputes.

[31] See s II(A) above.

[32] See sub-s III(C) below for a more detailed exploration of substantiality in music copyright law.

B. The *Arnstein* Test and its Nominalist Implications

In music borrowing cases, music nominalism inevitably breeds uncertainties when deciding what can be individuated as a protectable unit comprising creative elements from a borrowed work. Against this backdrop, I will show the landmark 1946 ruling in *Arnstein v Porter* by the USA's 2nd Circuit Federal Court represents one of the most difficult but influential ontological struggles with music borrowing in Anglo-American copyright law. The majority ruling, authored by the legal realist judge Jerome Frank, has left an interesting nominalist legacy[33] for music borrowing, whose legal and ontological significance will be explored here.

In *Arnstein*, the destitute plaintiff songwriter Ira Arnstein (1879–1956) sued the established and commercially successful musician Cole Porter (1891–1964) after a series of litigations against other Tin Pan Alley composers. Arnstein alleged Porter illicitly accessed and copied his works. Arnstein's claim was denied at the trial court as his story of Porter hiring 'stooges' to steal his music from his apartment was too strange or 'fantastic' to be true.[34] However, at the appellate court, Judge Jerome Frank disagreed with the trial court by reminding that 'sometimes truth is stranger than fiction' and the plaintiff Arnstein should not be denied the opportunity of having a full jury trial for finding facts that could possibly lead to copyright infringement (however small the chance of the plaintiff's success was). Most significantly, Frank crafted the so-called Arnstein test, which would become hugely important (and controversial) for adjudicating music-borrowing-related copyright infringement cases. According to Frank, the Arnstein test comprises two 'separate elements', known as (i) 'copying' and (ii) 'improper appropriation':

> In applying that standard here, it is important to avoid confusing two separate elements essential to a plaintiff's case in such a suit: (a) that defendant copied from plaintiff's copyrighted work and (b) that the copying (assuming it to be proved) went so far as to constitute improper appropriation.[35]

Unsurprisingly, these two elements also have nominalist implications that need to be spelt out. First, the element of 'copying' requires an individual work to be independently created rather than 'caused' by an earlier musical work. This is to ensure that an original work comes from identifiable authorial origins. This is the place where nominalism meets the Romantic aesthetics, which has put individual creators firmly on an authorial pedestal since the late eighteenth century in the Western world.[36] Nominalism and Romanticism share an ontological obsession with individuality. For nominalism, creative works gain their individuality by having reasonably definable boundaries. As mentioned above, the boundary of a Goodmanian musical work is defined and fixed by music scores. For Romanticism, individuality means the authorial autonomy defined by a creator's unique personality. This would only be possible when an author makes an independent creation without copying from an earlier work.

After the first element of the Arnstein test (ie copying) is proven, what needs to be established for the second element is 'improper appropriation', which will eventually lead to the establishment of copyright infringement.[37] Frank pointed out that not all copying was illicit; some could

[33] Famous music borrowing cases that were influenced by *Arnstein* include *Bright Tunes Music Corp v Harrisongs Music, Ltd* (1976) 420 F supp 177; *Three Boys Music Corp v Bolton* (2000) 212 F 3d 477; *Williams v Gaye* (2018) 895 F 3d 1106.

[34] *Arnstein v Porter* (1946) 154 F 2d 464. For Arnstein's life as a musician and copyright litigant, see G Rosen, *Unfair to Genius: The Strange and Litigious Career of Ira B Arnstein* (Oxford University Press, 2012).

[35] *Arnstein v Porter* (n 34) 468. For a critique of this test, see also J Bennett, 'We Can Work It Out: Methods in Forensic Musicology', ch 4 of this volume.

[36] For the development of Romanticism and copyright law, see Woodmansee's foundational work: M Woodmansee, 'The Genius and the Copyright: Economic and Legal Conditions of the Emergence of the 'Author'' (1984) 17 *Eighteenth-Century Studies* 425.

[37] Frank also calls the second element 'illicit copying' or 'unlawful appropriation'. *Arnstein v Porter* (n 34) 468.

be 'permissible'. To distinguish 'permissible copying' from illicit copying was a matter of fact that needed to be tried by juries: 'Whether (if he copied) defendant unlawfully appropriated presents, too, an issue of fact.'[38] Judge Frank therefore prescribed a lay listener test for adjudicating issues related to illicit copying. The question depends on 'whether defendant took from plaintiff's works so much of *what is pleasing to the ears of lay listeners*, who comprise the audience for whom such popular music is composed, that defendant wrongfully appropriated something which belongs to the plaintiff' (emphasis added).[39]

When dealing with improper appropriation, Frank put lay listeners' judgement over musical experts' testimonies. The fulcrum of the balance was put on 'what is pleasing to the ears of lay listeners' rather than experts' forensic musical analysis, which was dismissed as 'irrelevant'.[40] Frank's music nominalism is slightly more radical than Goodman's nominalism. It moves away from the Goodmanian composer-centric ontology[41] towards a listener-centric one. By putting emphasis on 'what is pleasing to the ears of lay listeners', it created two different tiers of music nominalism: one based on cold forensic dissection mastered by a selected group of music experts and another based on lay listeners' more direct and less mediated responses to music. The former is about rationally construing the individuality of music creations from music experts' point of view, while the latter comes from listeners' pleasure-based and non-intellectual appreciation of popular music as consumer products. Interestingly, Frank's nominalist commitment to listeners' auditory pleasure may inadvertently stray into the firing line of the social theorist Theodor Adorno, who criticised music consumers' 'regression of listening' in the contemporary age of mass culture.[42] This is made obvious by Judge Clark, who, in his dissenting opinion, called Frank's majority opinion 'anti-intellectual and book-burning'[43] right because of Frank's scepticism of experts' music analyses and endorsement of non-expert listeners' auditory-pleasure-based judgement.[44]

C. (Im)permissible Borrowing and the Sorites Paradox

Both of the elements in the Arnstein test need to be calibrated through the quantitative or qualitative measurement of *music similarity*, the concept of which has long been elusive and difficult to apply in music borrowing copyright disputes. Conceptually, it is important to differentiate music similarity into two types: the first is what Latman calls 'probative similarity',[45] which infers copying, while the second is 'substantial similarity', which establishes improper appropriation after the first is proven.[46] These two types are different not in *musical* terms, but in *legal* terms.

[38] ibid 472–73.

[39] ibid 473.

[40] ibid 468.

[41] As is shown above, Goodman's nominalist ontology is focused on music scores and it is compatible with the so-called *Werktreue* (fidelity to work) ideology.

[42] TW Adorno, 'On the Fetish Character in Music and the Regression of Listening (1938)' in A Arato and E Gebhardt (eds), *The Essential Frankfurt School Reader* (Blackwell, 1978) 286.

[43] *Arnstein v Porter* (n 34) 478.

[44] In the age of social media, music consumers' 'regressive' listening habits are becoming ever more visible with online streaming services such as Spotify. The task of fully analysing Frank's music nominalism from an Adornoian perspective is beyond the scope of this chapter, but I intend to research it in the future. For Adorno's view on musical nominalism, see M Jay, 'Adorno and Musical Nominalism' (2016) 43 *New German Critique* 5.

[45] A Latman, 'Probative Similarity as Proof of Copying: Toward Dispelling Some Myths in Copyright Infringement' (1990) 90 *Columbia Law Review* 1187.

[46] It is worth noting that Frank did not use these two terms for labelling the two prongs of the Arnstein test; the labels were only used later by either Frank himself or others after the *Arnstein* ruling. See ibid 1191–204.

In a music borrowing dispute, a complaining work and a defending work are identified with the same constellation of similar musical (eg melodic, harmonic, rhythmic or other) features, but they play two rather different legal functions. The first-type similarity corresponds to the first element of the Arnstein test, and it plays a 'probative' function for establishing that a defending piece has *copied* a complaining piece. Latman defines 'probative similarity' as one 'that under all the circumstances justifies an inference of copying'.[47] The proving of probative similarity does not necessarily lead to copyright infringement, because this type of similarity may be too trivial or insubstantial to prove such infringement. It is the second type – ie substantial similarity – that makes a defendant liable. Furthermore, substantial similarity can be proven on its own without the use of probative similarity if copying could be proven otherwise.[48] In other words, probative similarity is not the only route to prove copying and there is no need to have what Frank calls 'double-purpose' music similarity to prove both copying and improper appropriation:

> In some cases, the similarities between the plaintiff's and defendant's work are so extensive and striking as, without more, both to justify an inference of copying and to prove improper appropriation. But such *double-purpose* evidence is not required; that is, if copying is otherwise shown, proof of improper appropriation need not consist of similarities which, standing alone, would support an inference of copying. (emphasis added)[49]

The second element of the Arnstein test assesses how *substantial* the amount of copying needs to be in order to constitute copyright infringement. It is worth noting Frank did not explicitly use the term 'substantial' in *Arnstein*, but he mentioned it in a later case, where he argued that copying needed to be 'so "material" or "substantial" as to constitute unlawful appropriation'.[50] Applying the Arnstein test to music borrowing, one can tell that not all music borrowing will be actionable copyright infringement, and all borrowing activities must already involve some degree of copying (which can be either conscious or subconscious). Only substantial borrowing – ie those borrowing activities that take what is regarded as substantial – would constitute improper, illicit or unlawful appropriation. From a forensic musicological perspective, Bennett believes that Frank's two elements are artificially separated, but they can be combined into a single reformulated question surrounding substantiality: 'is a substantial part of a protectable element of Song B copied from Song A?'[51]

Although I agree that Bennett's reformulation is conceptually clearer and more helpful for forensic musicological practice, this deceptively simple question regarding substantiality does not entirely dispel the ontological problem that copyright law needs to struggle with. This is because substantiality is an inherently unstable and unpredictable product constructed by modern copyright's nominalistic quest for individuating elements of existing works for protection. Nominalistically speaking, there can be an almost unlimited number of ways of doing such individuation. The use of substantiality for finding copyright infringement can often be more indeterminate than that of the 'work' concept for establishing copyright subsistence. A copyrighted 'work' in question is likely to have a reasonably fixed textual boundary, which is created by its own author(s) and known to the public when this work is completed. When a musical work in question is composed, its boundary can be drawn by having either a *symbolic* representation (eg music scores) or a *sonic* representation (eg recorded performances) of the music. In contrast, what amounts to a 'substantial' part in a musical work is unlikely to be specified at the time when

[47] ibid 1190.
[48] For example, a party may explicitly acknowledge that there has been copying of or access to an earlier work.
[49] *Arnstein v Porter* (n 34) 469.
[50] Frank wrote this only a few days after the *Arnstein* ruling: *Heim v Universal Pictures Co* (1946) 154 F 2d 480, 487.
[51] See Bennett, ch 4 of this volume.

the musical work is scored or recorded (nor does it need to be). The uncertainty and indeterminacy surrounding substantiality concerns not just the defending music borrower, but also the complaining composer, who is unlikely to be absolutely certain whether the part of their work that has been taken is considered substantial or not until the issue is fully litigated.

The uncertainty surrounding substantial borrowing as improper appropriation is not simply a legal puzzle, but should also be seen as resulting from the age-old ancient Greek paradox known as the 'sorites paradox', which concerns all things with fuzzy boundaries. There are numerous formulations of the sorites paradox, which is also known as the 'paradox of the heap'.[52] Here is a commonly told version of the paradox: suppose there is an extremely small heap of sand, with only 1000 grains. If someone keeps taking one grain at a time from this heap, then at what point will this heap cease to be a heap? It is relatively certain that we can regard 999 or 998 grains still as a heap, albeit a smaller one than the original, but would we treat just nine or eight grains as a heap? What about 10, 20, 30 or 40 grains? Where is the cut-off point? Are we able to find such a threshold point at all?

To nominalistically preserve the individual identity of score-based music, Nelson Goodman provides one of the most notorious solutions in attempting to solve or avoid the sorites paradox in the music ontological context. Goodman's music nominalism prescribes a stringent requirement demanding all music performances to comply strictly with a music score, which is held to be the primary device to individuate music creation. If a performer plays one single scored note wrong from Beethoven's Fifth Symphony, then this minor non-compliance would disqualify this performance from being called a member of the compliance class in a work known as Beethoven's Fifth Symphony. Goodman argues:

> If we allow the least deviation, all assurance of work-preservation and score-preservation is lost; for by a series of one-note errors of omission, addition, and modification, we can go all the way from Beethoven's *Fifth Symphony* to *Three Blind Mice*.[53]

In short, Goodman's approach to musical works is indeed driven by a fear of the sorites paradox, because he is worried that a gradual relaxation of his score-centrism may cause the eventual loss of individuality of a given musical work. Goehr points out that Goodman's strategy here is to avoid stipulating 'arbitrary cutoff points' and this is consistent with his music nominalism: 'It is designed also to prevent overlap between works, sharply individuating one from another; hence [Goodman's] fine-grained specification of syntactic and semantic conditions made consistent with his strict nominalist and extensionalist commitments.'[54]

Goodman's theoretical analysis does not go beyond a nominalist account of musical work, because it fails to delve further into ontological issues related to *music similarity* and *improper appropriation*. Understandably, music borrowing and copyright law is not a focus of Goodman's philosophy of art, but I believe it is necessary to reveal a similar paradoxical conundrum surrounding *substantial borrowing*, though there can be no easy doctrinal solution to this paradox.

The sorites paradox also exists in music borrowing because there exists a spectrum between *de minimis* borrowing and substantial borrowing, and the former is legally permissible while the latter is not. For example, a musician is certainly allowed to legally borrow two consecutive notes

[52] The Greek word *soros* simply means 'heap'. D Hyde and D Raffman, 'Sorites Paradox' in EN Zalta (ed), *The Stanford Encyclopedia of Philosophy* (Summer edn, 2018) https://plato.stanford.edu/archives/sum2018/entries/sorites-paradox/; see also Goehr's analysis of the sorites paradox and Goodman's view on music scores and performances. L Goehr, 'Three Blind Mice: Goodman, McLuhan, and Adorno on the Art of Music and Listening in the Age of Global Transmission' (2008) 35 *New German Critique* 1.

[53] Goodman, *Languages of Art* (n 11) 186–87.

[54] Goehr (n 52) 4.

from a previous work. But if he subsequently borrows one more note at a time into a melodic sequence, so the borrowed melody is incremented by three, four, five and more notes, at what cut-off point will this borrowing become substantial and thus illicit? Interestingly, the widespread urban myth that one can legitimately borrow fewer than eight sequential notes without risking copyright infringement is not just legally untrue,[55] but also blissfully unaware of the soritical nature of music borrowing.

What makes soritical music borrowing even more perplexing (and the eight-note urban myth more inadequate and irrelevant) is non-melodic borrowing.[56] Think about harmonic borrowing with vertically stacked notes. Suppose a musician borrows a two-note chord, which is highly likely to be legitimate. Then he grows the chord by borrowing one more note at a time. At what cut-off point will this harmonic borrowing become substantial enough to be illicit? Would three, four, five or six notes in a harmony infringe? How about borrowing Wagner's Tristan chord? Suppose Wagner's copyright is still hypothetically valid; would the borrowing of the four vertically stacked notes comprising F, B, D♯ and G♯ in the Tristan chord constitute substantial borrowing?[57] Going beyond melodic and harmonic borrowing, there remains more uncertainty when coming to other types of borrowing activities, some of which are more exotic than others.[58] Again, this is due to the nominalistic mode of modern copyright, which is pressured to individuate as many units of creation as possible in an ever more litigious environment. Just like the attempt to distinguish a sand 'heap' from a 'non-heap', all music borrowing litigations are essentially soritical battles, which aim to push and fix the fuzzy boundary between substantial copying and insubstantial appropriation.

To conclude this section, it is worth discussing briefly the nominalist legacy left by *Arnstein* for later music borrowing. The implications of the *Arnstein* case are twofold. First, the kind of nominalism manifested in *Arnstein* boosts the ethos of possessive individualism, which has become increasingly dominant among music creators since the mid-twentieth century. This individualistic ethos is certainly marked by Arnstein's own firm belief that he was a mistreated and isolated 'genius', whose music everyone wanted to steal.[59] Without this belief, it would have been impossible for Arnstein to persistently launch a host of quixotic legal battles against almost the entire American popular music establishment (including famous musicians such as Cole Porter, Irving Berlin and George Gershwin) of his time, with *Arnstein v Porter* in 1946 being his final lost battle. This possessive individualistic ethos is also congruent with the Romantic aesthetics, which has put individual creators on an authorial pedestal and arguably given rise to the modern author-centric copyright law of the West.[60] Interestingly, Judge Frank, in his 1949 book *Courts on Trial*, also suggested that romanticism (as opposed to classicism) could be compatible with nominalism that celebrated individuality: 'Ultra-romanticism is, indeed, nominalism applied to human beings.'[61] With this nominalist-romantic mindset, Frank did not shy away from the idea that craziness and genius could go hand in hand with some exceptional individual creators:

[55] Bennett has done a great job in demystifying this eight-note urban myth in ch 4 of this volume.

[56] Fishman argues that music copyright should concern itself mainly with melodic copying, though music is more than just melodies. JP Fishman, 'Music as a Matter of Law' (2018) 131 *Harvard Law Review* 1861.

[57] According to Kivy as quoted above, there seems to be non-trivial substantial labour involved to 'discover' the Tristan chord, though Kivy vehemently denies music creatorship: 'the discovery of that chord required the labor of more than one lifetime'. Kivy (n 3) 118.

[58] These borrowing activities may range from rhythmic borrowing, to borrowing of chord progressions and even to borrowing of styles, feels or grooves. For types of borrowing, see Burkholder's typology in ch 2 of this volume.

[59] Rosen (n 34).

[60] See Woodmansee (n 36); P Jaszi, 'On the Author Effect: Contemporary Copyright and Collective Creativity' (1992) 10 *Cardozo Arts & Entertainment Law Journal* 293.

[61] J Frank, *Courts on Trial: Myth and Reality in American Justice* (Princeton University Press, 1949) 402.

> There have been partly crazy men who have been artistically creative: Nietzsche ended up in a bathouse, and so did Swift. Moreover, there have been cases where men have been treated unfairly as to some particular matter and have then gone nutty.[62]

This largely explains the nominalist-romantic rationale assumed by Frank's ruling against a summary judgment but in favour of a jury trial,[63] which intended to give Arnstein (a potentially 'crazy' genius) the largest possible benefit of the doubt.

The second implication of *Arnstein* is on the soritical nature of music borrowing copyright litigations. Akin to what happens in a typical sorites paradox, it is hard for any copyright legal doctrine to specify a clear cut-off point between permissible borrowing and improper appropriation. It would be unfair to solely blame copyright law for this level of vagueness or lack of clarity; the problem should also be seen as an ontological one that appears in non-legal fields as well. Music nominalism incentivises music creators to claim ownership rights in individuated units of creation, and there can be almost an unlimited way of constructing such individuality when coming to music borrowing. Given the inherently unstable and unpredictable individuality of protectable materials in music borrowing litigation, copyright law will need to continue this ontological struggle to legally distinguish between a soritical sand 'heap' and a 'non-heap'. In other words, all music borrowing disputes will continue to be adjudicated on a case-by-case basis as there is no such mythical eight-note cut-off point that can magically tell permissible borrowing apart from illicit appropriation.

IV. Coda: From 'Music Borrowing' to 'Music Returning'

This chapter explores the two competing ontological forces – music Platonism and nominalism – and their respective implications on music borrowing and copyright law. It shows that the nominalist mode has gained dominance in shaping the metaphysics behind modern copyright, which intends to protect particularised and individuated music creations. However, a nominalistic system of copyright law should not be immune from criticism. Radical nominalism tends to breed an overly individualistic copyright regime by propertising those generic music expressions that should have been in the intellectual commons. Copyright law needs to heed Theodor Adorno's caution against any radicalised form of music nominalism in the contemporary art world.[64] This is because extreme nominalism is likely to travel too far ontologically by not just disenchanting Platonism, but also remythologising individuality.[65] Radical nominalism, when coupled with possessive individualism in modern consumer culture, would inevitably make previously permissible music borrowing practice much more difficult as music copyright litigants would always be incentivised to forge new ways of individuating borrowed elements.

In this scenario, I propose that the current copyright regime governing music borrowing needs to be reinvented by animating the concept of 'music returning' to avoid radicalised nominalism. It is often forgotten that when Johann Mattheson first tackled 'music borrowing'

[62] Quoted in Rosen (n 34) 225.

[63] Balganesh offers a detailed analysis of the rationale behind the Arnstein ruling and Frank's jurisprudential motivation for making such a decision: S Balganesh, 'The Questionable Origins of the Copyright Infringement Analysis' (2016) 68 *Stanford Law Review* 791.

[64] For a summary of Adorno's account on, and critique of, music nominalism, see Jay (n 44).

[65] Jay calls extreme nominalism 'magical nominalism', which creates its own new myths about individuated forms of photographic art. The photographic magical nominalism can also be applied in the music context. M Jay, 'Magical Nominalism: Photography and the Re-Enchantment of the World' (2009) 50 *Culture, Theory and Critique* 165.

in his 1739 treatise *Der vollkommene Kappellmeister*, he also coupled this concept with the idea of 'music returning': 'Borrowing is permissible; but one must *return* the thing borrowed with interest, ie one must so construct and develop imitations that they are *prettier and better* than the pieces from which they are derived' (emphasis added).[66]

Mattheson believed it was legitimate to 'borrow' if a borrower could return with 'better and prettier' creations. As Mattheson himself did not specify in detail how this returning might legally operate under copyright law, I think this can be achieved through a 'copyleft' mechanism, which is already prevalent in the contemporary free and open-source software (FOSS) community. The basic idea of copyleft is to have software code 'borrowers' return their publicly released code modifications back to the original coylefted software repository to ensure an unbroken chain of freely available source code in an intellectual commons.[67] Loosely following this model, music returning does not have to be the repatriation of borrowed materials back to any individual original musicians; rather, it can be done through contributing those 'prettier and better' secondary creations to a music commons. Here I do not argue that all secondary creations need to be returned in this way; one needs only to return those creations that borrow from what becomes generic or commonplace music materials to justify their borrowing.[68] Of course, to forge a legal doctrine for facilitating music returning coupled with music borrowing cannot be a panacea for all the ontological problems encountered by music copyright so far. However, just like the concept of 'public domain', which needs to be reified,[69] the concept of 'music returning' also needs to be concretised or turned into an ontological *thing* first before it can be fully realised as a legal doctrine. As there has been a conspicuous lack of a discursive framework for music returning, I thus call for one that would ontologically help to facilitate music borrowing under copyright law for the purpose of nurturing and enriching music creativity in a shared music ecosystem.

[66] J Mattheson, *Johann Mattheson's Der Vollkommene Capellmeister: A Revised Translation with Critical Commentary* (EC Harris trans, UMI Research Press, 1981) 298.

[67] Chen Wei Zhu, '"Copyleft" Reconsidered Why Software Licensing Jurisprudence Needs Insights from Relational Contract Theory' (2013) 22 *Social & Legal Studies* 289.

[68] In this scenario, to craft a genre theory of music copyright is going to be helpful. For a discussion of a general genre theory of copyright, see O Rachum-Twaig, 'A Genre Theory of Copyright' (2016) 33 *Santa Clara High Technology Law Journal* 34.

[69] This is the argument made by Boyle as a pre-emptive measure against the enclosure of intellectual commons. J Boyle, *The Public Domain: Enclosing the Commons of the Mind* (Yale University Press, 2008).

4

We Can Work It Out: Methods in Forensic Musicology

JOE BENNETT

In most countries, musical works are protected by copyright. It follows, then, that in situations where musical borrowing is inappropriate (ie plagiarism), a copyright may be infringed and litigation may follow. Music copyright infringement cases are preoccupied with a core question, which in its simplest layperson form might be expressed as: 'Is Song B copied from Song A?' In *Arnstein v Porter*,[1] Judge Frank divided the question into two parts:

> [There are] two separate elements essential to a plaintiff's case [in a copyright infringement suit]: (a) that defendant copied from plaintiff's copyrighted work and (b) that the copying (assuming it to be proved) went so far as to constitute improper appropriation … Each of these two issues – copying and improper appropriation – is an issue of fact.[2]

The so-called Arnstein test (or court practices derived from it) is still in use today, and has been much criticised for demonstrating 'skepticism towards rules, judges, and the law'[3] and for revealing 'issues surrounding the application, or even misapplication, of musical expert testimony'.[4] I suggest that it is speciously simplistic in artificially separating 'copying' from 'improper appropriation'. Innocent musical borrowing is ubiquitous in popular music, due to the widespread use of commonplace elements (for example, the back-beat snare drum, certain chord progressions,[5] genre-typical choices of instrumentation and conventions of song form). Popular music is a constrained art form, featuring many common tropes and meta-characteristics.[6] So, rather than simply identifying what Judge Frank called the 'fact' of copying, the work of a forensic musicologist might be better expressed by incorporating both of the *Arnstein* elements into the more nuanced question: 'Is a substantial part of a protectable element of Song B copied from Song A?'[7]

[1] *Arnstein v Porter* (1946) 154 F 2d 464. Songwriter Ira Arnstein famously sued Cole Porter for allegedly copying fragments of melodies from the former's own songs.

[2] ibid.

[3] S Balganesh, 'The Questionable Origins of the Copyright Infringement Analysis' (2016) 68 *Stanford Law Review* 791.

[4] KM Leo, *Forensic Musicology and the Blurred Lines of Federal Copyright History* (Lexington Books, 2020) 90.

[5] J Covach, 'Form in Rock Music' in D Stein (ed), *Engaging Music: Essays in Music Analysis* (Oxford University Press USA, 2005); M Hirsch, 'Striking a Chord' *The Boston Globe* (31 December 2008) http://archive.boston.com/ae/music/articles/2008/12/31/striking_a_chord/; *The Axis of Awesome: 4 Chords* (2011) www.youtube.com/watch?v=oOlDewpCfZQ&feature=youtube_gdata_player.

[6] J Bennett, 'Collaborative Songwriting – the Ontology of Negotiated Creativity in Popular Music Studio Practice' (2011) *Journal of the Art of Record Production* issue 5, www.arpjournal.com/asarpwp/collaborative-songwriting---the-ontology-of-negotiated-creativity-in-popular-music-studio-practice/.

[7] Latman argues that courts have consistently misunderstood the adjective 'substantial', applying it to the first part of the Arnstein test (fact of copying) instead of the second (was the copying inappropriate?). I take issue with this view,

In this chapter, I will argue that forensic musicology (FM) practice can answer this question by combining comparative musical analysis and repertoire research, contextualised within an understanding of how songwriters and composers create and how listeners hear. In doing so, I shall identify the methodological and phenomenological traps into which courts and juries can fall and suggest ways in which these can be anticipated and circumvented.

I. Forensic Musicology Practices

Scholarly discussion of FM has focused almost exclusively on historical music copyright infringement litigation cases.[8] This is understandable, because court records represent the only public record of the development of the field, and most musicologist reports beyond those quoted in court documents are unavailable to researchers, due to non-disclosure agreements. In reality, only a fraction of the work of a forensic musicologist consists of expert testimony for infringement litigation. Most FM analyses never reach a courtroom, but rather are simply confidential consultancies for a commercial client – either a potential plaintiff who has noticed the similarity between their Song A and a more recent Song B or a potential defendant who wishes to know whether their Song B might be considered plagiaristic of Song A (or any prior work).

Commissioning clients typically require their consultant musicologist to provide an opinion on two interdependent questions, which are subtly different from those posed in *Arnstein*: (i) is the similarity we hear likely ascribable to plagiarism, as opposed to independent creation (IC), and (ii) are the similar elements unique to Song A or are they commonplace? As I shall argue, these questions bring with them epistemological challenges, some of which can be addressed through robust analytical methodology, repertoire research and professional integrity, and others that may remain problematic due to the nature of copyright law and the subjectivity of music listening.

In my own experience as a commercial forensic musicologist (since 2007), projects fall into three main categories: musical work comparison; audio sample analysis; and soundalike analysis.[9]

A. Musical Work Comparison

A musical work (MW) comparison attempts to ascertain whether perceived similarity between Song A and Song B is more likely ascribable to improper copying (plagiarism) or to coincidence (IC). These similarities often focus on the song's main vocal melody or on prominent topline instrumental parts, as do most music copyright infringement cases since the nineteenth century.[10] The simplest form of analysis is a comparative transcription, where the respective melodies are aligned vertically above each other, with highlighting of congruent pitches, rhythms

but only because I disagree with the false binary that the Arnstein test itself attempts to establish. A Latman, '"Probative Similarity" as Proof of Copying: Toward Dispelling Some Myths in Copyright Infringement' (1990) 90 *Columbia Law Review* 1187.

[8] Leo (n 4); J Bellido, 'Forensic Technologies in British Music Copyright' in S Hamilton et al (eds), *Sensing the Law* (Canadian Initiative in Law, Culture, and Humanities, 2014); D Begault, H Heise and C Peltier, 'Forensic Musicology: An Overview' in M Brookes and DR Begault, *Proceedings of the 54th AES International Conference on Audio Forensics* (Audio Engineering Society, 2014).

[9] These services are described, with variations of wording, in the websites and promotional materials of most professional forensic musicologists, eg forensicmusicologist.com (Alexander Stewart, USA), oxendale-music.co.uk/ (Peter Oxendale, UK), jfmusicservices.com/services/ (Judith Finell, USA), www.musiodata.com/services-fees (Sandy Wilbur, USA) and my own joebennett.net (Joe Bennett, USA).

[10] C Cronin et al, 'Music Copyright Infringement Resource' (*Music Copyright Infringement Resource*, 2021), https://blogs.law.gwu.edu/mcir/; M Osteen and PK Saint-Amour, 'Rhythm Changes: Contrafacts, Copyright, and Jazz Modernism' [2010] *Modernism & Copyright* 98; JP Fishman, 'Music as a Matter of Law' (2017) 131 *Harvard Law Review* 1861.

and underlying chords (ie harmony). This method has been in use in US infringement litigation since the mid-1800s, as Katherine Leo[11] attests:

> By the middle of the [nineteenth] century, courts had settled on similarity as the central inquiry for infringement cases as applied to all protectable works. Thus, a piece of music, or any other copyrightable work, was believed to have infringed on another work if the two pieces were sufficiently similar as to indicate copying.
>
> … Most expert witnesses approached the similarity inquiry as locating the extent of musical congruence, predominantly through note-by-note melodic comparison usually conducted separately from the harmonic and formal dimensions of the song.

Comparative analysis is usually accompanied by repertoire research, in which the musicologist will investigate whether the similar elements from Song A were unique to it or whether earlier works exist that contain the same musical elements. This additional repertoire can be used to counter any spurious accusation of plagiarism because, in the words of prominent US musicologist Sandy Wilbur: 'If the combination of similar elements can be found in prior art, the original elements cannot have originated in either of the works being compared.'[12]

Like the two aforementioned questions (plagiarism versus IC and unique versus commonplace), the two methods are interdependent: comparative analysis identifies the extent of the objective similarities and repertoire research subtracts the commonplace elements. When the commonplace elements are removed, the comparative analysis can be re-evaluated so that only copyright-protected similarities remain. This is simple enough conceptually, but can be challenging in practice, as I shall address later.

A notable recent example of MW comparison in litigation is *Gray v Hudson*, in which pop singer Katy Perry's hit 'Dark Horse' was alleged to have been copied from a Christian rap song entitled 'Joyful Noise'. The case was helpfully summarised in Judge Smith's opinion, at the conclusion of the defendants' successful appeal:

> [Plaintiffs] claim that a repeating instrumental figure – in musical terms, an ostinato – in Hudson's song 'Dark Horse' copied a similar ostinato in plaintiffs' song 'Joyful Noise'. After a trial centering around the testimony of musical experts, a jury found defendants liable for copyright infringement and awarded $2.8 million in damages. The district court vacated the jury award and granted judgment as a matter of law to defendants, concluding principally that the evidence at trial was legally insufficient to show that the Joyful Noise ostinato was copyrightable original expression.
>
> We affirm. Copyright law protects 'musical works' only to the extent that they are 'original works of authorship'. 17 USC § 102(a). The trial record compels us to conclude that the ostinatos at issue here consist entirely of commonplace musical elements, and that the similarities between them do not arise out of an original combination of these elements. Consequently, the jury's verdict finding defendants liable for copyright infringement was unsupported by the evidence.[13]

Although the defendants' musicologist's analysis is not in the public record, we can infer from their appeal that they successfully used prior art research to demonstrate that HORSE[14] was created independently of NOISE, when they state:

> The only claimed similarities between the two works are a small number of indisputably commonplace elements in the works' ostinatos and the undisputed evidence at trial established the many differences between both the ostinatos and the works as a whole.

[11] Leo (n 4) 14.

[12] S Wilbur, 'Music & Musicology Services & Fees' (Musiodata, 2021), www.musiodata.com/services-fees.

[13] *Gray v Hudson* (2022) 28 F 4th 87.

[14] In my own reports, after initially identifying the respective works, I use the typographical convention of subsequently referencing them with an uppercase unique noun from the title, eg HORSE. I prefer this for clarity; other common abbreviated title styles include a single word in quotes 'Horse', in italics *Horse* or full title in quotes 'Dark Horse'.

The two alleged musical similarities at issue in *Gray* were the ostinato (Figure 4.1) and the 'beats', ie the underlying backing track. For this discussion, I shall dispense with the beats' similarities, as the court did. There are very few cases in US legal history whereby beat similarities alone[15] have been enough to infer copyright infringement, because no two beats are exactly alike (except in cases of audio sampling) and because many beats are similar in their rhythmic design.

Figure 4.1 Gray v Hudson ostinato comparison. Dark Horse is originally in the key of Bb minor; in keeping with my use of key compensation, it is shown here transposed down one semitone (-1) aka one half-step, for clarity of comparison

Of more interest, for our discussion of listener phenomenology, are the pitch matches between the ostinatos. When HORSE and NOISE are played one after the other, the melodic congruence is obvious; the songs' respective two-bar ostinatos (short melodic sections) share six exact-match pitches, with identical rhythmic values. The similarity is exacerbated by the (I would argue irrelevant) fact that they share similar synthesiser sounds, played staccato. We can easily imagine that a jury might have considered these similarities to be subjectively compelling.

In Figure 4.1, we can see that 12 of the 16 notes in HORSE are identical, in terms of pitch and rhythmic values, to the equivalent notes in NOISE. To a non-musician, perhaps even to a hopeful plaintiff, this might appear to be evidence of plagiarism. But to a songwriter, it is quickly obvious that such a simple idea (playing quarter-notes starting on the third note of the minor scale, repeating the same note for a whole bar, then playing an adjacent note on the keyboard and maintaining the same pulse) is such a simple compositional gesture that it could have easily been undertaken independently by two separate song-writing teams. This hypothesis is supported by a classroom exercise I use in my FM classes at Berklee College of Music, where most students have experience of song writing and some are song-writing majors. On hearing the Gray ostinatos one after the other, a large majority of the class state confidently that they believe the similarity to be a coincidence, ie the opposite inference to the jury's conclusion in the lower court's original verdict. Further, students often express amazement or outrage that Gray was ever litigated because, to them, the accusation of plagiarism is so obviously musically unfounded. As relatively experienced songwriters, they are already able to subtract commonplace elements from protectable expression. This tacit knowledge is acquired over years of immersion in popular music creative practice. Juries, unfortunately, do not have access to this knowledge. All too often, they infer, often incorrectly, that copying is the most likely explanation for the similarity they hear.[16]

As the Appellate Court in *Gray* eventually found, neither the beats nor the ostinatos were sufficiently original to be considered protectable expression. But the fact that the jury initially found for plaintiffs demonstrates the challenge of listener perception in music copyright infringement litigation: how can a non-expert listener separate the commonplace from the protectable?

[15] A notable rare exception is Jessie J's 'Price Tag', which allegedly copied the breakbeat one-bar drum part of an earlier work 'Kimba Ku'. *New Old Music Group, Inc v Gottwald* (2015) 122 F Supp 3d 78.

[16] J Lund, 'An Empirical Examination of the Lay Listener Test in Music Composition Copyright Infringement' [2012] SSRN 2030509, http://papers.ssrn.com/sol3/papers.cfm?abstract_id=2030509.

The answer, of course, is that they must rely on expert testimony. But, as Leo and others[17] have noted, since the nineteenth century it has been possible for plaintiffs and defendants alike to find 'hired guns', ie experts who are willing to manipulate methodology in their clients' favour.[18] The duelling experts issue remains common to this day, and cannot easily be addressed because there are no formal guidelines or professional organisation for FM practitioners, as Fishman and Garcia observe: '[E]very expert with whom we spoke could think of no … networking outlet: no formal professional organization, no annual conference, no series of happy hours or meet-ups'.[19]

I agree with Fishman and Garcia's implication that such an organisation would be helpful to the field. It could provide several possible benefits for copyright owners and courts, including the establishment and codification of agreed methodologies, the vetting and accreditation of members to ensure experts are suitably skilled and qualified, and a set of ethical standards of evidence-based objectivity that might go some way towards countering the hired gun issue.

Musical Work Comparison: Typical Musicologist Workflow

- Client provides musicologist with access to Song A and Song B and identifies the similarity at issue.
- Musicologist undertakes comparative key-compensated[20] topline and harmony transcription to highlight similarities and differences between Song A and Song B.
- Musicologist identifies elements common to both works, such as instrumentation/production and melodic or lyric fragments.
- Musicologist researches repertoire (ideally that predates Song A), to identify the extent to which the similar elements between the works are commonplace or else are unique to Song A and Song B.
- If a large amount of similar repertoire is found – for example, if a melodic fragment is identified in numerous other works – this might be considered supportive of an IC hypothesis.
- Musicologist provides a report, which either states that the similarity is probably due to IC (no protectable elements of Song A appear identically in Song B) or that the similarity is likely evidence of plagiarism (Song B contains similarities of unique protectable elements that were originated by the composers of Song A, which is taken to be evidence of copying).

B. Audio Sample Analysis

Audio sample analysis is primarily concerned with the authentication of audio; that is to say, to detect whether the apparent audio sample in a sound recording (SR) is in fact taken from an

[17] [1884] *Medico-legal Journal* 146. Cited in Leo (n 4) 16.

[18] In *Gray*, the plaintiff's expert had a PhD in musicology, but with specialisms in ragtime, musical theatre, hammered dulcimer and Irish folk music – and no apparent experience of popular song writing or the commercial music industry. A strange choice, perhaps, and arguably a demonstration of the need for a professional organisation for FM experts.

[19] J Fishman and K Garcia, 'Authoring Prior Art' (2022) 75 *Vanderbilt Law Review* 1159.

[20] Key compensation is the practice of transcribing both works in the same musical key, regardless of the keys in which they were originally performed, notated or recorded. It is a ubiquitous practice in musicologist reports, in and out of the courtroom (it appears in Arnstein and most other MW cases). A more recent equivalent approach uses the sound recordings – the musicologist manipulates digital audio in software so that both works play back in the same key (and sometimes at the same tempo). Although some commentators (eg Begault) have criticised audio manipulation on the grounds that it tampers with the evidence, I consider this practice to be defensible – indeed, essential – because it enables non-expert listeners to hear 'like for like' without the distraction of different keys making the works sound more subjectively different than they actually are.

earlier SR. It deals with a different copyright from MW analysis, because the MW and the SR are protected separately in copyright law.[21]

Because infringement of an SR copyright requires that the defendant has *mechanically* copied the audio from the original source, making a *re-recording* of the source material is a viable creative strategy for a samplist, because it is technically a new SR so cannot infringe the copyright of the earlier one (although any musical work similarities would need to be treated separately). This has been a common practice[22] in the music industry since the 1990s, partly for economic reasons; pioneering hip-hop super-producer Dr Dre 're-recorded the majority of the samples he used with live musicians … [because] samples were becoming too expensive to clear'.[23]

From the musicologist's perspective, audio sample analysis culminates in a binary outcome – either the source of the sample in SR(B) is SR(A) or it is not. But although the expression of this opinion is simple, the methodologies to achieve it reliably can be highly technical and complicated, including visual waveform or spectrum analysis,[24] audio phase cancellation (alignment of the recordings to discover exact overlaps)[25] and intricate attempts to reverse-engineer the likely creative processes used by the defendants.[26] In some situations, it is possible to use anomalies in the earlier recording as a naturally occurring 'copyright trap'; this method was used in *Naxos v Salmon*, an SR infringement case in which my own expert analysis was used to ascertain whether defendant's recording of Vivaldi's *Four Seasons* was a digital copy of plaintiff's. Judge Lord Glennie summarised the process in his opinion:

> [the expert] proceeded to look at audible anomalies in the recordings, such as bowing scrapes and crunches in the string section, rattles from the harpsichord, unexplained random noises and disturbances within the recording venue, breathing sounds, clicks and other noises.[27]

For all its technical complexity, sample analysis is arguably the most straightforward aspect of FM practice, because it leads to a yes/no conclusion which, if reliably obtained, cannot be undone or challenged through lay listener perception, legal arguments or reductive methodology.

Since the early 1990s, when the practice of sampling became more common in popular music – particularly hip-hop – there has been an attendant rise in sample detection expert practices in SR-related infringement litigation; notable cases include *Grand Upright Music v Warner Bros Records Inc*,[28] *Salsoul v Chiccone*[29] and *Bridgeport Music v Dimension Films*.[30] Sampling case

[21] J Bennett and S O'Connor, 'Determining the Composition' in *Oxford Handbook of Music Law and Policy* (Oxford University Press USA, 2021), www.oxfordhandbooks.com/view/10.1093/oxfordhb/9780190872243.001.0001/oxfordhb-9780190872243.

[22] J Morey, 'Copyright Management and Its Effect on the Sampling Practice of UK Dance Music Producers' (2013) 3 *IASPM Journal* 48.

[23] J Brown, *Dr Dre in the Studio: From Compton, Death Row, Snoop Dogg, Eminem, 50 Cent, the Game, and Mad Money: The Life, Times, and Aftermath of the Notorious Record Producer, Dr Dre* (Colossus Books, 2006) 64.

[24] Begault et al (n 8).

[25] Musicologist Alexander Stewart provides a brief overview of some of the technical methods used in sample detection. A Stewart, 'Been Caught Stealing: A Musicologist's Perspective on Unlicensed Sampling Disputes' (2014) 83 *University of Missouri at Kansas City Law Review* 339.

[26] For a recent example of my own work in this area, see Judge Oetken's description of my sample detection methods, cited in *Hines v W Chappell Music Corp*, No 20-CV-3535 (JPO) (SDNY 8 June 2021).

[27] *Naxos Rights International Limited v Project Management (Borders) Limited + Keith Joseph Salmon* Outer House, Court of Session [2012] CSOH 158.

[28] *Grand Upright Music v Warner Bros Records, Inc* (1991) 780 F Supp 182. Rapper Biz Markie sampled four bars of piano/bass/drums from Gilbert O'Sullivan's song 'Alone Again (Naturally)'.

[29] *Vmg Salsoul, LLC v Ciccone* (2016) 824 F 3d 871. Madonna's 'Vogue' sampled a single 0.23 s horn hit from an earlier work, 'Love Break'.

[30] *Bridgeport Music, Inc v Dimension Films* (2005) 410 F 3d 792. NWA sampled a two-second excerpt of a guitar riff from Funkadelic's 'Get Off Your Ass and Jam'.

law is at an interesting point at the time of writing (2022). *Bridgeport* held that a sample of any length was copyright infringement, effectively reducing the *de minimis* sample-length threshold to zero for creators with Judge Guy's famous words, 'Get a license or do not sample'; the *Salsoul* verdict allowed for a very short (0.23 s) horn sample to be considered *de minimis*, although Judge Silverman's dissent, quoting *Bridgeport*, stated 'I would hold that the de minimis exception does not apply to the sampling, copying, stealing, pirating, misappropriation – call it what you will – of copyrighted fixed sound recordings'. Given that *Bridgeport* was in the Sixth Circuit and *Salsoul* in the Ninth, the USA currently has a circuit split in this matter, leaving the very real possibility that the hallowed halls of the US Supreme Court may one day ring out to the sounds of Funkadelic, Madonna and N.W.A, to decide once and for all the extent to which musicians can sample audio.

Sample Authentication: Typical Musicologist Workflow

- Client provides musicologist with access to the sound recordings and identifies the timestamp of SR(A) and SR(B) where the alleged similarity occurs.
- Musicologist imports both SRs into software for comparative analysis. If the samples are at different pitches/tempos, digital time stretching and pitch shifting may be used to compare like with like.
- Musicologist applies various comparative technical methods to establish the provenance of the sample in SR(B), such as phase cancellation, visual waveform or spectrogram analysis, anomaly spotting and reverse-engineering possible processes used by the alleged samplist.
- Musicologist provides a report, which states whether the source of the audio sample in SR(B) is SR(A).

C. Soundalike Comparison

A soundalike is an intentional attempt by a composer to make a musical allusion to a song, artist or style whilst creating a sufficiently original composition to avoid accusations of copyright infringement. They are common in film & TV, and particularly advertising, where the director may have briefed a composer to create the 'feel' of a pre-existing track to accompany moving images (this is known as a 'reference track' in the industry). In their least controversial form, soundalikes are simply genre pieces, combining production, instrumentation and arrangement in such a way as to evoke a cultural trope – think honky-tonk up-tempo piano for a comedy chase scene; twanging mouth harp, slow human whistling and reverbed rubato claves for a Western's gunfight showdown; the soaring unison strings of lovers reunited; or the urgent root-5th trumpet fanfare of a news anchor's theme tune. These compositional ideas are undoubtedly based on (maybe even 'borrowed from') earlier works, but they are not copyright-infringing because they are not unique to any *single* work. It follows, then, that as the number of works alluded to diminishes, so the possibility of copyright infringement increases. A soundalike is at its most problematic when it intentionally and identifiably alludes only to a single work – usually the reference track.

In a soundalike comparison, musicologists are often hired towards the end of the media production process, before the soundalike is made available to the public, though occasionally they can be used after the media are released, should a dispute arise. The purpose of such a pre-emptive analysis is to highlight any inappropriate similarities between the soundalike and the reference track and, if any are found, to recommend that the composer make changes.

The methodology here is in two parts and is like the approach used in MW analyses; indeed, it could be seen as modelling a courtroom scenario, to demonstrate or test how a jury might perceive a particular similarity. First, the new track and reference track are compared note-for-note for congruence, typically using just the vocal or instrumental topline and underlying harmony. Usually there is no issue here, because most professional media composers know not to copy melodic and harmonic material from earlier works – it is an unwritten rule that has held fast in the industry for many decades. The second part of the analysis is to situate the soundalike in its cultural context through repertoire research, usually with the aim of demonstrating that it is truly a *scènes à faire* genre piece that uses commonplace musical ideas found in more than one work. To expand on the earlier film trope example, a scene for a TV ad featuring a cowboy bar fight might include honky-tonk piano music, created by a professional media composer to the director's brief. The musicologist's role would be to demonstrate that the piano part was dissimilar to any *specific* work (comparative melodic analysis), but rather featured genre-based characteristics broadly, like in several works (repertoire research).

In one recent project (2022), I was commissioned by a media production company to undertake a comparative analysis of a custom-composed rock track that had been used in TV ads. The company had been approached by a well-known rock artist, who believed that the TV ads represented unauthorised use of one of their compositions. My musicologist's report provided a comparative analysis of the works, which found no melodic or harmonic congruence. The report then used repertoire research to demonstrate that the works only sounded similar because they featured genre-typical uses of instrumentation, tempo, rhythmic feel and guitar techniques – elements that appear in many works. My conclusion suggested that the complaining party would be unlikely to be able to demonstrate plagiarism, because the similar elements are commonplace (and therefore not individually protectable by copyright). The musicologist's report was then used to enable the client to refute the spurious claims of the rock artist.

Musicologists' analyses of soundalikes, or any pre-release works, are common practice in the media production process, and in my own experience represent the most common type of activity for FM practitioners; clients treat it as a form of due diligence or insurance, whereby a comparatively small cost can risk-manage the possibility of future litigation. I speculate that this practice is partly responsible for the relative scarcity of soundalike-related case law, such disputes having been pre-subtracted from court action due to what some law scholars call the selection effect.[31] A rare but significant recent example of media music in litigation can be found in *Eight Mile Style v New Zealand National Party, et al*,[32] in which a media composer had created an alleged soundalike of Eminem's 'Lose Yourself' for a TV advertising campaign (and, perhaps foolishly, had entitled their soundalike 'Eminem Esque').[33] The respective musicologists used different approaches: the plaintiff's expert (a Dr Ford) used a holistic methodology, suggesting that a combination of individually non-protectable elements had contributed to 'striking similarity' between the works, whereas the defendant's expert (a Dr Zemke) used repertoire

[31] 'Because straightforward or easy applications of legal rules are rarely litigated, the cases that come to a court are predominantly and disproportionately ones that are in some way hard. The litigated hard cases thus represent a biased sample of all legal events, a phenomenon typically referred to as the selection effect': FF Schauer, *Thinking Like a Lawyer: A New Introduction to Legal Reasoning* (Harvard University Press, 2009) 13.

[32] 'Eight Mile Style v New Zealand National Party, et al | Music Copyright Infringement Resource', https://blogs.law.gwu.edu/mcir/case/eight-mile-style-v-new-zealand-national-party-et-al/.

[33] The plantiffs prevailed, with their solicitor Adam Simpson describing the decision as 'a warning to sound-alike music producers and their clients everywhere'. Reuters, 'Music Rights Specialist Backs National over 'Eminem Esque'' (*RNZ*, 26 October 2017), www.rnz.co.nz/news/national/342383/music-rights-specialist-backs-national-over-eminem-esque.

research to demonstrate that the similar musical elements were musical tropes that appeared in many prior works. The tendency of (some) expert musicologists to select methodologies – or, worse, to cherry-pick evidence – to help bolster a client's case is a manifestation of the hired-gun phenomenon,[34] and is so common in the commercial world that I now include an objectivity clause in my own client contracts.

Soundalike Comparison: Typical Musicologist Workflow

- Client provides the pre-release media music (Song B) as an audio file, and audio recordings of any reference work/s (Song A) used by the composers.
- Musicologist undertakes comparative key-compensated topline and harmony transcription to highlight similarities and differences between Song B and reference works.
- Musicologist identifies elements common to both works (elements of instrumentation/ production and melodic or lyric fragments).
- Musicologist researches repertoire that predates Song A to identify the extent to which the similar elements between the works are commonplace or else unique to Song A and Song B.
- Musicologist provides a report, which either states that no action is needed (no protectable elements of Song A appear in Song B) or recommends compositional changes before release (Song B contains similarities of protectable elements).

Although all three categories of similarity (musical work, sampling and soundalikes) appear in historic and current litigated cases, the majority are MW disputes, and most commonly involve fragments of vocal melodies, or 'toplines'. I suggest that there are several reasons for this. First, partial melodic similarity is difficult to prove or disprove, meaning that these cases are more likely to reach litigation due to the selection effect. Second, melodies are among the lowest time-bandwidth data we can perceive in a pop song, with melodic pitch events occurring around three to eight times per second; by contrast, we can perceive high-frequency timbral (tonal) characteristics in music at up to 20,000 cycles per second and can identify sound recordings within 0.2 seconds,[35] meaning that coincidental partial exact-match similarities are possible in melodies but are mathematically impossible in SRs. Third, melodic copying is uncommon (and is, in fact, frowned upon) in the song-writing community. It is something of a truism that coincidental melodic similarity is much more common than many people believe, whereas songwriters plagiarising melodic fragments is much less common.

As stated previously, most of the work of musicologists is pre-emptive to, or preventative of, actual litigation.[36] Commercial clients want to seek confirmation of whether a similarity is indicative of copying, either to inform them of whether litigation is likely/advisable or else to try to prevent it. A soundalike composer may want reassurance that their composition is, in fact, a genre piece, and does not copy protectable elements from the reference track; if the similarity is deemed by the musicologist to be 'too close', the composer can make changes to the soundalike before it is released. A songwriter who notices a topline similarity between their own song and a later one may require the musicologist to comment on the extent to which the similarity is ascribable to copying (of a protectable element), to inform them of whether litigation is viable.

[34] Leo (n 4).

[35] DJ Levitin and PR Cook, 'Memory for Musical Tempo: Additional Evidence That Auditory Memory Is Absolute' (1996) 58 *Perception & Psychophysics* 927.

[36] Leo (n 4) 22.

Conversely, a songwriter who finds themselves unfairly accused of plagiarism may ask a musicologist to undertake repertoire research to demonstrate that the similarity between the works is due to shared commonplace elements and IC – showing that the works are simply stylistically similar and/or that the melodic similarity is a coincidence. Even the simple yes–no outcome of a sample analysis is more often used to inform commercial negotiations between the parties without necessarily proceeding to litigation. A client whose work has been sampled by a well-known artist is usually very pleased to receive a musicologist's report authenticating the sample because it gives them powerful leverage in the business negotiations that may follow, especially when the later work has already been commercially successful. All the scenarios I describe here are workaday activities for forensic musicologists, and in my own experience represent most client commissions.

II. Methodologies and Epistemologies

Following the logic of *Arnstein*, if the first question in any music copyright dispute is 'Did copying occur?', then it is also the first question – possibly the most important question – in forensic musicology. But how can we know whether copying has taken place? Only on very rare occasions in infringement litigation is there an admission of copying by the defendant. One notable such outlier is *Bridgeport Music, Inc v Dimension Films*,[37] where defendants N.W.A cheerfully admitted sampling two seconds of audio from Funkadelic's 'Get Off Your Ass and Jam' in their later song '100 Miles and Runnin''. But *Bridgeport* was a sample-based infringement case, and sampling is almost always simpler to demonstrate/disprove than other forms of musical plagiarism because it is a binary – the sampling either occurred or not. Given that SR cases are the only scenarios in which such a binary can be so starkly drawn, this is another area in which *Arnstein*'s simplistic emphasis on the 'fact' of copying fails to account for the full complexity of musical authorship, especially today, when many composers deal with elements of timbre and production, conflating the MW and the SR as creative objects.[38]

But in most situations – in fact, in almost every music copyright litigation case in history – defendants deny that the subjective similarity between the works is the result of plagiarism, instead arguing that it is due to IC. How, then, might we use music analysis to differentiate between coincidental similarity and plagiarism?

A. The First Step: The Similarity Proxy

In this section, I will address the epistemological difficulties in answering the copying/IC question definitively (as all musicologists' clients would prefer). As philosophers and behavioural psychologists have long held, we cannot know the mind of another person, and can only infer others' knowledge or intentions by observing their behaviours. It is rarely possible to identify from the works alone exactly how any creative gesture was achieved, still less the intent behind it. We can only observe the similarity evident in the works and use extent-of-similarity (what Leo calls 'musical congruence' and Latman calls 'probative similarity'[39]) as a proxy for

[37] *Bridgeport Music v Dimension Films* (n 30).
[38] Bennett and O'Connor (n 21).
[39] Leo (n 4); Latman (n 7).

likelihood-of-copying. I shall refer to this as the *Similarity Proxy*, and it is used to answer the first step in FM's process: *is the extent of similarity between the works likely to be evidence of copying?*

The Similarity Proxy is based on the conceptual principle that the greater the extent of the similarity, the less the likelihood that it could have arisen through IC. This makes mathematical sense. If we toss a coin once, the probability that it will land on tails is 0.5 (50 per cent, or one in two). But if we toss a coin three times, the probability of tossing heads, then tails, then heads again is 0.125 (12.5 per cent, or one in eight). In music, as a time-based art form, the choices available to composers between any consecutive musical events are much greater than two. It follows, then, that any very long melody that is identical to any pre-existing very long melody is likely to be evidence of plagiarism, especially if the underlying harmony is identical. Ergo, the likelihood of any similarity between long melodies being ascribable to IC decreases exponentially with every added note in the melodic chain.[40] And the exponential mathematics need not be limited to a single linear domain such as melody. Any musical arrangement that uses the exact same parameters as an earlier work in terms of instrumentation, musical form, musical key or tempo, for example, provides increasingly strong circumstantial evidence of copying as more similarities are added, even if such elements are themselves not protectable by copyright.

The principles of the Similarity Proxy are instinctively understood by musicians and may be even tacitly assumed by courts and lay listeners. This is perhaps the reason why many songwriters believe the urban myth that there is a legally defined *de minimis* number of consecutive pitches that can legitimately be copied before the copyright police knock at one's door. A rare example of this common musicians' fallacy being publicly aired is the following interview with *Wicked* composer Stephen Schwartz, where he describes the melodic content of the 'Unlimited Theme' that underpins several of the songs in the stage musical:

> What I thought was amusing (and I wondered if people would get it, and of course people did), is that it's the first seven notes of 'Over the Rainbow' … The reason that that's a joke is because *according to copyright law, when you get to the eighth note, then people can come and say, 'Oh you stole our tune'.* And of course, obviously it's also disguised in that it's completely different rhythmically. And it's also harmonised completely differently … but still it's the first seven notes of 'Somewhere Over the Rainbow'. (emphasis added)[41]

But notwithstanding any such misunderstandings of copyright's principles, the Similarity Proxy has always been the main method by which musicologists, courts and musicians address the copying/IC binary. And although it is arguably defensible as an approach, it does not take account of the fact that not all copying is plagiarism and not all plagiarism is copyright infringement.

III. The Second Step: Commonplace Elements

The copyright doctrine of *scènes à faire* holds that certain elements of a creative work may not be protected by copyright, because they are commonplace. FM does not necessarily concern itself with this doctrine in its pure form, ie genre tropes. Rather, it investigates *scènes à faire* in a less literal sense – comparing the works to commonplace rhythms, chords and (particularly) melodic

[40] E Selfridge-Field, 'Substantial Musical Similarity in Sound and Notation: Perspectives from Digital Musicology' (2015) 16 *Colorado Technology Law Journal* 249.

[41] C de Giere, interview with Stephen Schwartz, 'Wicked's Musical Themes' (*c*2004), www.musicalschwartz.com/wicked-musical-themes.htm.

fragments. If, for example, the writer of Song B hears an electronic dance music (EDM) Song A that opens with a 'four-on-the-floor kick drum'[42] (a bass drum, playing beats one, two, three and four of each bar, like a metronome), they can legitimately copy this drum element in their own Song B, and even admit to doing so, because the four-on-the-floor expression was not created by the composer of Song A. It is a staple element of genre in disco and EDM, and is commonplace in popular music.

This raises the next methodological step for FM; *once we have established the extent of the similarity, we must subtract the commonplace elements.* From my conversations with other forensic musicologists, it appears that all of us have experienced many approaches by hopeful potential plaintiffs, convinced that a musical element of their Song A (for example, a chord loop, a drum part, a lyric fragment and particularly a short melodic fragment) has been wilfully copied by a later songwriter in the successful hit Song B. The client's position, in many cases, is quite sincere; they genuinely believe, like many juries, that plagiarism is the only explanation for the subjective similarity between Song B and Song A. In most such cases, the analysis demonstrates to the disappointed client that the similar elements in question are common to many works, and that there is no copyright to protect. Some musicologists (including myself) try to avoid taking on such projects, because they are usually without merit and because clients are rarely comforted by the fact that the analysis has helped them to avoid expensive and fruitless litigation.

IV. Repertoire Research, Prior Art and the IC Hypothesis

Even though musicologists are expert listeners with a wide knowledge of repertoire, we cannot simply state that we believe an element is commonplace or unique – to do so would clearly be *argumentum ab auctoritate* (the 'argument from authority' fallacy[43]). To demonstrate to others (eg clients, courts, juries) that any similarity between Song A and Song B is coincidental, we must produce evidence that the relevant similar elements do, in fact, appear in other works: ideally, but not essentially, works that predate Song A. I shall call this the *Prior Art Proxy*, where the existence of a musical element in many works demonstrates that it is something that composers might create independently of each other. In my experience, it is most useful when applied to short melodic fragments – typically one to four bars of music.

Much of the history of music copyright litigation in the USA consists of disputes over such fragmentary melodic similarity.[44] In these scenarios, the plaintiff has noticed that part of their melody of their Song A is like part of the defendant's Song B. Such similarities are almost never exact, and very rarely are the melodic chains more than four bars in length. In *Arnstein* itself, the accusations against Porter all related to fragmentary non-exact melodic similarity; most of the fragments consisted of only a few consecutive pitches, none of which aligned exactly in terms of rhythmic values, harmonic context and bar placement. It is not difficult to see why the district court initially dismissed the case.

[42] *Four-on-the-Floor – That Disco Beat!* (directed by Auckland Philharmonia Orchestra, 2018), www.youtube.com/watch?v=8_NiMAEsP14.

[43] D Walton, 'Appeals to Authority', *Informal Logic: A Pragmatic Approach*, 2nd edn (Cambridge University Press, 2008), www.cambridge.org/core/books/informal-logic/appeals-to-authority/F455E1D4279677917F379D9464A76060.

[44] 'We found that courts' interest in prior art typically comes up where the plaintiff's claim centers on a short fragment, rather than on similarities that permeate the entire work': Fishman and Garcia (n 19) 25.

Figure 4.2 'A Modern Messiah' versus 'Don't Fence Me In' – melodic fragment similarity

To illustrate the IC hypothesis in litigation, Figure 4.2 is my transcription of one example from *Arnstein*, where Porter is accused of copying a five-note melodic fragment from the plaintiff's 'A Modern Messiah' (1934) in his hit song 'Don't Fence Me In' (1934). In preference to the rather chaotic and selective comparative methodology employed by Arnstein himself, I have aligned the melodies in proper context here, so it is clear that the five-note fragment in question comes at a different point in the musical phrase and in a different harmonic context, meaning that there are no congruent pitches anywhere between the works – not even the certainly coincidental five pitches that Arnstein identifies. I have been rather generous to Arnstein's argument here, by transcribing both examples in 6/8 time (FENCE is originally notated in 4/4), in the same key and removing the piano accompaniment, so we are left only with the simple topline on which the plaintiff's argument was based.

In my view, Arnstein's approach, in all his lawsuits, represents outrageous methodological bias – he manipulates the musicology to support his complaint, rather than applying objective comparative analysis to test the likelihood of plagiarism versus IC. Arnstein's selective transcriptions are perhaps the most egregious examples of what Leo calls 'a melocentric approach that privileged pitch and interval relationships over rhythmic context'.[45] When comparative transcription is applied reductively enough, it is easy to find coincidentally similar short fragments of melody.[46]

If such an obviously meritless case as *Arnstein* were to occur today (and the equally illegitimate claims against Katy Perry in *Gray* demonstrate that this is possible), I argue that the defendant's musicologist would simply need to find the short melodic fragments from the plaintiff's work in other works (ideally but not necessarily prior works) to demonstrate IC via the Prior Art Proxy. With such a simple pitch sequence as the mi–re–do–re–mi found in Arnstein's 'A Modern Messiah', this would be a simple matter. I offer the first five notes of the nursery rhyme 'Merrily We Roll Along', for example.

Fishman and Garcia[47] provide an unprecedentedly detailed discussion of the development of prior art usage in music copyright litigation, including interviews with several currently active musicologists and analysis of over 50 musicologist reports used in litigation. They posit that the use of prior art research is a relatively new practice, partly driven by the small number of forensic musicologists in the field, noting that: 'Generally, it was the defendant's expert who defined the universe of prior art at issue. Plaintiff-side experts, by contrast, tended not to mention specific

[45] Leo (n 4). I would like to thank Dr Leo for providing me with scans of the original Arnstein court documents, including the composer's own notes and comparative transcriptions.

[46] The level of reductiveness used in a court analysis is an acknowledged issue in copyright infringement suits; verdicts can turn on the extent to which the works are separated into their constituent elements, because '[to] dissect the works at issue into separate components and compare only the copyrightable elements … would result in almost nothing being copyrightable because original works broken down into their composite parts would usually be little more than basic unprotectable elements': *Boisson v American County Quilts and Linens, Inc* (2001) 273 F 3d.

[47] Above n 19.

prior art references except to rebut what the opposing expert had argued.'[48] I agree with their speculation about the reasons for the increased focus on repertoire research among defendants, the most important of which is that they serve to 'evaluate whether [a musical] element is creative or mundane'.

In the case of MW analysis, I posit that a prior art search is essential in evaluating whether a given similarity is due to IC or plagiarism. This is not simply to modulate substantiality, nor even to eliminate *scènes à faire* (which are often considered genre-specific),[49] but rather to test – and demonstrate – the extent to which IC is probable. If Song A contains a melodic fragment that appears in many prior works, this either supports the hypothesis that Songwriter A copied it from a prior source or (more likely) that the fragment is *just the kind of thing songwriters do*, otherwise known as IC. And, of course, in either scenario, Song B would not infringe a copyright. To address the *scènes à faire* genre issue from the opposite perspective, if melodically similar ideas are found in several works in *unrelated* genres, we might reasonably infer that the similarity is coincidental precisely *because* these composers are unlikely to have had access to each other's work. I am aware that my view contradicts the oft-expressed view in copyright scholarship that prior art is irrelevant and unnecessary because of the high bar for infringement, but I suggest that melodic similarity is a special case, due to the prevalence of coincidental fragmentary similarity in music composition, particularly in pop songs. When coincidental similarity occurs through IC, prior art research is, I suggest, the most robust methodology for rebutting spurious accusations of infringement.

For a recent example of the effectiveness of prior art in support of an IC hypothesis, let us look at opposing views from two of the most popular music analysis YouTube channels – Rick Beato and Adam Neely – as they respond to the announcement of a lawsuit[50] against pop songwriter Dua Lipa alleging that her song 'Levitating' copied four bars of melody from an earlier song 'Live Your Life'. Both YouTubers are accomplished musicians and songwriters, with comprehensive knowledge of music theory and pop repertoire. Beato does not mention any earlier works, and simply states 'they're virtually identical … what are the chances?';[51] Neely finds a number of antecedent equally similar melodies, and takes the opposite position: 'Levitating did not come from Live Your Life [and] both songs draw on prior art … things that other musicians had done beforehand'.[52] The division could not be clearer: one analysis does not use prior art, and finds the melodic similarity to be clear evidence of plagiarism; the other finds the melodic fragment in prior art, and draws the opposite conclusion.

The Beato/Neely example demonstrates that the plaintiff's case can appear strong based on similarity alone, unless and until prior art demonstrates that the IC hypothesis is a more likely explanation for the similarity. A recent example of this scenario in litigation can be found in *Smith v The Weeknd*,[53] where the defendant's song 'I Need To Love' was alleged to have copied a three-bar melodic fragment from an earlier work 'A Lonely Night'.

[48] ibid 31.

[49] ibid 14.

[50] *Christopher Edward Cope et al v Warner Records, Inc et al* [2022] District Court for the Central District of California, Western Division 2:22-cv-01384-SSS-AS.

[51] *Dua Lipa vs Reggae Band Lawsuit: Let's Compare!* (directed by Rick Beato 2022), www.youtube.com/watch?v=XT3DghWbk2A.

[52] Neely also speculates that '[the plaintiff] probably couldn't find a musicologist to go to bat for them'.

[53] *Smith v Weeknd* [2020] Dist Court, CD California CV 19-2507 PA (MRWx).

Figure 4.3 Excerpt from musicologist report in *Smith v Weeknd*

In the initial complaint, the plaintiff's musicologist boldly stated 'In this investigation and analysis I have found substantial similarities that *in my opinion can only be the result of copying*' (emphasis added).

Given the subjectively surprising extent of the pitch–rhythm–harmony similarity in *Smith*, melodic plagiarism seems entirely plausible *until the prior art is considered*. One prior art example given by the defendants for the non-originality of the phrase in bar 1 is the opening melody of the Bond theme 'The World Is Not Enough'[54] ('clear to me' versus 'not en-ough'); an even more compelling example for the entire phrase is the bridge section of Blondie's 'Heart of Glass', which apart from its major-key tonality, is otherwise almost identical to plaintiff's 'A Lonely Night' in pitch and rhythm.

Figure 4.4 Additional works cited in *Smith v Weeknd* (my transcription)

In Figure 4.4, I have transcribed[55] all four works mentioned in the case to show how the defendants used prior art to demonstrate that the apparently striking similarity between the plaintiff's NEED

[54] I would also offer the opening three-note melodic phrase from the verse of Delaney & Bonnie's 'Groupie (Superstar)' (1969), which uses the same pitches, rhythmic values and underlying harmony in the first bar.

[55] In this transcription, I have used the plaintiff's musicologist's apparent methodology (Figure 4.3), of allowing for one-sixteenth note worth of leeway as the threshold for rhythmic congruence. I suggest his approach was rather generous

and the defendant's LONELY was due to IC, and/or that both works could have used HEART or WORLD as inspiration. We can see that the similar line in bar 2, 'get that funny …'/'baby girl I …', is almost identical to the equivalent line in HEART ('what I find is …').

The defendants admonish the plaintiff's expert for bad methodology: 'Plaintiffs and their expert simply ignored the prior art that has the same or similar melody', and go on to assert that their own prior art search is evidence of IC: 'Because the claimed similar melody appears in hugely popular songs before … I Need to Love, it very well also could arise [in I Need to Love and A Lonely Night] if the two works had been created independently.'

V. Music Perception, Formal Fallacies and Solutions

I would argue that there are four reasons that the use of juries creates a finding-of-facts problem in music copyright infringement litigation. First, nonexpert listeners cannot easily distinguish between protectable and commonplace musical elements. Second, non-copyrightable musical characteristics – particularly key, tempo and instrumentation – can affect the perceived similarity of two pieces of music.[56] Third, when considering melodic similarity, it is all too easy to combine the base rate fallacy[57] with the prosecutor's fallacy[58] by underestimating how much music is generated,[59] and therefore to misjudge how common a particular melodic fragment may be in music generally. And fourth, melody represents the lowest-bandwidth data in musical composition, meaning it is statistically prone to coincidental similarity and therefore IC.[60] In each case, there is the risk that poor practices by expert musicologists – whether applied through bad methodology or, worse, deliberately manipulated in a hired-gun scenario – can sway a jury incorrectly in the plaintiff's favour.

To counter these issues, the most important practical step that could be taken is a set of agreed replicable FM methodologies, combining objective comparison with prior art contextualisation, possibly managed by some sort of membership organisation for FM practitioners. Such an organisation could publish an ethics code, where musicologists would agree in advance with their clients (as some already do[61]) to provide objective analysis, rather than support their clients' positions regardless. Most usefully, a raising of the *de minimis* threshold for melodic plagiarism (whether enshrined in copyright law or, more likely, evolved through case law) would enable courts to avoid wasting time and money litigating specious complaints, particularly for

to the plaintiff; my own method would have been to identify only exact rhythmic matches (which would have resulted in a lower level of apparent similarity in the notation). As in the plaintiff's filing, my highlighted notes in red represent rhythmic and pitch matches with the plaintiff's song NEED. In the transcription of HEART (the earliest work of the four), I have also coloured one note in pink to represent the diatonically different pitch on the second syllable of 'pleas-ing', which is a semitone higher than that found in NEED due to HEART being in a major key and NEED being minor.

[56] Lund (n 16).

[57] ie 'Failure to consider background information in situations in which it is actually very relevant': M Bar-Hillel, 'The Base-Rate Fallacy in Probability Judgments' (1980) 44 *Acta Psychologica* 211.

[58] 'The prosecutor's fallacy occurs when someone incorrectly believes that the probability of a random scientific match is equal to the probability that the defendant is innocent': M Conklin, 'The Effectiveness of Bayesian Jury Instructions in Mitigating the Defense Attorney's Fallacy' (2018) 9 *Houston Law Review: Off the Record* 73.

[59] T Ingham, 'Over 60,000 Tracks Are Now Uploaded to Spotify Every Day. That's Nearly One per Second' (*Music Business Worldwide*, 24 February 2021), www.musicbusinessworldwide.com/over-60000-tracks-are-now-uploaded-to-spotify-daily-thats-nearly-one-per-second/.

[60] It is interesting to observe that in more than 150 years of US case law, only a handful of plaintiffs have ever identified an exact-match melodic similarity of more than two bars of music.

[61] 'As an expert witness, my charge is not to take sides in these debates, but rather to offer unbiased and objective analyses that attempt to keep these analytical strands separate and clear': Stewart (n 25).

the mostly meritless fragmentary melodic similarity cases that are so problematic for juries and defendants. Taken together, these steps would enable the courts to get back to preventing genuine music copyright infringement and would help creators to make new work, free of the ever-present threat of litigation. This worthy goal was recently summarised by Ed Sheeran,[62] shortly after he prevailed against an opportunistic melodic-fragment plaintiff[63] in the UK's High Court in 2022:

> It's really damaging to the songwriting industry. There are only so many notes, and very few chords used in pop music. Coincidences are bound to happen … and I hope that this ruling means in the future baseless claims like this can be avoided … Hopefully we can all get back to writing songs, rather than having to prove that we can write them.

If Sheeran's wish is granted, this might result in more songs, less litigation and fewer work opportunities for forensic musicologists like myself. I say this is a price worth paying.

[62] *Ed Sheeran Statement in Response to His Victory in the UK High Court* (directed by Ed Sheeran), www.instagram.com/p/CcANzfhjaHL/.

[63] *Sheeran, et al v Chokri, et al* [2022] UK High Court of Justice EWHC 827 (Ch) (England).

5

Forensic Musicology in Action: A Personal Perspective

GUY PROTHEROE

I. Background

Through the 35 years in which I have been an expert witness in matters of music copyright – a forensic musicologist – I have been approached many times by people involved in music saying they would like to find out how to become one themselves. They have included performers in many musical genres, some working professionally and some enthusiastic amateurs, as well as students still training, composers, journalists and some people who think they know a lot and their opinions are important. I have always explained there are only two (overlapping) routes: (i) you have a leading academic position in music and musicology, generally as a professor in a leading university, college or other academic institution; or (ii) you have already been working in the profession intensively for some years in relevant areas as a performer, composer, arranger, etc with notable success and reputation.

Until the 1980s, only category (i) had appeared in the UK as experts: their testimony relied nearly always on reports containing transcriptions into musical notation of the works in question – normally just of the sections of the works where there was contention – and detailed analyses in words and notated musical examples showing comparisons between them, identifying similarities and differences; though occasionally recordings of the originals were also played in court.

Since the early days of the recording of music, disputes over music and copyright have been one of the most difficult areas for the courts, because music only exists as sound in time. Even when music was traditionally created by composers writing down every note, with literary instructions as to how it should be played, there could still be considerable differences between performances; but it was only when music began to be recorded that there was literally a 'record' of precisely what the musical work was, as contained in a sound recording.

Music cannot be 'frozen', as it were: only specific elements can be 'nailed down', especially because, in the field of popular music, where most of the litigation arises (because that is where the bulk of the money is), most composition of music is done not by composers writing music down in notation, but by performing live, recording and teaching the music to other performers, who may or may not contribute to the development of the musical work themselves.

There is an old saying: 'First the hit, then the writ.' When there is a big hit, often very many less successful, and/or older, songwriters are jealous and, if they hear anything like something they have written themselves, they can well get the idea that they have been copied. Also, some leading artists gather a reputation for copying other people's songs (whether they have or not) and the claims start flooding in. Very occasionally there may be grounds for a claim, but generally the grounds are just in their imagination. Although a few cases end up in court, the vast majority are either aborted or settled out of court. One of my hardest jobs is often the following scenario: (i) an artist/record company/music publisher approaches me enthusiastically with a potential claim; (ii) I analyse the merits of the claim thoroughly, and conclude there is not enough in common to constitute, in my opinion, any potential legal infringement at all, or at least there is no good chance of their winning a claim – far more likely they will waste a fortune pursuing it; and (iii) then I try to persuade them to drop it! If they persist, I suggest they consult another expert – which has happened, though I am not aware that any such claim has succeeded. (Any out-of-court settlements, abortions, etc remain, of course, confidential, so I cannot refer herein to any of the legion of opinions I have given in this respect – some involving as much work as cases which have gone to court.)

II. Introduction: Chariots of Fire

I first became involved as an expert in music copyright back in 1987 through a sound-alike: it was a video commercial for Clarks Shoes children's trainers, and the commercial featured children running along the beach at St Andrew's in Scotland. This was copying directly the imagery of the title sequence in the film *Chariots of Fire*, with music by Vangelis. They cut the video to the Vangelis music, then approached Warners, Vangelis's publishers, for the right to use it. They didn't agree a price, so the agency approached an EMI music company for a sound-alike. Warners and Vangelis's management were, of course, on the lookout, and a writ was issued the morning after its first showing. EMI then tried to defend themselves by threatening to counter-sue Warners – they bought the copyright of a Greek piece of music by the composer Stavros Logarides, who had previously brought an unsuccessful claim in the Greek courts – Logarides claimed Vangelis had copied his song 'City of Violets' in 'Chariots of Fire'.

The prime expert witness on the music for Vangelis was Dr Geoffrey Bush, already established in the field in my category (i) above – a leading composer, teacher and professor. He had also pioneered the role of forensic musicologist in several prominent cases, starting in 1960 with a claim of plagiarism in a song by Vera Lynn. Bush brought into court a piano to demonstrate the musical elements aurally (in parallel with musical notation), and later played gramophone records in court as well.[1] (Geoffrey Bush was, incidentally, a great enthusiast of crime fiction, and even co-wrote some himself – a great background for getting involved in the forensics of music!)

I had been working with Vangelis since 1975 as an arranger, singer, lyricist and conductor on many albums and films; I had also transcribed into musical notation Vangelis's music as required as, like most popular music composers since that time, he did not read music. Vangelis's team

[1] J Bellido, 'Popular Music and Copyright Law in the Sixties' (2013) 40 *Journal of Law and Society* 570.

then further employed me in this case as an expert on his music. (Prior to this, Vangelis and I had had discussions: he wanted me to teach him how to read and write in music notation, and in return he would teach me to speak Greek – I have always been involved in Greek music and culture. But after very careful thought I turned the idea down, as I was very concerned that his trying to think about music from the angle of notation would be harmful and restrictive to his natural instinctive way of composing. I am certain this was true – and so my spoken Greek is still not good!)

I undertook a detailed examination of all Vangelis's earlier music, to establish what evidence there might be in the way of 'prior art' in his own compositions, and I also investigated other earlier music in general for similarities.

When one writes a musicological report for presentation in court, one is required to state exactly one's qualifications, both academic and experiential, to justify one's appearance as an 'expert' on the matters in contention. If there is any weakness in one's claims in this respect, the opposing leading counsel will attempt, up front, to discredit one's credentials to the judge before getting on to cross-examination of the report.

I had won a scholarship to Oxford to read music, and therefore had the academic disciplines and background generally required for expert witnesses, and up until shortly before the court case had for several years been employed by the BBC as Music Presentation Editor.

In the Vangelis case, I worked with Geoffrey Bush in extending the techniques he himself had pioneered. I researched the material in common (essentially just four notes over one chord change) throughout the history of music and also in Vangelis's earlier music. I found many very similar phrases throughout his compositions – and, indeed, precisely the same figure and notes in a song he had written and recorded in 1969.

I show here two examples from my report as an illustration. As is usual, I made notated comparisons in parallel of the two themes in question, transposing 'Chariots of Fire' down a semitone into the same key that Logarides had used, C major (as is usual in such written comparisons, for visual simplicity). As can be seen, there is only a succession of four notes in common between them: the pitches F–G–A–G, in different rhythms. The Logarides piece was entitled (in English translation) 'City of Violets', and is shown with the 'Chariots of Fire' example notated in Figure 5.1.

Figure 5.1 Comparison of the 'City of Violets' and 'Chariots of Fire' melodies

In the Vangelis composition, unlike the Logarides, the melodic fragment first occurs at the very beginning of the melody, after only one quaver (on C), therefore immediately creating a movement in the theme, and giving an essential dynamic significance to the subdominant shift. Unlike the fragment in the Logarides, which occurs twice in the four bars of the melody, in the Vangelis it occurs three times: only the second appearance coincides in position with the first Logarides position (a). In addition the Vangelis melody is rounded off by a falling triplet figure (b) derived from the fragment.

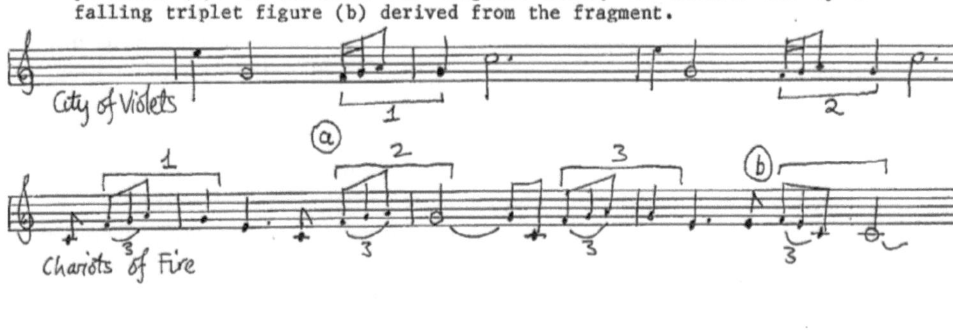

In Vangelis's song 'Wake Up', dating from 1969, the opening vocal melody begins as in Figure 5.2. This contains the same four-note unit and rhythm (and chords) as in 'City of Violets', which was written many years later, and is an illustration of why Vangelis did not need to copy from Logarides.

Figure 5.2 Vangelis's song 'Wake Up', bars 1–2

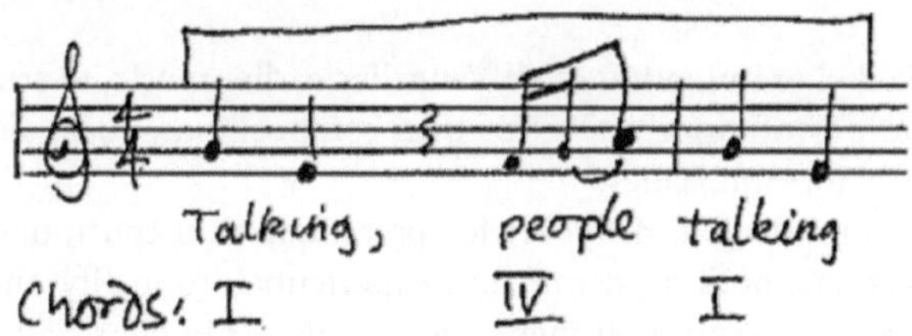

I rather deluged the judge with supplementary notated examples also recorded on cassette, compiled in date order, with a written commentary on the relevance of each (indeed, 215 examples!). The judge did make the comment that my report as a result was very long, to which I replied, 'I apologise, my lord, but I was encouraged to prolixity by an enthusiastic Greek!' (in fact, Vangelis's manager). But the judge was obviously interested and, as much quoted in the press coverage, he asked if someone could 'lend me a Sony Walkman', so he could study the recordings in his own time.

Also, we brought into court some of Vangelis's keyboards so that he could demonstrate how he composes – when writing music for film, generally improvising to the film on screen, without reference to any other music. There was contention that Logarides, on a visit to London, had played his piece to Vangelis in his studio. Quite by chance, I had been with Vangelis on each occasion Logarides had been there – Vangelis had left each time before Logarides started playing (saying he was not interested in Logarides and his music), and I left with him, so I was a witness of fact also (which led to even fiercer cross-examination, and for me something of a baptism of fire!).

This rather long introduction to my chapter I hope gives a context as to how such matters can be handled in court, and what the role of forensic musicologists is in that situation. After this case, which we won with much media coverage (largely because Vangelis had won an Oscar for his music score to *Chariots of Fire*), I began to get requests for my opinion on musicological matters from lawyers, publishers, record companies – and, indeed, directly from musicians and musical groups. I have given opinions on several thousand matters since, while maintaining my performing career in music, mainly as a conductor of both 'classical' art music from medieval times to the avant-garde and popular music of many countries and cultures, as noted above, which constantly informs the knowledge and experience I can bring to the field of forensic musicology.

As a result, I have been involved as an expert in most of the UK cases which have since gone to court, and have also given opinions within other disputes, both in the UK and internationally. Often there are several joint claimants or defendants, and sometimes, when there is, for example, a main publisher, there are also sub-publishers who want a separate opinion for their own reference, to see if their scenario is the same as that of the main publisher. There are very few major disputes in the UK and the USA in which I have not been engaged to give an opinion.

Some of the judgments in the UK courts have resulted in much commentary, mainly in legal journals, etc. I deal with this aspect in the following sections, beginning with the, as it were, classic claim of *plagiarism* (as in 'Chariots of Fire' above): 'he/she has copied my song'.

III. Plagiarism

An early example of the court's dealing with a claim of plagiarism was in the case of *Francis, Day & Hunter Limited and Another v Bron* (1963, in which Dr Geoffrey Bush appeared as an expert).[2] While the extent of similarities between the two songs was agreed between the experts, it was unclear to the court as to whether these similarities were the result of either conscious or unconscious copying or were complete coincidence. Had it been concluded that the defendant had known the earlier song, it is likely a verdict of plagiarism might have been found; but because of the uncertainty, the case was dismissed.

There have been several cases in the USA where a song has been deemed by a court to be an infringement but later the verdict has been overturned in the appeal court – and this overturn has not been the result of any further expert witness contribution. Most plagiarism claims are settled out of court, so the actual contributions by experts remain confidential and are not made public.

These days, with modern broadcasting, the internet, etc, it is much more often the problem for the defendant to convince the court, beyond reasonable doubt, that they have *not* heard the contested work, which can be very difficult if not impossible to prove.

A famous case in the 1970s which was settled in court (in the USA) was *Bright Tunes Music Corp v Harrisongs Music*,[3] when George Harrison was accused of copying, in his song 'My Sweet Lord', from Ronald Mack's 'He's So Fine'. Again, the experts agreed essentially on what was in common and what was not. Harrison's expert, the renowned musicologist Harold Barlow (known internationally for his published indices of themes of major classical instrumental and vocal works), 'acknowledged that, although the two motifs were in the public domain, their use here was so unusual that he, in all his experience, had never come across this unique sequential use of these materials'. Although the court accepted that Harrison had indeed copied 'He's So Fine', the judge commented 'I do not believe he did so deliberately. Nevertheless, *My Sweet Lord* is the very same song as *He's So Fine* with different words.' After the trial was over, the judge chatted with George Harrison's lawyer and said: 'I actually rather *like* both songs'. Harrison's lawyer responded immediately: 'What do you mean, *both* songs? You just ruled that they are one and the same!'. To which the judge desperately replied: 'What I mean is, I like the *one* song – but with the two sets of lyrics!'.

It was noted that the judge in this case was also a composer (his works include a three-act opera, and he had conducted orchestras). Despite this fact and his conclusion, the actual similarity between the two songs relates only to the main melodic phrases of both the verse and chorus sections of each song, where there are some short distinctive successions of pitches which are clearly similar; apart from this, the songs are independent, including the chord sequences, form, style and lyrics.

The case that more recently 'put the cat among the pigeons' was the claim in the USA against Pharrell Williams and Robin Thicke that their song 'Blurred Lines' infringed the copyright of Marvin Gaye in his 1977 song 'Got To Give It Up'. The original 2015 verdict of the jury in the district court of copying was affirmed in 2018 by the Ninth Circuit Court of Appeals.[4] In the original trial, there was great dissent between the parties as to the extent of any similarities between

[2] *Francis Day & Hunter v Bron* [1963] Ch 587 (Eng).

[3] *Bright Tunes Music Corp v Harrisongs Music, Ltd* (1976) 420 F Supp 177 (Dist Court).

[4] Quagliariello J, 'Blurring the Lines: The Impact of Williams v Gaye on Music Composition' (2019) 10 *Harvard Journal of Sports and Entertainment Law* 133.

the songs, and it was argued that Gaye's experts had cherry-picked small musical elements, too insubstantial to have any copyright protection, to play to the jury, in order to make them appear substantial elements in the songs. I have not heard what those elements were, but I was commissioned at the time by an interested party to give my own opinion, which was that there was no substantial similarity between the songs at all in terms of musical content, though I agree there is some similarity in style and sound. Apart from the behaviour of the defendants in court, a crucial problem in this case was that the judge only permitted the jury to hear renditions of the notated sheet music played in parallel with edited versions of the Gaye sound recording. (This whole area has subsequently been analysed and dissected in detail by the media and the law.)

When the case came later to the Ninth Circuit Court of Appeals in California, two of the judges were in agreement with the jury's verdict and one was against. The dissenting judge came to a radically different conclusion from the other two on the principle that complex musicology issues in copyright cases like this are beyond the scope of many federal judges. I would add to this that, if such issues are beyond the scope of judges, how should they be left to a jury of lay people to decide? The decisions of the original judge in this case as to how the music should be presented to the jury would not, I believe, be agreed with or approved by any experienced musicologist as being a fair or balanced way of comparing the essential and relevant copyright content of the two musical works contained in the recordings.

The Court of Appeals also had much discussion as to whether the first court should have considered the musical recording for the Gaye song or just the written sheet music that had been deposited with the Copyright Office, since the development of recording most popular music has been, and is, created directly in sound, rarely needing any formal notation as such (apart generally from lyrics to songs being written down). Nor do a lot of composers and performers of contemporary popular music know how to read or write music notation – there is no need: the process is irrelevant and potentially disruptive to their creative process (as I have noted in relation to Vangelis above). So, with regard to plagiarism, notation is only one aspect of a musical work. In court cases, it is the choice of individual experts (often pressured by their instructing lawyers) as to what elements they do and do not include in the notation in their reports, and it is their interpretations of what is the precise relevant musical material heard in the actual recording.

It is generally agreed within the music industry that the verdict in the 'Blurred Lines' case, if taken seriously, is potentially very dangerous to the whole field of creativity, not only in music. (Though of course there can be genuine major and original elements in a sound recording beyond the actual notes contained in the musical work, including the sound and style, which could be argued to be substantial parts in the 'sonic' work contained in the sound recording – of which, more later.)

IV. Parody

Another area in which I have also given opinions is that of parody. Often musical parodies occur in the soundtracks to videos, where fun/ridicule or criticism is being made of a particular artist or situation. The original artist may be parodied visually in the video or in a particular scenario, and music and/or lyrics may well be adapted into a parodied version to accompany it. Or the parody may be purely aural. It should be noted that parodies are generally created primarily for the purpose of creating fun at the expense of the original author(s), rather than making money.

My role has been to examine the musical work contained in the parody, and the lyrical work where relevant, and to assess, as standard, whether a 'substantial part' of the original work has been copied in the parody (without licence, that is). Of course, if not enough of the original work has been referred to, the listener will not form the aural link, so the parody is pointless. The UK Copyright Act currently states 'Fair dealing with a work for the purposes of caricature, parody or pastiche does not infringe copyright in the work'.[5] I read that this area of copyright is under discussion on several forums, with proposals being made for the revision of the associated legislation.

V. Joint Authorship

A very active field in music litigation in recent years has been the joint authorship of musical works, by members of musical groups other than the main songwriter(s) and arrangers, and there have been several conflicting judgments in this area.

By way of example, there were two judgments on these issues in 1999 and 2002 which have often since been compared in legal journals and commentaries. The first was *Hadley v Kemp*,[6] concerning the group Spandau Ballet, and the second was *Robert James Beckingham v Robert Hodgens*,[7] concerning the group the Bluebells. I was the expert for one of the parties in each case.

Gary Kemp was credited as the songwriter for all except one of the Spandau Ballet songs on which there were claims in this action. In this court case, three other members of the group claimed they were joint owners of the copyright in the songs on five of the group's albums. (Gary's brother Martin, the bass guitarist in the group, kept out of it.) Gary Kemp's method of creating the songs was to compose them complete by himself, then to teach them to the rest of the group. A problem, when it came to court, was that Kemp had not recorded or notated the songs before teaching them to the band. The argument presented by the claimants in court was that there were differences in musical content were between the version he taught the band and the version on the final recording. Furthermore, to achieve copyright in law, a musical work must be recorded in some material form (generally a notated score or a recording). Prior to writing my report, I went through each song with Kemp, who explained in detail exactly what he originally composed and what was different on the recordings – which, in most cases, was nothing substantive. My analysis and commentary on this was run through in court by counsel with each of the claimants. When Tony Hadley, the vocalist, was asked what he did beyond what Kemp told him to sing, the most he aspired to was 'Sometimes I held onto a note longer than he told me to'. In relation to the contribution of the drummer, John Keeble, I had stated I was not an expert on drumming, and recommended a leading drummer with whom I was acquainted to provide a report on this aspect, which was an important element in the case.

All the claims were sorted in the judgment; but there was one matter in the judgment which has subsequently caused some controversy amongst lawyers. This was in the song 'True', regarding a saxophone improvisation by Steve Norman in the 16-bar bridge section. My notation of this solo in my report is shown in Figure 5.3.

[5] www.gov.uk/guidance/exceptions-to-copyright#parody-caricature-and-pastiche.

[6] [1999] EMLR 589.

[7] *Beckingham v Hodgen* [2002] EWHC 2143 (Ch); *Hodgens v Beckingham* [2003] EWCA Civ 143.

Figure 5.3 Spandau Ballet's 'True' saxophone solo in the bridge section

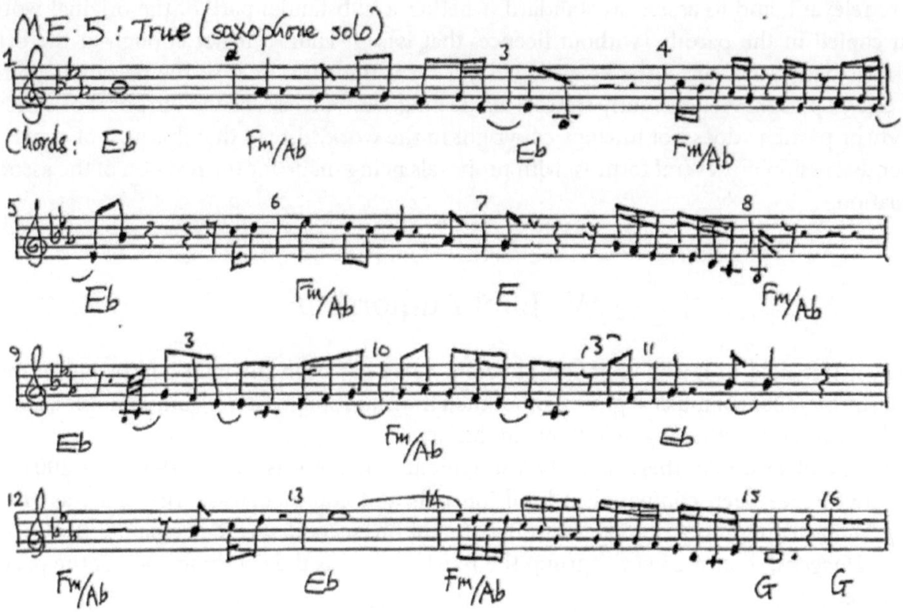

I was asked by my instructing lawyers to opine as to whether this passage constituted a 'substantial part' of the musical work. It was, in my opinion, an anonymous and unmemorable line of music. The judge agreed with me in my musical opinion, stating in his judgment that, 'In order to be a joint author a person must first establish that he had made a significant and original contribution to the creation of the musical work', and concluded in this case that he had not. The judge also concluded that, overall, in this claim, the memories of Gary Kemp of the circumstances were 'more likely to be reliable' than those of the claimants.

The Bluebells case again concerned a solo instrumental line, this time in the introduction to the song 'Young at Heart' and played on violin by Bobby Valentino, who was brought in for the purpose as a session player. My transcription in the report of Valentino's opening riff is presented in Figure 5.4.

Figure 5.4 The Bluebells' 'Young at Heart' opening violin riff

I was retained as the expert for the writer of the song, Robert Hodgens, who stated he had devised the solo line and, indeed, had played it on guitar to Valentino by way of instruction. Before the trial, he recorded himself on video playing what he claimed to have been his 'original' version

of the riff, for the purpose of illustration in court. In Figure 5.5 is my own transcription of what Hodgens played (on guitar) in his video, which is musically similar overall to what Valentino played, but has many differences in detail. (This example was handwritten as I had to transcribe it in counsel's office while the trial was running in court.)

Figure 5.5 The Bluebells' 'Young at Heart' opening riff as played by Robert Hodgens

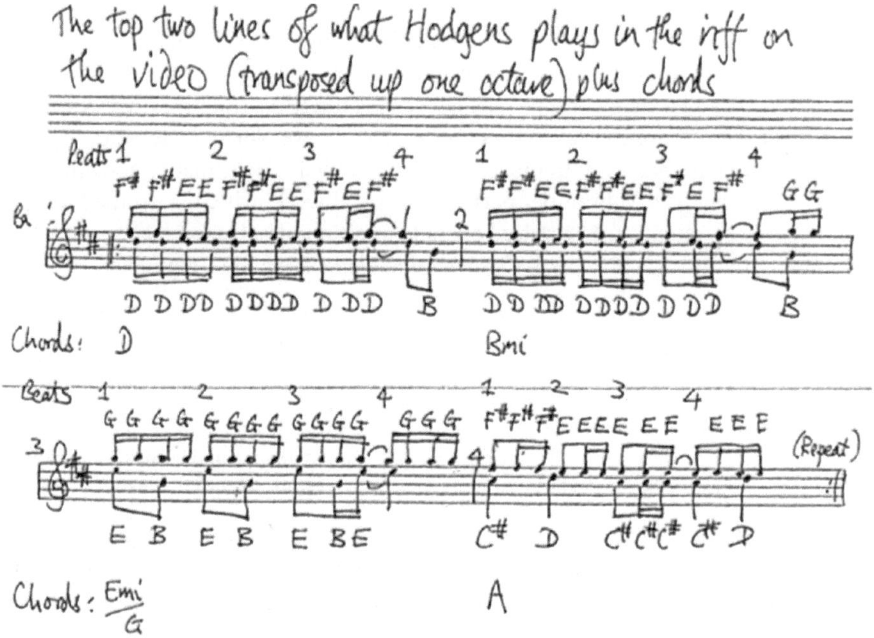

The judge included my own transcriptions of both the violin and guitar versions as annexes to his judgment and stated that he was not convinced that Hodgens's evidence on this was accurate. Furthermore, he noted that both experts considered 'the violin riff memorable and catchy'.

Another element was that Valentino had not made a claim of joint authorship until 15 years after the release of the recording. In the judgment, a matter of difference between the experts was noted:

> Mr Chandler, who was called by Mr Valentino, was of the view that to be found to have wrongly denied a coauthor a credit to which he was entitled was not harmful … Mr Protheroe thought that such a finding would be seriously harmful to a composer in his dealings with recording companies … I prefer Mr Protheroe's evidence which seems to me to accord more with common sense.

It can be gratifying when, on occasions, an expert's observations on music industry practice are noted and have the potential of affecting subsequent disputes on such matters (even if in this instance my objective comment was not in favour of my client's argument!).

The findings for Bobby Valentino in this matter were reflected in the judgment in a court case soon after concerning the song 'A Whiter Shade of Pale' by Procol Harum. The keyboard player Matthew Fisher was successful in his claim of joint authorship in the song for his organ solo introduction. I was initially involved in this case.[8]

So case law in these matters, including the Bobby Valentino/Bluebells case, has clearly established on balance that if anyone makes a contribution to a musical work which is of sufficient skill

[8] *Fisher v Brooker & Ors* [2009] UKHL 41 (House of Lords).

and labour, and is original in the sense that it comes from the contributor, they will be entitled to a copyright interest in the musical work concerned and to a share of the publishing income.

These judgments in the Spandau Ballet and Bluebells cases have subsequently often been discussed as a pair, many suggesting that the judge in the Spandau Ballet case got it wrong and that the one in the Bluebells case got it right. If one listens to these recordings in purely *musical* terms, without considering legal issues, I believe most musicians would concur that, whereas the saxophone riff is anonymous and unmemorable (although it fulfils its function in the structure of the song), the violin riff is indeed notable and memorable (though it is also highlighted by its appearance at the opening of the track). This focuses on a dichotomy between musical assessments by musicians and legal assessments of music by lawyers. A question amongst the lawyers has been: who composed the saxophone notes in these bars? It was Steve Norman, not Gary Kemp. This is correct; but the problem that arises in most music cases, as here, is the matter of defining precisely what material qualifies as a 'substantial part' of a musical work, which is deemed to be 'more a matter of quality than quantity'. A standard overall definition of 'substantiality' used in the courts is to be found in the authoritative book *Copinger and Skone James on Copyright*:

> As to whether a substantial part of a musical work has been copied, the question remains whether the alleged infringement has made use of a substantial part of the skill, labour and taste of the original composer. It is common practice in music copyright cases to call expert evidence to identify and explain the significance of similarities and differences between the works. Although the court is often helped by such evidence, the issue of substantial part does not depend solely on a note for note comparison but must be determined by the ear as well as by the eye, for the most uneducated in music can recognise that an altered work of music is, in effect, the same as or is derived from the original work.

In a court of law in the UK, it is generally not the verdict of 'the most uneducated in music', or even a jury in this role: it is the verdict of the judge, putting himself in this position. (In fact, some judges have an intimate knowledge of music – which I have found can on occasion be a problem, when their decisions appear to be influenced by their own personal perceptions of the music, and sometimes override the musical opinions of the experts on both sides!) Fundamentally, any judgment of substantiality in music must be subjective. It is easy to measure and calculate objectively the *quantity* of elements in a musical work, ie how much they are used, in terms of duration, and also to map their *prominence*, etc (though that factor has to be partly a matter of subjective reasoning), but it is not easy to measure their aesthetic *quality*, which is inevitably and fundamentally abstract.

There is also the persisting concept of *de minimis* in terms of what qualifies as copyright material, for which the threshold in UK law has historically been at a very low level. This can confound the business of experts trying to advise their clients in advance on the potential outcome of a particular claim: it is unpredictable at what levels the relative issues of substantiality and *de minimis* will be interpreted, which can vary greatly, and are often influenced by the most recent case law.

VI. Libel: The James Bond Theme

Another case which provides a parallel about potential joint authorship was a claim of libel by Monty Norman against the *Sunday Times*: *Monty Norman and Times Newspapers Limited* (which, being a libel case, qualified for a jury trial).[9] The claim concerned the theme music for the first James Bond film, *Dr No*. The *Sunday Times* quoted John Barry as saying he had composed the

[9] Queen's Bench Division 1997 N No 728.

'James Bond Theme'; Monty Norman sued for libel, claiming he had composed it. The details of this case are irrelevant here, but suffice it to say that Monty Norman provided a melody line, which he had previously written, and John Barry was commissioned to orchestrate it. Barry adapted the melody line, gave it to electric guitar (played at the bottom of its range by Vic Flick) and composed around it the whole 'James Bond Theme', as it has been known ever since, which contains large amounts of other musical material. I was the expert for the *Sunday Times*, John Barry, etc.

Monty Norman provided in evidence of his original theme a single sheet of manuscript paper containing a sketch of a melody line. In Figure 5.6, I have copied the first 12 bars, marked 'MN sketch', and have added above each staff in this figure the alphabetical names of all the pitches to assist in reading.

Figure 5.6 Melodies in Monty Norman sketch, vocal recording and 'James Bond Theme'

Monty Norman's melody was originally designed for a song in a projected musical entitled *A House for Mr Biswas*, which was never completed. He also provided to the court a video clip from a CNN programme in which he sang the first bars of the song, entitled 'Bad Sign, Good Sign'. I have notated this, together with the lyrics, as the middle line in Figure 5.6, identified as 'MN vocal'.

In the third stave in Figure 5.6, I have notated the opening guitar melody as it appears in John Barry's arrangement. I have transposed Barry's low guitar line up the interval of a minor 10th, so that it appears at the same pitch at which Norman sang his melody.

As can be seen, the pitches in the first two bars of each are the same, with rhythmic variations, and these patterns repeated identically in bars 3–4, where the vocal line ends. Bar 6 is almost the same in the MN sketch and JB theme; they then both rise higher in bars 7–8. MN continues differently, ending in bars 11–12 with a rising figure. A similar sort of figure, but higher and with different notes, is seen in JB in bars 7–8.

So, Barry has used the basic pattern of the opening two bars from Norman, repeated several times and then varied. This two-bar figure is the only element substantively in common. 'Bad Sign, Good Sign' has no chords below; the full 'James Bond Theme' features rich harmonies, with the famous rising–falling chord sequence in the opening bars, before the main melody begins. Also 'James Bond Theme' is heard a 10th lower in pitch and played at almost twice the speed of Norman's singing, and, of course, the character and style are entirely different.

In court, there was some muddy definition as to what the 'theme' in question was. Norman's melody line was just that – a theme consisting of a line of individual notes (with lyrics) and nothing else; Barry's production was a complete musical work. In the early days of registration of popular music for copyright, all that was entered was the top melody line – of a song or an instrumental piece; but that process had been long outdated. The jury in the Bond case were played the Norman melody, as sung solo by Monty Norman without any accompaniment, then the melody as it appeared in the Barry arrangement, and they decided it was essentially the same melody line (tune) – which was true, in terms of the theme's opening repeated figure. But it was what Barry had done to it by way of development – making a complete musical work – together with the iconic orchestration and resulting sound which made it unforgettable and one of the greatest film themes. The expert for Monty Norman, the renowned classical musicologist Dr Stanley Sadie, opined (regarding the complete 'James Bond Theme') that, 'in the absence of any evidence deducible from it that Mr Barry's role was larger than the traditional one of arranger, that Mr Norman must be regarded as the composer of *The James Bond Theme*'. I countered with my opinion, that 'I believe the musical work *The James Bond Theme* is substantially more the creative work of John Barry than of Monty Norman'. My own opinion and recommendation, as presented in court, was that, in terms of music copyright, John Barry should have been credited as a joint author of the music, and the equitable solution would have been a copyright share of the royalties – which I still believe to be correct, musically.

So the level described here is again a matter of *de minimis* and, viewing this as a musician, it seems to me that if the 'James Bond Theme' case had been one concerning a claim of joint authorship by John Barry, on such precedents he would probably have won easily. I can only conclude that the reason Monty Norman won was because (i) it was a different sort of claim – libel; and (ii) there was also a jury, and how much of the music was presented to them was an issue.

VII. Copyright Arising in New Editions of Historical Musical Works

Another major court case in which I appeared as an expert concerned new editions of historical works, and the nature and extent of the copyright arising for the editor – a major issue in this field which had not been tested in court before: *Hyperion Records Ltd v Sawkins*.[10] The composer

[10] *Hyperion Records Ltd v Sawkins* [2005] EWCA Civ 565.

in this case was Michel-Richard de Lalande (1657–1726), who was principal court composer at Versailles under both Louis XIV and Louis XV. Lalande is still well known these days for shorter instrumental works, but his large-scale choral orchestral works had mainly not been published in modern performing editions. In 2001, Hyperion Records Limited recorded on a compact disc a number of these latter works performed by a leading group specialising in French baroque music, Ex Cathedra, with the scores prepared by the Australian musicologist Lionel Sawkins, the world expert on Lalande. For this project, Sawkins transcribed the works into modern musical notation, which involved editorial work and decisions he considered were required. The policy of the commissioner of this work, the director of Hyperion, was, however, never to pay copyright royalties in respect of musical works which were deemed to be out of copyright by virtue of their age.

In the judgment of the court case, the Honourable Mr Justice Patten stated:

> The central issue for me to determine in this action is whether the production of a new performing edition of the score of an existing composition is capable of vesting in the editor copyright in the musical work, as recorded in the score which is produced.

The expert on behalf of Dr Sawkins was – again – Dr Stanley Sadie, who himself had prepared some performing editions of Lalande's works 40 or so years earlier. I appeared as expert for Hyperion Records: as part of my Oxford music degree, I had studied French baroque music, and had also been a performer (as a singer) in several recordings and concerts of music from this period with leading conductors and groups, so had a good overall knowledge of the history and the intricacies of interpreting the original notation from the period. At the start of Dr Sawkins's appearance in the witness box, he 'accepted that his aim was, so far as possible, to reproduce faithfully Lalande's work'. It was put to him 'that the more successful he was at doing this, the more likely it was that he would have produced something close to what the composer had himself originally created' – hence potentially not producing any new copyright material. I examined every bar of music in the scores and compared them with the contents of the original manuscripts. There were also modern editions of a few of the works predating those by Sawkins, which I also examined and compared. From this research, I identified exactly which elements Dr Sawkins had created that were not already in the original editions (or in the preceding modern ones), and was instructed then to assess whether, in my opinion, his work in each of these pieces demonstrated enough appropriate skill and labour to constitute copyright material.

What Sawkins had added was largely, in terms of the overall bulk of his work, a matter of adding to the scores some extra 'figured bass' (an eighteenth-century shorthand that adds figures below the musical notes and chords). The original scores contained much in the way of such figures; Sawkins had added such extra figures as he considered helpful to the keyboard player (and, as I demonstrated, the keyboard player in the Hyperion recordings had written many further figures into his own score, for his own convenience).

'Figured bass' was added, in baroque music, to the bass line (the basso continuo), which is most often played on harpsichord or organ (or harp, lute, etc) and often doubled by some string or other single-note instruments. The keyboard player's part contained only the bass line, with figures below to indicate which chord is needed to be played above. If there are several instruments or voices scored above, all the figures are doing normally is providing a quick shorthand describing the chords appearing in the full score, to save the player needing to read or play from a copy of the full orchestral/choral score. So, no original creativity is required to write the figures, and such additions are often referred to as just 'clerical' – including by Dr Sadie in his report: 'a largely clerical task'. But if there is only a solo part above, or there are just a few, the keyboard player (or editor) might need to choose or invent appropriate chords to fit (filling in missing notes), which is a creative activity. In my opinion, such creative additions constituted a distinct minority in the Sawkins editions (which, as I commented, was not a criticism of Sawkins – merely that not many were needed).

Figure 5.7 is a scan of the opening from one of the Lalande scores: the instrumental parts in bars 1–8 of 'Sacris solemniis S74'.[11] The lowest part is the bass, with numbers below defining chords.

Figure 5.7 Lalande's opening of 'Sacris solemniis' with figured bass (Lionel Sawkins's transcription)

To demonstrate how 'figured bass' works, in Figure 5.8 I have re-notated the same 8 bars above, and have added the alphabetical pitch names of each note. (In the example, the viola parts are notated, as usual, in alto clef; below I write them in treble clef, which is much more familiar to most people.)

Figure 5.8 Lalande's opening of 'Sacris solemniis' with figured bass (Protheroe's transcription)

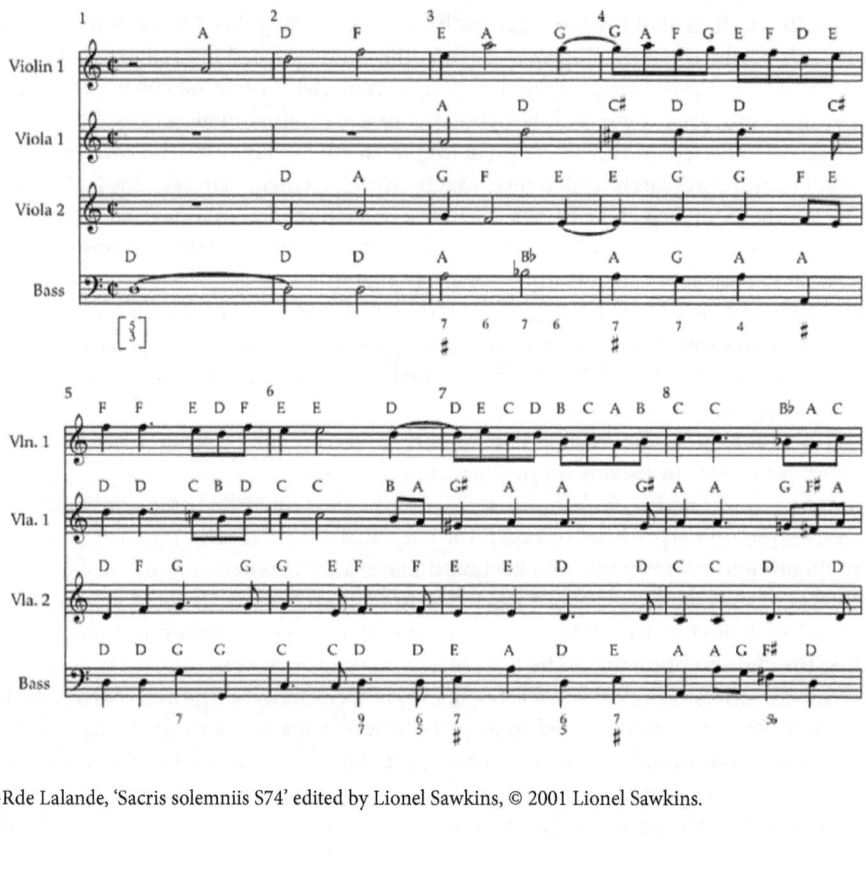

[11] M-Rde Lalande, 'Sacris solemniis S74' edited by Lionel Sawkins, © 2001 Lionel Sawkins.

Here are a few comments to explain this. When there is no number below a bass line note, this means that it is a 'root position' chord, which means the pitches in the chord are three steps and five steps above the bass note. So, in bar 1, the pitches above the bass note D are F and A. (Because this is the default basic chord, it is generally not written as 5–3 above; hence I have added this in bar 1 in brackets.)

There are four crotchet beats in each bar. In bars 3 and 4, the notation on beat 1 under the bass note A is 7 over #. 7 is seven pitches above A, which is G, as in viola 2. The sharp (#) means C sharp, indicating a chord of A major. (The C sharp is not actually notated in the chord in bar 3, but this chord here would be obvious to any performer, and is known as 'A major 7'.) In bar 3, under beat 2 is marked 6: this is the note F in viola 2, six steps above the bass note A. So, the figures denote the main chords in this passage. There are also short 'passing notes' within the beats in the upper parts, as in the violin 1 line in bar 4, but these do not change the essential chords in these places.

Further to this analysis, I was instructed to examine whether the *new* 'editorial interventions' that had been added to the score by Dr Sawkins had been included in the performances recorded on the CD. I examined every detail in this respect and concluded that where there had been such editorial decisions, most had indeed been included in the recordings.

The judgment found, in relation to most (but not all) of the works, that the extent of the work of Dr Sawkins did indeed attract copyright. (My personal conclusion agreed with this judgment.) And, of course, there were many other issues raised in court relating to circumstantial elements, including disputes concerning who had agreed what and when, and concerning Dr Sawkins's terms of contractual engagement on the project – such issues as form part of most cases in court.

The subsequent judgment of the Appeal Court supported the verdict of Mr Justice Patten, quoting many of the useful precedents that are taken into consideration in the courts concerning copyright law,[12] which have also helped to produce a new definition of what actions made by editors of historical music create a copyright. (I believe that such factors should potentially by extension also apply to arrangers – speaking as one myself!) In ¶56, Mummery LJ wrote that

> it is wrong in principle to single out the notes as uniquely significant for copyright purposes and to proceed to deny copyright to the other elements that make some contribution to the sound of the music when performed, such as performing indications, tempo and performance practice indicators, if they are the product of a person's effort, skill and time, bearing in mind, of course, the 'relatively modest level' of the threshold for a work to qualify for protection.

Again, the low level of creativity and originality needed to qualify for copyright protection is stated.

So, the work of a forensic musicologist (if they can demonstrate to the court appropriate expertise in the subject) can cover the whole field of music, and most of the methodology and techniques are relevant throughout – as demonstrated in the following subject areas.

VIII. Advertising Music

A major regular part of my musicological activities has been, and continues to be, advising on music for advertising – mainly for television, but also for cinema, radio, etc. Some issues are

[12] *Hyperion Records Ltd v Sawkins* [2005] EWCA Civ 565 (Court of Appeal Civil Division).

straight claims of copyright infringement in screened/broadcast commercials, but I am also very often involved at the front end of the process, when music tracks – 'jingles' – are being devised for inclusion in the commercials.

A standard scenario is that companies approach an advertising agency to devise and create advertising material for their products and/or services. Sometimes the client may have some specific ideas, which they discuss with the agency, or they may leave it to the creative team at the agency to come up with ideas. When an audio/visual advert is planned, there is most often some pre-existing music associated, and often the first demos of the advert have a 'temp' music track attached, to which the video (or just audio, if a radio commercial) is edited. On some occasions, when the clients are very keen, a licence to use the original recording may be obtained. Sometimes, however, they may not get the original rights holders to agree, for reasons of money or because the rights holders do not want to be associated with the product. In this case, it may be decided instead to commission a new, independent music track – or to instruct a music production company ('jingle company') to come up with something like the temp track, but without infringing copyright! The jingle company will then come up with several demos for consideration.

This is where I have come in, several hundred times, often instructed directly by the advertising agency, or otherwise by the jingle company, which these days is frequently instructed by the agency to provide an indemnity that what they have written is not infringing copyright of the original work. (But if the track they submit does not relate aurally to the previous work, it will probably be rejected by the agency anyway.) Of course, the jingle company cannot provide a legal indemnity (only a court of law can do that), so instead I am asked to examine the demos, and to opine as to any potential copyright problems arising. If I find that there are any, I analyse what the essential aspects of the original track that have attracted its use are (beyond, of course, the original musical material), and suggest suitable revisions of it, so that the new track makes the same impact but will not be perceived by the audience as either a copy of the original or an adaptation of it. So, this is a matter, in accordance with the Copyright Act, of being able to copy 'an idea' but not the particular 'expression of the idea'. To protect myself, I only approve a music track if it fulfils completely what I regard as the copyright requirements, and it is in my opinion an independent work in terms of copyright law. Of course, I, too, cannot provide an 'indemnity' in this respect; but I am not aware of any occasion where a musical jingle which I have approved has gone 'on air' and there has subsequently been a challenge. (Furthermore, I have written jingles myself several times, and I would obviously not risk the possibility of a claim against me, which would hardly benefit my professional reputation – hence sometimes my commission as composer!)

One amusing instance regarding revision and adaptation occurred about 15 years ago, when I was engaged by a rap artist who had been engaged as a vocalist on a TV commercial, for which a demo had already been written. It was agreed that he would update the rap lyrics in the music track – he was an expert on 'ragga' (dancehall reggae), which was the style of the music. He then demanded rights as a joint author of the lyrics, but the jingle company would not agree, so he sued. At the appropriate stage in the proceedings, I, and my opposing expert Peter Oxendale (the two of us have been the experts in most UK disputes this century), gave our opinions before the judge in chambers. At the end, the judge said 'I do not think I could claim to be expert on the matter of lyrics in rap; but I think neither Mr Protheroe nor Mr Oxendale would claim to be so either. However, on balance I have to say I agree with Mr Protheroe!' Very nice of him – but the point here is that it is possible to apply one's forensic methods and skills developed in the field of musical works to other aspects of copyright as well.

IX. Single Joint Expert

I have once appeared in court as a Single Joint Expert, which was a curious situation. The claimant said that the chorus sections in a song he had composed had been copied in a song by the defendant, to the extent that it represented an infringement of copyright. The claimant had written his own extensive analysis identifying where he believed there was copying. The defendants produced in response a report by the musicologist Peter Oxendale containing a detailed analysis of both songs and of all the issues raised by the claimant. The claimant then wrote a detailed rejection of Mr Oxendale, to which Mr Oxendale was instructed to make another detailed response. When the matter came to court, I was appointed as Single Joint Expert, wrote my own detailed report and was questioned on my findings in great detail in the witness box. As it happened, I agreed thoroughly with almost every detail in Peter Oxendale's reports – the claimant found this very hard to stomach, but that was my objective opinion.

X. Piracy and Sampling

Early on in my forensic musicology career, in the 1990s, I was instructed by the IFPI (International Federation of the Phonographic Industry) to examine recordings which it was suspected were pirate copies of original recordings. The originals were provided to me on compact disc, analogue cassette, DAT (digital audio tape), reel-to-reel, vinyl disc and video cassette. The suspected pirate copies were nearly always on CD and had generally the same track listing (sometimes in a different order, or sometimes compilations from several different albums) but claimed to be different recordings of the same songs. Together with a recording engineer colleague, Simon Weir, with whom I have worked ever since, we developed a methodology for comparing recordings – known as A:B Testing.

The methodology had two main stages: (i) direct aural comparison, including unique vocal events (like breathing patterns, consonants, etc), unique instrumental events (specific playing techniques, vibrato, modulation), unique background or environmental events (noises from instruments, clicks, hums) and unique live performance events (audience noises, traffic, aeroplanes, etc); and (ii) the employment of phasing techniques: synchronising recordings in parallel (using vari-speed), then testing for phase cancellation, etc.

The phasing technique was essentially very simple: I started by listening to the original recording mixed into mono in my left headphone and the potential copy in the right headphone. Figure 5.9 shows my original handwritten illustration.

Figure 5.9 A:B Testing stage 1

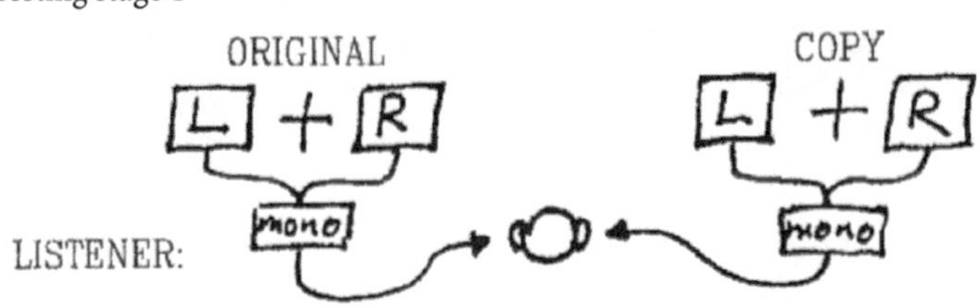

I would then use vari-speed to adjust the audio in the right channel (which also automatically made a change of pitch). If the two recordings ran together, synchronised and in phase, all the common elements would be heard as a stable image in the centre of one's head, and any different elements would be apparent on the left or right. At this point, I would switch both tracks back into stereo, so left and right are superimposed in each, then switch the phase of the copy into reverse, as illustrated in Figure 5.10.

Figure 5.10 A:B Testing stage 2

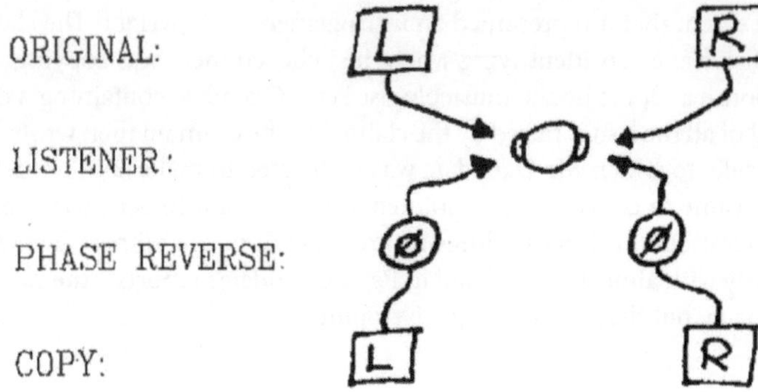

If the second recording is, indeed, a copy of the first, there will be considerable (if not complete) cancellation of sound, demonstrating that the fundamental audio components of the original and the copy are the same.

I undertook investigation of several thousand sound recordings in this respect. The methodology we developed enabled in most cases very fast assessment, and it was also very efficient, early on, at helping to identify illegal sampling. However, as the years progressed, digital technology in music production leapt ahead rapidly and, in relation to attempts at piracy, it became much easier to hide such copying.

A technique I later developed with the same engineer was that of spectographic analysis, comparing the content of two different recordings visually, not by looking at the waveforms, but by analysing the frequency content against time. Two examples follow which Simon Weir has prepared for me for the purpose of demonstrating this technique. They appear here in black and white – the original images are in full colour, revealing in detail similarities and differences of frequencies, timings, intensities, etc. Figure 5.11 shows the waveforms of two recordings in stereo (left channel above, right channel below), the claimed copy on the left (showing multiple echoes of an alleged sample) and the original sample on the right.

Figure 5.11 Spectographic analysis example 1

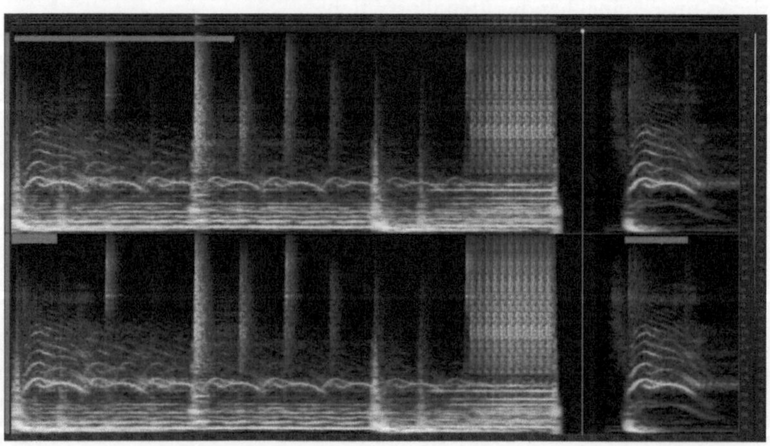

Figure 5.12 zooms in on the first instance of the sample in the claimed copy (left) and the original sample (right), comparing the unique spectrographic 'fingerprint'. In the original analysis, there were detailed comments on very specific technical aspects, such as harmonics and instrumental timbres.

Figure 5.12 Spectographic analysis example 2 (zoomed in)

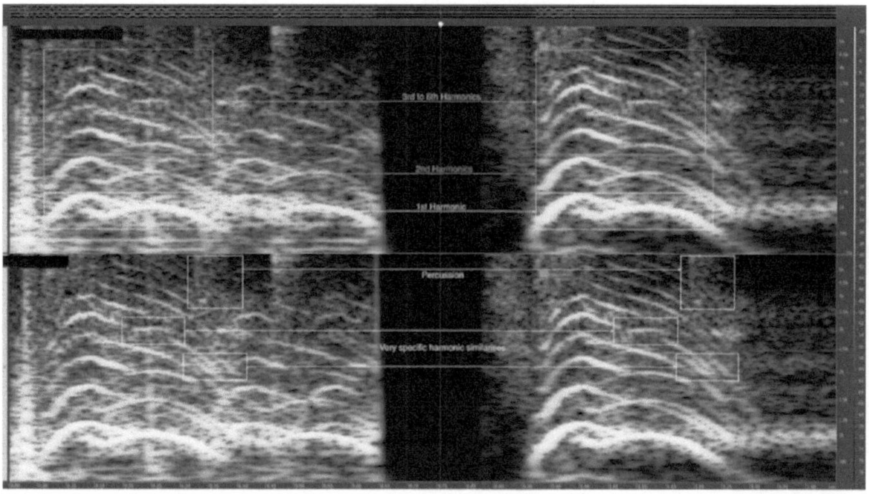

Further to this, we have demonstrated piracy by using spectrographic analysis where, in parallel to the sound cancellation test described above (A:B Testing), we have printed out the spectrograms of each recording (or a section of each) on transparency. If they are the same recording, one can slide one transparency over the other and see just the one image, as they are identical (including all the spectrum of colours). This is a strong visual demonstration of copying.

Although I have my own digital studio system, which I use for all my own investigations on copyright issues and also for my own writing and arranging, the digital techniques that are now standard have become so sophisticated and advanced that generally, when I am asked to give forensic evidence in relation to disputed sampling, I pass the matter of scientific proof of sampling to one of my engineer colleagues (with all of whom I often work as a live performing musician, including Simon Weir). These colleagues analyse the recordings and provide technical reports. If there are issues arising over whether what has been sampled represents (i) a substantial part of the original *musical work* in the recording (ie a publishing issue) and/or (ii) a substantial part of the original *sound recording*, then I am often asked to opine further. (But it seems to be generally accepted these days that *any* copying from a sound recording constitutes an infringement – a matter of *de minimis* again.)

XI. Miscellaneous

I have also been involved in many matters which are not in the direct field of forensic musicology, but which need my knowledge and experience to clarify issues. One example was my being engaged in 2008 as a consultant on a new UK karaoke game show series devised by

ITV productions, *Who Dares, Sings!*[13] I was brought in to check on and research all aspects of the format and operation of the show, and to be present at all recordings (which was a major undertaking) in order to protect ITV against any claims from Ofcom of unfair or 'untransparent' operation within the show – there had been several notorious cases just before between Ofcom (the Office of Communications, the government-approved regulatory and competition authority for the broadcasting, telecommunications and postal industries of the UK) and the BBC concerning game show and quiz rigging.

XII. Musicologists and Court Appearances

Because music exists essentially just as a matter of sounds in time, which is the perception of any listener, it has always been a considerable problem for the law to define in legal terms. Regarding plagiarism, in the Court of Appeal judgment in *Hyperion Records Ltd v Sawkins*, as discussed in section VII above, Mummery LJ very helpfully stated (¶¶53–54):

> Music must be distinguished from the fact and form of its fixation as a record of a musical composition … But the fixation in the written score or on a record is not in itself the music in which the copyright subsists … The fact that in musical copyright the sounds are more important than the notes in the text is recognised, for example, in the approach to infringement. The test of substantial reproduction is not a note-by-note textual comparison of the scores. It involves listening to and comparing the sounds of the copyright work and of the infringing work.

One problem which arises in musical disputes, and which is inevitable, is that, in contrast to lawyers, music experts – defined as forensic musicologists for this purpose – inevitably listen to music primarily as musicians. (I sang in my father's church choir from the age of six, and my whole career throughout has primarily been as a performer and writer, in many musical styles and cultures.)

Of course, to be a useful and efficient forensic musicologist, one needs to have a good working knowledge of how the law works in this area, and to have a reasonable knowledge of legal precedents and judgments in the field of music concerned in the relevant action (otherwise much time can be wasted). Or, if the matter is an area which has not arisen before in music litigation, it can be helpful to the lawyers if the expert can identify elements involved in previous case law which might have some relevance. (That is one advantage of employing musicologists already experienced in the field of litigation.)

So, in a dispute concerning music, the musicologist naturally approaches the music from the angle of musicology, an intellectual discipline of its own, whereas the lawyer, trained in primarily in law, approaches it from the angle of law – they may have some musical experience, but it is very unlikely to be professional. This aspect is generally dealt with early on, by the lawyers refining the questions which the witness is instructed to address – though I ensure that my instructing solicitor and barrister are aware of views I may have on matters which are not in my instructions (this is matters of opinion, not fact), but which I might be called on to address in my cross-examination.

Such matters are generally dealt with, and often arise, in the process of 'proofing' the witness's evidence. On occasion, shortly before I am due to appear in the witness box, I am given a live mock cross-examination by my own leading counsel, to ensure there are no loose threads in my

[13] https://en.wikipedia.org/wiki/Who_Dares,_Sings.

evidence, my memory of what is in it and any new ideas which might occur to me during this process. This can be very intensive and gruelling – there is no mercy shown, just because we are on the same side; but it certainly helps concentrate the mind!

To finish, there can be lighter moments in court for an expert. On one occasion, when my evidence was being discussed, I was sitting with our lawyers prior to my appearance in the witness box. The judge asked our barrister if the expert Mr Protheroe was in court, to which the reply was affirmative. 'Could you point him out to me?' 'Yes, my lord: he's the one with the natural wig!' (my having grey, curly hair). And I was referred to thus in a later case also, when the judge said, 'I see your expert is the one with the natural wig'. Getting recognised and remembered can be useful!

On another occasion, the plaintiff, just before going into court, sacked his legal team (and me along with it), and led his own case (for several days). When he mentioned musicology, the judge said, 'I see your expert is in court: Mr Protheroe' (I had gone to watch and was sitting in the public benches, just behind the defence lawyers). To this, the plaintiff replied that his expert now was his studio engineer and named him. The judge addressed the defence legal team: 'Does the court know Mr X?' To which the reply was 'No, my lord'. 'Does Mr Protheroe know Mr X?' To which my reply, through the lawyers, was 'No'. It was remarked on subsequently that the judge should not be asking someone on the public benches. But he and I knew each other well, through previous court appearances and indeed personal friendship. I guess that lent some credibility to my status as an expert!

XIII. Conclusions: Looking Forward

As the years, musical tastes and technology move on, the matter of defining what elements constitute copyright material in musical works becomes harder. In the heady days of avant-garde electronic music, in which I was involved from the 1960s with composers like Karlheinz Stockhausen, most of the public perceived such music (if they heard it) as just 'noise', and the description of music as 'sound organised in time' was indeed appropriate (because, in essence, that is what all music consists of anyway).

It took longer for popular music to reach the same area sonically: indeed, older generations may perceive much of the latest electronic pop music as predominantly noise. But there is huge popularity at least among younger generations for music which does not fit into the traditional definitions used in the field of copyright.

The new technologies also muddy the separation of the roles of composer, performer and, indeed, producer. From the time of George Martin producing the Beatles, with the technological developments in digital studio recording and engineering, an inspired producer can transform the sound and impact of a band and of individual artists, both by their technical supervision of recording sessions and their relationships with and influences on the artists.

In the creation of hip-hop, rap and similar genres, there is often no need at all to go into a recording studio, as all the elements required to construct a song (and, indeed, achieve a hit) are available on a laptop, with downloads of drum samples, etc. Probably only the main vocal needs to be 'original' (and perceived as such), containing lyrics delivered in rhythmic patterns, very often in speech style without any pitched melody, in terms of notes. And often such songs are created by just one person sitting in a home studio, fulfilling all the traditional roles.

Furthermore, such tracks, which are often hugely popular, can contain nothing identifiable in the traditional sense as a 'musical work'. Nevertheless, clearly the whole resulting track must qualify for copyright, as the result of time, skill and labour, although often, I believe logically it should be regarded as a combined musical/lyrical work. (It can make little sense, in many rap tracks, to separate music and lyrics into separate copyrights, as so often the lyrics are created to fit into the rhythmic patterns employed by the rapper, such rhythmic patterns being part of the musical work rather than literary.) If there are lyrics, they can at least be written down and their potential copyright value can much more easily be assessed – this arises most often when there are claims of plagiarism of lyrics. But if the (musical) backing track is left by itself, with the rap removed, there is generally very little for a forensic musicologist to nail as a 'substantial part' of the musical work – unless there is a very identifiable musical 'hook' in the track (which may well have been copied from a sample anyway).

So, while traditional composing continues, both in the classical and commercial fields of music, the forensic musicologist still has a role to play. But the future appears unpredictable, until the law catches up with the new music technology. This, of course, includes the whole new area of AI (artificial intelligence), creating new musical works independent, or largely independent, of human composers: how will copyright operate in this new world of music and sound? We experts await, anxious and intrigued, for legal developments in this area.

6

Borrowing from Traditional Culture: Ownership and Commodification of Traditional Music from a Cultural Custodianship Perspective

ANTHONY CK KAKOOZA*

I. Introduction

I will start this chapter by defining the key terms that are discussed throughout this chapter. The goal is to provoke the reader into connecting the dots between culture and its manifestation, particularly with regard to traditional music, in intellectual property (IP). This is achieved by providing an understanding of music borrowing from a cultural borrowing perspective.

A. Culture

Culture is looked at herein as a form of identity that connotes the sharing of certain common beliefs and experiences within a restricted setting.[1] It is otherwise understood as the idea of community. It is therefore through culture that humanity can draw up differences around the world, in the way people live and engage with one another.

Culture is, as such, part and parcel of traditional cultural expressions (TCEs). TCEs, which are also referred to as expressions of folklore, relate to the form or representation of traditional cultures (such as traditional song, performance, oral narrative or graphic design).[2] Traditional music is therefore an aspect of TCEs and is used interchangeably as such throughout this paper. The term 'traditional' can be misleading and is often erroneously considered as archaic. However, TCEs involve a living body of knowledge that goes through a sort of metamorphosis as it is

* This chapter is an improved version of a presentation titled 'Turning Culture into Property: Africa's Dilemma', which was made by the author at the Institute of African Development, Cornell University, Ithaca, NY, on 7 March 2019.

[1] Culture has also been simply defined as the characteristics and knowledge of a particular group of people, encompassing language, religion, cuisine, social habits, music and arts. See www.livescience.com/.

[2] WIPO, *Intellectual Property Law Handbook* (2004). See also Intergovernmental Committee on Intellectual Property and Genetic Resources, Traditional Knowledge and Folklore, 23rd Session, Geneva, 4–8 February 2013, 'Glossary of Key Terms related to IP and Genetic Resources, TK and TCEs', Document WIPO/GRTKF/IC/23/INF/8 (2 November 2012) www.wipo.int/edocs/mdocs/tk/en/wipo_grtkf_ic_23/wipo_grtkf_ic_23_inf_8.pdf.

passed on from one generation to another. Each stage in the evolution of traditional music adds on another element of creativity. This chapter will thus address the challenge of whether such new elements of creativity can be appreciated as copyright belonging to an individual or whether they still serve as traditional music that is owned by the whole community.

The next sub-section highlights the appreciation of property in what is considered as the Western perspective (which is basically the developed world), as well as in the perspective of ethnic communities. The key discussion therein is as to whether traditional music, which is part of culture, also constitutes property to generate a measure of controlled access and utilisation.

B. Property

The term 'property' has been explained as being a bundle of rights.[3] Property rights include possessory rights and rights of transfer.[4] Such concepts are, however, quite peculiar within the understanding of traditional music. This is because in the appreciation of property in itself and the rights accruing with it, the difference between custodians of traditional music and the developed world is in how one looks at the protectable element that gives value to the concept of property. Susan Scafidi guides us in understanding that difference. She states that: 'For Intellectual Property, the intangible element is an idea; for cultural products, the intangible element may be an expression of community beliefs, values, aesthetics, or practices.'[5]

It therefore follows that protection of property in copyright, in music for instance, focuses on protecting how an idea has been expressed; whereas protection of property in traditional music focuses on the belief system and societal norms.

This different mindset as to what is protected further explains why the individual is the focus of protection in the Western concept of property while the community is the driving factor in the protection of traditional music.

John Locke, in his *Two Treatises on Government*,[6] provides the argument that ownership and commodification of property in copyright is assigned to individuals on the premise that they have exerted some effort and labour into the creation of such property. The theory also posits that creativity in the establishment of IP springs from utilising what is already freely available to all, ie what 'nature hath provided', and then turning it into something that all are in a position to enjoy, as long as the creator of the new property is rewarded for his effort, or what 'he hath mixed his labour with'. Such reward relates to the enjoyment of economic and moral rights by creators in the copyright industry.

This theory, however, does not fit in well with property perspectives under TCEs. This is because although TCEs are freely available for all to use, the freedom for such usage is not necessarily premised on what 'nature hath provided' but is derived from a cultural heritage that is passed on through generations. Secondly, such freedom to use such cultural practices falls within the parameters of the ethnic community from which they are derived, and not to foreigners. In some respects, communities exercise sacred norms through which a class system dictates which members of the community are free to practice certain cultural expressions, as is discussed later in this chapter.

The element of comparisons of TCEs with copyright falling into the public domain once the duration of protection expires is also disregarded by ethnic communities. This is because if TCEs are regarded as public domain works, then access to such TCEs is free for all without recognition

[3] R Cooter and T Ulen, *Law and Economics*, 6th edn (Addison-Wesley, 2012) 73.

[4] S Shavell, *Economic Analysis of Law* (Fountain Press, 2004) 5.

[5] S Scafidi, *Who Owns Culture? – Appropriation and Authenticity in American Law* (Rutgers University Press, 2005) 31.

[6] Book II, ch V (1690), adapted from JE Cohen, LP Loren, RL Okediji and MA O'Rourke, *Copyright in a Global Information Economy*, 3rd edn (Aspen Publishers, 2010) 11.

and observance of the sacred rites and value systems attached to the cultural heritage. Creating a new sense of ownership and commodification of what has originally been seen as traditional music can risk creating a cultural devaluation of the traditional music.

Competition within the music industry is ever growing and plays a role in influencing those in the copyright industry to tap into traditional music in the commodification of new forms of music. On the face of it, this would seem socially and legally acceptable, based on the fact that traditional music, in most jurisdictions, is not regulated by any written laws. However, there are concerns that need to be considered in the ownership and commodification of traditional music, as the next section presents.

II. Custodianship and Underlying Conflicts in the Utilisation of Traditional Music

A. The Concept of the Tragedy of the Commons

The existence of inadequate regulatory mechanisms to manage the utilisation of TCEs plays a large role in the misappropriation and inefficient use of TCEs, inclusive of traditional music. Garrett Hardin points out in 'The Tragedy of the Commons' that if property is not well defined, it will be subjected to ill use, and that if no one owns or has an interest in the resource, it will be overused.[7] Borrowing from traditional music and the eventual creation of copyright in such musical works is something that is undertaken by both members and non-members of the custodial communities. This is mainly because of an inadequately structured legal regime at the international and regional levels as well as, in some jurisdictions, the national level. However, we need to first appreciate what custodial communities are.

B. The Custodians of Culture

The custodians of culture, in the context of this chapter, relate to indigenous people. A helpful definition of indigenous people is drawn from Article 1 of the 1989 International Labour Organization Convention (No 169) Concerning Indigenous and Tribal Peoples in Independent Countries.[8] It defines indigenous and tribal peoples as persons with definitive social, cultural and economic conditions that distinguish them from other persons.

This definition relates 'tribal peoples' to 'social, cultural and economic conditions'. Where such conditions regulate the way of life of such people, it is indicative of the attachment that they have to their culture as custodians. Custodians of culture, and particularly custodians of traditional music, are thus the whole membership of the ethnic community by virtue of their culture, which constitutes part of their identity and way of life.

It is estimated that there are more than 476 million indigenous peoples around the world in some 90 countries, with the biggest concentrations in Asia and the Pacific, followed by Africa.[9] The prevalence of traditional music in such jurisdictions is therefore premised on the dominance of custodial communities therein.

[7] G Hardin, 'The Tragedy of the Commons' (1968) 162(No 3859) *Science* 1243, https://science.sciencemag.org/content/sci/162/3859/1243.full.pdf.

[8] 27 June 1989, 1650 UNTS 384 (entered into force 5 September 1991), www.ilo.org/dyn/normlex/en/f?p=NORMLEXPUB:12100:0::NO::P12100_INSTRUMENT_ID:312314.

[9] See 'IFAD and Indigenous Peoples', www.ifad.org/english/indigenous/index.htm.

A key challenge, then, is to determine who enforces against abuse when traditional music is [mis]appropriated by others. A case in point that highlights the difference in property rights between TCEs and copyright is that of the Hezhe community in China. In 2003, the Beijing Higher People's Court passed a decision in a case involving a dispute over the originality of a song between a modern composer and the ethnic Hezhe minority.[10] A musician by the name of Guo Song and two others had composed a song in 1962 known as 'Wusuli Chantey', which was inspired by studies Song had conducted in the area where the ethnic Hezhe lived.[11] On 12 November 1999, an international folk song festival was organised in Nanning City in which the performance of 'Wusuli Chantey' by Gui Song was featured.[12] After its performance, a presenter announced that the song was an original composition, even though it had initially been presented as an adaptation from traditional Hezhe folklore.[13]

In reaction, the local government of the ethnic Hezhe people, acting as representatives of the Hezhe indigenous community, instituted a claim in the Beijing People's Second Intermediate Court, asserting that Guo's 'Wusuli Chantey' was derived from their centuries-old folklore, which belonged collectively to the ethnic Hezhe and for which they sought protection under copyright law.[14] The Second Intermediate Court agreed, reasoning that 'Wusuli Chantey' should be identified as a derivative work of the Hezhe folklore rather than as an original composition and that future use of the song should attribute originality to the Hezhe people.[15] On appeal, the Beijing Higher People's Court confirmed the earlier court's judgment on 17 December 2003.[16] The lower court's decision was based on Articles 6[17] and 12 of the 1990 Copyright Law of the People's Republic of China (as amended in 2001). Article 12 stipulates copyright protection for adaptations without prejudice to copyright in pre-existing work.[18]

Although the song was identified as derivative of the Hezhe people's folklore, the Higher People's Court did not give any specific mention to the abuse of the right to attribution or entitlement of the Hezhe community to part of the royalties from the song. It is also important to note the relevancy of the local government, which acted as a voice for the Hezhe community where they could not collectively defend their communal ownership of the traditional music.

C. Custodianship over Property Rights in Traditional Cultural Expressions

In a previous study related to the context in this chapter,[19] investigations were conducted in Uganda to gauge different perspectives on the issue of custodianship and ownership of property rights in Uganda's traditional music. The interviewees included IP lawyers, traditional elders,

[10] D Zografos, *Intellectual Property and Traditional Cultural Expressions* (Edward Elgar, 2010) 42, citing 17 December 2003 Decision of the Beijing Higher People's Court in Case No 246 (2003)(final)(2006) 37 IIC 482–87.

[11] ibid.

[12] ibid.

[13] ibid.

[14] ibid.

[15] ibid.

[16] ibid.

[17] ibid 44. Zografos notes that 'Article 6 provided that measures for the protection of copyright in works of folk literature and art should be formulated separately by the State Council. The State Council, however, never implemented such measures.'

[18] See https://wipolex.wipo.int/ru/text/466295.

[19] This author conducted empirical research between June 2012 and December 2013 on the use of traditional folklore in copyright mainly in Uganda.

musicians and music promoters. Notably, all the subjects interviewed asserted confidently that no ethnic community leader could lay a claim, either individually or in a representative capacity, to traditional music – or any other TCE, for that matter.[20] This dispels any conclusions that the custodians or authorities over cultural matters, inclusive of TCEs, are the leaders of the ethnic communities.

This finding also means that an ethnic community leader in Uganda would not automatically have the right to rely on that position to prevent any community member from using TCEs that are attributed to their ethnic community. For instance, in response to the question as to whether permission is required from traditional or community leaders before using TCEs, Dr Mercy Mirembe Ntangaare[21] responded by stating that: 'I reject permission because the traditional leaders do not own – even if you are the King of Buganda, you do not own the folk music in the Kingdom.'

Furthermore, in the case of a rap song titled, 'You Want Another Rap?', which is attributed to and was performed by President Museveni, Dr Mwangusya Ndebesa, who filed an objection against copyright registration in the song by the President, stated:[22]

> There is no body who is actually known out there that is there to protect the cultural music … I did myself attempt to stop the President from appropriating the traditional music, but that was purely individual. No body mandated me to do it.

These opinions are evident of the self-accountability that members of ethnic communities have over their TCEs, as each member is a custodian of the TCE.

It is therefore evident that the custodians of the so-called property rights in culture cannot commodify it to the extent of depriving others of it since it is something that many members of society (and not necessarily the ethnic community from which the TCE emanates) have partaken in developing it into its current form.

D. Can Custodianship of TCEs Go Beyond the Community Members?

As a custodian of cultural expressions from his community, Dr Ndebesa felt it was his right to take up action with a view of saving his community's TCEs. In 2010, during the run up to the presidential elections, when Uganda's President, General Yoweri Kaguta Museveni, came up with a rap song derived from two poems from the Ankole Community in western Uganda, Dr Ndebesa filed an opposition to copyright registration of the rap song.[23] In her ruling, the then Registrar of Copyrights[24] dispelled Dr Ndebesa's argument that the President's rap song was

[20] The traditional elders interviewed were: Andrew Benon Kibuuka (a clan head in the Buganda Community and drama artist – interviewed on 18 July 2013); Aloysius Matovu Joy (a traditional elder in the Buganda Community and drama/music artist – interviewed on 20 July 2013); Joel Isabirye (Buganda traditional elder, traditional musician and Professor of Performing Arts, Kyambogo University, Uganda – interviewed on 18 July 2013); Mwangusya Ndebesa (History Lecturer, Makerere University and traditional elder in the Ankole Community – interviewed 19 July 2013); John Jean Barya (Law Professor, Makerere University and traditional elder in the Ankole Community – interviewed 26 July 2013); and Augustine Mutumba (a clan head in the Buganda Community and Senior Government Medical Officer – interviewed on 20 November 2013).

[21] Dr Mercy Mirembe Ntangaare is an Associate Professor of Drama/Theatre at Makerere University. She is also a playwright and folklorist. At the time of the interview, she was the Chairperson of the Board of Trustees of the Uganda National Cultural Centre (interviewed on 26 July 2013).

[22] See: In the Matter of an Application No 25 of 2010 for registration of Copyright by Yoweri Kaguta Museveni in the song 'You want another rap' and In the Matter of an Objection by Mr Mwambusya Ndebesa and Dr Katono Nzarwa Deo.

[23] ibid.

[24] Ms Mercy K Kainobwisho was, the time, the Registrar of Copyrights that handled this matter.

not original. She reasoned in her ruling that 'the transformation of a folksong is to my mind an original creation which as expressed constitutes a derivative work … the idea seems obvious but the expression is original'. She thus ruled to the effect that the President's rap song was a derivative work which by selection and arrangement of its content constituted original work and was thus entitled to copyright protection by virtue of section 5(1) of the Copyright and Neighbouring Rights Act of Uganda.[25] She noted, however, that

> copyright in a derivative work covers only the additions, changes or other new material appearing for the first time in the work and does not extend to any pre-existing material and does not prevent anyone else from using the existing work for another derivative work.

In summing up her ruling, the Registrar stated that:

> I am aware that the objectors were under the impression that the applicant was attempting to monopolize a piece of heritage of the Banyankole/Bakiga. I hope that they can now rest assured that the heritage of the aforementioned people can still be enjoyed by anyone and has not in any way been misappropriated but instead can now be enjoyed by anyone including the young generation whom, I hazard to say, may relate to the applicant's new arrangement of the said works.

From this ruling, it would ideally follow that under the copyright law regime, any person, whether a member of a custodial community or not, can generate copyright out of derivative versions of traditional music.

E. Violation of Property Rights in TCEs

Ordinarily, in a copyright legal environment, the liability rule makes it easy to identify and enforce against a person or entity that violates the property rights of the copyright owner. This is because copyright has an identifiable owner of the IP and the parameters of such ownership are clearly laid out, which is not the same case with TCEs.

Susan Scafidi asserts that:[26]

> Who can assert a right to define the normative use of a cultural product; or who may give permission to copy a cultural product [?] The issue of control does not arise when source-community members have exclusive possession of their cultural products and use them in consensual manner. Rather, conflict may appear in the case of contested or nonconforming use by source-community members or in the case of any use by nonmembers.

This assertion lays out how violation of property rights in TCEs reveals itself in the process of commodification of culture. As already pointed out above, all community members are owners of TCEs by virtue of their allegiance to a community. There is no concern as to how they use or profit from such TCEs as long as they conform to the cultural norms, religious values or sacred rites that attach to the TCE that they are using. As such, cause for concern arises only in two situations: (i) when the community member breaches the cultural values of the TCE through its use; or (ii) if a non-community member uses the TCE.

It is therefore important to analyse how such violations come about under the two different categories.

[25] The Copyright and Neighboring Rights Act, No 13 of 2006, s 5 provides for works entitled to Copyright Protection.
[26] Scafidi (n 5) 53.

(i) *Violations of TCE Property Rights by Community Members*

In instances where violations of TCEs are orchestrated by a community member through appropriation of community folklore, no monetary compensation is shared with the community. In any case, this would hardly amount to a violation because there is no deprivation of property and the user is as entitled to the TCEs as any other community member. Nonetheless, where communities inevitably turn their TCEs from being identified as culture into commodities, other community members consider such acts as violations – with no legal basis to such claims, save for jurisdictions where this is backed up by the law.

Where cases are likely to arise from such considered violations of property rights, it is naturally easier to establish a claim based on economic loss than on the tainting of cultural values. With or without realising it, ethnic communities have supported the conversion of their cultures into commodities while fighting against the violation of their property rights in TCEs. Arguably, this has never been their intention. Michael F Brown highlights this point[27] when he states that:

> A tidy separation of property and privacy is impossible within a market system that turns identity into a commodity. When persons or groups choose to commercialize their identity for economic gain, courts are less likely to accept the argument that unauthorized use of that identity undermines their dignity. Identity (in the sense of moral integrity and worth) and personality (in the sense of a social marker with commercial potential) coexist in a highly unstable relationship.
>
> This volatility helps explain why indigenous peoples' complaints about the appropriation of elements of their cultures often jump from the abstract language of human rights to narrowly framed demands for monetary compensation. The difficulty of keeping the two issues separate is often misinterpreted as evidence that what indigenous peoples really care about is the economic value of their cultures. Even when grievances are presented entirely in terms of a group's desire for dignity and self-respect, capitalism imbues them with a mercantile logic that is difficult to suppress.

As such, whereas ethnic communities would be satisfied by a property rule that can guarantee protection of their cultural values, the market dictates otherwise. Ultimately, without intent or purpose, the liability rule overshadows the property rule. The liability rule is a legal relief in the sense that it favours compensation for what the communities would consider as harm already done – in this sense, lost royalties; whereas the property rule is an equitable relief in that it looks into preventing future acts that could inflict further harm to the community[28] – and in that sense, it includes an erosion of the cultural values that the communities hold sacred.

The question is thus how does one establish a connection between violation by members and the abuse of cultural values? There are a variety of possible responses. However, Milton Wabyona[29] throws some light on the matter when he explains that ethnic communities will accept a musician's work if he borrows from a folk song and does it well, following the right procedures. Wabyona also adds that:

> I think where the problem comes in is, we have had so many masquerades in the music industry because they want money. They eventually end up doing things haphazardly and they are not bringing out the true picture, so definitely people are going to complain.

[27] MF Brown, *Who Owns Native Culture?* (Harvard University Press, 2003) 38.

[28] Shavell (n 4) 95.

[29] Milton Wabyona is a specialist in African music composition and performances, and Executive Director of Uganda Heritage Roots. He is a lecturer in the School of Performing Arts at Makerere University, Uganda. He was interviewed on 16 July 2013.

As such, the influence of the so-called masquerades on the social scene who are purely focused on the monetary rewards could negatively impact the value in the TCEs that they derive their music from. This is particularly so if their music sends out the wrong message that devalues educative and socially uplifting cultural norms in TCEs. Mwangusya Ndebesa[30] has a succinct way of putting it: 'if the music is looked at merely for entertainment value, not for preservation [of culture] value, [then] we are losing out'.

The preservation of cultural values is therefore still highly esteemed in certain circles despite the gradual commodification of TCEs. When Steven Rwangyezi – a non-member of the Baganda community – was criticised by traditional leaders in the Buganda community with regard to his use of the traditional *amaggunju* dance[31] in one of his folklore entertainment group's performances,[32] he stressed that the issue of monetary compensation never came up. The community were only concerned about the preservation of the cultural values attached to the original dance, that is, the fact that the original dance was meant to be performed for only the king and within his palace.[33]

(ii) Violations of TCE Property Rights by Foreign Persons

In the absence of a *sui generis* legal system for TCEs, the IP legal system has been relied upon to the greatest extent possible in addressing the violation of property rights in TCEs. In 'Facing the Music: Traditional Knowledge and Copyright', Bryan Bachner[34] gives a critical review as to the extent at which Western-styled IP plays a role in the commodification of traditional music. He points out the imbalance between ethnic communities, which demand better recognition and protection of their traditional musical expressions, and the Western world, which recognises such works as public domain and therefore free for all to use. He then provides case studies on a number of famous controversies between individual copyright ownership and claims of misappropriation by traditional music rights holders, such as:[35] (i) the case of 'Mbube' or 'The Lion Sleeps Tonight', which involved a conflict between the South African family of the late Zulu song writer Solomon Linda and the use of a song by Disney Enterprises, Inc; and (i) the case of 'Song of Joy' or 'Return to Innocence', which involved the appropriation of traditional music from the Ami People of Taiwan by a rock group called Enigma on their 1993 album *Cross of Changes*. A detailed discussion of these cases follows.

(a) 'Mbube' and the Zulu Community in South Africa

The song 'The Lion Sleeps Tonight' had achieved international fame long before it was incorporated into the Walt Disney animated film *The Lion King* in 1994, making it an even bigger international hit. The first studio version of this song was introduced under the title of 'Mbube' (a Zulu word for 'Lion') by a South African Zulu migrant worker and entertainer by the name of

[30] See n 20 above.

[31] The amaggunju dance is a traditional folklore from the Buganda kingdom that was historically preserved as a performance for the Buganda king. See O Bichachi and M Nakisekka (eds), *The Kings of Buganda and the Roots of a 700-Year-Old Kingdom* (Fountain Publishers, 2011) 15.

[32] Steven Rwangyezi is proprietor of the Ndere Dance Troupe based in Kampala, Uganda. He was interviewed in July 2013.

[33] Bichachi and Nakisekka (n 31).

[34] B Bachner, 'Facing the Music: Traditional Knowledge and Copyright' (2005) 12(3) *Human Rights Brief* 9, http://digitalcommons.wcl.american.edu/hrbrief/vol12/iss3/3/.

[35] ibid.

Solomon Linda in 1939.[36] He assigned his rights to Gallo Records in South Africa. Eventually, the song found its way to the USA and was assigned to a music publishing company called Folkways. It first went to a folksinger by the name of Pete Seeger (who changed the title to 'Wimoweh', which was a corruption of the Zulu word *Uyimbube*, or 'he is the lion'). Then this song, went to, amongst others, a group called The Tokens. These derivative versions of the song were hugely successful worldwide without any royalties being paid to the Solomon Linda estate by virtue of copyright assignments based on US copyright law.[37]

The family of Solomon Linda eventually filed a suit in South Africa in 2004 against Disney Inc (*Griesel NO v Walt Disney Enterprises Inc and Others*) for rights over the 'Mbube' song.[38] The case was eventually withdrawn and settled out of court. Generally, the terms of the settlement were to the effect that the Linda family would receive payment for past uses of 'The Lion Sleeps Tonight' and an entitlement for future royalties from its worldwide use.[39] It is estimated that by that time the song had earned over $15 million in composer royalties worldwide.[40]

Deborah Wassel's study on 'African Folk Music in Dual Systems of Law' looks at Western exploitation of traditional African music.[41] She traces the history of the 'Mbube' song after it gained popularity in South Africa and states: 'Mbube and its subsequent covers were so popular that approximately "[150] artists eventually recorded the song." It was "translated into languages from Dutch to Japanese," and was featured "in more than [13] movies."'[42]

It is noteworthy, however, that although Solomon Linda was the first to perform 'Mbube' in a studio, his song was also inspired by, and derived from, Zulu folklore.[43] At the time, South Africa did not have a guiding legal framework as to how to address TCE usage by foreign persons.[44] Whereas it was easier for Solomon Linda's family to be compensated for the use of the song, the same would not apply for the Zulu community, which has custodial interests in the folklore. In this sense, then, there is no evidential economic outcome to the ethnic community where the folklore, which earned millions in royalties from the different derivative versions after its commodification, could have benefited the community in one way or another.

(b) 'Return to Innocence' and the Ami People of Taiwan

Another matter in which the elements of communally raising a claim to royalties would have been challenging relates to the successful single 'Return to Innocence' by a rock group called Enigma

[36] O Dean, 'Copyright in the Courts: The Return of the Lion' [2006] *WIPO Magazine* Issue 2, www.wipo.int/wipo_magazine/en/2006/02/article_0006.html. Dr Owen Dean, of South African law firm Spoor and Fisher, personally directed the litigation on behalf of the Linda family against Walt Disney Enterprises Inc.

[37] Independent Lens, *A Lion's Trail*, www.pbs.org/independentlens/lionstrail/.

[38] ibid.

[39] ibid.

[40] Above n 36.

[41] D Wassel, 'From Mbube to Wimoweh: African Folk Music in Dual Systems of Law' (2009) 20 *Fordham Intellectual Property, Media & Entertainment Law Journal* 289. For the original Solomon Linda version, see www.youtube.com/watch?v=mrrQT4WkbNE; for the *Lion King* version, see www.youtube.com/watch?v=s6qCD1rO_BQ; for the Peter Seeger/The Weavers version, see www.youtube.com/watch?v=77VUYPVMtWY.

[42] Wassel (n 41) 2, citing S LaFraniere, 'In the Jungle, the Unjust Jungle, a Small Victory' *New York Times* (22 March 2006) A1, www.nytimes.com/2006/03/22/international/africa/22lion.html?r=1&scp=3&sq=solomon%20linda&st+cse.

[43] ibid. See also comments following Miriam Makeba's performance of the original 'Mbube' at www.youtube.com/watch?v=U6AAtKmx6Qk&feature=related, where it is mentioned that the original version of 'Mbube' has been sung for centuries within the Zulu community.

[44] In February 2014, the South African government signed into law the Intellectual Property Laws Amendment Act, No 28 of 2013, which was published in Government Gazette No 37148 of 10 December 2013. The aim of this law is to, inter alia, 'provide for the recognition and protection of certain manifestations of indigenous knowledge as species of intellectual property'. It was further supplemented in 2019 by Act No 6 of 2019 on the Protection, Promotion, Development and Management of Indigenous Knowledge Act, 2019.

on their 1993 album *Cross of Changes*. Bryan Bachner[45] provides an analysis of the appropriation of traditional music from the Ami people of Taiwan, which takes up a substantial part of the song. While on a cultural exchange programme in Paris, Kuo Ying-nan, a member of the Taiwanese Ami ethnic community, performed the folk song 'Jubilant Drinking Song' with his wife across Europe at the invitation of the French Cultural Ministry. Without their knowledge, the performances were recorded and distributed on CD by the French Cultural Ministry. The licence to the music productions was eventually purchased by a German Music producer, Michael Cretu, who was accredited with the creation of the musical project called Enigma and the production of the *Cross of Changes* album. The Ami song was incorporated into the heart of the single 'Return to Innocence'.[46]

Kuo Ying-nan and his wife sued Cretu for the rights to the song and later settled out of court for an undisclosed amount of money.[47] Just like with the Solomon Linda case, it was easier for these particular individuals to pursue their claim under copyright infringement as opposed to the source community pursuing a claim over the use of its musical expression. The case also emphasises how easy it is for economic rights to play into the hands of individuals that have used derivative versions of TCEs from their own communities. Generally, the enforcement of property rights in culture is much easier when there is a transformation through the ownership and commodification of cultural expressions.

It naturally follows from the above examples that if a member of an ethnic community makes use of the community's folklore as part of his own musical expressions, the resulting royalties are his entitlement. Copyright law, which supports this view, shows that this would be so regardless of whether the musician has made any alterations to the original folklore or not. All that matters here is that the TCE has been performed by someone and placed in a fixed form. This makes it more a work of copyright as opposed to traditional music.

What is also fascinating about the above two case studies is that although they mainly highlight violations of TCE property rights by foreign persons, the exposure of the traditional music outside of the community environs was instigated by community members. Nonetheless, without the involvement of specific persons coming out and laying claim to property rights over traditional music that had been commoditised by outsiders, the practice – in these particular cases – would have gone on unabated.

It is also noteworthy that there have been instances where community members that benefit financially from the commodification of traditional music tend to pass on some of the economic benefits to their respective ethnic communities. In the case of Kuo Ying-nan, after their claim was successful, it is reported that he and his wife used the compensation money to benefit their local community through the establishment of a foundation to preserve their culture.[48] The same goes for a group of music artists based in the UK known as the Ganda Boys. This group is composed of two Ugandans, called Denis Mugagga and Daniel Sewagudde, as well as British musician and record producer Craig Pruess.[49] The Ganda Boys' style of music is a fusion of well-known traditional music mainly from the Buganda community in Uganda, with some English verses. Economic gains have been made from such music fusions that are protected by copyright law. For instance, a copy of the Ganda Boys' *Bakisimba* album that is purchased online costs US$10, while a CD goes for $12.97.[50] The Ganda Boys have been able to use some of the proceeds from

[45] Bachner (n 34) 10; see also www.youtube.com/watch?v=Rk_sAHh9s08.

[46] ibid.

[47] RF Roper, 'Taiwanese Settle Lawsuit Claiming Their Original Composition Was Stolen; They Will Now Set Up Foundation' (*Business Wire*, 23 June 1999).

[48] ibid.

[49] See http://gandaboys.com/.

[50] ibid.

their music to benefit local communities in Uganda. According to their website, they founded the Ganda Foundation in 2009 with the goal of providing better healthcare and educational services, as well as other life-improving projects for impoverished Ugandans.[51]

It can therefore be argued that there is some benefit in having community members involved in the commodification of traditional music as long as this does not overstep the sacred norms of the custodial communities. In situations where the ownership and commodification are entirely undertaken by foreign elements, this is more of a misappropriation of culture, with no guaranteed economic or social benefit to the source community.

In *Who Owns Native Culture?*, Michael F Brown gives an exposé of the exploitation of TCEs from vulnerable ethnic communities for economic gain.[52] He argues that, in some instances, the appropriators believe that by carrying out their acts of TCE misuse as far away from the source community as possible, they will probably not get noticed.[53] Brown highlights a study report by Steve Feld, an anthropologist and ethnomusicologist who tracks traditional musical expressions among an ethnic group in Central Africa that are known as Pygmies in the West.[54] In order to fully capture the way in which the TCE is appropriated from the community, the following excerpt is taken from Brown's study:[55]

> First recorded systematically in the 1950s, the distinctive intervals and timbre of Pygmy music soon worked their way into the Afrocentric jazz of the 1970s (Herbie Hancock's *Headhunters* album), then into the emerging genres of world music and electro-acoustic music of the 1970s (the work of Egberto Gismonti and Brian Eno, among others), then, perhaps inevitably, into the pop diva Madonna's album Bedtime Stories in the 1990s. The most significant recent appearance of Pygmy music is a cameo role in the bestselling album Deep Forest, ostensibly created by French musicians but based heavily on material taken from field recordings of indigenous music. Deep Forest sold more than two million copies, and its music has been featured in advertisements for products ranging from skin cream to sports cars. Although the CD's producers claim that some of the proceeds from the album find their way back to the tribal people whose voices and instruments figure in it, Feld could find no evidence that Pygmy populations benefited financially from the album's success.[56]

From the following excerpt, it is possible that the Pygmy community is not only left out in the cold in terms of economic benefit derived from commodification of their traditional music, but they also have no knowledge about such misappropriation taking place or, worse still, anyone to speak out for them. As argued previously, such scenarios are mainly brought on by the absence of adequate legislation to deal with commodification of TCEs. The next section lays out recommendations for addressing this situation.

III. Proposals on Addressing the Commodification of Traditional Music

As this chapter has laboured to show, culture is part and parcel of society and communities grow as their cultures develop. Unfortunate as it may seem, the foreign intrusion into the way

[51] ibid.
[52] Brown (n 27).
[53] ibid.
[54] ibid.
[55] ibid.
[56] Ibid, citing S Feld, 'Pygmy POP: A Genealogy of Schizophonic Mimesis' in *Yearbook for Traditional Music, 1996* (International Council for Traditional Music, 1996) 1–35. For promotional information about the creators of Deep Forest, see www.sonymusic.fr/deepforest/.

communities enjoy the expression of their cultures also leads further to the growth of such cultures. What matters is the direction such growth is taking. We should therefore not be looking to come up with regulatory measures that stifle the growth of culture, more specifically traditional music; rather, the focus should be on *how to* process the ownership and commodification of cultural expressions. As such, the following recommendations can be considered.

A. Establishment of a *Sui Generis* Legislation on the Utilisation of Culture

Regional regulatory measures have been put in place that address the utilisation of culture. Such regulatory frameworks are crafted in such a way that they bring out unique (*sui generis*) enforcement mechanisms that are not necessarily like intellectual property regulation but are aligned with principles on the protection of creativity and innovation coming from communities as opposed to individuals. One regional instrument that is worth mentioning is the 2010 Swakopmund Protocol on the Protection of Traditional Knowledge and Expressions of Folklore. This instrument is important for member states of the Africa Regional Intellectual Property Organization (ARIPO) in highlighting ways in which such countries can work with traditional communities in enhancing and protecting their TCEs.

The Swakopmund Protocol, which falls within the framework of ARIPO, came into force on 11 May 2015.[57] As of 31 December 2020, ARIPO has 20 member states, but not all of them have signed and ratified the Protocol yet, including Uganda. Nonetheless, the positive influence of the Protocol has already been felt through the enactment of domestic *sui generis* legislations on the protection of traditional knowledge and TCEs in some ARIPO member states such as Kenya and Zambia. Most of the provisions in such legislations are, to a large extent, guided by the principles in the Protocol.

Countries with ethnic communities should thus position themselves into coming up with *sui generis* legislations that provide for the administration and utilisation of TCEs to create an organised and balanced system of ownership and commodification of cultural expressions. This should be in such a way that the laws cater for the safeguarding and preservation of culture at the same time as creating orderly utilisation of the same in a way that fosters socioeconomic development.

B. Recognition of TCEs as a Value Asset

Communities and their host governments need to recognise cultural expressions as a form of economic enhancement. Various examples abound with regard to how traditional music, for instance, has been transformed into copyright and has generated immense profits for the individual owners. Communities need to tap into this by establishing contractual arrangements on access and benefit sharing, like the licensing regimes in place for users of IP rights where there is no outright transfer of ownership. The royalties generated from such use of TCEs can be used in turn to lift the socioeconomic status of the custodial communities, especially when they exercise self-determination in the way their TCEs are utilised by outsiders.

[57] www.aripo.org/entry-into-force-of-the-aripo-swakopmund-protocol-on-the-protection-of-traditional-knowledge-and-expressions-of-folklore/. For a copy of the Swakopmund Protocol, see www.cbd.int/doc/measures/abs/msr-abs-aripo-en.pdf.

Such contractual arrangements with TCE users can also involve the reliance on principles of 'prior informed consent': any person who seeks to commodify a cultural expression must go through a structure of consent guided by the community from which the cultural aspects are borrowed. In this way, the community also ensures that the cultural norms and sacred rites in their cultural expressions are safeguarded.

C. Documentation of TCEs

TCEs are generally passed on from one generation to another through word of mouth, as exhibited through musical or dance performances, sharing of folk tales and so on. It can therefore be a matter of concern in advocating for documentation of TCEs, with the fear being that this will stagnate the growth of TCEs. However, this recommendation can be carefully handled to ensure that folklore is documented in terms of safeguarding its origins and linkage to certain communities. Otherwise, most commodification of culture is simplified by the fact that where traditional music exists only in the oral form, those that borrow from it and commodify it have been easily able to obtain copyright protection without the need to compensate the custodial communities. Worse still, they present the risk of placing injunctions on custodial communities against their utilisation of such cultural expressions through environments where courts of law recognise only copyright as opposed to cultural expressions.

The documentation process can therefore include the creation of a data centre for the storage of cultural expressions and the utilisation of research institutions in the gathering, documenting and study of culture.

To erase the risk of cultural stagnation in traditional music, national governments can also invest into cultural festivities that explore and highlight the rich heritage of indigenous communities. Such festivities can be like the traditional circumcision events performed annually in eastern Uganda. Borrowing from the way the government in Brazil invests in the Brazilian carnival and how China also invests into cultural activities surrounding the New Year, such festivities attract a lot of tourists and boost the local economies. In the same vein, such festivities derail private commodification and cultural theft by instead promoting the culture in the local jurisdictions.

IV. Conclusion

The ownership and commodification of culture highlights the richness in cultural diversity among ethnic communities. It is unfortunate that many such communities are the most vulnerable and impoverished globally, yet there would be so much socioeconomic potential in store for them were they to have a direct hand in the utilisation of their culture. This involves boosting awareness of the values obtainable against cultural expressions beyond what is appreciated within the customary parameters of such communities. Foreign entities and individuals that have had the upper hand against communities in creating new forms of ownership and commodification of culture have thrived mainly on the ignorance of those communities. Changing this landscape therefore requires a concerted effort involving public and private stakeholders working hand in hand through unique regulatory regimes in the administration and utilisation of their cultural expressions.

However, as this chapter has highlighted, 'music borrowing' is intertwined in many ways with 'cultural borrowing' through the connection between copyright and folklore. A reformation of copyright regimes is thus necessary to formalise this structure through a *sui generis* legislation to generate smooth borrowing from culture to further develop the music industry.

PART II

Analysing Music Genres and their Relationship with Copyright

Section A: General

7

Pop and the Musical Unconscious

JOSE BELLIDO*

I. Introduction

It is often claimed that pop music is a genre predicated on a distinctively fleeting musical catchiness, an unmistakable youth appeal and a certain disdain for the establishment. As an indicator of what was to come, these attributes are interesting because pop ended up becoming the musical genre that attracted more legal controversies than any other. While it might be possible to trace legal disputes affecting pop artists regarding the originality of facial make-ups, the illegitimate release of album covers or the rise of merchandising controversies over brand exploitation, copyright became the pre-eminent legal device in the historical narrative that defined pop music. The law of copyright has often been called upon to deal with contractual quarrels over royalties, piracy and plagiarism, and the great variety of legal claims raised or defended by pop artists was epitomised by the history of the band in which the genre is frequently claimed to be rooted – The Beatles.

Pop music has attracted so much copyright litigation because, as a forensic musicologist ironically observes in this volume, 'that is where the money is'.[1] The well-known US case in which former Beatle, George Harrison, was sued for copyright infringement seems to confirm this premise.[2] Money appears to have been the main trigger for the dispute. Gold discs, celebrity stardom, catchy songs and musical similarities constituted the common elements that brought this and many other controversies over musical properties into the courts. In this specific instance, the judge ruled that Harrison had subconsciously copied the plaintiff's composition. From a legal perspective, it is the resonance of this judgment that is remarkable. It is often mentioned in textbooks, conferences and scholarly articles.[3] Although some domestic courts have pointedly declined to follow the decision as it came from another jurisdiction, this has not stopped lawyers

* Thanks to Ross Carder, Anastasia Karel, John Maher, Mike Faulkner, Nathalie Barton, Jacqueline Santora Zimmerman, Chris Gardner, Piyel Haldar and Randall Redman.

[1] See G Protheroe, 'Forensic Musicology in Action: A Personal Perspective', ch 5 of this volume.

[2] *Bright Tunes Music Corp v Harrisongs Music Ltd* 420 F Supp 177 (SDNY 1976). For this case and many other pop music controversies, see the Music Copyright Infringement Resource (Columbia Law School and the George Washington School of Law) at https://blogs.law.gwu.edu/mcir/.

[3] WM Landes and RA Posner, *The Economic Structure of Intellectual Property Law* (Harvard University Press, 2003) 88; J Waldron, 'From Authors to Copiers: Individual Rights and Social Values in Intellectual Property' (1992) 68 *Chicago-Kent Law Review* 841, 882; D Vaver, 'Creating a Fair Intellectual Property System for the 21st Century' (2001) 10 *Otago Law Review* 1, 8; S Corbett, 'Creative Commons Licenses, the Copyright Regime and the Online Community: Is There a Fatal Disconnect?' (2011) 74 *MLR* 503, 508; T Aplin and J Davis, *Intellectual Property. Text, Cases and Materials* (Oxford University Press, 2021) 201.

and legal scholars from repeatedly referencing it.[4] One reason for this insistence is that the case exemplifies an infringement arising from an unintentional act of borrowing.[5] At first glance, this type of borrowing appears paradoxical, but it serves to highlight that pop music is a genre especially inhabited by the unconscious.[6] In fact, the judge himself committed a Freudian slip after his judgment, referring to the two songs as if they were distinct.[7] Although the decision remains a frequent trope in copyright scholarship, the mechanisms by which the case came to judgment have received far less attention. The legal proceedings, the evidence and the events that took place in the courtroom and afterwards have been eclipsed by a normative discussion around the nature and scope of copyright liability.[8] While the doctrinal impulse is a logical reaction to a type of borrowing that seems to blur the legal distinction traditionally made between copyright and patents, the problem is that it often conflates the descriptive with the normative, thus foreclosing other lines of enquiry.[9] This is regrettable, not only because the musician himself described the experience as a 'nightmarish' week in court,[10] but also because an excessive focus on the regulatory question obscures several recurrent features that tend to characterise pop music's encounters with the law.

This chapter traces some of these characteristics by revisiting the details of the dispute, and its associated procedural difficulties, which spanned over two decades. On the one hand, it argues that media influences on human agency tend to shape the way pop music comes to be thought of and imagined in copyright law. On the other hand, it offers an alternative reading of copyright litigation and adjudication beyond the debates of experts. Despite the heavy emphasis on forensic musicologists, primarily because they tend to narrow and stabilise an analytical framework for comparison and judgement, there is much more to be said about the associations between pop music and copyright. Looking beyond the musicological expertise offers a starting point to trace connections that made pop music significant as both a legal and a cultural phenomenon.

II. Hearing

What does popular music mean? How can it be measured? Through sales? Peer recognition? Followers? Cult status? Or does it depend on people still recalling a song despite the passing of time? It is telling that trials involving pop music often begin with attempts to measure popularity and success.[11] The concept of 'the popular' is problematic because of the ambiguity of the term and its changing connotations.[12] In that sense, and for the record, is music popularity not

[4] This can be seen in Canadian, British and Australian copyright cases, eg *Gondos v Hardy* (1982) 64 CPR (2d) 145, 38 OR (2d) 555 (Canada); *Drynan v Rostad* (1994) 59 CPR (3d) 8 (Canada); *Michael Mitchell v British Broadcasting Corporation* [2011] EWPCC 42 (UK); *Universal Music Publishing Pty Ltd v Palmer* (No 2) [2021] FCA 434 (Australia).

[5] 'George Harrison Guilty of Plagiarizing, Subconsciously, a '62 Tune for a '70 Hit' *New York Times* (8 September 1976) 42.

[6] P Szendy, *Hits: Philosophy in the Jukebox* (Fordham University Press, 2012) 32–42.

[7] D Pedler, *The Songwriting Secrets of the Beatles* (Omnibus Press, 2003) 637; J Blaney, *George Harrison: Soul Man* (Paper Jukebox, 2016) 116; B Harry, *The George Harrison Encyclopaedia* (Virgin Books, 2003) 279.

[8] CL Alden, 'A Proposal to Replace the Subconscious Copying Doctrine' (2008) 29 *Cardozo Law Review* 1729.

[9] R Metzger, 'Name that Tune: A Proposal for an Intrinsic Test of Musical Plagiarism', (1985) 5 *Loyola of Los Angeles Entertainment Law Review* 61.

[10] The legal ordeal had such an impact on him that it featured in one of his subsequent songs; see G Harrison, *I, Me, Mine* (Chronicle Book, 2002) 340; R Cromelin, 'Lawsuit Inspires Harrison's Song' *Los Angeles Times* (21 November 1976) 93; G Giuliano, *Dark Horse. The Secret Life of George Harrison* (Pan Books, 1991) 166.

[11] See, eg the British copyright case of *Fisher v Brooker & Ors* [2006] EWHC 3239 (Ch) paras 1 and 3 (Blackburne J): 'one of the most successful popular songs of the late, 1960s … [it is] no exaggeration to say that with the passage of time the song has achieved something approaching cult status'.

[12] J Derrida, *Eyes of the University. Right to Philosophy 2* (Stanford University Press, 2004) 175–84.

self-evident?[13] Antoine Hennion suggests that pop songs 'have no need to justify their existence; they exist in their own right, and their sales figures are the only claim to legitimacy they need'.[14] However, establishing what is known of and about the popularity of songs constitutes an important frame of reference in juridical practice.[15] While it might look like a mere fact-finding exercise, it is in reality particularly significant in copyright litigation narratives concerning pop music.[16] The reasons are twofold. First, measuring exposure serves as a springboard for copyright infringement tests that hinge upon access (or causal connection).[17] Second, success ratings and mass consumption indexes allow for the argument that pop songs might have become part of our collective musical unconscious, thus paving the way for the possibility of unintentional musical borrowings. In an era in which music is everywhere, from muzak to Spotify, this possibility exists, enhanced by media saturation and exploitation. However, the predicament in court lies not only in establishing the popularity of a song, but also in the need to prove that the defendant had probably heard it. Indeed, the admissibility of chart popularity indexes was one of the contentious issues in the case against George Harrison.

The hearing began at the Foley Square courthouse in downtown Manhattan in the last week of February 1976.[18] As the plaintiff introduced the first exhibits, the defence attorney, Joseph J Santora, raised an objection against one of them.[19] There was no problem with copyright registrations, depositions or even record sleeves tendered. The main complaint concerned music charts and their probative weight. Their character as out-of-court statements, and hence hearsay evidence, was the subject of some initial legal deliberation. Given the statistical significance of the charts as an index of popularity, their reliability and admissibility were problematic, as they would encourage in the mind of the judge a plausible scenario whereby, as one expert witness in the trial mentioned, 'you can't escape it'.[20] How is it possible not to be exposed to a song if it has been played extensively on air? This assumption echoes the emblematic notion of a radio pop hit, an earworm that has lodged itself in your head, whether it was wanted or not. Even if you did not particularly like it, or did not deliberately tune in to hear it, there it was, and it was impossible to avoid.[21] It would influence you even against your will. Although the objection against charts was partially overcome by the issuing of a subpoena to a staff member of *Billboard*,[22] the defence

[13] According to Umbreit, 'it would be better to treat popularity value as the primary element in copyright': see KB Umbreit, 'A Consideration of Copyright' (1938) 87 *University of Pennsylvania Law Review* 932, 953.

[14] A Hennion, 'The Production of Success. An Anti-Musicology of the Pop Song' (1983) 3 *Popular Music* 59, 162.

[15] See, eg the US copyright cases *Packson v Jobete Music* 1967 [unreported]; *Devin Copeland v Justin Bieber et al*, 789 F 3d 484 (4th Cir 2015); *Williams v Gaye*, 895 F 3d 1106, 1116 (9th Cir 2018).

[16] In the British case of *Francis Day & Hunter v Bron* [1963] Ch 587, this question of how to figure out the factor to achieve a high place in the Hit Parade was put to expert witnesses such as Geoffrey Bush and Stanley Smith-Masters. See 'English Evidence: Francis, Day, & Hunter v Bron' in RG21 – Records of the District Court for the Eastern District of PA, Civil Action, File 27800, National Archives and Records Administration (NARA) Archives.

[17] *Carew v RKO Radio Pictures* 43 F Supp 199 (1942); *Ellis v Diffie* 177 F 3d 503, 506 (6th Cir 1999); see generally MB Nimmer and D Nimmer, *Nimmer on Copyright* (Matthew Bender, 1963) 604–05 ('Copying by the defendant').

[18] George Harrison was represented by Hardee, Barovick, Konecky & Braun. The reason was that one of the partners was David Braun, a well-known music lawyer who had represented Bob Dylan and Neil Diamond. Interview with Stephen Ross, 3 March 2022.

[19] *Bright Tunes-Music v Harrisongs Music Ltd et al*, transcript of the hearing, 14–16 (docket 71-CV-602); Box 5449; RG 21; Records of the US District Court for the Southern District of New York, Civil Action, National Archives and Records Administration (NARA) (hereafter 1976 hearing transcript).

[20] David Greitzer (on cross-examination), 1976 hearing transcript (n 19) 102.

[21] Learned Hand explained this in the following manner: '[E]verything registers somewhere in our memories, and no one can tell what may evoke it … Once it appears that another has in fact used the copyright as the source of this production, he has invaded the author's rights. It is no excuse that in so doing his memory has played him a trick'. See *Fred Fisher, Inc v Dillingham*, 298 F 145, 147–48 (SDNY, 1924).

[22] Constance Bewen (direct examination), 1976 hearing transcript (n 19) 154–60. Bewen was the supervisor of the steno pool at Billboard Publications.

attorney continued arguing against their use on the basis that 'an entry in *Billboard* is not the same as a certified Government document in this sort of thing'.[23]

It is important to highlight that music charts and record listings were invoked and displayed repeatedly throughout the proceedings.[24] As the lawyer in the parallel action brought against Harrison in England observed, one of the difficulties in the trial preparation was to obtain 'a blackboard and easel to hang the charts from, but we are continuing our efforts in this connection'.[25] While charts served to build a discourse about the currency and purported popularity of the plaintiff's song, and therefore the chance that Harrison had heard it, their centrality also set up the argument of unconscious borrowing. It is notable how many pop music copyright cases continue to be tied to framing strategies that use music charts as a springboard for an argument.[26] As Ken Barnes has explained, record companies loved the various music charts, largely because they enabled them to differentiate songs and develop advertising campaigns so they could 'create a success story for a record'.[27] As music charts served the dual purposes of data collection and product promotion, they represented marketing devices to capture audiences and incentives to buy a record using a teaser. However, the rising importance of charts to buttress legal cases had an unintended consequence, namely their influence in reducing the plausible explanation of substantial similarities to the following hypothetical dichotomy: coincidence or unconscious copying.

In this specific case, 'He's So Fine', the popular song by The Chiffons that the plaintiff, Bright Tunes, alleged had been infringed by Harrison, had been top of the charts in 1963.[28] George Harrison's song, 'My Sweet Lord', had also topped the charts in the early 1970s.[29] The similarity between the songs seemed obvious, as the experts demonstrated extensively in court.[30] However, among the expert testimonies introduced by the defendant was a witness somewhat different from the typical musicologist. Harrison's defence called on an ethnomusicologist who specialised in gospel.[31] The point was to move the analysis from forensic musicology to another musical perspective. This shift relied on the definition of ethnomusicology as 'a branch or separate field, actually, depending on who you speak to, of musicology. We prefer as ethnomusicologists to think of it as a separate field totally from musicology'.[32] This particular witness provided evidence highlighting how 'My Sweet Lord' was to be interpreted as deriving not from the plaintiff's work, but from a religious and spiritual allure based upon musical improvisations and mantras. The very title of the song suggested that characteristic, which was enhanced by a repetition of Christian and Hindu mantras ('hallelujah' and 'Hare Krishna') to praise the Lord.[33] While neither

[23] ibid 160.

[24] George Harrison (cross examination), 1976 hearing transcript (n 19) 258–59.

[25] Ray Palmer, Davenport, Lyons & Co to John Gardner, 22 June 1976; John Gardner Papers (hereafter JGP).

[26] See, eg *Three Boys Music Corp v Bolton*, 212 F 3d 477 (9th Cir 2000); *Pharrell Williams et al v Bridgeport Music et al*, No 15-56880 (9th Cir 11 July 2018).

[27] K Barnes, 'Top 40 Radio. A Fragment of the Imagination' in S Frith (ed), *Facing the Music. Essays on Pop, Rock and Culture* (Mandarin, 1990) 41. The specific relationship between music charts and pop music is explored in C Belz, *The Story of Rock* (Oxford University Press, 1969) 17–20; EA Hakanen, 'Counting Down to Number One: The Evolution of the Meaning of Popular Music Charts' (1998) 17(1) *Popular Music* 95.

[28] *Bright Tunes Music Corp v Harrisongs Music Ltd* 420 F Supp 177, 179 (SDNY 1976); see also S Soocher, *Baby, You're a Rich Man. Suing the Beatles for Fun & Profit* (University Press of New England 2015) 178.

[29] JM Greene, *Here Comes the Sun. The Spiritual and Musical Journey of George Harrison* (Bantam Books, 2006) 226.

[30] Some music journalists, like Peter Jones, had already identified similarities between the songs; see P Jones, 'Mirror Pick' *Record Mirror* (24 July 1971) 16.

[31] David Simpson Butler (direct examination), 1976 hearing transcript (n 19) 479–519; see also A Clayson, *George Harrison* (Sanctuary Publishing, 2001) 354.

[32] Butler (direct examination), 1976 hearing transcript (n 19) 480.

[33] Harrison (direct examination), 1976 hearing transcript (n 19) 203.

the plaintiff nor the judge felt that this testimony was relevant, it is nevertheless remarkable, as it was aimed at prompting the argument that musical genres and traditions could determine that songs that are substantially similar, analytically or forensically, might nevertheless be culturally, and thus musically, different.

This blind spot has not gone unnoticed. For instance, Richard Elliot has recently considered how the legal case focused almost exclusively on 'plagiarism of melodic motifs, with little reference to lyrics beyond their syllabic value'.[34] By placing such an emphasis on melodic motifs, the court was constrained by its own search for musical equivalences, missing the connections between words and melodies that transcend them.[35] It is clear that the mantras were not original and could not be subject to copyright protection, but Harrison was arguing that, at the point of recording and composing the song, they were its most important determiners.[36] Indeed, this way of fashioning the argument relied on defining Harrison's song as an invocation, whose choruses depicted a search for immediate contact with God and Krishna, introducing a Sanskrit prayer and shifting the analysis of musical similarities to a genealogical enquiry about its provenance. Although the point was not successful in avoiding copyright liability, it was significant in the assessment of damages. The consequence implied here is that there might be different gradations of musical borrowing.[37] According to the defence attorney, the infringement was partial as it did not touch upon the lyrics and some aspects of the tune; hence, 'any award to the plaintiff should be on that basis alone commensurate and be even less than a 50 per cent'.[38]

A. Sotto Voce

One of the interesting features of the case is that George Harrison himself was called to give evidence and became the central object of attention in the courtroom. Although it is possible to see the influence of forensic experts in dissecting the songs, Harrison's testimony was pivotal, not only because the judge accepted its credibility, but also because, in doing so, he implied that Harrison neither intended to copy nor was conscious of having done so. How did Harrison copy? How did he compose? What did he have to say? As the decision depended on the view that copying was not deliberate, Harrison's testimony and his demeanour seem to have won the judge's sympathy to enable the peculiar finding of inadvertent copying. What those who attended the trial still remember is that 'there was a peacefulness and humility about him and I think the Judge recognized this, especially when George was testifying and demonstrating on his guitar the notes and chords he used in composing "My Sweet Lord"'.[39]

Harrison was often labelled 'the quiet one' of the Beatles, and the transcript of the hearing confirms that personality trait.[40] Both in examination and cross-examination, Harrison's

[34] R Elliott, 'So Transported: Nina Simone, "My Sweet Lord" and the (Un)folding of Affect' in M Thompson and I Biddle (eds), *Sound, Music, Affect. Theorizing Sonic Experience* (Bloomsbury, 2013) 81.

[35] See, eg EJ Huntley, *Behind that Locked Door. George Harrison: After the Break-Up of the Beatles* (Xerostar Holdings, 2002) 67.

[36] This can also be seen in his conversation with Mukunda Goswami in AC Bhaktivedanta Swami Prabhupada, *Chant and Be Happy. The Power of Mantra Meditation* (The Bhaktivedanta Book Trust, 1997) 32–35; see also O Harrison, *George Harrison. Living in the Material World* (Editions de la Martinière, 2011) 280.

[37] One particularly enlightening essay on the gradation is P Nettl, 'Musical Kleptomaniacs' *The Etude* (February 1947) 66.

[38] *ABKCO Music, Inc v Harrisongs Music*, transcript of the hearing (docket 71-CV-602) 35; Box 5526; RG 21; Records of the US District Court for the Southern District of New York, Civil Action, National Archives and Records Administration (NARA) (hereafter 1979 hearing transcript).

[39] Correspondence with Joan Chiarini, February 2022; interview with Bob McKay, February 2022.

[40] See, eg A Clayson, *The Quiet One. A Life of George Harrison* (Black Bear, 1991).

testimony came across as rather odd and he was frequently interrupted with requests to raise his voice.[41] Instead of delivering a robust testimony, his voice was so soft as to be on occasion almost inaudible. This was nowhere better displayed than in the response he gave to the request to describe how he composed his music. This question of authorship was of considerable significance because, as many other pop musicians mentioned in the trial, he did not read music.[42] As Harrison stated,

> there is no particular way to write a song from my point of view, and also from most people that I know who compose songs. I mean it can come either with just an idea driving in a car, just by playing about on an instrument I can get an idea just by a rhythm, hearing a rhythm. You could write a song to that police siren outside if you want to …[43]

While this reference, connecting what was happening outside to the inside of the courtroom, illustrated an openness to transforming and absorbing anything into music, it also evidenced a distraction and a difficulty when it came to pinpointing exactly where inspiration might emerge.[44] It is no coincidence that a recurring problem in pop music copyright relates to disputes about joint authorship precisely because of that empirical difficulty to which George Harrison testified in court.[45] And yet, when he was trying to explain it, he was interrupted again:

> *Q:* Mr Harrison, can you raise your voice just a little bit so I can hear you? The windows are open, and the sirens you are talking about, the sound make it difficult. You mentioned something like sound, you hear sounds. You mentioned the police siren a moment ago, and you said that that at times can cause you to compose a song. Can you think offhand of an example or two where you have composed a song in that fashion?[46]
>
> *A:* I mean, for example, the police car was just going. And that is a rhythm, straight away, so all you need, I mean on one example I was on a holiday in Sardinia, and the house I was staying in had a water pump that I think was for circulation of a swimming pool. It was in a shed, and the rhythm that the water pump was making, I composed a song just starting from that rhythm.[47]

Somewhat cryptic, perhaps, but indicative of sound as the starting point for musical inspiration. For Harrison, music was 'something I hear and I feel'.[48] Curiously, this description echoes the way in which David Byrne has recently explained his view of musical creativity,[49] and seems to confirm Lionel Bently's observation that 'in popular music, it is sounds that matter'.[50] Harrison testified at length at the trial, bringing a guitar to the courtroom and performing musical demonstrations directly relating to the issue of how he composed 'My Sweet Lord'.[51] Although illustrations and musical renditions by expert witnesses had been a recurring feature of copyright litigation,[52] it was not so common to see a defendant demonstrating methods of composition in court via

[41] George Harrison (direct examination), 1976 hearing transcript (n 19) 164, 170, 176, 178 (recalled), 329.

[42] Harrison (direct examination), 1976 hearing transcript (n 19) 189.

[43] Harrison (direct examination), 1976 hearing transcript (n 19) 176.

[44] See, eg M Cable, *The Pop Industry. Inside Out* (WH Allen, 1977) 138–50.

[45] In fact, the judge also speculated that the infringing song, 'My Sweet Lord', was coauthored with another musician, Billy Preston; see *Bright Tunes Music Corp v Harrisongs Music Ltd* 420 F Supp 177, 180 (SDNY 1976).

[46] Harrison (direct examination), 1976 hearing transcript (n 19) 176.

[47] ibid 177.

[48] Harrison (cross-examination), 1976 hearing transcript (n 19) 278.

[49] D Byrne, *How Music Works* (Canongate, 2013) 210.

[50] L Bently, 'Authorship in Popular Music in UK Copyright Law' (2009) 12 *Information, Communication and Society* 179.

[51] Harrison (direct examination), 1976 hearing transcript (n 19) 184, 196.

[52] Perhaps the most famous of these expert witnesses was Sigmund Speath, known as the 'tune detective', who was reported singing, tapping his feet and playing the piano on his multiple court appearances. See *Rich v Paramount Pictures, Inc* [Civ No 20256 Second Dist, Div One, 15 February 1955]; F Waring, 'In Memory of Sigmund Speath' *Music Journal* (1 January 1967) 25; S Speath, 'Musical Plagiarism' (1936) 173 *Harper's Magazine* 329; GA Rosen, *Unfair to Genius. The Strange and Litigious Career of Ira B Arnstein* (Oxford University Press, 2012) 101–18.

a musical instrument.[53] Introducing an instrument into proceedings was significant, not only because it shifted the perception beyond the printed score, but also because it reinforced the quality of pop music as a genre primarily defined by playing.[54] Evidence scholars like Gerald Nokes had already highlighted that 'a musical instrument may be both seen and heard, though once the sound of words is in question, as with a gramophone record of a song played in court, the border between real and other evidence requires delineation'.[55] What is also interesting in the context of that border between real and other evidence is Harrison's specific selection of musical instrument. While it would later become obvious why he chose a guitar, the fact is that music copyright lawsuits until then had been characterised by the prominence of the piano as the ideal vehicle to demonstrate points in dispute.[56] The sovereignty of the piano as an evidential tool had been such that some lawyers went further, giving advice as to the type, characteristics and positioning of the instrument to be brought to the courtroom:

> [A]n upright [piano] is preferable to a spinet, for it has a superior courtroom presence and afford a convenient platform for exhibits and sheet music. Because the piano is useful in emphasizing or demonstrating elements of testimony, it should be positioned as near as possible to the witness stand and the court reporter, so as to minimize interruption to the flow and cohesiveness of the presentation'.[57]

The court performance seems to have proved exactly what Harrison had previously revealed in his testimony, namely, as recalled by his attorney, 'that neither he nor any of the other Beatles read music, and that they were all "jungle musicians" who operate[d] strictly by sound'.[58] Although such unorthodox evidence could have irritated the judge, there is no trace in the transcript of that reaction. Quite the opposite, in fact. According to Harrison's attorney, the judge 'sincerely and strongly believed that it was his original composition and not an infringement'.[59] While this reading of the decision is debatable, it is nevertheless accurate to suggest that Harrison's unusual testimony enabled the judgment that his copying was unconscious rather than deliberate and wilful.[60] The judge concluded that his

> subconscious knew it already had worked in a song his conscious mind did not remember … Did Harrison deliberately use the music of 'He's So Fine'? I do not believe he did so deliberately. Nevertheless, it is clear that 'My Sweet Lord' is the very same song as 'He's So Fine' with different words, and Harrison had access to 'He's So Fine'. This is, under the law, infringement of copyright, and is no less so even though subconsciously accomplished.[61]

[53] Although it was not common for defendants to demonstrate musical abilities, there was a long history of evidential practice whereby plaintiffs performed different instruments (eg violin and piano) in court to support their case; see *Arnstein v Edward B Marks Music Corp* 11 F Supp 535 (SDNY 1935); *Arnstein v Edward B Marks Music Corp* 82 F 2d 275 (2d Cir 1936); 'Song Writer Plays Piano for Court' *New York Times* (7 March 1939) 25; Rosen, *Unfair to Genius* (n 52) 119–45.

[54] It is no surprise, then, that the dichotomy between authorship and performance is often blurred in pop music; see R Arnold, 'Are Performers Authors?' (1999) 21 *European Intellectual Property Review* 464.

[55] GD Nokes, 'Real Evidence' (1949) 65 *Law Quarterly Review* 57, 64.

[56] *Wilkie v Santly Brothers, Inc* 91 F 2d 978 (2nd Cir 1937); *Allen v Walt Disney* 41 F Supp 134 (SDNY 1941); *Jones v Supreme Music Corp* 101 F Supp 989 (SDNY 1951); *Northern Music Corp v King Record Distributing Co* 105 F Supp 393, 400 (SDNY 1952); *Rich v Paramount Pictures, Inc* [Civ No 20256 Second Dist, Div One, 15 February 1955].

[57] JS Clark, 'Copyright Litigation' in MD Kraft (ed), *Using Experts in Civil Cases* (Practising Law Institute, 1977) 146.

[58] JJ Santora, *Bright Tunes v Harrison (1971–1998)* (unpublished memoirs, 1999) 2, Santora Zimmerman archive (hereafter SZ).

[59] Joseph J Santora (affidavit), 1979 hearing transcript (n 38) 214–15.

[60] 'It is apparent from the extensive colloquy between the court and Harrison covering 40 pages in the transcript that neither Harrison nor (Billy) Preston were conscious of the fact that they were utilizing the "He's So Fine" theme': *Bright Tunes Music Corp v Harrisongs Music Ltd* 420 F Supp 177, 180 (SDNY 1976); see also 'Harrison Guilty' *Variety* (8 September 1976) 82; 'George Harrison Guilty of Plagiarism' *Billboard* (11 September 1976) 21; 'Subconscious Plagiarism Infringes Copyright' (1977) III(2) *Art & the Law* 6.

[61] *Bright Tunes Music Corp v Harrisongs Music Ltd*, 420 F Supp 177, 181 (SDNY 1976).

For that finding to be arrived at, however, there was a preliminary step, a causal trajectory where the possibility of copying was established. The rhetorical strategy pushed by the plaintiff consisted of privileging music charts to document a chance or possibility of copying.

A key moment in Harrison's cross-examination reflects the legal strategy to establish a causal relation between the litigants. It came when Harrison was asked if he had heard the plaintiff's recording, described by the plaintiff's attorney as a hit radio song in England. When Harrison denied having heard the song, he was confronted with the UK charts in which the plaintiff's song appeared 'virtually at the same time as the Beatles' own recordings'.[62] Again he denied being aware of this fact, but was asked to scroll down the charts to state the ranking position in which both were listed.[63] Bringing Harrison to read aloud the coexisting time frame of popularity eventually helped to link his testimony to that plausibility sought by all copyright plaintiffs: the opportunity to copy. Music charts produced this potentiality in and of themselves, allowing their perspective, their qualitative measurement, to be produced in court. Seeing radio charts in this way gradually advanced the argument from the question of *timing* towards the issue of the *manner* in which the copying could have taken place, shifting the question of access towards that of awareness. This could be rephrased, as some copyright agencies and index-hunters had already flagged in the 1960s, as inadvertent copying.[64] The unfortunate effect of media exposure was the production of an echo of a memory that could not necessarily be intentionally recalled. The music was stored in the head, coming out accidentally years later. In that sense, the introduction of radio charts tied together to musical resemblances raised the spectre of unconscious copying.

Given that radio popularity caused a degree of subjectivation, the mass medium could equally prompt a collateral effect – the production of accidental similarities and innocent infringers. It is no surprise that several scholars have focused on these unintended effects in their attempt to develop normative solutions to fix what they conceive as copyright 'accidents'.[65] This doctrinal shift could help to solve the puzzle of liability. Ascribing agency and responsibility using moral or fault-based credentials could be taken to imply not only bureaucratic standards (instead of rules) governing the possibility of copyright infringement, but also the act of unconscious copying, defined as 'a sin of neglect rather than intention'.[66] One can add here that, in any case, Harrison did not have any sense of guilt; nor did he feel redeemed or reconciled by the decision. His concern was that he could not understand 'how the courts aren't filled with similar cases – as 99 percent of the popular music that can be heard is reminiscent of something or other'.[67] Curiously, a subtle link between unintentional hearing, ubiquity and the unconscious had already become explicit a couple of decades earlier. The Muzak company had based its success on the premise of disseminating music to be heard but 'not listened to'.[68] Recorded music had been franchised to restaurants, elevators, banks, factories, transatlantic aeroplanes and a variety of places to be easily assimilated unintentionally by workers and consumers.[69] Its omnipresence was

[62] Harrison (cross examination), 1976 hearing transcript (n 19) 258.

[63] ibid.

[64] 'Rencontres, réminiscences, plagiats' *SACEM, Bulletin d'information de la société des auteurs compositeurs et éditeurs de musique* (April 1965) 30.

[65] See, eg O Bracha and PR Goold, 'Copyright Accidents' (2016) 96 *Boston University Law Review* 1025, 1038.

[66] R Posner, *Little Book of Plagiarism* (Pantheon Books, 2007) 97.

[67] 'My Sweet Lord' in F Bronson, *The Billboard Book of Number One Hits* (Billboard, 1985) 286; see also M Brown, 'A Conversation with George Harrison in *Rolling Stone*, 19 April 1979' in A Kahn (ed), *George Harrison on George Harrison. Interviews and Encounters* (Chicago Review Press, 2020) 271.

[68] J McDermott, 'If It's To Be Heard but Not Listened To, It Must Be Muzak', box 215, folder 9, John Steiner Collection, University of Chicago Library.

[69] Another way of expressing this was to refer to Muzak as 'somnambulist' music. See William Benton to Ethel Maclean, 18 July 1949, William Benton papers, box 226, folder 5, University of Chicago Library.

such that Anthony Haden-Guest wrote that 'Muzak will attend your birth in (for instance) the Mercy Home, Carolina; and your death in (for instance) the Nelson Funeral Home, Arkansas, or a crematorium in Birmingham'.[70] Although there might be some obvious differences between the copyright decision under discussion and Muzak, there is, nevertheless, an interesting shared premise, typified in the way Muzak was described as 'music for the subconscious'.[71]

B. Money

It is remarkable how the musicological analyses avoided the subject of economic success, given that much of the emphasis in the dispute was on the connection between copyright and money – how to trace it, whether and when to settle, how to account for it. The protracted legal controversy involving 'My Sweet Lord', which had started in the early 1970s, affected Harrison's subsequent ventures, such as the recording of an album tellingly entitled *Living in a Material World* (1973) and the establishment of the Material World charitable foundation, which used copyright royalties as a way to fund humanitarian projects.[72] It took more than five years for the copyright dispute to reach the courts as the plaintiff, Bright Tunes, had financial difficulties and had gone into receivership.[73] After the liability hearing in August 1976 had found Harrison liable of a copyright infringement, the next legal hurdle was the calculation of damages.[74] How could one assess the damage caused by a subconscious copying? How to account for an unintentional liability? Interestingly, the question raised again the issue of popularity, shifting the focus from the media to the legal remedy, and from access to the plaintiff's song to the success of the defendant's infringing composition. The shift in the legal process meant turning the eye to the role of popularity in record sales, live performances and radio airtime.[75] Although this might be disregarded as a mere bean-counting exercise, the peculiarity of the infringement (unconscious or unintentional) required a certain calibration in the estimation of damages.[76] As the judge himself pointed out, 'had I earlier found that Harrison deliberately plagiarized the music, I would award the entire earnings of "My Sweet Lord"'.[77]

The assessment of damages was further complicated by the fact that the infringing song, 'My Sweet Lord', was a big hit, so there was a need to consider its worldwide reach, the different sublicensing agreements and the existence of infringement claims pending or settled in other jurisdictions.[78] While radio stations used individual songs in their programmes and playlists,

[70] A Haden-Guest, *Down the Programmed Rabbit-Hole* (Hart-Davis MacGibbon, 1972) 12.

[71] L Lader, 'Music That Nobody Hears' [September 1950] *Nation's Business* 58; Ronald H Coase papers, box 84, folder 3, University of Chicago Library.

[72] George Harrison chronology, March 1973, box 40; George Harrison visit 13 December 1974, Sheila R Weidenfeld Files, Gerald R Ford Presidential Library; Harry (n 7) 278.

[73] JC Self, 'The "My Sweet Lord"/"He's So Fine" Plagiarism Suit' [1993] *9/10 Magazine.*

[74] 'Good Lord! It's the Same Old Song' *Melody Maker* (18 September 1976) 30.

[75] *ABKCO Music, Inc v Harrisongs Music Ltd* 508 F Supp 798, 800 (SDNY 1981).

[76] Huntley (n 35) 165.

[77] *ABKCO v Harrisongs* (n 75) 804.

[78] In fact, a similar infringement action brought in England by the British copyright assignee of 'He's So Fine', The Peter Maurice Co Ltd, began in January 1974 and was settled out of court in 1977. The hearing date was distanced off due to the heavily congested state of the court lists in England, so it ended up being scheduled after the American liability case was decided, facilitating the ground for a negotiated agreement between the parties; see Palmer to Gardner, 5 April 1976; JGP (n 25). Although there is obviously no law report, the first expert approached by the claimant for advice, Geoffrey Bush, declined the possibility to participate in the case for the plaintiff, saying 'he could never believe that a former Beatle could have infringed any copyright, either consciously or unconsciously', and acted instead for the defendant (Harrisongs); see J Bellido, 'Popular Music and Copyright Law in the Sixties' (2013) 40 *Journal of Law and Society* 593. The expert

record companies had become increasingly album-orientated since the early 1950s.[79] This difference in the way the musical commodity circulated raised the problem of the calculation of its value, and apportionment of damages from a copyright perspective.[80] If radio time was easy to track, the impact factor and the value of a song in an album was significantly more difficult to ascertain.[81] For example, how much money was derived from an infringing song that was included in an album alongside other tracks? This question not only referred to *All Things Must Pass*, on which the infringing song was originally released, but also affected albums such as *The Concert of Bangladesh* (1971) and *The Best of George Harrison* (1976), on which 'My Sweet Lord' had been also included.

Here the law hesitated between a mechanistic theory of profits, whereby cuts or tracks in an album were considered equally in the treatment of royalties, and a more subjective appreciation of the significance of the infringing piece in those albums, based on the consideration that the most popular song was the crucial factor contributing to sales.[82] Either way, the accounting exercise in respect of the income from the infringing song was even more vexing in respect of the other two albums. On the one hand, a significant aspect of *Bangladesh* was that the presence of other musicians such as Bob Dylan and Ravi Shankar could explain its popularity and sales.[83] The difficulty with the second album was not only the fact of its release after the copyright judgment, but also its special character as a compilation of previous hits, therefore making it even more difficult to assess profits attributable to the infringing song.

Another way in which the law tried to deal with the lack of legal definition of the notion of popularity was by enlisting the evidential assistance of copyright collecting societies, such as the Performing Rights Society (UK) or Broadcast Music, Inc (USA), as their role was to monitor the exploitation of musical works from their repertoire. While the production of paper records relating to performances has an evidential weight in the tracing of money routes, the significance of collecting societies in these narratives is also derived from other administrative decisions. After a legal controversy is flagged up, they tend to temporarily freeze royalty accounts until a dispute is resolved.[84] As copyright litigation in pop music is costly and tends to be prolonged over years or decades, the effect of such an internal administrative decision over the financial lives of musicians and music publishers is weighty. In taking this stance, collecting societies often steer the parties towards settlement and mediation. This could also explain how some cases never reach the courts, therefore partly answering Harrison's question as to how come the courts were

musicologist approached subsequently by the plaintiff in England, John Gardner, thought that resemblance between the songs was unassailably precise, making it 'a cast-iron case'; see Gardner to Irene Bull, 29 April 1993, 'Love Hurts folder', JGP (n 25). However, after the settlement out of court, Gardner received a letter from Geoffrey Bush in which he said, 'meaningfully, that all the Court Ushers and Reporters, chairwomen and odd bods were strongly of the opinion, after listening to the records, that there was no resemblance between the songs!': Gardner to Palmer, 6 July 1977, JGP (n 25).

[79] The market for records dramatically changed the course of music publishing after the Second World War and recordings became the major way in which music was communicated. '[T]he introduction of the LP album which could include twelve songs instead of the two previously available on singles created opportunities for the use of six times as many songs although the unit price per song to the consumer remained about the same': L Feist, 'Notes for the Bicentennial. 300+ Years of American Music Publishing', Leonard Feist papers, box 4, folder 5, New York Public Library, Library for the Performing Arts, Music Division.

[80] RS Rosen, *Music and Copyright* (Oxford University Press, 2008) 238–39.

[81] *ABKCO v Harrisongs* (n 75) 804. The judge used the Broadcast Music, Inc monitoring of air play by disc jockeys to estimate the value of each song from the album *All Things Must Pass*.

[82] Huntley (n 35) 165–67.

[83] G Cannon, 'The Bangladesh Concert Records' *The Guardian* (4 January 1972) 8. On the tax and legal problems of the Bangladesh album, see Clayson, *George Harrison* (n 31) 311–19.

[84] 'Plagiats', *SACEM, Bulletin d'information de la société des auteurs compositeurs et éditeurs de musique* (February 1967) 26–27.

not filled with similar cases. The opportunity to encourage mediation did not arise in this case. Although Harrison and his publishing company, Harrisongs, were affiliated to different societies, such as the PRS, the composer of the song owned by the plaintiff, Ronnie Mack, was not a member of a collecting society.[85]

C. Trust

Often lost in the doctrinal analysis of the decision are the specific procedural details that made the case even more remarkable. The switch from liability to damage incidentally revealed operations before and after the trial in a way that characterised the pop music industry throughout the 1970s. It not only showed how royalties, past and future, could be estimated, but also how entangled relationships and arrangements between musicians and agents could cloud the issue, even to the point of influencing the very possibility of a legal dispute. These dealings, negotiations and arrangements were fundamental in commercialising pop. For example, business agents and managers mediated the transfer of music into recordings and their circulation around radio and television stations, contributing to their popularity.[86] As essential as they were in codifying copyright into business, these relationships tended to be brittle and ephemeral, somehow mirroring the genre itself, brief by its very nature and characterised by the splitting up of bands or the meteoric rise and downfall of music trajectories.[87] One of the consequences of this volatile environment was that, once these relationships started to crumble, acrimonious legal disputes ensued. These breakdowns are intriguing and yet somehow strangely ordinary at the same time, particularly because loyalties were tied to royalties as a way to reimburse agents for negotiating record contracts and promoting artists.[88]

Shortly before this case moved to the damage phase, the Beatles' notorious former business manager, Allen B Klein, acquired both the copyright interest of the plaintiff and the damage claim against Harrison.[89] In doing so, his company, ABKCO, replaced the original plaintiff in the proceedings. The move appeared to signal the typical side-switching, back-stabbing reaction of a disgruntled former manager – in this case, one well known for his litigious character.[90] It looked like a strategy developed after the judicial outcome, so the swap was accepted by the court and ABKCO continued the damage proceedings against Harrison in relation to the unconscious copyright infringement.[91] However, as Klein's lawyers had advised Harrison previously, this substitution meant not only that he was sued by his former manager, but ironically that this

[85] Ruth Beltram, PRS to Paul Adler, ASCAP, 6 October 1986, PRS archives (Harrisongs).

[86] Rogan's discussion of different types of managers in pop history is particularly interesting. According to Rogan, the function of the pop manager in the 1960s was somewhere between 'the hard businessman, the medical doctor and the dedicated schoolteacher'. J Rogan, *Starmakers and Svengalis: The History of British Pop Management* (Trans-Atlantic Publications, 1988) 266.

[87] J Fielding, 'Insight: The Toughest Wheeler-Dealer in the Pop Jungle' *Sunday Times* (13 April 1969) 1–2.

[88] In the UK, Salmon LJ provided a telling depiction of the significance of management in pop music: 'Almost anything a manager might do, however harmless or trivial, could induce hatred and distrust in a group of highly temperamental, jealous and spoilt adolescents'. See *Denmark Productions Ltd v Boscobel Productions Ltd* [1968] 3 WLR 841.

[89] 'Agreement between Bright Tunes and ABKCO Music, Inc, 13 April 1978'; *ABKCO v Harrisongs* (n 75) 803.

[90] F Goodman, *Allen Klein: The Man Who Bailed Out the Beatles, Made the Stones and Transformed Rock & Roll* (Eamon Dolan/Houghton Mifflin Harcourt, 2015) 278. This seems to be confirmed by the number of legal cases that the firm got involved in after the well-known disputes that Klein had against the Rolling Stones, the Beatles and the Kinks. See, eg *ABKCO Music, Inc v Stellar Records, Inc* 96 F 3d 60, 62 n 4 (2d Cir 1996); *ABKCO Music, Inc v LaVere* 217 F 3d 684 (9th Cir 2000); *ABKCO Music & Records Inc v Jodorowsky* [2002] All ER (D) 304 (Feb).

[91] Harry (n 7) 276.

was 'one of the few times in American litigation where one party was responsible for the pleadings on both sides of a case'.[92] Significantly, the discovery proceedings opened another line of inquiry – the way the manager might have influenced the circumstances under which the initial controversy arose. The key point here, beyond the typical legal trivialities, is that it laid bare the different rationales before and after a trial. Klein (or ABKCO) did not come on the scene after the copyright litigation but had been in contact with the plaintiff at the early stages, that is to say, when the settlement negotiations were taking place.[93] In fact, Harrison's attorney, Joseph J Santora, recalled how the very same process server involved in the Beatles' break-up case against Klein was the one who served the legal papers on Harrison.[94] In any case, the vital issue was that covert interference and the breach of fiduciary duty could have contributed to the failure of the settlement negotiation between Harrison and Bright Tunes, and hence enabled the legal dispute to ensue.

Was this the main trigger of the dispute? What might have happened had Klein not intervened? Although it was not possible to ascertain with absolute certainty whether the copyright case would or would not have taken place without Klein's breach of fiduciary duty, the notable feature here is how money and information were considered as gatekeepers to the law. The disclosure of financial information had the likely effect of having influenced the negotiation by prejudicing the very possibility of a settlement.[95] One of the problems of such conclusion is that it turns the copyright decision upside down, revisiting the controversy before the litigation. Would not settlement have been the preferred vehicle to resolve a dispute that culminated in an unconscious copying judgment? With the benefit of hindsight, yes. However, that possibility was surely off the table because of the breach of fiduciary duty. What could be the legal remedy in a lawsuit that would probably not have taken place without such illegality? This conundrum was addressed by the decision of the district court in 1981, which held that Harrison remained the owner of the copyright in the infringing song, 'My Sweet Lord', and required ABKCO and Allen B Klein to turn over the rights and profits acquired from the original plaintiff in relation to the original song. This meant that a constructive trust was imposed in favour of Harrison.[96] Two years later, the Court of Appeals for the Second Circuit affirmed the judgment of the lower court in the two main issues, namely, ownership by Harrison of the copyright in 'My Sweet Lord' and the constructive trust requiring ABKCO to transfer the rights and profits acquired by it in relation to the original composition, 'He's So Fine'.[97] Although the litigation continued for a decade, also taking into account foreign settlements and redefining the scope of the trust,[98] this twist epitomises the elasticity of the encounter between pop music and copyright, riddled with ambiguities and professional conflicts.[99] Judged in the context of its time, it exemplifies a special type of legal irony, particularly if one compares it to the emphasis on percentages and proportions whereby statistical evidence and expert musicological analysis framed the relationship in the courtroom. In the end, the songwriter who had been found liable for copyright infringement ended up becoming the owner of the song he had infringed.[100]

[92] Santora, *Bright Tunes v Harrison* SZ (n 58) 2.

[93] *ABKCO v Harrisongs* (n 75) 803.

[94] Santora, *Bright Tunes v Harrison* SZ (n 58) 1.

[95] Bertolt Brecht had already suggested this issue in relation to his copyright litigation. See J Bellido, 'Experimenting with Law. Brecht on Copyright' (2020) 31 *Law and Critique* 127.

[96] *ABKCO v Harrisongs* (n 75) 803.

[97] *ABKCO Music, Inc v Harrisongs Music Ltd*, 722 F 2d 988 (2d Cir 1983).

[98] 'Now Harrison Sued in UK' *Music Week* (2 July 1977) 4; 'Harrison Settles Out of Court' *Music Week* (9 July 1977) 4.

[99] The final iterations of the legal controversy were *ABKCO Music, Inc v Harrisongs Music Ltd* 841 F 2d 494 (1988) and *ABKCO Music, Inc v Harrisongs Music Ltd* 944 F 2d 971 (1991).

[100] B Southall, *Pop Goes to Court* (Omnibus Press, 2008) 56; Goodman (n 90) 241.

III. Conclusion

Although the case was decided almost half a century ago, it has become representative – indeed, virtually prophetic – of a certain oddity in the genre-specific dynamics between pop music and copyright law. How could someone copy while denying having heard a popular song? How could anyone deny hearing a song when we are all surrounded by music in a media-saturated world? Are forensic musicologists the final arbiters in explaining what we can hear and what we cannot remember? Has copyright law inevitably become the province of expert listeners? The case left some interesting questions up in the air while somehow anticipating what was yet to come.[101] One of the very few points on which almost all copyright scholars seem to agree today is that the law needs to be reimagined. On the one hand, contemporary legal scholarship focuses on the necessity of interpreting exceptions and defences to copyright infringement broadly – especially the treatment of quotations – extending the purely textual paradigm into popular media such as music, film and television. On the other hand, more pop music plagiarism cases have reached the courts, reiterating the problems highlighted in this chapter.

Uncannily, as the Harrison controversy dealt with musical consciousness and memory, it was only a matter of time before science fiction narratives took it as source material. Most jurisprudents and legal historians would be indifferent to this reference and might even be alarmed by it – perhaps rightly so. However, from the vantage point of science fiction, we can transcend historiographical or doctrinal interpretations and examine anxieties generated by such cases. In a short story entitled *Melancholy Elephants* (1984), Spider Robinson introduces the Harrison case in a conversation set in Washington, DC between two characters, a lobbyist and a politician, in the context of a bill that would extend the copyright term. According to the lobbyist, plagiarism lawsuits like the Harrison case had become a plague.[102] In fact, she mentions a stream of lawsuits that came in its aftermath – copyright controversies involving Yoko Ono, the John Lennon estate and many others that, more often than not, ended up being settled.[103] In a chaotic and bewildering technological age dominated by copyright clearances, musical fact-checkers and claims routinely settled, the story is interesting because it invites the reader to reflect on borrowing, creativity and the illusion of originality that copyright instils in its subjects.

What does it mean to reflect on the encounter between the popular and copyright law in an increasingly technologised and mass mediated world? What was the seminal desire elicited by pop in all its aspects? Unlike other musical genres, pop music democratised compositional procedures, creating a celestial backdrop of highs and lows around authorship, while at the same time becoming subservient to the record industry. This combination of stardom, creativity and law had particular effects on the way we link copyright to our capacity to dream, remember and forget. One of the characters in the science fiction narrative mentioned above speculates about the spell of originality fading away if copyright continued to be extended by legislation when we consider the increase in life expectancy. For what would be the function of copyright if distant memories and musical resemblances could easily be retrieved by the legal system? Seeking to

[101] Immediately after the decision, Ringo Starr commented that Harrison had been 'very unlucky. There's no doubt that the tune is very similar but how many songs have been written with other melodies in mind? … he was very unlucky that someone wanted to make it a test case in court': R Coleman, 'Starr Trek' *Melody Maker* (2 October 1976) 17.

[102] S Robinson, *Melancholy Elephants* (Penguin Books, 1984) 12–13; see also J Oswald, 'Bettered by the Borrower: The Ethics of Musical Debt' in C Cox and D Warner (eds), *Audio Culture: Readings in Modern Music* (Continuum, 2004) 131–37.

[103] Most of these controversies are also mentioned in R Palmer, 'The Pop Life. Today's Songs, Really Yesterday's?' *New York Times* (8 July 1981) 21.

avoid the hassle and the vertigo of plagiarism allegations, a well-known pop musician recently decided to start documenting his compositional forays. This would certainly produce a sort of artificial repository for the memory, a documentary of entire recording processes to avoid being caught by an appeal to the unconscious or a reference to accidental copying. Here we see record keeping imagined as a kind of witnessing in pop composition and song writing, a strategy to make a record of composing, writing a song or, indeed, making a record. Although claiming to be an innovative strategy for solving copyright problems, such self-documenting and archiving might not actually be so new. In fact, they can be traced to arrangements that tied pop music to marketing and advertising promotions. In that sense, there is nothing particularly innovative in documenting behind-the-scenes creative processes, since not only is it part of our everyday experience in social media, but rather – and perhaps more interestingly – it resembles the urban legend of copyright protection that involved sending a certified sealed letter with the material to one's future self, so that there existed a stamped and sealed envelope containing the manuscript, album or score.[104] However, once again, the record does not speak for itself. A notable passage in *Melancholy Elephants* shows that the illusion (or delusion) of originality is probably more problematic, hypnotic and mysterious than it seems at first glance:

> My husband wrote a song for me, on the occasion of our fortieth wedding anniversary. It was our love in music, unique and special and intimate, the most beautiful melody I ever heard in my life. It made him so happy to have written it. Of his last ten compositions he had burned five for being derivative, and the others had all failed copyright clearance. But this was fresh, special – he joked that my love for him had inspired him. The next day he submitted it for clearance and learned that it had been a popular air during his early childhood, and had already been unsuccessfully submitted fourteen times since its original registration. A week later he burned all his manuscripts and working tapes and killed himself.[105]

[104] Although this scheme, often called 'poor man's copyright', was recommended as early as the 1950s, it is not a coincidence that it became particularly ubiquitous in 'How to Make It in the Pop Music' business literature of the 1970s. See, eg 'So You've Written a Song!' (1955) 9(2) *Changing Times – The Kiplinger Magazine* 45; K McNeel and M Luther, *Songwriters with a Touch of Gold* (Will Martin Publishing, 1976); LP Wilbur, *How to Write Songs That Sell* (H Regnery, 1977) 52–53; JG Erickson, ER Hearn, ME Halloran and S Riklin, *Musician's Guide to Copyright* (Scribner's, 1979) 17.

[105] Robinson (n 102) 16–17.

8

'Do the Right Thing' or 'Fight the Power?': Hip-Hop Music, Sampling and Copyright Law

JOYCE LEE AND MARC MIMLER

I. Introduction

Hip-hop music has become one of the most popular music genres. In 2018, hip-hop and rap music topped the league of total music consumption in the USA, at 21.7 per cent.[1] This number reflects hip-hop's influence not only on a wide audience, but also on other genres of music. Hip-hop music is now a global phenomenon and is performed worldwide in various languages in addition to English, such as French, German, Chinese, Spanish and Turkish. To some extent, defining hip-hop as only a genre of music would be a mistake. Rather, it encompasses a much wider array of cultural practices, with diverse forms of expressions.[2] As such, hip-hop has become a certain lifestyle that an increasing number of people around the world embrace.

The focus of this chapter is the tension between copyright law and sampling, a core element of hip-hop music creation. The drama surrounding The Sugar Hill Gang's 'Rapper's Delight' embodies the apotheosis of such tension. First released in 1980, 'Rapper's Delight' was one of the very first commercially successful hip-hop tracks.[3] The success, however, came with the threat of copyright infringement lawsuit by the members of Chic. The members of Chic argued that the bassline of their song 'Good Times' distinctively featured in 'Rapper's Delight' by the Sugar Hill Gang. It should be noted that Rapper's Delight did not sample the recording of 'Good Times', but used a replay of the notorious bassline.[4] After hearing the track, Nile Rodgers and Bernard Edwards of Chic threatened the Sugar Hill Gang with legal action based on copyright infringement. Ultimately, they settled; it was agreed that Rodgers and Edwards would also be credited as songwriters of 'Rapper's Delight'.[5,6]

[1] www.statista.com/statistics/310746/share-music-album-sales-us-genre/.

[2] M Katz, *Capturing Sound: How Technology Has Changed Music* (University of California Press, 2010) 126.

[3] J Okpaluba, 'Digital Sampling and Music Industry Practices, Re-spun' in K Bowrey and M Handler (eds), *Law and Creativity in the Age of the Entertainment Franchise* (Cambridge University Press, 2014) 79.

[4] A Said, *The Art of Sampling – The Sampling Tradition of Hip-Hop/Rap Music & Copyrights Law*, 2nd edn (Superchamp Books, 2015) 338; J Demers, *Steal This Music: How Intellectual Property Law Affects Musical Creativity* (University of Georgia Press, 2006) 92.

[5] TW Joo, 'Remix without Romance' [2011] *Connecticut Law Review* 415, 427–38.

[6] In an interview, Rodgers said the following: 'Our music to us was sacred. I certainly didn't mind somebody jamming with us on stage live. But to record it and not put our names on it and then make a lot of money. I think that the record was so big it might have been even bigger than "Good Times". At least it was more exciting as it felt like a new Art form': 'The Story of Rapper's Delight by Nile Rodgers' (RapProject.tv, retrieved 12 October 2008) www.youtube.com/watch?v=t-SCGNOieBI.

Before delving into the tension between copyright law and sampling, this chapter will provide context to sampling, the most essential practice of hip-hop musicians in developing their tracks. For that purpose, the chapter will lay out the evolution of hip-hop music from its inception in the 1970s in New York City's Bronx to its current status as one of the most commercially successful genres of music. The chapter will then look at the pertinent copyright issues surrounding hip-hop music. On this particular point, the chapter will analyse this issue in relation to law of the USA and the EU, as they provide a good amount of case law and serve as a good comparative set.

II. A Brief History of Hip Hop

Hip-hop originated in the USA. More specifically, it originated in the Bronx, one of New York City's five boroughs. The spirit of taking initiatives motivated hip-hop musicians to take on creative ventures throughout the genre's development. The origin of hip-hop music can be traced back to a party held by the Jamaican-American DJ Kool Herc in 1973,[7] where he created the 'Merry-Go-Round' technique.[8] The break part, a heavily percussive segment of the records he was playing, was particularly popular with the dancing crowd, which would get ecstatic when the break occurred.[9] He first selected passages of his liking and cut them out to create isolated beats carrying bass and percussion alone.[10] These short instrumental break records, known as 'breakbeats', often lasted less than a second and had to be repeated multiple times to be used. Kool Herc then lined up two record players to produce a continuous flow of breakbeats and created his own unique musical collage.[11] Later, Grandmaster Flash took it even further to orchestrate a table with multiple record players, which enabled him to check the flow of his breakbeats even before it was delivered through the loudspeakers.[12]

Ever since its birth in the 1970s, hip-hop has served as an outlet for the disenfranchised, namely the Black community, to deliver social commentaries in the form of popular art and entertainment. As such, hip-hop naturally embraces the ideology of the civil rights movement and black freedom struggle through and after the pertinent era in the USA.[13] The common topics addressed by hip-hop artists include racial and class inequalities, discrimination, drugs, police brutality and the usurpation of individual rights in the country. Nowadays, these topics concern not only African Americans in the USA, but also other oppressed groups of people around the world[14] who are actively providing cross-cultural elements to the recipe of hip-hop. In the context of US history, hip-hop's criticism on social injustice has been repeatedly produced by a number of Black leaders, including Malcolm X, Martin Luther King, Jr and Angela Davis, among various artists.[15] The rebellious spirit of hip-hop is well reflected in 'Whitey On the Moon', released in 1970 by Gil Scott-Heron. The artists here portrayed in lyric the vivid contrast between the poverty of African American society and NASA's lunar missions:[16]

[7] Said (n 4) 11.
[8] J Chang, *Can't Stop Won't Stop: A History of the Hip-Hop Generation* (Picador, 2005) 79.
[9] J Vernon, *Sampling, Biting, and the Postmodern Subversion of Hip Hop* (Palgrave Macmillan, 2021) 13.
[10] F Neumann, 'Hip Hop: Origins, Characteristics and Creative Processes' [2000] *The World of Music* 51, 59.
[11] JA Williams, *'Rymin' and Stealin'' – Musical Borrowing in Hip-Hop* (University of Michigan Press, 2013) 23.
[12] Neumann (n 10) 60.
[13] DP Alridge, 'From Civil Rights to Hip Hop: Toward a Nexus of Ideas' [2005] *Journal of African American History* 226, 226.
[14] ibid 228.
[15] J Demers, 'Sampling the 1970s in Hip-Hop' [2003] *Popular Music* 41, 50.
[16] ibid 43–44.

> I can't pay no doctor bills, while whitey's on the moon
> Ten years from now I'll be paying still, while whitey's on the moon
> You know, the man just upped my rent last night, cause whitey's on the moon
> No hot water, no toilets, no lights, but whitey's on the moon
> I wonder why he's upping me', cause whitey's on the moon?

The hip-hop movement is thus built on the civil rights movement and the Black power movement. It is noteworthy, though, that hip-hop breaks with politics and social visions of the previous Black popular movements. However, despite a view criticising hip-hop's detachment from the civil rights ideology in the post-1970s, it still serves as a powerful tool for youths to find their voices and to come up with a powerful counter-narrative against social inequalities across the globe.[17] The message of positivity has been replayed, referenced and reinvented by hip-hop artists of the following generation.[18] Hip-hop's repertoire thus continues to carry inspiring messages encouraging self-esteem for young people, addressing issues of racial injustice, and promoting the much-needed sense of community. Its emphasis on purposeful optimism has been one of the genre's most salient features from early on and is well reflected on the mission statement of the Hip-Hop Summit Action Network (HSAN). This non-profit organisation is 'dedicated to harnessing the cultural relevance of Hip-Hop music to serve as a catalyst for education advocacy and other societal concerns fundamental to the well-being of at-risk youth throughout the United States'.[19]

III. The Artistic Features and Practices of Hip-Hop Music

Music is only one form of expression of hip-hop culture. It is more of a lifestyle highlighting distinctive features and practices that have been interacting with and transforming one another. Hip-hop consists of four distinctive features or elements:[20] (i) DJing; (ii) rapping or MCing; (iii) breaking; and (iv) graffiti. All these movements are linked to the same geographical space, where artists often engage in more than one of the aforementioned features of hip-hop.[21] Breaking, more widely known as breakdance, was usually performed at 'gigs', or performances, and was most prominent at early hip-hop parties.[22] Contemporary graffiti[23] as another artistic expression linked to the hip-hop lifestyle was equally developed in New York in the 1970s. Even though these two elements fused into their own sub-cultures, this chapter will not discuss them in further detail, as they are not tangential to music.[24]

[17] Alridge (n 13) 226, 228; H Osumare, 'Keeping It Real: Race, Class, and Youth Connections through Hip-Hop in the US & Brazil' [2015] *Humboldt Journal of Social Relations* 6, 6.

[18] DP Alridge, 'From Civil Rights to Hip Hop: Toward a Nexus of Ideas' [2005] *Journal of African American History* 226, 227.

[19] P Butler, 'Much Respect: Toward a Hip-Hop Theory of Punishment' [2004] *Stanford Law Review* 983, 994.

[20] Katz (n 2) 126; TM Evans, 'Sampling, Looping, and Mashing … Oh My!: How Hip Hop Music is Scratching More Than the Surface of Copyright Law' [2011] *Fordham Intellectual Property, Media & Entertainment Law Journal* 843, 852.

[21] Williams, *'Rymin' and Stealin'* (n 11) 22–23.

[22] JG Schloss, '"Like Old Folk Songs Handed Down from Generation to Generation": History, Canon, and Community in B-boy Culture' [2006] *Ethnomusicology* 411, 413.

[23] I Miller, 'Hip-Hop Visual Arts' in JA Williams (ed), *The Cambridge Companion to Hip-Hop* (Cambridge University Press, 2015) 32–41; Said (n 4) 13–16.

[24] See further M Iljadica, *Copyright beyond Law – Regulating Creativity in the Graffiti Subculture* (Bloomsbury Publishing, 2016); E Bonadio (ed), *The Cambridge Handbook of Copyright in Street Art and Graffiti* (Cambridge University Press, 2019); IK Johnson, 'Hip Hop Dance' in Williams, *The Cambridge Companion to Hip-Hop* (n 23) 22–31.

DJing as an element of hip-hop music was made possible by turntables becoming more than just a means to reproduce music but instruments in their own right. While DJing is possible with only a single turntable, the combination of two turntables initiated by Kool Herc allowed the DJ to loop a particular part on a record repeatedly. These parts were often instrumental parts, ie 'breaks', to which b-boys and girls (ie breakdancing performers) would showcase their moves.[25] While Kool Herc was the first DJ to use turntables as an instrument, it was Grandmaster Flash who first touched the top of records and created various techniques that became staples in hip-hop DJing.[26] Some DJs took yet another approach to make breakbeats last longer by physically turning the record to repeat them multiple times.[27] The by-product of this process was scratchy noise from the turning, which was picked up and arranged to add a rhythmic texture to the music. This technique is called 'scratching'; it was developed by Grand Wizzard Theodore in the mid-1970s in the Bronx[28] and became one of the most iconic sounds of hip-hop DJing.

The aim of DJing in the beginning was to create a continuous musical beat that was recognisable[29] because the music was used at jams to get the crowds dancing. This explains why records from funk and disco music which had noticeable breaks were used in the early days and DJs obtained large collections of records which contained the desired sounds, commonly referred to as 'crate digging'.[30] Before the introduction of digital files, battle records were created which contained many brief desirable samples and sounds for DJing and scratching.[31] The introduction of Digital Vinyl Systems (DVS) along with samplers and synthesisers widened the scope for creating music. As hip-hop evolved as a musical genre, DJs would utilise increasingly diverse types of records from eclectic musical sources for their creation. Afrika Bambaataa, for instance, started using the instrumental portions of songs by a variety of groups such as Aerosmith, the Monkees and Kraftwerk. Similarly, Run DMC covered Aerosmith's 1975 song, 'Walk This Way', to create one of the first crossover tracks featuring musical elements from rock, pop and hip-hop. The subgenre of jazz hip-hop was further developed by artists such as Jungle Brothers, A Tribe called Quest and De La Soul, who prominently used jazz instrumentation within their composition.[32] This diversification of musical sources and creative desire to improve the quality of the beats transformed hip-hop from mere accompaniment to dance to pleasurable listening sensation by itself.[33] Such transformation also advanced the multidimensionality of the genre, as hip-hop earned global appeal. The sampled material itself would borrow more often from traditional music of worldwide communities, as seen in Turkish hip-hop in Germany using samples from traditional Turkish music.[34]

The other element of hip-hop is rap, or microphone checking, ie MCing. Rapping arguably derives from 'toasting',[35] a verbal performance that is derived from the old African tradition of storytelling.[36] Said identifies three forms of African American toasting as 'signifyin''-, 'radio

[25] Katz (n 2) 125.

[26] Said (n 4) 19–20.

[27] Neumann (n 10) 59.

[28] Katz (n 2) 125; Vernon (n 9) 15.

[29] Said (n 4) 17–18.

[30] KF Hansen, 'DJs and Turntablism' in Williams, *The Cambridge Companion to Hip-Hop* (n 23) 42, 49.

[31] ibid 42, 49.

[32] CJ Farley, 'The Construction of Jazz Rap as High Art in Hip-Hop Music' in Williams, *The Cambridge Companion to Hip-Hop* (n 23) 47–72.

[33] Said (n 4) 70.

[34] Demers, *Steal This Music* (n 4) 89.

[35] Neumann (n 10) 59.

[36] A Price-Styles, 'MC Origins: Rap and Spoken Word Poetry' in Williams, *The Cambridge Companion to Hip-Hop* (n 23) 11.

DJ'- and 'hustler' toasts, all of which influenced rapping in hip-hop.[37] James Brown's music and Lightnin' Rod's album *Hustler's Convention* are commonly considered the most influential works for early rap.[38] Initially, rapping or MCing was only functional and subsidiary to DJing.[39] However, this changed gradually over time. The complexity of the rhymes also evolved as MCing grew to embrace more serious themes, such as crimes and violence, compared to the nursery rhymes and much lighter subject matters from the early days. In the beginning, DJs would be the protagonists, as jams were the main attraction to the public; MCs simply played supportive roles of adding an accompaniment to the DJs' music. However, the roles and dynamics between DJs and MCs reversed over time. The first commercial hip-hop track, 'Rapper's Delight' by the Sugar Hill Gang,[40] shifted the focus from the DJs to the rappers. The move away from jams to radio and recorded music arguably added to this development as well.[41] As MCing started to feature as the predominant element of hip-hop, rapping, albeit mistakenly, has often been regarded as an equivalent for hip-hop itself.[42]

IV. Sampling as a Constitutional Element of Hip-Hop Music

Sampling is not simply a feature of hip-hop, but rather constitutes the essence of music composition of hip-hop.[43] Many famous hip-hop tracks contain recognisable samples from other tracks. Examples include Vanilla Ice's 'Ice, Ice, Baby', which sampled the bass line from 'Under Pressure' by David Bowie and Queen, and Coolio's 'Gangsta's Paradise', which sampled Stevie Wonder's 'Pastime Paradise'. In addition, Ice Cube, in 'It Was a Good Day', also used a pitched sample of the main bassline of the Isley Brothers' 'Footsteps in the Dark', and Kanye West used a slowed down sample from Curtis Mayfield's 'Move on Up' in his song 'Touch the Sky'. Other samples are not as easily recognisable but are nevertheless important for the genre, such as the break by percussionist Clyde Stubblefield in James Brown's song 'Funky Drummer', which became one of the most sampled pieces ever.[44] Its consistent presence in the hip-hop canon made sampling a constituent part of the genre and a vehicle of expression for hip-hop artists. It has also assumed a role as an instrument of reference, providing 'a reaffirmation of the musical and cultural lineage of hip-hop itself' as hip-hop further evolves.[45] Sampling as a form of musical composition, however, is not a creation of hip-hop. Sound collages were used in earlier compositions, and have been an important form of expression within the fine arts and other musical genres.[46] Finally, as sampling technology became more ubiquitous, digital sampling has become a feature of musical composition for musicians of various genres, such as pop and electronic music.

[37] Said (n 4) 23–27.
[38] ibid 27.
[39] Price-Styles (n 36) 11, 13–14.
[40] Evans (n 20) 855.
[41] Said (n 4) 49–54.
[42] ibid 40.
[43] Advocate General Szpunar noted in his opinion in *Pelham*: 'It is true that, in musical genres such as hip hop or rap, sampling plays a special role which provides not only the means of creation, but also constitutes an artistic process in itself'. Case C-476/17 *Pelham and Others* Opinion of AG Szpunar, 12 December 2018, para 93.
[44] The website 'whosampled.com' currently lists that 'Funky Drummer has been sampled in 1760 tracks': www.whosampled.com/James-Brown/Funky-Drummer/.
[45] Demers, 'Sampling the 1970s' (n 15) 56.
[46] K McLeod and P DiCola, *Creative License: The Law and Culture of Digital Sampling* (Duke University Press, 2011) 26–74.

The practice of sampling entails 'the digital incorporation of any pre-recorded sound into a new recorded work'.[47] The technology allows the digital sample to be altered once it has been created. It can be manipulated in numerous ways, by changes to the tempo or pitch, or by reversing, cutting, looping and layering the sound,[48] thus enabling a multitude of creative options in incorporating it within a new track. The use of samples in hip-hop can be traced back to its very inception, where breakbeats, which were continuously played using turntables, formed constituent parts of the genre. This form of beat making, where many beats derive from a pre-existing record, is essential to understanding the use of samples in hip-hop. The above-mentioned practice of 'crate digging', ie obtaining a large selection of records to be played often by churning through record stores and flea markets, became an important practice of DJs.[49] Finding and retrieving obscure and rare pieces would not only generate new beats, but would also gain respect from the audience and wider community. It also shows the ability of the producers as listeners to perceive 'musical possibility in a song, to listen for connections that may not currently exist in the song, to perceive aural spaces where they might not be obvious'.[50]

Digital sampling in hip-hop music composition taps into the practice of looping breakbeats. Rather than repeatedly switching back and forth between two turntables, the loop was created digitally. The inception of sampling in hip-hop is linked to DJ Marley Marl, who discovered digital sampling almost by mistake.[51] He not only was the first person to fully grasp the potential of sampling for composition, but started customising the sounds by not only using the break, but also other parts of a record.[52] The practice became widely used by artists as the technology improved and became more affordable in the mid- to late 1980s,[53] and this is the era that it often referred to as the golden age of sampling in hip-hop. Albums such as Public Enemy's *It takes a Nation of Millions to Hold Us Back*, De La Soul's *3 Feet High and Rising* and the Beastie Boys' *Paul's Boutique* were created in this period.[54] All of these albums are canonised parts of hip-hop and made extensive use of samples.

The commercial success of hip-hop, however, brought an end to that golden, or 'Wild West', era of sampling due to heightened scrutiny by the music industry.[55] By the early 1990s, the legal landscape had changed, with an increasing number of lawsuits surrounding hip-hop music. The heightened risks for not clearing samples clearly impacted hip-hop music composition. One notable example relates to the next albums of the above-mentioned hip-hop pioneers, which contained far less sampling than in the golden age.[56] For instance, the Beastie Boys' album *Check Your Head* had far fewer samples than its immediate predecessor, *Paul's Boutique*.[57] Artists reacted to the rise of litigation on samples in different ways: while some artists were able to afford to pay royalties to clear samples,[58] others started to employ more obscure sources for their samples,

[47] Katz (n 2) 147.

[48] ibid 148.

[49] McLeod and DiCola (n 46) 22.

[50] V Chang, 'Records That Play: The Present Past in Sampling Practice' [2009] *Popular Music* 143, 147.

[51] AS Muhammad and F Kelley, 'Marley Marl on the Bridge Wars, LL Cool J and Discovering Sampling' (NPR, 12 September 2013) www.npr.org/ss/microphonecheck/2013/09/11/221440934/marley-marl-on-the-bridge-wars-ll-cool-j-and-discovering-sampling.

[52] Said (n 4) 59.

[53] JA Williams, 'Intertextuality, Sampling, and Copyright' in Williams, *The Cambridge Companion to Hip-Hop* (n 23) 206.

[54] McLeod and DiCola (n 46) 20–26.

[55] ibid 26–30.

[56] A Sewell, 'How Copyright Affected the Musical Style and Critical Reception of Sample-Based Hip-Hop' [2014] *Journal of Popular Music Studies* 295, 302.

[57] McLeod and DiCola (n 46) 27–28.

[58] Demers, *Steal This Music* (n 4) 97.

ie crate digging through indie music recordings or niche foreign record shops,[59] in the hope of avoiding litigation. Others used the approach the Sugar Hill Gang used for 'Rapper's Delight' and used re-performances of the sought sample or manipulated the sample beyond recognition (ie 'chopping' or 'flipping' a sample),[60] while others gave up on sampling completely.

While increased litigation has affected the use of sampling in hip-hop music, it has far from faded away. The wider use of source material led to new creations that extended beyond the initial source material of funk and soul albums. Notable, for instance, is the underlying sample from Towa Tei's and Bebel Gilberto's electronic music track 'Techonova' within 'Find a Way' by A Tribe Called Quest. Other examples are Us3's use of Herbie Hancock's famous jazz piano chords in 'Cantaloop Island' in their track 'Cantaloop Island (Flip Fantasia)'[61] and MC Solaar's use of Serge Gainsbourg's 'Bonnie and Clyde' sample. A contemporary example is the creative use in Kendrick Lamar's 'Duckworth' from the award-winning album *Damn*, where the track producer 9th Wonder skilfully intertwines samples from different musical genres. Finally, it should be noted that this reuse and recontextualisation has not only created new music, but has also raised new interest in the sampled pieces.

V. Sampling and the Law

Sampling is important not only for hip-hop music – it has become a crucial element of making music generally. The rising commercial importance of sampling is displayed by the fact that a third of the top 100 albums of 1999 contained samples, a significant increase from the only eight of the top 100 albums in 1989.[62] The rising success of hip-hop music, however, increased the scrutiny of sampling, as mentioned above. Technological advancement enabled the detection of even less recognisable samples in order to build a case on copyright infringement. This deployment of legal action has led, as some commentators lament, to a decrease of creativity in hip-hop composition, and the end of the golden age of hip-hop[63] was heralded with the seminal decision in *Grand Upright v Warner Brother Records*.[64] Having to clear samples would restrict their use and make creation of new works impossible, and record labels became risk averse in publishing works containing uncleared samples.[65] Other commentators do not regard this higher degree of scrutiny by copyright holders in relation to sampling as preventative. Copyright law did not and could not prevent hip-hop artists from sampling.[66] Samples could be cleared, and issues resolved.

[59] H Campos, 'Sampling in Hip-Hop: Art or Theft?' (TCS, 24 October 2020) www.tcs.cam.ac.uk/sampling-in-hip-hop-art-or-theft/.

[60] Sewell (n 56) 298.

[61] Hancock embraced digital sampling as a form of musical composition early and allowed Us3 the use of the sample from Cantaloop Island – S Vaidhyanathan, *Copyrights and Copywrongs: The Rise of Intellectual Property and How It Threatens Creativity* (NYU Press, 2001) 150–51. In an interview, Hancock said that '"Cantaloop" gave my composition new life, and it still sounds hot': K Grow, 'History of Us3's Bold Jazz–Rap Breakthrough "Cantaloop (Flip Fantasia)"' (*The Spin*, 24 October 2013) www.spin.com/2013/10/us3-cantaloop-flip-fantasia-herbie-hancock-lou-donaldson/.

[62] Evans (n 20) 857.

[63] Vaidhyanathan (n 61) 144; Demers, *Steal This Music* (n 4) 97; Said (n 4) 71.

[64] The 1991 case *Grand Upright Music Ltd v Warner Brothers Records, Inc* 780 F Supp 182 (SDNY 1991), which involved Biz Markie admitting using a sample from Gilbert O'Sullivan's song 'Alone Again' in his song 'Alone Again', arguably marks the end of the Wild West days of sampling, with the court's opinion opening with the 7th of the Old Testament commandments 'Thou shall not steal' – McLeod and DiCola (n 46) 132.

[65] McLeod and DiCola (n 46) 28.

[66] Butler (n 19) 990.

Having cleared samples could also be regarded as not just 'doing the right thing' in a legal sense, but also a form of affirmation that the original creator permitted the use.[67]

While sampling is seen as a creative and indispensable process in relation to hip-hop, it is also regarded as the most contentious one from a copyright perspective.[68] In copyright diction, a sample constitutes a literal copy of a sound recording (phonogram) and an unauthorised reproduction would constitute an infringement.[69] Moreover, a sample will also copy the musical composition encapsulated within the phonogram. But, aside from this legal subsumption, the use of samples is not only a distinctive but rather an essential element of hip-hop music. Much of the original shared cultural code of hip-hop stressed recycling or remixing more than creating 'out of whole cloth'.[70] It thus provides for interesting inquiries into the core of copyright law doctrine: are samples mere appropriation of someone else's work which ought to be banned by the law? Or are they rather used transformatively in creating new works built upon the blocks left by previous creators which ought to be fostered? Does it matter that only a fraction of a recording or musical composition is taken for the assessment of copyright? How far does the scope of copyright reach? Does recognisability of the sampled original work in a new work affect the inquiry of infringement or the application of limitations or exceptions thereof? Would this signify that the sampler wishes to create a dialogue with the work or the semiotic features this work stands for, thus being covered by freedom of expression? The courts have had several opportunities to analyse sampling within the copyright context, as will be discussed below.

A. Copyright and Sampling under US Law

The practice of sampling, ie copying and using segments of another artist's work, is generally prohibited under US copyright law, as only a copyright holder has the exclusive right to reproduce the copyrighted work in copies or phonorecords.[71] However, for public policy purposes, courts have been avoiding such draconian illegalisation of sampling through legally recognised exceptions, such as de minimis use[72] and fair use.[73] Early disputes in relation to sampling, which involved the use of samples by the Beastie Boys, De la Soul and Vanilla Ice, were settled outside the courtroom.[74] The first case to be decided by a court in the USA was the above-mentioned *Grand Upright Music v Warner Bros Records*, the decision of which held that sampling could constitute copyright infringement. The succeeding case law was not coherent as to its approach as some courts were willing to assess the 'relationships between appropriating and appropriated works on a case-by-case basis'[75] and assessed the matter by applying de minimis standards, substantial similarity tests and fragmented literal similarity tests.[76]

In desperate need for a reliable legal doctrine, the US Court of Appeals for the Sixth Circuit issued the highly controversial and often criticised opinion in *Bridgeport Music, Inc v Dimension*

[67] Okpaluba (n 3) 95.
[68] Said (n 4) 1.
[69] Agreement on Trade-Related Aspects of Intellectual Property Rights (TRIPS), Art 14(2).
[70] Butler (n 19) 990.
[71] 17 USC §106.
[72] *Campbell v Acuff-Rose Music, Inc* 510 US 569.
[73] 17 USC §107.
[74] Demers, *Steal This Music* (n 4) 93; McLeod and DiCola (n 46) 131–32; Sewell (n 56) 296.
[75] Demers, *Steal This Music* (n 4) 95.
[76] L Zucchino, 'Sound Familiar? Digital Sampling is taking Center Stage' [2022] University of Miami Business Law Review 295, 306.

Films on 3 June 2005.[77] What was at issue in this case was a mere two-second sample consisting of a three-note guitar riff from the Funkadelic's 'Get Off Your Ass and Jam', which was repeated about 15 times and appeared at five different places in the defendants' (NW.A) song '100 Miles and Runnin''.[78] Before appeal, the US District Court for the Middle District of Tennessee had already summarily judged for the defendant and concluded that there was no actionable infringement because the copying was de minimis.[79] On appeal, however, the US Court of Appeals for the Sixth Circuit reversed the district court's grant of the defendants' summary judgment.[80] The Sixth Circuit reasoned that § 114(b) of Title 17 of the United States Code (USC) grants exclusive rights to reproduce sound recordings to copyright holders regardless of the amount copied and that any amount of copying of sound recording is actionable copyright infringement in the absence of a licence to sample.[81] To reach this conclusion, the Sixth Circuit intentionally ignored well-established legal analyses of de minimis use and fair use, debasing the very goal of 'promot[ing] the Progress of Science and useful Arts'.[82] The Sixth Circuit's refusal to apply de minimis analysis is based on an erroneous claim that the analysis applies only to musical composition copyright cases.[83] Such abandonment of de minimis analysis in sound recording copyright cases is unsupported by the language of the 17 USC § 114(b) and legislative history.[84] 'The "practice of digitally sampling prior music to use in a new composition should not be subject to any special analysis".'[85]

Unlike the presumption the court relied on in *Bridgeport*, nothing in the language of 17 USC § 114(b) suggests that de minimis analysis should not apply to sound recording copyright cases. It is true that 17 USC § 114(b) grants exclusive rights to the sound recording copyright owner to copy and prepare derivative works of the sounds from his own recording. However, the language of the statute does not seek to grant sound recording copyright owners absolute and foolproof rights against de minimis copying. In fact, the statute clearly states:

> The exclusive right of the owner of copyright in a sound recording under clause (2) of section 106 is *limited* to the right to prepare a derivative work in which the actual sounds fixed in the sound recording are rearranged, remixed, or otherwise altered in sequence or quality. (emphasis added)[86]

Accordingly, a court cannot rely on the language of the statute to neglect de minimis analysis in cases where the copying at issue is of a sound recording. The language of the House Report No 97-1476 also implies that Congress intended courts to apply de minimis analysis in sound recording infringement cases.[87] The report points out that since 17 USC § 114(b) extends the statutory protection only to the actual sounds of a sound recording, 'infringement takes place whenever all or *any substantial portion* of the actual sounds that go to make up a copyrighted sound recording are reproduced' (emphasis added).[88] As such, it requires courts to apply de minimis analysis in sound recording infringement cases.

[77] 410 F.3d 792 (6th Cir 2005) (*Bridgeport Music* 2005).
[78] *Bridgeport Music, Inc v Dimension Films* 230 F Su2d 830, 839 and 841 (MD Tenn 2002).
[79] ibid 842–43.
[80] *Bridgeport Music* 2005 (n 77).
[81] ibid 800–01.
[82] US Constitution, Art I, § 8, cl 8.
[83] *Bridgeport Music* 2005 (n 77) 801–02.
[84] J Schietinger, 'Bridgeport Music, Inc v Dimension Films: How the Sixth Circuit Missed a Beat on Digital Music Sampling' [2005] *DePaul Law Review* 209, 232.
[85] Brief of Amicus Curiae RIAA, 9, *Bridgeport Music, Inc v Dimension Films* 410 F.3d 792 (6th Cir 2005) (Nos 02-6521, 02-5738) (citing MB Nimmer and D Nimmer, *Nimmer on Copyright*, § 13.03[A][2], 13–50 (2004)).
[86] Schietinger (n 84) 233; 17 USC §114(b).
[87] Schietinger (n 84) 233.
[88] HR Rep No 94-1476.

The Sixth Circuit supported its perfunctory creation of a bright-line rule by reasoning that it was required to create judicial efficiency in sound recording copyright infringement cases.[89] The court's logic is based on an assumption that the affirmative defence of fair use is neither applicable nor necessary in sound recording copyright cases.[90] Nevertheless, there is no language in House Report No 97-1476 to support that Congress intended to allow courts to treat sound recording copyright cases any differently from others when it comes to applying fair use.[91] The House Report clearly states that 17 USC § 107 'is intended … not to change, narrow, or enlarge [the fair use doctrine] in any way',[92] supporting that fair use shall be treated as a defence available for all types of copyright infringement cases. The House Report acknowledges that while § 107 'endorses the purpose and *general* scope of the judicial doctrine of fair use' (emphasis added), it is ultimately up to the courts to make decisions by taking into account 'the endless variety of situations and combinations of circumstances … during a period of rapid technological change'.[93] Such language seems neither to allow any special treatment of sound recording copyright cases nor to justify a bright-line rule at the cost of 17 USC § 107. The Sixth Circuit's justification in *Bridgeport* is therefore flawed,[94] as pointed out by subsequent cases.

In *VMG Salsoul v Ciccone*,[95] for example, the Ninth Circuit squarely declined to follow the reasoning of *Bridgeport*, stating that it found '*Bridgeport*'s reasoning unpersuasive'.[96] Disagreeing with the Sixth Circuit, the Ninth Circuit held that Congress did not eliminate the de minimis exception to copyright infringement claims of sound recordings in 17 USC § 114(b).[97] The subject of this copyright infringement case was the song 'Vogue' by the pop star Madonna. The plaintiff, VMG Salsoul, LLC, claimed that a segment from its song, 'Love Break', was taken, modified and incorporated into 'Vogue' without permission.[98] The segment consisted of a mere 0.23-second horn hit of four notes in the key of B-flat.[99] Reversing the lower court's grant of summary judgment in favour of Madonna, the Ninth Circuit initiated its discussion of the case by establishing the de minimis use as a required analysis to be done. It stated that 'for an unauthorized use of a copyrighted work to be actionable, the use must be significant enough to constitute infringement'.[100] The Ninth Circuit accordingly rejected the plaintiff's request to follow the bright-line rule of the Sixth Circuit, and further emphasised that the long-standing judicial trend clearly compels courts to apply de minimis analysis 'throughout the law of copyright, including cases of music sampling'.[101] The Ninth Circuit further criticised the Sixth Circuit's reading of both the statutory language and legislative history of 17 USC § 114(b), and stated that correct reading reveals that Congress intended to limit the rights of a sound recording copyright holder, as confirmed by the legislative history behind it.[102] It is thus not surprising that the Ninth Circuit characterised the decision in *Bridgeport* as 'illogic'[103] and its interpretation as '[resting] on a logical fallacy'.[104]

[89] *Bridgeport Music* 2005 (n 77) 802.
[90] Schietinger (n 84) 235.
[91] HR Rep No 94-1476.
[92] ibid.
[93] ibid.
[94] *Bridgeport Music* 2005 (n 77); Schietinger (n 84) 235.
[95] 824 F.3d 871 (9th Cir 2016).
[96] ibid 874.
[97] ibid 874.
[98] ibid 875.
[99] ibid 875.
[100] ibid 877; see also Ringgold v Black Entm't Television, Inc, 126 F.3d 70, 74–75 (2d Cir., 1997).
[101] *VMG Salsoul* (n 95) 881; also see 388 F.3d, 1195.
[102] *VMG Salsoul* (n 95) 883.
[103] ibid 884.
[104] ibid 884; *Nimmer* § 13.03[A][2][b], 13–61.

As the Ninth Circuit acknowledged, its decision in *VMG Salsoul* would lead to 'different levels of protection in different areas of the country, even if the same alleged infringement is occurring nationwide'.[105] The circuit split may result in forum shopping in cases regarding sampling under US Copyright law, which will have to be resolved by either Congress or the Supreme Court.[106]

B. Copyright and Sampling under EU Copyright Law: The 'Metall auf Metall' Litigation

Similar to the situation in the USA, the practice of sampling has been subject to the scrutiny of copyright law in Europe. In the context of copyright law within EU member states, the so-called InfoSoc Directive[107] is the relevant piece of legislation and yardstick. Like other EU Directives in copyright law, it aims to harmonise the copyright legislation of EU Member States.[108] Of particular relevance for this chapter is the fact that Member States must provide phonogram producers with the right of reproduction and the making available right.[109] Additionally, Article 5, paragraphs 2 and 3 of the InfoSoc Directive provide a closed list of exceptions which EU Member States may optionally provide within their copyright law. Copyright law, however, is not a unitary EU right but remains national law, despite the various EU Directives on this subject matter. This added complexity is wonderfully underlined by the 'Metall auf Metall' litigation: it was not only the first sampling case before German courts,[110] and led to one of the major copyright cases before the Court of Justice in recent years; it also showcases how courts appear to struggle to appropriately assess the cultural practice of sampling under the practice of copyright law.

(i) The Litigation in Germany

The underlying litigation that culminated with the decision of the Court of Justice of the EU (CJEU) in 2019[111] commenced as long ago as 1999. Moses Pelham, a hip-hop producer and performer, used an approximately two-second sample that derived from the track 'Metall auf Metall' from the 1977 album *Trans Europa Express* by the famous German electronic music pioneers Kraftwerk. Unaware of its origin, Pelham slowed the two-second segment down, looped it and used it for the track 'Nur Mir' performed by the German artist Sabrina Setlur, which was released in 1997. Members of Kraftwerk sued Pelham for infringement of their phonogram producer's right pursuant to § 85 of the German Authors' Rights Act.

The case made its way twice to Germany's highest court on civil matters, the German Federal High Court (Bundesgerichtshof; BGH). In its first judgment, the BGH initially found for the claimants and discarded the appealed Higher District Court of Hamburg's obiter dictum that using 'tiniest portions' of a sound recording for the purpose of sampling could escape copyright

[105] *VMG Salsoul* (n 95) 886.

[106] MS Morrissey, 'A Music Industry Circuit Split: The De Minimis Exception in Digital Sampling' [2022] *University of Richmond Law Review* 1436, 1452–56.

[107] Directive 2001/29/EC of the European Parliament and of the Council of 22 May 2001 on the harmonisation of certain aspects of copyright and related rights in the information society [2001] OJ L167/10.

[108] InfoSoc Directive, Art 2c).

[109] InfoSoc Directive, Art 3 Nr2b).

[110] C Zhang, '"Sampling" Is Freedom of Art: The German Federal Constitutional Court Deliberates on the Acceptability of Music Sampling in the "Metall auf Metall" Case' [2017] *Computer Law & Security Review* 870, 871.

[111] Case C-476/17 *Pelham and Others* Judgment of the Court (Grand Chamber), 29 July 2019.

infringement.[112] Apparently realising the vast scope of protection given to right holders, it held that sampling could by analogy fall within free use pursuant to § 24(1) of the German Authors' Rights Act, which allows the free use of a work without the author's authorisation,[113] thus working as an exception to the right of the phonogram producer.[114] The provision, however, would not apply where the sample could have been created independently, ie without reproducing a phonogram.[115]

In its second judgment, the Federal High Court added that some deliberations on the fundamental rights positions of the parties were enshrined within the German constitution, the Basic Law. The Court, however, noted that the freedom of arts pursuant to Article 5, paragraph 3 Basic Law in using the sample to create a new musical work itself might be based on economic interests. Thus, it would not encompass the use of the entrepreneurial endeavours of others even under the most favourable economic conditions imaginable.[116] Any practical doubts as to what would constitute an independently created sample were dismissed laconically by the Court, which said that such uncertainty 'must be accepted'.[117] The advice given to producers wishing to use samples was to acquire the corresponding rights from the phonogram producers of the original recording, create the sound themselves 'or – if they consider this effort to be too high and not economically viable – refrain from taking it over entirely'.[118]

Questioning the practical application of the Federal High Court's guidance on when sampling would be legal and holding that it would de facto make sampling impossible, Pelham appealed to the highest German Court, the Federal Constitutional Court. The Constitutional Court's discussion is particularly relevant as it showcases the impact of a shift of perspective, ie away from the habitual right–exceptions conundrum that so many copyright and intellectual property (IP) right decisions face.[119] Being a constitutional court, it first outlined the involved interests that needed to be balanced towards one another, ie the guarantee of property by the phonogram producer on the one hand and the freedom of artistic expression of those wishing to conduct an artistic discourse by using samples on the other. It also outlined that the rules of the Copyright Act (ie the exclusive right, its scope and limitation) would serve to balance these interests encapsulated in the clashing fundamental right positions. In order to ensure that such collisions are appropriately accommodated, the principle of practical concordance needs to be applied: this aims at ensuring that both fundamental rights positions are safeguarded as far as possible.[120]

Importantly, the Constitutional Court stressed that such a balancing exercise cannot be conducted from the perspective of one fundamental right only, but rather must relate to balancing two equally protected fundamental right positions. This approach, which has also been

[112] *Metall auf Metall* GRUR 2009, 403, para 14.

[113] § 24 (1) of the German Author's Rights Act (*Urhebergesetz*, UrhG) states: 'An independent work created in the free use of the work of another person may be published and exploited without the consent of the author of the work used.'

[114] The court arguably did so in order to offset the otherwise wide-reaching exclusive rights enjoyed by the Phonogram producers over sound fragments, even though they were not required to meet the originality requirement: M Senftleben, 'Flexibility Grave – Partial Reproduction Focus and Closed System Fetishism in CJEU, Pelham' [2020] *International Review of Intellectual Property and Competition Law* 751, 755.

[115] The Higher District Court of Hamburg, which was tasked to assess the case, after hearing expert evidence, again came to the finding that an average phonogram producer would have been able to reproduce the sequence in question independently in the year 1997 – OLG Hamburg, 'Urheberrechtsschutz für Soundsamples' [2011] GRUR-RR 396, 400–01.

[116] BGH: Benutzung eines fremden Tonträgers – Metall auf Metall II MMR 2013, 464, para 23.

[117] ibid para 24.

[118] ibid para 24.

[119] MD Mimler, '"Metall auf Metall" – the German Federal Constitutional Court Discusses the Permissibility of Sampling Music Tracks' [2017] *Queen Mary Journal of Intellectual Property* 119, 126.

[120] AF Lescano, 'Kritik der praktischen Konkordanz' [2008] *Kritische Justiz* 166, 167; T Hoeren, 'Was bleibt vom Urheberrecht im Zeitalter von Filesharing und Facebook?' [2012] *Zeitschrift für Europarecht* 2, 8.

applied by the European Court of Human Rights (ECtHR) in its IP-related decisions,[121] breaks with the tradition of regarding IP protection as the rule, stipulating that any third-party use of the IP would need to be permitted only exceptionally. The Constitutional Court provided an important analysis on the point of whether the preceding courts had adequately acknowledged Pelham's artistic freedom. In its deliberations, the Court, for instance, held that in curtailing the phonogram producer's fundamental right to property, the courts would need to apply an art-specific approach that would entail the acknowledgement that an adoption of works within one's own creation would constitute a form of artistic expression. Practically, this approach would need to guide courts in interpreting and applying exceptions and limitations to copyright and would widen their scope in comparison to non-artistic uses of a copyright-protected work. Where artistic uses would only minimally encroach on the copyright holder's interest to exploit the work, then the latter would need to make way for artistic freedom.[122]

The Constitutional Court underlined that sampling would be covered by the fundamental right of freedom of arts, which was also acknowledged by the German Federal High Court. It noted, however, that the very narrow interpretation regarding the permissibility of sampling as promoted by the BGH's decision would have significant ramifications for artists, in particular in the field of hip-hop music, as it would require sample producers to leave the creator with limited choices: to either ask for a licence or to reproduce the sequence themself. However, only being able to resort to one of these alternatives would curtail the users' artistic freedom, a point not sufficiently acknowledged by the BGH.[123] Having to resort to licensing would entail the possibility of the right holder refusing to this, and the fact that the fee is largely determined by the right holder would make the situation complex where many different samples were used. The transaction costs and limited catalogue of sample databases would be of only limited use, according to the Court.[124]

Finally, the Constitutional Court delivered a striking blow to the BGH's deliberation regarding the reproducibility of samples, ie the litmus test for permissible sampling. Samples were a key element of hip-hop music and the Court compared them to collages, where the use of an original work plays a similar role. Thus, the art-specific approach promoted by the Constitutional Court mandates acknowledgement of the original sequences used in hip-hop music. Additionally, reproducing sequences of samples may be very laborious, and the question remains whether they could actually be reproduced identically – which might have such a chilling effect that artists refrain totally from using samples.[125] Kraftwerk's position would only be impaired to a minimal extent, as the two works were not in competition with each other. The loss of licensing revenue would not be significant, and the Court noted that § 85 UrhG was provided to tackle piracy, not as a ground for generating licensing revenue.[126] Permitting the use of samples would also not necessarily amount to the loss of such revenue where the works are not in direct competition. Thus, the case was handed back to the BGH.

(ii) 'Metall auf Metall' before the Court of Justice of the EU

The InfoSoc Directive became applicable on 22 December 2002, which meant that any assessment of whether some relevant uses of the 'Metall auf Metall' sample by Pelham were infringing

[121] eg A Donald, *Case of Ashby Donald and others v France* App no 36769/08 (ECtHR, 10 January 2013).
[122] Bundesverfassungsgericht BVerfG 1 BvR 1585/13, para 86.
[123] ibid para 98.
[124] ibid para 98.
[125] ibid para 100.
[126] ibid para 104.

or not would thereafter need to conform with the Directive.[127] Therefore, the BGH decided to stay the proceedings and referred several questions to the CJEU as sole arbiter on EU law by means of a preliminary reference. The BGH queried, inter alia, whether taking a sequence from one phonogram and transferring it to another would constitute infringement.[128] Additionally, the German court sought to clarify whether the German doctrine of free use, which it applied through analogy, would be consistent with EU law as the Directive would currently not provide for an equivalent provision as to whether sampling would fall within the quotation exception pursuant to Article 5(3)(d) InfoSoc Directive and to what extent the rights contained within the Charter on Fundamental Rights of the European Union need to be taken into account.

The Court applied a literal interpretation of the right of reproduction, which allows the right holder to 'authorise or prohibit direct or indirect, temporary or permanent reproduction by any means and in any form, in whole or in part'.[129] The Court, therefore, followed the guidance of the Advocate General's opinion (and that of the BGH), by holding that 'the reproduction by a user of a sound sample, even if very short',[130] would constitute a reproduction 'in part' of that phonogram and would fall within the exclusive right. This would be necessary to guarantee the high level of protection enshrined within the Directive's recitals and safeguard the producer's investment against appropriation.[131] The Court then applied fundamental rights considerations. It re-established that IP was not inviolable and should rather provide for a fair balance between the interests of the right holders and 'the interests and fundamental rights of users of protected subject matter as well as of the public interest'.[132] In this context, the Court acknowledged that sampling would constitute a form of artistic expression, thus being protected under the freedom of the arts pursuant to Article 13 of the EU Charter on Fundamental Rights. But in comparison to the wide scope given to artistic freedom by the German Federal Constitutional Court, the CJEU held that it could only be exercised where a sample would be used 'in a modified form unrecognisable to the ear, in a new work'.[133] However, it rejected the Advocate General's opinion, which found that there would be no de minimis threshold for the reproduction of phonograms,[134] thus leaving a small amount of wiggle room for musical sampling.

In relation to whether sampling could be covered under 'free use' as suggested by the BGH, the CJEU reiterated that it would constitute an 'inherent limitation to its scope of protection, based on the idea that it is not possible to conceive of a cultural creation without that creation building upon the previous work of other authors'.[135] The CJEU, however, noted that the relevant catalogue of exceptions and limitations of the InfoSoc Directive would be exhaustive. It would jeopardise the Directive's purpose to harmonise copyright law in view of the proper functioning of the internal market, whereby 'Member States were free to provide for such exceptions and limitations beyond those expressly set out in Directive 2001/29'.[136] Senftleben laments this approach and would rather have seen free use as an inherent limitation of the scope of protection

[127] The referral also sought to ascertain whether an extract of a phonogram is a 'copy' of that phonogram for the purposes of Directive 2006/115 (Rental and Lending Rights Directive).

[128] *Pelham and Others* Judgement of the Court (n 111) para 21.

[129] Art 2(c) InfoSoc Directive.

[130] *Pelham and Others* Judgement of the Court (n 111) para 29.

[131] Recitals 4, 9 and 10, InfoSoc Directive.

[132] *Pelham and Others* Judgement of the Court (n 111) para 32.

[133] ibid para 31.

[134] *Pelham and Others* Opinion of AG Szpunar (n 43) paras 28–33.

[135] *Pelham and Others* Judgement of the Court (n 111) para 56.

[136] ibid para 64.

rather than a limitation/exception that would need to be assessed by the legislative straitjacket[137] of Article 5 InfoSoc Directive.[138]

The CJEU also found that the subject matter of sampling would not necessarily fall within the possibility of quotations for purposes such as criticism or review if they relate to a work or other subject matter pursuant to Article 5(3)(d) of the InfoSoc Directive. The Court followed the AG's opinion that a musical work may fall within the scope of the provision. A quotation would be given where

> use, by a user other than the copyright holder, of a work or, more generally, of an extract from a work for the purposes of illustrating an assertion, of defending an opinion or of allowing an intellectual comparison between that work and the assertions of that user, since the user of a protected work wishing to rely on the quotation exception must therefore have the intention of entering into 'dialogue' with that work.[139]

Thus, this could apply where the 'sound sample [is] taken from a phonogram which is recognisable to the ear in that new work'[140] but not where it is not possible to identify the work concerned.[141]

C. Analysis

Courts on both sides of the pond have quickly found that even short passages of samples can fall within the reproduction right and thus be subject to the authorisation of right holders. This is not surprising; the interesting point is how the courts provide leeway to allow certain forms of sampling without seeking authorisation. As sampling often relates to considerably small elements of another work/phonogram, the de minimis doctrine under US copyright law would be able to cover many forms of sampling. Arguably, the *Bridgeport* decision, which denied the applicability of this doctrine on judicial efficiency, provided a blunt and quite cynical approach to addressing the matter.[142] Unsurprisingly, this approach was ignored outside the 6th Circuit, as noted by the 9th Circuit in the *VMG Salsoul* decision.[143] In contrast to the court in the *Bridgeport* decision, the 9th Circuit applied a holistic and teleological statutory construction of copyright law in order to discern congressional intent.[144] It also took every opportunity to criticise the *Bridgeport* approach[145] leading to the aforementioned circuit split. Of course, many forms of sampling may also fall within fair use where sampling is used as parody, such as in the case of the famous decision *Campbell v Acuff-Rose Music* by the US Supreme Court.[146] In the absence of a Supreme Court decision, it has been suggested that applying the fair use doctrine would provide a middle ground to address sampling to address the circuit split,[147] as conducted by the Court of the Southern District of New York in *Estate of Smith v Cash Money Records, Inc.*[148]

[137] InfoSoc Directive, Recital 32 ('This Directive provides for an exhaustive enumeration of exceptions and limitations to the reproduction right and the right of communication to the public').

[138] Senftleben (n 114) 760.

[139] *Pelham and Others* Judgement of the Court (n 111) para 71.

[140] ibid para 72.

[141] ibid para 73.

[142] The court held that 'the music industry, as well as the courts, are best served if something approximating a bright-line test can be established': *Bridgeport Music* 2005 (n 77) 798–99.

[143] *VMG Salsoul* (n 95) 881.

[144] TB Burns, 'And They Sayin' It's Because of the Internet: Applying the De Minimis Exception to Digital Sound Sampling in the Wake of VMG Salsoul, LLC v Ciccone' [2018] *Drexel Law Review* 445, 477.

[145] Zucchino (n 76) 312.

[146] 510 US 569.

[147] Zucchino (n 76) 318–21.

[148] The court found that the use of a 35 seconds spoken segment by jazz artist Jimmy Smith by hip-hop artist Drake in the song 'Pound Cake/Paris Morton Music 2' is protected fair use due to altering the wording. *Estate of Smith v Cash Money Records, Inc* 253 F Su3d 737 (SDNY 2017).

The German approach, which would have subsumed certain unauthorised samples under free use and its flexibility in balancing the interest of the involved parties, was carried to the grave by the *Pelham* decision. This currently leaves unauthorised sampling between a rock and a hard place under EU copyright law. On the one hand, unrecognisable samples may fall outside the scope of copyright infringement, while otherwise they might be covered by the quotation exception where they are recognisable. But trying to navigate between these two criteria regulating the scope of permissible sampling has its pitfalls. Recognisability, of course, leads to the question of how this assessment would be conducted and by whom. How could an objective test be possible if it will inevitably have subjective variations? In order to maintain sufficient scope for artistic freedom, this assessment ought to be conducted by the ears of the average music consumer. Thus, the approach taken by the CJEU may allow sound collages which incorporate a large number of often small sound fragments.[149] Recognisable samples may then fall within the quotation exception, thus ensuring freedom of expression.[150] The scope of the quotation exception remains uncertain as the Court laconically stated that this would depend 'on the facts of the case'.[151] The Court did not follow the Advocate General's copyright maximalist approach, which compared samples to the paint and brushes of a painter that would need to be purchased,[152] thus comparing 'apples and oranges'.[153] So, a sufficiently broadly interpreted quotation exception could cover an array of samples.

Aside from resorting to permitted uses, exceptions or other limitations of the exclusive rights, artists can resort to clearing the samples they use. This would be the way to 'do the right thing' according to the court in *Bridgeport*, which suggested that the new artist 'Get a license or do not sample'.[154] However, the costs for clearing samples can constitute an obstacle according to several commentators.[155] Sample clearing can involve several copyrights held by different parties,[156] and the more samples require clearing the more the situation is exacerbated, which then can lead to hold-up costs.[157] Other costs relate to opaque pricing and search costs, which arise when a sampler seeks to identify the relevant right holder. This is an easier task for artists who are signed for big labels than for those signed by independent labels,[158] which do not have a large back catalogue themselves.[159] In some cases, some artists will refuse to clear samples up front,[160] while, according to Sewell, other right holders behave like 'sample trolls' whose business model is set to extract money from licensing or litigation.[161]

The impact of sample clearing in the aftermath of *Bridgeport* for the creation of hip-hop music has been mixed. Some authors have lamented the restraints that sample clearing poses,[162] which marked the end of the golden era of hip-hop. Indeed, some studies show that highly influential

[149] Senftleben (n 114) 757–58.

[150] C Geiger and E Izyumenko, 'The Constitutionalization of Intellectual Property Law in the EU and the Funke Medien, Pelham and Spiegel Online Decisions of the CJEU: Progress, but Still Some Way to Go!' [2020] *International Review of Intellectual Property and Competition Law* 282, 289.

[151] *Pelham and Others* Judgement of the Court (n 111) para 72.

[152] *Pelham and Others* Opinion of AG Szpunar (n 43) para 52.

[153] BJ Jütte and JP Quintais, 'The Pelham Chronicles: Sampling, Copyright and Fundamental Rights' [2021] *Journal of Intellectual Property Law & Practice* 213, 216.

[154] *Bridgeport Music* 2005 (n 77).

[155] Evans (n 20) 862.

[156] ie the phonogram/sound recording and that of the underlying musical composition.

[157] Said (n 4) 349.

[158] McLeod and DiCola (n 46) 161.

[159] Okpaluba (n 3) 86.

[160] Said (n 4) 350.

[161] Sewell (n 56) 297.

[162] Said (n 4) 353.

hip-hop artists relied on less sampling in their post-1991 recordings.[163] Joo, however, argues that *Bridgeport* merely confirmed an already prevalent business practice.[164] Sewell, on the other hand, states that these developments have not necessarily decreased the creativity, but have altered the approaches taken by producers and artists.[165] This mirrors Okpaluba's finding that many new innovations with regard to digital sampling[166] were applied by some artists by recreating samples with studio musicians and synthesisers in order to avoid clearing costs for sound recordings.[167] Where the sample is altered sufficiently, this might even avoid the need to seek a licence for the musical composition.[168] For some artists, however, recreating samples may not be artistically desirable since the original samples would also create a 'purer' sound in comparison to the reproduction – a point which has resonated within the *Pelham* decision by the German Federal Constitutional Court. A different approach was taken by artists such as Danger Mouse with *The Grey Album*. He resorted to 'fighting the power' by releasing a sample-heavy album on the internet. While this has not generated income for him, it has provided exposure.[169]

VI. Conclusion

Much of this chapter has discussed copyright law's assessment of sampling. It has showcased that the increased scrutiny of copyright law after the 'Wild West' days of hip-hop music did alter practices in the composition of hip-hop music. Providing an answer as to whether this was for the better or worse for the genre is beyond the scope of this chapter. The current regulatory situation presents itself with sample clearing being a commonly used practice now which, however, requires reform. This entails a simplification of the sample clearing process in order to make it as widely accessible and feasible as possible for hip-hop and other sample artists alike. Clear and tiered pricing depending on quantity and quality of the sample would also be beneficial. Compulsory licences have also been mooted as a part of the solution where voluntary licensing fails.[170]

Additionally, the current industry practices need to factor in free uses of samples that copyright law may provide, such as the de minimis doctrine and fair use in the USA and the interplay of no-recognisability and quotation right under EU law. Standards as to when a sample would be de minimis or considered unrecognisable would make the application of these free uses easier. It would go against copyright policy if the legislative will to keep some reproductions outside of the exclusive right of right holder were to be omitted. This point calls for clarification of the law by courts and possibly also legislators. The discussed case law showcases, however, that courts have often struggled to adequately address sampling as an essential form of artistic expression within hip-hop music. In some cases, it almost appears that courts have discriminated against sampling in comparison to other forms of copying[171] by ignoring the nature of sampling as a laborious, creative and transformative cultural expression.

[163] Okpaluba (n 3) 96; Sewell (n 56).
[164] Joo (n 5) 428–29.
[165] Sewell (n 56) 316.
[166] Okpaluba (n 3) 96.
[167] Sewell (n 56) 298.
[168] ibid 298.
[169] McLeod and DiCola (n 46) 19; Okpaluba (n 3) 97–98.
[170] Demers, *Steal This Music* (n 4) 142.
[171] McLeod and DiCola (n 46) 16.

Such ignorance ought to be avoided and has wider ramifications for IP policy as it calls for appropriately assessing exceptions and limitations to exclusive rights. From a socio-legal perspective, the exclusivity which the legal system provides in the form of copyright law can inhibit the communicative discourses within other societal systems, such as that of the arts.[172] Such clashes between different societal systems can be accommodated through the creation of limitations of rights within the legal system enabling these other discourses. To minimise regime clashes, Teubner argues that the relevant other societal discourse would need to be heard before the legal decision on the collision of discourses is made.[173] This is where the assessment of the fundamental rights position becomes useful as it mandates courts to take all positions and interests into account and thus avoids one-sided approaches.[174]

[172] D Wielsch, *Zugangsregeln* (Mohr Siebeck, 2008) 46–48.
[173] G Teubner, 'Altera Pars Audiatur: Law in the Collision of Discourses' in R Rawlings (ed), *Law, Society and Economy* (Oxford University Press, 1997) 170.
[174] Wielsch (n 172) 66–81.

9

Understanding the Creative Processes, Musical Borrowing and Copyright Protection of the Electronic Dance Music Industry

NICOLA LUCCHI

I. Introduction

This chapter aims to increase understanding of the practice of music borrowing in the field of electronic dance music (EDM). After explaining the creative practices that are common in the EDM community (such as mashups, samplings, bootleg remixes and DJ mixes), the chapter discusses the critical arguments for and against copyright protection for this particular genre of music. The chapter concludes with a series of open questions and some arguments for solutions to adapt current copyright laws to ensure the survival of new genres of music and to encourage the creative practices and original expression of electronic music creators.

Electronic dance music, also referred to by the acronym EDM, is a form of music intended for dancing often in nightclubs, discos or at parties.[1] It encompasses a wide range of music produced over the last 30 years.[2] It emerged from the remains of disco in the urban dance clubs of Detroit and Chicago in the early 1980s.[3] The genre quickly spread across the USA and around the world.

Electronic dance music is usually inspired by independent composers and producers and then played by disk jockeys (DJs) in discos or at raves, concerts and festivals. EDM typically puts together different selections of tracks using a digital audio workstation, moving seamlessly from one recording to the next. In the UK and mainland Europe, EDM is more commonly referred to as 'dance music', or simply 'dance'.[4] It can be described in terms of many subgenres, such as techno, house, trance, trip-hop, ambient or drum 'n' bass.[5] Electronic dance music comes in many

[1] On the general features of electronic dance music, see, eg J Merrich, *A Short History of Electronic Music* (Arcana, 2021); D Sofer, 'Categorising Electronic Music' (2020) 39 *Contemporary Music Review* 231; C Aryandari, '"Ora Minggir Tabrak" Electronic Dance Music (EDM), a Montage of the Time-Image' (2019) 5 *Journal of Urban Society's Arts* 87; D Warner, *Live Wires: A History of Electronic Music* (Reaktion Books, 2017); ME Halick, 'What Can You Teach With Electronic Dance Music? A Music Teacher's Guide to EDM' (2016) 30 *General Music Today* 4; S Lau, *Popular Music in Evangelical Youth Culture* (Routledge, 2012); A Hugill, 'The Origins of Electronic Music' in N Collins et al (eds), *The Cambridge Companion to Electronic Music* (Cambridge University Press, 2011) 7.

[2] See Halick (n 1).

[3] See Aryandari (n 1) 90; E Mazierska et al, *The Evolution of Electronic Dance Music* (Bloomsbury, 2021).

[4] See the entry 'Electronic dance music', Wikipedia, https://en.wikipedia.org/wiki/Electronic_dance_music.

[5] See MJ Butler, *Unlocking the Groove: Rhythm, Meter, and Musical Design in Electronic Dance Music* (Indiana University Press, 2006) 40 et seq.

forms and styles. As a genre, it is generally up-tempo music created with software and electronic machines such as synthesisers, drum machines, keyboards, samplers, sequencers and computers.[6] So, today, the acronym EDM is something of a catch-all term for music that is danceable but does not fit into any other category. Consequently, as long as it has a dance vibe, a piece of electronic dance music might appear somewhere under the EDM label. The bad news is that this makes it almost impossible to analyse the genre in any particular musical sense, and it is only possible to make some very broad generalisations.

II. The Principal Constituent Elements of EDM

As the name implies, electronic dance music is created with electronic technologies using few or no musical instruments or traditional sound devices, and has a fast tempo suitable for dancing (120–150 beats per minute and higher).[7] The sound of EDM is often intentionally 'unnatural', using drum machines, synthesisers, sequencers and samplers.[8] The most commonly used effects include 'compressors, limiters, noise gates, transient designers, equalizers, reverb, and distortion'.[9]

EDM arrangements, commonly referred to as 'tracks', can vary in length, but are generally substantially longer than other popular music.[10] Furthermore, there are no 'standard chord progressions, cadences, or phrases, and no predetermined length or shape'.[11] EDM also typically does not make use of a text, lyrics or other verbal components to convey its meaning.[12] On the contrary, it is created by adding and removing layers of repetitive patterns called 'loops'.[13] Normally these recurring repetitions manifest themselves in different ways: 'not only in loops, but also in sequences and ultimately within the structure of a complete track, as embodied in the form of a continuously revolving record'.[14] As this is a dance-based genre, rhythm is crucial and it is important to never lose the beat.[15] Live performance and improvisation are fundamental elements of the genre and tracks are often originally created 'generically' and possibly 'remixed' by disc jockeys.[16] Many tracks also contain intro and outro sections that provide smooth transitions: 'Stereotypically, these intro/outro sections have a thin musical texture' that allows for a seamless transition between successive tracks.[17] In this way, the music and dance are never interrupted.

III. Originality in Electronic Dance Music Production

Like all creative endeavours, new musical creations are essentially based on the existing body of previous works and forms of expression. In order to strike a balance between the need for artists to be protected from infringement and the need to allow other artists to access and use cultural

[6] See Aryandari (n 1) 89.
[7] See Butler (n 4) 34.
[8] ibid 64.
[9] See Halick (n 1) 5.
[10] ibid 4.
[11] ibid.
[12] See Butler (n 4) 11.
[13] See Halick (n 1) 5.
[14] See Butler (n 4) 90.
[15] See Halick (n 1) 5.
[16] ibid.
[17] ibid.

material so that they can continue to express their creativity and create original works of art, copyright does not protect certain elements that can be freely used by anyone. The basis of copyright protection is undoubtedly originality, but the concept of originality is not a simple question in copyright disputes in the music field. It becomes even more complex with phenomena such as sampling, remixing and mashup, because the original work is not only an influencing factor at the base of the creative process, but a real 'material' source of the sound patterns used in the new musical work. Normally, under these circumstances, copyright law expects one to obtain prior approval to use copyrighted works unless exceptions apply to allow this taking. However, as other scholars have pointed out, this often does not happen in today's practice, as transaction costs almost always exceed the potential financial gain from content use.[18] Moreover, many users create content simply for non-commercial reasons 'as a form of personal creative expression'.[19] The question that arises here, then, is whether there are some components or features in recorded music that can be taken from an existing recording and combined in a new work without infringing the relevant rights of the original author.

The peculiarity of EDM lies in the fact that the boundary between record production and music composition is practically non-existent, as both dimensions are fully integrated into one single process.[20] In addition, since most EDM artists perform live as disc jockeys and play sound recordings for the audience, the production and sound design of these records is of great importance.[21] Another peculiarity of this type of music is that it normally includes sounds and elements that simply cannot be notated using traditional or conventional notation systems. This particular aspect is relevant here because the current law 'does not recognize the process of making a sound recording or the recording practice as musical practice in the compositional sense'.[22]

Generally, a musical work conventionally comprises three distinct elements: melody, rhythm and harmony.[23] To compose a musical work, one must make a significant contribution to all or some of these elements, especially melody. It is important to keep in mind, however, that much musical expression today is 'created through the use of music technology through recording practice – that is, through the creation of sound recordings'.[24] Although they do not traditionally contribute to the musical work, what record producers and sound engineers do during recording practice may be highly original and creative musical expression.[25] Sound design is really important as part of an EDM producer's creative process, and is normally integrated into the composition. For example, if you write a great melody, you also need to design a unique synth sound that reflects that melody.[26] For musicians in particular, the use of electronic and digital technologies in music production has led to 'new ways of composing music, new concepts of musical sound';[27] at the same time, musicians have been transformed into 'individuals whose knowledge and skill in the uses of the recording studio, and the various technologies associated with it, have become as important as their knowledge of music, style, or vocal and instrumental

[18] See D Rosen, 'Electronic Dance Music, Creativity, and User-Generated Content – A Canadian Perspective' (2014) 26 *Intellectual Property Journal (Canada)* 153, 154.

[19] ibid.

[20] ibid.

[21] ibid.

[22] ibid.

[23] See J Martineau, *The Elements of Music: Melody, Rhythm and Harmony* (Wooden Books, 2008). See also Butler (n 4) 11–12.

[24] See Rosen (n 18) 157.

[25] ibid.

[26] ibid 157.

[27] See S Frith, 'Technology, Creative Practice and Copyright' in S Frith and L Marshall (eds), *Music and Copyright*, 2nd edn (Routledge, 2004) 139.

performance'.[28] Finally, when electronic dance music artists perform live, they deal in advance with mixing, selecting and adapting tracks, theme songs and sound effects to suit a particular acoustic performance, and they produce their own tracks to meet certain sound standards.[29]

Based on all the arguments above, it seems clear that the production of electronic dance music, although produced through a rather unconventional creative process, places a remarkable value on original expression through recording practice. In particular, even though EDM may contain elements that can be notated through traditional means, EDM producers often show a high degree of creativity and originality in the stages of recording practice.[30] Recording practice is only ostensibly a technical matter; on the contrary, it can also be tremendously artistic to the point of being considered 'a complete, self-sufficient musical language', as well as 'the dominant musical language of popular music communications'.[31] Specifically, in EDM composition, what people do to make a record (ie their recording practice) is actually incorporated into the composition phase.

IV. Remixes, Samplings, Mashup and Edits

Dance music has always relied on musical techniques closely related to the creative process, namely the sampling, the remix, the rework, the re-edit, the mashup and the bootleg: 'From the first incarnation of mixing two records' on two turntables to create a third mashup, to the development and associated increasing power of samplers and audio workstations.[32] It is fair to say that without sampling, dance music would be very different and perhaps would not exist at all.[33]

Sampling is normally considered as an electronic technique used by music composers 'in which physical sound waves are converted into binary digital units and used to recycle sound fragments originally recorded by other musicians'.[34] New musical works are created by transforming these fragments and integrating them into a new musical composition. Digital sampling is a very common compositional technique in EDM, but this practice has increasingly come into conflict with the law. A remix or a rework is essentially the result of altering an original track in some way to create a different version by adding, removing or changing various elements within the song. A bootleg is basically an unofficial remix and refers to anything that is illegal (ie done without the copyright owner's permission).[35] A mashup simply combines two or more songs to create a new version:[36] for example, by overdubbing the backing track of one piece of music with the vocals of the other.[37] Mashups are not only useful for live performances, but are also often

[28] ibid.

[29] See Rosen (n 18) 158.

[30] ibid.

[31] J Hodgson, *Understanding Records: A Field Guide to Recording Practice* (Continuum, 2010) viii (noting how recoding practice is a technical affair, to be sure … but it is also immensely artistic).

[32] See R Snoman, *Dance Music Manual*, 2nd edn (Focal Press, 2009) xiii.

[33] ibid.

[34] See T Reilly, 'Good Fences Make Good Neighboring Rights: The German Federal Supreme Court Rules on the Digital Sampling of Sound Recordings in Metall auf Metall' (2012) 13 *Minnesota Journal of Law, Science & Technology* 153, 157.

[35] Originally, 'classic' bootleg recordings were those that contained an unauthorised copy of a commercially unreleased performance. Then the term became an all-encompassing word that, when applied to electronic music, refers to an unofficial or unauthorised production – usually a remix or mashup of another artist's work.

[36] Another term commonly used to describe a mashup is 'edits'.

[37] See A Power, '15 Megabytes of Fame: A Fair Use Defense for Mash-ups as DJ Culture Reaches Its Postmodern Limit' (2007) 35 *Southwestern University Law Review* 577, 579 (defining the mashup as a type of sampling that consists of a vocal track from one song digitally superimposed on the instrumental track of another).

available online for instant listening and/or free downloading on popular and ubiquitous music service platforms (eg soundcloud,[38] bandcamp,[39] beatport[40] or mixcloud[41]). Finally, an edit or re-edit is the alteration – usually done by a DJ – of the arrangement of a track to fit the DJ set or style, or for some other purpose (eg to make the introduction longer or to remove a section of the song).

Legally speaking, sampling is not allowed without the consent of the copyright holders of the musical works or sound recordings that are the subject of the sampling. Sampling in EDM, however, is considered an area of activity that does not readily conform to a clear set of rules. In the practice of sampling in EDM, the samples are often 'small pieces of audio: a kick drum, a clap, a drum kit, or a single chord'.[42] Indeed, 'many of these samples appear without clearance in a large number of EDM recordings'[43] and go essentially unnoticed by copyright holders. In fact, it has been noted that EDM producers have been using commissioned sample CDs for over two decades.[44] Yet many producers still knowingly use copyrighted samples without permission. It should be emphasised, however, that most of the times EDM producers do not even know the exact original source of their samples. They build up libraries of thousands of audio samples over time from a variety of sources, including copyrighted sound recordings, sample packs and samples they create themselves.[45] It can thus be argued that in these circumstances the copyright infringement in unintentional.

As for the practice of remix or re-work, it is hard to say whether mixing together someone else's music might violate the composer's moral right of integrity. To succeed with such a claim, a composer would have to show that their reputation or honour was damaged or impaired by the mix. This could often be difficult. Also, under copyright laws, remixes are considered a 'derivative work', meaning a new work grounded on an original one.[46] This means that – legally speaking – a permission from the upstream creator is needed. It should, moreover, be noted that a mix or remix may be considered a 'musical work' in its own right.[47] Thus, if the mix or remix was recorded, it is protected by copyright – regardless of the copyright in the material used for the mix.[48] However, permission from the copyright owners of all 'underlying' music and recordings is also usually required.[49]

EDM users and creators often take advantage of copyrighted materials and appropriate them by creating mashups, bootleg remixes and DJ mixes, for example, and offering them for

[38] https://soundcloud.com/.

[39] https://bandcamp.com/.

[40] www.beatport.com/.

[41] www.mixcloud.com/.

[42] See Rosen (n 18) 160.

[43] ibid.

[44] ibid 160 (observing how producers may use signal processing to manipulate the original sample beyond the point of detection. Sometimes they leave the original sample intact, combining it with other elements in their production to make it difficult to detect. It is quite a challenge to prove that a kick drum or clap was sampled, as they undergo sonic changes through recording practice. You would have to examine the producer's computer and the original source files to find concrete answers).

[45] ibid.

[46] See S McDonald, 'Copyright and Electronic Dance Music Production: What Are the Legal Risks to Producers? (2014) *Intellectual Property & Technology Forum at Boston College Law School* 1, 2.

[47] See I McDonald, *Music and Copyright* (Australian Copyright Council, 2014) 42.

[48] ibid (noting that 'someone rapping over a mix or remix generally owns the copyright in their rap, but a freestyle rap is only copyrighted if it was recorded in some way – for example, if it was written down, recorded to tape, or stored on a digital device').

[49] ibid (eg a publisher who gives a disc jockey permission to remix a track or publish a rap version of a song he has published may also require that he assign to him the copyright in the work created: this is also generally the case with arrangements of musical works).

download online. These informal practices are quite common and 'serve as important gap fillers in our copyright system'.[50] Basically, these practices and habits flourish because copyright law has many loopholes and 'gray areas that cannot possibly be filled or clarified quickly enough to keep up with the enormous number of uses of copyrighted works that occur every day'.[51]

In fact, in the EDM community, there are two categories of work on which these musical techniques are based: commissioned work (or work for hire, ie created on specific request), when a DJ is purposely asked to arrange a remix for an already existing song;[52] and non-commissioned mixes, which are in principle created illicitly, without a licence or prior agreement. Indeed, DJs are often invited to create a remix or an adaptation for an already recorded and written piece of music by singers, bands or other DJs.[53] In these cases, the DJ and artist whose song is to be remixed negotiate and conclude a contract commissioning the DJ to do the job. When the remix is finalised, the original artist retains the copyright to the new mix, while the DJ receives the agreed-upon price for the work.[54] This means that remixers who wish to claim copyright for their remixes should state so in the agreement by which an artist commissions the remixer to create a creative remix of a song controlled by the same artist.[55] On the other hand, a non-commissioned mix is created without any licence or permission from the copyright holders over the upstream content. This is unfortunately the most problematic and common scenario in the EDM creative practice: it is well known that obtaining permissions for the use of copyrighted material is often a laborious and time-consuming process that involves locating the many creative individuals who own the copyrights and other rights that must be authorised for the reuse of all the pre-existing material required for sampling and remixing. In addition, this process involves high transaction costs and a large amount of time that is often required to release a sample or obtain permission for an official remix.[56] The exact outcome of the negotiation to acquire a licence is based on a wide variety of factors involving the fame of the remixed artist, the sampling artist and the sampled work. The price of the licence may then depend on many other factors.

In short, sample pricing is somehow opaque and difficult to predict prior to negotiations. Consequently, artists who do not have a high profile and do not have the financial means to pay for a sample are often unable to comply with all the copyright formalities.[57] Moreover, the way the relevant licensing procedure is normally structured can put samplers in a highly inferior bargaining situation. Typically, the sampler first creates their work, then subsequently seeks to obtain the authorisation to exploit a sampled work. This means that the sampler is obliged to first invest money, time and effort in the design and creation of the new work, including the sample, even

[50] See E Lee, 'Warming Up to User-Generated Content' (2008) 5 *University of Illinois Law Review* 1459, 1461.

[51] ibid 1461 (noting how 'formal copyright licenses might fill some of these gaps, but high transaction costs often make licenses cost-prohibitive or ineffective, so sometimes copyright holders even prefer informal practices over formal licenses').

[52] See D Passman, *All You Need to Know About the Music Business*, 10th edn (Simon & Schuster, 2019) 309.

[53] See J Sayers, 'The Wrong Mix: Electronic Dance Music and its Copyright Problem' (2014) Law School Student Scholarship paper 566, 16.

[54] See Passman (n 52) 307 (explaining the functioning of a work for hire).

[55] A recent US court ruling clarifies the question of copyright in a remixed track. The case involves a Russian electronic dance musician and DJ (Artem Stoliarov) who filed a lawsuit in the US District Court for the Central District of California alleging that Marshmello's song 'Happier' copied the synthesiser melody from his 2014 remix of OneRepublic's 'I Lived'. Marshmello – an American electronic music producer and DJ – won the case, as the court ruled that the Russian DJ had contractually waived the rights to the remix composition and therefore had no cause of action. For further commentary on this case, see E Bonadio and A Tanwar, 'Music Remixing and Copyright Ownership in Arty v Marshmello' (2021) 43 *European Intellectual Property Review* 747.

[56] See Rosen (n 18) 162. In order to save time, major labels usually outsource the clearance process to a number of specialist sample clearing houses.

[57] ibid.

at the risk of facing an excessive economic demand or the prospect of rejection of the licence. If licensing is not a viable or feasible option, the sampling artist may attempt to disguise the sampling in the hope of avoiding discovery by the copyright owner and thus avoiding any possible copyright infringement claims.

It is worth noting that many EDM creators, especially those who are just starting out, often use remixes made without the official permission of the artist whose work was sampled to gain fans and attention, and to show off their talent for production and composition. Unauthorised covers or remixes are generally accepted as part of the EDM subculture and left largely untouched or unchallenged.[58] Normally, they tend to differ significantly from the original recordings, making it difficult for copyright infringement detection systems, such as those used by many online platforms, to detect them and automatically remove the infringing content. Many scholars[59] believe that an unambiguous regulation prohibiting any unlicensed or unauthorised practice of sampling is too restrictive and may have the negative effect of limiting the scope for creative expression in certain musical genres.

The question, then, is whether sampling can be regarded as equivalent to a new form of composition that uses sounds rather than notes as raw material and is therefore forced to exploit previous pieces of music, albeit in an original and transformational way. However, there is also another school of thought that argues otherwise, ie that there is no evidence that requiring licensing of samples would limit creativity, and that it is therefore reasonable in most cases to grant copyright holders full control over the use of their sound recordings.[60] Regardless of which argument one chooses as a starting point, scholars of both schools of thought concur that the current legal regime does not offer well-defined boundaries for when a certain case of tort sampling should be permissible.[61]

Clearly, this situation raises fundamental problems for the effectiveness of copyright that should be addressed: if artists and creators are afraid of or discouraged from creating new music because they fear legal action, the original intent of copyright is de facto diluted because it means that it is not able to fully protect all the creative aspects of the music industry. It can thus be argued that sampling and mashup seem to fall within the broader tradition of musical borrowing. Indeed, music creators use works from the past to build a musical tradition, to challenge the assumptions of the originals through criticism, to attract listeners to the new work with familiar materials and to challenge the very concept of originality.[62] In all cases, music makers consciously borrow, and listeners find great pleasure in hearing and discovering these references.[63] All these

[58] ibid 167.

[59] See eg S Vaidhyanathan, *Copyrights and Copywrongs: The Rise of Intellectual Property and How It Threatens Creativity* (New York University Press, 2001); L Lessig, *Remix: Making Art and Commerce Thrive in the Hybrid Economy* (Penguin, 2008) 77 (noting that the current system does not enable protection for both remix artists and original artists); J Demers, *Steal This Music: How Intellectual Property Law Affects Musical Creativity* (University of Georgia Press, 2006); OB Arewa, 'From JC Bach to Hip Hop: Musical Borrowing, Copyright and Cultural Context' (2006) 84 *North Carolina Law Review* 547; J Boyle, *Public Domain. Enclosing the Commons of the Mind* (Yale University Press, 2008); K McLeod and P DiCola, *Creative License. The Law and Culture of Digital Sampling* (Duke University Press, 2011).

[60] See eg MA Pote, 'Mashed-Up In Between: The Delicate Balance of Artists' Interests Lost amidst the War on Copyright' (2010) 88 *North Carolina Law Review* 639; E Harper, 'Note, Music Mashups: Testing the Limits of Copyright Law as Remix Culture Takes Society by Storm' (2010) 39 *Hofstra Law Review* 405; Reilly (n 34).

[61] It is worth noting, however, that there are empirical studies that have shown that the act of sampling significantly increased sales of original works that were sampled in the year following the release of the new work compared to the year before. See WM Schuster, 'Fair Use, Girl Talk, and Digital Sampling: An Empirical Study of Music Sampling's Effect on the Market for Copyrighted Works' (2013) 67 *Oklahoma Law Review* 443 (establishing a positive correlation between the use of hip-hop samples in derivative works and the purchase of the songs from which the samples are taken).

[62] See CE McLeish, '"The Future is Medieval": Orality and Musical Borrowing in the Middle Ages and Online Remix Culture' (Master's thesis, University of Western Ontario).

[63] ibid.

exchanges 'take place in society, orally, in musical sounds, without the need for notation'.[64] Therefore, copyright law, which is best suited to written pieces of music, can limit the oral practice of borrowing by controlling the kinds of statements that music creators can make.[65]

V. Conclusion

EDM artists practise original creative appropriation by placing the sound of other recordings at the centre of each composition. However, current practices of creative appropriation in the EDM community still have some grey areas that need to be addressed and overcome so that users and creators who wish to both consume and create content are not left in the dark about their rights and the limits they encounter when interacting with creative content.

Every new form of artistic expression creates numerous copyright problems. Some of these problems arise immediately, while others develop as the particular art form gains popularity or is altered by technological advances. Copernican changes in sound recording, copying and transmission systems have fundamentally changed not only how popular music is disseminated and how people consume it, but also how music is produced and created. Paradoxically, despite all these creative changes in musical expression, copyright law has been slow and inconsistent in adapting to ensure the survival of new musical genres and the continued dissemination of new works.

This chapter has shown that there are numerous open questions, but the fundamental issue of most concern to electronic music composers – and one that deserves to be investigated in more depth – is whether their works can be protected by copyright and the extent to which they may infringe copyrights of others. For example, unauthorised remixing is still a grey area in copyright law. Even assuming non-commercial intent, unauthorised remixes often lead to commercial success for an artist. Indeed, an unauthorised remix would constitute infringement under both fair use laws in the USA and EU copyright law, as substantial portions of the original work are often taken. However, at the centre of all these musical creative practices (whether the sound manipulations and mixing techniques of audio engineers or the looping and layering practices of sampling artists) 'is the transformative power of new technologies when used creatively by technologists'.[66]

Music has evolved from its beginnings in myriad ways. Copyright law should be reformed to better accommodate the exchange of the digital remix culture.[67] What makes EDM music particularly interesting – more so than any other type of participatory remix or any previous version of musical borrowing – is that it draws almost exclusively on pre-existing music, which

[64] ibid 21.

[65] ibid 22.

[66] See A Barron, 'Introduction: Harmony or Dissonance? Copyright Concepts and Musical Practice' (2006) 15 *Social & Legal Studies* 25, 26 (observing how conventional performers and composers have benefited from refocusing their practices on the transformative and productive potential of new technologies. In this sense, while some practices associated with new technologies appear to be the negation of older forms of musical practice (as well as the negation of copyright), in reality they do not completely negate or replace older forms of practice, but rather displace them and force us to redefine our notions of creativity and originality).

[67] In a general perspective of regulatory changes, it is interesting to note a recent decision of the Dutch Supreme Court that held that DJs own phonographic rights (neighbouring rights) in their home-produced recordings – not the record labels that commercially release them. Dutch Supreme Court (de Hoge Raad) *Spinnin' Records v Martin Garrix* ECLI:NL:HR:2021:1923. For a comment on this decision, see PB Hugenholtz, 'DJs Are Phonogram Producers, Says Dutch Supreme Court' (*Kluwer Copyright Blog*, 31 January 2022) http://copyrightblog.kluweriplaw.com/2022/01/31/djs-are-phonogram-producers-says-dutch-supreme-court/.

argues for a particular form of creative expression and leaves it in a controversial area of copyright law. Moreover, EDM's existence is currently threatened by the increasing adoption of algorithmic regulatory systems that screen content for alleged copyright infringement. Artists make valuable contributions to the community when they can borrow parts of existing works – contributions that should be adequately protected, given their importance to musical discourse.[68]

The music industry is one of the creative industries that must adapt to change and make the necessary transition. The creative process and sharing methods of music have now become very easy and available to everyone. The legal loopholes can be addressed, for example, by introducing new forms of exceptions and limitations to copyright protection to encourage the creative practices and original expression of electronic music creators. Another option on sampling discussed in the USA is the possibility to obtain a compulsory licence for sampling 'under which the copyright holder loses the right to deny permission for certain specific uses'.[69] An additional possibility, which also has the advantage of being more compatible with European copyright traditions, could be the introduction of a compulsory licence only for related rights.[70] The adoption of such a model could allow the use of material protected by intellectual property without, or even against, the prior consent of the copyright owner, as long as the use meets certain required specifications or standards. One thing is certain, however: the existing licensing system reflects the economic power of the music industry and rights holders, not the original aim of copyright. Restricting original expression certainly does not contribute to the development of art in society. It is therefore necessary to craft a legal way to support user-generated content such as that created by the EDM community and to share this kind of work, probably recognising creative appropriation as a form of original expression.

[68] See McLeish (n 62).

[69] See McLeod and DiCola (n 59) 225.

[70] See A-K Kaila, 'Music Plagiarism, Sound Recordings and the Future of Transformative Musical Works' (Master's thesis, HELDA, 2015) 92, https://helda.helsinki.fi/handle/10138/156017 (noting that such systems already exist in some jurisdictions for the licensing of cover songs).

[68] [illegible]

[69] [illegible] Kaila, [illegible]

[illegible]

10

How Jazz Persists at the Periphery of Copyright

KATHERINE M LEO

I. Introduction

'Like all good things, jazz is inherently at odds with what is around it ... It will never rule, for its nature is to subvert'.[1] For over 100 years, collaborative, cumulative creative practices in jazz have been misaligned with US copyright law. Decades of federal statutory requirements predicated on notated sheet music and exclusive notions of authorship have served to legally marginalise jazz.[2] While in some instances jazz musicians have obtained copyright protection for their music, often their compensation has been diminished by complex statutory provisions that favour compositional novelty over arrangement, borrowing and revision. Reduced protection for arrangements and pre-1972 sound recordings, coupled with commonly unfair publishing and recording contracts,[3] as well as limited legal and professional agency,[4] all served to alienate many jazz creators, who had little, if any, recourse if their music was misappropriated. In lieu of effective formal protection, jazz and its communities have nevertheless persisted, due at least in part to the development of normative practices that have at times adapted to, and at others subverted, formal copyright laws.

In spite of jazz serving as a beacon for essential music copyright problems, genre-specific legal scholarship about it is sparse prior to the mid-1990s.[5] Attention paid specifically to creative practices in jazz, which are to varying extents indistinguishable from other American vernacular music, has tended to reframe legal evaluations of originality in light of arrangements and improvisation;[6] and to model 'higher order'[7] ontological questions intent on locating

[1] B Scott, 'The House with the Heart' in R Gottlieb (ed), *Reading Jazz: A Gathering of Autobiography, Reportage, and Criticism from 1919 to Now* (Vintage Books, 2014) 454.

[2] See, eg OB Arewa, 'Creativity, Improvisation, and Risk: Copyright and Musical Innovation' (2011) 86 *Notre Dame Law Review* 1829, 1842; J Griffin, 'Copyright in Music: A Role for the Principles of Reverse Engineering' (2010) 30 *Legal Studies* 653.

[3] See, eg B Ward and P Huber, *A&R Pioneers: Architects of American Roots Music on Record* (Vanderbilt University Press, 2018) 310; S DeVeaux and G Giddins, *Jazz*, 2nd edn (Norton, 2015) 55.

[4] See, eg KJ Greene, '"Copynorms", Black Cultural Production and the Debate over African-American Reparations' (2008) 25 *Cardozo Law Review* 1180, 11855–89.

[5] But see S Turk, 'Copyrights and Jazz Improverisation: Creativity Unprotected' (1992) 1 *University of Baltimore Intellectual Property Law Journal* 66; JZ King, 'The Anatomy of a Jazz Recording: Copyrighting America's Classical Music' (1990) 40 *Copyright Law Symposium* 277; M Nelson, 'Jazz and Copyright: A Study in Improvised Protection' (1972) 67 *Northwestern Law Review* 216.

[6] See, eg JR Zoesch, '"Discontented Blues": Jazz Arrangements and the Case for Improvements in Copyright Law' (2006) 55 *Catholic University Law Review* 867; 'Jazz Has Got Copyright Law and That Ain't Good' (2005) 118 *Harvard Law Review* 1940; SR Wilson, 'Rewarding Creativity: Transformative Use in the Jazz Idiom' (2003) 4 *University of Pittsburgh Journal of Technology Law and Policy* 1.

[7] A Kania, 'New Waves in Music Ontology' in K Stock and K Thomson-Jones (eds), *New Waves in Aesthetics* (Palgrave, 2008) 32.

jazz 'works'[8] across recordings, notation systems and live performances.[9] Some scholars have offered myriad solutions to what are often cast as shortcomings in existing statutory and common law, while others have instead presented cross-disciplinary critiques to recast these problems as rooted in fundamentally exclusionary policies.[10] Comparatively little attention has been paid, however, to how jazz musicians have responded.

The present chapter aims to fill this gap by modelling genre-specific copyright issues for jazz and the normative practices jazz musicians have developed as a result. Section II seeks to circumscribe the nature of jazz as a musical genre by tracing central narrative themes according to cumulating repertories, creative techniques and performer identities. Section III then considers the history of statutory copyright revisions and legal disputes involving jazz to demonstrate how the music and its performers have been forced out of the centre of federal copyright protection. The chapter then divides borrowing practices in section IV between those involving copyright-protected sheet music, including provisions for arrangements, contracts and licensing, and the distribution of what became known as 'fakebooks'; and in section V, those that involve borrowing through improvisation. Normative policing of improvisational borrowing seeks to balance protections for individual performer originality with limited access intended to promote sequential creativity and stylistic homage.[11] Penalties for violating these norms rarely align with formal legal relief, instead constituting severed relationships and even ostracisation, which can be professionally catastrophic. Through this interdisciplinary investigation, this chapter shall demonstrate how jazz has persisted at the periphery of US copyright law.

II. What Is Jazz?: Circumscribing a Genre

To the perennial question 'What is jazz?', the apocryphal answer is typically 'if you have to ask, you'll never know'.[12] Despite over a century of analysis and description by musicians, authors, poets, historians, critics and fans, jazz seems to evade classification. As a set of social and musical practices shared across overlapping creative communities, jazz relies on understandings that may be at times consciously accessible while at other times not.[13] For this reason, jazz is often represented through imperfect, oppositional discourses intent on reconciling concurrent styles, histories and identities.

Broad jazz histories usually rely on coalescing notions of a repertory comprised of approximately 200–300 'standards', mostly drawn from commercial popular songs, including those derived from Broadway musicals and Hollywood films, as well as newly composed tunes and evolving 'metadiscographies'[14] of them.[15] By analysing this repertory, many historians aim to

[8] A Kania, 'All Play and No Work: An Ontology of Jazz' (2011) 69 *Journal of Aesthetics and Art Criticism* 391, 392 (noting that the work concept in music has multiple meanings, typically 'referring to the primary focus of appreciation').

[9] L Mann, 'If It Ain't Broke … Copyright's Fixation Requirement and Cultural Citizenship' (2011) 34 *Columbia Journal of Law and Arts* 201, 202; 'Jazz Has Got Copyright' (n 6) 1940; G Donat, 'Fixing Fixation: A Copyright with Teach for Improvisational Performers' (1997) 95 *Columbia Law Review* 1363.

[10] See, eg O Arewa, 'A Musical Work is a Set of Instructions' (2014) 52 *Houston Law Review* 467; Greene (n 4); CG Hines, 'Black Musical Tradition and Copyright Law: Historical Tensions' (2005) 10 *Michigan Journal of Race and Law* 463. But see Mann (n 9) 228–29 (cautioning against the social costs of revising existing copyright laws).

[11] See, eg EA Posner, *Law and Social Norms* (Cambridge, Harvard University Press, 2000) 12–35.

[12] See, eg S DeVeaux, 'Constructing the Jazz Tradition' (1991) 25 *Black American Literature Forum* 525, 528.

[13] Kania, 'All Play and No Work' (n 8) 392.

[14] B Epperson, 'Uncertain and Unverifiable: Jazz Metadiscography and the Paradox of Originality' (2008) 39 *ARSC Journal* 215, 216.

[15] See R Witmer, 'Jazz Standard' (Grove Music Online, 2003).

generate narratives of stylistic progress according to musical qualities, such as evolving improvisatory practices or rhythmic 'feels', notable techniques of individual performers and economic orientations to live performance, publication and recording.[16] These often broad surveys tend to periodise jazz history, locating its origins in American vernacular genres primarily associated with African and Black American communities – chiefly blues and ragtime – during the early twentieth century. Early jazz previously has been labelled with the increasingly pejorative term 'Dixieland'; it is understood to have grown into so-called 'hot' and 'sweet' styles of big bands, with swing as a commercial pinnacle, followed by a post-World War II divergence from popular mainstreams into more avant-garde peripheral styles, including bebop, post-bop, cool, modal, fusion, free, and eventually postmodern collage and 'trad' nostalgia.[17] Although often described first according to musical conventions and innovations, notions of jazz style are necessarily intertwined with narratives of racial identities, especially the unique experiences of African and Black Americans.[18]

In an effort to create narrative coherency across the twentieth century, however, style-period approaches to jazz history often contribute to the construction of exclusive musical canons that tend to oversimplify by eliding diverse, fragmented and concurrent stylistic influences and performers.[19] Attempts to classify jazz according to its 'identity, function, and racial character … and the shifting ideological terrain on which one encounters them',[20] can do more to delimit than bound the style. As a result, some histories resort to a politics of exclusion: understanding jazz by what it is not.[21] For example, fusion might be excluded because of its renewed interest in commercial imperatives, as well as its stylistic instrumentation, audio production techniques and complex, syncopated rhythmic patterns more common to commercial rock or funk.[22]

Creative commonalities do exist across styles and periods, including sequential practices such as musical borrowing that typically involve the harmonic progressions and melodic fragments from the choruses of 'standard' repertory. Borrowing sometimes entails direct quotation; at other times, it entails interpolating new musical ideas into pre-existing ones. As trumpet virtuoso and bebop bandleader John Birks 'Dizzy' Gillespie described:[23]

> We'd take the chord structures of various standard and pop tunes and create new chords, melodies, and songs from them. We … added substitute chords to songs like *Night and Day, How High the Moon*. When we borrowed from a standard, we added and substituted so many chords that most people didn't know what song we really were playing.

Contrafacts, or new melodies layered over pre-existing and often well-known chord progressions, are common. For example, Figure 10.1 aligns the harmonic progressions and melodies of Gillespie's 1944 hit 'Groovin' High' with the 1920 song 'Whispering', popularised by Paul Whiteman and his Ambassador Orchestra, to demonstrate its contrafact relationship.

[16] See generally T Gioia, *The Jazz Standards: A Guide to the Repertoire* (Oxford University Press, 2012).

[17] See generally DeVeaux and Giddins (n 3); T Gioia, *The History of Jazz*, 3rd edn (Oxford University Press, 2021); BW Peretti, *The Creation of Jazz: Music, Race, and Culture in Urban America* (University of Illinois Press, 1994).

[18] See, eg M Tucker and TA Jackson, 'Jazz' (Grove Music Online, 30 June 2020); D Ake, *Jazz Cultures* (University of California Press, 2002) 11–28 ('For many, jazz has played an especially strong role in representing "blackness" in America … it remains irrefutable that most the genre's most influential players have originated from African-diasporic communities').

[19] The literature on jazz canons is vast. See, eg K Gabbard, 'Introduction: The Jazz Canon and Its Consequences' in K Gabbard (ed), *Jazz Among the Discourses* (Duke University Press, 1995) 1–28.

[20] Tucker and Jackson (n 18).

[21] DeVeaux (n 12) 528.

[22] ibid 528.

[23] E Southern, *The Music of Black Americans: A History*, 3rd edn (Norton, 1997) 491; DeVeaux and Giddins (n 3) 306–08.

The non-identical, yet similar, harmonic progressions can be seen by comparing the summative 'lead sheet' chord symbols for the harmonies above each notated measure.[24] The 'Groovin' High' melody significantly diverges from the 'Whispering' melody, revealing the musical complexity that Gillespie and other mid-century jazz musicians introduced.

Figure 10.1 Lead sheet comparison of 'Whispering' and 'Groovin' High'

[24] The term 'lead sheet' refers to 'a score, in manuscript or printed form, that shows only the melody, the basic harmonic structure, and the lyrics (if any) of a composition'. R Witmer, 'Lead Sheet' (Grove Music Online, 2001). Lead sheet symbols for harmonies can vary. See M Hoffman, 'Just Play the Changes: An Aesthetic Inquiry into the Notation and Interpretation of Chord Symbols' (1998) 98 *Twentieth Century Music* 1.

'Rhythm changes', or the harmonic progression from the chorus of George Gershwin's 1936 tune 'I Got Rhythm', is another famous example of jazz borrowing, appearing in contrafacts such as Ellington's 'Cotton Tail', Charlie Parker's 'Anthropology' and 'Dexterity', Thelonious Monk's 'Rhythm-a-Ning' and Sonny Rollin's 'Oleo', among many others. Figure 10.2 aligns the choruses of Parker's 'Anthropology' with Gershwin's 'I Got Rhythm' to reveal different melodies despite nearly identical harmonic progressions.

Likewise, Charlie Parker's 1948 tune 'Marmaduke' borrows from Fats Waller's 1928 'Honeysuckle Rose'. Each contrafact introduces new melodies and sometimes altered forms, but all employ the similar borrowing technique of using the harmonic progression from an earlier composition. Borrowing need not be complete, as in the case of Charlie Parker's 1947 composition 'Scrapple from the Apple', which borrows music from both 'I Got Rhythm' and 'Honeysuckle Rose'. Such borrowing practices relied on shared repertory knowledge among musicians to facilitate sequential creativity and variation across performances.

Figure 10.2 Lead sheet comparison of 'Anthropology' and 'I Got Rhythm'

2 Anthropology/I Got Rhythm

Another quintessential, yet ephemeral, characteristic of jazz is improvisation.[25] Notions of improvisation may include a completely unprompted, novel idea, but also acts of musical borrowing or quotation, realisation and transformation of existing musical ideas.[26] In some instances, improvisation involves seemingly spontaneous creation; but more commonly, it entails

[25] See G Peters, *The Philosophy of Improvisation* (University of Chicago Press, 2009) 146 (quoting Derek Bailey); see also ibid 9 (quoting British improviser Neil Sorrell, who describes the inherent problems in defining improvisation 'because of its extensive and vague applications to music … because of its usage in everyday speech, conveying something that is insufficiently prepared and of no lasting value'); Mann (n 9) 204–05 ('Improvisation is easy to name, but hard to describe').

[26] See Berliner, *Thinking in Jazz* (University of Chicago Press, 1994) 221.

a musician approaching a performance with some predetermined material combined with more immediate or 'freshly conceived' ideas.[27] Improvised performances, therefore, can be classified as fleeting expressive works, unfolding in the moment and different each time they happen. Improvisation often introduces layers of meaning based on 'invoking and reworking' elements of various 'standards'.[28] Borrowing via direct quotation or allusion is critical to imbuing a performance with intertextual meaning and establishing a performer's musical identity, both of which rely on shared repertories and histories known among performers and listeners alike.[29]

Oral histories, documents, recordings and transcriptions provide essential evidence of jazz, but they tend to raise as many questions as they might answer. Oral histories often focus on recollections of performances and musician interactions, which emphasise flexible creative networks predicated on skill, virtuosity, repertory and originality. Recordings, written arrangements and solo transcriptions serve to partially document this music, but likewise present issues for identifying creator(s) and their creations – compositions, arrangements and improvisations – as works.[30] Considerable jazz scholarship has been devoted to tracing relationships between recordings, notation and performances,[31] both in the abstract and in relation to creative networks of performers and repertories. Similar investigations have considered the relationship between popular commercial songs and elaborate arrangements of them created by various musicians for their ensembles, as well as recordings that increasingly featured extended improvisations captured across multiple takes. The problematics of documentation, when combined with cumulating creative practices and the complexities of musical identity, render any essential description of jazz imperfect.

III. Centre and Periphery: Copyright Problems for Jazz

Perennial questions surrounding the nature of jazz intersect with enduring legal questions regarding copyright protection of it: where does the composition end and an arrangement of it begin? What, and how much, revision and reorganisation is necessary to constitute creativity? What is the relationship of live performance to recordings, or even notation, and which one best represents the musical work as intellectual property? Which 'take' of a recording is definitive of the work as intellectual property according to the creator(s) and their communities?[32]

These questions became apparent the moment jazz emerged as a commercially viable genre in 1917, shortly after the enactment of the 1909 US Copyright Act, which revealed the music to be at odds with the newly overhauled statute.[33] Although the music was ostensibly eligible for federal protection, creative processes in jazz obscured boundaries necessary to objectify it into copyrightable intellectual property. Published sheet music required by the formalities of the 1909 Act offered at best incomplete representations of music understood more fully through live or

[27] See ibid 496.

[28] See I Monson, *Saying Something: Jazz Improvisation and Interaction* (University of Chicago Press, 1997) 96, 190; see also JP Murphy, 'Jazz Improvisation: The Joy of Influence' (1990) 18 *Black Perspectives on Music* 7, 9.

[29] See, eg Monson (n 28) 97–127.

[30] See J Rasula, 'The Media of Memory: The Seductive Menace of Records in Jazz History' in Gabbard, *Jazz Among the Discourses* (n 19) 134; see also Kania, 'All Play and No Work' (n 8) 391.

[31] See, eg J Dodd, 'Upholding Standards: A Realist Ontology of Standard Form Jazz' (2014) 72 *Journal of Aesthetics and Art Criticism* 277; Kania, 'All Play and No Work' (n 8) 391; JO Young and C Matheson, 'Metaphysics of Jazz' (2000) 58 *Journal of Aesthetics and Art Criticism* 125.

[32] See generally G Solis, '"A Unique Chunk of Jazz Reality": Authorship, Musical Work Concepts and Thelonious Monk's Live Recordings from the Five Spot, 958' (2004) 48 *Ethnomusicology* 315; see also Epperson (n 14) 215.

[33] See KM Leo, 'Early Blues and Jazz Authorship in the Case of the 'Livery Stable Blues'' (2020) 12 *Jazz Perspectives* 311.

recorded performance.[34] Reliance on written notation disfavoured protection for improvisation, but, due at least in part to the newly codified compulsory mechanical licence,[35] jazz musicians could not turn to recordings as a practical alternative.[36]

Communal creative practices presented further legal problems for determinations of authorship, originality and rights allocation. While many musical ideas were shared and revised freely, it remained unclear what content was reserved and by whom when professional relationships dissolved. Bitter, long-standing disagreements over copyright control between bandmates and collaborators resulted.[37] Few of these disputes escalated to litigation, and of those that did, most were dismissed or settled out of court, leaving little trace of common law discourse. Rather than provide much-needed statutory interpretation to recentre jazz in these instances, presiding judges often responded with low aesthetic valuations of jazz, to the detriment of musicians seeking to enforce their rights.[38]

Federal lawmakers appear to have recognised as early as the 1920s a need to revise copyright statutes in ways that protected recorded sound, especially for ephemeral and at best partially notated genres, including jazz.[39] As songwriter Bobby Troup later explained in his 1967 Senate testimony in favour of updating federal copyright law to address this concern:[40]

> Jazz is much more than just printed notes. In many cases, it is the complete lack of printed notes. The creativity of jazz is what jazz is all about. It is the taking of the bare 'framework' of a tune – the basic chord progressions – and then using this skeleton to weave an original melody that becomes a creation in itself. This is a creation that belongs to only one individual: the musician who created it.

Recordings would not be classified as a category of protectable work in the USA until the 1971 Sound Recordings Act, and even then, they could not represent the underlying musical composition until revisions introduced by the 1976 Act. This lag in adapting to technological advancements in recorded sound extended across the entirety of jazz's prominence as a commercial genre,[41] and it would not be until the 2018 Music Modernisation Act that pre-1972 recordings could be eligible to receive even partial retroactive protection.[42]

[34] See 35 Stat 1075, §§9, 18, 25–32 (superseded 1976).

[35] For a history of the compulsory mechanical licence, see, eg K Leo, 'The Legal Legacy of the Player Piano and the Origins of the Mechanical License' in CH Wolter (ed), *Player Pianos in Early 20th-Century Life* (University of Illinois Press) (forthcoming).

[36] See Arewa, 'Set of Instructions' (n 10) 534.

[37] For example, the Original Dixieland Jazz Band copyrighted 'Barnyard Blues', which was contested by jilted bandmates Alcide Nunez and Raymond Lopez. See Leo, 'Early Blues and Jazz Authorship' (n 33) 6–8. 'Tiger Rag' was contested by Dominic 'Nick' LaRocca and 'Jelly Roll' Morton. See, eg V Caporaletti, *Jelly Roll Morton, the 'Old Quadrille' and 'Tiger Rag'* (P Del Lungo trans, Libreria Musicale Italiana, 2011) 51–72. After their personal and professional breakup, Lillian 'Lil' Hardin sought copyright control of 'Struttin' with Some Barbeque' from Louis Armstrong, but both musicians claimed to have composed the song. See J Berrett, *The Louis Armstrong Companion* (Schirmer Books, 1999) 402–05; Gioia, *Jazz Standards* (n 16) 409.

[38] See, eg *Hart v Graham* Equity Case File 914 (ND Ill 1917) ('no living human being could listen to that result on the phonograph and discover anything musical in it'); *Berlin v Daigle* 31 F.2nd 832 (5th Cir 1929) ('musical compositions such as these popular songs, set to "jazz" or syncopated tunes, can only be classified … [as] only the common, garden variety of musical compositions'). Legal scholars have noted that such valuations can be unavoidable. See RK Walker and B Depoorter, 'Unavoidable Aesthetic Judgments in Copyright Law: A Community of Practice Standard' (2015) 109 *Northwestern University Law Review* 343.

[39] See, eg Staff of Subcommittee on the Judiciary, 86th Congress, 2nd Session, Copyright Law Revision Study No 26 (1961) 21, 25 (Barbara A Ringer).

[40] Hearings on Senate Bill 597 Before the Subcommittee on Patents, trademarks and Copyrights of the Senate Committee on the Judiciary, 90th Congress, 1st & 2nd Sessions (1967) 831 (Robert Troup).

[41] See J Demers, *Steal This Music: How Intellectual Property Affects Musical Creativity* (University of Georgia Press, 2006) 23; Berliner (n 26) 477–79.

[42] See 'CLASSICS Act', HR 5447, Title II (2018).

Borrowing practices among jazz musicians presented similar incongruences with the 1909 Copyright Act, which had not fully realised protection for sequential creativity. While the Act did extend protection to 'compilations or abridgements, adaptations, arrangements, dramatizations, translations, and other versions of works in the public domain',[43] it did not codify a derivative work provision until the 1976 Act. While this late-twentieth-century provision allowed for a separate work copyright for sequential creativity common among jazz communities, only musical content that could be demonstrated to be both new and protectable was covered and the derivative work rights holder was still beholden legally to the rightsholder of the first composition copyright.[44] Likewise, the statutory affirmative defence of fair use through classification of borrowing or arrangement as 'transformative' would not be available to jazz musicians until the 1990s.[45] The provisions were not retroactive, and as a result, musicians whose creativity emphasised revision over novelty did not receive equitable legal protection compared to those musicians who created works considered new.

As a result of inadequate statutory protection and dismissive judicial opinions, jazz was pushed swiftly away from the centre of federal copyright protection predicated on the 'visual bias'[46] of written notation, exclusive authorship and ownership, and limitations on protection for sequential creativity. In this legal space, jazz that conformed to statutory requirements remained protectable, while non-conforming jazz, regardless of the significant creative labour involved, usually was not. This system forced jazz to a periphery of protection where musicians could not necessarily rely on legal remedies to enforce control over their music.

IV. Borrowing from Copyright Holders

Shared repertories and lineages of intertextual borrowing are central to creativity in jazz, yet these same practices raise fundamental questions regarding standards of originality necessary for copyright protection and practical ones regarding registration, licensing and copying. For arrangements and later performances of 'standards', the federal copyright system offered channels to facilitate authorised borrowing from copyright holders. Often promising far from equitable compensation, however, these provisions favoured copyright holders of pre-existing musical compositions at the cost of rewarding the creativity of jazz arrangers. These kinds of legal expenses motivated savvy record companies and musicians to adapt. One practice involved borrowing to dodge incurring royalty commitments, especially when creating new recordings.[47] Another involved the increasingly widespread unauthorised copying and distribution of copyrighted 'standard' repertory in what became known as 'fakebooks'. Their proliferation reveals jazz musicians not simply adapting to, but subverting, the legal system that failed to accommodate their creative practices.

A. Arrangements and Derivative Works

While jazz musicians create many new compositions, their arrangements of commercial popular 'standards' have served both as a creative format and a practical necessity for jazz

[43] Copyright Act of 1909. § 7.
[44] See, eg King (n 5) 298–300.
[45] See generally 'Jazz Has Got Copyright' (n 6) 1940–61; Wilson (n 6).
[46] Arewa, 'Set of Instructions' (n 10) 481.
[47] See, eg Berliner (n 26), 477; DeVeaux and Giddins (n 3) 306–08.

performances.[48] Commonly built on theme-and-variation forms, arrangements usually borrow a main melody – often from the chorus of a popular song, which provides 'the head' of the tune – and harmonic progression from a pre-existing, usually copyright-protected, 'standard'. In so doing, arrangements offer individualised realisations orchestrated for ensembles that also create musical space for soloistic improvisation.[49] Arrangers typically develop their own musical styles, preserving or altering to varying extents the melodic, harmonic and rhythmic profile of an existing composition. Elite jazz groups sometimes even retain full-time arrangers, such as Billy Strayhorn's tenure with the Duke Ellington Orchestra (1939–67), whose sophisticated interpolations of 'standards' and original compositions were often as well known as the bandleaders and star soloists.

Provided they meet the low legal standard for originality, arrangements are subject to copyright protection according to provisions codified in the 1976 Copyright Act as 'derivative works', or 'a work based upon preexisting works … which as a whole, represent an original work of authorship'.[50] For music in this category, protection only extends to new contributions, thereby excluding elements protected under the previous copyright. Profits made from derivative works are thus split between the holder of the arrangement rights and the holder of the first composition copyright.[51] While this division might seem equitable by compensating the first copyright holder for use of their music, in effect, it inequitably preserves the right to create arrangements in the pre-existing work by requiring arrangers to seek permission.[52] It furthermore inequitably recognises the creativity of the arranger, especially for arrangements that deviate considerably from the pre-existing composition. As a result, derivative work provisions can seem to disincentivise sequential creativity central to musical genres such as jazz.[53]

While more than simply practical orchestration that facilitated the next performance, these arrangements remain intertwined with their pre-existing models, rendering it difficult to separate new from old if questions of infringement are raised.[54] Evaluating arrangements according to a 'substantially new and original' legal standard has proven problematic for courts since the nineteenth century, yet almost no published case specifically involves the pervasive practice in jazz. *Tempo Music Corp v Famous Music Corp*, over the song 'Satin Doll', offers a notable exception; however, the disagreement between the Ellington and Strayhorn estates focused on a standard of originality for the purpose of determining authorship rights in sequential versions of the song.[55] Scholars have offered myriad solutions to problems inherent in determining originality in arrangements, many of which propose a reduced standard that allows arrangers to

[48] Although some scholars have argued for multiple meanings to the notion of a jazz arrangement, it is most recognised as a 'written-down, fixed, often printed and published version of a composition, usually for one of the various standard ensembles (jazz orchestra, big band, small group, etc': G Schuller, 'Arrangement' (Grove Music Online, 2001); see also Zoesch (n 6) 867 fn 4.

[49] See, eg T Owens, 'Forms' (Grove Music Online, 2003).

[50] 17 USC § 101 (2000 & Sup 2002) amended by 17 USCA § 101 (West Sup 2005); see also MB Nimmer and D Nimmer, *Nimmer on Copyright* (LexisNexis, 2005 edn) vol 1, § 3.01, 3–4 ('A work is not derivative unless it has substantially copied from a prior work'). But see 17 USC § 103(a) ('protection for a work employing preexisting material in which the copyright subsists does not extend to any part of the work in which such material has been used unlawfully').

[51] See 17 USC § 103(b) (derivative work copyright 'is independent of, and does not affect or enlarge the scope, duration, ownership, or subsistence of, any copyright protection in the preexisting material').

[52] See ibid (limiting the copyright in a derivative work 'only to the material contributed by the author of such work, as distinguished from the preexisting material employed in the work').

[53] See Arewa, 'Set of Instructions' (n 10) 534; Zoesch (n 6) 873; 'Jazz Has Got Copyright' (n 6) 1944–45.

[54] See Zoesch (n 6) 895–99.

[55] *Tempo Music v Famous Music* 838 F Su162 (SDNY 1993); see also K Leo, '"That's My Satin Doll": Authorship, Originality, and the Copyright Dispute over "Satin Doll"' (2020) 27 *Blue Light: Journal of the Duke Ellington Society of the United Kingdom* 16, 16.

seek greater recognition of their creations.[56] Others have proposed redefining derivative works to focus on protecting what new content was added, rather than what pre-existing content was borrowed from an earlier copyrighted musical work.[57]

B. Borrowing to Avoid Copyright Obligations

Limited compensation for the creation of derivative works did offer recompense to musical composition copyright holders, especially the composers of what become jazz 'standards'. The mechanical licence likewise ensured that composition copyright holders were compensated when jazz musicians produced recordings of copyright-protected music. Yet record companies and jazz musicians found ways to avoid these copyright royalty obligations through musical borrowing.

It was not uncommon for companies to impose repertory control over the 'standards' that musicians selected to record, often based on agreements with publishing houses and artists that held composition copyrights. Some companies went so far as to create their own publishing affiliates and to require recording artists to 'sign over' their copyrights, which later could include extemporaneous improvisation captured on record.[58] Other companies even 'prefer[ed] to re-record new versions of pieces whose publication rights they already own[ed] and release[d] them on different albums rather than record new pieces that obligate[d] them to pay royalties'.[59] In response to these inequitable contract practices, some musicians began to compose their own original material, and fewer formed their own publishing houses and recording companies to retain control over their music.

These legal-economic conditions were one of several reasons for the proliferation of contrafacts; that is, to avoid licensing fees and create newly protectable compositions.[60] Charlie Parker's borrowing of the harmonic progression of Ray Noble's 1938 tune 'Cherokee', which he transformed into the bebop 'standard' tune 'Ko Ko', is a famous example.[61] Because of its new melody and greater formal space left for improvisation, 'Ko Ko' did not constitute an arrangement, but rather a new composition. Such intertextual borrowing complicates the boundaries between copyrightable works and ownership of them, but it also reveals keen legal adaptability among jazz musicians and record companies.

C. Fakebooks and Criminal Infringement

The gradual accretion of jazz 'standards' was aided by radio director George Goodwin's 1942 release of the Tune-Dex, a card catalogue of main melodies to popular songs, along with their accompanying harmonic progressions notated in shorthand, as well as their publishing information.[62] Initially intended as a reference for musical selection, subscribers paid for a copy of the catalogue with the promise of monthly updates. To avoid the risk of the cards replacing sheet music purchases, Goodwin entered into strict licensing agreements with music publishing

[56] See generally Zoesch (n 6).

[57] See 'Jazz Has Got Copyright' (n 6) 1953–56.

[58] See Berliner (n 26) 478.

[59] Berliner (n 26) 478.

[60] See J Patrick, 'Charlie Parker and Harmonic Sources of Bebop Composition: Thoughts on the Repertory of New Jazz in the 1940s' (1975) 2 *Journal of Jazz Studies* 3, 11; King (n 5) 287 (discussing the economic reasons for selecting musical content to record); Berliner (n 26), 479 n.32.

[61] See DeVeaux and Giddins (n 3) 307–08.

[62] See B Kernfeld, *The Story of Fakebooks: Bootlegging Songs to Musicians* (Scarecrow Press, 2006) 2–5.

companies to limit the total number of card copies for each song. The emergence of 'cocktail combos', or small ensembles hired to perform the latest commercial hits in venues from hotels and restaurants to private events, provided the Tune-Dex with a second market populated by musicians in need of a vast repertory from which to 'fake' performances of requested songs. Using the Tune-Dex, a musician could efficiently practice a song – or even look up one at a venue – perform its recognisable melody then rely on summative lead sheet chord symbols, like those appearing in Figures 10.1 and 10.2, to realise the harmonic progression as a frame for improvisation. By the end of the 1940s, unauthorised copies of the Tune-Dex began being distributed with little regard to the two copyright warnings printed on each one of the cards.[63]

Tune-Dex cards were soon replaced by 'song books', or similar collections in more portable formats. Unauthorised reproductions of these collections led to a series of FBI investigations, as well as civil and criminal suits against 'gangster' publishers brought by copyright-holding publishing houses and the federal government.[64] As then-Assistant US Attorney Thomas A Baer explained: 'The entire purpose of these books is to reproduce copyrighted sheet music in a form for musicians so that the musicians will not have to buy the copyrighted sheet music from the copyright proprietor.'[65] Books containing as many as 1000 song fragments could be purchased for about $25 – it was a 'brainless choice' for musicians to invest.[66] No legitimate music publisher ever attempted to produce a similar collection as a means to compete. Copies of these collections became so pervasive, simultaneously with the rise of bebop styles reliant on only skeletal formal and harmonic shorthand as the basis for extended improvisation, that musicians soon began to refer to them as a sort of repertory bible, vital to a performer's professional success.[67]

As production of song collections proliferated, not to mention the criminal infringement such activities incurred, the collective name evolved to 'fakebooks', at least in part 'because musicians have to devise their own rhythm and harmonies to go with the printed melody line'.[68] Fakebooks were published in a variety of formats, from reproductions of Tune-Dex cards to hand-cut-and-pasted collections from published sheet music, where the creator would remove the left-hand piano part and retain only the right-hand melody with chord symbols above and lyrics below, which then could be mass photocopied.[69] Other collections contain slight alterations to harmonic progressions and melodies, ostensibly to distance the copy from the copyrighted original or to reflect normative creative revision practices. While some fakebooks have retained the harmonic key of the songs as copyrighted, other collections have been transposed to accommodate so-called 'transposing' instruments, such as trumpets and saxophones common in 'cocktail combos'.

During legal investigations, the first authorised 'fakebook' was published in 1963, and by the 1970s, large-scale song collections, some titled 'real books', were published with appropriate

[63] See ibid 39.

[64] See *Santly-Joy, Inc v Chicago Aligraphy & Lithographing Company et al* Civil Case file 50C 1060, Records of the US District Court, Northern District, Eastern Division, RG 21, Records of US District and Circuit Courts, NARA-Great Lakes Region (Chicago); *US v Bert Rose* Criminal Case 66 Cr 25, Records of the US District Court of the Southern District of New York, RG 2, Records of US District and Circuit Courts, NARA-Northeast Region (New York City); *US v Irwin Rosenburg and Melvin Gershun* Criminal Case 62 CR 284, Records of the US District Court, Northern District, Eastern Division (Chicago), RG 21, Records of US District and Circuit Courts, NARA-Great Lakes Region; *US v Jules G Slapo, Sidney Rogoff, Leonard Bidney and E and E Bindery Service, Inc* Criminal Case 66 Cr 691, Records of the US District Court of the Sothern District of New York, RG 21, Records of US District and Circuit Courts, NARA-Northeast Region (New York City). See also Kernfeld (n 62) 51–73.

[65] Kernfeld (n 62) 52.

[66] ibid 52–53.

[67] ibid 67.

[68] ibid 83 (citing the *New York Times*).

[69] ibid 83.

copyright acknowledgements for each song according to proper licensing and royalty agreements.[70] Even in the present day, however, distribution of unauthorised fakebooks continues, with musicians understanding the legal and professional stakes of possessing such collections. Perhaps more stealing than borrowing – at least according to music publishers and composition copyright holders – the proliferation of 'fakebooks' revealed jazz communities subverting a legal system ill-suited to their creative practices.

V. Borrowing from Each Other: Normative Practices for Improvisation

Improvisation is considered 'the heart and soul of jazz',[71] yet it is not protected by federal copyright. Despite some legal arguments that improvisation falls within copyrightable subject matter, its variability and oral ephemerality still do not align with the federal copyright system and its continued reliance on written notation.[72] Even jazz musicians who publish transcriptions of their solos rarely, if ever, receive adequate royalties due to derivative works provisions,[73] because improvised music relies to varying extents on precomposed melodies, chord progressions and forms, as well as recognisable 'stock' motives.[74]

Because creative practices in jazz promote a balance of individual expression and community collaboration, musical control and acknowledgement matter to jazz musicians. In lieu of an adequate legal solution that protects improvised musical content, jazz musicians confront a considerable creative risk in improvising.[75] They instead have devised normative regulations to protect individual creativity while subjectively permitting limited amounts of musical borrowing, which at times might seem to mirror interest-balancing between protection and access in formal copyright law. These practices can take the form of establishing community values through education, such as promoting originality within a stylistic lineage, but it can also involve severe penalties, such as professional ostracisation. Although hierarchies among musicians do exist, often based on seniority and merit, there are no designated individuals responsible for conducting policing efforts – everyone is expected to hold each other accountable.

A. Acceptable Borrowing

Regardless of the legal risks entailed, borrowing is not only prevalent, but essential, to creativity in jazz, especially during improvisation. Borrowing serves as a means for musicians to situate themselves in relation to their musical lineage and to demonstrate their own interpretive creativity. In many instances, 'borrowing discrete patterns or phrase fragments from other improvisers … is expected'.[76]

Improvisatory borrowing can occur from a variety of sources, beginning with simple variation of a pre-composed melody of a 'standard' tune,[77] but also includes 'the kinds of things everybody

[70] ibid 121.
[71] G Schuller, *Early Jazz: It's Roots and Early Development* (Oxford University Press, 1968) 58.
[72] See, eg Arewa, 'Set of Instructions' (n 10) 472, 494; Turk (n 5) 67–69.
[73] See, eg 'Jazz Has Got Copyright' (n 6) 1945–46; King (n 5) 277, 294–96; Turk (n 5) 71–72.
[74] See Arewa, 'Set of Instructions' (n 10) 531–32.
[75] See, eg Mann (n 9) 206; Arewa, 'Creativity, Improvisation, and Risk' (n 2) 1829.
[76] Berliner (n 26) 101.
[77] See DeVeaux and Giddins (n 3) 39.

plays',[78] such as an archetypal blues riff or a melodic introductory or concluding motive or 'tag'. These smaller musical motives are so well known that they are held communally among musicians, even if they were once associated with individual musicians or 'standards'. Idiosyncratic distinctions nevertheless are drawn between borrowing deemed 'unoriginal' versus improvisation where the performer establishes their roots through such practices by conserving an earlier style.[79] As multi-instrumentalist Arthur Rhames explained:[80]

> The great players always give homage to their predecessors by recalling certain things that they did. They give it in appreciation and in understanding of the validity of their predecessors. Being able to quote from songs and solos is always part of a mature artist because he's aware of the contribution of others and its impact ... Something that is really valid is timeless.

For example, saxophonist Anthony Braxton described a 'post-Parker continuum', tracing 'Charlie Parker's music as a point of departure and within that vocabulary [musicians] try to make something special happen, people like Cannonball Adderley – they can still be original'.[81] Later generations of musicians are expected to achieve a masterful balance between rooting themselves stylistically to these lineages and musically innovating within them to represent their own perspective. Musicians may perform the same standard repertory with music that remains recognisable to discerning listeners, therefore, but which is rarely played precisely the same as any other musician.

Discerning content available for borrowing from content that is off-limits requires experience. New performers are excused, at least temporarily, from the high pressure of continual invention by being allowed to borrow more from other musicians. Pedagogical emphasis on listening to recordings and live performances and studying transcriptions by exemplary musicians is common, and a certain amount of borrowing reflects such apprenticeships.[82] Jazz musicians are taught to collect a variety of short melodic, rhythmic or harmonic motives, known as 'vocabulary, ideas, licks, tricks, pet patterns, crips, [and] clichés',[83] to use during improvisation, some of which the musician is expected to create on their own, while others may be harvested from predecessors or enlightening performance experiences.[84] A master jazz musician's 'personal sound is commonly the precise object of imitation for learners. It is a clearly discernible, all-encompassing marker of an individual artist's identity.'[85]

Students nevertheless are taught early 'to make an imprint of your own',[86] and to avoid doing things the way other players do:[87] 'Many students block their imaginations because they're afraid of being unoriginal ... Ordinary people asked to improvise will search for some "original" idea because they want to be thought clever. They'll say and do all sorts of inappropriate things.'

Young musicians may borrow, but they must tread lightly so as not to disturb the creative identity of their fellow performers. Brief melodic or rhythmic motives considered 'signature' or unique to a soloist can be off-limits to some but available to others, especially in mentor–mentee relationships.[88] Some borrowing practices can stretch across generations and creative networks,

[78] Berliner (n 26) 102.
[79] See Berliner (n 26) 103–04, 254–55.
[80] Berliner (n 26) 103–04 (quoting Rhames).
[81] A Braxton, 'Biography' in Gottlieb, *Reading Jazz* (n 1) 329.
[82] See, eg Monson (n 28) 126.
[83] Berliner (n 26) 102; see also DeVeaux and Giddins (n 3) 23.
[84] See, eg G Lees, 'The Poet: Bill Evans' in Gottlieb, *Reading Jazz* (n 1) 422 ('Bill had his clichés, as every jazz musician does. But they were very much his. Many pianists have adopted them, and still more have tried').
[85] Berliner (n 26) 124–25.
[86] ibid 121, 251–55.
[87] Peters (n 25) 97 (quoting Keith Johnstone).
[88] See Berliner (n 26) 103.

where musicians borrow material from their mentor, who themselves borrowed from another performer. The ultimate goal, however, is for each jazz musician to develop an original creative perspective. As trombonist Curtis Fuller explained, 'I would rather be an extension than a retention.'[89]

B. Unacceptable Borrowing

Considering their own searches for individualised improvisatory styles, most jazz musicians view borrowing as an ethical matter.[90] When compared to federal copyright standards, community norms for borrowing are equally subjective regarding the quality and quantity of available content. Like *de minimis* and transformative use exceptions, brief melodic or rhythmic fragments may be borrowed, and even expected, for certain 'standards', depending on the musical context. These small but sometimes priceless motives have been considered 'gems: so simple anyone can play them, yet so fully capable of generating emotional and physical exultation'[91] as to generate masterful improvisation. What is acceptable when performing one 'standard' or for one improviser is not acceptable for another, and performers must be entuned to the expectations of their community so as not to face perilous professional consequences.

Uncreative musicians, or those performers who borrow too much from others without inserting their own new or transformed expressions without permission, develop bad professional reputations. They can eventually become unwelcomed in jazz communities, ultimately risking professional ostracisation.[92] Concerns about unoriginality can become so significant among improvisational performers that it can be crippling. Jazz trumpeter Miles Davis famously felt 'panicked trying to be different, trying to continually change and be modern.'[93]

While excuses are often made for students, these concessions regarding originality do not last forever. Jazz musicians typically identify unoriginality by the formulaic, simplistic or predictable nature of an improvised solo.[94] Soloists who use conventional jazz vocabulary, such as formulaic endings or recognisable melodic phrases from famous recordings, demonstrate an unacceptable lack of creativity.[95] As bassist Don Pate described: 'Someone may play something obvious and predictable and you know right away what he's doing. [The soloist is] so simple-minded, they're embarrassing to listen to.'[96] This kind of moral shock at what would be considered a lack of creativity has significant consequences. During one rehearsal, for example, a bandleader is said to have interrupted a new performer's solo, aghast at its lack of originality: 'Everyone plays phrases like that on a Spanish tune. If you can't think of anything else to play, let's play a different tune.'[97]

[89] Berliner (n 26) 121 (quoting Curtis Fuller).

[90] See, eg Berliner (n 26) 121.

[91] DeVeaux and Giddins (n 3) 23.

[92] See, eg Berliner (n 26) 253–55 (explaining values in originality and success in the professional community among jazz musicians).

[93] A Pepper, 'Art Pepper' in Gottlieb, *Reading Jazz* (n 1) 279.

[94] Jazz trumpet player Winton Marsalis 'has been criticised for sounding like an encyclopedia of jazz trumpet styles, from Miles Davis's melancholy to Louis Armstrong's growls to Fats Navarro's liquid phrasing to Clifford Brown's clarity to Dizzy Gillespie's puckishness': L Porter, *Jazz: A Century of Change* (New York, Schirmer, 1997) 254. The division between replicating other artist's styles and a performer developing their own sound within a performing tradition is blurry. 'If you play trumpet and you don't sound like Miles or Dizzy or Clifford or Fats, you're probably not playing jazz,' Marsalis argued. 'If you don't sound like somebody else, you sound like nothing': ibid 254.

[95] See Berliner (n 26) 254.

[96] Berliner (n 26) 253. Pate distinguishes between successful soloists, like Miles Davis and Lester Young, whose soloing style was marked by its simplicity, and 'corny' performers who are using basic, seemingly uncreative practices.

[97] Berliner (n 26) 254.

Eventually, such unoriginality might slow down a rehearsal and shrink the band's repertory, ultimately threatening the band's economic viability if the unoriginal soloist is present.[98]

Other jazz musicians might ostracise uncreative players by creating music so theoretically abstract that only the most highly skilled and connected players can 'keep up'. As drummer Kenny Clarke explained, mid-century bebop performers, including Thelonious Monk, would purposefully create new, more complex rhythms and harmonic progressions in order to[99] 'discourage the sitters-in at night we didn't want … When we started playing these different changes we'd made up, they'd become discouraged after the first chorus and they'd slowly walk away and leave the professional musicians on the stand.'

These behaviours served to prevent certain musicians from entering the community, but also to protect one's own content. Cornetist Joe Oliver allegedly 'would hold back particular tunes and alter his ideas as a soloist when he noticed musicians in the audience who he felt were inclined to steal from him'.[100] Even in the present day, jazz musicians expect one another to have a sophisticated knowledge of tradition, repertory and music theory. Soloists who cannot creatively adapt alongside other performers can be excluded.

While jazz musicians can, and have, used the US copyright system to the extent it applies, considering its limitations, they have developed normative practices to regulate borrowing. Decisions regarding the quality and quantity of permissible or impermissible borrowing seem to mimic formal copyright standards, as well as the subjective nature by which such decisions are weighed. These commonly shared practices are taught to students, even as they are permitted temporarily to cross otherwise unacceptable boundaries in the name of learning the shared repertory, traditions and practices common to jazz communities. Although they imperfectly serve generations of jazz musicians, such normative practices have allowed jazz to preserve creativity in lieu of formal legal protection.

VI. Conclusion

Genre-specific study of jazz reveals the music, and its creators, to be at odds with federal copyright law. Part of the reason for this antagonistic relationship is long-standing gaps in legal protection generated by copyright policies that favour written notation, novelty and exclusive authorship. In some instances, such as arrangements, transcriptions and post-1972 recordings, jazz musicians have met legal requirements either by securing at least marginal protection for their works or by adapting to avoid royalty fees. In others, musicians have intentionally subverted copyright laws, as in the proliferation of fakebooks. Where creativity celebrated in jazz communities falls entirely outside the scope of formal legal protection, as for improvisation, jazz communities have developed their own normative practices to regulate creativity and preserve individual styles. As a result, jazz has persisted at the periphery of copyright.

[98] Berliner (n 26) 254–55.

[99] J Stewart, 'No Boundary Line to Art: "Bebop" as Afro-Modernist Discourse' (2011) 29 *Journal of American Music* 332, 338. Berliner offers a similar account, noting that Monk and Gillespie 'would perform 'complex variations on chords … to scare away the no talent guys': Berliner (n 26) 469 fn 18.

[100] Berliner (n 26) 469 fn 18 (interview with Buster Bailey).

11

Confronting an Extractive Racialised Genre System: Black Lives Matter, Royalty Recovery and Musical Reparations

OLUFUNMILAYO B AREWA AND MATT STAHL

I. Introduction

The political-economic practices of commercial music production may be plausibly analogised to a relation of plunder and redistribution, clothed in and (legally) legitimated by recording and publishing contracts. For African Americans, this was particularly true during the pre-Civil Rights era. During that time, entrepreneurs and companies that offered recording, song writing and publishing contracts to African Americans were able to take advantage of social-structural contexts of considerable societal racial exploitation and violence targeted at African Americans. Further, for all artists prior to (and even during) the digital era, the realities of the commercial recording industry have left open few alternative paths to a recording career other than those largely determined by recording companies. For many artists, this lack of alternatives meant that taking a bad deal was generally preferable to no deal at all.

The US commercial recorded music industry has long been a socially extractive industry with racial characteristics. Here, varied experts, including recording scouts, industry executives and other intermediaries, have frequently operated as seekers after and discoverers of rich seams of unrefined music: they secure rights of exploitation through contracts; and they extract, refine and market uncountable varieties, seizing on and pumping as much value as possible out of the most productive and marketable sources. In a 2004 interview, Marshall Chess, son of Chess Records founder Leonard Chess, recalled his experience of the Chess Records headquarters when a new Chess record became a hit: 'The excitement of a hit was the closest thing I've seen to looking at those old movies where they get the oil gushers.'[1]

> That's how it used to be when you got a hit. It was just amazing; it would be going like a wave going across the country. Records would break, and the phones would start ringing. We'd yell up and down the hall, like 'Detroit 13,000!' I mean, you'd be running and running trying to get the pressings, and it would just roll across the country.[2]

[1] J Broven, *Record Makers and Breakers: Voices of the Independent Rock'n'roll Pioneers* (University of Illinois Press, 2005) 123.

[2] ibid 123.

Chess Records was one of several independent music labels that exploited a vacuum left by major recording companies. Between 1945 and 1955, these indie labels specialised in commercial music made by African Americans, with marketing targeted at African American communities.[3] The development of this 'race' record market segment led such companies to record African American artists in varied genres, including blues, R&B and rock 'n' roll, with a focus on recording artists performing genres categorised as 'black'.

Marshall Chess's 'oil gusher' metaphor highlights the prospecting/extraction dynamic that can be seen at work in several phases of the commercialisation of African American music. In this chapter, we focus on the controversies that can erupt when a creator or bearer of valuable music – a performer or composer – questions the legitimacy of an extracting agent – a record company owner or music publisher – or resists their terms. For example, Little Richard recalled confronting Don Robey about his treatment as an artist contracted to Robey's Peacock Records: 'He jumped on me, knocked me down, and kicked me in the stomach. It gave me a hernia that was painful for years. I had to have an operation. Right there in the office he beat me up.'[4] Years later, according to James Salem, Robey's partner Evelyn Johnson called Little Richard's allegations '"flat, bald-faced lies", but she does remember Robey slapping him once'.[5] In 1985, a television news reporter doing a story on royalties asked singer Hank Ballard (writer of 'The Twist' and other hit songs, long under contract to King Records) 'What happened to your publishing rights?' Ballard responded 'publishing rights? At that time, they didn't allow blacks to have publishing. If you went to a record company and even mentioned publishing, out the door you'd go.'[6]

Many African American artists have pursued restitution by contracting with 'royalty recovery' experts. Yet this tactic has often had perverse results: these experts work for a piece of the action, typically 30–50 per cent, in some cases not just of royalties recovered but of all royalties owed the artist after the royalty recovery contract was signed. For many of these experts' clients, this relation exchanged one extractor for another. Further, much royalty recovery litigation has been between royalty recovery experts and their clients. We contextualise this form of redress to contribute to a historical account of previous restitutive efforts on behalf of African American artists, as well as to highlight potential booby traps in contemporary plans for reform.

II. Black Lives Matter, the Black Music Action Coalition and the Move for Musical Reparations

The dynamics of music industry extraction and configurations of industry intermediaries are perhaps changing during the digital era.[7] However, recent events and the emergence of the Black Lives Matter (BLM) social movement have highlighted the continuing racialised nature of industry institutional configurations and dynamics. The BLM social movement emerged as a Twitter hashtag in July 2013 following the acquittal of George Zimmerman for the 2012 shooting death of African American teenager Trayvon Martin.[8] BLM received significant additional visibility

[3] J Karp, 'Blacks, Jews, and the Business of Race Music, 1945–1955' in R Kobrin (ed), *Chosen Capital: The Jewish Encounter with American Capitalism* (Rutgers University Press, 2012) 141.

[4] C White, *The Life and Times of Little Richard, the Quasar of Rock* (Da Capo Press, 1994) 37.

[5] J Salem, *The Late Great Johnny Ace and the Transition from R&B to Rock 'n' Roll* (University of Illinois Press, 2001) 70.

[6] 'West 57th, September' (television series episode) produced by Martyn Burke (CBS News, 1985).

[7] OB Arewa, 'YouTube, UGC, and Digital Music: Competing Business and Cultural Models in the Internet Age' (2010) 104 *Northwestern University Law Review* 431.

[8] AB Tillery, 'What Kind of Movement is Black Lives Matter? The View from Twitter' (2019) 4 *Journal of Race, Ethnicity and Politics* 297.

following the 25 May 2020 murder of George Floyd, one of numerous African Americans killed in the USA in recent years during encounters with law enforcement.[9] Facilitated by digital age technologies, BLM has been described as an 'Internet-driven civil rights movement'.[10]

In 2020, attendance at BLM protests in the USA made BLM the largest social movement in US history.[11] BLM has had a broad impact in the USA and globally, extending to areas far beyond events that led to its emergence. BLM is a decentralised social movement for which Twitter has been indispensable.[12] BLM has drawn attention to systemic racism with a goal 'to eliminate the racial injustice which permeates and surrounds a wide variety of places in society'.[13] For African American performers and music professionals, linking this impetus to long-standing concerns with the recording industry was a short step.

African American musical forms have long been a key source of musical innovation, and a succession of African American musical genres, from ragtime to rap, have 'stamped themselves indelibly on the lives of generation after generation … [as] the most important tributary flowing into today's music', which is a function of 'the exceptional vitality, creativity, and power of musicians working within these idioms'.[14] Yet 'tributary' also names the relationship of a subject population obliged to pay regular tributes to a conquering ruler. From the dawn of the recording industry, African American innovators in music have been exploited in myriad ways in line with a dominant gold rush impetus in the recording industry in which varied intermediaries sought to harvest value from African American culture within broader approaches built upon an ethos of extraction. Past and present exploitative practices have affected a broad range of musicians, not just African American ones. However, the fundamental role of African American musical genres in musical innovation, pervasive exploitative borrowings from African American music and musicians, societal status of many African Americans and contexts of official white supremacy in which the US recording industry took form have led to exploitation having an outsized impact within African American communities.

Exploitation has also occurred in contexts, particularly in the pre-Civil Rights era, in which entertainment was one of the few socially sanctioned avenues of work for many African Americans other than servitude:

> Long after slavery had ended, African Americans could not escape servitude, having few if any other alternatives for employment … There are many reasons for this dearth of options, but prominent among them is the assumption of the utilitarian nature of black people based on the conviction of black inferiority, and an accompanying resistance to reconceptualizing the potential for anything else for blacks.[15]

Music critics and historians have often noted parallels in the regimes of sharecropping and the recording industry.[16]

[9] DM Clayton, 'Black Lives Matter and the Civil Rights Movement: A Comparative Analysis of Two Social Movements in the United States' (2018) 49 *Journal of Black Studies* 448.

[10] J Eligon, 'One Slogan, Many Methods: Black Lives Matter Enters Politics' *New York Times* (18 November 2015) www.nytimes.com/2015/11/19/us/one-slogan-many-methods-black-lives-matter-enters-politics.html.

[11] L Buchanan, Q Bui and P Jugal, 'Black Lives Matter May Be the Largest Movement in US History' *New York Times* 3 July 2020) www.nytimes.com/interactive/2020/07/03/us/george-floyd-protests-crowd-size.html.

[12] Tillery (n 8).

[13] Clayton (n 9).

[14] S McClary, 'Rap, Minimalism, and Structures of Time in Late Twentieth-Century Culture' in C Cox and D Warner (eds), *Audio Culture: Readings in Modern Music* (Continuum, 2004) 289.

[15] MI Jordan, *African American Servitude and Historical Imaginings: Retrospective Fiction and Representation* (Palgrave Macmillan, 2004) xiv.

[16] N Carr, *Utopia is Creepy and Other Provocations* (WW Norton, 2016) 30–31. See also F Tharpe, 'Steve Stoute on Disrupting the Culture, the Grammys, and the Coming "Revolution in Music"' (*Complex*, 20 December 2018) www.complex.com/life/2018/12/steve-stoute-disruptor-interview.

In recent years, particularly since the 2020 murder of George Floyd, a BLM epistemology has proliferated across many sectors of American life, returning public attention to forms of institutionalised racism. Inspired by concerns raised by BLM about racial injustice, the non-profit Black Music Action Coalition (BMAC) was founded in June 2020 to 'ensure that the music business – which is arguably kept afloat by black music and black creators – continues to combat systemic racism beyond a fleeting moment of uproar and activism'.[17] The inequities that are the focus of the BMAC include the terms of industry contracts and the composition of industry senior management, executives and board members.

A 2021 report from the University of Southern California Annenberg Institute Inclusion Initiative highlights the broad lack of inclusion across all segments of the music industry:

> In conclusion, the findings in the report show that a lack of inclusion in the music industry is not the problem of one company or one sector. It involves the entire community of artists, executives, agents, managers, publicists, distributors, and even the audience. Thus, creating a more inclusive industry requires the insight, input, and effort of all.[18]

The BMAC embodies BLM in its 2020 challenges to music industry institutions to get right with African American performers, composers, industry professionals and audiences. In January 2021, in response to public demands for accountability on the part of music corporations, Berlin-based BMG announced results of an internal audit of its artist contracts.[19] Although BMG seemingly acknowledged and owned up to racialised contracting practices, the data released by BMG gave little insight into underlying biases and their impact. BMG also promised further, as yet unidentified, action.

Industry approaches to systemic racism have been neither sustained nor comprehensive. As the 2021 BMAC *Music Industry Action Report Card* notes: 'The music business has been confronted about practices which marginalize Black artists and executives before, and those confrontations usually lead to some organizational or financial changes, but those changes don't last.'[20] BLM has reinvigorated debate about reparations across sectors of the economy; BMAC has been at the forefront of calls for reparations in the music industry. BMAC was also part of a coalition of groups that formed part of the Why We Can't Wait Coalition, which issued a statement in 2021 urging the US Congress to immediately act on the Federal Slavery Reparations Bill.[21] Others, including Jeff Tweedy, singer and guitarist for the American alternative rock band Wilco, have also called for reparations in the music industry.[22]

[17] S Hissong, 'Meet the Music Industry's New Black Music Action Coalition' *Rolling Stone* (22 June 2020) www.rollingstone.com/pro/news/black-music-action-coalition-record-industry-1018726/.

[18] SL Smith, C Lee, M Choueiti et al, 'Inclusion in the Music Business: Gender & Race/Ethnicity Across Executives, Artists & Talent Teams' (USC Annenberg Inclusion Initiative, June 2021) https://assets.uscannenberg.org/docs/aii-inclusion-music-industry-2021-06-14.pdf.

[19] BMG refers to BMG Rights Management GmbH, also known as the 'new' BMG. This 'new' BMG, founded in 2008, is a music publisher, record label and subsidiary of the private multinational media conglomerate Bertelsmann. 'The Success Story of the New BMG' (24 March 2021) www.bertelsmann.com/media/news-und-media/downloads/bmg-milestones.pdf.

[20] Black Music Action Coalition 2021. Music Industry Action Report Card, 4, https://www.bmacoalition.org/musicindustryreports.

[21] 'Why We Can't Wait Coalition Statement Urges Immediate Congressional Actions on HR 40/S.40, the Federal Slavery Reparations Bill' (30 July 2020) www.hrw.org/sites/default/files/media_2021/11/Coalition%20Letter%20-%20Why%20We%20Cant%20Wait%20-%20US%20Congress%20Should%20Pass%20Reparations%20Bill%20HR%2040.pdf.

[22] J Bernstein, 'Why Jeff Tweedy Is Calling for Reparations in the Music Industry' *Rolling Stone* (20 July 2020) www.rollingstone.com/music/music-features/jeff-tweedy-reparations-royalties-racism-interview-1024524/.

III. Blues and R&B (and Country) as Racialised Music Genres

The music industry has long been criticised for racialised music genre categories that have placed African American artists in categories reserved for music classified as 'black'. Contemporary genre categories in music reflect a historical legacy of racial classifications. Racial classifications, which have been used in the USA since the early days of its formation,[23] have long been an integral part of the marketing of recorded music. Music genres are constructed categories that may be taken for granted or assumed to be natural ones. The recording industry has shaped not only genres, but also the types of music different musicians could record. We draw attention to two interlocked, mutually reinforcing problems associated with racial genre classification: the naturalisation of 'black' and 'white' musical forms and ways this antinomy has licensed and justified racialised exploitation. African American artists appear to be 'black' before they are 'artists'.

In the early days of the commercial recording industry, industry participants had to create new markets for new recording technologies. Music soon emerged as a key application of recording technologies. Early acoustic technologies limited what could be recorded due to the limited range of early recording technology.[24] These limitations contributed to a search for things to record that led to engagement with an emerging body of African American popular music.

Blues is a distinctively American musical form and one of the most important of such forms. It arose in the early twentieth century and became a crucial sector of the recording industry in the 1920s, comprising an important element in other musical forms, including jazz, country music, R&B and rock 'n' roll. Blues is a 'definable body of musical elements or traits inherited from both African and European traditions, that forms the foundational language of much twentieth-century American musical style'.[25] Blues music has roots in African music, African American folk and work songs, and European musical traditions.[26] It is typically identified by a characteristic 4/4 syncopated or offbeat phrasing rhythmic structure, a musical mode that may incorporate flatted thirds and sevenths, and lyrics in a three-line stanza in which the second line repeats the first (AAB).[27]

As is the case with other African American-influenced musical genres, blues music has traditionally reflected an aesthetic based on borrowing and other types of copying, 'which has significantly contributed to the dynamism and widespread reach of blues as a musical form', highlighting 'the inability of current dominant copyright perceptions of music to encompass musical practice in blues and other living musical traditions that reflect borrowing and improvisatory practices'.[28] Since the early twentieth century, blues has been a key source for much of popular music, including R&B and rock 'n' roll.

Dominant recorded music business practices, as they developed during the early roots music recording era, of which the blues was a key aspect, have continued long after the peak of blues music popularity. Music industry institutional structures continue to be based in practices

[23] K Prewitt, 'Racial Classification in America: Where Do We Go from Here?' (2005) 134(1) *Daedelus* 5.

[24] M Chanan, *Repeated Takes: A Short History of Recording and Its Effects on Music* (Verso, 2005) 50.

[25] RJ Ripani, *The New Blue Music: Changes in Rhythm & Blues, 1950–1999* (University of Mississippi Press, 2006) 16.

[26] ibid 4–9.

[27] P Oliver, *Songsters and Saints: Vocal Traditions on Race Records* (Cambridge University Press, 1984) 1–9; GP Ramsey, *Race Music: Black Cultures from Bebop to Hip-Hop* (University of California Press, 2004) 113; Ripani (n 25) 16–61; E Southern, *The Music of the Black Americans: A History*, 3rd edn (WW Norton, 1997) 334–36.

[28] OB Arewa, 'Blues Lives: Promise and Perils of Musical Copyright' (2010a) 27 *Cardozo Arts & Entertainment Law Journal* 602.

rooted in earlier eras that reflect models based to a significant degree on exploitation rather than partnership.[29] Early blues was initially distributed largely through sound recordings of African American musicians for African American audiences manufactured and sold by white-owned companies. Although blues sound recordings were based on a continuing live blues performance tradition, the types of recordings that were distributed by companies marketing so-called 'race' records (of which blues formed an important segment) were significantly influenced by cultural assumptions and hierarchies of race. African American artists have often faced double exploitation. Within existing forms of exploitative business and legal norms, African American artists have suffered forms of racial exploitation that have both deprived them of ownership of their creative works and subjected them to business and legal norms that continue to the present day to be organised around an ethos of segregation and exclusion based on race.

The term 'race records' had been used since Mamie Smith's 1920 bestselling Okeh recording of 'Crazy Blues'. In 1949, the recording industry changed the 'race' music category to rhythm and blues, or R&B: 'The term *Rhythm and Blues* came into use in the late '40s after *Billboard* magazine substituted it for *race*'.[30] Terms such as 'race' music, R&B and, more recently, 'urban' music are marketing terms that have been applied to a broad range of music whose most significant commonality – as far as marketers were concerned – was the race of its performers and targeted market.[31] For example, at its emergence, R&B was not a pristine or unitary phenomenon, but a 'conglomerate of many different musical styles', including blues shouting, jump blues, blues ballads, country blues, vocal groups and gospel music.[32]

Racialised genre categories and recording industry marketing and business practices are important background factors in considering copyright treatment and contractual practices involving the blues and R&B genres. The continuing impact of racialised music genre categories remains a pressing issue, not least because their naturalisation justifies racially disparate treatment past and present. Ironically, responding to pressures about racial injustice following the murder of George Floyd, in June 2020 the Grammy Awards decided to rename the 'Best Urban Contemporary Album' as the 'Best Progressive R&B Album'.[33] The term 'urban', however, remains in the Latin music space.[34] This seeming change just repeats racialised categories of the past and highlights participants' widespread difficulty in attempting to confront racialised industry categories and other forms of exclusion and discrimination.

The recording industry's race-based genre categorisation system has a significant and continuing impact on African American musicians. African American musicians in the popular music arena are usually assigned to record chart categories considered to be 'black'.[35] In contrast, white performers typically start out on the pop charts.[36] In the past, construction of charts themselves reflected subjective assumptions about race that could diminish how charts accounted for the success of artists in 'black' genres.[37] This was evident when *Billboard* began using Nielsen

[29] M Stahl and O Arewa, 'Accounting for Injustice: AFTRA, Work and Singers' Royalties' in SM O'Connor (ed), *Oxford Handbook of Music Law and Policy* (Oxford University Press, 2021) 202.

[30] A Shaw, *Honkers and Shouters: The Golden Years of Rhythm & Blues* (Macmillan, 1978) xv.

[31] Ripani (n 25) 6.

[32] ibid 6.

[33] G Suarez, 'The Grammy's Still Don't Get It' (*Vulture*, 20 June 2020) www.vulture.com/2020/06/grammys-urban-category-essay.html.

[34] ibid.

[35] R Garofalo, 'Industrializing African American Popular Music' in PK Maultsby and MV Burnim (eds), *Issues in African American Music: Power, Gender, Race, Representation* (Routledge, 2016) 81.

[36] ibid 81.

[37] TJ Dowd and M Blyler, 'Charting Race: The Success of Black Performers in the Mainstream Recording Market, 1940 to 1990' (2002) 30 *Poetics* 87.

SoundScan data in 1991. The staggered implementation of SoundScan data led to inconsistencies between different *Billboard* charts. The SoundScan data also revealed that hip-hop had a far larger market share than was apparent under the old subjective reporting system, in which *Billboard* contacted certain record stores to determine song popularity for the purpose of constructing industry charts.[38]

Early recording industry business and marketing executives focused their efforts on what they considered to be 'authentic' black music, which for them meant blues, not string band music. Black string bands were thus excluded from 'race' music catalogues because they played 'hillbilly' music and from 'hillbilly' music catalogues because they were not white.[39] A few black 'hillbilly' musicians made careers within country music, notably harmonica player DeFord Bailey, the first African American country music star.[40] However, most black string bands were not able to get recorded, leading the black string band tradition to come 'close to disappearing'.[41]

The segregation of most African American musicians to music genres categorised as 'black' affects the shape and reception of music that might be created or recorded by African American artists. In the 1980s and 1990s, African American performers of rock music formed an activist organisation, the Black Rock Coalition, to contest this deep-seated divide. In Maureen Mahon's analysis, these musicians faced a catch-22: they were 'at once too black to be real rockers' and 'not black enough because they rock'.[42]

Race-based genre distinctions pervade the music industry and influence choices about marketing, booking and other aspects of the industry. Racialised categories have a significant impact on creators and other music industry participants and shape creative spaces in critical ways. Musicians still face pressure to fall within race-based industry silos. African American country star Mickey Guyton, for example,

> found that many people would attempt to silo her, calling her an R&B artist rather than acknowledge her legitimacy as a country musician … 'With Black women, we're supposed to be just R&B', she [Guyton] said. 'That is where everybody's comfortable putting us in'. In 2018, Guyton sang 'Caught Up in Your Storm' for the film 'Forever My Girl'. She distinctly remembers a group of white men loudly yelling during her performance, 'That's R&B! That's R&B!' She had to start over. 'There's a video of me singing it, and that was the day that it happened', Guyton said. 'Because I was a girl and because I was Black, they felt that they could do that, say that, and they were very, very rude about it. But I don't care. I'm here. Sorry, not sorry'.[43]

In late 2018, African American rapper, singer and songwriter Lil Nas X released the country rap hit single 'Old Town Road'. 'Old Town Road' became a viral meme on the video-sharing social networking service TikTok. The song went on to be number one on the US *Billboard* Hot 100 record chart for 19 weeks, which at the time was longer than any song since the chart originated in 1958. In addition to appearing on the *Billboard* Hot 100, 'Old Town Road' appeared on the Hot R&B/Hip Hop chart, a chart typically for music categorised as 'black', and the Hot Country Songs chart. In March 2019, *Billboard* announced that 'Old Town Road' was to be removed from the Hot Country chart.[44] Thus, even today, African American musicians who cross into genres

[38] SC Watkins, *Hip Hop Matters* (Beacon Press, 2006) 35–37.

[39] E Wald, *Escaping the Delta: Robert Johnson and the Invention of the Blues* (Amistad/HarperCollins, 2004) 47.

[40] RK Oermann, *Behind the Grand Ole Opry Curtain: Tales of Romance and Tragedy* (Center Street, 2008) 242–50.

[41] CK Wolfe, 'Hillbilly Fever, The Lost Tradition of Black String Bands' [May/June 2002] *No Depression* 112, www.nodepression.com/the-lost-tradition-of-black-string-bands/.

[42] M Mahon, *Right to Rock: The Black Rock Coalition and the Cultural Politics of Race* (Duke University Press, 2004) 162.

[43] RE Samuel, 'Mickey Guyton Is Carving a Path for Black Women in Country Music' (*Huffpost*, updated 11 November 2021) www.huffpost.com/entry/mickey-guyton-black-women-country-music_n_618ab716e4b055e47d80c592.

[44] E Leight, 'Lil Nas X's "Old Town Road" Was a Country Hit. Then Country Changed Its Mind' *Rolling Stone* (26 March 2019) www.rollingstone.com/music/music-features/lil-nas-x-old-town-road-810844/.

considered to be white may be guided to categories largely reserved for music considered to be 'black' and that typically derive from the original 'race' music category: 'This problem is not exclusive to country. In the music industry, rock and pop are also still thought of as music by, and for, white people.'[45]

The experiences of Mickey Guyton and Lil Nas X in the country music space reveal the degree to which the apparently natural 'whiteness' or 'blackness' of a musical genre is actively (re)produced.[46] Country music has long presented itself as a white music genre,[47] notwithstanding its evolution from racially mixed musics and African American musical influences.[48] Relaxation of such racial genre policing could undermine the legitimacy of what Maureen Mahon calls popular music's 'racialized political economy'.[49]

IV. Music, Race and Exploitation

Racial ecosystems of exploitation are reflected in at least two major problems evident in terms received from and practices connected to economic arrangements. First, African American artists in varied circumstances have received lower compensation and stated royalty rates. In addition, many African American artists have not been and are still not being paid the compensation to which they are contractually entitled. In this section, we outline key elements of these two problems.

A. Lower Stated Royalty Rates

The 2020 BMG audit revealed that African American musicians have often received lower stated record royalty rates (royalties associated with sales and licences of sound recordings). In December 2020, BMG announced the results of its audit of historical labels that it had acquired. The BMG audit was inspired by BLM, racial justice protests after the murder of George Floyd, and the activities of the BMAC. Audits such as the one undertaken by BMG are certainly a step in the right direction. However, the results of the audit, as reported in media sources, suggests that we have a long way to go in terms of audits that are transparent and that reveal the magnitude of exploitation that African American artists have experienced.

The full BMG study does not appear to have been widely released. The findings as reported in the news media were: 'BMG has found that four of the 33 labels in its historic acquired catalogues show "statistically significant differences between the royalties paid to Black and non-Black artists".'[50] Notably, however, this reporting is not sufficiently transparent. It appears to suggest

[45] ibid.

[46] J Hamilton, *Just Around Midnight: Rock and Roll and the Racial Imagination* (Harvard University Press, 2016); K Hagstrom Miller, *Segregating Sound: Inventing Folk and Pop Music in the Age of Jim Crow* (Duke University Press, 2010).

[47] R Thomas, 'There's a Whole Lot O'Color in the "White Man's Blues": Country Music's Selective Memory and the Challenge of Identity' (1996) 38 *Midwest Quarterly* 81.

[48] JR Neal, *The Songs of Jimmie Rodgers: A Legacy in Country Music* (Indiana University Press, 2009) xiii; D Peckhold (ed), *Hidden in the Mix: The African American Presence in Country Music* (Duke University Press, 2013); A Randall, 'Lil Hardin to Lil Nas X: The Genius of Black Country' in *Rivers of Rhythm: African Americans and the Making of American Music* (National Museum of African American Music, 2020) 131–51.

[49] Mahon (n 42) 106.

[50] M Stassen, 'BMG Publishes Results of Historic Royalties Review, Pledges Action and Invites Other Labels to Probe for Evidence of Racial Disadvantage' (MusicBusinessWorldwide, 18 December 2020) www.musicbusinessworldwide.com/bmg-pledges-action-on-results-of-historic-royalties-review/.

that the magnitude of the royalty differences between black and non-black artists relates to small numbers (only four out of 33 or some 12 per cent of labels had such lower compensation). The public revelations, however, give little or no indication as to the actual magnitude of these royalty differences for the artists involved. Most importantly, the revelations do not reveal the key information that one would need to know to assess the impact of reduced royalties paid to black artists: what total number and percentage of black artists across all labels received lower royalties regardless of the number of labels involved or whether the labels were segregated or had black and non-black artists.[51]

BMG's acquired historical recorded catalogues include recordings on 33 labels by 3163 total artists, with 1010 black artists (31.9 per cent).[52] Fifteen of the 33 labels include both black and non-black artists, which suggests that the other 18 labels may perhaps be segregated,[53] although it is difficult to determine exact breakdowns, given the publicly reported numbers. Of the 15 labels that had both black and non-black artists, a quarter had statistically significant lower royalty rates for black artists: 'in the case of four labels there was a statistically significant negative correlation between being black and receiving lower recorded royalty rates, a difference ranging from 1.1 to 3.4 percentage points'.[54]

The BMG study is an important starting point for identifying lower stated royalties for African American artists, but may be incomplete in important ways. The reported data from the study highlight the importance of greater transparency, but also raise questions. For example, what is the racial composition of the 18 labels that did not include both black and non-black artists and that may perhaps be segregated? If these labels are segregated in that some may have all black artists and some all non-black artists, what are the royalty rates among the different labels? The data released by BMG also lacks other demographic data, including information about royalties and gender, which may reflect a doubly negative impact on artists who are black and female. It would also be helpful to understand the magnitude of the impact of the royalty differential. For example, how many of the 1010 black artists in the BMG-acquired catalogues were in the four labels with the discrepancies or in labels with statistically significant lower royalty rates?

In addition, other provisions may be important in determining artists' contractual rights other than those related to stated royalty rates. Reports about the BMG disclosures do not give a sufficiently comprehensive overview of the legal and economic terms of contracts with the 1010 African American artists who signed contracts with BMG historic labels. The disclosures also do not give sufficient information about how these provisions compare with those of other contracted artists.

B. Non- and Under-payment of Contractual Record Royalties

In addition to lower stated royalty rates, African American (and other) artists have experienced persistent difficulties in getting royalties paid to them. Difficulties in getting paid often relate to

[51] The terms 'black' and 'white' are not capitalised in this chapter. As Kwame Anthony Appiah has noted, both black and white are categories that reflect 'historically created racial identities'. KA Appiah, 'The Case for Capitalizing the B in Black' *The Atlantic* (18 June 2020) www.theatlantic.com/ideas/archive/2020/06/time-to-capitalize-blackand-white/613159/.

[52] Stassen (n 50).

[53] C Cooke, 'BMG Calls on Industry to Follow Its Lead to Tackle Discrimination in Old Record Contracts' (*Complete Music Update*, 21 December 2020) completemusicupdate.com/article/bmg-calls-on-industry-to-follow-its-lead-to-tackle-discrimination-in-old-record-contracts/.

[54] ibid.

problems with royalty accounting and recording firms' manipulation of royalty accounting.[55] In the 1980s and 1990s, Howell Begle, a pro-bono attorney working on behalf of Ruth Brown, Joe Turner, the Clovers and many other 1950s R&B acts, found evidence that Atlantic Records had larded performers' royalty accounts with debits in the form of packaging and other charges not allowed by their contracts, and neglected to monitor, account for or pay Ruth Brown's (and possibly other artists') foreign record royalties for over 10 years.[56] When Ruth Brown stopped recording for Atlantic Records in 1963, the company declared that she owed them tens of thousands of dollars in unrecouped cash advances and other monies the company paid on her behalf. Until Begle made his discoveries public, Atlantic denied that their own accounting practices contributed to Brown's negative royalty account balance, her 'debt' to the company.

In a recent case involving the late soul artist Johnnie Taylor, Sony was said to be writing off that singer's debt (or negative royalty account balance) so that Taylor's family could receive royalty payments.[57] Howell Begle's research threw into question the bromide that R&B recording artists' negative royalty account balances (like Johnnie Taylor's supposed 'debt') were due to performers' poor financial discipline.[58] Ruth Brown and Howell Begle's 'royalty reform' activism gathered steam in the mid-1980s and culminated about 10 years later with several major and minor record companies acknowledging historical and continuing injustices, zeroing out negative royalty account balances, updating their accounting practices and in some cases raising royalty rates from the one to five per cent standard of the 1950s to the 10 per cent standard of the 1980s.[59]

The patterns of institutional behaviour that are suggested in the recent BMG study, brought to light in Ruth Brown and Howell Begle's royalty reform work and recently evinced in news accounts of Johnnie Taylor's persisting negative royalty account balance with Sony, all hinge on historical problems associated with *record royalties*, royalties to be paid to artists on retail sales of recordings to the record-buying (or cassette- or CD-buying) public. When journalistic coverage of a recording artist speaks of a *royalty rate*, reference is being made to the formula by which a record company determines how much it will credit a recording artist per unit sold. For most artists addressed by Brown and Begle, a typical royalty rate would have been around one to five per cent; this is likely the case with most of the artists covered in the BMG study whose contracts predate 1965. Problems of record royalties relate to distinct patterns of unequal treatment, evident, for example, in artists in some genres being offered lower rates than artists in other genres, as well various ways companies have avoided paying even those lower rates.

V. Dispossessive Music Publishing Practices in Blues and R&B

Problems with record-royalty accounting are also associated with a distinct but closely related system of extraction, one where race and genre also play very significant roles: music publishing

[55] Stahl and Arewa (n 29).

[56] M Stahl, 'Tactical Destabilization for Economic Justice: The First Phase of the 1984–2004 Rhythm & Blues Royalty Reform Movement' (2015) 5 *Queen Mary Journal of Intellectual Property* 344.

[57] J Bernstein, 'He Scored the First Platinum Hit. 45 Years Later, His Family Is Fighting for Every Penny' *Rolling Stone* (2 November 2021) www.rollingstone.com/music/music-features/johnnie-taylor-fonda-bryant-sony-royalties-1241773/; D Brown, 'Late Soul Singer's Family Fights with Sony to Get Rid of His Debt' (WSOC-TV 9, 10 November 2021) www.wsoctv.com/news/local/late-soul-singers-family-fights-with-sony-get-rid-his-debt/6IFBCCFOGFFTNLNUNK4AUXHUKU/.

[58] Stahl (n 56).

[59] ibid.

in the recorded music industry. A pattern of publishing practices emerged in the early 1920s with the development of relations between record companies, African American singers and instrumentalists, African American record buyers and a new cohort of intermediating figures: the talent scouts/music publishers now generally known as 'A&R' (artist and repertoire) people.[60] People in this role, frequently lauded as risk-taking pioneers, continue to fascinate historians of the recording industry.

A. The Mechanical Right

The booming recording industry of the 1920s took advantage of 1909 Copyright Act provisions that allowed companies to make a mechanical reproduction (phonorecord) of a musical composition 'without the consent of the copyright owner provided that the person adhered to the provisions of the license'.[61] The compulsory mechanical licence provisions had stringent requirements, including statutory minimum royalty rates. These requirements meant that compulsory mechanical licences under the 1909 Act were not widely used.[62] Mechanical licences were often privately negotiated, with the statutory minimum royalty rates typically being a ceiling for them.[63] Statutory minimum rates were two cents per copy from 1909 until the 1976 Copyright Act came into force on 1 January 1978.[64]

By the late nineteenth century, US copyright law gave copyright owners exclusive rights to reproduce and distribute their copyrighted works,[65] including in the case of music through sale of sheet music, to translate and dramatise such works[66] and to publicly perform them.[67] Those seeking to make reproductions, distribute copyrighted works or undertake public performance of musical compositions thus required the permission of the copyright owner, which typically required receiving permission (or a licence) from the copyright owner for the use of the musical composition. Such licences usually entailed payment of royalties to the copyright owner.

The 1909 Act created additional rights for copyright owners of musical compositions for *mechanical reproductions* of such compositions, including through piano rolls and recorded cylinders and discs. These rights were, however, made subject to a compulsory licence framework due to concern about the monopolisation of these mechanical rights by a single company.[68] To prevent such monopolisation and foster competition among manufacturers,[69]

[60] To avoid anachronism and glorification, we use the less-loaded term 'intermediary' hereinafter.

[61] Statement of Marybeth Peters, The Register of Copyrights before the Subcommittee on Courts, The Internet and Intellectual Property of the House Committee on the Judiciary, United States House of Representatives, 108th Congress, 2nd Session, 11 March 2004, www.copyright.gov/docs/regstat031104.html.

[62] ibid.

[63] ibid.

[64] ibid.

[65] In 1831, the first general revision of the US Copyright Act extended copyright protection to musical compositions: Copyright Act, Washington DC (1831). L Bently and M Kretschmer (eds), *Primary Sources on Copyright (1450–1900)* www.copyrighthistory.org.

[66] In 1870, Congress extended the Copyright Act of 1831 to translations and dramatisations of musical compositions: Copyright Act, Washington DC (1870). ibid.

[67] In 1870, Congress also extended the Copyright Act of 1831 to public performances of dramatic works. ibid. In 1897, Congress extended the Copyright Act of 1831 to public performances of musical compositions: US Copyright Amendment Act of 1897, Copyright Act (Public Performance of Musical Compositions), Washington DC (1897). ibid.

[68] Peters (n 61).

[69] House of Representatives Report No 60-2222, 6 (1909).

the 1909 Act provided that 'whenever the owner of a musical copyright has used or permitted or knowingly acquiesced in the use of the copyrighted work upon the parts of instruments serving to reproduce mechanically the musical work, any other person may make similar use of the copyright work' by following procedures laid out in the 1909 Act,[70] or by negotiating privately with the owner of the copyright. A House of Representatives Report for the 1909 Act identifies varied types of mechanical reproduction, including discs, plates, cylinders, strips, perforated rolls and phonographs. This report notes that:

> It is not the intention of the committee to extend the right of copyright to the mechanical reproductions themselves, but only to give the composer or copyright proprietor the control, in accordance with the provisions of the bill, of the manufacture and use of such devices.[71]

As of 1965, somewhat late in the period surveyed here, 'no legitimate record company ha[d] ever [exercised] the compulsory license provisions of the Act. In every instance the record company obtain[ed] an agreement with the publisher because of certain benefits derived irrespective of the Act'.[72] These benefits included, for example, the possibility that a star artist would record a new version of a previously recorded song (cover song) and, by selling hundreds of thousands or millions of records, generate revenue through mechanical and performance royalties from uses of the musical composition. Such cover songs could also increase interest in the song and thus improve the likelihood that the song would be recorded and released in new versions by other companies in the future. The potential benefits of cover songs could also induce rights holders to accept reduced mechanical royalties or even create agreements where the record company would pay no mechanical royalties until a certain record sales threshold was reached. Agreements like these enabled record companies to structure agreements to avoid or minimise having to deal with mechanical licences.

The 1909 Copyright Act's compulsory licence provisions created a framework for two related developments that are important to our story of genre-related business practices in the US recording industry. The first was the emergence in the 1920s of a new kind of entrepreneurial publisher, an intermediating figure who brokered relations between African American music performers and composers and the companies who demanded new recordings to market to African American music consumers. According to Ward and Huber, these intermediaries 'often earned most of their income in the recording industry from controlling copyrights'.[73] The second development was the merging of record manufacturing and music publishing in the development of record companies' 'in-house' (or affiliated or subsidiary) publishing companies. According to Arnold Shaw, himself a publishing professional in blues and R&B during the postwar period, recording company executives developed business techniques 'to reduce royalties paid to song-writers and publishers'.[74] Each of these phenomena became systematised around the extraction of copyrights and/or claims of copyright ownership by recording company-owned publishing companies, whether through transfers of publishing rights from composers or through executives' full or partial claims of authorship.

[70] 1909 Copyright Act, Pub L No 60-349, 35 Stat 075 (4 March 1909), §1(e).

[71] House Report (n 69) 9.

[72] W Whiting, 'Compromise to Correct Result: Retention and Modification of the Compulsory License in Proposed Copyright Law Revision' (1965) 53 *California Law Review* 1528.

[73] B Ward and P Huber, *A&R Pioneers: Architects of American Roots Music on Record* (Country Music Foundation Press, 2018) 90.

[74] Shaw (n 30) 200.

B. Race Records Producing and Publishing in the 1920s

By the 1920s, thanks in part to the popular 1910s compositions of WC Handy and the staggering sales of Mamie Smith's 1920 record 'Crazy Blues', a 'blues and jazz bonanza' was underway.[75] From that time until the early 1930s, the business of 'race' records was quite profitable.[76] Companies such as Paramount, Okeh, Vocalion and Brunswick Records manufactured and sold recordings by rural and city-dwelling African American performers. According to William Barlow, 'there were close to 15,000 race records released by the industry [during this period]; approximately 10,000 blues titles, 1,750 gospel titles, and 3,250 jazz titles'.[77] These were white-owned companies that soon came to depend on intermediaries who could recruit and record African American performers whose recordings they could market to African American audiences.

At the same time, it is not at all clear that these companies prioritised copyright acquisition or exploitation; some seem to have understood their business solely as manufacture and sale of tangible wares, not proprietorship of intellectual property rights. The conditions existed, therefore, for the emergence of intermediaries who could (i) locate and recruit vocalists and instrumentalists to provide recordings needed by record manufacturers, and (ii) register the copyright to any copyrightable works not already protected by copyright (or secure rights to registered works) that such performers recorded. Ward and Huber emphasise the centrality of this mode of extraction to the establishment of the recording industry: 'these practices constituted the vital financial lifeblood – as well as the dark heart – of the interwar roots music recording business'.[78]

J Mayo 'Ink' Williams, Perry 'Mule' Bradford, Clarence Williams, Ralph Peer, Polk Brockman, HC Speir and other entrepreneurs, seeing an emerging mass market in sound recordings, positioned themselves to siphon off royalties flowing from rights in copyrighted musical compositions. They recruited performers to make recordings that Paramount, Okeh, Vocalion, Brunswick and other companies could manufacture and sell. These music producers prioritised securing copyrights to musical compositions – sometimes on behalf of the companies, but often for themselves alone – by buying the composition from the performer on the spot, by licensing it for shared revenue or by simply claiming it without explaining or disclosing anything.

The workings of the mechanical royalty set early record producers 'on a feverish search, not just for new talent to record but also, more specifically, for new talent with original material that might be copyrighted'.[79] These miners in a cultural gold rush operated on a piece-of-the-action basis. In 1923, Polk Brockman started copyrighting and publishing the blues songs of performers whose recording he supervised, later branching out into 'hillbilly' music; 'My sole interest', he said, 'was in the mechanicals and recordings'.[80] In 1965, William Whiting observed that 'a significant part of the income of the music industry is derived from mechanical reproduction'.[81] Recent research into the practices of intermediaries like those discussed here sheds new light on how this principle played out in racialised terms.

Ralph Peer is best known for his recruitment and recording of 'hillbilly' performer-composers like the Carter Family and Jimmie Rodgers. However, Peer had witnessed the blues windfall of Okeh Records while working for that company in 1920, when they released Mamie Smith's

[75] W Barlow, 'Cashing In: 1900–1939' in JL Dates and W Barlow (eds), *Split Image: African Americans in the Mass Media*, 2nd edn (Howard University Press, 1990) 33.
[76] Ward and Huber (n 74) 90.
[77] Barlow (n 76) 33.
[78] Ward and Huber (n 74) 91.
[79] ibid 93.
[80] ibid 100.
[81] Whiting (n 73).

blockbuster 'Crazy Blues'. Moving to Victor Records in 1926, Peer made a deal to recruit and record race and hillbilly acts in exchange for a piece of the action. Victor Records seems to have been unconcerned with music publishing, and Peer claimed publishing rights on virtually all the material he recorded. According to David Suisman, 'Peer understood that every record that came out had in it a lucrative "mechanical right" to exploit',

> and in 1926, when he went to work for Victor as a producer, he negotiated for the company to sign over to him all the copyrights of the recordings whose sessions he organized, in lieu of receiving any salary. Victor, believing Peer foolish to negotiate such a deal, gladly agreed, but Peer knew what he was doing. In the second quarter of 1928 alone, he earned close to $250,000. Concerned that Victor would get wise to the amount of money he was taking in, he then set up several publishing companies for cover, which by the 1930s and '40s had expanded into a multimillion-dollar international publishing empire.[82]

One of the publishing companies Peer developed in this context is now known as Peermusic. It remains family-run and maintains a catalogue of over 250,000 pop music compositions.[83]

J Mayo Williams was another influential intermediary and contemporary of Peer. Williams worked for Paramount, Brunswick and Decca Records during the late 1920s and early 1930s, typically without a salary and without an official position, recruiting performers and recording new masters for the companies in exchange for rights in compositions. 'I never had no salary contract, nothing like that because I would get mine from the royalties from the songs.'[84] In a 1970s interview, Williams said

> 35% of the artists sold off their composition outright for a flat proposition … Not only did the publishing company receive all the royalties from the compositions they owned outright, but they stood to make a lot if another company made a record using that composition.[85]

According to Robert Springer, Williams's 'name appeared as author or coauthor of about half the compositions registered. From 1928 to 1932, State Street Music [the publishing company Williams had founded] deposited 500 songs in the race series of both labels.'[86] Sara Filzen writes that Williams 'once described himself as being about "fifty percent honest"'.[87] As Ward and Huber write, 'Virtually all the artists Williams signed and recorded for Paramount, Brunswick, and Decca [in Williams' own words] "received a flat fee … I don't know of a single one that was on a royalty basis"'.[88]

Peer and Williams exemplified a novel mode of extraction built around the social process of recording in a racially stratified socio-legal context. According to Kenney,[89] independent recruitment and contracting of artists by Williams, who was African American and one of the most successful producers of his era, enabled the companies to whom he supplied recordings and performers to show that they employed no African Americans in managerial positions. This further permitted white company officers to avoid dealing directly or publicly with the African American artists on whose unique services and copyrightable compositions they depended.

[82] D Suisman, *Selling Sounds: The Commercial Revolution in American Music* (Harvard University Press, 2009) 175.

[83] www.peermusic.com/; A Paine, 'We Are Family: Peermusic's Mary Megan Peer Takes Over as CEO' *Music Week* (11 December 2020) www.musicweek.com/publishing/read/we-are-family-peermusic-s-mary-megan-peer-takes-over-as-ceo/082183.

[84] Ward and Huber (n 74) 91.

[85] ibid 103.

[86] R Springer, 'Folklore, Commercialism and Exploitation: Copyright in the Blues' (2006) 26 *Popular Music* 33, 37 (citation omitted).

[87] S Filzen, 'The Rise and Fall of Paramount Records' (Winter 1998–99) 82 *Wisconsin Magazine of History* 114.

[88] Ward and Huber (n 74) 103.

[89] WM Kenney, *Recorded Music in American Life: The Phonograph and Popular Memory, 1890–1945* (Oxford University Press, 1999).

C. In-House Blues and R&B Publishing in the 1950s

The 'rise of the independents' – the scores of little record companies that sprang up in post-war American cities to record African American musicians and market to African American consumers – is a story that has been told many times from many different perspectives.[90] Scholarly and other histories of blues and R&B companies, entrepreneurs, songwriters and performers often highlight music publishing as a major concern in this business ecosystem. The most successful independent companies had their own in-house or affiliated publishing companies, and many of those companies made it a requirement that a new performer signing a recording contract also sign a publishing contract assigning publishing rights to the company's publisher. James Salem writes that 'the independent record companies that survived the transition from r&b to r&r in the 1950s … did so on the strength of their publishing subsidiaries'.[91]

'The traditional publisher–composer relationship,' writes Roger Wallis,[92] 'assumes close ties between creator and [publisher, as creator's] representative, with the publisher being entirely independent of the recording industry.' This idealised model does not adequately describe the operations of the intermediaries discussed in the previous section. It also does not explain publishing activities undertaken by postwar blues and R&B record companies. Many blues and R&B entrepreneurs, having gained music industry experience before starting their own record companies, entered into record manufacturing and music publishing in close succession, as, for example, did Art Rupe with his Specialty Records and Venice Music Publishing and Syd Nathan and his King Records and Lois Music. Publishing subsidiaries were most profitable when major national companies had their mainstream white pop stars record cover recordings of songs whose publishing rights the regional independents held. The independent companies' publishing subsidiaries would receive the mechanical royalties owed by the major companies on each copy of the cover record they sold.

The well-documented practice of covering, as was undertaken in the early 1950s, is widely understood as a racialised extractive process whereby the major record companies re-recorded songs originated (if not written) by African American artists and released these re-recordings within months or even weeks of the original independent release. Cover recordings by mainstream white pop singers were frequently able to capture the upward chart momentum of the original recording, effectively capping the original's sales and geographical spread, as radio DJs and record retailers prioritised relations with richer companies over imprecations from original artists and their advocates. This system very often gave the white performer (Pat Boone, Georgia Gibbs, Elvis Presley, Ernie Ford and so on) a national hit. It was the performers of the original recordings, especially those who could claim no authorship credit, who were most negatively affected here.[93] As Don Snowden writes, the in-house publisher arrangement 'was a situation ripe for exploitation since an artist was completely dependent on the publisher and record company to supply accurate information that would let the performer know what was going on'.[94]

[90] See, eg Shaw (n 30); GC Altschuler, *All Shook Up: How Rock'n'Roll Changed America* (Oxford University Press, 2003).

[91] Salem (n 5).

[92] R Wallis, 'Copyright and the Composer' in S Frith and L Marshall (eds), *Music and Copyright*, 2nd edn (Routledge, 2004) 109.

[93] See the interview with LaVern Baker in C Deffaa, *Blue Rhythms: Six Lives in Rhythm and Blues* (Da Capo Press, 1996) 174–216. Baker was a singer recording for Atlantic Records in the 1950s, whose songs were repeatedly covered by Mercury Records' white pop singer Georgia Gibbs.

[94] W Dixon and D Snowden, *I Am the Blues: The Willie Dixon Story* (Da Capo Press, 1989) 185.

By owning or co-owning in-house publishing companies, record manufacturers such as Chicago's Chess Records could effectively pay themselves all or most of the mechanical royalties. Muddy Waters, Howlin' Wolf, Chuck Berry and dozens of other African American artists were under contract to Chess in the 1950s and 1960s. Chess Records's historian Nadine Cohodas outlines how this worked for Chess and its affiliated publisher Arc Music, formed in 1953:

> The four Arc principals [Leonard and Phil Chess and their partners Gene and Harry Goodman] agreed that Chess would pay the one-penny 'mechanical' fee on the sale of [songs first released on] Chess Records directly to the writer. But Arc would not get the other penny even though it was publisher of the song. That penny would remain at Chess ...[95]

In other words, Chess Records would pay to Arc Music no part of the two cents per song per record that they could otherwise have been required to pay an independent publisher. Chess instead kept both cents on the understanding that the record company would pay the writer's share of the mechanicals to the writer 'directly'.[96] Chess would not pay mechanicals to Arc Music even on cover versions released on Chess's labels; it was as if there were no publisher at all in this situation. Arc Music would only receive mechanical royalties when the song at issue was re-recorded and released by another label. Thus, Arc Music played little immediate role in the day-to-day experiences of the many Chess song-writing artists whose songs were not covered by artists recording for non-Chess companies.

D. Royalty Recovery – Ambivalent Restitution

Varied R&B and blues musicians, including Willie Dixon, Robert Johnson and McKinley Morganfield (Muddy Waters) and their heirs, may have experienced multiple levels of exploitation over time, including through *royalty recovery*.[97] Royalty recovery is a restitutive model that emerged in the 1970s whereby white experts with industry experience and connections, including Scott Cameron and Chuck Rubin, worked to recover copyrights or royalty rights, most often for African American artists, frequently ending up in conflict (if not in litigation) with their clients. In the case of the estate of early blues artist Robert Johnson, for example, Johnson's heirs assigned to Steve LaVere, a music historian, the rights to photographs of Johnson and other memorabilia and copyright to Johnson's works in exchange for 50 per cent of any royalties earned by LaVere for their use.[98] Artists often experienced significant difficulty when they sought to terminate contracts with royalty recovery experts, leading to extensive royalty recovery contract litigation. The Johnnie Taylor case referred to above, the Robert Johnson case and other cases involving estates of artists highlight the intergenerational consequences of exploitative music industry practices, which have likely contributed to the racial wealth gap. Royalty recovery cases and disputes about music industry contracts and accounting underscore the critical need for more extensive analysis of experiences of African American litigants in commercial litigation involving music industry contracts.

One distinguishing feature of royalty recovery practitioners is a persistent, long-term financial interest in the outcome of their royalty recovery activities. Such interests were evident in

[95] N Cohodas, *Spinning Blues into Gold: The Chess Brothers and the Legendary Chess Records* (St Martin's Press, 2012) 80.

[96] Willie Dixon makes it seem like that 'direct' payment system was a means by which Chess could demand kickbacks as a condition of making any payments to Dixon: Dixon and Snowden (n 95) 199–200.

[97] M Stahl and O Arewa, 'Willie Dixon, Muddy Waters, and Commercial Litigation: The Intergenerational Impact of Royalty Recovery Cases' (unpublished manuscript).

[98] *Anderson v LaVere* 895 So 2d 828, 831 (Miss 2004).

Cameron's disputes with the Dixon family, and later the disputes of Cameron's surviving spouse Elizabeth with the family of Muddy Waters.[99] Chuck Rubin and his Artists Rights Enforcement Corporation (AREC) have been parties to numerous lawsuits against their own clients. Royalty recovery practitioners' suits against their clients amount to another extractive system, a *shadow industry* of contracts upon contracts, extractions upon extractions, operating in the asymmetrically racialised gaps and ambiguities that have characterised the music industry of the twentieth century.

VI. Conclusion

Black Lives Matter and the Black Music Action Coalition returned public attention to the 'racialized political economy'[100] of the American recording industry. BMG's 2020 self-audit confirmed BLM and BMAC arguments, albeit in an obscure and insufficiently transparent fashion. In this chapter, we have tried to show some of the core factors at work for a century in the production and reproduction of the recording industry as an extractive system with racial characteristics. There is much still to learn about how the following factors (and others) interacted: the construction of racialised music genres; the formation of copyright law's categories and boundaries with respect to music; and the development of roles, resources and institutions in the twentieth-century recording industry.

Since the early days of the recording industry, widespread use of racial categories and differential compensation based on race have intensified the impact of pervasive exploitative borrowings from African American musicians and culture. Although borrowing is a characteristic aspect of African American-influenced music, these exploitative borrowings underscore the impact of broader sociocultural contexts. A BLM epistemology emphasises that all these factors and relations unfolded in a context of official and thoroughly normalised white supremacy. In the worlds of American popular music, white supremacy contained and supported fascination with African American music and performers, an economic interest in African American consumers' growing purchasing power and a readiness to recruit, classify and exploit African American performers and repertoires to the hilt.

Racialised practices of value extraction by means of appropriation and/or control of copyrights and publishing rights exemplified and undergirded this fluid articulation of laws, norms and practices, particularly as they operated in the margins of early twentieth-century US society and its burgeoning entertainment industries. As Mayo Williams and Ralph Peer did in the 1920s, so the Chess family and other entrepreneurs secured ownership and/or control of copyrights and publishing rights in the margins of the post-war US recording industry. These entrepreneurs secured massive windfalls by licensing their copyright-protected material to major national companies able to market it to mainstream white audiences, while maintaining contractual control of the originating artists and composers signed to their regional, specialised recording and publishing companies.

Almost certainly under multiple pressures, many African American artists were stripped of their copyrights, knowingly or unknowingly, by representatives of white-owned companies in a political-legal regime of white supremacy. Political philosopher Charles Mills quotes a 1969 article from the journal *Foreign Affairs*: as late as the 1940s,

[99] Estate of McKinley Morganfield Deceased, 18th Judicial Circuit Court, DuPage County Illinois.
[100] Mahon (n 42) 146.

> [t]he long-established patterns of white power and nonwhite non-power were still the generally accepted order of things. All the accompanying assumptions and mythologies about race and color were still mostly taken for granted … white supremacy was a generally assumed and accepted state of affairs in the United States as well as in Europe's empires.[101]

Kenney writes that the 'purchase of copyright' – and, as we have suggested, its appropriation through other methods – 'was a widespread procedure in the race record business, and it continues to provide a basic factual reference point for African American accusations of musical exploitation in the United States'.[102] For African American performers and composers in a turbulent, insecure industry, the ready cash offered by a Mayo Williams or Polk Brockman for a recording session and/or property in the song may well have been more appealing than 'hypothetical sums that might come their way in the future',[103] particularly given a social context where continuing exploitation was likely to be an accepted norm. This notion that 'a bad deal is better than no deal' arises in much of the primary and secondary literature.

In the 1970s and 1980s, many of these artists (by this time at retirement age) and/or their heirs sought overdue compensation, often signing contracts with royalty recovery experts like Chuck Rubin, Scott Cameron and Steve LaVere. These second-order intermediaries' whiteness, music industry knowledge and industry contacts enabled them to recover publishing and record sales royalties. Yet these recoveries came at very high prices; in many cses, these experts' contracts with clients including Huey 'Piano' Smith, Carl Gardner, Willie Dixon, Muddy Waters and the heirs of Robert Johnson were even more onerous and extractive than the artists' original recording and publishing contracts. It is not surprising that a large proportion of the lawsuits in which, for example, Chuck Rubin and his successors were parties in suits against AREC's own clients.

Our concern here has been to illustrate how the recording industry's extractive system is historically constituted such that the racialised incentives that attracted and rewarded extractors like Williams, Peer and the Chess brothers and others remain operational. This extractive system provides the basis for royalty recovery as a shadow extractive industry, an industry of contracts on contracts. The American recording industry's stubborn racial-genre segregation and the racialised system of economic incentives persist and, we believe, must be considered in the development of strategy and tactics for reforming the recording industry's racialised practices.

[101] Quoted in C Mills, *The Racial Contract* (Cornell University Press, 1997) 27.
[102] Kenney (n 89) 119.
[103] Springer (n 87) 39.

12

'Not like Pyrates': Borrowing, Copyright and Creativity in the Eighteenth Century

ANN VAN ALLEN-RUSSELL

I. Introduction

Even in the eighteenth century, there had long been an established tradition of crafting new works out of existing music through borrowing, transformation, imitation or allusion.[1] Such practices were not considered an infringement of a composer's intellectual property, but were a common compositional strategy that young composers were encouraged to adopt as a facet of developing their style, using transformative imitation to seed their creativity. Burkholder notes that 'making old music new is at the very centre of our musical tradition'[2] and that this practice 'has its own traditions and its own history'.[3] However, if plagiarism[4] (as we understand it today) was not a material concern of composers of this period, piracy of printed works was. The growth in the commodification of printed music in eighteenth-century England spurred composers to protect their creative outputs – their artistic property – from wholesale theft by unscrupulous publishers and led to a legal and economic revolution in musical ownership.

Drawing on Burkholder's typology and techniques of uses and reuses of existing musical material, this chapter focuses on examining how this particular compositional strategy was understood as a common practice at the time and on identifying the various methods of borrowing employed by eighteenth-century composers via a snapshot of some key exemplars from the period, considering not only what was borrowed or recycled and how it was transformed within a new work, but also *why* was it borrowed. Conversely, the subject of piracy – the unauthorised printing and dissemination of musical works – and the relational difference between it and creative borrowing must also be considered, and how it drove composers such as Arne, Geminiani and JC Bach to assert their right of authorial property over their printed work and reap the benefit of their mental labour, leading to the establishment of musical

[1] JP Burkholder, 'The Uses of Existing Music: Musical Borrowing as a Field' (1994) 50 *Notes* 858.

[2] JP Burkholder, 'Making Old Music New: Performance, Arranging, Borrowing, Schemas, Topics, Intertextuality' in V Kostka, PF DeCastro and WA Everett (eds), *Intertextuality in Music: Dialogic Composition* (Routledge, 2021) 84; JP Burkholder, 'Borrowing' (Grove Music Online, 2001) www.oxfordmusiconline.com/grovemusic/view/10.1093/gmo/9781561592630.001.0001/omo-9781561592630-e-0000052918.

[3] Burkholder, 'The Uses of Existing Music' (n 1) 861.

[4] 'Plagiarize' is defined as '1. 'take and use (the thoughts, writings, inventions, etc. of another person) as one's own. 2. pass off the thoughts etc. of (another person) as one's own … Latin *plagiarius* kidnapper': 'Plagiarize' in D Thompson (ed), *The Concise Oxford Dictionary of Current English* (Clarendon Press, 1995) 1043.

copyright. This nascent legal protection did not mark an end to borrowing, but provided the impetus for a long evolution of legal and social consideration of music as intangible property under the strict control of its creator.[5]

II. The Uses of Existing Music, Structures or Borrowed Ideas During the Eighteenth Century

Burkholder asserts that 'the use of existing music as a basis for new music is pervasive in all periods and traditions';[6] in the eighteenth century, the reworking, revising, transforming and imitating existing ideas (musical and otherwise) was seen as a common practice and an accepted part of the creative paradigm.[7] Just as early eighteenth-century literary critics of the English Augustan period,[8] such as John Dryden (1631–1700), Jonathan Swift (1667–1745), Joseph Addison (1672–1719) and Alexander Pope (1688–1744), and, later, the painter

[5] The full and fascinating history of the evolution of musical copyright is one I will set aside here, it having had a thorough exploration by several authors: D Hunter, 'Music Copyright in Britain to 1800' (1986) 67 *Music & Letters* 269; J Small, 'The Development of Musical Copyright' in M Kassler (ed), *The Music Trade in Georgian England* (Routledge, 2011) 233–386; RJ Rabin and S Zohn, 'Arne, Handel, Walsh, and Music as Intellectual Property: Two Eighteenth-Century Lawsuits' (1995) 120 *Journal of the Royal Musical Association* 113, doi.org/10.1080/02690403.1995.11828226; OB Arewa, 'From JC Bach to Hip Hop: Musical Borrowing, Copyright, and Cultural Context' (2001) 84 *North Carolina Law Review* 547; S Rogers, 'The Use of Royal Licences for Printing in England, 1695–1760: A Bibliography' (2000) 1 *The Library* 133, doi.org/10.1093/library/1.2.133; A van Allen-Russell, 'Documents Relating to Bach vs Longman and Lukey' in E Warburton (gen ed), *The Collected Works of Johann Christian Bach, 1735–1782*, 48:2 (Garland 1999) 577–82; A van Allen-Russell, '"For Instruments Not Intended": The Second JC Bach Lawsuit' (2002) 83 *Music & Letters* 3.

[6] Burkholder, 'Borrowing' (n 2).

[7] The following studies explore the various uses of existing music as an influence of one composer over another or one work over another, or as an aspect of the compositional process from the seventeenth to the twentieth century. This is by no means an exhaustive list of sources. Y Balmer, T Lacôte and CB Murray, 'Messiaen the Borrower' (2016) 69 *Journal of the American Musicological Society* 699, www.jstor.org/stable/26417270; G Barnett, 'Handel's Borrowings and the Disputed "Gloria"' [2006] *Early Music* 34; G Buelow, 'The Case for Handel's Borrowings: The Judgment for Three Centuries' in S Saide and A Hicks (eds), *Handel: Tercentenary Collection* (UMI Research Press, 1987) 61–82; Burkholder, 'Making Old Music New' (n 2) 68–84; D Cranmer, 'Handel Borrowings' (1981) 122 *The Musical Times* 524; C Croukamp, 'Borrowing and Action in Mozart's Instrumental Music' (DPhil thesis, University of Oxford, 2011); H Fromm, 'JS Bach in the Twenty-First Century: The Chapel Becomes a Larder' (2008) 60 *The Hudson Review* 543; CM Girdlestone, 'Rameau's Self-Borrowings' (1958) 39 *Music & Letters* 52; WD Gudger, 'A Borrowing from Kerll in "Messiah"' (1977) 118 *The Musical Times* 1038; A Hicks, 'Handel [Händel, Hendel], George Frideric' (Grove Music Online, 2001) www.oxfordmusiconline.com/grovemusic/view/10.1093/gmo/9781561592630.001.0001/omo-9781561592630-e-0000040060; H Meconi (ed), *Early Musical Borrowing* (Routledge, 2004); D Humphreys, 'Something Borrowed' (1997) 138 *The Musical Times* 19, doi.org/10.2307/1004029; MJ Lee, 'The Art of Borrowing: Quotations and Allusions in Western Music' (DMA thesis, University of North Texas, 2016) digital.library.unt.edu/ark:/67531/metadc849772/m2/1/high_res_d/LEE-DISSERTATION-2016.pdf; D McCaldin, 'Haydn as Self-Borrower' (1982) 123 *The Musical Times* 177; N Nettheim, 'How the Young Schubert Borrowed from Beethoven' (1991) 132 *The Musical Times* 330, doi.org/10.2307/966281; I Payne, 'Telemann's Musical Style c 1709–c 1730 and JS Bach: The Evidence of Borrowing' (1999) 30 *Bach: Riemenschneider Bach Institute* 42, www.jstor.org/stable/41640474; I Payne, 'Another Händel Borrowing from Telemann? Capital Gains' (2001) 142 *The Musical Times* 33, doi.org/10.2307/1004680; I Payne, 'A Tale of Two French Suites: An Early Telemann Borrowing from Erlebach' (2006) 147 *The Musical Times* 77; JE Sawyer, 'Irony and Borrowing in Handel's "Agrippina"' (1999) 80 *Music & Letters* 531; MA Smart, 'In Praise of Convention: Formula and Experiment in Bellini's Self-Borrowings' (2000) 53 *Journal of the American Musicological Society* 25; S Taylor, *The Indebtedness of Handel to Works by Other Composers: A Presentation of Evidence* (Cambridge University Press, 2014); JO Urmson, '"Messiah" Borrowings' (1967) 108 *The Musical Times* 142, doi.org/10.2307/953942; JT Winemiller, 'Recontextualizing Handel's Borrowing' (1997) 15 *Journal of Musicology* 444, doi.org/10.2307/764003; S Wollenberg, 'Handel and Gottlieb Muffat: A Newly Discovered Borrowing' (1972) 113 *The Musical Times* 448; S Zohn and I Payne, 'Bach, Telemann, and the Process of Transformative Imitation in BWV 1056/2 (156/1)' (1999) 17 *Journal of Musicology* 546.

[8] English Augustan period: 1660 restoration of Stuart monarch to 1740s, with the deaths of Pope and Swift.

Sir Joshua Reynolds (1723–92), espoused the use of imitation or borrowing as a primary means or 'common property'[9] in developing style, taste and expression in poetry, drama, literature and art, so the use of existing musical material, models and ideas from the distant past or more recent times was an accepted practice of the creative compositional process.[10] Education during the eighteenth century was 'grounded in Classical approaches to learning',[11] formed on rhetorical and oratorical works of Aristotle, Cicero and Quintilian, and had as one of its key pedagogical tenets the concept of imitation or use of existing ideas or models to help students develop their rhetorical style and expression, and seed their creativity.[12] In dispensing advice to his students, Quintilian makes much of the importance of imitation[13] when crafting their work:

> [It is] from these authors [of ancient Greek culture], and others worthy to be read, must be acquired a stock of words, a variety of figures and the art of composition. Our minds must be directed to the imitation of all their excellences, for it cannot be doubted that a great portion of art consists in imitation – for even though to invent was first in order of time and holds the first place in merit, it is nevertheless advantageous to copy what has been invented with success. Indeed, the whole conduct of life is based on the desire of doing ourselves that which we approve in others.[14]

Literary critics, theorists, writers and artists of the period advocated the imitation and emulation of ideas and models from both past and more recent writers or artists as best practice in developing a writer's or painter's style, expression and taste.[15] There was little in the way of disapproval of the practice of those who employed the works of others as models, allusions or even overt citations within new contexts. However, unmitigated copying (plagiarism) from sources was a concern that started to enter the debates in the mid-eighteenth century regarding excesses of imitation and its legitimacy as an aspect of creativity. There was an expectation that borrowing would be considered and measured, and would serve to spark new creative works, rather than be used to claim credit for others' efforts.[16] Also, the imitation should not be a direct mapping of the original source within a new work; it had to be transformed in some way during the creative process. Quintilian tells his students that 'it is dishonorable even to rest satisfied with simply equalling what we imitate. For what would have been the case, again, if no one had accomplished more than he whom he copied?'[17] He continues, instructing them that the borrowed material needed to be in some way transformed through the application of the student's own invention to the new work:

> If we take a view of all arts, no one can be found exactly as it was when it was invented … for certainly nothing does improve by imitation only … exact likeness is attended with such difficulty that not even nature herself has succeeded in contriving that in the simplest objects, and such as may be thought most alike, shall not be distinguished by some perceptible difference.[18]

---

[9] J Reynolds, *Discourses* (P Rogers ed, Penguin, 1992) 153, 278; G Buelow, 'Originality, Genius, Plagiarism in English Criticism of the Eighteenth Century' (1990) 21 *International Review of the Aesthetics and Sociology of Music* 119.

[10] Buelow, 'Originality, Genius, Plagiarism' (n 9) 120; A Bosker, *Literary Criticism in the Age of Johnson*, 2nd edn (W Heffer & Sons, 1954).

[11] Buelow, 'Originality, Genius, Plagiarism' (n 9) 119.

[12] ibid 119; JJ Murphy and HC Wiese (eds), *Quintilian on the Teaching of Speaking and Writing: Translations from Books One, Two and Ten of the Institutio Oratoria*, 2nd edn (Southern Illinois University Press, 2016) 132–36.

[13] Murphy and Wiese (n 12) 125 fn 1.

[14] ibid 132.

[15] Buelow, 'Originality, Genius, Plagiarism' (n 9); E Nitchie, 'Longinus and the Theory of Poetic Imitation in Seventeenth and Eighteenth Century England' (1935) 32 *Studies in Philology* 580; Reynolds (n 9).

[16] Winemiller (n 7) 488; Nitchie (n 15) 585, 591.

[17] Murphy and Wiese (n 12) 133.

[18] ibid 133.

Pope remarks that borrowing was 'merely a matter of following tradition, of making use of our inheritance from our ancestors'.[19] Still, the reimagination of that 'inheritance' is an element of the creative process:

> [T]hat writers, in the case of borrowing from others, are like Trees, which of themselves would produce only one sort of Fruit, but by being grafted upon others may yield variety. A mutual Commerce makes Poetry flourish; but then Poets, like Merchants, should repay with something of their own what they take from others; not, like Pyrates [*sic*], make prize of all they meet.[20]

Edward Young (1683–1765), who was more a proponent of originality than imitation,[21] still employed this specific transformative form of imitation in his own prose, writing in 1730 'we must exert [the original's] energy in subject and designs of our own'.[22] The painter Sir Joshua Reynolds strongly argued in his *Discourse VI* (1774) that an artist needed to be 'conversant with the inventions of others'[23] and that invention is 'the child of imitation'.[24] In *Discourse XII* (1784), the painter notes that 'The daily food and nourishment of the mind of an Artist is found in the great works of his predecessors'.[25] In fact, Reynold's own practice involved various degrees of borrowing and modelling paintings on earlier masters, but employing the borrowed elements in a completely different manner to the original.[26]

> It is vain for painters or poets to endeavour to invent without materials on which the mind may work, and from which invention must originate. Nothing can come of nothing.[27]
>
> After you [the student] have taken a figure, or any idea of a figure, from any of those great Painters, there is another operation still remaining, which I hold to be indispensably necessary, that is, never to neglect finishing from nature every part of the work. What is taken from a model, though the first idea may have been suggested by another, you have a just right to consider as your own property.[28]

Reynold's level of extensive borrowing found him accused of plagiarism.[29] However, this aspect of Reynold's creative process was defended by his friend, the English writer and politician

[19] Nitchie (n 15) 583–84.

[20] Alexander Pope to William Walsh (2 July 1706): 'I wou'd beg your Opinion, too, as to another point: it is, how far the Liberty of borrowing may extend? I have defended it sometimes by saying, that it seems not so much the Perfection of Sense, to say things that had never been said before, as to express those best that have been said oftenest; and that Writers, in the Case of borrowing from others, are like Trees, which of themselves would produce only one sort of Fruit, but by being grafted upon others, may yield variety. A mutual Commerce makes Poetry flourish; but then Poets, like Merchants, should repay with something of their own what they take from others; not, like Pyrates [sic], make prize of all they meet. I desire you to tell me sincerely, if I have not stretch'd this Licence too far in these Pastorals? I hope to become a Critic by your Precepts, and a Poet by your Example. Since I have seen your Eclogues, I cannot be much pleas'd with my own; however, you have not taken away all my Vanity, so long as you give me leave to profess myself yours, &c': *Letters of Mr Pope and Several Eminent Persons, From the Year 1705, to 1735*, vol I (London, 1735) 54; also cited in G Sherburn (ed), *The Correspondence of Alexander Pope*, vol 1 (Clarendon Press, 1956) 19–20.

[21] '*Imitation* are of two kinds; one of Nature, one of Authors: The first we call *Originals*, and confine the term *Imitation* to the second … *Imitators* only give us a sort of Duplicates of what we had, possibly much better, before; increasing the mere Drug of books, while all that makes them valuable, *Knowledge* and *Genius*, are at a stand': E Young, *Conjectures on Original Composition*, facs edn (first published 1759, Leeds, 1966) 9–10.

[22] E Young, *Imperium Pelagi. A Naval Lyrick: Written in Imitation of Pindar's Spirit. Occasion'd by His Majesty's Return, September 1729. and the Succeeding Peace* (Lawton Gilliver, Homer's Head against St Dunstan's Church, Fleetstreet, 1730) 2.

[23] Reynolds (n 9) 151.

[24] ibid 154.

[25] ibid 273.

[26] Reynolds (n 9) 153–54; E Wind, *Hume and the Heroic Portrait: Studies in Eighteenth-Century Imagery* (J Anderson ed, Clarendon Press, 1986) 74.

[27] Reynolds (n 9) 158.

[28] ibid 278.

[29] Wind (n 26) 69–73.

Horace Walpole (1717–97), who argued that Reynold's borrowings were transformed 'pictorial quotations',[30] not direct copies.

> Sir J Reynolds has been accused of plagiarism for having borrowed attitudes from ancient masters … [But] when a single posture is imitated from an historic picture and applied to the portrait in a different dress and with new attributes, this is not plagiarism but quotation: and a quotation from a great author, with a novel application of the sense, has allowed to be an instance of parts and taste; and may have more merit than the original.[31]

Just as borrowing was seen as a normative aspect of the creative process by writers, literary critics and artists, so too did contemporary music critics and theorists consider the practice of using existing music as a basis for, or within, new works as a common aspect of compositional strategy.[32] German composer, singer, music theorist and Handel's close friend Johann Mattheson (1681–1764) notes in his treatise, *Kern melodischer Wissenschaft* (1737), that some composers would 'gladly snatch a foreign idea from the mass of things that fall under their hands, of which often not two notes are their own'.[33] In her biography of Handel, Marshall makes similar observations to those of Quintilian, Pope and Reynolds, in that the use of existing music was far from an anomaly in new works. Marshall stresses that 'Existing music was a huge vocabulary … capable of endless combination and arrangements to suit different ideas and plans',[34] and that quite often new compositions contained borrowed material just as literary works (and paintings) would draw on works by predecessors or coevals.[35]

Writing in 1740, Mattheson describes various reasons why a composer might utilise existing musical ideas ranging from a musical earworm stuck in one's mind to the intentional use of an idea:

> 1. Sometimes a composer will use another composer's ideas by accident, simply because he cannot remember where he had heard the music originally 2. However, some composers have an almost perfect, much more gifted ability to remember music, which must be most convenient (he says) for them. 3. That when a composer's borrowed idea receives a good working-out, it must please the music's inventor and true owner. 4. That this practice is of no disadvantage to the composer of the original idea, but rather a special honour when a famous person comes upon his ideas and makes from them a true basis of his own music.[36]

Likewise, the important distinction between imitation and outright plagiarism made by art and literary critics was also the subject of discussion among eighteenth-century music theorists and critics. As part of a composer's development, Mattheson recommends borrowing musical ideas and imitating models as a means of stimulating the creative process. The borrowed and imitated

[30] ibid 69.

[31] Reynolds (n 9) 381 endnote 6.

[32] Buelow, 'The Case for Handel's Borrowings' (n 7) 68; Burkholder, 'The Uses of Existing Music' (n 1) 862; Burkholder, 'Making Old Music New' (n 2) 68.

[33] J Mattheson, *Kern melodisher Wissenschaft* (Hamburg, 1737) 128. Quoted in JH Roberts, 'Why Did Handel Borrow?' in Saide and Hicks (n 7) 86.

[34] J Marshall, *George Frederick Handel* (Sampson Low, Marston & Co, 1883) 35. 'Existing music was a hug vocabulary of words and phrases, capable of endless combinations and arrangements to suit different ideas and plan, and it was no more expected of a new composition that it should contain none but original themes, than it would be required of a literary work to contain an original proverb or aphorism in every paragraph. Hitherto, ownership had been acquired or conferred in virtue of treatment, and it was really not till Beethoven's time that the principle of property in ideas became generally recognized.' Also cited in Sadie and Hicks (n 7) 84.

[35] Marshall (n 33) 35.

[36] J Mattheson's *Grundlage einer Ehren-Pfote* (1740) quoted in Buelow, 'The Case for Handel's Borrowings' (n 7) 63.

material must nevertheless be of good quality ('only fine models are chosen'), and be transformed or reimagined in some way ('not however copied and stolen … most is fetched out of this source for invention').[37] Furthermore, Mattheson instructs that 'borrowing is permissible; but one must return the thing borrowed with interest, i.e. one must so construct and develop imitations that they are prettier and better than the pieces from which they are derived'.[38] This advice is similar to that given by Pope in his 1706 letter on transforming the 'inheritance' from one's predecessors, and that of Reynold's, where the artist's daily food and nourishment is found in the great works of their predecessors. Mattheson further stipulates that while there may be those who do not need to borrow existing music as they have 'enough resources of [their] own' that they 'need not begrudge' those who do employ this technique, nevertheless, to the theorist, this applies to a minority of composers.[39]

> [A]s even the greatest capitalists are given to borrowing money, if they see special advantages or benefit in this. The last *loco testimoniorum* is most useful in music when one quotes in a certain way a song by someone else which is known to virtually everyone, as for example church hymn, etc, so that the quoted material would serve as proof of confirmation, as *citatium* or *allegatum;* this then is sometimes very beautifully expressive and can be seen as a good invention, especially if such quoted phrases seem to come at the right moment and are developed with diligence and reflections. Thus ends this very brief report or assay on how the familiar *loci topici* or sources of inventions, in so far as they are taken from oratory, can also perform unusual service in musical composition.[40]

The music historian Charles Burney (1726–1814), too, focuses on the uses of existing music as part of the creative process, writing of one of the more well-known prolific borrowers of the eighteenth century – George Fredrick Handel.[41] Burney opens the section 'Character of Handel, as a Composer' in his 1785 *Account of the Musical Performance in Westminster Abbey* by explaining that producing a 'wholly and rigorously new'[42] composition is impossible and that even the best composers 'avail [themselves] of the best effusions, combinations, and effects, of his predecessors; to arrange and apply them in a new manner'.[43] In addition to benefiting from the musical material of others, Burney explains what Marshall distils in her Handel biography: that self-borrowing also provides musical ideas from which to enrich a new work – 'to add, from his own source, whatever he can draw, that is grand, graceful, gay, pathetic, or, in any other way, pleasing'.[44] In other words, taking that existing material and recrafting in a variety of

[37] EC Harriss, *Johann Mattheson's Der Vollkommene Capellmeister: A Revised Translation with Critical Commentary* (UMI Research Press, 1981) 298.

[38] ibid.

[39] ibid.

[40] ibid.

[41] Details of Handel's borrowing is discussed in the next section.

[42] C Burney, *An Account of the Musical Performances in Westminster Abbey, and the Patheon in Commemoration of Handel* (London, 1785) 39.

[43] ibid 39.

[44] ibid. 'I know it has been said that Handel was not the original and immediate inventor of several species of Music for which his name has been celebrated; but, with respect to ORGINALITY, it is a term to which proper limits should be set, before it is applied to the productions of any artist. Every *invention* is clumsy in its beginning, and Shakespeare was not the first writer of *Plays*, or Corelli the first composer of *violin Solos*, *Sonata*, and *Concertos*, though those which he produced are the best of his time; nor was Milton the inventor of Epic Poetry. The scale, harmony, and cadence of Music, being settled, it is impossible for any composer to invent a GENUS of composition that is *wholly and rigorously* new, any more than for a poet for form a *language, idiom and phraseology*, for himself. All that the greatest and boldest musical inventor can do, is avail himself of the best effusions, combinations, and effects, of his predecessors; to arrange and apply them in a new manner; and to add, from his own source, whatever he can draw, that is grand, graceful, gay, pathetic, or, in any other way, pleasing.'

ways, transforming within a new context. Still, as Winemiller highlights, some early eighteenth-century pedagogical texts instruct students to avoid 'uncritical copying' of material.[45] It would not be until the nineteenth century that allegations of 'musical felonies' were levelled against Handel,[46] although Johann Joachim Quantz (1697–1773) opines in his *Versuch einer Anweisung die Flöte traversiere zu spielen* (1752) that 'young and untutored' Italian opera composers tended to be less ethical in their borrowing as they

> imitate each other, copy each other's works, or even present another's work as their own, as experience will show, especially if such instinctive composers find it necessary to seek their fortune in foreign lands. They bring along their inventions not in their heads but in their luggage.[47]

All these viewpoints have a common perspective when it comes to using existing material in literature, art and music: that it was an accepted (and often encouraged) practice, and that borrowing was considered an aspect of a writer's, artist's or composer's tool kit in crafting new works – a practice whose focus, however, is not a direct or uncritical copy of borrowed ideas and structures, but a transformed imitation of style and expression within a new context. Imitation is the impetus for the creative process that feeds originality.

III. *Ex Nihilo Nihil Fit:*[48] Exemplars of Borrowing in Eighteenth-Century Music

The previous section contextualised the uses of existing material by eighteenth-century writers, poets, painters and musicians as a common means to seed innovation and creativity. Drawing upon Burkholder's approach to developing a typology of procedures, this section explores the types of uses of existing music commonly employed by eighteenth-century composers. With no claim that this is anything near an exhaustive exploration of the topic, this snapshot will illustrate the variety of approaches by composers of the period.[49] Some exemplars are well known, while others are more recent discoveries; overarching categories that appear to be accepted norms in the uses and reuses of existing music: Efficiency, Education and Homage/Influence.

One composer closely associated with the reuse of existing music is George Frederic Handel (1685–1759). Not only have scholars over the last several decades forensically studied Handel's practice of reworking, revising and reimagining existing musical material of his own music and that of others, but so had contemporaries such as Burney, Scheibe, Mattheson and some of his fellow composers.[50] Friedrich Zachow (1663–1712), Handel's teacher, encouraged

[45] Winemiller (n 7) 449.

[46] FW Horncastle, 'Plagiarism' (1822) IV *Quarterly Musical Magazine and Review* 142. Horncastle accuses Handel of plagiarising from an array of composers and himself and declares that he should be 'brought up to the *Harmonic Old Bailey*, where [he is] to receive the reward of [his] crimes by *verdict* of a jury of *critics*'. Horncastle's intention was to advise young composers on what 'shallows' they must avoid in a 'moral world'.

[47] JJ Quantz, *On Playing the Flute*, trans. Edward R Reilly, Second edition (Boston: Northeastern University Press, 1985) 20.

[48] 'Nothing comes of nothing.' Reynolds (n 9) 158.

[49] Winemiller (n 7) 454.

[50] Harriss (n 37); C Burney, *A General History of Music: From the Earliest Ages to the Present Period (1789)*, vol 2 (F Mercer ed, Harcourt, Brace & Co, 1935); W Crotch, *Substance of Several Courses of Lectures on Music* (London, 1831) 93–94, 121–22; Roberts (n 33) 83; Payne, 'Another Händel Borrowing' (n 7) 33–42.

the young composer to feed his creativity by imitating, modelling and drawing on musical ideas of other composers, past and present, as a means to crafting his own style (similar to Reynolds's advice to young painters on developing their own style drawing upon others' works), a compositional strategy the composer continued to employ throughout his career.[51] Several years after Mattheson's notable points in his *Kern melodisher Wissenschaft* on how a composer might utilise existing musical ideas, music critic and theorist Johann Adolph Scheibe (1708–76) wrote explicitly on Handel's (and Johann Adolph Hasse's) use of existing music by other composers, and specifically that of the highly regarded opera composer Reinhard Keiser (1674–1739):

> Our Reinhard Keiser was in his time an outstanding composer, and inexhaustible in the invention of musical ideas. Handel and Hasse, those famous men who gave honour to Germany in Italy and England, have – especially the former – often used his ideas, and in doing so fare well. They understood so well how to apply their art to these ideas that under their hands they are changed to new and original thoughts. Mattheson and Telemann have corroborated this more than once, and I cannot doubt it from other available reports I have had.[52]

An example of Handel's borrowing from Keiser is found in Polyphemus's aria 'O Ruddier than the Cherry', from *Acis and Galatea* (1718), HWV 49. In this aria, Handel draws from Keiser's aria 'Wann ich dich noch einst erblicke', sung by Agrippina from his opera *Janus* (1698),[53] along with several other works by Keiser borrowed by Handel in *Acis and Galatea*, employing Keiser's musical ideas in an 'innovative fashion'.[54] Handel's use of this borrowed music is far from the simple modelling of one melody to another: instead of borrowing the vocal melody of 'Wann ich dich noch einst erblicke', Handel instead takes Keiser's jagged ostinato bass line and recrafts it into the all-familiar lively melody of 'O Ruddier than the Cherry'.[55] As Winemiller argues, Handel's recontextualising of Keiser's ostinato figure 'significantly alters and expands the original musical function of the borrowed material' from accompaniment to the main musical idea.[56]

A well-known set of examples of Handel's self-borrowing are from the oratorio *Messiah* (1741). The choruses 'And He Shall Purify', 'His Yoke is Easy' and 'For unto Us a Child Is Born' are all modelled on musical ideas drawn from the Italian cantatas *Quel fior che all'alba ride*, HWV 192 (*c*1739) and *No, di voi non vo'fidarmi*, HWV 189 (1741), which were produced just prior to *Messiah*. However, as with the composer's use of Keiser's musical material, these are not straightforward cases of note-to-note self-borrowing as there is a considered recrafting of the music from the cantatas for two singers into the four-part, multi-voiced *Messiah* choruses. For example, the first movement of *Quel fior che all'alba ride* is the basis for 'His Yoke is Easy',[57] with the duet

[51] Buelow, 'The Case for Handel's Borrowings' (n 7) 62. '[B]orrowing (the use of existing material) played an immensely important role in Handel's creativity': D Hunter, *The Lives of George Frederic Handel* (Boydell Press, 2015) 223.

[52] J Scheibe's *Über die musikalische Composition* (1773) quoted in Buelow, 'The Case for Handel's Borrowings' (n 7) 64.

[53] Winemiller (n 7) 455; D Dugaw, 'Parody, Gender, and Transformation in Gay and Handel's "Acis and Galatea"' (1996) 29 *Eighteenth-Century Studies* 353.

[54] Winemiller (n 7) 454.

[55] GF Handel, 'O Ruddier than the Cherry' *Acis and Galatea*, HWV 49 (1718), 47, http://vmirror.imslp.org/files/imglnks/usimg/9/9f/IMSLP318860-PMLP44359-haendel_acis_and_galatea.pdf.

[56] Winemiller (n 7) 457–58.

[57] However, as now established by Cummings, the origins of the tune for some of these iterations is a Buxtehude organ work, Praeludium in G minor, BuxWV 163, which was composed between 1675 and 1685. G Cummings, 'Lübeck to London: A Much Travelled Fugue Subject' (2007) 53 *Händel-Jahrbuch* 331. Hunter posits that Handel may have learned the theme either from a manuscript copy or hearing the work performed when he was in Lübeck in 1703. Hunter, *The Lives of George Frederic Handel* (n 51) 222–23.

material reworked for the four-part chorus, weaving the original two-part exchange into a layered contrapuntal text for large chorus with orchestra, with melodic and rhythmic adjustments made to follow the English text.[58] Handel also models 'And He Shall Purify' on the final movement ('L'occaso ha nell'aurora') of the same cantata. Much of the existing material of 'L'occaso' – the melody, countermelody and bass line, and the imitative exchange between the vocal parts – is retained; Handel, however, alters and expands the borrowed material, such as finessing the existing contour of the melody to create the rapid passagework familiar to many choruses and solos in *Messiah*.[59] The composer also adapts the rhythm and melodic contour at points, especially at the cadences, to reflect the different text settings.[60]

With the second Italian cantata, *No, di voi non vo'fidarmi*, Handel takes the opening movement's theme, with its spirited dialogue between the two vocal parts, and the bass line for the chorus 'For unto Us a Child Is Born'.[61] Besides making use of the existing music, Handel maintains the dialogic structure of the duet by pairing different voices of the four-part chorus throughout the opening section (one of the upper vocal parts and a lower one with the borrowed music, for example). However, there is always a transformative element as part of the creative process: in this instance, new musical material is integrated with the unison section 'And his name shall be called, Wonderful, Counsellor, the mighty God, the everlasting Father, the Prince of Peace'.[62]

Handel was by far not the only composer to recycle or borrow musical ideas. One of Handel's lifelong friends, Georg Philip Telemann (1681–1767), often self-borrowed as well as reworking material from other composers, including Biber, Rameau and JS Bach, as well as Handel.[63] Conversely, Bach and Handel also borrowed from Telemann – according to Payne, Telemann's and Bach's borrowings from each other were a means of exploring and learning new compositional techniques and genres.[64]

One genre that was particularly ripe for emulation – and was all the rage at the time – was the nascent Italian solo concerto of the early eighteenth century as defined by Torelli, Corelli and Vivaldi.[65] JS Bach was one of Antonio Vivaldi's best students, even though Bach never travelled to Italy (in fact, he never left Germany) nor ever met Vivaldi. Vivaldi's concertos were widely published during the period,[66] and Bach had access to copies, particularly Vivaldi's Op 3 and 4 sets,[67] and transcribed at least nine of the concertos: three for solo organ (BWV 593, 594 and 596) and six for solos for harpsichord (BWV 972, 975, 976, 978, 980 and 1065), the latter six transcribed

[58] GF Handel, *Quel fior che all'alba ride*, HWV 192 (c1739) https://s9.imslp.org/files/imglnks/usimg/9/95/IMSLP237355-WIMA.7c10-hwv_192.pdf; GF Handel, *Messiah* (1741) part I, https://s9.imslp.org/files/imglnks/usimg/4/4d/IMSLP10705-Part_1a.pdf.

[59] Handel, *Quel fior che all'alba ride* (n 58).

[60] ibid; Handel, *Messiah*, part I (n 58).

[61] Hunter, *The Lives of George Frideric Handel*, 231. GF Handel, *No, di voi non vo'fidarmi*, HWV 189 (1741) https://s9.imslp.org/files/imglnks/usimg/0/0f/IMSLP202910-WIMA.b124-hwv_189.pdf; Handel, *Messiah*, part I (n 58).

[62] Handel, *Quel fior che all'alba ride* (n 58); Handel, *Messiah*, part I (n 58).

[63] Payne, 'Another Händel Borrowing' (n 7) 33; Payne, 'Telemann's Musical Style' (n 7) 43–44.

[64] 'Bach reworked Telemann's material … Bach deliberately borrowed material from Telemann, which he then subjected to his own compositional processes': Payne, 'Telemann's Musical Style' (n 7) 63; S Zohn and I Payne, 'Bach, Telemann, and the Process of Transformative Imitation in BWV 1056/2 (156/1)' (1999) 17 *Journal of Musicology* 571.

[65] A Hutchings et al, 'Concerto' (Grove Music Online, 2001) doi.org/10.1093/gmo/9781561592630.article.40737.

[66] Vivaldi's concertos were published in Amsterdam by Estienne Roger in 1711. R Rasch, 'Roger, Bach and Walter: Musical Relations between Amsterdam and Weimar' (2019) 69 *Tijdschrift van de Koninklijke Vereniging Voor Nederlandse Muziekgeschiedenis* 88.

[67] M Boyd, *Bach, Master Musician*, 3rd edn (Oxford University Press, 1994) 74.

from Vivaldi's well-known collections *L'estro armónico*, Op 3 (1711) and *La stravaganza*, Op 4 (1716).[68] While it is now thought that Bach's transcriptions may not have been solely for self-education,[69] it was in Vivaldi's Op 3 set that Bach encountered a new compositional concept and 'musical thinking'.[70]

To focus on a single example, Bach's Concerto in F major for Harpsichord, BWV 978 (1713–14) is a transcription of Vivaldi's Violin Concerto in G major, Op 3, No 3, RV 310 (1711). Here Bach follows Vivaldi's score fairly closely, retaining some of the features of the original concerto, including the ritornello form, the well-defined melodic contours and the solo-tutti opposition (in thematic contrast, harmonic schemes and scoring) that articulate the form and produce dramatic effects.[71] However, Bach's transcription is far from a direct note-for-note transfer from violin concerto to keyboard concerto – we can see Bach 'returning the thing borrowed with interest'[72] as he adapted Vivaldi's work to his own compositional processes, including integrating contrapuntal textures as well as transposing the key of Vivaldi's original to one more suited to the range of keyboards Bach used.[73] The opening ritornello alone provides a sampling of Bach's transformative invention of Vivaldi's material.

Bach tried to match Vivaldi's virtuosic violin solos with equally flashy keyboard solos, even if the idiomatic differences and techniques and often limited keyboard range required Bach to change the original figuration. Vivaldi's Op 3, No 3 opens with the solo violin and the ripieno's upper strings playing the ritornello's first motive in unison in bar 1, while the lower strings (violas, cello and bass) join in in bar 2, providing harmonic support in the form of repeated quavers. In his transcription, Bach has the harpsichord's right hand play the original ritornello's first motive alone. However, instead of emulating Vivaldi's simple accompaniment pattern, which started in the second bar, Bach adds a new line that is an imitation of the right hand's opening motive at the octave, with the newly composed contrapuntal approach demonstrating Bach's 'take' on the original piece. Throughout the concerto, Bach often rewrites passages to enrich the texture, particularly the bass lines, which were more simple and less contrapuntal in Vivaldi's version. In BWV 978, Bach transforms Vivaldi's simple repetitive quaver bass line in bars 7–11

[68] Bach's concertos that are transcriptions of Vivaldi's: BWV 593 (organ concerto after Vivaldi's Op 3, No 8 = RV 522); BWV 596 (organ concerto after Vivaldi's Op 3, No 11 = RV565); BWV 972 (harpsichord concerto after Vivaldi's Op 3, No 9 = RV 230); BWV 975 (harpsichord concerto after Vivaldi's Op 4, No 6, RV 316); BWV 976 (harpsichord concerto after Vivaldi's Op 3, No 12 = RV 265); BWV 978 (harpsichord concerto after Vivaldi's Op 3, No 3 = RV 310); BWV 1065 (concerto for four harpsichords after Vivaldi's Op 3, No 10 = RV 580). C Wolff and W Emery, 'Bach, Johann Sebastian' (Grove Music Online, 2001) doi.org/10.1093/gmo/9781561592630.article.6002278195.

[69] H Schulze, 'JS Bach's Concerto-Arrangements for Organ: Studies or Commissioned Works?' (1972) 3 *Organ Yearbook* 4.

[70] C Wolff, *Bach: Essays on His Life and Music* (Harvard University Press, 1991) 74–75.

[71] A Vivaldi, *L'estro armonico*, Op 3, 52–73, https://s9.imslp.org/files/imglnks/usimg/d/d6/IMSLP272378-PMLP06105-L'Estro_Armonico_-_Libro_Primo.pdf; JS Bach, Concerto in F major, BWV 978 (1713–14) 101–07, https://s9.imslp.org/files/imglnks/usimg/8/85/IMSLP05917-Bach_-_BGA_-_BWV_978.pdf.

[72] Harriss (n 37) 298.

[73] Bach transposed the original key of Vivaldi's concerto down a tone from G major to F major for his transcription; he did this with several of his transcription of Vivaldi concertos. This was primarily to address the issue of the restricted range of the keyboards Bach used. In the first movement of Bach's transcription (BWV 978), the harpsichord used by the composer did not extend to d''', an essential note in Vivaldi's Op 3, No 3, for example. In bars 3 and 4 (and later bars 18 and 19) of Op 3, No 3's first movement, d''' appears often; transposing it down a tone to F major shifts the dominant to C, a note within the range of Bach's keyboard. Bach also employed transposition to clarify parts that were often in the same register in the original. In the opening section of the first movement of BWV 978, Bach takes the reiterated quaver bass line notes (as found in bars 3–6 and throughout the movement) and places every other note an octave higher. This more clearly defines the bass line function within the sonority of the harpsichord. See scores for Vivaldi Op 3, No 3 and Bach's Concerto in F major, BWV 979 listed above; H Shanet, 'Why Did JS Bach Transpose His Arrangements?' (1950) 36 *Musical Quarterly* 186.

of the Allegro's opening ritornello by arpeggiating the harmony, creating a driving contrapuntal texture with the primary melodic material. With the first solo section starting in bar 12, this shifts back to the original quaver rhythm while still maintaining the arpeggio pattern. Bach later integrated and expanded the ideas and principles learned from transcribing Vivaldian concertos to his own distinctly original instrumental concertos, most notably the six Brandenburg Concertos BWV 1046–51.

So far, I have explored using existing music as a means of learning a new compositional aesthetic or generating new works based on material from oneself or others to further develop one's craftsmanship or musical thinking as an artist. There are, however, also composers who made use of existing music to reflect a level of influence or homage, or as an element of novelty within their works.

Handel's borrowings from Keiser (mentioned earlier) may well also be Handel tipping his hat to Keiser, who was a well-respected composer at this early point in Handel's career.[74] Another composer significantly influenced by a senior coeval was Wolfgang Amadeus Mozart (1756–91), who developed a lifelong friendship with, and admiration for, Johann Christian Bach (1735–82) during the Mozart family's 15-month stay in London (1764–65) when Mozart was only eight years old. During this period, JC Bach became a central influence on Mozart's musical development, and it is thought that Mozart produced his earliest symphonies under the guidance of Bach at the time.[75] In fact, Bach had a lasting impact on Mozart that can be traced into his mature works.

JC Bach's compositional style reflected the Italian *galant* style that was the fashionable musical trend of the time,[76] a compositional style that Mozart's father, Leopold, was keen to have his young son develop.[77] Bach's direct influence can be seen in several genres, including a set of Mozart's early piano concertos K 107, Nos 1–3 (1772), the aria 'Marten aller Arten' from Act II of *Die Entführung aus dem Serial* (1782) and the andante from Mozart's Piano Concerto No 12 in A major, K 414/385p (1782).

As a young composer advancing his compositional techniques and skills, Mozart looked to JC Bach as a model for composing concertos. Among his earliest endeavours in this genre, Mozart transcribed three of Bach's Opus 5 solo keyboard sonatas (Op 5, Nos 2–4) into the keyboard concertos, K 107 (Nos 1–3). In each of his three concertos, Mozart copied Bach's solo sonatas note for note, mastering the way Bach crafted lyrical themes, tasteful embellishments and harmonic schemes, as well as how Bach employed contrasting themes in sonata-form movements. Essentially, with Bach's keyboard sonatas, the 16-year-old Mozart already had a basic structure that followed the sonata principle,[78] which he could transform into concertos by adding new instrumental ritornellos or tutti sections (here scored for a modest ensemble consisting of first and second violins and cello) and adding light string accompaniment to the existing keyboard sonata material, creating the familiar alternation between the solo and tutti sections of an instrumental concerto. The ritornellos crafted by

[74] Hicks (n 7).

[75] Wyzewa and Saint-Foix posit that Mozart … felt [JC Bach] influence soon after the family arrived in London. It was at first combined with other influences, but "increasingly, until 1768 and beyond, it replaced the influence of the father and of Schobert, *so that John Christian Bach became the only, the true teacher of Mozart*"': H Gärtner, *Johann Christian Bach: Mozart's Friend and Mentor* (RG Pauly trans, Amadeus Press, 1994) 211.

[76] D Heartz, *Music in European Capitals: The Galant Style 1720–1780* (WW Norton, 2003) 904–20.

[77] 'He [Leopold] gave Wolfgang free rein, even encouraging him to return to John Christian Bach, the one person to whom the boy was strongly attracted as a musician and a human being': Gärtner (n 75) 214.

[78] C Rosen, *Sonata Forms* (Norton, 1988).

Mozart consist of repeating Bach's music, introducing the main melodic ideas, which are then played by the solo.[79]

An example of influence and indirect borrowing can be seen in two mature works by Mozart. Mozart models his aria 'Marten aller Arten' from Act II of *Die Entführung aus den Serail* (1782) on JC Bach's aria 'Infelice! In van m'affanno' from Act II of *La clemenza di Scipione* (1778), a powerhouse soprano aria with elaborate concertante parts for flute, oboe, violin and cello, and bravura vocal writing. However, Mozart does not borrow actual existing music from the aria; instead, he imitates the structure, unique scoring and orchestration, texture and virtuosity of 'Infelice!'. Mozart employs the instrumental sections – enlisting the same wind instrument as in Bach's aria – in a manner similar to Bach, having them function as a ritornello that is juxtaposed to the vocal line throughout the aria.[80] Instead of directly quoting or embellishing existing music, Mozart uses Bach's material as a point of departure from which to craft his tour de force aria.

Mozart's Piano Concerto No 12 in A major, K 414/385p (1782), also reflects Bach's continued influence. The central theme of the concerto's second movement directly – but not identically – quotes the theme from the second movement of Bach's opera overture *La calamita de' cuori* (before 1763). The theme is transformed with nuanced changes to the rhythm and harmony of the viola and cello parts, although Bach's original orchestration is retained and the borrowed melody is distinctly recognisable from the start of the movement.[81] The inclusion of this theme could also have been Mozart memorialising Bach, who had died on 1 January 1782, shortly before Mozart's work was composed.[82] Mattheson notes 'That this practice [of quotation] is of no disadvantage to the composer of the original idea, but rather a special honour when a famous person comes upon his ideas and makes from them a true basis of his own music'.[83]

IV. 'Musical Felonies': Piracy and Copyright

I have explored various uses of existing music by composers, how this strategy was an accepted part of the creative paradigm and the important distinction between uses of existing material for transformative imitation and the unacceptable *untransformative* imitation of work to garner benefit that was due to the writer, artist or composer. But where were the bounds of acceptable usage? And where did composers draw the line?

[79] JC Bach, Keyboard Sonatas Op 5 (1766) https://s9.imslp.org/files/imglnks/usimg/6/6a/IMSLP284471-PMLP09626-JC_Bach_-_Six_Sonatas_Opera_5_(Welcker).pdf; WA Mozart, Concerto in E-flat, K107, No 3 (1772), https://imslp.hk/files/imglnks/euimg/2/2f/IMSLP26420-PMLP58730-Mozart_KV_107-3_Piano_concerto_in_E_flat_after_JC_Bach.pdf; Mozart, Concerto in G, K 107, No 2 (1772), https://imslp.hk/files/imglnks/euimg/a/ae/IMSLP26419-PMLP58730-Mozart_KV_107-2_Piano_concerto_in_G_after_JC_Bach.pdf; Mozart, Concerto in D, K 107, No 1 (1772), https://imslp.eu/files/imglnks/euimg/2/2a/IMSLP26418-PMLP58730-Mozart_KV_107,_3_Piano_concertos_after_JC_Bach.pdf.

[80] JC Bach 'Infelice! In van m'affanno, Act II, *La clemenza di Scipione* (1778) 111–28, https://s9.imslp.org/files/imglnks/usimg/c/c0/IMSLP338428-PMLP546132-jc_bach_clemenza_scipione_2.pdf; WA Mozart, 'Marten aller Arten', Act II, *Die Entführung aus den Serail* (1782) 123–59, https://s9.imslp.org/files/imglnks/usimg/6/66/IMSLP365237-PMLP15322-WAMozart_Die_Entführung_aus_dem_Serail,_K384_WAMWS5B7N15.pdf.

[81] JC Bach, *Six Favourite Overtures in 8 Parts for Violins, Hoboys, French Horns, with a Bass for the Harpsicord and Violonecello Compos'd by Sigr Bach, London. Printed for I Walsh in Catharine Street in ye Strand* (1763) https://s9.imslp.org/files/imglnks/usimg/b/b0/IMSLP370640-PMLP598620-jcb_6_fave_overtures00pugn_parts.pdf; W A Mozart, Concerto in A, K 414/385p (1782), https://imslp.hk/files/imglnks/euimg/2/26/IMSLP534109-PMLP15367-Mozart,_Wolfgang_Amadeus-NMA_05_15_3_01_KV_414_scan.pdf.

[82] Letter to his father dated 10 April 1782. E Anderson (ed), *The Letters of Mozart and His Family*, 3rd rev edn (Macmillian, 1985) 799–800.

[83] Mattheson's *Grundlage einer Ehren-Pfote* (1740) quoted in Buelow, 'The Case for Handel's Borrowings' (n 7) 63.

The eighteenth century was also a crucial period for the history of music as a commodity, with composers gaining control over how their music was copied, printed and disseminated. So, where composers such as Arne,[84] Geminiani,[85] Pyle,[86] JC Bach,[87] Abel[88] and Storace[89] 'drew the line' was not at borrowing, but at outright piracy: the production or selling of unauthorised copies or arrangements of works by publishers without the consent (or sometimes even the knowledge) of their creators.[90] The fundamental principle was that borrowing material is acceptable if it is transformed; the untransformative imitation of work in order to reap benefit (pecuniary or otherwise), as noted above, is unacceptable. And so, the composers went to law.

Although use of each other's material for creative purposes was considered acceptable by composers, the wholesale publication of a composer's work by publishers without an agreement was not. Unfortunately, this was a common practice at the time and composers had few legal protections against such predation. A survey of legal suits between *c*1728 and 1792[91] reveals that the primary concern for both composers and publishers was the printing or importing and selling of unauthorised copies or extracts of musical works; or breach of exclusivity contracts.[92] For example, the composer Francesco Geminiani launched a legal action in the early 1730s (thought to be one of the earliest)[93] against music publisher John Walsh to prevent the production of an unauthorised edition of Gemininani's *Six Concertos … Opera Seconda* (1732).[94] In another case, composers JC Bach and Carl Friedrich Abel filed three Bills of Complaint in Chancery against London music publishers and sellers James Longman and Charles Lukey,

[84] *Arne v Roberts and Johnson* (1741, unreported), The National Archives, UK [hereafter TNA] C11/2260/7; see also Rabin and Zohn (n 5).

[85] J Hawkins, *A General History of the Science and Practice of Music*, vol 5 (T Payne, 1776) 247, https://s9.imslp.org/files/imglnks/usimg/a/a9/IMSLP337343-PMLP544570-generalhistoryof05hawk.pdf. Also noted in Rabin and Zohn (n 5) 112–13.

[86] *Pyle v Falkener* (1774, unreported), TNA C12/2082/42 and C33/442. This case centres on the executor of printer John Walsh Jr's estate, John Pyle, who sued the bookseller Robert Falkener for producing unauthorised prints of works by Handel, Arne, Maurice Green and Isaac Bickerstaffe. Rabin and Zohn (n 5) 113.

[87] Transcriptions of core records housed at TNA associated with *Bach v Longman* can be found in van Allen-Russell, 'Documents Relating to Bach vs Longman and Lukey' (n 5).

[88] *Abel v Longman* (1773, unreported), TNA C12/71/6.

[89] *Longman v Storace* (1788, unreported), TNA C12/1703/11; *Storace v Longman* [1788] ER 170: 1069 (2 Camp 27), TNA C12/618/12; *Storace v Longman* (1789, unreported), TNA C12/623/35.

[90] For the definition of 'plagiarize', see n 4.

[91] A sampling of legal actions pursued in the English courts between *c*1728 and 1792 include *Geminiani v Walsh* (*c*1731–32, unreported); *Arne v Roberts and Johnson* (n 84); *Bickerstaff v Thorowgood* (1765, unreported), TNA E112/1596/730; *Bickerstaff v Fought* (1769, unreported), TNA C12/1026/2; *Bickerstaff v Roberts* (1769, unreported), TNA C12/1026/3; *Abel v Longman* (1773, unreported) TNA C12/71/6; *Bach v Longman* [March 1773] ER 98: 1274 (2 Cowp 623) (first suit), TNA C12/71/22; *Bach v Longman* (May 1773, unreported) (second suit), TNA C12/71/22; *Pyle v Falkener* (1774, unreported), TNA C12/2082/42; *Thompson v Falkener* (1776, unreported), TNA C33/446; *Longman v Babb* (1784, unreported), TNA E133/82/26; *Clasuss v Longman* (1785, unreported), TNA C217/134; *Rennett v Longman* and *Rennett v Thompson* (1785, unreported), TNA E133/104/67; *Storace v Longman* [1788] ER 170: 1069 (2 Camp 27); *Storace v Longman* (1789, unreported); *Forster v Longman* (1791, unreported), TNA E133/54/54–55; E133/54/55; E127/1746/4924 E112/1724/4329; *Forster v Longman* (1792, unreported), TNA E133/54/55; *Skillern v Broderip* (1792, unreported), TNA C12/185/34. See also a 'Summary of Legal Cases' in Kassler (n 5) 507–24.

[92] *Forster v Longman* (1791); see also NA Mace, 'Haydn and the London Music Sellers: Forster v Longman & Broderip' (1996) 77 *Music & Letters* 527.

[93] Rabin and Zohn posit that the dispute may have happened in 1731 or 1732. Rabin and Zohn (n 5) 112–13.

[94] There is no extant copy of this Chancery suit in the National Archives, but this dispute is relayed by John Hawkins in his *A General History of the Science and Practice of Music* (1776). One of the reasons that a record of this legal action was not made is that, according to Hawkins, 'Walsh compounded the matter [settled with Geminiani] and the work was published under the inspection of the author'. Thus, some sort of out-of-court agreement was made, probably before Geminiani filed a Bill of Complaint. Hawkins (n 85) 247.

charging them with the unauthorised publication, arrangements and distribution of several of their compositions.[95]

In short, composers wanted what writers had been progressively gaining throughout the eighteenth century: the right to control and benefit from their creative output, including pecuniary benefit, recognition as the rightful creator of the works and control over dissemination of those works. But what intellectual property rights did composers have in England during Bach's time? As John Small explains rather succinctly in his article on the first Bach lawsuit, there were three legal grounds a composer could use as the basis for a copyright infringement suit: the Copyright Act 1710, the common law or a royal warrant.[96]

A royal warrant or privilege was available only by royal grant or application, giving the holder exclusive rights to print, copy, sell and distribute their work. This allowed rights holders to recoup their initial financial outlay and gain some profit without fear of competition. Being the recipient of a royal privilege could also add prestige; noting the royal connection as Music Master to the Court or as a recipient of a royal privilege on the title page added the implication of the monarch's endorsement, and thus could increase sales and lead to new commissions. But even this protection was limited; most privileges were granted to protect newly written works before first publication and were not intended to protect a composer's entire output.[97] Privileges were also generally only issued for a limited time and, as a 'gift of the Crown', they could be revoked at any time.[98] Abel had been granted such a privilege in 1760, as had JC Bach in 1763,[99] but royal warrants were generally only issued for a limited time – in the case of both Bach and Abel, for a period of 14 years – and the right of the Crown to grant these privileges was itself not on firm legal footing, and thus offered little help to composers.

The Act for the Encouragement of Learning, or the Copyright Act 1710 (also known as the 'Act of Anne'), gave an author, or their assigns, 'of any Book or Books already composed, and not printed and published' exclusive publication rights for 14 years from the time of a book's first publication. If the author was still alive at the end of this period, the copyright would automatically be extended for another term of 14 years, giving an author a total of 28 years of copyright.[100] The key aspects of this Act were that it limited the length of copyright and, most importantly, gave the author the copyright to their own material. Unfortunately for composers and music publishers, the Act made no specific mention of music, only of 'Books and other Writings', and the legal basis for composers was again tenuous.

Before the Act of Anne, copyright was protected by common law and was considered unlimited in time because writings, at this level, were considered the intellectual property of the author, or to whomever they sold the rights. It was left to the courts to decide whether material was copyrighted under common law (in perpetuity) or under the Copyright Act (for 14 or 28 years only).

[95] Bach brought two of the legal proceedings. His first suit, filed on 18 March 1773, concerned two keyboard sonatas, one in G major for solo keyboard (sold by Longman & Lukey as *A New Lesson for the Harpsichord or Piano Forte …*) [CW A 10b] and one in F major for keyboard and viola da gamba [CW BN 6b]. The second lawsuit, which concerns the three Op 9 symphonies, was filed two months later, on 6 May 1773. The following day, Abel began his legal proceedings against Longman & Lukey regarding a set of three trios for violin, cello and bass. van Allen-Russell, 'For Instruments Not Intended' (n 5).

[96] J Small, 'JC Bach Goes to Law' (1985) 126 *The Musical Times* 526.

[97] Hunter, 'Music Copyright in Britain to 1800' (n 5).

[98] This information is also noted in A van Allen-Russell, 'Stop Copying My Music!: The Emergence of Musical Copyright in England' (*The Avid Listener* blog, 28 July 2020) theavidlistenerblogcom.wordpress.com/2020/07/28/stop-copying-my-music-the-emergence-of-musical-copyright-in-england/.

[99] Bach's royal warrant, TNA SP44/375, 98–99; Abel's royal warrant, TNA SP44/374.

[100] ER 1: 837 (2 Bro PC 129).

Unfortunately again for both authors and composers, the courts eventually decided that the Act of Anne superseded common law, and the limited term protection would prevail.[101]

A more practical option was used by JC Bach, who countered an unauthorised edition already published – in this case by Robert Bremner, in 1766 – by issuing a so-called 'corrected' edition himself and placing an advertisement stating that the other edition was faulty.[102] This was only of limited effectiveness in most instances, however, and meant that the composer would essentially have to spend both their time *and money* producing their own editions to compete with the unauthorised ones on the market, and those producing the unauthorised versions would still profit.[103]

When Bach and Abel filed their Bills of Complaint against Longman and Lukey in 1773, therefore, it was in the context of an environment with very limited options for composers to protect their own material from misuse. Their arguments focused on presenting their compositions as an expenditure of mental labour and intellectual capital (ideas) in creating goods which belonged to them – ie the printed music – and the injury caused by the unauthorised publication and selling of these works since they could not reap the profits from their labour. This can be seen in the language of their complaints: they each emphasise that the specific works listed had been 'with *great study, labour and expense composed*' and that the works are 'solely of your Orator's *composing and writing, and his absolute and exclusive right and property*'[104] and they '*are the composition writing estate and property* of your said Orator'.[105] Thus, by the selling of pirated copies, Longman and Lukey harmed (or 'wounded') the profits of the two composers: a form of intruding on a particular right.[106]

Initially, in their legal actions, Bach and Abel relied primarily on their royal warrant or privileges and, tacitly, common law protection of their compositions. When this approach failed[107]

[101] *Donaldson v Beckett* [1774] ER 1: 83 (2 Bro PC 129), which ruled that the Copyright Act 1710 negated common law.

[102] Bremner, who published three of Bach's symphonies as part of his Periodical Overture series, got off lightly when he issued an unauthorised edition of Bach's overture in D major as No 15 in the series. *To be continued Monthly The Periodical Overture In 8 Parts, Composed by Sigr Giovanni Cristiano Bach Number XV. Price 2sh London Printed and Sold, by R: Bremner, the Harp and Hautboy, Opposite Somerset-House in the Strand.* RISM A/I B253. DW Jones, 'Robert Bremner and The Periodical Overture' (1978) 7 *Soundings* 66, 72. In this case, Bremner advertised the work on 1 July 1766 in the *Public Advertiser*, and by 4 August JC Bach had placed a notice informing the public that '[t]his overture, having been printed as periodical Overture No 15, and not being correct, the Author thought it proper to have it printed right. To be had at Welcker's Music Shop in Gerrard Street …'. *An Overture in eight Parts Composed by Sigr Giovanni Cristiano Bach London Printed and Sold at Welcker' Musick Shop in Gerrard Street St Ann's Soho Where may be had all the above Author's Works.* RISM A/I B252. Interestingly, neither the Bremner (pirated) nor the Welcker (authorised) edition is error-free; in fact, they are virtually identical. This suggests that Bach was concerned more with Bremner's piracy of the work than with the accuracy of the edition. See also van Allen-Russell, 'For Instruments Not Intended' (n 5) 8.

[103] van Allen-Russell, 'Stop Copying My Music!' (n 98).

[104] van Allen-Russell, 'Documents Relating to Bach vs Longman and Lukey' (n 5); Charles Frederick Abel's first Bill of Complaint, *Abel v Longman*, TNA C12/71/6.

[105] 'the Defendants … have lately in the name of your Orator but without you Orator's Licence and consent printed, published and sold for a very large profit divers copies' of the said compositions … all which actings, [*sic*] doings and pretences that said James Longman and Charles Lukey and Company are contrary to Equity and good conscience and manifestly tend to your Orator's great wrong and injury': van Allen-Russell, 'Documents Relating to Bach vs Longman and Lukey' (n 5); Charles Frederick Abel's first Bill of Complaint (n 104).

[106] Writing in *An Argument in Defence of Literary Property*, printed on 5 February 1774, Francis Hargrave notes that if pirated or unauthorised copies were being sold, the 'right is *wounded* [and] affected' because of the fact that "the profits, which would otherwise arise from the exercise of the right, are *diminished*; and the intruding on this *particular* right is as much a *trespass*, a *tort*, a *fraud*, a *violence*, a *damage*, as an invasion of any *other* incorporeal property can be': F Hargrave, *Argument in Defence of Literary Property* (London, 1774) 19; L Bently and M Kretschmer (eds), *Primary Sources on Copyright (1450–1900)*, www.copyrighthistory.org.

[107] One of the reasons for the failure of their initial legal approach was that an aspect of *Millar v Taylor* questioned the Crown's right to grant privileges in which it did not have a vested interest, asserting that it could not grant a privilege that would create a monopoly for printing, interfering with free market trade. Examples of works in which the Crown was said to have an interest included *Statutes* and *The Book of Common Prayer*. ER 98: 201 (4 Burr 2303).

(as did a petition to Parliament), the composers' counsel explicitly introduced the Act of Anne as a *new* basis for granting relief, forcing the Court of Equity to refer the first of JC Bach's two suits to the King's Bench as any legal ruling would establish a key point of law. At long last, in June 1777, the ruling of the King's Bench did establish that music was protected under the 1710 Copyright Act. The ruling declared that:

> Music is a science; it may be written; and the mode of conveying the ideas, is by signs and marks. A person may use the copy by playing it; but he has not right to rob the author of the profit, by multiplying copies and disposing of them to his own use. If the narrow interpretation contended for the argument were to hold, it would equally apply to algebra, mathematics, arithmetic, [and] hieroglyphics. All these are conveyed by signs and figures. There is no colour for saying that music is not within the Act ... we are of opinion, that a musical composition is a writing within the Statute of the 8th of Queen Anne ...[108]

The change in the legal tack and the language used indicate a deliberate shift in not only the legal approach, but the understanding of the issue of music as intellectual property. The original approach focused on the use of what limited privilege the composers held (or believed they held) as granted to them personally by the Crown. As the arguments became more wedded to the debates concurrently taking place by booksellers, the concept of music as a form of writing – and thus a 'labour of the mind and production of the brain' – became more central to their approach; the suits were no longer just about mere pursuit of compensation for wrongful use of specific pieces of music, but rather about resolving the fundamental legal principle of ownership of both the physical property and the 'labour of the mind', thus establishing their right to control the use of all their music, for the present and in the future. Bach and Abel may not have been the driving force behind the concept of writing as property, but their efforts established music as both writing *and* property at a time when it was considered to be neither.

The establishment of musical copyright because of the Bach and Abel suits did not mark an end to borrowing of existing material by composers, but it was perhaps the beginning of the end, setting off a long evolution of legal and social consideration of music as intellectual property under the strict control of its creator. Borrowing continued to be a source of innovation to various extents up to the present day, and existing works continue to spur new ones in new and innovative ways (as the current use of sampling demonstrates).

[108] King's Bench Hearing, 10 June 1777. ER 98: 1274–75 (2 Cowp 624).

Section B: Americas

13

Remix, Reuse and Reggae: Creativity and Copyright in Jamaican Music

ENRICO BONADIO AND BRYAN KHAN

I. Introduction: A Very Brief History

What makes the story of the rise of reggae music so fascinating are the circumstances in which the genre evolved. It seems to have been birthed by a cosmic alignment of the right social and cultural factors, rather than an anticipatable evolution of existing cultural institutions. Unlike neighbouring islands, which had hosted vibrant creole musical cultures since the nineteenth century, a formal music scene was not a major component of the Jamaican cultural landscape until the mid-twentieth century.[1] The Jamaican people, however, always had a poetic, vibrant and expressive creole culture, which seemed to just need the right circumstances to channel into a revolutionary artistic movement.

Jamaican folk music takes the form of 'mento', a style partially related to the 'calypso' of the more southern Caribbean islands, but distinct in its instrumentation. In fact, many early mento records from the 1940s and 1950s were marketed as 'Jamaican calypso'.[2] However, in the 1940s, the Jamaican music scene was much less developed than that of the other islands. It was comprised mostly of jazz musicians playing American jazz and rhythm and blues standards for tourists and the upper class.

The popular trend in the youth culture was American 'jump blues', an up-tempo form of blues which evolved from boogie-woogie and swing music, and would later come to influence the birth of rock 'n' roll and modern R&B. The infrastructure for musical entertainment was limited – the country was not developed enough for personal record players, live entertainment venues or record stores to be common. It is within this setting that the quintessential Jamaican institution evolved to fill this gap – the 'sound system'.[3] Sound systems were assemblies of amplifiers, speakers and turntables which were designed to be mobile discotheques, bringing live entertainment to the youth wherever they might choose to gather. Sound systems would evolve into their own social and cultural phenomenon, where each system had an associated crew and an entire informal economy associated with its mobilisation through the streets.

[1] P Manuel and M Largey, *Caribbean Currents – Caribbean Music from Rumba to Reggae*, 3rd edn (Temple University Press, 2016) 180, 187.

[2] R Hitchins, *Vibe Merchants: The Sound Creators of Jamaican Popular Music* (Routledge, 2014) 16.

[3] Manual and Largey (n 1) 187.

In this competitive environment, a few systems and proprietors rose to dominate the 1950s scene and earn great social influence. The history of reggae can never be told without explicit reference to some of the most prominent of sound system proprietors – Arthur 'Duke' Reid, Clement 'Sir Coxsone' Dodd and Prince Buster.

At the centre of a sound system's popularity was the repertoire of records that it had access to play. Sound system selectors kept close guard of their records so that rivals could not figure out what records it possessed, and their 'mic men' or deejays hyped the crowds in parties which were held in the streets or makeshift dancehalls. Official labels were often scratched off records to prevent spying, and operators would write in their own identifying details. Competition had multiple dimensions – loudness, a selector's deejaying ability, a mic man's hype skills and, of course, having access to the best and latest records. Innovativeness and creativity would drive the construction of bigger and better speakers, and the natural charisma of Jamaican youth would drive the hype and skills of deejays and mic men. The constraint, however, remained access to American records, which were costly and difficult to come by. This was made even more challenging by trends in American popular music, which began to shift to rock 'n' roll and soul music by the 1960s.[4]

The inevitable solution was for sound system proprietors to invest in their own studios, and act as small-scale record labels. Duke Reid's Trojan Sound System evolved into the Treasure Isle Label, and Coxsone Dodd's Downbeat Sound System evolved into Studio One. These studios would recruit musicians to perform songs – generally covers of the popular American songs of the day – often producing a single copy of a record ('dubplate' or 'special') on an acetate disc, without mass production on vinyl. So, each sound system would have its own unique stream of recorded songs. As the market grew, copies of successful records would also be sold publicly through retail channels.

The next phase of Jamaican music centred around a simple but revolutionary musical trend. Performing musicians on melodic instruments such as the guitar or horns began to place more and more emphasis on the 'upbeat', whilst the rhythm section of drums and bass maintained a strong and consistent groove. And so the musical force known as 'ska' was born. While musicologists debate the exact origins of this rhythmic twist,[5] this shift most certainly transformed Jamaican music from amateur renditions of popular American songs, especially R&B, to an entirely new, expressive genre.

The proliferation of ska music coincided with Jamaica's independence in 1962 and provided a soundtrack for the young, aspiring nation. With the rise of the popular local art form, recordings moved away from mere renditions of existing songs, and original compositions began to reflect the challenges of poverty and lack of social mobility in the urban jungles of Kingston. Subsequently, by 1966, the tempos had begun to slow down, giving rise to 'rocksteady', an intermediary genre between ska and reggae.

Reggae music was later poised to take over the world. It provided a cultural voice from the developing world in an era where self-determination and independence movements were thriving, and counter-cultural art and philosophy was the popular youth culture of the Western world. The genre attracted the attention of major British record labels such as Island Records (founded in Jamaica by Chris Blackwell in the early 1960s), which would go on to invest heavily in promoting and exporting Jamaican music to the wider world. The early 1970s then saw reggae develop into a global phenomenon on its own. In particular, 1972 saw two important events, first

[4] ibid 189.
[5] ibid 190.

with the release of the film *The Harder They Come*, starring Jimmy Cliff, which would become a cult cinema classic with a reggae soundtrack, and second with the signing of Bob Marley to Island Records. The decade also saw continued musical innovation at home. Sound system deejays would play instrumental recordings from the B-sides of records, while their mic men would improvise (or 'toast') over the music. At the same time, sound engineers (such as the pioneer King Tubby) and studio producers (especially Lee Perry) began experimenting with new production and remixing techniques, applying filters, heavy reverb and echo effects to existing recordings to achieve surrealist soundscapes, giving rise to the genre of 'dub'. Throughout the 1970s, reggae music assumed more conscious, militant and revolutionary connotations, with lyrics openly embracing Rastafarianism, including references to black liberation and repatriation to Africa. This is the so-called 'roots reggae', a genre characterised by the dropping of the bass drum emphasis, which typically falls on the first beat of a measure ('one drop beat').[6]

Sadly, by the end of the 1970s, the social and cultural boom that coalesced around reggae music began to collapse. The eccentric and eminent producer Lee Perry allegedly burnt down his famous Black Ark studio in 1979, and Bob Marley – the face of the global reggae movement – died in 1981. Jamaica experienced extremely violent general elections in the 1970s and then once again in 1980 which saw mass gang violence fuelled by political rivalries. Local musical trends shifted away from roots reggae, and by the mid-1980s, dancehall became the dominant youth culture soundtrack, with its glorification of violence, urban gang culture and overt sexuality. Reggae's global relevance nevertheless still held strong, influencing burgeoning musical movements all over the world from punk rock, two-tone, and drum and bass in England to hip-hop in the urban hubs of the USA, reflecting the cultural impact of Caribbean migrants to these areas.

Today, reggae and its progeny maintain a strong global presence, with a multitude of international scenes in which it has fused with other indigenous art forms. All over the world, reggae music remains a constantly recognised and respected genre of popular music, as well as a reflection of Jamaican cultural identity.

II. Enabling Creativity: Market Dynamics

A. Role of the Sound System

The unique role of sound systems contrasts with many of the assumptions that one might hold about how new artistic movements form. The sound system began as an entrepreneurial endeavour by simply acting as a mobile discotheque for playing recorded music. It quickly developed into an art form of its own, with sound system design and deejaying embodying unique creative skills. In that setting, traditional musical performance was almost an afterthought, much less actual musical composition.

Actual musical performance was originally limited to studios, and live bands only played an important role at a later stage when the genre had grown and artists would tour outside of Jamaica. This is most certainly an inversion of the more common story, where live performance fuels a new art form, which is only later documented in recorded form. In the early days of ska, rocksteady and reggae, it is the recorded form that took precedence. Furthermore, records were produced to give sound systems a stream of new content to play, rather than to create a

[6] ibid 192.

physical product to sell to consumers. Playing pre-released songs on sound systems gave labels a unique mechanism to test the popularity of a song and determine if mass production for retail was commercially viable. Unique acetate pressings were produced to enhance the reputation of a sound system through exclusivity in access to musical works and recordings. Thus, recorded music as a sound system product can be seen as the antithesis of mass production of commercial records.[7] As summarised by Toynbee, industry organisation and innovation were largely determined by this specialised form of end use (public performance of records for sound system dancers).[8]

Even after recordings were made more widely available through retail, the practice of producing 'specials' would persist, whereby an artist would record a version of a song which promoted a specific sound system. While this practice became particularly prevalent in the 1990s dancehall scene, examples can be found from the earliest days of ska. For example, the early ska song 'On the Beach' by Owen Gray (circa 1961, Coxsone Records) contains the refrain 'I was dancing to the music of Sir Coxone the Downbeat, on the beach'.

This tradition continues to today, with reggae and dancehall artists recording short promotional clips for deejays and sound systems. Recording 'dubplates' has even grown into an industry of its own, with studios and managers specialising in acting as intermediaries between performing artists and clients such as radio stations or even commercial advertisers. It is a common practice for Caribbean artists to include time in their touring schedule to visit local studios to 'cut' exclusive 'dubplate' endorsements for local clients and earn further income. Often, promotional dubplates use the melodic hook of an artist's popular hit, working the name of the client into the lyrics, which often boast of their superiority over competitors. However, while the artist is the performer who made a melodic line popular, they are not necessarily the author or owner in the copyright sense. Furthermore, dubplates might be performed on the musical bed of the original song or a popular instrumental. Recording dubplates therefore involves a musical reproduction which is not necessarily authorised in copyright terms but is nevertheless a culturally accepted practice.

As mentioned, another notable aspect of early sound system culture was the practice of physically scratching off the labels of records so that competitors could not ascertain a selector's repertoire. In modern copyright law, 'technological protection measures' (TPMs) are mechanisms used to prevent unauthorised use and maintain the integrity of 'rights management information' (RMI), which is necessary for copyright administration. From the perspective of the original rights holders, label scratching may be compared to an infringement of their RMI and a possible violation of their moral right of attribution, as the information necessary to determine the authors, performers and record labels is intentionally destroyed. Deejays removing this information and scribbling in their own reference codes could also be considered akin to a form of TPM. The measure in this case protects the sound system's exclusivity in access to and ownership of the specific record. In fact, the exact collection of records owned by sound system would likely constitute a 'trade secret' in modern intellectual property (IP) law – the information is valuable because it is secret, it is known by a limited number of persons and the sound system takes explicit steps to keep this information secret.

[7] Hitchins (n 2) 33.

[8] J Toynbee, 'Reggae Open Source: How the Absence of Copyright Enabled the Emergence of Popular Music in Jamaica' in L Bently, J Davis and J Ginsburg (eds), *Copyright and Piracy: An Interdisciplinary Critique* (Cambridge University Press, 2010) 358.

B. Producers, Performers and Contracts

The standard model in Western popular music is that a songwriter composes a song and uses a publisher to seek out record labels that wish to have the song performed and recorded. In some cases, songwriters would themselves be performers seeking out recording contracts. The assumed logic is that competition in song writing and performance is what drives musical creativity in the commercial setting of popular music. The evolution of Jamaican music inverts this model, as development of the industry was driven by competition in the distribution of music through sound system communications, not competition between artists and performers themselves.

As the sound system proprietor became a recording studio owner, they essentially functioned as small-scale record labels, seeking out new performers and assembling house bands to support recording sessions. By owning both sound systems and recording studios, proprietors monopolised both the channels of music production and its distribution, and thus held significant economic, social and cultural power.

In the early ska era, producers would find performers to do localised versions of existing songs recorded in the USA. As the industry progressed, producers would work with artists to produce original compositions. Record producers usually did not pay artists (or at least pay them appropriately well), and the concept of contractual agreements was unfamiliar to young singers, many coming from the impoverished settlements of Kingston. While most studios had a standing ensemble of supporting performers as a 'house band', session musicians often worked with different studios and producers. In principle, musicians were sometimes contracted as part-time employees to a single studio or label, but in practice, they moved between projects fluidly.

As argued by Toynbee,[9] in this setting it was the labour market conditions and not the IP that were the driver of creativity. This is not to say, however, that IP played no role. Cunning producers would take advantage of the open creative social norms and performers' lack of education and would register foreign copyrights for original compositions in their own names. Distribution agreements with foreign record labels like the English Blue Beat Records and Trojan Records helped not only in the popularisation of ska and reggae in foreign markets, but also in providing a source of revenue for local studios and sound systems. What was created was thus a dual attitude to copyright – the local market operated as if copyright did not exist, while in foreign markets, producers entered into licensing agreements. The legitimacy of these licensing agreements, however, was questionable, as producers presented themselves as the sole owners of the copyrights, irrespective of actual authorship and the creative roles played by performing artists.

We can draw insights into these practices from the *Oh Carolina* case. The song 'Oh Carolina' was originally recorded by the Folkes Brothers, produced by Prince Buster and released on his Wild Bells label in 1960. The song was later covered by Shaggy in 1992 and became an international hit and one of the most popular reggae pop songs of the 1990s. Litigation ensued before the UK courts between Greensleeves (the label and publishing company to which Shaggy was attached), John Folkes and Prince Buster concerning authorship of the song. Prince Buster claimed that he composed the song and was entitled to any ensuing royalties. John Folkes, however, claimed that he had written the song as a teenager in 1958, had been denied royalties or any contractual agreement with Buster and had only obtained a payment of £60 after a confrontation between the two. The court accepted John Folkes's version of the events, ruling that he was the sole composer and that his 1993 copyright assignment to Greensleeves Publishing was valid. In its judgment,

[9] ibid (generally).

the court took specific note of Prince Buster's 'unattractive behaviour', where he 'appeared to be willing to take the chance on an incorrect registration in the full knowledge that he was not, contrary to the relevant entry, the sole composer'.[10] This case exemplifies the exploitative practices employed by record producers in the early Jamaican music industry, where composers were denied rightful recognition of their authorship, performers were denied reasonable remuneration and access to contractual certainty, and producers made false declarations in copyright registration systems for their illegitimate benefit.

Frustrations regarding insufficient compensation became such a common theme in the ska and rocksteady industry that the premise of the 1972 film *Harder They Come* was that Jimmy Cliff's character turns to crime after he is paid only $20 for his best song.

III. Traditions of Borrowing

While market conditions in both creative labour (performing artists) and distribution (sound systems) produced the enabling environment to drive creativity, the development of the art form itself centred around a permissive culture of musical borrowing. Toynbee describes Jamaican musicians as prolific copiers, open with their imitation, which is understood as a perfectly legitimate method for creating new music.[11] In this environment, although IP rights played a minor role, there was still a strong competitive advantage to being the first to market with a new sound.[12] As such, the industry produced a very high rate of musical innovation facilitated by traditions of musical borrowing.

Generally, the sentiment was that competing musicians and producers understood that objecting to others using 'their' creative output was not reasonable, as the resulting growth of the market was in everyone's best interests.[13] Even competitors Coxsone Dodd and Duke Reid, whose intense rivalry shaped the history of ska and reggae, would cooperate with each other when needed.[14] In this way, the development of the industry was characterised by a 'dynamic blend of competition and cooperation', and the absence of a major role for conventional IP norms.[15]

A. Versioning

The clearest form of musical borrowing in reggae is the practice of 'versioning', in which local artists would record their own versions of popular songs. Indeed, it is this practice that facilitated the birth of the local recording industry and created the foundation for it to grow and for producers and recording engineers to develop their technical skills. These versions were generally created with neither concern for attributing credit to the original songwriters nor the seeking of formal authorisation, much less the payment of any royalties.

Versioning was so widespread that there would often be several versions of the same song released around the same time – each with its own unique performance details.[16] For example, in 1976, there were no fewer than 25 versions of the song 'I'm Still in Love with You', performed

[10] *Greensleeves Records Ltd & Anor v Melodisc Music Ltd & Ors* [1993] CH G 4177 – High Court of London.
[11] Toynbee (n 8) 365.
[12] ibid 362–63.
[13] ibid 370.
[14] D Katz, *Solid Foundation: An Oral History of Reggae* (Bloomsbury, 2012) 71.
[15] Toynbee (n 8) 359.
[16] D Hebdige, *Cut'n'mix: Culture, Identity and Caribbean Music* (Routledge, 1987) 12.

by different artists in rotation, on the Jamaican market.[17] Hebdige speaks about versioning in the context of quotation, where a song takes on a new life with each version, as new musical elements are brought in by different performers. Versioning is therefore democratic as no one artist has the final say, no version is treated as definitive and everyone has an opportunity to contribute.[18]

While the dominant trend was versioning and covering without legal consequence, there have been a few notable cases of copyright litigation for unauthorised versioning since the early 1980s. The story of reggae producer Joe Gibbs has become an infamous anecdotal example of this. The song 'Someone Loves You Honey' was written by Don Devaney and popularised by a 1978 recording by country artist Charlie Pride. In the tradition of reggae versioning, Joe Gibbs produced a rendition of the song performed by JC Lodge and released by Gibbs's Belmont Records in 1980. After this version became a hit, Gibbs was sued by the original rights holders, which supposedly resulted in such financial loss that he had to close his operations in Miami and return to Kingston.[19]

Versioning would result not only in otherwise obscure R&B songs becoming major hits in Jamaica, but also in ska breaking into international markets. A particularly important example is the 1950s pop song 'My Boy Lollypop', which was first recorded by Barbie Gaye in 1956. The song was re-recorded by Jamaican teenager Millie Small in London 1964, and became the first major international ska hit and one of the best selling reggae–ska records of all time. Another classic example is the rocksteady version of 'You Don't Love Me', performed and recorded by Dawn Penn in 1967. Penn was introduced to the song by Coxsone Dodd, who had imported the original blues record 'You Don't Love Me' (recorded by Willie Cobbs in 1960, and itself an adaptation of Bo Diddley's 1955 'She's Fine She's Mine') to play in his sound system. Penn later re-recorded a dancehall version in 1994 which became an international hit. While the lyrics and melody of this song clearly derive from versioning, the international success of the song led to disputes between Dodd (original producer of the 1967 version) and Steely and Clevie (producers of the 1994 version) regarding the rights in the arrangement and musical backing track.[20]

The tradition of versioning later evolved into the covering of classic ska, rocksteady and reggae songs, particularly in musical scenes emerging in the 1970s. Notable examples include Eric Clapton's 1974 'I Shot the Sheriff', covering Bob Marley and the Wailers' hit of 1973; UK punk legends the Clash covering Junior Murvin's 1976 'Police and Thieves' in 1977; and American new wave/punk band Blondie versioning the Paragons' 1967 'Tide Is High' in 1980. More extensively, the entire genre of 'second wave ska' (or 'two-tone') that emerged in the UK was based on versioning first generation Jamaican ska songs.

B. The Role of Riddims

In typical popular music, a song is composed of an instrumental musical bed and a vocal performance – a 'riddim' and a 'voicing', in the parlance of Jamaican music. Over time, reuse of the same musical riddims has become a cornerstone of the Jamaican music scene. In fact, the notion of the riddim has taken on the status of an art form itself, and the riddim is seen as its own autonomous creative entity.[21] Famous riddims like the Real Rock Riddim have been used on

[17] ibid 87.

[18] ibid 14.

[19] This story is related in various accounts of the career of Joe Gibbs. See, eg 'Joe Gibb: Celebrated Jamaican Record Producer' *The Guardian* (29 April 2008).

[20] Hitchins (n 2) 136.

[21] See generally P Manuel and W Marshall, 'The Riddim Method: Aesthetics, Practice, and Ownership in Jamaican Dancehall' (2006) 25 *Popular Music* 447.

hundreds of recordings and are so instantly recognisable that they are synonymous with reggae itself. While the practice is mostly associated with dancehall music, the riddim method traces back to practices of musical reuse in early ska. For example, the music and lyrical theme of 'Stop that Train' (allegedly recorded by the Spanishtonians in 1965) was reinterpreted by several other ska and reggae artists, and its backing music has now risen to the status of a riddim. Over time, the riddim method has also become standard in other modern Caribbean musical genres, such as Trinidadian soca.

This practice partially emerged from sound system culture in several ways. There was high demand for new songs and a need for fast turnover in recording to enable sound systems to compete. However, recording was – and still is to an extent – an expensive and time-consuming endeavour, especially when it involves the coordination of multiple session musicians playing live instruments for accompaniment. Furthermore, a producer would not know if a new record would be a hit until there was an opportunity to test a pre-release version with sound system audiences. These factors all give the producer an incentive to reuse instrumental tracks with new voicings by different performing artists. Additionally, the practice of publishing records with an instrumental B-side – popularised in the early 1970s – created pools of instrumental tracks that performers could (re)use. One commentor suggests that use of riddims became so prolific that by 1983, almost no Jamaican recording had a completely original rhythm track, so restrictions on riddims could not be allowed as this would endanger the very existence of the sound system model.[22]

An even more important influence was the emergence of 'toasting', pioneered by several deejays in the 1960s (such as Sir Lord Comic and King Stitt) and 1970s (including U Roy). Toasting is the practice of improvising short, rhythmic phrases over a record played by a selector, often in a monotone fashion that contrasts with traditional singing. The practice likely draws from West African traditions of call and response chants, and partially evolved from mic men simply hyping up the audience. Young performers would wait next to a sound system selector for a chance to be passed the mic and display their toasting skills. The practice grew from toasting a few phrases on existing songs, to voicing on instrumental B-side tracks, to recording these performances in the studio – which would become the new genre of dancehall. A useful illustrative example is the 1976 recorded song 'Natty Rebel' by U-Roy. In 1976, the roots reggae band the Gladiators recorded a version of 'Soul Rebel' (originally written and recorded by Bob Marley and the Wailers in 1970). U-Roy recorded his toasts on top of the Gladiator's version to create 'Natty Rebel', with the Gladiators' original vocals still underneath the track, treating the entire recording as a musical bed.

The use of riddims democratised the music scene in several ways. It made recording more affordable as a pre-existing musical bed is used, while both established artists and newcomers have access to the same riddims for voicing. As riddims are often named after the first (or biggest) songs which use them, being first to voice on a riddim creates a sort of first-to-market advantage, where subsequent reuse would reinforce the popularity of the first song, rather than competing with it. In this creative system, (re)use of riddims is not only allowed, but actively encouraged.

It was even common for competing producers to re-record ('re-lick') their own versions of popular riddims, particularly with Coxone Dodd's Studio One catalogue.[23] This was perhaps

[22] S Daynes, *Time and Memory in Reggae Music: The Politics of Hope* (Manchester University Press, 2011) 772–73.

[23] Okpaluba suggests that local producers were not so tolerant of other's re-licking their riddims, and this drove competition between producers to remake and update riddims and release them first. J Okpaluba, 'Free-Riding on the Riddim'? Open Source, Copyright Law and Reggae Music in Jamaica' in Bently et al (n 8) 380. In particular, rivalry between Channel One and Studio One led to a constant race to re-lick riddims in the absence of copyright enforcement: Manuel and Marshall (n 21) 463.

tolerated by major local producers as demanding compensation for re-licked riddims would validate the anger of musicians and vocalists frustrated at the lack of royalties. A cunning producer might seek to manage a delicate balance between the practice of open copying locally and obtaining profitable international publishing licences less immediately visible to the public. Furthermore, re-licking of riddims can be seen as a sign of respect for high-quality work, which boosts the reputation of the producer and the prestige of the original version.[24]

An interesting (albeit unintended) result of the riddim model is that a mechanism is created for songs to be co-marketed and co-distributed. In a dancehall or radio setting, selectors/deejays 'juggle' songs, meaning that they play several songs on the same riddim in sequence and use their skills in mixing to seamlessly fade from one track into another, essentially creating a lengthy medley. In this way, songs on the same riddim are complementary to one another, rather than being in direct competition.

While the practice of riddim reuse might seem to parallel the practices of mixtape production and sampling in hip-hop music, it differs in a few ways.[25] In reggae, the use of another producer's beats is not framed as an act of appropriation, but rather an act of participating in a collective art form. Furthermore, while hip-hop is a genre based heavily on sampling, the social norm in hip-hop is that it is taboo to sample a record which another producer has already sampled. Thus, hip-hop producers intentionally search for obscure records to sample. This contrasts sharply with reggae and dancehall, where repeated sampling of the same works is the cultural norm.

C. A Commons of Musical Motifs

All musical genres are defined by common stylistic elements of instrumentation, arrangement, performance techniques and overall aesthetics. In some cases, there might also be certain musical motifs which are commonly and repeatedly reused. Common elements might range from abstract non-copyrightable performance ideas to specific copyright-eligible melodies and lyrical phrases. The history of reggae music reflects social norms of musical borrowing, where such elements are used and reused across different generations of artists paying homage to the roots of reggae and its associated subgenres.

In essence, over time, a 'common pool' of musical elements has emerged from which all artists are free to draw. These motifs often originate as elements of specific songs or riddims which achieve the status of iconic works, and are subsequently and repeatedly reused and transformed. Even where the original elements are copyright protectable, repeated creative reuse eventually leads to them becoming transformed into genre-specific common motifs. In contrast with modern Western attitudes of individual authorship, social norms acknowledge the cumulative nature of creativity which historically drove the evolution of reggae music, and this process does not just operate on the level of individual works borrowing from other individual works. Repeated borrowing creates networks of thematic and overlapping interrelations which create a distinctive continuity within the genre itself.

[24] D Howard, 'Copyright and the Music Business in Jamaica – Protection for Whom? Revista Brasileira do Caribe' (2009) IX(18) *Brasília* 503, 514.

[25] Vaidhyanathan discusses how Caribbean migrants to New York influenced the culture of hip-hop, and notes that the practice of versioning can be seen as a direct influence on rap music's tradition of sampling. S Vaidhyanathan, *Copyrights and Copywrongs: The Rise of Intellectual Property and How it Threatens Creativity* (New York University Press, 2001) 136.

(i) 'Stalag 17' and 'Bam Bam'

To illustrate this phenomenon, we take the example of the iconic Stalag Riddim. The riddim traces back to an instrumental track titled 'Stalag 17', which was composed and performed by Ansel Collins and released in 1973 by Winston Riley on his Techniques Records label. Several years before, in 1966, reggae icons the Maytals released a song called 'Bam Bam'. While 'Stalag 17' was not based on 'Bam Bam', the two songs are structured around repeated bass lines with similar rhymical structures. The rhythm section of 'Stalag 17' was sampled to form what would become Riley's Stalag Riddim, one of the most recognisable reggae riddims of all time.

In 1982, the song 'Bam Bam', performed by Sister Nancy, was released by Riley on Techniques Records. The hook of Sister Nancy's 'Bam Bam' drew on the vocal refrain of the Maytals' song of the same name and was voiced on the Stalag Riddim. The song has since taken on a life of its own, becoming one of the most iconic tracks in reggae history, and has been sampled endlessly in different genres. In the sub-genre of dub, the song has become a common backbone for dub remixing practices as its own art form.

Yet another classic reggae song on the Stalag Riddim is Tenor Saw's 'Ring the Alarm', released in 1985 under Techniques Records. The refrain of 'Ring the alarm, another sound is dying' has become an iconic phrase encapsulating sound clash culture and has been reused by several artists across musical genres, from hip-hop artist Mos Def to post-hardcore band Fugazi. Aside from the massive success and influence of 'Bam Bam' and 'Ring the Alarm', the Stalag Riddim itself has become iconic, and has been repeatedly deconstructed, recreated and reproduced over the decades by different producers in different genres of music.

The riddim's influence is so deep that the very bass line around which it is structured has been effectively transformed into part of the common pool of stock reggae grooves. Though the melody is simple and generic, its rhythmic structure has become a defining template for reggae bass lines.

A slightly modified version of the 'Stalag 17' bass line is the main element in the Bam Bam Riddim, whose name alludes to a connection not only with the Stalag Riddim, but the original 'Bam Bam' song by the Maytals. The most popular song on the Bam Bam Riddim is 1992's 'Murder She Wrote' by Chaka Demus & Pliers, produced by Sly and Robbie. Pliers – half of the group Chaka Demus & Pliers – even recorded his own version of the Maytals' original 'Bam Bam' in 1992, on the same Bam Bam Riddim that the hit 'Murder She Wrote' was performed on.

With these series of performances and recordings, Ansel Collins's 'Stalag 17' and the Maytals' 'Bam Bam', two distinct and separate works, became intertwined through the organic evolution of musical themes based on creative borrowing, facilitating new generations of works which draw indirectly from their influence. This is a prime example of how elements of distinct works form part of a greater continuity of musical themes within reggae music, with a significance that transcends the original works from which they are derived. This is particularly important for a cultural setting that embraced social authorship, where continuity between recordings is more important than isolated originality.[26]

(ii) Interpreting Reuse of Elements

Reuse of musical elements represents homage to the original artist where there is clear attributability, and where the reuse is closer to the 'source' of the original work both culturally and stylistically. The further the original and reuse are, however, the more likely the reuse is to be seen

[26] Toynbee (n 8) 359.

as drawing on a musical common rather than homage. Vocal melodies – which are inherently more closely connected to a particular artist than instrumental elements – are also more associated with homage, while bass lines and grooves are the most likely musical elements to form part of the reggae commons.

In this regard, one can observe that this kind of reuse tends not to be within a sub-genre of the same era, but between newer genres and the predecessors that influenced them. Elements of ska and rocksteady are reused in roots reggae, elements of roots reggae are reused in dancehall and elements of dancehall are reused in hip-hop. This creates a sort of inter-generational thematic continuity and cultural legitimacy across various genres associated with or inspired by Jamaican music. The nature of creative borrowing is therefore not only direct, but also indirect and cumulative, with an impact that goes much beyond the boundaries of the genre of reggae itself.

IV. Enabling Creativity: Social Dynamics

A. Anti-Babylon Ethics

The history of reggae is intertwined with the cultural system of the Rastafari religion.[27] While Rastafari had existed in Jamaica since the 1930s, its growth coincided with the development of reggae music. Rastafari was originally rejected by the musical establishment, which, like wider Jamaican society, saw Rastafarians as esoteric social outcasts. For example, it is said that Duke Reid forbade Rastafari lyrics from being recorded in his studio. Over time, however, Rastafari would have a musical influence on reggae, infusing African Kumina rhythms into song arrangements. The Rastafari percussionist Count Ossie was recruited by Prince Buster and came from the camp he founded on the Wareika Hills to play drums on Buster's recordings. His drumming performance can be heard on the above-mentioned Folkes Brothers' 1959 'Oh Carolina' record. By the 1970s, reggae had become intertwined with Rastafari culture, and common lyrical themes grew out of this association, such as messages of black identity, peace and harmony, and the consumption of cannabis.

Inherent in the culture of roots reggae was a message of decolonisation and black liberation which manifests in the rejection of 'Babylon' – a term used by Rastafarians to refer to oppressive institutions such as colonial power structures, the police and the Catholic Orthodoxy seen as responsible for trans-Atlantic slavery. Repudiation of Babylon is therefore not just a lyrical theme, but an ethical position, and to 'burn/chant down Babylon' is not just a political imperative, but an artistic goal in a space where culture is inherently political. It is this anti-Babylon ethos that would reinforce the lack of contractual relationships between composers, performers and producers. While such free-spirited relations allowed for artists to maintain their cultural values and freedoms, they facilitated producers' unethical and often exploitative business practices.

In the lawsuit started by Aston 'Family Man' Barrett against the Marley estate and Island Records regarding the contractual arrangements for royalties between the members of Bob Marley's band the Wailers, the High Court of London in 2006 noted that 'The Wailers were, on the whole, not interested in business or contracts'. Commenting on payment arrangements between the band, Wailers guitarist Junior Marvin stated that he did not approach Marley because the band was about 'One Love' and not the 'Babylon style of making money'.[28]

[27] For an overview of the Rastafari religion and its links to Jamaican culture and history, see B Chevannes, *Rastafari: Roots and Ideology* (Syracuse University Press, 1994).

[28] See the decision in *Barrett v Universal-Island Records Ltd* [2006] EMLR 21, para 84.

An aversion to contractual agreements was thus common across the reggae industry (with some exceptions), and spreading the message of self-determination and one love[29] provided an intrinsic motivation for creativity without the need for the commercial incentives enabled by copyright and contracts.

On the issue of cultural and political values, the anti-imperialist, liberation-based ethos of Rastafari had strong anti-capitalist undertones, especially in the Cold War environment of the 1960s/70s. Furthermore, Orthodox Rastafari came from a tradition of communal living which places focus on collective responsibility and notions of community. Rastafarians themselves, however, reject convention political labels, as 'isms' and 'schisms' themselves are seen as tools of Babylon. These values may have had a social role in reinforcing the practices of open musical borrowing, where asserting private rights on an individual basis would be viewed as a Babylonian act. In this setting, the Western capitalistic notion of copyright and individual authorship would certainly not fit within the cultural framework of vintage Jamaican music, particularly the subset associated with Rastafari.

While these anti-property ethics may have contributed to cultural and creative progress, they also created future problems for the industry. Many prolific recording artists, including Bob Marley himself, died with no will and many children, creating a messy web for both copyright and succession law to sort out.

B. Dispute Settlement

While legal cases were not a common feature of the early Jamaican music industry, disputes between artists and producers most certainly existed. As in any community, conflicts might result from perceived disingenuous imitation, pure competition or failed business relationships. In many cases, however, these conflicts were resolved through music itself, further fuelling creative dynamics.

(i) Lee Perry v Joe Gibbs

One example is the well-known feud between producers Joe Gibbs and Lee 'Scratch' Perry. In fact, Lee Perry had a history of feuding with other producers, and previously had a dispute with Duke Reid's claim to authorship of Stranger Cole's 1962 ska hit 'Rough and Tough'.[30]

Perry and Gibbs had worked together in the mid-1960s, but after some disagreement, Perry left to form his own label, Upsetter Records. The new label's first release was a 1968 song authored and performed by Perry himself titled 'People Funny Boy'. The song was a parody of the Pioneers' recently released 'Long Shot', using the song's melody and lyrical structure. 'Long Shot' was in fact a song that Perry had helped craft for Gibbs, which made Gibbs very financially successful from the Pioneers' success.[31] 'People Funny Boy' is a direct attack on Gibbs for his perceived unappreciative ways, and innovatively contains a sample of a baby crying, which is interpreted as making fun of Gibbs.

[29] 'One Love' is an expression in Rastafarian/Jamaican culture which refers to the ethos of peace, love, harmony and inclusion. The phrase was very much popularised by Bob Marley and the Wailers' song of the same name, first published in 1965.

[30] Katz, *Solid Foundation* (n 14) 53, 56.

[31] D Katz, *People Funny Boy: The Genius of Lee 'Scratch' Perry* (Payback Press, 2000) 66.

Shortly after the release of 'People Funny Boy' in the same year, Gibbs released an answer song in the form of 'People Grudgeful' under his own moniker 'Sir Gibbs'. Both songs are landmarks of early reggae recordings, solidifying the evolution from rocksteady to reggae, and indeed 'People Funny Boy' is one of the first examples of the loose-feel drum groove that would come to define reggae music. In the tradition of versioning, Gibb's 'People Grudgeful' borrows the melody, vocal phrasing and lyrical structure of Perry's 'People Funny Boy' (a lot of which was, in turn, derived from 'Long Shot'). While Perry sings a chorus refrain of 'Why, why, people funny bwoy?', Gibbs sings 'Why, why, people grudgeful bwoy?', and the lyrics of Gibbs's verses are also a direct response to the lyrics in Perry's verses.

(ii) Prince Buster v Derrick Morgan

Another quintessential example of dispute settlement through music is the feud between producer Prince Buster and the 'Ska King' Derrick Morgan. Morgan originally worked with Buster, but left him to work with upcoming producer Leslie Kong, whose payment of £20 per song was twice what Buster was offering. In 1962, Morgan recorded the song 'Forward March', which celebrated Jamaican independence and became a major success for Kong. Prince Buster was infuriated and accused Morgan of giving Kong songs that Buster had helped develop, and specifically claimed that the saxophone solo in 'Forward March' was stolen from Prince Buster's song 'They Got to Come'.

Buster launched his attack with the 1963 single 'Blackhead Chinaman', which featured racially antagonistic lyrics criticising Morgan, a black West Indian, for affiliating himself with a producer of Chinese descent. The first line, 'You done stole my belongings and give to your China man', confirms that the trigger for the dispute was an allegation of unauthorised musical copying. Morgan responded with the 1963 song 'Blazing Fire', and so began a series of singles released by Prince Buster and Kong in which Morgan and Buster attacked one another. On some occasions, the songs directly referenced each other in title and lyrics, such as Prince Buster's 'Praise Without Raise', to which Morgan responded with 'No Raise No Praise', both from 1963.

The feud eventually caused growing social problems, as crews of rude boys (urban youths) supporting either side would clash, leading to physical violence on the streets. The Jamaican government would eventually step in and coordinate a staged photoshoot to make it appear that Prince Buster and Derrick Morgan were close friends, and that the entire feud was just in good fun.[32] As with many aspects of the 1960s Jamaican music scene, it is difficult to separate truth from legend. It is sometimes speculated that the Buster–Morgan feud was never real in the first place and was just an elaborate ruse to promote both artists' music.

(iii) Violence and Thuggery

The tradition of dispute settlement through musical exchange underscores that legal mechanisms did not have a place in the early Jamaican music industry. This tradition is also seen in other Caribbean musical forms such as calypso, and urban genres inspired by West African and Caribbean diasporas such as hip-hop. Responding through music is an opportunity to showcase one's lyrical skills, dominate the opponent and boost one's own reputation. In the early ska–reggae scene in which sound system following was the economic and creative driving force, reputation was particularly important.

[32] Katz, *Solid Foundation* (n 14) 54.

As interesting as musical dispute settlement is, violence always had – and continues to have – an unfortunately major role in Jamaican musical culture. It was not uncommon for disputes over plagiarism to spill over into physical fighting. For example, one story suggests that the Wailers and organist Glen Adams accused Niney the Observer of copying the structure of Bob Marley and the Wailers' song 'Duppy Conqueror' in Niney's hit 'Blood and Fire', and an ensuing fight resulted in Niney being hospitalised.[33] More generally, in the 1990s dancehall scene, clashes (live lyrical battles) between artists would sometimes erupt into violence where loyal followers held rival gang affiliations.

The links between music and violence can be traced back to the early days of ska and the sound system culture. Sound system proprietors would employ thugs to protect their systems, records and parties against sabotage by rivals. As sound system proprietors became record producers, thuggery was used to defend their dominating status. Producers would notoriously pay the recording artist very little for their recording efforts, and if a singer protested to a producer such as Coxsone Dodd, 'he might flash his gun or have his enforcers teach the bwoy a lesson'.[34] In the legal dispute between Prince Buster and John Folkes regarding the authorship of 'Oh Carolina', the court even took explicit note that threats of violence from Prince Buster would have hindered the Folkes Brothers' ability to enforce their rights.[35] In an environment in which contractual agreements and intellectual property licences were not common, threats of violence often regulated the relationships between producers and artists.

V. Copyright Law in Jamaica

A. The Role of the Imperial Copyright Act

While the UK Copyright Act of 1911 automatically extended to Jamaica as part of the British Empire, the UK Copyright Act of 1956 did not.[36] After independence in 1962, Jamaica did not implement a modern copyright framework until the Copyright Act of 1993. Thus, for the entirety of the development stages of ska, rocksteady and early roots reggae, the 1911 UK Copyright Act was the applicable law.

Under the 1911 Act, the 'employer as first copyright owner' principle applied very broadly. It covered not just formal employment relationships, but also any 'contract of service or apprenticeship', even where there was no formal or permanent employment relationship. Today, unlike most modern Commonwealth copyright legislations, the Jamaican Copyright Act of 1993 does not contain a statutory provision on employee-ownership, and the first owner is always the author, perhaps as a legislative overcorrection for the 1911 provisions that applied for so long.

Understanding the applicable law allows one to reflect on the legitimacy of prevailing practices in the early ska and reggae industry. Record producers would certainly be the legitimate

[33] D Katz, 'Niney the Observer's Lucky 13: The Greatest Tracks of an Unsung Reggae Hero' (*Factmag.com magazine*, 2012) www.factmag.com/2016/02/19/niney-the-observer-reggae-best/14/.

[34] Manuel and Largey (n 1) 191.

[35] *Greensleeves* (n 10) 26–27.

[36] D Daley, 'Shades of Grey: Uncovering the Century Old Imperial Imprint on Jamaica's Modern Copyright Act' in U Suthersanen and Y Gendreau (eds), *A Shifting Empire: 100 Years of the Copyright Act 1911* (Edward Elgar Publishing, 2013) 174–75.

owners of the rights in sounds recordings under both the old (1911 UK) and new (Jamaica 1993) legislations. Pre-1993 ownership of musical compositions is, however, more complex and depends on whether (i) producers contracted artists to compose and record songs or (ii) artists recorded pre-composed songs, and the service provided to the producer was not composition but just studio performance.

Retaining ownership of commissioned works while underpaying authors would have technically been legitimate, though unethical. However, falsely purporting to be the owner of another's existing compositions would have been fraudulent. As the law always required copyright assignment to be done in writing, a producer could 'purchase' an artist's labour for a studio performance, but not the rights in a pre-existing original composition unless there was written assignment. On this issue, Daley suggests that the practices of false accreditation to producers, diverted royalties and conflicting authorship claims result from the 1911 Act's provisions on commissioned works and lack of moral rights protection.[37]

B. The Overextension of Protection Terms

In 2015, the Jamaican Parliament passed the Copyright Amendment Act, 2015, which extended the standard term of protection from 50 years to 95 years after the death of the author, giving Jamaica one of the longest copyright terms in the world. Sound recordings also now enjoy protection for 95 years. Classic works and recordings from the golden ages of ska, rocksteady and roots reggae will hence enter the public domain in foreign countries much earlier than at home in Jamaica.

The formalisation of intellectual property practices in Jamaica (especially after the 1993 Act) resulted in the liberal attitudes towards musical borrowing no longer dominating the industry. Allowing classic works to enter the public domain would at least legitimise the notion of a common pool of musical ideas from that time which are now free to be (re)used. The term extension, however, undermines the current generation of musicians' ability to reuse and remix in the same manner that facilitated the development of the industry in the first place between the 1950s and 1980s.

This is concerning because longer terms do not incentivise more creativity; rather, they have negative effects on creative freedom. Furthermore, the shift in attitudes creates a barrier to sampling, interpolation and reuse of classic riddims – even legitimately – where authorship and ownership are improperly documented. Rather than promoting creativity and managing orphan works, the term extension possibly exacerbates the problems of indeterminate ownership.

The Jamaican legislature did not choose the option of 'material reciprocity' or 'comparison of terms', where protection of foreign works is limited to the shorter term of the country of origin. As both local and foreign works attract longer protection, the term extension does little for revenue generation in the local market. While legacy rights holders will be able to earn local royalties for a longer period, commercial users also need to pay foreign rights holders for a longer time. The predicted patterns of net royalty outflows are thus unchanged, while no new royalty inflows are created as the longer term is not reciprocated in foreign markets.

[37] ibid 200–01.

C. The Role of Copyright in a Historical Context

Perspectives on the role of copyright in the development of Jamaican music are embodied in the debate between Toynbee and Okpaluba.[38] In essence, Toynbee argues that 'reggae music would never have emerged had copyright been implemented on the island'.[39] Okpaluba responds by highlighting how different creative practices have different copyright implications and rejects Toynbee's analogies. Power and Hallenkreutz also suggest that formalisation of intellectual property is good for the Jamaican music industry, as the previous lack of institutional infrastructure led to under-investment and a fragmented industrial organisation.[40]

In assessing these debates, the claim that there was an absence of copyright protection in Jamaica during the golden era of ska and reggae is sometimes overstated. Not only was the UK Copyright Act of 1911 applicable in Jamaica since 1913, but that Act was surprisingly modern, particularly compared to pre-1976 US copyright law. The Act provided for public performance rights, a term of life plus 50 years, separate rights for musical works and sound recordings, and the protection of both published and unpublished works, but did not require publication notices or other formalities. The issue is thus not an absence of copyright protection, but rather an absence of copyright enforcement.

The sound system model is one based around communication to the public (or public performance) of pre-recorded musical works. In principle, compliance with performance rights licences from collective management organisations would have created a mechanism for at least some revenues from sound system events to be redistributed to local authors and composers. This would, however, require proper attribution and registration of song-writing credits. Without proper attribution, performance royalties would simply just flow from sound system operators (users of works) back to the illegitimate rights holders (producers who are also sound system operators). There would thus be no redistributive effect. Proper attribution of authorship was hence an issue that precluded collective management capacity. Even if collective management was strong, it is unlikely that there would have been much compliance with collective licences in the first place, given sound system proprietors' proclivity for criminal intimidation.

When it comes to versioning foreign works, this practice was usually unauthorised and amounted to blatant infringement. However, it allowed the industry to develop its technical and creative capacity to then later flourish into a major international exporter of cultural output. It provided a stock of pre-composed songs that could be quickly adapted to ska and recorded in the early days of record-driven sound system competition.

In terms of riddim use and reuse of local musical elements, however, irrespective of the applicable law, these practices are regulated through the social norms of collective authorship and permitted creative reuse. The questions of whether copyright protection exists and whether creative borrowing is socially permitted are thus separate considerations. While a lack of copyright enforcement certainly contributed to the creative norms of open reuse, the existence of copyright itself does not necessarily prohibit the emergence of such norms.

[38] See generally Toynbee (n 8); Okpaluba (n 23).

[39] Toynbee (n 8) 357.

[40] D Power and D Hallencreutz, 'Profiting from Creativity? The Music Industry in Stockholm, Sweden and Kingston, Jamaica' (2002) 34 Environment and Planning A 1833.

Perhaps the most harmful copyright violations were the practices of producers. While permissive borrowing allowed the industry to develop, unfair business practices meant that producers appropriated most of the profits by expropriating the rights of composers and performers. Here, the issue is the complex question of legitimate ownership and assignment of composition rights, and the impact of the overbroad provisions of the 1911 Act regarding commissioned works. Ownership of publishing rights is especially important given the practice of versioning and riddim reuse, where several versions of a composition are recorded and published. Value is concentrated in the musical composition itself more than the sound recording, and monetisation of the social value of a work is spread over several versions and voicings, each with its own sound recording rights. The structure of the Jamaican industry is thus unique in that the stakes are even higher when it comes to ownership of composition and publishing rights, as opposed to master and sound recording rights.

Looking at the historical context, however, the true driver of creativity in the golden age of ska and reggae was not copyright, but rather labour market conditions. As sound system owners diversified into becoming music producers and studio owners, they held strong control over the means of both recording and distributing music. Even if copyright norms were formalised, producers would likely still have the bargaining power to make composers and performers assign their rights in exchange for upfront fees, rather than receive continuous royalties under joint-ownership claims or more favourable licensing agreements. As such, even if strong copyright norms clarified legal authorship and proper attribution, labour market conditions would still drive the contractual agreements on how ownership is subsequently assigned. What should have been formal written contracts enforced through law often took the form of informal oral agreements enforced through market power and thuggery. However, the underlying power imbalances which characterise these contracts would remain unchanged, so the actual final ownership arrangements would not have necessarily been that different in an environment of formalised copyright.

The labour market setting for backing musicians also played a role in overall notions of social authorship. The evolution of Jamaican music is marked by a sort of continuity between recordings, particularly because of a balance between musical innovation and musical reuse. Both practices were at least partially driven by musicians, some of whom would come to play on hundreds of recordings. It is therefore inevitable that common musical tropes would emerge, where the same musicians record different tracks with their own performance nuances and stylistic expressions. Where musicians of a generation influence one another – a natural part of the evolution of any popular music genre – these influences often operate as stylistic elements under the threshold of copyright originality. More importantly, where accompanying musicians themselves explicitly reuse musical elements, the non-enforcement of rights was likely beneficial in allowing the creative labour market to function, especially where rapid turnover of new music drove the sound system competition and thus market development.

Overall, the debate on musical development and copyright in Jamaica points in two directions. On one hand, there is a view that a lack of copyright norms facilitated sustained poverty amongst artists and performers who were artistically but not financially successful. On the other hand, a lack of copyright allowed creativity to flourish and for the recording music industry to develop into a major cultural force. These views are not in conflict. The issue of author/performer remuneration is an issue of proper attribution, determination of authorship, and contractual ownership arrangements for specific works and recordings. The issue of free creative borrowing, however, is a narrower issue of cultural constraints on the enforcement of reproduction rights of musical works.

VI. Conclusion

Jamaican ska, rocksteady and reggae music tell a story like no other music genre in the world. This music evolved and rose to be a global cultural force in a matter of a few decades, without building on any significant existing foundation of a domestic recording industry. Both market development and musical innovation took place at a remarkably rapid pace. This is certainly an anomaly, as the genre is seen by the larger global community as an indigenous art form, with strongly establish musical, cultural and aesthetic traditions.

This rise was most certainly facilitated in part by a lack of copyright enforcement – at least by modern standards – which allowed for free and open creativity and the nurturing of domestic musical talents. This legal setting was, however, not the only factor. Labour market conditions between sound system proprietors, record producers and performers played a major role, particularly in the environment of an unequal developing society. Similarly important was the unique cultural setting of a newly independent island state. The result was a musical art form that embraced open traditions of musical borrowing and reuse and that thrived in defiance of the standard narrative of copyright as a necessary incentive. Unfortunately, unethical business practices by sound system proprietors turned into record producers resulted in unfair distribution of the gains from the industry's rapid growth.

More recently, new tensions have arisen as Jamaica aims to leverage its position as a global cultural exporter to its economic advantage. While the future of the once permissive norms of musical borrowing is uncertain, the cultural impact of ska, rocksteady and reggae are forever embedded into global popular cultural, and strongly tied to notions of Jamaican – and, by extension, Caribbean – identity.

Katz suggests that Jamaican music is constantly undergoing cycles of renewal, and the quest for new innovative sounds continues.[41] Hebdige similarly refers to roots of Caribbean music as being in a state of constant flux and change.[42] Collective Jamaican society rightfully feels as if its cultural contributions to the world were not rewarded proportionately. These sentiments should, however, be understood in a much wider creative, social and political context, with a need for responses which balance the goals of commercialisation and cultural innovation. Through shared values of social authorship, cumulative creativity and innovation through remix, a global musical and cultural phenomenon emerged and continues to evolve. The challenge for the current generation of artists is now to reconcile changing attitudes to intellectual property with these values and traditions.

[41] Katz, *Solid Foundation* (n 14) 416–17.
[42] Hebdige (n 16) 10.

14

Rhythm and Melody Sans Humanité: Copyright and the Development of Calypso Music

BRYAN KHAN

In the collective mind of Western pop culture, the romanticised idea of the 'Caribbean' invokes specific aesthetical stereotypes. Images of golden sand beaches and pristine blue shorelines are conjured to the sounds of distinctly 'Caribbean' music. This music is often the sounds of reggae, the steelpan or calypso. While reggae has become a powerful symbol for Jamaican culture on the global stage, steelpan and calypso music are associated with its sister nation state, Trinidad and Tobago. While many Caribbean islands have a musical form like calypso, Trinidad has a celebrated claim as 'The Land of Calypso'.[1]

Like its more successful cousin reggae, calypso music has its roots as an art form that builds on the Caribbean's African heritage. Kaiso – a predecessor to (or rather, an alternative name for) calypso – has an even more pronounced social role in the society of Trinidad and Tobago, and parts of the Eastern Caribbean. Trinidad and Tobago has the largest (pre-Lenten) Carnival celebrations in the Caribbean Region, and calypso music is the historical soundtrack to these celebrations. Calypso and soca music (a modern dance music derived from calypso) fuel the creative economy centred around the Carnival season, its parades and the hundreds of parties surrounding it.

I. A Brief Account of Historical and Cultural Roots

As calypso has a deep and complex history, we present here just a brief account of a few factors to set the stage.[2] For simplicity, we focus on three key traditions which are important for the development of the art form – *chantwell*, *kalinda* and *canboulay* – all of which are linked to colonial experiences and resilience through slavery on the island of Trinidad.

The chantwell is essentially an incarnation of the West African tradition of the *griot*. Both chantwell and griot serve a key role in the community as preservers of oral histories, communicating tradition and stories through poetry and song, and improvising chants of praise and satire

[1] J Guilbault, *Governing Sound – The Cultural Politics of Trinidad's Carnival Musics* (University of Chicago Press, 2007) 22.

[2] For a comprehensive history of calypso music, see G Rohlehr, *Calypso and Society in Pre-Independence Trinidad* (Gordon Rohlehr, 1990).

to facilitate intra-community social dialogue. The traditions continued after Emancipation, with chantwells singing *lavways* (call-and-response chants in French creole) in the setting of ritualised stick-fighting (kalinda).

In the post-Emancipation period, former slaves and indentured workers were prohibited from participating in the pre-Lenten activities associated with French aristocrats. In response, canboulay, originally having roots as an Emancipation festival, evolved into a grassroots 'Jamette Carnival' for the emancipated classes, carrying on the traditions of chanting, drumming and singing.

In the 1880s, the colonial powers outlawed many aspects of these creole traditions, including kalinda stick-fighting and percussion. This led to the Canboulay Riots of 1881, whose re-enactment now forms part modern Carnival celebrations. In response to the banning of traditional drumming, bamboo cuttings were used as percussion instruments, leading to the tradition of *tamboo bamboo*. Tamboo bamboo bands would march through communities beating not only bamboo pieces, but also metal objects, like biscuit pans and dustbin covers. Over time, metal oil drums were repurposed and tuned to produce melodic notes, and so the tradition of the *steelpan* was born. Just like bands of roaming chantwells and stick-fighters, early steelbands were seen as thuggish troublemakers provoking social disruption.

While these specific traditions are rooted in Afro-Caribbean heritage, the evolution of calypso music is certainly a product of complex cultural interactions, and draws on Spanish and French influences, as well as Afro-Caribbean reinterpretations of European traditions. Given the rich cultural setting in which it exists, calypso music is better understood as not just a genre of music, but also as a constituent component of the Trinidadian Festival Arts, alongside stick-fighting, steelpan and, of course, Carnival parades.

At the turn of the twentieth century, calypso music became more formalised and recognised as an indigenous art form. As English took over French creole as the dominant language, kalinda chants evolved into early 'oratory form' calypso, backed by string arrangements influenced by the music of neighbouring Venezuela. The first identifiable recordings were done in New York in 1912, and by the 1930s, American record labels like Decca and RCA Victor showed interest in recording calypso music for export. In a prime display of the art form's tendency for meta-commentary, the history of calypso music as a recorded art form is perfectly summarised in the song 'Where Kaiso Went' by veteran calypsonian Brother Valentino.

Calypso flirted with international success in the 1950s largely thanks to the Jamaican-American pop star Harry Belafonte, who popularised mass-market versions of calypso and West Indian folk songs for North American and European audiences. Belafonte's 1956 album *Calypso* was the first LP to sell over a million copies. Films like *Calypso Heat Wave* (1957) helped to spread the romanticised image of calypso music, and the genre was capitalised on by white American entertainers and served as a new source of expression for the African-American community.

Iconic calypsonian The Mighty Sparrow sang a song titled 'No More Rockin' (No More Rollin') in 1959, celebrating the fact that calypso appeared to have dethroned rock 'n' roll as the dominant popular American music genre of the day, and might be seen as a response to Nat King Cole's 1957 'When Rock and Roll Come to Trinidad'. This celebration was, however, short lived, as calypso was never able to maintain its global presence as a popular art form, especially when compared to the phenomenal success of its cousin, reggae. Calypso nevertheless made an important contribution to global world music and continues to do so in its modern incarnation as soca, which is a major cultural export of the Caribbean, and in particular Trinidad and Tobago.

II. The Aesthetics of Kaiso: Oratory and Melody

A. Schools of Thought on Artistic Characteristics

The unique cultural context of calypso music has given rise to two broad schools of thought on the essence of the art form.

The more traditional view sees calypso as fundamentally an oratory art form, reflecting the music's roots in griot and chantwell traditions. Under this view, musical accompaniment is merely the vehicle for the expression of calypso, and the central artistic character of calypso is embodied in lyrics. Indeed, calypso is often described as a form of 'musical poetry'. The alternative school of thought is naturally that calypso, like any other popular musical genre, is defined by both lyrics and instrumentation as artistic elements.

These two competing views are not totally unknown to copyright law, where different jurisdictions take on different definitions of 'musical work'. In defining the subject matter of copyright, Article 2 of the Berne Convention refers to 'musical compositions with or without words'. In the USA, copyright law defines a musical work to include accompanying words,[3] while in the UK, the statutory definition excludes words.[4]

Conceptually, the boundaries of a 'work' would depend on the creative process through which it is authored. If lyrics are written without melodic accompaniment, they should be understood as a 'literary work', akin to a poem. When those lyrics are later put to music, then a new work is created – a musical work – which is a derivate work of the initial literary work. The principles of joint authorship also apply, whereby separate copyrights might be given to different creative collaborators where their independent contributions might amount to independent original works. This is indeed sometimes the case of lyrics and musical accompaniment, where a single unified object of property is only recreated through the contractual arrangement on co-ownership of the joint work (ie a single song with lyrics and music). Seeing calypso as fundamentally a lyrical art form is thus not at all inconsistent with the norms of copyright law.

B. Oratory: The Calypsonian as a Newscaster

The primacy of lyrical content is important in understanding the role of the calypsonian as a reincarnation of the West African griot, serving the role of community storyteller and oral historian. In this tradition, the calypsonian takes on the role a newscaster, opinion leader and grassroots public intellectual.

This tradition was particularly pronounced in the golden age of calypso, when colonial power structures denied most of the working class access to platforms for public discourse. While calypsonians often sing songs of love, romance and male bravado, they are best known as commentators on the news of the day and contentious social issues. Even songs filled with ribaldry, satire and irreverence have an underlying, albeit often indirect, social commentary, and lyrics which focus on double entendre are insights into social and gender relations.

[3] USC 17 § 102.
[4] UK CDPA 1988, § 3.

Songs with more direct social and political lyrics not only communicated news and political developments to a population that might have limited literacy, but also framed the issues in ways that resonate with the working class.[5] Noted ethnomusicologist Peter Manual describes calypso's textual focus as both its strength and its weakness – the focus on current local issues allows the art form to flourish as a 'dynamic form of grassroots folklore', though it limits its potential appeal across time and outside of Trinidad.[6]

An example is the 1945 song 'Commission's Report' by prolific golden age kaisonian Atilla (Raymond Quevedo). This song communicates the details of The *Report of West India Royal Commission*, which was an inquiry into the 1934–39 labour riots throughout the British West Indies that reported on the poor living conditions in the colonies. In a similar vein, King Radio's 1950 song 'Sedition Law' sang of colonial abuses of civil liberties and restrictions on free speech. Social tensions manifested in the conflict between calypsonians and the Colonial Secretary, which sought to censor calypsos and required that all lyrics be submitted for approval before they could be sung. Commenting on this, Atilla sang the song 'Banning of Records' (1938), which itself was inevitably banned.

It is thus no surprise that calypso played a vital role in the social and political development of Trinidad and Tobago, but also that many calypsonians themselves often formalise their political involvement by transitioning into electoral politics. Atilla himself was the first calypsonian to serve in public office, being elected to the Port-of-Spain City Council in 1946 and to the Legislative Council of Trinidad and Tobago in 1950. There is even the polarising tradition of some calypsonians making entire careers serving as oratory campaigners for specific political parties, a trend which peaked during the political tensions of the 1990s. Party-supporting calypsonians might be rewarded with positions on state boards should their side come to power.

During national elections in Trinidad and Tobago, it is common practice for parties to hire popular calypsonians to write endorsement songs and perform them in campaign advertisements and rallies. In other cases, a calypsonian's public contributions through music can be so influential that they directly affect the political tides themselves. One prominent example is the song 'Sinking Ship' by Gypsy, released for the 1986 General Election. Armchair historians often credit this song with channelling the collective frustrations of the national community, resulting in the unseating of the ruling party for the first time in the country's post-independence history. Gypsy later went on to serve as a Member of Parliament for both rival national parties at different times in his career.

C. Melody: Sources of Musical Inputs

Despite its self-proclaimed nature as an oratory art, calypso as a genre reflects a very deep musical tradition, with various rich sources of melodic influence.

As already noted, kalinda stick-fighting chants are an important source of melodic structure and phrasing. Another important source is Orisha chants – the ceremonial songs of the Caribbean manifestation of the West African Yoruba religion. Orisha represents not only linkages to the elements of African traditions which persevered throughout the atrocities of slavery, but also a connection to calypso's orientation as an art form of resistance. In 1917, the British Colonial

[5] For a comprehensive discussion on the politics of post-independence calypso, see L Regis, *The Political Calypso: True Opposition in Trinidad and Tobago 1962–1987* (University of the West Indies Press, 1999).

[6] P Manuel, *Caribbean Currents: Caribbean Music from Rumba to Reggae*, 3rd edn (Temple University Press, 2016) 237–38.

Authorities implemented the 'Shouter Prohibition Ordinance', which banned the practice of 'Obeah' and the Spiritual Baptist faith. This outlawing of Baptist and Orisha drumming is reminiscent of the outlawing of canboulay drumming a few decades earlier.

While kalinda and Orisha represent musical influences in the form of heritage and folk traditions, calypso also draws melodic influence from a wider range of ethnic and cultural inputs. The island of Trinidad is just 11 kilometres away from the closest point of the Venezuelan mainland, so Venezuelan folk music traditions also serve as inputs into calypso. One early forerunner of the genre was Lionel Belasco, a composer and pianist whose prolific work in the early twentieth century was an important predecessor to calypso, and who was known to draw influence from Venezuelan music. Furthermore, calypsonians would also often draw on colonial sources, and were particularly influenced by British tastes for melodic composition.

One more important source of influence is Trinidad's relationship with the neighbouring Caribbean islands to its north. In 1783, while Trinidad was still under Spanish rule, the 'Cedula of Population' decree opened the island up to immigration of largely Catholic French Caribbean people, introducing a new cultural and linguistic dimension to the country's social composition. Intra-Caribbean immigration patterns, particularly from the smaller Eastern Caribbean islands, would continue to be a major social influence in Trinidad well into the twentieth century, given the island's position as the second largest economy and country in the British West Indies.

Indeed, the early 1900s was a period when folk song melodies from all over the West Indies contributed to the development of Trinidadian calypso.[7] The popular lore suggests that calypsonian King Radio, who worked on the docks of Port-of-Spain, would deliberately mingle with the crews of ships arriving from other islands to learn their native folk songs and later rearrange them into popular calypsos.[8]

So, like many hybrid New World art forms, appropriation and adaptation are important processes for the development of calypso. However, despite the rich variety of influences, the core musical palette of calypso was traditionally seen as somewhat limited. Atilla asserted that there were only 12 basic calypso rhythms (melodies), which are repeatedly reused. During the 1930s and 1940s, the common practice was to use the known melodies of the day and simply add new text.[9] A more reasonable estimate is that in the 1950s, calypso music likely was based on about 50 traditional melodies, which were constantly reworked.[10]

These observations support the idea that calypso in its earlier twentieth century form, was fundamentally a lyrical art form, where melody and accompaniment were secondary creative expressions. Perhaps this continued reuse of common musical themes allowed focus to be placed on lyrics and reinforced the role of calypso as a forum for political debate.

D. Musical Performance as Contestation

While the calypsonian's compositions reflect their role as a chantwell, their oratory skills are most directly manifested in the art form of *ex-tempo*. In ex-tempo, calypsonians extemporaneously compose and perform lyrics on the spot, often in the setting of a calypso tent where they are in competition with another calypsonian.

[7] Rohlehr (n 2) 60.

[8] R Quevedo, *Atilla's Calypso: A Short History of Trinidad Calypso* (University of the West Indies, 1994) 100.

[9] K Warner, *Kaiso! The Trinidad Calypso* (Three Continents Press, 1982) 21.

[10] C Charles, 'Calypso Music: Identity and Social Influence – the Trinidadian Experience' (Doctoral Thesis, Universiteit Leiden, 2016) 96.

These lyrical battles are a predecessor to similar practices in Jamaican dancehall music and American hip-hop. Reputation is key to an artist's success, and reputation is formed by paying dues in these settings of contestation. Like a dancehall or hip-hop artist, a calypsonian who is unable to perform on the spot and dominate a challenger has no legitimacy in the prevailing cultural system, no matter how good their pre-composed or recorded music might be. Like these other forms of musical battle, masculine pride is on full display during ex-tempo, and lyrics are crafted to boast of one's own abilities and to demean the challenger. The ex-tempo stage is thus in many ways an incarnation of the 'gayelle' (stick-fighting ring).

Calypsonians often adopt sobriquets to reflect larger-than-life personas, using honorific titles appropriated from colonial hierarchies (eg Lord Invader, Lord Kitchener) or epithets that reflect their commanding presence (eg Mighty Sparrow, Mighty Bomber), or likening themselves to an aggressive animal (eg Growling Tiger, Roaring Lion). Each calypsonian has their own unique cadence when engaging in 'calypso war', which defines their own personal style.

For contestation to be fair, the same backing music is used by both challengers. Different melodies have been used for ex-tempo, but over time the definitive melody has become 'Sans Humanité'. The French words *sans humanité* are often pronounced as 'santimanitay' and translate to 'without mercy', reflecting the weaponisation of improvised lyrics. These words would be used to complete a performance of a Sans Humanité verse, sometimes being replaced by alternatives of similarly confrontational refrains such as 'my intention is war'.

It is hard to truly convey the iconic status of the Sans Humanité melody, and its power to invoke calypso history and culture in any setting. It might be an exaggeration to say that this single melody literally shaped Trinidadian society. However, this is at least symbolically true in that calypso traditions shaped the national social and political landscape, and it is around this melody that the essence of the tradition coalesces. While the exact origins of the Sans Humanité melody are uncertain, authoritative calypso historian Gordon Rohlehr suggests that it is influenced by Catholic litanic chants.[11] No matter the origins, this melody represents one of the most important Traditional Cultural Expressions of Trinidad and Tobago, and one whose consistent reuse is central to calypso music.

Figure 14.1 Generic Sans Humanité melody

III. Pan-Caribbean Recontextualisation

Given intra-Caribbean migration patterns and the spread of cultural influences throughout the West Indies, it is no surprise that many folk songs are claimed as national traditions in multiple islands. As a result, calypso represents not just a reflection of cultural identity in Trinidad and

[11] Rohlehr (n 2) 58.

Tobago, but also a point of intersection for other related indigenous Caribbean musical forms. Indeed, before the popularisation of Jamaican ska and reggae music, Jamaican mento (folk music) was often marketed as 'Jamaican calypso', as mento and calypso share common thematic and cultural roots.

The result is a sort of intercultural dialogue through shared traditions which emerges through the recontextualisation of works. Folk songs are performed with similar lyrics but take on different meanings in different contexts. The process allows for the emergence of a loose pan-Caribbean aesthetic and folk music tradition, while allowing individual islands to retain their own senses of national culture. It creates a commons of Caribbean folk music standards, while still allowing considerable room for individual performers to reinterpret works around established themes.

A. 'Sly Mongoose'

A prime example of this phenomenon is the song 'Sly Mongoose'. This song is often claimed as a Trinidadian calypso, but certainly has Jamaican roots. Multiple Caribbean islands, even French-speaking Guadeloupe, claim 'Sly Mongoose' as their own.[12]

The first known recording of this song was by Sam Manning in the mid-1920s, and it was made popular through a recording by Trinidadian calypsonian Lord Invader in 1946. However, other versions are known to have been recorded in different parts of the Caribbean, such as the 1935 recording 'Slide Mongoose Slide' by the Nassau String Band in the Bahamas. The song has now become something of a calypso standard, being constantly performed and recorded by calypsonians and by performers influenced by calypso or calypso-adjacent genres.

Almost all renditions use some version of the lyrics 'Sly Mongoose, your name gone abroad' as the main refrain or chorus. Typical versions of the song use the verse lyrics 'Mongoose go inna Bedward's kitchen, take out one of his big fat chicken, put it inna his waistcoat pocket, Sly Mongoose'. In these lyrics, 'Bedward' refers to Alexander Bedward, a Jamaican Revival Church preacher who had a large following in the late nineteenth and early twentieth century. Bedward had infamously gathered his followers to demonstrate that he could fly from a tree, only to fall and injure himself and many observers. He was later admitted to a mental asylum, where he died in 1930. His legacy as a folk curiosity is immortalised in various forms, such as the mento song 'Dip Dem Bedward', which sings of Bedward's purported healing powers.[13] 'Sly Mongoose', in its form as a Jamaican folk song, is another such musical account of Bedward's legacy, where he is likened to a thieving mongoose as a comment on his dishonest character. The refrain 'your name gone abroad' communicates that Bedford's notoriety had been reported beyond Jamaica's borders.

The version of the song recorded by Sam Manning in 1925 tells a different story, also involving Bedford. In this version, the 'sly' character (possibly a well-known Jamaican government official) attempts to win the affection and sexual attention of one of Bedward's daughters, leading to scandal. The song begins with the line 'Listen to the story why mongoose fly from Jamaica', which refer to the scandal of the character having to flee Jamaica.

Another account suggests that in the US Virgin Islands of St Thomas and St Croix, the relationship between the mongoose and Ms Bedford alludes to a sexual relationship between a house cook and master, or between a mistress and a worker.[14] In some Eastern Caribbean versions,

[12] ibid 102.

[13] O Lewin, *Rock It Come Over – The Folk Music of Jamaica* (University of the West Indies Press, 2000) 32.

[14] MJ Soule and M Lieth-Philip, *Zoop Zoop Zoop: Traditional Music and Folklore of St Croix, St Thomas, and St John, Liner Notes* (New World Records, 1993).

reference is made to a raid on 'the white man's kitchen' instead of 'Ms Bedward's kitchen'. In these versions, the story is further adapted by changing the refrain to 'the dogs know your name' rather than 'your name gone abroad'.[15]

In Guyana, the song is also embraced as a folk song. As Guyana is a larger, more rural continental space than the islands of the Caribbean, the problem of the mongoose as a pest that steals chickens is interpreted even more literally. Here, it is useful to note how the mongoose came to be such a symbol in Caribbean folk cultures. The 'mongoose' was introduced in many islands of the British West Indies in 1870s to control rat populations in sugar plantations. Over time, however, they developed a reputation for attacking domestic chickens and land crabs. The analogy of the 'mongoose' as a cunning pest thus has strong roots in West Indian colonial experiences. The Jamaican folk song 'Mahngoose a Come' features a mongoose as representing an admirer who seeks to chastise a character named Dory and compete for a female character's attention. The musical call 'Mahngoose a Come, Dory' was then repurposed by labourers to indicate that the master was near, so the gang should appear to be busy.[16]

In Trinidad, the song has yet another meaning and history. After arriving in Trinidad through an intra-Caribbean shipping crew, a version of 'Sly Mongoose' was sung by calypsonian Houdini in a calypso tent in 1921.[17] It became so popular that it was sung by most Carnival bands in 1923, perhaps making this song the first 'Road March' (a coveted title given to the most popular song performed during a year's Carnival parades). Rohlehr comments on the irony that the first modern Trinidadian Road March is actually a Jamaican song that defied Carnival bands' resistance to singing the same choruses as their rivals.[18]

In 1941, Houdini defeated Mighty Growler, Mighty Destroyer and Lord Invader in a calypso competition hosted in the USA. Despite this success, Houdini was not well respected among the calypso fraternity in Trinidad and was seen as a trickster who was not a genuine calypsonian. In response, Lord Invader penned a version of 'Sly Mongoose', and relates the story of the American calypso competition, casting Houdini as the mongoose character. This version, recorded in 1946, uses the chorus refrain of 'Sly Mongoose, only dog know your name', suggesting that Houdini is not worthy of any fame or renown. Here, the reference to going into 'the white man's kitchen' can be interpreted as a reference to entering an American competition, and the stealing of the chicken refers to illegitimately stealing the winner's title. Note that Lord Invader also reuses the melody of 'Sly Mongoose' in another song, called 'Old Time Cat-O'-Nine', which was recorded in 1945.

B. 'Brown Skin Girl'

Another example of a song that takes on different meanings in different performance contexts is the calypso standard 'Brown Skin Girl'. The chorus of this song is always some form of the lines 'Brown skin girl stay home and mind baby … I'm going away in a sailing boat, and if I don't come back, stay home and mind baby'. Various versions of the song appear in folk music collections of several Caribbean countries, including the Bahamas, Jamaica, Grenada, Guyana, and Trinidad and Tobago.

[15] *Lord Invader Calypso in New York*, Liner Notes (Smithsonian Folkway Recordings, 2000).

[16] W Jekyll, *Jamaican Songs and Story: Annancy Stories, Digging Sings, Ring Tunes and Dancing Tunes* (Folklore Society, 1904) 277.

[17] Quevedo (n 8) 16.

[18] Rohlehr (n 2) 117.

The origins of this song trace back to the Grenadines.[19] As the islands of the Eastern Caribbean are smaller, there have always been fewer opportunities relative to larger economies like that of the more industrialised Trinidad. There is thus a long tradition of migrants from the Eastern Caribbean moving to the larger islands looking for jobs, to send income back to their families at home. In this context, 'Brown Skin Girl' tells the story of a young man who is 'going away on a sailing boat' to seek employment on a different island, as he advises his partner to stay at home and take care of the couple's child. The traditional version of the song sometimes ends with the line 'and if I don't come back, throw away the damn baby', giving the song dark undertones of a fragile Caribbean masculinity centred around a presumption that without a male figure present, child-rearing is not possible.

The song was recorded by King Radio in 1947, with verses criticising American soldiers based in Trinidad during WWII who would impregnate local girls, then leave the 'blue-eyed babies' without fathers. In this version, the refrain 'I'm going away on a sailing boat, and if I don't come back, stay home and mind baby' is sung through the perspective of the American soldier fleeing responsibilities, rather than the young Caribbean father seeking new opportunities. This change in context alters the narrative of the song as well as its fundamental emotive tone. It is King Radio's version of the song that was later popularised by Harry Belafonte.

Later versions by the Mighty Terror and Lord Invader tell the story from yet another angle. The narrative is of a man being 'trapped' by illegitimate claims of paternity. In these versions, the chorus of 'brown skin girl stays home and mind baby' is used to demean the female character and dismiss her false paternity claims. The refrain of 'I'm going away on a sailing boat, and if daddy don't come back, stay home and mind baby' confirms the singer's intention to leave in a metaphorical rather than literal boat.

The King Radio version is generally considered to be the definitive version of the song, so almost all published recordings of 'Brown Skin Girl' credit the author as Norman Span (King Radio's legal name). As King Radio died in 1970, the song only entered the public domain very recently in jurisdictions with a copyright term of 'life plus 50 years', while in much of the world that has a longer term it is still (supposedly) under copyright protection.

C. Implications of Musical Recontextualisation

The above examples of 'Sly Mongoose' and 'Brown Skin Girl' show that within the cultural system of calypso music, a pan-Caribbean folk repertoire is formed where the same works are recontextualised in different settings. Thus, it might be the case that even where a song has an identifiable author (and is even possibly still copyright-protected), it is still treated like a folk song for others not only to re-perform, but also to re-contextualise and transform.

The implication for intellectual property law is that it becomes unreasonable to pursue efforts to protect Caribbean folk songs as Traditional Cultural Expressions at the national level. A few Caribbean countries of note contain folklore provisions in their national copyright laws (Dominica, Barbados, and St Kitts and Nevis),[20] though no such provisions exist in Jamaica or Trinidad and Tobago.

[19] Quevedo (n 8) 18.

[20] See §§ 2 and 18(8) of the Copyright Act of the Commonwealth of Dominica; §22 of the Copyright Act of Barbados; and §22 of the Copyright Act of St Kitts and Nevis.

It is not unreasonable to suggest that calypso standards that have become pan-Caribbean folk songs might qualify as a form of folklore under these provisions, as multiple communities claim these works as part of their inter-generational cultural heritage. Furthermore, these works evolve in a way that reflects both community authorship and joint authorship across multiple communities; the traditional expression is not the individual versions of works authored by specific artists, but rather the common thematic elements and collective creativity that manifest in a shared cultural and social identity. It is only where an additional requirement of having 'unknown authorship' exists that the application of folklore protection provisions to these works might be limited.

Any viable attempt to protect this specific form of Caribbean folk music would thus require coordination between the individual countries who stake a claim to the traditions. Caribbean folk music is simply too great to be constrained by the national borders of small states, and Trinidad, as the home of calypso, is inevitably at least one point of its convergence. Furthermore, there is the incongruence of vesting in any government such rights in folk songs which largely developed from anti-establishment traditions.

IV. Attitudes Towards Authorship and Ownership

Attitudes towards authorship and ownership are shaped by calypso's complex socio-cultural context. Social authorship manifests in how works draw from common folk melody sources. However, the role of the calypsonian as a larger-than-life character with exaggerated posturing places a strong emphasis on the individual performer. A calypsonian does not just perform a calypso as a musical work but performs in a theatrical manner, which includes body language, facial expressions, intonation and crowd interactions.

Understanding this duality means again tracing the calypsonian's roots back to the chantwell – an individual whose performance was a manifestation of a communal spirit. The chantwell would sing kalinda chants to encourage their community's stick-fighter and to intimidate rivals. This role evolved into the leader of a carnival band who would coordinate the singing of proto-calypso chants amongst the members of the band. As such, the calypsonian's role as a key participant in the Carnival arts reflects a complex interplay between individual personalities and collective participation. The 'yard' in which pre-Carnival rehearsals took place was fundamentally a communal space before being transformed into commercial calypso 'tents' which the public could access.

Moving into the era of calypso as a more structured and distinct genre, the art form is very much based on individual reputation, while still embracing some norms of social authorship. Key motifs are built upon between artists, and social authorship in the form of 'follow-on creativity' can be found throughout the corpus of classic works.

For example, Lord Kitchener's 1946 'Jump in the Line' won the title of Road March that year, and uses a melody that resembles the earlier song 'Calypso Behind the Wall', made popular by the Growler. A few years later, Lord Invader penned his own version of Lord Kitchener's 'Jump in the Line', about playing Carnival in New York City, and 'Labor Day (Jump in the Line)' was released in 1955. The Lord Invader version was made further popular by Jamaican mento singer Lord Flea, who also widely performed a version called 'Shake Shake Senora', which was recorded and released in 1957. While the phrase 'Jump in the line' pre-dates Lord Kitchener's song (and, for example, appears in the early kalinda-based calypso song 'J'ouvert Barrio'), the refrain 'Jump in the line and move/shake your body in time' evolved into a common motif in calypso music.

'Jump in the Line' ultimately became an international hit when Harry Belafonte released his own version in 1961 inspired by Lord Flea called 'Jump in the Line (Shake, Senora)'. It has since been covered and sampled by several artists in different genres of music.

It is also common for melodies to be reused from generation to generation. For example, the melody of the proto-calypso song 'Caroni Swamp' (credited to Phil Madison) is reused by Lord Beginner in his 1940 Road March 'Run You Run (Adolf Hitler)', which is a WWII remake of Inventor's WWI song 'Run You Run (Kaiser William)'. It is not uncommon for a single artist to reuse their own melodies. Both the Mighty Sparrow and Lord Kitchener – two of the most popular and celebrated calypsonians of all time – are known to have done precisely that at various points throughout their careers.

Roaring Lion – a calypsonian known for his unique experimentation – reused the same melody derived from the 'Congo Bara' chant in both the songs 'Baboolala' and 'Netty Netty', the latter of which won the Road March in 1937. 'Netty Netty' is a calypso classic, but is itself surrounded by contested authorship, as both Roaring Lion and the Mighty Unknown claim to have composed the song.[21] While the tradition is for a calypsonian to write their own lyrics and at least basic melody, the calypso lore is full of stories of ghostwriting and exchanges of songs. Sometimes songs are purchased from a writer, and conflicts arise when the same song is sold to more than one singer.[22]

Attitudes towards authorship and ownership have, however, become much more formalised over time. The calypso fraternity and the organisations that represent the Carnival arts are key institutional players who lobby for stronger respect for intellectual property and better remuneration for local creatives. Of course, calypso's true form would not be apparent without an example of its own self-commentary on the issue of copyright and remuneration. In the 1990 song 'She Want Me to Sing in She Party', calypsonian Scrunter sings 'She wha meh to sing in she party, and doh wanna pay meh no money; Ah say dahlin I cah do that, it is against the Copyright Act'.

V. The Elusive Notion of Arrangement

Turning to the issue of 'originality' and creativity in musical composition, one of the most remarkable features of calypso is the central role played by the 'arranger'. While the arranger is an important creative agent in many musical genres, their role in calypso music is unique.

Generally, the assumption of copyright law is that 'arrangement' implies creating a new 'derivative work' by adapting an existing musical work with added original creativity. The Berne Convention confirms that copyright holders have an explicit right over adaptations and arrangements of their work (Article 12), and that new arrangements of music are copyright-eligible without prejudice to the original works (Article 2(3)).

In Western European 'classical' music, an arranger might coordinate the process of orchestration by mapping musical parts and roles in an overall composition, depending on the size and formation of the ensemble. In jazz music, the process of arranging involves reinterpreting an existing composition through creative choices like reharmonisation of chords and alterations in structure.

In calypso, however, the arranger plays a role in developing the initial composition itself and is more akin to a coauthor or creative producer. The arranger is seen as a creative facilitator for

[21] Warner (n 9) 21.
[22] Manuel (n 6) 245.

the primary composer, who is often – but not necessarily – a calypsonian who has composed lyrics and an overarching melody. Firstly, an arranger might assist in refining the core melody and hook of a song, and help the composer in developing a rudimentary idea into a more substantial melody. Secondly, the arranger assists in developing the accompanying instrumentation for a song, such as the guitar chords and bass line. Thirdly, the arranger might transcribe the music into musical notation, so that it can be performed by the house band in a calypso tent.

The process of writing accompaniment and transcription became even more complex after the 1950s, as musical parts written for brass sections became more central to the sound of calypso. Such brass parts reinforce the melodic hook of a song and provide structural definition by delineating verses and choruses. Where a song's core might be based on a variation of established stock melodies and chord progressions, these brass arrangements often become defining features rather than secondary supporting elements.

Most traditional calypsonians were also guitar players, and the chord progressions used in the genre are very specific in defining the overall aesthetics of the art form. Calypso guitar goes beyond simple choices of major and minor chords, and involves strategic use of diminished, augmented, sevenths or inversions of chords. These subtle choices allow the arranger to develop an accompaniment which compliments the story being told by the calypsonian, by controlling the emotive tone of the music. Their role is the bridge between the two schools of thought regarding the framing of calypso as primarily an oratory art form or a musical art form. Well-known and skilled arrangers are the behind-the-scenes technical artisans that balance the art form's orientation as a performance art with appropriate musical complexity. The arranger is thus able to transform the established pool of stock melodies into more substantial musical compositions. As such, despite its history of repeated reuse of common melodies, the corpus of calypso music over the decades shows a remarkable degree of musical depth.

Until the 1980s, a single arranger would normally be hired by a calypso tent to arrange the accompaniment for all performed calypsos, and so had a significant influence on the art form.[23] Prolific arrangers might work on hundreds of songs over their careers. The most renowned arrangers might even be associated with the sounds of certain time periods in calypso history, such as Frankie Francis in the 1960s or Art De Coteau in the 1970s. Of course, there are criticisms of the perceived trend of calypsonians becoming less skilled composers and having an over-dependence on the talents of arrangers. In Chalkdust's 1988 song 'Two Chords and Leston Paul', he mocks the simplified formulas used by 'quack' calypsonians, who deliver songs with little creativity and rely on just 'two chords' and a skilled arranger.

These roles suggest that under copyright law, the arranger is likely a joint author. This is especially true where the arranger is building on a stock melody provided by the calypsonian, and their creativity transforms the public domain folk melody into an original expression. However, under the cultural system of calypso, the arranger is considered not a songwriter, but rather a facilitator. Their role is seen as more of an intermediary who might be the beneficiary of performers' related rights, rather than a joint author in the copyright sense. This attitude is certainly linked to the concept of calypso as a story-telling art form, where lyrics have primacy over musical accompaniment and even melodic structure. There is thus a divergence of how we frame the dichotomy of authorship and performance in the legal space of copyright and related rights law, on the one hand, and within the cultural norms of calypso, on the other. The fundamental issue is again what we understand the core 'work' to be in the copyright sense. While copyright law might define a musical work as an original melody 'with or without accompanying words', a traditional calypsonian might see the work as words 'with or without accompanying music'.

[23] Guilbault (n 1) 138.

Another part of this phenomenon is likely the importance of tradition and notions of authenticity in the art form. Calypso music is meant to be performed primarily in a live setting, where the calypsonian is centre stage and supported by the house band of a calypso tent. Even in modern times, many calypsos might not be recorded in studios, but are fixed only through archives of live broadcasts of national competitions.

Modernisation of music production and a shift towards a focus on recorded music certainly reframes the role of the arranger. In a studio setting, the arranger is more likely to be seen as a joint author rather than a facilitator and performer, as the context of how the music is performed and presented to the audience is fundamentally different than that of the tent. Indeed, arrangements for royalty splits among co-songwriters are the norm when it comes to calypso's modern incarnation as soca music. However, for more traditional calypso music, the notion of authenticity still places the calypso tent as the primary performance forum, where the lyricist is the primary author and the arranger is a facilitator. These attitudes do indeed appear to be reflected in how works are registered and managed with the collective management organisations in the Caribbean.

A. Arrangement in Pan

To truly understand calypso music, it is always important to position it in the wider context of the Trinidadian Festival Arts. Both calypso and the steelband play a central role in Carnival celebrations. Traditionally, chantwells would lead community groups of revellers who sing call and response songs, as well as play the drums, tamboo bamboo and steelpan. As such, there was always an important role for an arranger, who would interpret the popular calypso songs of the day to be played on pan.

In modern times, Carnival bands are more coordinated at an entrepreneurial level, with music being provided by mobile sound system trucks which accompany a band's parade route. Like calypso, where national competitions are central to the art form, the main forum for steelpan music has become the national Panorama competition, which first started in 1963.

Steelband groups compete in classes based on the size of the ensemble and the number of players, and perform an arrangement of one of the popular calypsos of the season. The success of a calypso might be judged not only in terms of reception amongst Carnival bands and masquerades, but also how popular it is as a choice for the steelband arrangers.

Pan arrangement is a complex skill involving the various dimensions of rearranging a pre-existing work in Western music. The arranger adds new compositional elements, reharmonises chord structures, interpolates elements of multiple works and creates complex dynamics throughout the arrangement. Given calypso's oratory focus, the pan arranger's challenge is to adapt the story-telling process without the aid of lyrics and words.

The arrangement is then transcribed and distributed to different sections of the band to learn the respective parts – or, in the case of many famous arrangers who do not possess formal training, the parts are taught directly by rote. As a large band can have more than 100 players, the arranger works with dedicated 'section leaders' and 'drill masters' to coordinate the logistics of practice.

Pan arrangement is thus a remarkably creative process, where some of the deepest complexities of Caribbean music are on display. Arrangements are transformative, and the work produced is unquestionably an original creative composition in its own right. Renowned arrangers like Len 'Boogsie' Sharpe and Jit Samaroo are celebrated as champions of the art form and Trinidadian musical icons.

As Panorama formally institutionalised the relationship between calypso and steelpan, the context of calypso composition evolved. Some calypsonians began to compose songs with a higher degree of musical complexity, where the lyrics tell steelpan-themed narratives. These songs are written specifically to be arranged on pan, as opposed to primary performance in calypso tents or during Carnival parades. Famous songs in this tradition include Shadow's 'Bassman' (1974), Scrunter's 'Woman on the Bass' (1979) and Lord Kitchener's 'Pan in A Minor' (1987).

From a copyright law perspective, made-for-pan calypsos represent a whole new creative dynamic as works are authored with the explicit intention of facilitating follow-on creativity and the production of derivative works. As the performance context shifts, the dynamics of creativity shift to a form of uncoordinated joint authorship between the calypsonian and the pan arranger. In this process, the work is reshaped from the calypso form, in which the lyrics are central, to the steelpan performance form, which is instrumental, thus representing a sort of inversion of the primacy of lyrics over musical accompaniment.

Surprisingly, the cultural system is such that there is generally no formal assertion of proprietary rights over original steelband arrangements. There is no tradition of arrangers claiming copyright in arrangements as derivative works, or of individual steelband members claiming related rights as performers. Arrangements are not registered with local collective management organisations, and any royalties generated from live performances flow only to the composers of the original calypsos that were (re)arranged. Although immense creativity and labour are put into creating and practising original arrangements, they are intended to be one-time transient performances for the national competition (even if they are recorded live), as opposed to permanently fixed works with a life of their own.

While patrons support their favoured steelband side or arranger, the value added by their original arrangements is not formally captured as a form of intellectual property. Rather, it is prestige, reputation, tradition and community spirit that drives creativity in and dedication to the art of steelpan. Investment is facilitated by corporate sponsorships, and creative labour is motivated by cash prizes in the national competition and direct arranger fees. How this lack of assertion of rights in arrangements and performances affects investment in the art form is, of course, an entirely separate question. Nevertheless, it certainly seems that the steelpan culture and creativity thrive without formalised exclusive rights over arrangements as derivative works.

VI. 'Rum and Coca-Cola'

Many of the concepts discussed above can be observed in the story of the song 'Rum and Coca Cola' – perhaps the most important case that connects the worlds of calypso and copyright law.

The Calypso Craze of the 1950s was a mixed blessing. While it placed Caribbean culture on the global stage, the sanitised and polished form of calypso made popular by Harry Belafonte disconnected calypso from its socio-political roots. Political lyrics used as contextual commentary on colonial experiences and poverty were displaced by idealistic and romanticised images of an island paradise. Brooding minor keys and complex narrative chord structures were replaced by jovial major keys, as nuanced lyrical cadence was replaced by a forced syncopation unfamiliar to North American singers.

Just as Caribbean folk songs are 'recontextualised' in different settings throughout the region, calypso became 'decontextualised' as it entered American popular culture, and no song was decontextualised as drastically as 'Rum and Coca Cola'.

A. Lord Invader v the Yankee Invaders

During WWII, England rallied resources from all over its colonial empire to assist in the war effort. In 1940, Britain gave the USA 99-year leases to lands throughout the Caribbean to establish military bases, and the military base established in Chaguaramas essentially converted the northwest peninsula of Trinidad into an extension of the American war effort.

Tens of thousands of American troops were deployed to an island of just about half a million inhabitants. Social tensions were inevitable. The perception that has persisted is that American soldiers stationed in Trinidad enjoyed lavish lifestyles facilitated by the strength of the US currency, the culture of the island, access to local rum and women, and the absence of active warfare. As King Radio sang in his version of 'Brown Skin Girl', 'Now the American made an invasion, we thought it was to help the island, until they left from here on vacation'.

The sentiments of the time are best captured in the first verse of Lord Invader's 1943 hit 'Rum and Coca-Cola':

> Since the Yankees came to Trinidad
> They have the young girls going mad
> The young girls say they treat them nice
> And they give them a better price

The chorus then contains the iconic refrain 'Both mother and daughter, working for Yankee dollar'. The song speaks of American soldiers using their money to solicit sex from local girls, and the effects on social and gender relationships in Trinidad. As aptly put by none other than Atilla, the song 'described in a few short verses what it would have taken a sociologist pages and pages to accomplish'.[24]

After 1945, the Americans left behind a legacy of social disruption and exploitation. The end of the war, however, facilitated the spread of calypso all over the world. American soldiers returned home with memories of calypso music and their time in Trinidad. On the other side of the Atlantic, the presence of the Windrush Generation in London allowed calypso to complement its cousin genres of ska and reggae in reshaping the landscape of British music in the 1960s.

In September 1943, American entertainer Morey Amsterdam travelled to Trinidad to perform for American soldiers. After returning to the USA, Amsterdam claimed to have written a song called 'Rum and Coca-Cola'. The song was published by Leo Feist Inc, and recorded by the popular boogie-woogie sister trio the Andrews Sisters in October 1944. The Andrews Sisters' version became a massive hit and was one of the best-selling American records of the 1940s.

The music of Amsterdam's version is virtually identical to Lord Invader's version. Changes to the lyrics, however, distort the meaning of the song. Lord Invader's verses referring to infidelity and local women leaving their husbands are replaced with sanitised verses about tropical romance. The line 'and they give them a better price' was changed to 'make Trinidad like paradise', painting the American soldier as a romantic hero rather than a corrupting invader. The song was totally stripped of its social criticism and was thus 'decontextualised' despite its massive international success. There is also a deep irony in a song criticising the American military presence on a colonial island being popularised by performers remembered in American popular culture for lifting the nation's spirits during the war.

[24] Quevedo (n 8) 77.

Two separate copyright lawsuits arose from the success of Rum and Coca Cola: (i) *Khan v Feist*[25] and (ii) *Baron v Feist*,[26] the former in relation to the words of the song, the latter in relation to the music.

B. *Khan v Feist*

In *Khan v Leo Feist, Inc* (1948), the Southern District of New York found no difficulty in finding infringement of the song's lyrics. Most of the court's attention was dedicated to technical issues of standing and assignment validity. As a result, the case ended up being an important precedent which validated oral agreements for copyright assignments under British law, albeit one made by a non-British court.

In its judicial opinion, comments from the court show a surprisingly sophisticated understanding of calypso's cultural context. In attempting to define calypso, references were made to calypso lyrics as a source of news and social commentary, how this creative expression is linked to the experience of the audience and local context, and the practices of melodic reuse and audience participation.

C. *Baron v Feist*

The second case – *Baron v Leo Feist* (1948) – was filed before the same district court as the first and concerned the musical accompaniment and melody of 'Rum and Coca-Cola'.

A summary of the facts as found by the court are as follows. In 1906, prominent West Indian pianist Lionel Belasco composed the music and lyrics of a song called 'L'Annee Passee' ('last year'). The lyrics were in patois (as were most early calypsos of that era) and told the story of a high society girl turned streetwalker after a failed inter-class relationship. Much later, in 1941, Belasco worked with singer Massie Patterson in New York, and the two secured a contract with music publisher Maurice Baron in 1943 to publish a collection called *Calypso Songs of the West Indies* containing 'L'Annee Passee'.

It is in 1943 that Lord Invader composed 'Rum and Coca-Cola' and was performing it in Trinidad. He sang the song to a tune he had learned from a member of Belasco's early group of musical friends, who were taught the song 'L'Annee Passee' around 1906.

Amsterdam claimed that he never heard the song while in Trinidad, and had only once heard a soldier singing the words 'Rum and Coca-Cola kill the Yankee soldier' to a tune like the American folk song 'It Ain't Gonna Rain No More'. Amsterdam then met with singer Jeri Sullivan, who sought out Paul Baron to compose accompanying music. Paul Baron's claims are that his inspiration came from various sources, including a song called 'King Jaja' (a West Indian folk song closely associated with Barbados, whose verse bears much melodic resemblance to 'Rum and Coca-Cola'). Despite a heated trial where almost every material issue of fact was under dispute, the court easily found that Amsterdam and Paul Baron fabricated their story and had lifted the music of 'Rum and Coca-Cola' from Lord Invader.

One line of argument put forward by the defence was that the melody for 'L'Annee Passee' was in the public domain, and thus the Maurice Baron copyright protected only Belasco's original

[25] *Khan v Leo Feist, Inc* 70 F.Su450 (SDNY 1947).
[26] *Baron v Leo Feist* 78 F.Su686 (SDNY 1948).

arrangement (and not the underlying core melody). In articulating their positions, both sides indirectly invoked the two competing schools of calypso: the defence contended that calypso uses a commons of folk melodies and focus is on originality in lyrics, while the plaintiff stressed the importance of melody and lyrics.

During the trial, Belasco testified that the original lyrics translate to 'Last year I was a little girl, I was a little girl at my mother's home; this year I am a streetwalker'. When Maurice Baron was transcribing harmonies for the song, he made a dramatic arrangement choice by harmonising with an 'unessential discord to a chromatic chord', to match the pathos of the original lyrics.[27]

The same dissonant chord is found in Amsterdam's version as a resolution to the fourth bar, where the word 'glad' is sang. It was argued that, from a compositional point of view, there is no justification for that odd choice, and this is strong proof of copying. This underscores the unique role of arrangement in calypso music, and demonstrates that in 'decontextualising' the song, composers from outside of the culture are unable to command the sophisticated compositional tools of the genre.

Another source of contention was the wording used in registering the copyright for *Calypso Songs of the West Indies*, as well as the foreword for the book. The court ultimately found that these points had no bearing on the legitimacy of Belasco's authorship. However, the use of certain terms like 'transcriber-arranger', 'lyrics collected' and 'collectors of (calypso)' are examples of the unique conceptions of authorship within calypso culture. These points also alluded to the unique context of Caribbean folk music, where songs can be seen as traditional standards, even if they are relatively new and can be traced to a living author.

D. Legacies of Rum and Yankees

The cases were inevitably appealed, with Feist losing in both.[28] In retrospect, the popular narrative celebrates that Belasco and Lord Invader were able to win their infringement claims against Amsterdam and Feist. An obvious but important observation is that although Lord Invader admitted to using Belasco's melody and music, Belasco seemed to have taken no issue with this.

The two cases would have certainly required some coordination between the two parties in managing the proceedings. After the appeals, private settlements were reached simultaneously as neither winning party opted for court-determined damages. Such coordination would have been necessary in the eyes of Feist Publishing, who negotiated cash settlements in return for retaining copyrights in the entire work that is 'Rum and Coca-Cola'. Any outcome where Feist would relinquish the copyright in either the lyrics or music, but not the other, would not be economically feasible for a large music publisher whose core business is music licensing. In the eyes of the local community, however, the story is often told in a way that implies that Lord Invader was done an injustice by not having the copyright of the song rightfully (re)assigned to him.

As for Belasco, while he is celebrated as a talented musician and seminal figure in the history of calypso music, there is a perception that he too was an appropriator. Belasco was formally trained and came from a middle-class creole background. His model was ultimately to take the folk melodies of his youth from all over the Caribbean (and neighbouring Venezuela) and formalise adaptations which could be registered as American copyrights. This is, of course, not to

[27] L Nizer, *My Life in Court* (Doubleday, 1961) 238–54.

[28] *Khan v Leo Feist, Inc* 165 F.2d 188 (CA.2 1948); *Baron v Leo Feist* 173 F.2d 288 (CA.2 1949).

say that much of Belasco's prolific work was not his own composition. However, the belief today is that 'L'Anne Passe' was originally a French Caribbean folk song from Martinique.[29]

In the 1946 song 'Yankee Dollar', Lord Invader followed up his massive hit by singing about how things in Trinidad have gotten much harder since the end of the war, and the local women now make less income soliciting. Taking a longer view of the history of calypso, the theme of Yankee-linked prostitution is eventually brought to closure with the Mighty Sparrow's 1956 Road March 'Jean and Dinah', one of the most iconic songs in all of Trinidadian culture. The song tells the story of women struggling to make ends meet after the American base was closed, resulting in more blatant public prostitution. In this new reality, with the threat of American competition gone, local male bravado returns with full force as 'the Yankees gone, and Sparrow take over now'.

VII. Conclusion

In this chapter, we have explored various dimensions of calypso music. It is a genre that is characterised by a unique relationship between instrumentation and lyrics, which, in turn, creates an important synthesis between its aesthetic and social functions. It also reflects tensions between social authorship as a modern folk art and the prominence of the individual artist in forums of entertainment and contestation. Practices of musical borrowing and unique creative dynamics facilitate calypso as a vehicle for political discourses and context-specific social messages, while a common pool of simple folk melodies from diverse cultural sources are brought to life by nuanced notions of arrangement.

The development of calypso music is further linked to the emergence of a broader pan-Caribbean folk music tradition. Thus, Trinidadian calypso, like Jamaican reggae, is a collective art form which reflects uniquely Caribbean experiences and attitudes. As articulated by Hebdige, in Caribbean music 'the collective voice is given precedence over the individual voice of the artist or the composer'.[30]

Calypso music is a music genre that not only has a deep and complex history of its own, but is also situated within the even more complex setting of the various Festival Arts which constitute Carnival celebrations. Its unique systems of arrangement, performance and participation suggest that the art form is much more than just a creative phenomenon: it is a fundamental mode of expression embedded into the society of Trinidad and Tobago, and the wider Caribbean. While the art form's presence on the stage of global popular culture has waned since the boom of the post-war Calypso Craze, its modern incarnation as soca music is growing rapidly as a musical genre that celebrates Caribbean identity by fusing both modernity and tradition. Regardless of how the context of the music changes over time, calypso continues to play an important role in the cultural and social landscape of Trinidad.

[29] Quevedo (n 8) 14.

[30] D Hebdige, *Cut 'n' Mix: Culture, Identity and Caribbean Music* (Routledge, 1987) 11.

15

Pholourie Bina Chutney: Copyright and Cultural Identity in Indo-Caribbean Music

BRYAN KHAN

I. Introduction

The Caribbean region is home to a wide range of indigenous musical art forms, from Jamaican reggae to Afro-Cuban jazz, which have become associated with the identity and aesthetics of the region's islands. One of its indigenous genres, *chutney*, is very different in its position within the wider cultural landscape of the West Indies. Chutney music is little known outside of its core demographic and is not a particularly celebrated art form. However, it nevertheless plays an important social and cultural role in the ethnically diverse fabric of the Southern Caribbean.

While the scale of the chutney scene is relatively small, it has developed within a much more compact cultural space, allowing for its unique creative norms to develop in a more concentrated and rapid manner. Interestingly, the genre's development has been relatively recent, meaning that its cultural norms and creative dynamics are still evolving and adapting. Nevertheless, the genre – particularly its modern incarnation as *chutney soca* – has become a growing sector with surprising commercial value and is legitimately an important element of the Caribbean music industry.

Slavery was officially abolished in the British Empire in 1833, though formerly enslaved people still faced exploitation under apprenticeship until 1838. After Emancipation, the British Authorities turned to a system of indentured servitude to find new sources of labour to continue agricultural production in the colonies. The British considered various sources of labour, but the system eventually centred on labour from then British India. The Dutch government also signed a contract with the British to supply labourers to Dutch Guyana (now the Republic of Suriname).

Under indentureship, over two million Indian labourers were transported to European colonies between 1838 and 1920. As a result, a large Indian diaspora grew in the Pacific Islands (Fiji), the Indian Ocean islands (Réunion and Mauritius), South Africa and the West Indies. In the West Indies, the demographic presence of the Indian diaspora is most strongly felt in the south of the Caribbean, and in particular the countries of Trinidad and Tobago (35 per cent of the population), Guyana (40 per cent) and Suriname (27 per cent). In all these countries, the relationships between the diverse ethnic groups would come to emerge as a primary factor in social organisation and domestic politics.

Unlike enslaved peoples of African origin, Indian immigrants came to the Caribbean with their language, culture, religion and traditions relatively intact. These traditions evolved over time, and chutney music emerged as a hybrid expression, incorporating elements of Old World culture, post-indentureship diasporic experiences and the wider post-Emancipation creole culture with which it was in proximity.

While chutney music is also associated with Guyana and Suriname, the discussions here generally often focus on the art form's history in Trinidad and Tobago, as this is the country in which the genre's complex cultural and creative system evolved most acutely.

II. The Development of Chutney

A. Migrant Roots

Indentured workers in the Caribbean generally came from the northern Bhojpuri region of India. Bhojpuri was thus the common language of the Indian labourer, and the music of these migrants consisted of Bhojpuri folk and devotional songs. They brought with them musical instruments from the mainland, which included drums such as the *dholak* and *tabla*, and melodic instruments such as the *harmonium*. Working on the plantations throughout the colonies, a percussive instrument called the *dhantal* evolved, which is a long steel rod adapted from oxcarts and struck rhythmically with a horseshoe.

Many different specific folk music traditions were invoked or adapted in the New World, such as *chowtal* (seasonal pre-Holi songs), *biraha* (narrative songs) and devotional *bhajans* in Hindi. A major component of Bhojpuri folk songs was songs associated with specific life-cycle events, such as weddings and births. During the *chathi* and *barahi* (sixth and twelfth days after a child's birth), slow folk songs called *sohar* would be performed, but as the evening got lively, faster 'breakaway' songs would be played. The breakaway songs would also be performed on key nights associated with pre-wedding rituals. The separate but related tradition of *tān* singing (or 'tent singing') would come to be known locally as 'classical Indian music', evolving into its own hybrid form and based on devotional sources.

B. The Hindu Wedding

While some of the migrants were Muslim, Hindu religious practices formed a major component of social identity for the majority. One particularly important practice is the ceremonial structure of the Hindu wedding, which is an elaborate affair often lasting several days, and an important cultural institution.

On the Friday night before the wedding, the families of the bride and groom gather at their respective homes and prepare for the wedding. This night is known as the *maticoor* night, where the ceremonial 'patching of the laawa' is conducted (the parching of rice, which is later exchanged in the wedding ceremony). The activities at the bride's residence are particularly vibrant. The gathered women sing and dance lewdly to improvisations based on folk songs associated with pre-marriage rituals. There were traditionally no (or very few) men present, perhaps only those who are there to play the supporting musical instruments – the dholak (a two-sided hand drum), harmonium (a small, hand-pumped organ) and dhantal. The older women would sing lewd songs to teach the bride-to-be about what to expect on the consummation night, often while miming sexual positions with a vegetable such as a *baigan* (aubergine). The tradition would evolve into improvised songs making fun of the bride or groom's families, such as 'Dulha Ke Maiya Chinar' (the groom's mother is a harlot).

By the 1940s–50s, traditional chutney music emerged out of this mixture of pre-wedding rituals, folk music and reconstituted religious traditions as a localised form of Indo-Caribbean expression. Breakaway songs were lifted from their original ceremonial context and brought into the public space. In Suriname, an almost identical fusion was taking place, with the genre of *Baithak Gana* evolving as a local Hindustani form of music pioneered and popularised by the harmonium player Ramdew Chaitoe and female singers like Bidjanwatie Chaitoe and Dropati. Baithak Gana shares its roots with the classical tān singing, but it manifested some of the characteristics of chutney (like faster tempos) at an earlier stage.

C. From Traditional to Modern Chutney

A major inflection point was the song 'Nani and Nana', composed by Trinidadian singer Sundar Popo in 1969. Popo grew up influenced by his mother, who would sing at Indian weddings. He is carded as the first to take the melodies of Bhojpuri folk music and mix them with English lyrics and more structured pop-music arrangements and instrumentation. As such, Popo is considered to be the father of chutney music. His songs such as 'Nani and Nani', 'Kaise Bani' and 'Scorpion Gyal' are defining songs of the 'classic chutney' era, and his lyrics would combine various elements of original themes, jovial balderdash and known breakaway verses.

In Trinidad, the television show *Mastana Bahar* was founded in 1970 to showcase Indian culture, giving the first major stage for Indian performances outside of localised village events. In 1971, only five of the 88t entries in the *Mastana Bahar* auditions were local compositions, with the rest being renditions of Indian film songs.[1] Popo's 'Nani and Nana', however, changed everything. He proved that Indian cultural expression did not need to be derivative of the motherland but could take an original and indigenous form.

During the 1980s–90s, chutney music continued to grow, and generally developed in two different but overlapping directions. In one direction, performers focused on maintaining cultural authenticity. This is the classic branch of modern chutney, largely coming from artists involved in the 'local classical music' tradition. These artists balanced the traditional aesthetics and melodies of chutney with more modern production tools, such as digital drum machines. Lyrics would be based on adaptations of devotional songs (bhajans), vignettes of Indian social and cultural life, or stock Indian narratives like Krishna teasing the cowgirls. This era of the genre is also characterised by family musical dynasties, where traditions and skills are passed down between generations and kept withing family networks. The songs 'Nanda Baba' (a devotion to Lord Krishna which has become a classic chutney standard) popularised by Anand Yankeran, and the classic hit 'Mousie', by his brother Rakesh Yankaran, exemplify these features.

In the other direction, performers fused elements of Indian instrumentation with the Afro-Caribbean rhythms of calypso and soca music. Bass guitar (or electronic bass lines) might be added to create a stronger rhythm section. This would represent an early incarnation of the genre of chutney soca, which is a modern bridge between the two previously distinct musical forms of calypso and chutney. An important purveyor of this strain was Babla and Kanchan, a husband-and-wife duo from India who initially began their singing careers performing Indian film songs. They re-recorded many local chutney songs written by Trinidadian and Guyanese composers, making these songs into major hits during the 1970s and 1980s for the international Indian diaspora.

[1] N Tejaswini, *Mobilizing India: Women, Music, and Migration between India and Trinidad* (Duke University Press, 2006) 95.

Unfortunately, most accounts of the history of chutney tend to understate the foundations laid by Surinamese and Guyanese artists, and misleadingly imply Trinidad as the genesis of the genre.

D. The Chutney Soca Explosion

In the 1990s, the genre would evolve to incorporate elements of soca – more explicitly, solidifying chutney soca as a contemporary art form – and securing a space for the Indo-community within the Trinidadian Festival Arts traditionally associated with Afro-creole traditions. Pioneers of the genre were Drupatee Ramgoonai, considered to be the 'mother of chutney soca', and the male singer Rikki Jai. A turning point was 1995, when the Chutney Monarch competition was established to compliment the International Soca Monarch and Calypso Monarch competitions. The chutney soca song 'Lotela' by Sonny Man became a major hit during the Carnival season of 1996, representing the first time a chutney song was widely celebrated by the entire national community.

Moving into the 2000s, trends in chutney soca would often follow the broader musical production trends in soca. Modern chutney soca is less dependent on traditional instrumentation, and synthesisers and digital instruments have largely replaced the melodic role of the harmonium and percussive role of the dholak. Melodically, the dominant practice that has emerged is that chutney soca songs borrow their melodies from Indian film songs. Chutney soca has now become a legitimate cultural export to cities like Toronto and New York, where large Indo-Caribbean diasporas reside, and artists are securing increasingly larger international tour schedules. Figure 15.1 is a stylised summary of the genre's evolution through different phases, each with progressively different influences from source material and instrumentation.

Figure 15.1 A styled account of the musical evolution of chutney

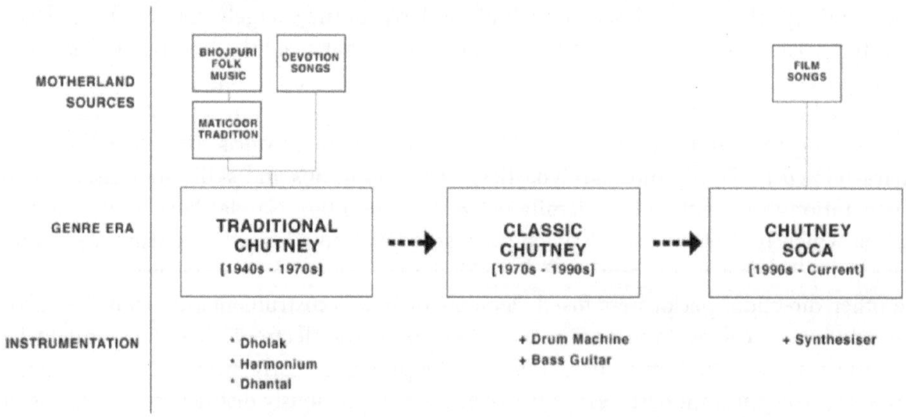

E. Socio-cultural Context

To truly understand chutney music, a few brief points must be made on its social context. The first is that the music represents an important nexus of post-colonial ethnic identity for Indo-Caribbean peoples, who felt historically marginalised from public life and the Afro-Caribbean forms of creole culture around which national identities coalesced.[2] Indo-Caribbean culture has thus often tended to be inward looking and insular, as it struggles to balance connections to the Old World with the formation of New World identities. Chutney music, however, especially chutney soca, has always attracted the ire of the conservative Indo-community, who see it as a morally corruptive force associated with the decline of Indian classical music and traditional Hindu values.

The politics of gender relations is also a defining theme. The roots of chutney are in a traditional space reserved for women, where they could freely express themselves through both words and dance, without the constraints of gendered social expectations. When chutney established itself as a popular art form, this freedom manifested in further empowerment of women, as a public space was created for men to be openly criticised. Rasika Dindials's 'Lazy Man' (circa 1997) is a prime example of a song in this tradition. When chutney soca exploded, these practices moved even more explicitly onto the public stage. This new stage integrates the participation of men and invites a renegotiation of gender identities through sexually provocative lyrics and dance.[3]

We should therefore understand traditional chutney as an inherently feminist movement, and chutney soca (particularly chutney soca dancing) as an anti-patriarchal expression. This is particularly pronounced as the traditional segregated dances from which chutney evolved were done largely by lower-class women, arguably one of the most historically oppressed sectors of society, who are now able to claim a space in national culture.[4] However, the rebalancing of gender roles in this setting has now become more complex. On the one hand, men breaking into the chutney space – particularly Sundar Popo in the 1970s – set the creative events in motion for the genre to grow, innovate and gain popularity. On the other hand, this involved male singers co-opting a space reserved for female liberation. As such, the complex relationship between male and female performers is a defining characteristic of the genre.

Class identity also forms an integral part of chutney culture, as well as its lyrical themes. Unlike the calypso and creole cultures which eventual gained the acceptance of the urban middle class by the independence era of the 1960s, chutney always perpetuated its rural roots and aesthetics. Nevertheless, calypso, steelpan and chutney were all born from impoverished working-class settings without the initial support of the petite bourgeoisie.

Chutney does not aim to push aesthetic, intellectual or technical boundaries, but rather emphasises identity, tradition and social dance. Traditional and classic chutney draws heavily on Hindu devotion and themes of everyday village life. Modern incarnations of the genre have, however, embraced and amplified a playful balance between self-commentary and self-indulgence. Chutney soca lyrics are almost exclusively based on one of four themes (i) *tabanka* (unrequited love), (ii) sexual inuendo, (iii) alcohol consumption (specifically rum) and (iv) marital infidelity (or 'horning' in Trinidadian parlance).

The themes of alcohol and infidelity reflect social symbolism rooted in colonial experiences. If Sundar Popo's 'Nani and Nani' is accepted as the first modern chutney song, then the dark themes of alcoholism and domestic abuse have characterised the genre since inception, as the song tells the story of a grandmother and an abusive alcoholic grandfather. Songs of rum and horning can be seen as self-aware meta-commentaries on social identity, where traditional chutney's

[2] CL Ballengee, 'Music Competitions, Public Pedagogy and Decolonisation in Trinidad and Tobago' (2019) 11(2) *South Asian Diaspora* 5.

[3] A Mohammed, 'Love and Anxiety: Gender Negotiations in Chutney-Soca Lyrics in Trinidad' (2007) Issue 1 *Caribbean Review of Gender Studies* 1, 39.

[4] P Manuel, *East Indian Music in the West Indies: Tan-singing, Chutney, and the Making on Indo-Caribbean Culture* (Temple University Press, 2000) 171, 195.

vignettes of village life are transformed into chutney soca's amplified self-aware caricatures. The result is a disarmament of colonial-era stereotypes through self-satire. The process also stands in rebellious defiance of the aristocracy, cultural gatekeepers and the Hindu Orthodoxy, through the embrace of frivolous lyrics and intentionally amateur and unpretentious approaches to composition.

III. Musical Characteristics and Creative Practices

A. Sources and Structure of Melody

For classic chutney, original melodies are rare, and the main source is Bhojpuri folk melodies and localised adaptations of the same. The stock of folk song melodies is very limited, however, even in their original setting, where the 'paucity of melodies' was documented by administrators in British India.[5] In the Caribbean setting, specific iterations of these stock folk melodies adapted over time, and many were made popular by the genre's progenitors. The result is not exact melodies, but rather general melodic phrases and keys which become established as standard, as the folk connections between specific melodies and narrative themes are lost.

Like other forms of Caribbean music, the continuous remaking of popular songs is central to the art form of chutney music. For example, it is almost a rite of passage for a male chutney artist to perform their own versions of Sundar Popo hits. This creates an interesting phenomenon, where these works may or may not be based on stock folk melodies but become strongly associated with a specific popular song. With consecutive cycles of reperformance and reinterpretation, new compositions can achieve this 'classic' status in less than a generation. It thus becomes extremely difficult to separate the popular repertoire of classics into 'folk songs' and works with known living authors. The boundaries between original folk songs and generational reinterpretations become blurred. The default attitude has thus become to treat many popular compositions as if they are in the public domain, even if they were created by identifiable living authors. In fact, versions of Sundar Popo's most popular songs have all been transformed into de facto stock melodies. Popo himself is documented as claiming that chutney artists who came after him all take 'his' melodies.[6]

Generally, the 'classic'-style melodies are defined by contiguous interval steps, which allude a simple character when combined with simple rhyming structures. Furthermore, a classic chutney melody almost always resolves to the tonic note at the end of the verse. This contrasts with pop music, where a verse melody often only resolves in the first note of the chorus, creating a sense of a verse being pulled into the chorus for resolution. The result is that the chutney melody can be delivered in more discreet sections (like a single verse only) and still achieve a sense of satisfactory resolution.

The perception of classic chutney's melodic simplicity is further reinforced by its instrumentation. The only instrumental melodic support comes from the harmonium, which has a relatively short scale and is played with only one hand, the other hand being used to pump air into the instrument. Additionally, the instrument lacks any of the sustained tonal drone that characterises

[5] As reported in ibid 94.

[6] TK Ramnarine, *Creating Their Own Space: The Development of an Indian-Caribbean Musical Tradition* (University of the West Indies Press, 2001) 39.

instruments such as the sitar used in other forms of Indian music. Hence, harmonium performances are typically scaled runs supporting key melodies. Where chords are used, they are typically simple triad chords. Additionally, performances are typically by a single vocalist without backup singers. This reinforces an overall perception of melodic simplicity, as performances lack any dimension of harmony.

Moving from classic chutney into chutney soca, melodies are routinely taken (interpolated) from foreign sources. In many cases, these sources are international pop songs, where melodies are reused even to the extent of creating local parodies. These interpolations are done without any concern for the infringement of copyright in the original works. However, by far the most significant phenomenon in interpolation is the use of melodies from Indian film songs (discussed in detail later).

B. Musical Structure and Arrangement

While all genres typically have common patterns for musical arrangement, classic chutney songs exhibit very specific and interesting structural features derived from their folk song roots. Essentially, melodies are broken up into single measure-long motifs, different combinations of which make up verses, chorus and instrumental breaks. The main hook of a song is the main motif, and it typically serves three functions: (i) the chorus melody; (ii) the second half of a verse and its resolution (where a melody very similar to the main motif is used); and (iii) an instrumental lead, to complete a chorus.

Instrumental measures are used to create spaces between verses and choruses, or to break up verses. Often, instrumental measures will be freestyled runs, and can modulate from minor to major (or vice versa) to create contrast and tension in terms of both key and melodic complexity. Where an instrumental run breaks up verses, the first part of the verse will not resolve, and only the second part (after the break) will resolve using a melody derived from the main motif. By doing this, the main motif's status as a hook is amplified by serving as both a chorus and a verse resolution. Choruses might even be of different lengths, as they form from different clusters of the key motifs and refrains.

An interesting implication of this structure is that although songs are in common time (4/4), song sections can emerge as clusters of three measures rather than four. We can see this structure in action in Table 15.1, which shows the structure of one chorus and verse of Sundar Popo's *Kaise Bani*.

Table 15.1 Excerpt of *Kaise Bani* arrangement

Chorus	Kaise banī, kaise banī	Chorus motif A
	Kaise banī, kaise banī	Chorus motif B
	Pholourie bin-a chatanī kaise banī	Chorus motif main
	(Instrumental break)	Chorus motif main
	Pholourie bin-a chatanī kaise banī	Chorus motif main
	(Instrumental break)	Chorus motif main
Verse	Ah' beating meh drum and ah singin' meh song	Verse motif A
	Ah' beating meh drum and ah singin' meh song	Verse motif A
	The only thing ah missin' is meh bottle of rum	Verse motif B

These arrangement techniques contribute to classic chutney's defining aesthetics. Variances in chorus structures and common resolutions between choruses and verses result in an overall arrangement that exhibits musical continuity, and almost makes the distinctions between verses and choruses arbitrary. Theses variances also give these songs a loose structure and quasi-improvised feel even through recorded music. These key features convey the simplistic impressions to the listener associated with classic chutney, while hidden behind surprisingly nuanced arrangements.

One last critical arrangement feature is important to point out. This is the very specific form of the classic chutney intro. The typical intro is some iteration of four specific successive elements: (i) an ascending harmonium run; (ii) landing on a sustained tonic chord; (iii) slowed acapella recitation of the main vocal refrain; and (iv) syncopated percussive stabs which break into the faster tempo of the main song. This intro arrangement is so specific, yet so common, that it is the one trope that can always be used to invoke the genre's sound.

Critics often comment that chutney lacks musical diversity. This is because of commonalties which are not only melodic (where particular parts of a song might sound similar), but also structural, where the overall aesthetic impression conveyed by different songs is the same. Indeed, all modern musical genres are defined by some common formulas for song arrangement. However, it is just that in the case of chutney, the arrangement formula is so specific and genre-defining that there is a greater potential for perceived homogeneity. Here, cumulative creativity is reflected in the fact that the genre as a whole can be seen as the cultural expression, rather than individual songs.

C. Picong and Response Songs

A feature that chutney has in common with other Caribbean popular music forms is the role of *picong* – friendly disputes through music. Picong songs are a subset of more general response songs, and the inevitably lyrical tradition in the chutney space is to sing of one's own sexual and romantic prowess with your opponent's lovers. A prime example is the 2003 hit 'Rum Till I Die' by Adesh Samaroo, which produced the response 'Right in Front Yuh Eye' by Devanad Gatoo and the counter-response 'Mash You Up' by Samaroo.

The chutney picong and response song model generally does not resolve genuine interpersonal disputes. Rather, they are playful yet competitive bouts where artists can boost their own profiles and popularity. When one artist's song becomes popular, other artists then have the opportunity to respond with their own song and create a musical dialogue, essentially free riding off the original work's popularity. This practice is not at all seen as exploitative, but rather an established and welcome part of chutney culture. It thus democratises the popularity of major hits and represents a form of potential social authorship.

A particularly endearing form of picong is response songs which play off gender divisions. Typically, a male artist would have a successful song, and a female artist will release a response song which invokes the wider theme of male–female conflict. For example, after the 2009 Chutney Soca Monarch-winning song 'Radica' by Kenneth Salick (where Salick sings of his actual wife Radica leaving him), Rawltee Ramroop responded with the song 'Ah Had Ah Right To Leave And Go', re-singing the song from the perspective of Radica. In another example, chutney soca artist KI released the popular 2009 song 'Catch Meh Lover', about catching his lover Sunita cheating on him with a girl named Nadia. Guyanese singer Princess Anisa responded with the song 'Tek Sunita (Nadia's Reply)', singing from the perspective of the Nadia character, boasting of romancing the Sunita character away from KI.

These songs are interesting as they are particularly striking examples of collective authorship. The dialogue created between songs is not just one of confrontation, but one of actual narrative continuity where characters are developed through different lyrics. They also create a platform for equal gender participation in the genre, as they are typically responses from less well-known female artists to successful hits from male artists. The social commentary espouses female empowerment, and the 'battle of the sexes' trope reflects the genre's roots of picong in the maticoor night setting, where the families of the bride and groom poke fun at each other in private. More importantly, these songs represent female artists reclaiming chutney music as a fundamentally female space.

Unlike general picong response tracks, which reuse the original song's lyrical themes and phrasing, male–female responses take identical musical form, with only the lyrics changed. This is again done without any concern for the copyright in the original song, and the possibility of such responses is understood as part of the culture. Generally, response songs are seen as a compliment that further boosts the popularity of the original song (as well as the reputation of the respondent). In a chutney party, it is typical that if the deejay plays one of these hit songs, it will be followed by the response track.

One final form of response song is the parody response. In this model, a successful song is repurposed with new lyrics that reference the original words and theme, but not necessarily in the format of picong.

D. Medley and Remix Versions

Another typical feature of chutney music is making local versions of popular 'English' songs (ie any song that comes from outside of the 'Indian' artistic space). In the chutney scene, an important entity is the 'crossover band', which uses live electric instruments, and is typical entertainment at parties and weddings. These bands play songs from a mixed 'Indian' and 'English' repertoire, and the lead singers perform pieces of different songs depending on the crowd's mood, often blending them together into a single fluid performance. This inevitably results in the incorporation of hooks and elements from popular songs into local chutney songs in the live performance setting.

This practice has translated to bands recording these 'remix' mashups for radio play and advertising purposes, although they are generally not released as commercial records. The range of covered music is wide and includes any 'English' songs that the local audience would enjoy, from reggae, dancehall, calypso and soca to American pop and radio rock. Typically, verses from Indian film songs will be inserted into these covers between the English verses and choruses, to create an English–Indian medley. Again, these derivative works are created with no attention to copyright implications.

While this practice has historically been a promotional tool, there is evidence that it is becoming a more formalised creative format, as evidence by the 2022 hit single 'The Indian Anthem' by chutney artist Anil Bheem. This song combines elements of the classic Jamaican dancehall (Bam Bam Riddim and Hot This Year Riddim) with the song 'Suhani Raat' from the 1949 film Dulari (which is so popular it is often referred to as the 'Indian Anthem' within the Indo-Trinidadian community).

E. Versioning and Reperformance

In chutney, it is common for artists to record their own versions of popular songs that have achieved classic hit status. This is usually done without permission from the original songwriter, as classic-style chutney songs are perceived as free to be reused. During Carnival time, it is standard procedure for soca and chutney soca bands to learn all the popular songs in rotation for that season and perform pieces of them live. This practice does not necessarily raise copyright issues as the songs are not recorded, and the live performances are covered by the blanket licences secured by event organisers from collective management organisations.

Another Carnival season trend is that of the chutney remix–re-release. If an artist has had a hit within the chutney community, they often later release a remix of the song featuring a soca artist and remarket the song as a chutney soca version to a wider audience. This practice has allowed chutney and soca artists to reach each other's audiences through collaboration. It is particularly popular with artists who wish to keep their orientation as a classic-style chutney artist, as it allows them to reach a soca audience without explicitly pivoting to writing chutney soca songs. The remix–re-release can also be used by an artist whose previous offering was not successful and opts to re-record a new version of the same song featuring a more established artist to re-market the song.

F. 'Gunga Ghana'

The song 'Gunga Gana' (also Gunga Ghana or Gunga Ganna) is a remarkable case study in the creative norms of chutney. The song was released by Trinidadian Dubraj Persad in 2015 and follows the template of modern chutney production. The lyrics use localised Bhojpuri and translate to a criticism of 'singers of dumb songs' and the chutney music industry in general. The song gained only moderate traction until a remix featuring popular chutney artist Ravi B became extremely popular after its release in 2019.

Chutney veteran Hemlata Dindial released her own version as a response song, called 'Ghana Gunga' (reversing the original track's title). Dindial found herself in receipt of a legal complaint from Persad's attorneys, who alleged 'illegal reproduction of original melody containing key words and phrases'.[7] According to the attorneys representing Dindial, the response song contained an 'original idea, creative work and contains completely different words to Persad's song, with the exception of four "common words"'. Ironically, but not surprisingly given the closeness of the chutney community, the complainant's attorney was also a chutney artist, who has released several recordings in recent years using the same practices of liberal remix and creative borrowing that define the genre.

In response to the conflict, Hemlata Dindial's sister Rasika Dindial (a legendary chutney singer, and co-writer of Hemlata's song) released the song 'Kach Kach'. She sharply criticises Persad for stirring up conflict and abusing the picong tradition to make money, and implies that he is trying to make a name without paying his dues. In suggesting that Persad should 'worship his helper and guru' (likely Ravi B, who is famous for interpolating melodies), Dindial is advising that Persad should respect chutney's cultural norms. Overall, while 'Kach Kach' did not rise to the mass popularity of 'Gunga Gana', its lyrical content can be seen as coming to the defence of the social and creative norms of musical borrowing, and the ethos of collective ownership and social authorship. Copyright enforcement is simply not part of this system of norms.

Further responses followed, such as the songs 'Is a Hurricane Love' and 'Gunga Gawaiya' by Hemlata herself. Singer Aaron Jewan Singh released a song titled 'Gunga Ghana Kuchur' that directly commented on the conflict between Persad and Hemlata Dindial. Guyanese traditional chutney artist Rajesh Dubraj also released a song called 'Durga Gana', performing a bhajan for Mother Durga using the 'Gunga Ghana' melody.

[7] 'Chutney Bacchanal over "Gunga Gana"' *Trinidad Express* (3 May 2019).

While the legal conflict seems to have fizzled, the 'Gunga Gana' dispute is a great example of *Gaari* (picong battle). In a Western setting, we might expect an artist threatened with copyright infringement to be very measured and careful about making comments which might prejudice their position regarding an ongoing legal dispute. However, we see both Rasika and Hemlata Dindial making bold public statements through their music. Rasika comes to her sister's defence by criticising the complainant and Hemlata shows bold opposition to the very accusation of copyright infringement, while third party artists comment from a distance. In the eyes of the performing artists, reputation and the court of public opinion are the forum in which disputes are settled, rather than the formal judicial system. Regardless of whether Persad's claim had legal merit, his pursuit of that claim violated the revered culture of the industry. In doing so, he suffered potential damage to his reputation and credibility within the chutney fraternity.

IV. Chutney Soca and Bollywood Interpolation

In the unlikely case that the reader is unaware, Bollywood refers to the Hindi-language film industry based in Mumbai and is the largest film production sector in the world. While other regional Indian film industries exist (such as the Bengali 'Tollywood'), in the international forum, 'Bollywood' is often used as a reference to the Indian film industry generally. In the typical Bollywood film format, film and song are inseparable, as narratives are told using elaborate song-and-dance numbers interspersed throughout the film. In this format, a successful film and a successful film soundtrack are largely one and the same, and the contemporary music industry is inextricably linked with the film industry.

A. Bollywood Interpolation

The practice of chutney soca borrowing melodies is not new, as classic chutney had always borrowed melodies from old Indian sources such as bhajans and film songs. In modern chutney soca, however, the practice has essentially become standard protocol, as melodies are borrowed from both contemporary and old films, regardless of whether they are well known or obscure to the diaspora. In the classic chutney setting, only the melodies were borrowed, as the Hindi lyrics were changed to localised Bhojpuri. As both languages are foreign to most listeners in the Caribbean, the practice would not necessarily invoke a sense of appropriation. With modern chutney soca, however, Hindi film lyrics are replaced with English and local dialect, invoking a sense of cultural degradation in the eyes of many purists, especially given the frivolity of the new lyrics.

This practice has become so widespread that it has now become a defining feature of modern chutney soca. Melodies are taken wholesale from film songs to be used as chorus hooks, with lyrics sometimes even adapted to mirror the phonetic structures of the original Hindi lyrics. Verse melodies are generally simpler and less important in the context of making a seasonal hit, and these melodies may also be copied or might be original. The practice is also done openly and unapologetically. Indeed, most chutney soca hits since the 2000s have been authored using this technique, where melodies are not just similar, but identical, and borrowing is done without concern for copyright infringement. The scale of this practice is hard to convey and identifying source melodies has become something of a prideful pastime of many Indo-Caribbean music aficionados. Some popular examples from the last two decades are given in Table 15.2, many of which were winners of the Chutney Soca Monarch title.

Table 15.2 Examples of Bollywood-sourced melodies

Song (artist, year)	Source song (film, year)
Mr Shankar (D'Hitman, 2005)	*Jai Jai Shivshankar* (Aap Ki Kasam, 1974)
Rum Is Meh Lover (Ravi B, 2006)	*Akela Hoon Mein* (Baat Ek Raat Ki, 1962)
Bring It (Hunter, 2008)	*Chahoonga Mein Tujhe* (Dosti, 1964)
Jep Sting Naina (Hunter et al, 2008)	*Jabse Tere Naina* (Saawariya, 2007)
Radica (Kenneth Salick, 2009)	*Ek Masoom Sa Chehra* (Zinda Dil, 2003)
Barman (Rikky Jai, 2010)	*Dil Mera Ek Aas Ka Panchhi* (Aas Ka Panchhi, 1961)
Spanner (D'Hitman, 2010)	*Husn Hai Suhana* (Coolie No 1, 1995)
Ah Drinka (Ravi B, 2010)	*O Saathi Re* (Muqaddar Ka Sikandar, 1978)
Single Forever (KI, 2012)	*Dekhta Hai Tu Kya* (Krazzy 4, 2008)
Bread (Ravi B, 2014)	*Chane Ke Khet Mein* (Anjaam, 1994)
Same Gyul Twice (KI, 2016)	*Jab Gori Ne* (Bulandi, 2000)
Balkisoon (Omardath Maharaj, 2016)	*Aye Mere Dil-E-Nadan* (Tower House, 1962)
Budget (Ravi B, 2017)	*Mohan Ki Muraliya Baja* (Mela, 1948)

Many of these examples illustrate not only that the melodies are borrowed, but also the exact phonetic phrasing of the original refrains is approximated with the choice of new words. For example, in the song 'Mr Shanker' the refrain 'Listen Mr Shanker …' approximates the phonetic sound of the original 'Jai Jai Shivshankar'. In the song 'Rum is Meh Lover', the original lyrics 'Akela Hoon Mein' are even included to complete the refrain. One of the most interesting examples is perhaps in the song 'Jep Sting Naina', whose title and refrain is a particular choice of local words which mirror the phonetics of the original title and refrain 'Jabse Tere Naina'. That song is performed by an all-star group of chutney artists, and even begins with a recital of the original source song's verse.

An important finding is that there appears to be no social norm in which an artist claims or enjoys exclusivity to a borrowed melody, even if they are the first to use it or make it popular. For example, Guyanese singer Terry Gajraj released the song 'Aye Mere Dil E Nadan (Why you leave and gone)' in 2009, several years before that film melody was popularised by the song 'Balkisoon' in 2016. There is still, however, some incentive to search for unused or obscure melodies from the seemingly endless archives of Indian film music, as there is some reputational advantage to be the first artist to popularise a melody.

A new, emerging trend seems to be deliberately pointing the public to the original source of the film melody. For example, Raymond Ramnarine's 'Mohan Ke Muraliya' was released in 2017, in response to Ravi B's Chutney Soca Monarch-winning 'Budget'. It is essentially a chutney soca reperformance of the 1948 song from which the 'Budget' melody is sourced. We can interpret this form of response song as not just calling out the first artist, but attempting to compete with them in terms of vocal ability rather than typical chutney response song formats, as authentic performances of such film songs are technically challenging tasks.

In another example, Ravi B's 2021 'Ek Haseen (Party Hard)' (with Dubraj Persad) combines two hooks: (i) an English party-themed soca hook; and (ii) a performance of the song 'Ek Haseen Sham Ko Dil Mera Kho Gaya' from the 1967 film *Dulhan Ek Raat Ki*. Instead of directly interpolating the melody with new words, the actual film song verses are performed, and part of the original song title ('Ek Haseen') is directly used. In this case, the performer deflects any accusation of trying to pass off the film melody as original, as the audience is pointed directly to the original source.

The practice of Bollywood melody reuse has caused much controversy in the chutney community (and, indeed, wider Caribbean music industry), where two camps exist – one that believes that borrowing film melodies should not be allowed and one that believes that the practice is legitimate. The practice has been a dividing point in the organisation of the annual Chutney Soca Monarch competition, and the awarding of its significant cash prize. Popular artists have come out in support of both sides of the debate. In 2013, singer Raymond Ramnarine won the Monarch title, but chose not to re-enter in 2014 due to delays in prize payment, and also disappointment that Bollywood melodies were allowed.[8] The run-up to the 2017 competition saw public protests from various artists who lamented the use of Bollywood melodies in the competition as their use undermined their own original efforts.[9] In response, international chutney soca star Rikki Jai publicly supported the practice.[10] It has not been uncommon in the last few years to also see letters to the editor in local papers complaining about the practice. Several smaller alternative competitions have been organised recently to promote 'authenticity and originality', where Bollywood melody use is not permitted.

Interestingly, the issue has even been alluded to by the judiciary of Trinidad and Tobago, where the ruling High Court judge in copyright matter (not involving chutney music) references a need to 'dissuade artists from merely copying melodies and lyrics from Africa and India'.[11]

B. The Phenomenon of Non-enforcement

The trend of chutney soca music's heavy reliance on interpolation of Bollywood melodies leads to a very interesting puzzle of infringement, enforcement and forbearance. The extent of melody use certainly constitutes substantive similarity for the purpose of establishing copyright infringement. There is also no reason to believe that the industry is unaware of the practice, as the connections between the Indian industry and the Indo-diasporic markets are strong. Bollywood has established licensing networks with film and television distributors throughout the Caribbean. Furthermore, prior to statutory amendments in 2012, Indian film songs were created on a work-for-hire basis, meaning that Bollywood producers owned the copyrights in both the films and the film songs.

Bollywood is a billion-dollar force, and chutney music has been steadily growing into a multi-million-dollar industry within the Caribbean and its own diaspora. The question thus arises as to why there seems to be no major precedent of Indian rights holders taking enforcement action against Indo-Caribbean musicians for what seem to be clear-cut cases of copyright infringement. Two possible explanations are offered here. The first is that the Bollywood industry itself is based on various practices of copying, thematic borrowing and social norms of collective ownership. The second is that even if Bollywood were a habitual enforcer, it would see it as economically rational to forbear against Indo-Caribbean musicians.

[8] 'Ramnarine Not Defending Trini Chutney Soca Title' *Stabroek News* (5 February 2014).

[9] 'Chutney Soca Singer Protests Use of Bollywood Melodies in Competition' *LoopTT News* (12 January 2017).

[10] 'Jai Supports Bollywood in Chutney/Soca' *Trinidad Guardian* (16 January 2017).

[11] *Full Blown Entertainment Company Ltd v Devon Matthews, Anson Soverall and Gem Radio Five Ltd* Trinidad and Tobago High Court of Justice, Claim No CV 2015-01073, delivered on 18 January 2017; para 85.

C. Bollywood and Commercial-Scale Plagiarism

The Bollywood industry has been notoriously criticised over the last decades for plagiarising Hollywood productions, with American films often being remade scene-for-scene, with film posters even recreated based on the originals. The films are, however, adapted for Indian audiences by adding song-and-dance routines and making other changes. There are endless examples of plagiarised films, and even many allegedly unauthorised adaptations of novels and books.

The practice has, however, come under threat somewhat since a series of enforcement actions began in the late 2000s. In 2009, Warner Brothers Studios took out notices in Indian newspapers, warning Indian film producers against making an adaption of the 2008 film *The Curious Case of Benjamin Button*.[12] One year earlier, Warner Brothers lost a bid before the High Court in Delhi to block the film 2008 film *Harri Puttar: A Comedy of Terrors* (on trademark grounds), due to its title being an obvious reference to the *Harry Potter* film series. The court ruled that the public would be able to tell Harri Puttar apart from Harry Potter.[13] Nevertheless, the film was a clear remake of another well-known Hollywood film, 1990's *Home Alone*. The biggest successful enforcement was perhaps a 2009 settlement of US$200,000 reached between Twentieth Century Fox and the producers of the film *Banda Yeh Bindaas Hai*, which was a Hindi remake of the 1992 Hollywood comedy *My Cousin Vinny*.[14]

One commenter's analysis suggests that Hollywood traditionally did not concern itself with enforcement for three reasons: (i) Bollywood's lack of profitability; (ii) India's developing country status; and (iii) traditionally distinct audiences for both types of films.[15] With India's economic growth and migration patterns, these trends are reversing, so enforcement is now a greater concern for American film producers. However, it is argued that Hollywood producers would likely have a hard time successfully litigating, as actual damages from infringement would be very difficult to prove.[16] When a film is 'Indianised', the new elements are what give it market value to an Indian audience. What constitutes substance in the Indian cultural space is very different from Western ideas of artistic aesthetics, as Western film focuses on narrative while Indian film focuses on the process of narrative. In this sense, both take the same format as audiovisual work, but plot serves a different role in Bollywood, secondary to aspects like costuming, dialogue, song, dance and pacing. Accusations of plagiarism – whether in film or music – thus largely imply judging non-Western art forms by Western artistic standards.

Bollywood's reputation for alleged plagiarism is not limited to film, as it is known to also copy international music (as well as local music from Indian artists) for its film songs. Enforcement actions have recently also become more common for film song infringements. A notable example is the successful 2017 injunction won by Canadian singer Loreena McKennitt against the song 'Aaro Nee Aaro' from the 2011 film *Urmi*, which plagiarised her songs 'Caravanserai' and 'The Mummers' Dance'.[17]

D. Caribbean Music in Bollywood

Bollywood has also been known to use Caribbean music. The 2012 film *Dabangg 2* features a version of none other than Sundar Popo's 'Kaise Bani'. Also in 2012, the critically acclaimed

[12] 'Bollywood's "Copycats" Get Warning from Hollywood' *Times of India* (12 April 2009).

[13] 'Hari Puttar Fails to Conjure Potter Magic' *The Guardian* (28 September 2008).

[14] 'BR Films Settles Plagiarism Charges with Fox' *Economic Times of India* (8 August 2009).

[15] H Basi, 'Indianizing Hollywood: The Debate over Copyright Infringement by Bollywood' (2011) 18 *UCLA Entertainment Law Review* 37.

[16] ibid 68.

[17] 'Urumi Song Issued Warrant for Plagiarism' *Times of India* (10 January 2017).

two-part film *Gangs of Wasseypur* featured a soundtrack heavily inspired by Bihari folk music, and several tracks that incorporated Indo-Caribbean chutney.

A particularly noteworthy incident involved the 'Father of Soca' Lord Shorty (later known as Ras Short I), who is celebrated in Trinidad and Tobago for helping to bridge the Indo–Afro cultural divide. His fusion of Indian elements with calypso set the early template for soca music and built on a long tradition of calypsonians experimenting with Indian themes since the 1920s. In fact, in his 1966 song 'Indian Singers', he incorporates the film song 'Ham Hai to Chand Aur Tare' from the 1959 film *Main Nashe Mein Hoon*.

Lord Shorty's 1976 anthemic 'Om Shanti Om' is a landmark in Trinidadian music and is essentially a Hindu prayer sung by an Afro-Trinidadian artist. The song was later remade without his authorisation and was used for the 1980 Indian film *Karz*. The film and song were a massive hit, and Lord Shorty was frustrated at his inability to earn royalties from the exploitation of his work. His own comments suggest that it was not possible to enter India to enforce rights.[18] The popular oral account is that this situation persisted because 'India had not signed the international copyright treaties'.

E. Copyright and Creative Norms

Indeed, before 1999, foreign works were not automatically protected under the applicable Indian Law – the 1957 Copyright Act – despite the country being party to the Berne Convention since 1928.[19] With the 1999 International Copyright Order, foreign works were finally afforded protection on reciprocal terms. This legislative reality certainly explains the deeply entrenched norms of plagiarism that define the Bollywood industry, and the inertia to modern attitudes of copyright compliance. This is further compounded by the general tensions between Western conceptions of 'originality' and private property rights and the centuries-old notions of communalism in the Indian arts and philosophy.

Bollywood is thus certainly conscious of its international reputation. It understands that it is not only a major rights holder, but also a major user of third parties' creative content. To engage in enforcement for the use of its melodies by Caribbean musicians would be a violation of its own norms of creative copying, and would be disruptive to the very basis of its own industry. As such, enforcement is limited to acting against non-creative infringements, such as unauthorised reproduction and distribution of physical copies of films, or unauthorised transmissions of cable broadcasts. This would explain why Indian rights holders aggressively enforce the distribution rights for films and television shows, but not the creative reuse of melodies by chutney artists.

F. Expressions of Indo-Caribbean Identity

Bollywood is a visibly present force in the Southern Caribbean, and imports of Indian film, television and music are major sources of entertainment for the local Indo-Caribbean public. In Trinidad, Guyana and Suriname, local cinema, radio and film rental clubs are all filled with Indian film content, and images of Bollywood stars are present in popular culture and media.

[18] 'What Connects Karz's "Om Shanti Om" to a Song by Lord Shorty, Inventor of Soca Music?' (*Film Companion* blog, 29 January 2019).

[19] § 13(2) of the 1957 Copyright Act.

Understanding this presence is necessary to understanding expressions of Indo-Caribbean identity. The traditional markers of culture have all undergone their own transplantation, adaptation and creolisation in the post-indentureship West Indies. Except for in Suriname (where Sarnami Hindustani is the third most spoken language), Bhojpuri and Hindi are not common languages outside of a few loan words which have entered the local lexicon. Indo-Caribbean religious practices and cuisine are also quite distinct from their original South-Asian sources. To the majority of the Indo-Caribbean community, enjoying Indian exports in the form of films, television shows and film songs is thus the only remaining direct cultural connection to the Indian motherland. Unlike classical Indian music and dance, which are art forms enjoyed only in certain class or high culture settings, film and film music are mass-produced commodities for mass consumption across social classes.

We should therefore see borrowing Bollywood melodies as a process of adaptation and creolisation, just as the other markers of culture have undergone. This process is dynamic, as a dialogue is created between the motherland and the diaspora through musical art forms. The practice solves the fundamental existential question for Indo-Caribbean culture, as it creates a form of expression that simultaneously reflects inherent 'Indianness' but also a self-defined sense of 'Caribbeanness'. The art form combines the strongest musical elements of both sides of the *kala pani* (the mythical dark waters between India and the New World) – indigenous Caribbean rhythms and Indian melodies.

In this setting of hybrid cultural identity, the Indo-Caribbean community creates its own space to define themselves through music and compensate for the perceived historical exclusion from national public life. The simple act of appropriating Bollywood melodies becomes central to facilitating this complex expression of identity. Unlike Bollywood's copying from the entire international pop culture repertoire, the Caribbean's copying is focused and has a defined cultural context where the use of music as a vector of identity takes priority over notions of 'originality'.

G. Rational Forbearance

As the Indo-Caribbean community represents an important market for Indian cultural products, it is in Bollywood's interest to promote the cultural framework that sustains demand for these imports.

Despite the lucrative growth of the chutney industry and a plethora of clear-cut cases for copyright infringement in musical works, Bollywood's position is one of 'rational forbearance'. The scale of Bollywood film, music and television exports is just so massive that lost licensing revenue for derivative musical works is considered a mere cost of doing business. Forbearance towards the use of melodies is a form of indirect investment in market access, as it reinforces a sense of ethnic and cultural identity in the Indo-Caribbean community and creates the cultural environment which drives demand for Indian cultural imports. This is especially true when what is borrowed is very old source material, given the rapid rate of turnover in the Bollywood industry, where new films and songs are constantly produced with short product life cycles.

If this explanation is valid, then it rebuts paternalistic attitudes to intellectual property compliance. It is not the business of third parties to criticise acts of infringement when rights holders themselves have a rationale for choosing not to enforce their rights.

H. Wider Interpolation of Film Music

Even further, we should understand how diverse the practice of Bollywood melody appropriation is across different cultures. Marcus describes the evolution of Bhojpuri folk music, and notes that, traditionally, a singer puts a poet's texts (*bol*) to a melody (*tarz*) using standard stock melodies which are linked to established themes. By the 1940s, however, film melodies became incorporated into performances as temporary mid-song substitutions.[20] The changing social context and the incorporation of film melodies to bridge modernity and folk art are certainly evocative of chutney's history.

In addition to the Southern Caribbean, Bollywood music is enjoyed in places like South Africa, Mauritius and Fiji, where there is a large Indian diaspora. Even outside of the diaspora, however, there are examples of melodic reuse. In the north of Nigeria, Bollywood films have been incorporated as an integral part of contemporary social life for Hausa people. Indian film songs have entered into the local cultural framework, and their melodies are used by religious singers, who change the words to sing praises to the Prophet Mohammed.[21] In Kenya and Tanzania, an indigenous music sub-genre called *Indian Taarab* exists, where Swahili words are set to Hindi film song melodies, with acute attention paid to approximating phonetic structures.[22] Both of these examples from the African continent demonstrate the cross-cultural appeal of Bollywood's undeniable mastery of both love story narratives and compelling melodies. Here, melodies are not recycled to make new derivative works, but, rather, are upcycled to create new forms of cross-cultural expressions.

I. In Defence of Interpolation

As a result of the hybridity of chutney soca as a genre, its trends often reflect those of wide soca music, including increasingly digitised instrumentation. The melodic role of the harmonium has long given way to stock digital synthesiser tones, and the dholak and dhantal – two instruments which are difficult by nature to mic, amplify and mix cleanly – have become replaced by sterile digital drum machine samples which attempt to approximate their traditional grooves. Chutney soca tempos have also slowed down, and the aesthetics have increasingly converged with those of soca.

With instrumentation playing a smaller role as a defining stylistic trait, melody becomes more central in defining the boundaries of the genre. Repurposing Bollywood melodies is thus an important creative tool for delineating between soca and chutney soca and for maintaining the delicate balance of ethnic expressions that define the Southern Caribbean music industry. The practice is thus useful, as it strengthens chutney soca's capacity to negotiate 'Indianness' and maintain its contributions to a multicultural society.

To defend the use of folk melodies but oppose film melodies simply because the latter are technically subject to copyright (albeit rights that the owners seem uninterested in enforcing) is to concede to Western values which are in contradiction with the creative dynamics of the

[20] S Marcus, 'Recycling Indian Film-Songs: Popular Music as a Source of Melodies for North Indian Folk Musicians' (1992) 24 *Asian Music* 101, 101–06.

[21] B Larkin, 'Indian Films and Nigerian Lovers: Media and the Creation of Parallel Modernities' (1999) 67 *Africa: Journal of the International African Institute* 406, 406–07.

[22] AJ Eisenberg, 'The Swahili Art of Indian Taarab: A Poetics of Vocality and Ethnicity on the Kenyan Coast' (2017) 37 *Comparative Studies of South Asia, Africa and the Middle East* 336, 342–43.

prevailing cultural system. In essence, the old commons of folk melodies have been depleted and new melodic sources are needed. Film melodies are an endless resource, and the rights holders do not object to their use. They serve the function of ethno-identity expression, arguably even better than folk melodies for the young generation, and exhibit much greater melodic complexity than folk melodies, thus breathing new life into the art form. Of course, the possibility of using these melodies in no way implies that creation of original melodies is not encouraged. It just provides access to another tool for continued musical expression and innovation.

The opposition to use of film melodies in chutney is based on a desire to maintain traditional authenticity. However, it is important to understand the evolving construct of 'folk' authenticity in a post-colonial setting. In traditional chutney, Bhojpuri folk melodies were already largely dissociated from their original contexts, where melodies are explicitly associated with specific narrative themes. Just as these melodies took on new cultural significance for the post-indentureship generation, the cultural associations of film melodies evolved for later generations who have a different relationship with their heritage and modern hybrid social identities.

Once preoccupations with assumed exclusive private rights are set aside, there is no functional difference between folk melodies and film melodies; the use of either can connote originality or a lack thereof, depending on the creativity of the artist and the perspective of the audience. Generations ago, the use of Hindi or Bhojpuri words was considered necessary for authenticity in expressions of working-class Indo-Caribbean culture. Film song melodies might now be considered as supplanting the role of language in lending authenticity. The reluctance to the use of film melodies today mirrors the reactions of purists in the 1970s who resisted Sundar Popo's incorporation of English into Indian musical expression. Needless to say, he has been vindicated by time and is now canonically celebrated as a pioneering innovator in Indo-Caribbean culture. Perhaps the chutney soca artists of today will enjoy the same vindication a generation from now.

V. Concluding Remarks

Chutney music has certainly come a long way from its roots in Bhojpuri folk music. In just two generations, it has come to form an important part of Indo-Caribbean culture in Suriname, Guyana and Trinidad, and is even part of the national cultural identity of Trinidad and Tobago as projected to the rest of the world. Chutney soca has become a cultural export to Indo-Caribbean migrants in urban hubs like Toronto, New York, Amsterdam and London, where it serves as an expression of even more complex secondary diasporic identity, as well as to places like South Africa, Fiji, India and other spaces where Indians and Indo-diaspora reside.

Chutney soca has also come to embody various critical social themes – female liberation, Indo-Caribbean ethnic identity, Caribbean multiculturalism and contemporary commentary on gender and class dynamics. At the same time, it is important to state the obvious, that the Indo-Caribbean community, like any other demographic, is not a culturally homogeneous group.

As an art form which has undergone its own gradual process of adaptation and creolisation, chutney music has thrived by establishing its own aesthetic boundaries and creative norms. As part of its cultural system, these creative norms are inseparable from the art form's significance. This is where discourse on copyright and plagiarism is too often disingenuous, as one cannot separate the rules of creativity from their social context. As such, one should not criticise creative actions from a perspective of copyright without understanding the implications of those actions not only on art and aesthetics, but on gender, ethnic and class identities. For example, the practice of male–female response songs is critical for enabling the genre's ability to serve as a forum for female liberation and challenge gender roles, even if this is a form of copyright infringement on the surface.

In terms of the reuse of melodies from Indian film songs, this practice creates an intercultural dialogue between a motherland and a far-removed diaspora, separated by a century of diverging social experiences. While the practice is very controversial, it deserves at least a fresh evaluation from this perspective. At the least, critics should not be so quick to accuse chutney soca artists of plagiarism, as the reuse of melodies lacks explicit intention to pass off the source material as their own. Rather, their use is part of a more complex form of hybrid expression which is remarkably effective at achieving the difficult task of negotiating seemingly conflicting cultural identities. In this regard, indictments of copyright infringement, especially where the Bollywood rights holders are unconcerned in enforcing those rights, seem very exaggerated, and even counterproductive in terms of cultural policy.

In many ways, the open creative norms of chutney draw similarities to other Caribbean genres, like reggae and calypso. Chutney is, however, unique in that the widespread musical borrowing is not just part of its historical development but of its current state, where creative norms are still under development. In the end, chutney music without creative reuse and remix would just be like pholourie without chutney – consumable, but lacking flavour and spice.

16

River Plate Tango: Appropriation, Borrowing and Innovation

MAXIMILIANO MARZETTI*

I. Tango, Traditional Cultural Expression of the River Plate

A saying states 'the tango is a sad feeling that is danced' (*el tango es un sentimiento triste que se baila*). The artistic manifestation of that feeling is manifold, the main ones are music, text and dance (aka *the tango triad*).[1] Today, internationally, tango is mainly associated with Argentina (Argentine Tango), however, Uruguay and Uruguayan artists also played a key role in its development. Thus, in this chapter I will use River Plate tango to encompass tango works and authors from both Argentina and Uruguay, whose capitals, Buenos Aires and Montevideo, respectively, are located on opposite sides of the River Plate (Río de la Plata). Nevertheless, due to the availability of sources, I will mainly refer to Argentine tango authors, works and laws in this chapter.

The conditions under which River Plate tango was conceived were unique, in time, place and mores. Buenos Aires and Montevideo are port cities, melting pots that received millions of European immigrants, particularly at the end of the nineteenth and early twentieth century. Half of the inhabitants of Buenos Aires in 1887 and of Montevideo in 1899 were born abroad.[2] Argentine and Uruguayan tango artists influenced each other, regularly crossing national boundaries.

In both countries, but more commonly in Argentina, the term *porteño* (port dweller) refers to the inhabitants of their port capital cities. Moreover, both countries speak a distinct variety of Spanish, *Rioplatense Spanish*, which has become the official language of River Plate tango. River Plate tango has become a Traditional Cultural Expression (TCE),[3] ie a medium through which specific communities express their customs, values and beliefs.[4] In 2009, pursuant to a joint nomination by the governments of Argentina and Uruguay, UNESCO recognised that River Plate tango met the requirements to be included in the *Representative List of the Intangible Cultural Heritage of Humanity*.[5]

* All translations from Spanish to English are by the author and follow a functional approach.

[1] Namely, *tango romanza* (instrumental music), *tango canción* (lyrics) and *tango milonga* (dance).

[2] H Ferrer, *El Tango, Su Historia y Evolución* (Editorial A Peña Lillo, 1960) 15.

[3] WIPO, Intergovernmental Committee on Intellectual Property and Genetic Resources, Traditional Knowledge, and Folklore: Thirty-Third Session (Geneva, 2017).

[4] WIPO, Intellectual Property and Genetic Resources, Traditional Knowledge, and Traditional Cultural Expressions (2020).

[5] UNESCO, Decision of the Intergovernmental Committee: 4.COM 13.01 (Abu Dhabi, 2009), https://ich.unesco.org/en/decisions/4.COM/13.01.

II. Impure Origins

For a long time, the official story posited that tango was the creation of melancholic European immigrants, which lent support to the myth of Argentina and Uruguay as white nations.[6] However, recent historiographic and musicological studies suggest that the influence of Afro-Argentines and Afro-Uruguayans on River Plate tango has been larger than previously thought.[7] Since the foundation of Buenos Aires in 1580, approximately 200,000 enslaved Africans arrived in Argentina. The Argentine census of 1778 estimated that 46 per cent of the population was of African descent.[8] In 1810, Buenos Aires counted 55,000 inhabitants, 8000 of whom had African antecedents (almost 15 per cent of the population). By 1870, Buenos Aires had approximately 178,000 inhabitants, of whom 80,000 were European immigrants (44,000 of them Italian), while Afro-Argentines remained at 8000. Over time, the population of African descent diluted among millions of European immigrants, like a drop in a gallon of water, but it did not disappear. Gradually, Afro-Argentines moved away from their traditional places and mixed with the rest of the population in a process of miscegenation.

The word 'tango' itself might come from African languages. Historical evidence suggests that during colonial times, the words *tangó* and *tambó* were indistinctly used to identify the place where black people gathered and danced to the sound of African rhythms. Whether these words are derived from a mispronunciation of the Spanish *tambor* (drums), an instrument commonly found in African rhythms, from Latin (*tangere*, to touch) or from the Congolese, Guinean or Sudanese deities from the Yoruba pantheon (*Shango* or *Xango*) remains disputed.[9] In any case, tango would become the word to identify a new musical genre born in the River Plate. Other words related to tango music, such as *milonga*, which today designates a traditional dance hall and a quicker-paced tango dance (*tango milonga*), may also come from African languages. In the Kimbundu language, milonga means *word* or *words*.

River Plate tango evolved in a process we may call today cultural appropriation. Some sources suggest that the late nineteenth-century *compadritos* (tough guys of creole origin) started to visit the places where Afro-Argentines gathered and began imitating their dances and movements.[10] Tango's characteristic *cortes y quebradas* (sudden stops, criss-crossing of legs and hip twists) may have originated in an exaggerated imitation of the movements the compadritos saw in the African tangos, more likely to mock them. Other foreign influences may have shaped the tango dance form. Compadritos dancing may also have been influenced by Cuban habaneras and Andalusian tangos (two musical genres also rooted in African rhythms).

[6] For an account of how the *white nation* myth minimised the influence of blacks in Argentine and Chilean history, see J González de Gispert, '"Aquí no hay negros": cómo se borró de la historia de Argentina y Chile el aporte de los esclavos y los afrodescendientes' (*BBC News Mundo*, 11 June 2019) www.bbc.com/mundo/noticias-america-latina-48508342.

[7] For Argentina, see C Chazelle, 'Tango: Des Origines Controversées' (2001) 31(1) *Cahiers Charles*; OG Brunelli, 'Bases para una aproximación razonable a la cuestión del componente afro del tango' (2017) 18 *Revista Argentina de Musicología* 91; NRO Oderigo and NP Cirio, *Latitudes Africanas Del Tango* (EDUNTREF, 2009); NP Cirio, *La Historia Negra Del Tango*, (Museo Casa Carlos Gardel, 2010); M Annecchia, A Martín and C Mercado, *Dimensiones Afro En El Tango. Tensiones Racializadas En Los Géneros Populares Del Río de La Plata* (Revista Antropologías Del Sur, 2017); D Díaz, *La Presencia de Los Afroargentinos En El Tango* (Escritos Musicológicos Tempranos, 2016). For Uruguay, see G Goldman, *Lucamba: herencia africana en el tango* (Perro Andaluz Editores, 2008).

[8] Ministry of Culture (Argentina), 'El Origen Afro de La Argentina' (18 July 2018) www.cultura.gob.ar/el-origen-africano-de-la-argentina_6165/.

[9] O Freixa, 'Tango Negro. Los Orígenes Afro Del 2 x 4' (5 December 2013) www.omerfreixa.com.ar/tango-negro-articulo-academico-publicado-en-el-portal-de-fundacion-sur-madrid/; WW Megenney, 'The River Plate "Tango": Etymology and Origins' (2003) 22(2) *Afro-Hispanic Review* 39.

[10] J Gobello, *Breve Historia Crítica Del Tango* (Corregidor, 1999).

Over time, dwindling numbers of Afro-Argentines felt intimidated, gradually abandoned their public places and continued their traditions behind closed doors. Of the original rhythms danced by Afro-Argentines and Afro-Uruguayans (African tango), only *candombe* has survived to this day, most ostensibly in Uruguay. The compadritos created *tango criollo* (creole tango), mixing African, American and European elements.

The last elements of River Plate Tango were added by the *gringos* (European immigrants, most of them from Italy and Spain), who added new instruments (most notably the accordion and piano) as well as elements from European ballroom dances, such as the couples' embrace (Polish polkas, mazurkas and Germano-Austrian waltzes). Germani estimates that, between 1856 and 1930, Argentina received 6,500,000 European immigrants.[11] Most of them lived in cramped *conventillos*, or tenement houses. In these houses, space was limited and privacy non-existent. Thus, the *conventillo* became a musical Babel, where the Neapolitans, Andalusians, Volga Germans and Poles sang their canzoni, zarzuelas, schottisches and mazurkas on the common patio. The *conventillo* became the brewing ground for River Plate tango.

Most of the European immigrants were men. Single and homesick, it is unsurprising that many of them flocked to brothels. It must be noted that at the time, prostitution was legal in both Argentina and Uruguay.[12] Brothels also contributed to delineating the contours of the tango genre. A particular type of brothel, where men could drink, play cards and dance with the waitresses (who also offered paid sexual services to the customers), was called a dance academy (*academia de baile*). The dance academies favoured by Italian immigrants were called *peringundines*, in reference to a dance from French Périgord popularised in Argentina by Genoese immigrants. *Peringundines* would also become associated with tango and its lyrics. Due to these shady origins, nationalist author Leopoldo Lugones wrote 'Tango, that reptile of the brothel' (*Tango, ese reptil de lupanar*). Anecdotal evidence suggests tangos were also played outside brothels. Since demand exceeded supply and brothel space was limited, men would queue outside on the streets. To amuse their clients while they waited, brothel owners would pay musicians to play on the street, where, for fun, men would dance with other men. The practice seemed not to have had a homosexual connotation. In one of his works, Borges evokes seeing couples of men dancing the tango on the streets because, he claimed, decent women at the time were unwilling to dance to such indecent rhythm.[13] At some point, tangos would also be performed at *sainetes* (a theatrical play of usually one-act, often comic, with a popular atmosphere and characters), increasing their popularity. The bawdy origins may also explain the abundant terminology in early tango lyrics alluding to prostitutes, brothels and pimps.[14] It is also probable that the Argentine elite heard the new rhythm in the brothels.

Thus, River Plate tango is the syncretic by-product of the African, American and European musical traditions that coalesced in two port cities in a foundational period of national identities. River Plate tango is not a pure breed but a mongrel, the by-product of cultural syncretism, both local and universal, yet unique.

The term 'cultural appropriation' refers to the use of arts, styles and objects of a non-dominant culture by members of the dominant culture, in ways that may be considered improper, disrespectful or disparaging by the former. Some authors claim cultural appropriation in the arts may

[11] G Germani, *Mass Immigration and Modernization in Argentina* (Studies in Comparative International Development, 1966).

[12] Prostitution was legal in Argentina from 1875 to 1934. For a history, see HN Zinni and RO Ielpi, *Prostitución y Rufianismo* (Homo Sapiens Ediciones, 2004). Prostitution remains legal in Uruguay to this day.

[13] JL Borges and M Kodama, *Borges Cuenta Buenos Aires* (Emecé, 2016).

[14] Some tangos titles refer to sexual organs ('El Choclo'), sexual acts ('El Fierrazo') or to the names of famous prostitutes ('Margot', 'Madame Ivonne', 'Ivette', 'Esthercita-Milonguita').

be unethical.[15] However, it is not necessarily illegal. From a copyright law perspective, cultural appropriation of works in the public domain is a legit and important phase of the creative process. Even borrowing from protected works, within some boundaries, is sometimes tolerated (the idea/expression dichotomy, the doctrine of *scenes à faire*, etc).

Seen with contemporary eyes, what creoles and European immigrants did to Afro-American cultural expressions may amount to cultural appropriation. However, such a process of cultural hybridisation led to the creation of a new and original genre, enriching the cultural heritage of mankind. The public domain, the *commons of the mind*[16] is a patchwork of expression coming from different cultures. Restrictive interpretations of cultural appropriation, by limiting the use of works in the public domain, may include constraint and chill creativity and innovation. River Plate tango could not have existed in a world that does not have some tolerance for cultural reappropriation. In such a world, there would not be California sushi rolls or NY pizza either, and what a sadder world it would be. Eventually, it is the role of musicology and historiography to trace the multiple origins of musical genres and pay homage to them. Copyright law, as a driver for human creativity, should set limits to censorship doctrines, regardless of their pretended higher moral ground.

III. Evolution and Innovation in Tango

The evolution of River Plate tango can be divided into four periods, namely: (i) the beginnings (1880–95); (ii) the Old Guard (*Guardia Vieja*) (1895–1925/30); (iii) the New Guard (*Guardia Nueva* 1925/30–50); and (iv) the Avant-Garde, aka tango nuevo or symphonic tango (1950–60/70).

Old Guard tango artists (*tangueros*) had little or no formal music training; most of them played by ear, accompanied only by Spanish guitars, and the lyrics referred to disreputable topics, such as criminals, prostitutes or dandies.[17] The New Guard was represented by sophisticated musicians, most of them with formal musical training. The formation of big bands, called typical orchestras (*orquesta típica*), characterised this phase of tango evolution, playing in front of large groups at social clubs and dance halls. During this period, the Argentine elite and even the Catholic Church finally accepted tango.[18]

The first tangos had no lyrics; they were purely instrumental. These were the tangos danced in brothels, academies and on the streets. Most tango historians agree that 'El Entrerriano' (1897), by Afro-Argentine musician Anselmo Rosendo Mendizabal, was the first River Plate tango. Others claim it was 'El Talar' (1894, though the date is contested). However, the first lyrical tango (*tango canción*) is thought to be 'La Morocha' (1905). Gregorio Ángel Villoldo wrote the lyrics to 'La Morocha' following the model of the Spanish *cuplé* (a style *en vogue* in the cabarets of Buenos Aries at the time). 'La Morocha', like many early tangos, refers to *gauchesco* themes, ie rural life.

The success of the River Plate tango is inextricably linked to technology. Tango took off at the same time as a number of (then) new technologies, like phonography and filmography. Technology made tango a mass phenomenon. The first phonographic recording in Buenos Aires was made in 1904. The transition from rural to urban topics is attributed to poet Evaristo Carriego,

[15] JO Young, *Cultural Appropriation and the Arts* (Blackwell Publishing, 2008); JO Young and CG Brunk, *The Ethics of Cultural Appropriation* (Blackwell Publishing, 2009).

[16] J Boyle, *The Public Domain: Enclosing the Commons of the Mind* (Yale University Press, 2010).

[17] Ferrer (n 2) 29 et seq.

[18] Apparently, somebody requested the pope (it is not clear whether it was Pius X, Benedict XV or Pius XI) to bless the River Plate tango. The pope either agreed or was unimpressed. See J Barsky, *El Tango y Las Instituciones: De Olvidos, Censuras y Reivindicaciones* (UAI Editorial, Editorial Teseo, 2016).

who was admired by Borges.[19] Carriego's poetry created a stylistic canon, elements that became commonplace in early tango lyrics. In copyright law parlance, Carriego provided the *scenes à faire*. Carriego's poem *El alma del suburbio* (*The soul of the suburb*) offers a catalogue of River Plate tango *topoi*, such as the longing for the old *barrio* (neighbourhood), the *cafetín* (a small coffee shop where old pals met) and knife fights among *guapos* (rascals but brave men). Also in this period, *Lunfardo*, the jargon of the River Plate underworld, began to permeate tango lyrics. Lunfardo was probably first used by criminals to avoid being understood by the police. Hence, many Lunfardo words refer to criminal activities or instruments such as *tombo* (police), *canusa* (prison) and *escruchar* (breaking and entering). Later, Lunfardo would be enriched by the pidgin spoken by the immigrants, adopting terms coming from Italian dialects (*farabute*, *jetatore*, *mufa*, *pelandrún*, *pibe*), French (*chiqué*, *gigoló*) and Portuguese (*descangayado*, *tamango*). Lunfardo words have passed into the common language of Argentines and Uruguayans.[20] However, there are tangos with little or no Lunfardo words, such as those by Alfredo Le Pera and Homero Manzi. New technologies such as phonographic recordings and sound films made it possible to extend the market for tangos to all of Latin America. This demanded a neutral Spanish with no Lunfardo words, equally understandable in Argentina, Peru, Colombia and Mexico.

The tragic undertones of River Plate tango lyrics are associated with Pascual Contursi. A son of Neapolitan immigrants, Contursi shifted the tone of tango lyrics from praising the courage of *gauchos* and *compadritos* to sorrowful stories of betrayal and love forever lost. Contursi was an innovative storyteller. His tango lyrics were self-contained stories approximately three minutes long.

Carlos Gardel is without a shadow of a doubt the most famous tango interpreter of all time. Gardel is the equivalent of Elvis Presley or Frank Sinatra in their respective genres. Gardel began his career as a folk singer in a duo with guitarist José Razzano, singing at the Armenonville cabaret in Buenos Aires in 1914. Technological innovations amplified Gardel's success. He recorded his first phonogram in 1913 (on which he sang only folkloric songs). Gardel's first recorded tango was 'Mi Noche Triste', in 1917. From that first tango recording until he died in a plane crash in Medellin in 1935, Gardel recorded hundreds of songs and played in dozens of films. NBC hired Gardel, making him the first international tango star for the Latin American market. In the 1921 film *The Four Horsemen of the Apocalypse*, Rudolph Valentino danced the tango on the screen. Quickly, the sensual Argentine dance captivated the puritan USA. It would not be an exaggeration to claim that the video clip was invented by tango artists and producers, as evidenced by the video recording of 'Yira Yira' in 1930, sung by Carlos Gardel, with lyrics by Enrique Santos Discepolo.

By the early twentieth century, River Plate tango had conquered Paris. Argentine entrepreneurs and bon vivants exported tango to the Parisian dance halls, where it was danced by Count Robert de Montesquiou and praised by Jean Richepin at the Académie Française in 1913. After succeeding abroad, tango was accepted by the Argentine elite on their own turf. Antonio De Marchi, an Italian impresario, produced to memorable tango shows, the first at Buenos Aires' Palais de Glace in 1912 and the other at the Palace Teatro in 1913.

River Plate tango avant-garde is indissociably related to Astor Piazzolla. Piazzolla was a musical revolutionary who, despite his many detractors, took tango to new heights. Piazzolla was born in Argentina but spent most of his childhood in the USA, where he became familiar with jazz. He was an accomplished bandoneon player, performing in the prestigious orchestra of Anibal Troilo. Piazzolla studied composition with Alberto Ginastera in Buenos Aires and Nadia Boulanger in

[19] JL Borges, *Evaristo Carriego* (M Gleizer Editor, 1930); NT Di Giovanni and S Ashe, *Evaristo Carriego: A Book about Old-Time Buenos Aires* (Dutton, 1984).

[20] DS González, 'El Lunfardo: ¿Un Habla de Delincuentes Que Quedó En El Pasado?' (2016) 42(1) *Revista de Filología y Lingüística de La Universidad de Costa Rica*.

Paris. His *new tango* (*tango nuevo*), unlike the tango of the Old Guard, was composed to be listened to in a theatre, not to be danced in a dance hall.

Piazzolla brought new influences to tango. Musicologists identified baroque[21] and jazz[22] influences in Piazzolla's compositions. Tango purists never accepted Piazzolla, among them Borges. Both authors coincided in the multimedia project *Historia del Tango* (Tango History), which was meant to span a series of four albums. For this project, Borges wrote the milongas 'Jacinto Chiclana', 'El Títere', 'A Don Nicanor Paredes' and 'Alguien le Dice al Tango'. The project did not go well. Piazzolla and Borges never understood each other.[23] In the end, only two albums and three songs from the third one were recorded.

In the 1960s and 1970s, the popularity of River Plate tango began to decline, replaced by foreign genres such as rock 'n' roll, pop music and, more recently, cumbia.[24] Contemporary Argentina and Uruguay tango is no longer mainstream. Nevertheless, the late twentieth century saw a tango revival, mainly in its danced form, spurred by Hollywood films such as *Scent of a Woman* (1992), *True Lies* (1994) and *Moulin Rouge* (2001),[25] and sustained by Argentine tango dancers who opened tango dance academies in the USA.[26] In the twenty-first century, new tango forms have appeared, like electronic tango, epitomised by groups such as Gotan Project, Electrocutango and Tanghetto. Electronic tango maintains the structural melodic features of traditional tango but introduces electronic instruments (most notably, the synthesiser) and digital music processing. In e-tango, traditional tango lyrics are replaced by repeated short couplets or onomatopoeias. Many E-tango groups exist in Argentina and abroad.

River Plate tango has begun to take roots in other latitudes and, like a flower transplanted to different soil and environment, it has mutated. Such is the case in Finland (*suomalainen tango*) or Italy (*tango liscio*). River Plate tango may be subject to a process of hybridisation in foreign lands similar, mutatis mutandis, to the one that created this genre in the first place.[27]

IV. Author's Rights in Argentina and Uruguay

This author found no documented evidence to suggest copyright law played any significant role in the genre's development, at least in its early stage. The River Plate tango consolidated as a new genre during a period in which there was no copyright law or, when the first copyright laws were passed, it was sparsely enforced. However, at some point, once the genre and the market for it have consolidated, and intermediary institutions have been set up (such as collective management organisations) legal rules play an important role in determining how economic benefits are distributed.

[21] OG Brunelli, *El Uso de Rasgos Del Barroco En Las Composiciones Populares de Astor Piazzolla*, IV Congreso de la Asociación Regional para América Latina y el Caribe de la Sociedad Internacional de Musicología, ARLAC/IMS(2019).

[22] OG Brunelli, 'La Incorporación Del Jazz a La Trama Del Tango En La Música de Astor Piazzolla', Coloquio Internacional 'Tango: Creaciones, Identificaciones, Circulaciones' (2011).

[23] OG Brunelli, 'Borges y Piazzolla: Un Desencuentro Por Milonga'. *Actas de Las Jornadas de Investigación Del Instituto de Literatura Hispanoamericana, XXVII* (Jornadas de Investigación Del Instituto de Literatura Hispanoamericana, 2015).

[24] P Semán and P Vila, *Youth Identities and Argentine Popular Music. Beyond Tango* (Palgrave Macmillan, 2012).

[25] RF Thompson, *Tango: The Art History of Love* (Vintage Books, 2006).

[26] M Gonzalez and M Yanes, *Tango: Sex and Rhythm of the City* (Reaktion Books, 2013).

[27] E Cámara De Landa, 'Hybridization in the Tango. Objects, Process, and Considerations' in G Steingress (ed), *Songs of the Minotaur. Hybridity and Popular Music in the Era of Globalization* (LIT Verlag, 2002).

A. The Early Years, 1853 to 1933

The Argentine Constitution of 1853, inspired by Juan Bautista Alberdi's influential work,[28] copied to a large extent the US Constitution of 1787.[29] This explains why the Argentine Constitution included in section 17 an Article[30] that emulates the US Constitution's *copyright* or *progress clause*.[31] Thus, the Constitution entitled authors to their *literary property*, including musical works.

Article 17 of the Argentine Constitution must be read together with former Article 67 subparagraph 16, which gave Congress the power to grant *temporary privileges and rewards of encouragement*. This allowed two possible interpretations, one of Article 17 alone (literary property as an absolute right) and another in conjunction with Article 67 subparagraph 16 (literary property as a utilitarian public policy tool). The second reading would prevail until the first decades of the twentieth century. Thus, until an effective copyright act was passed (which happened in 1933), the protection of an author's literary property would remain an unmet expectation. The absence of explicit legal rules and sanctions for copyright infringement may have incentivised borrowing and copying in early tango works.

Argentina's early copyright policy seems to be in stark contrast with its patent policy. Argentina enacted its first Patent Act (Act No 111) in 1864. However, the rationale for passing a patent act and not passing a copyright act may be the same. Vidaurreta[32] suggests Patent Act No 111 was passed quickly because it was seen as necessary to attract foreign capital and qualified human resources, and to foster technology transfer to the country (a utilitarian rationale). The Argentine founding fathers expected the legal monopoly and the promise of exceptional gains would lure foreign entrepreneurs into investing in Argentina.

Ripp[33] suggests the Argentine government delayed passing a *lex specialis* effectively protecting literary property also for utilitarian reasons. The Argentine government considered passing a copyright act contrary to the interests of a developing nation. At the time, most literary and scientific works read in Argentina were written by foreign authors. A copyright act would have protected the rights of foreign authors to the detriment of local citizens, ie there would be a net loss from a cost–benefit perspective. Without a copyright act and effective enforcement of the literary property of foreign authors, the price of works in Argentina became cheaper (a local publisher was able to publish any foreign work without paying royalties, competing in price among themselves and consequently lowering the price), thus increasing access to works, literacy and learning. However, this policy came at the cost of depriving local authors of protection for their literary property. This logic began to change only when the number of Argentine authors reached a critical mass that lobbied collectively for a copyright act that would benefit them. It is worth noting that the USA applied, mutatis mutandis, a similar policy, for the same reasons.

[28] JB Alberdi, *Bases y Puntos de Partida para la Organización Política de la República Argentina* (1852).

[29] JM Miller, 'The Authority of a Foreign Talisman: A Study of US Constitutional Practice as Authority in Nineteenth Century Argentina and the Argentine Elite' (1997) 46 *American University Law Review* 1483; M Gordon, 'Don't Copy Me, Argentina: Constitutional Borrowing and Rhetorical Type' (2009) 8(3) *Washington University Global Studies Law Review*.

[30] 'Every author or inventor is the exclusive owner of his work, invention, or discovery, for the term agreed by law' in Spanish, 'todo autor o inventor es propietario exclusivo de su obra, invento o descubrimiento, por el término que le acuerde la ley'.

[31] US Constitution, Art I, s 8, cl 8.

[32] GE Vidaurreta, *Historia Del Sistema Argentino de Patentes de Invención (1580–1863) Propiedad Intelectual En La Constitución Nacional – Antecedentes, Fuentes e Interpretación* (La Ley, 2007).

[33] HR Ripp, *La Postergación de La Regulación de Los Derechos de Autor En La Argentina : Desde La Constitución Nacional de 1853 a La Sanción de La Ley 11.723 de 1933, La Más Sagrada de Las Propiedades Sin Ley* (FLACSO, 2013).

The USA's first Copyright Act of 1790 excluded foreign authors from copyright protection – a situation that was not changed until 1891.[34]

Argentina promulgated its Civil Code in 1869, which contained no direct reference to literary property. The only indirect reference to paintings, sculptures, writings and prints (Article 2.335) referred to *specificatio*, a way of acquiring property based on Roman law.[35] This was a limited use provision to an author wishing to protect his literary and artistic property against an infringer.

Thus, for a long time, the only way for an author to protect his literary property was to invoke the Constitution's Article 17. However, this route was foreclosed to foreigners. Giuseppe Verdi assigned all economic rights for his opera *Otello* in Latin America to impresario Tito Ricordi. In 1895, the rights holder initiated a lawsuit to stop an infringing performance of *Otello* in Buenos Aires. The intervening judge denied the request, stating that Article 17 of the Argentine Constitution was only available to national authors.[36]

Well-known local authors were more successful at enforcing their rights. José Hernández, a famous Argentine author of the *gauchesco* genre, sued a publisher for unauthorised reproduction of his work *La Vuelta de Martín Fierro*. The intervening judge declared the Constitution's Article 17 directly applicable and the Civil Code's general principles applicable to (tangible) property rights. Hernández received 10,000 pesos in compensation.[37] This judicial doctrine was confirmed in later cases.[38]

Absent effective legal enforcement for authors' rights, the most common strategy to monetise their intellectual capital was to sell (assign) their works to publishers, phonographic producers and theatres. This implied that the authors had to create new works regularly to maintain a regular income stream. This system may seem unfair today, tilted in favour of the intermediaries, but it may have led to an explosion of creativity, given the large repertoire of early tango songs.

Boldrin and Levine suggested a similar hypothesis to explain Verdi's higher opera output before Italy passed an effective copyright law.[39] While legal entitlements improve authors' bargaining power vis-à-vis intermediaries, thereby increasing their profits, at the same time, it may reduce their incentives to create new works.

Anecdotal evidence suggests that during the early days of tango, borrowing and even verbatim copying were common practices among authors.[40] Ángel Villodo's 1905 tango 'La Morocha' (1905) was an evident copy of 1893 Orosman Moratorio's 'La flor del monte'.[41] Other times, an author's lyrics were modified without the author's authorisation, with satirical intention,

[34] For the US pirate past, see Z Khan, 'Copyright Piracy and Development: United States Evidence in the Nineteenth Century' (2008) 10(18) *Revista de Economía Institucional* 21; Z Khan, *Does Copyright Piracy Pay? The Effects of US International Copyright Laws on the Market for Books, 1790–1920* (National Bureau of Economic Research, 2004) NBER Working Papers 10271.

[35] The paintings, sculptures, writings and prints will always be reputed as main when the art has greater value and importance than the matter in which it has been exercised, and as accessories the table, canvas, paper, parchment or stone to which they are attached.

[36] *Ferrari A v Ciacchi C and co, re 'opera Otello'* 16 May 1865.

[37] *Hernández, José v Barbieri Brothers* 5 November 1884, affirmed by the Argentine Supreme Court on 24 November 1885.

[38] *Vedia v Moen* 20 April 1893 (unauthorised reproduction of an almanac); *Gutiérrez v Podestá and Scotti* 30 October 1897 (unauthorised performance of a play); *Renauld v Lava and others* 17 August 1899 (unauthorised reproduction of a map); *Correa v Estrada* 13 June 1901 (unauthorised appropriation of a map). Cited by CA Villalba and D Lipszyc, *El Derecho de Autor En La Argentina: Ley 11.723 y Normas Complementarias y Reglamentarias, Concordadas Con Los Tratados Internacionales, Comentadas y Anotadas Con La Jurisprudencia* (La Ley, 2001).

[39] M Boldrin and DK Levine, *Against Intellectual Monopoly* (Cambridge University Press, 2010).

[40] Gobello (n 10) 51.

[41] Orozco's first stanza begins, 'I am the sweet brunette, the one with the burning eyes' (in Spanish, 'yo soy la dulce trigueña, la de los ardientes ojos'), whereas Villoldo wrote, 'I am the brunette, with a fiery look' (in Spanish, 'yo soy la morocha, de ardiente mirar').

to mock the original author or an interpreter. So, there were sometimes two identical musical compositions with different lyrics, the original and the modified version, coexisted side by side. Sometimes, the altered version was more successful than the original one. This seems to have been the case with Domingo Espínola's satirical lyrics of 'Mi noche triste', recorded by Gardel. At least during the times of the Old Guard, these practices seem to have been tolerated. It is unclear if such tolerance was born out of a truly collaborative ethos or from the absence of effective legal redress.

Another common practice seems to have been to add lyrics to someone else's musical composition without permission. This may explain why some tango compositions have different lyrics, including famous ones like 'La Cumparsita'. Apparently, this was the modus operandi of Pascual Contursi, who added lyrics to tangos composed by other authors without always requesting their authorisation. Some lyrics were even collective works by anonymous authors. Early tangos had no lyrics. However, one or many anonymous authors added lyrics over time, and they became the canonical versions interpreted today. The names of these anonymous authors have been lost forever; however, their works live on. Without historical records, it is difficult to tell today which version was the original and which was the infringing one.

The weak enforcement of author's rights and literary property during the early phase of River Plate tango may have facilitated borrowing and copying between authors, cross-fertilisation and development of the nascent genre.

B. Clemenceau's Copyright Act

The first Argentine Copyright Act was born at the request of the French government. The year 1910 marked the first centennial of the Argentine nation. Among the invitees to the celebrations in Buenos Aires was French statesman Georges Clemenceau. Clemenceau had penned a dramatic work, 'Le Voile du bonheur', to be performed in Buenos Aires as part of the celebratory events. When Clemenceau found out that foreign works enjoyed no effective legal protection in Argentina, he urged the Argentine government to pass an act to protect local and foreign literary works. The Argentine government agreed, and thus the first Argentine Copyright Act No 7.092 (aka Clemenceau's copyright act) was passed in 1910.

Act No 7.092 granted copyright protection during the author's life and for 10 years *post mortem auctoris*. However, it did not regulate publishing contracts, nor did it refer to exceptions or limitations, or incorporate criminal offences in case of copyright infringement. Since it lacked teeth, it was rarely enforced. It was later amended by Act No 9.510 of 1914, without much success.

Case law suggests difficulties remained in enforcing the newly granted author's rights. In 1921, the rights holder of the musical works 'Mi Bandera' and 'El Garrotín' sued *Atlántida Magazine* for illegally reproducing the works in issues 76 and 79.[42] The claimant requested \$10,000 for compensatory damages (15 cents for each of the 60,000 infringing copies, plus a lump sum of \$1000 for moral damages). The defendant did not contest the facts, but objected to the basis for calculating the damages. The court sided with the rights holder since his work was reproduced without authorisation. However, the rationale for the decision was the general principles of the civil code, not the provisions of the Copyright Act. Moreover, the court limited the total award of damages to \$450. In doing so, the court disregarded the number of magazines sold and considered how many music sheets the author would have sold had the magazine not been published.

[42] Buenos Aires Civil Court of First Instance, 30 June 1921, *in re Sanchez Arista c Vigil* (published in *Patentes y Marcas*, 5 July 1921, 107).

The underlying rationale for the court's quantification of damages was to avoid overcompensating the victim (a general principle taken from the law of obligations). Moreover, the court rejected the claim of moral damages and allegations of a criminal offence.[43] The situation was not different on the other side of the River Plate. The first Uruguayan Copyright Act, No 3.956 (Ley de propiedad literaria y artística), was passed in 1912 but still excluded foreign authors. The *post mortem auctoris* term of protection was 25 years.

C. Copyright Act No 11.723

After several unsuccessful draft bills,[44] a new Argentine Copyright Act (Regimen Legal de la Propiedad Intelectual),[45] No 11.723, was promulgated on 28 September 1933 and published in the Official Gazette the day after. The new law resulted from the concerted lobbying efforts of local authors and collective management organisations, which began to be created in the early twentieth century.[46]

Unlike its predecessor, Act No 11.723 made copyright infringement a criminal offence. The Copyright Act's sections 71–74 added new criminal offences (copyright scam and fraud, unauthorised acts of reproduction, distribution and communication to the public of copyrighted works). Act No 11.723 established a copyright term equivalent to the life of the author plus 30 years *post mortem auctoris*. Subsequent modifications elevated this term to life plus 70 years *pos tmortem auctoris*. The 1933 Copyright Act, with some minor modifications, is still in force today.

For its part, Uruguay passed a new and stringent Copyright Act in 1937 (Ley de derecho de autor), No 9.739, which is still in force today. The creation in 1929 of the General Association of Authors of Uruguay (Asociación General de Autores del Uruguay) is considered a determinant factor in the passing of the new law. Act No 9.739 established a copyright term of life of the author plus 40 years *post mortem auctoris*, later extended to 50 years *post mortem auctoris* by Act No 17.616.[47]

D. The River Plate Paying Public Domain

It must be noted that Argentina, since 1958, and Uruguay, since 1937, are two of the few countries still enforcing a paying public domain (*domaine public payant*). According to the World Intellectual Property Organization (WIPO), under a *domaine public payant*, or paying public domain, a tax is imposed for the use of works in the public domain. Generally, the system works like a compulsory licence: the use is conditioned on payment of the prescribed tax but not upon

[43] 'Publication Non Authorisée de Deux Oeuvres Musicales Dans Une Revue. Dommage. Mode d'évaluation' (1922) 35(1) *Le Droit D'Auteur* 7.

[44] Introduced in 1918, 1923, 1925 and 1932, respectively.

[45] Despite its name, the act refers solely to copyright and neighbouring rights.

[46] The National Society of Authors, Composers and Publishers of Music (Sociedad Nacional de Autores, Compositores y Editores de Música) was created in 1918; the Society of Dramatic Author (Sociedad de Autores Dramáticos) in 1919; the Argentine Association of Authors and Composers of Music (Asociación Argentina de Autores y Compositores de Música) in 1921; and the Circle of Authors and Music Composers (Círculo de Autores y Compositores de Música) in 1930. The latter two entities merged and constituted the Argentine Society of Authors and Composers of Music (Sociedad Argentina de Autores y Compositores de Música) in 1936.

[47] See J Gemetto, 'Historia de la regulación del derecho de autor en Uruguay: una visión crítica' (Creative Commons Uruguay, 7 September 2015) www.creativecommons.uy/2015/09/07/historia-de-la-regulacion-del-derecho-de-autor-en-uruguay-una-vision-critica/.

securing a priori authorisation.[48] This implies that in these two countries, a tax must be paid to a state agency to reproduce, perform or broadcast a tango whose copyright has expired. In Argentina, the agency is the National Fund for the Arts (Fondo Nacional de las Artes), which exercises this right in perpetuity.[49] In Uruguay, the collection of the tax is entrusted to the Copyright Council (Consejo de Derecho de Autor). The tax may create an additional (and unnecessary) financial obstacle to the dissemination of tango works.[50]

E. Conservatism and Censorship

Most tango lyrics are rather conservative and few of them refer to extreme political ideals,[51] which may explain why tangos were rarely censored. However, there is a noteworthy exception. In Argentina in 1943, a military coup deposed President Castillo, and a military junta issued a Decree-Law ordering the modification of all tango titles and lyrics considered indecent, which at the time meant contrary to the nationalistic and catholic ideas of the military government.

Subsequently, with the stroke of a pen, references to prostitutes, criminals, alcohol, drugs, Lunfardo and even foreign words were expurgated overnight from tango lyrics and replaced with politically correct ones. Fearing political and economic reprisals, phonographic producers, radio stations and publishers modified hundreds of tango titles and lyrics without the authors' consent or respect for their moral right of integrity of the work.

Thus, titles like 'Shusheta' (a Lunfardo term for dandy) became 'El Aristócrata', and 'Comme il faut' (a foreign term) became 'Como se debe'.[52] The censorship was short-lived and ended in 1946. However, some tangos recorded during the censorship period with modified titles and lyrics became, over time, the canonical versions due to the loss of the original works.

F. A Rare Case of Arbitration Concerning Authorship

Domestic arbitration has rarely been a popular method to solve disputes in Argentina. However, a noteworthy exception concerns a famous tango.[53] In 1917, a Uruguayan student, Gerardo Hernán Matos Rodriguez, composed the music of 'La Cumparsita'. The same year, he assigned all economic rights to his work to Casa Breyer Hermanos in exchange for $50. In 1924, Ricordi Americana SA acquired Casa Breyer Hermanos and its entire catalogue, including

[48] WIPO Secretariat, 24 November 2010, Note on the Meanings of the Term 'Public Domain' in the Intellectual Property System with particular reference to the Protection of Traditional Knowledge and Traditional Cultural Expressions/ Expressions of Folklore, Intergovernmental Committee on Intellectual Property and Genetic Resources, Traditional Knowledge and Folklore, Seventeenth Session.

[49] The website of the National Funds from the Arts states 'the reproduction of a movie like Frozen, by Disney, must also pay [the paying public domain fee] since its story is an adaptation of The Snow Queen by Hans Christian Andersen, and the use of a work like Michelangelo's Creation of Adam in a video game, too': https://fnartes.gob.ar/como-nos-financiamos.

[50] For a law and economics perspective on the paying public domain, see M Marzetti, 'Paying for Works in the Public Domain? The "Domaine Public Payant" in the 21st Century' (2019) 2019(4)*Gewerblicher Rechtsschutz Und Urheberrecht, Internationaler Teil* 343.

[51] For a study of the few tango songs containing anarchic and socialist ideas, see J Campo, *Las ideas libertarias y la cuestión social en el tango* (Editorial Reconstruir, 2014).

[52] EJ Abálsamo, *Crónicas Del Tango: Sus Protagonistas, Las Anécdotas* (Editorial Del Cardo, 2006) 182 et seq.

[53] JM Aroca, 'El Arbitraje Sobre Los Derechos de Propiedad Intelectual de La Cumparsita. Un Ejemplo de Arbitraje' (2011) 10 *Teoría y Derecho: Revista de Pensamiento Jurídico* 333; JM Aroca, 'La Cumparsita: Una Fuente de Pleitos Contursi y Maroni vs Matos Rodríguez' [2016] *Ius et Veritas* 56.

'La Cumparsita'. In 1925, after a conversation with a lawyer, Matos Rodriguez discovered he had a cause of action to invalidate the 1917 assignment: at the time of signing the agreement, he was a minor; thus, the contract was null and void. In 1926, Matos Rodríguez settled with Ricordi Americana SA. To avoid a lawsuit, Ricordi Americana SA recognised Matos Rodríguez's economic rights over 'La Cumparsita' but retained full ownership over the musical composition. This deal was not good enough for Matos Rodríguez, who managed to renegotiate it in 1933. The new deal entitled Matos Rodríguez to receive half of the proceeds for any phonographic reproduction, synchronisation or performance of 'La Cumparsita' in Argentina and Uruguay.

As said earlier, Contursi habitually added his lyrics to other authors' musical compositions. In 1917, Contursi added lyrics to Matos Rodriguez's 'La Cumparsita' without the composer's consent.

In 1924, Pascual Contursi and Enrique Maroni wrote the *sainete* called *Un programa de cabaret*, in which Matos Rodriguez's 'La Cumparsita', with Contursi's lyrics, was included. The sainete was a huge success in Buenos Aires. Pascual Contursi and Enrique Maroni were considered joint authors of the 'La Cumparsita' lyrics (although the latter had nothing to do with it). In 1924, Matos Rodríguez had no rights over his musical composition. However, the situation changed after the agreement with Ricordi Americana SA in 1926. Then, Matos Rodríguez requested collective management organisations and theatres to prevent the performance or reproduction of 'La Cumparsita' having Contursi's lyrics. Matos Rodríguez's ban affected the Argentine musical industry, even Carlos Gardel's 1928 recording of 'La Cumparsita' with Contursi's lyrics.

Contursi died in 1942 and his rights passed to his widow, Hilda Briano, and his son, José María Contursi. In 1946, Hilda Briano, José María Contursi and Enrique Maroni collectively sued Matos Rodríguez. They claimed compensation and coauthorship rights for 'La Cumparsita'. In 1947, José Razzano, who had obtained all economic rights to Gardel's works, also sued Matos Rodríguez, seeking compensation for the proscription of the reproduction, distribution and performance of Gardel's 1928 rendition of 'La Cumparsita'.

Matos Rodríguez died in 1948, leaving his mother as his only legal heir. However, she was declared mentally insane, and her daughter, Ofelia Isis Matos, became her curator and the manager of her brother's rights. To end a protracted legal battle, Maroni, Contursi and Matos Rodríguez's heirs agreed to submit their dispute to the binding ad hoc arbitration by famous orchestra director Francisco Canaro. Acting as sole arbiter, not being a lawyer, Canaro agreed to solve the dispute according to the general principles of fairness (*ex aequo et bono*) and not according to legal rules. Razzano had already withdrawn from the lawsuit, for which he received money from Maroni and Contursi's heirs.

In the award, Canaro addressed whether Contursi's lyrics contributed to the diffusion and success of Mattos Rodríguez's composition of 'La Cumparsita'. He answered this question affirmatively. Therefore, Contursi and Maroni had to be compensated. In addition, Canaro included a scheme to distribute past and future profits from the song (performance, synchronisation, publishing and fixation rights).

Ricordi Americana SA, who also had rights to Matos Rodríguez's composition 'La Cumparsita', was not party to the arbitration. To avoid litigation, the parties to the arbitration and Ricordi Americana SA settled in 1952. After agreeing on a new distribution scheme for synchronisation, fixation and publishing rights, Ricordi Americana SA agreed to include the names of Maroni and Contursi together with Matos as joint authors.

V. Concluding Remarks

In this chapter, I have briefly described the origins, the inspirations and the evolution of River Plate tango and, to a lesser extent, the genesis of copyright law in Argentina and Uruguay. The history of River Plate tango is a complex skein of cultural appropriation and reappropriation, borrowing, musical and technological innovation. Different rhythms, genres and cultures contributed to its unique yet universal appeal. River Plate tango, as we know it today, is a hybrid genre that could not have existed without a dynamic process of cultural symbiosis and recombination by different ethnic groups and social strata of African, European and American elements during a unique period of Argentine and Uruguayan history. This brief study of the origins of River Plate tango suggests caution before demonising all forms of cultural appropriation, which, although based on legitimate reasons, may have the effect of chilling artistic creativity. A rich and free-for-all-to-take public domain is a key precondition for the creation of new works.

The evolution of River Plate tango also provides interesting insights into the conditions necessary for the emergence of copyright laws. Since their respective independences until 1933 in Argentina and 1937 in Uruguay, there was little enforcement of authors' economic and moral rights, and none for foreign authors. The absence of legal entitlements may have encouraged tango authors to produce new works regularly to assign them to intermediaries in exchange for monies to make a living, and to rely on social norms and alternative dispute resolution mechanisms to minimise or put an end to conflicts. Borrowing, imitation, misappropriation and even abusive contracting practices may have created the conditions for a higher rate of creativity and productivity among artists. What may be considered unfair from the perspective of individual authors may have been beneficial on a collective level, allowing River Plate tango to consolidate in a relatively short time as a sui generis genre. It was much later, once the tango genre had been well established, that local authors, interpreters and newly created collective societies lobbied for stronger copyright laws and enforcement.

Moreover, this chapter also confirms the thesis that developing nations' governments purposively favoured a weak author's rights policy at an early stage. Such a policy may pay off in developmental stages and absent international constraints by allowing local publishers to reproduce works at lower prices than otherwise due to the absence of exclusive rights (an institutionalised form of free-riding). Such a policy benefited the local population, which accessed low-priced literary, scientific and cultural works.

However, the pendulum shifts when national authors and interpreters reach a critical mass and organise around collective management organisations, and a local market for their works develops. Then, the benefits of enforcing copyright law outweigh its costs, even if consumers will have to bear most of the cost of the policy shift.[54] Law and economics scholarship suggests that granting copyright (property rights on literary and artistic works) increases the author's extrinsic incentives to generate new works, which increases the overall total welfare, at least if the duration of copyright is reasonably set.[55] However, the early development of the tango genre suggests that,

[54] This pattern seems coherent with the economic theory of property rights, according to which, mutatis mutandis, property rights are granted when the overall benefits of instituting and managing them outweigh their costs. See A Alchiam, 'Some Economics of Property Rights' (1965) 30(4) *Il Politico*; H Demsetz, 'Toward a Theory of Property Rights' (1967) 57(2) *American Economic Review*.

[55] WM Landes and RA Posner, 'An Economic Analysis of Copyright Law' (1989) 18 Journal of Legal Studies 325, 325–33.

even in the absence of extrinsic economic rewards, such as copyrights, many authors will continue to create new works, mainly moved by intrinsic motivation, such as aesthetic pleasure, art for art's sake, etc., or, from a less romantic perspective, if they can capture profits indirectly, by assigning their works or performing their works 'live'.[56]

Technology also played an important role in the consolidation and international success of River Plate tango. The recordings of Carlos Gardel were heard all over Latin America thanks to the phonogram and cinematographers.

From its origins to contemporary developments, River Plate tango has not remained a static genre. Rather, it is fluid, and in constant mutation. River Plate tango may have become a TCE of the River Plate, but has also become something larger. The future evolution of River Plate tango may happen beyond the geographical area where it was originally conceived.

[56] E Deci, *Intrinsic Motivation* (Springer US, 2012).

Section C: Europe

17

Ownership as Sharing: The Practices of Irish Folk Music

LUKE McDONAGH

I. Introduction

In this chapter, I examine Irish folk – or traditional – music through the lens of copyright law.[1] Irish folk music can be described as music from Ireland that is traditional in the sense of transmission or performance style, and which has developed in Ireland over the last three or four centuries.[2] As other chapters in this volume explore, folk music is usually categorised as pre-modern and is distinguished in historical practice from other forms of music by dependence on a process of person-to-person transmission (orality/aurality).[3] This oral/aural process differed – and continues to differ – from the written forms of learning and transmission common to, for example, Western classical music. However, today, many performers of folk music augment the traditional techniques of oral/aural transmission with learning aids (usually recordings or transcriptions).[4]

II. Irish Folk Music – Distinctive Characteristics

Irish folk music has several defining characteristics that make it distinctive. Many Irish melodies share similar motifs, meaning that there are many tunes that share similar, if not identical, melodic parts. Numerous older melodies have, via performance and transmission, 'branched off' into distinctive variants that are today performed as separate tunes.[5] For example, the famous reel 'Toss the Feathers' has at least four distinct versions and each version contains subtle but clear differences.[6] The existence of these shared melodic motifs, as well as identical tune parts, gives

[1] Although the terms 'folk' and 'traditional' are sometimes used interchangeably, the term 'traditional music' is preferable as it more clearly implies a process. Nonetheless, for the purposes of consistency with the other contributions to this volume, I refer to Irish folk music in this article.

[2] B Breathnach, *Folk Music and Dances of Ireland* (Irish Book Centre, 1978).

[3] L Ó Laoire, 'Fieldwork in Common Places: An Ethnographer's Experiences in Tory Island' (2003) 12 *Ethnomusicology Forum* 13.

[4] J Toynbee, 'Copyright, the Work and Phonographic Orality in Music' [2006] *Social and Legal Studies* 77.

[5] C Mac Aoidh, *Between the Jigs and the Reels* (Drumlin Publications, 1994) 42.

[6] Journalist and uileann piper Peter Browne refers to the different, distinct versions of 'Toss the Feathers' in his liner notes to *Matt Molloy, Matt Molloy* (Mulligan, 1977).

a unique character to Irish folk music – demonstrating continuity and variance at once. Adding to the distinctiveness of Irish folk music, there are several regional styles and innumerable individual ones. The eastern and western styles in County Clare are arguably as distinct from each other as they are from the styles of County Kerry and County Donegal.[7] Further to this, many performers developed their own individual styles.[8] In fact, the ability to add melodic variation and ornamentation to a tune is vital to each musician's individuality, making the improvisory practices of Irish traditional dance music comparable to jazz.[9]

III. Commercialisation and Commodification

The commercialisation of Irish folk music in Ireland can be traced to the boom in house dances and dance halls that occurred in the 1920s–1930s.[10] Until then, competitive and commercial concerns rarely arose. This changed somewhat in the more professional environment of the licensed dance hall and increased further with the popularity of the *céilí* bands that performed in such venues, bands that possessed a hybrid traditional–modern sound, featuring drums and the saxophone alongside traditional folk instruments such as the fiddle and flute. Later, the boom in pub sessions, from the 1950s–1960s onward, led to small-group playing in pub sessions overtaking the *céilí* band in popularity.

Commercialisation also occurred via the recording industry as it emerged in the USA in the early part of the twentieth century. Several recordings were made of Irish immigrant musicians, such as Michael Coleman and James Morrison, during the 1920s and 1930s – and these commercial recordings eventually found their way back to Ireland, where they proved influential. Post-WWII, the 1960s' folk revival led to a new boom in commercial recordings of Irish traditional music.[11] Folk music groups such as the Clancy Brothers and the Dubliners even had some success in the pop charts of the USA and UK. Irish folk melodies were recorded during the 1960s–1970s by successful groups such as the Chieftains, Planxty and De Danann. During the 1990s, Irish folk music became yet more commercialised, this time at the global level, as part of the 'world music' brand. This culminated in the transnational success of the musical *Riverdance*, which continues to tour the world today.[12]

By the dawn of the twenty-first century, Irish folk music, which had emerged as a communal, rural art form, could now become a privatised commodity in the music industry. Unsurprisingly, as the music became more commercially viable, some musicians became more professional-minded. Today, the most successful professional musicians of Irish folk music – such as Martin Hayes, John Carty or Matt Molloy – tend to release recordings either on their own labels or with the assistance of major distributors.[13] Professional or semi-professional musicians undertake

[7] LE McCullough, 'Style in Traditional Irish Music' (1977) 21 *Ethnomusicology* 85.

[8] See generally 'A Lilt All His Own', interview with Martin Hayes in *Fiddler Magazine* (Spring 1994) www.ceolas.org/artists/Martin_Hayes/interview/html.

[9] Musicians may incorporate variations they have heard from other musicians into their own arrangements and improvisations – as noted in M McCarthy, *Passing It On: The Transmission of Music in Irish Culture* (Cork University Press, 1999).

[10] Public Dance Halls Act 1935.

[11] B Whelan, 'Globalising Irish Music', www.ucd.ie/scholarcast/transcripts/Globalising_Irish_Music.pdf.

[12] https://riverdance.com.

[13] The most successful contemporary Irish traditional musician is Martin Hayes, who records and tours as a professional musician: www.martinhayes.com.

concert tours, stopping off at folk and traditional festivals around the world in countries as far apart as the USA, Australia and Japan. Yet, it is notable that the impact of the commercial scene on the majority of musicians – who are talented amateurs – has been minimal. The community has continued to thrive at the local level. Even the most commercially successful musicians attend local sessions and participate in community transmission at Irish festivals such as the Feakle Music Festival.[14]

What, then, of claims of copyright in works of Irish folk music?[15] In the sections that follow, I outline the key elements of international and national law as it applies to traditional Irish music.

IV. Music and Copyright Law at the International Level

The legal understanding of music under copyright has been shaped in part by developments at the international level.[16] Key here is the Berne Convention of 1886, which has been adopted by much of the global community and which provides an international framework for copyright in relation to musical works.[17] Many of its standards also form part of the 1994 TRIPS agreement within the World Trade Organization (WTO) system.[18] Berne protects 'musical composition with or without words' and 'dramatico-musical works', but does not define 'music' or 'musical composition'.[19] Indeed, there are surprisingly few definitions of 'musical work' in national and international copyright law. When, in 1994, the WTO TRIPS Agreement was negotiated, it merely adopted the terms of the Berne Convention and did not provide a further definition of musical work.[20] The WIPO World Copyright Treaty of 1996[21] does not even attempt to define it. Similarly, the relevant US legislation does not provide a definition.[22] What this may indicate is that legislative bodies, both national and international, accept that the terms 'music' and 'musical work' are inherently difficult to define (and/or that it is not necessary to define the terms strictly for copyright purposes).[23] As shown below, the UK courts have, over time, developed their own rich and useful definition of the musical work.

[14] www.feaklefestival.ie.

[15] L McDonagh, 'Exploring "Ownership" of Irish Traditional Dance Music – Heritage or Property?' (2022) 29 (special issue 2) *International Journal of Cultural Property* 183.

[16] See Berne Convention for the Protection of Literary and Artistic Works, 9 September 1886, S Treaty Doc 99-27, 1161 UNTS 3 (amended 28 September 1979) (hereinafter, Berne Convention).

[17] Universal Copyright Convention (1952). This was enacted to provide international protection standards for countries that were unwilling to accept certain terms of the Berne Convention. Today the Universal Copyright Convention is less relevant due to the requirement that countries accede to the TRIPS agreement for WTO membership. Universal Copyright Convention, 6 September 1952, revised at Paris 24 July 1971, 25 UST 1341.

[18] Agreement on Trade-Related Aspects of Intellectual Property Rights, 15 April 1994, Art 27(2), Annex 1C of the Marrakesh Agreement Establishing the World Trade Organization, 1869 UNTS 299 (hereinafter, TRIPS).

[19] Berne Convention, Art 2(1).

[20] Berne Convention, Arts 1–21 were adopted into TRIPS with no expansion of the definition of 'musical work'.

[21] WIPO Copyright Treaty (1996). The WCT was enacted primarily to address the issues surrounding copyright and digital technology, www.wipo.int/treaties/en/ip/wct/trtdocs_wo033.html#P51_3806.

[22] United States Copyright Act 1976, s 102(a)(2), www.law.cornell.edu/copyright/copyright.act.chapt1a.html#17usc102.

[23] When the Berne Convention was revised in 1908, it was decided that copyright should arise automatically; in other words, there should be no need for registration (though the USA retained a registration system until the 1970s): Convention for the Protection of Literary and Artistic Works (1908), Art 4. It was also agreed that the minimum term should be 50 years after the life of the author.

V. Defining the Musical Work in the UK and Ireland

The Imperial Copyright Act of 1911 brought the Berne Convention standards into UK law.[24] It was followed by the Copyright Act of 1956.[25] Yet, neither the 1911 Act nor the 1956 Act provided a definition of 'musical work'. However, the Copyright, Designs and Patents Act 1988 (CDPA) did so, stating that a musical work is 'a work consisting of music, exclusive of any words or action intended to be sung, spoken or performed with the music'.[26] Nevertheless, the statute does not define what amounts to a piece of 'music'.[27]

One advantage of the lack of a definition of music within the CDPA is that the courts have leeway to take a broad interpretation of what is encompassed by a musical work.[28] In this regard, the Court of Appeal decision in *Sawkins v Hyperion*[29] remains the most authoritative decision on the nature of the musical work in the UK and is the exemplar of the benefits of a flexible approach. In *Sawkins*, the claimant successfully argued that he owned the copyright in performing editions that he had prepared of public domain works originally composed by Michel-Richard Lalande during the early modern period. Mummery LJ remarked that 'the essence of music is combining sounds for listening to'.[30] Mummery LJ's statement is worth analysing:

> Music is not the same as mere noise. The sound of music is intended to produce effects of some kind on the listener's emotions and intellect. The sounds may be produced by an organised performance on instruments played from a musical score, though that is not essential for the existence of the music or of copyright in it … There is no reason why, for example, a recording of a person's spontaneous singing, whistling, or humming or improvisations of sounds by a group of people with or without musical instruments should not be regarded as 'music' for copyright purposes.[31]

Evidently, this notion of music is not limited to harmony or melody. Mummery LJ further opined that it would be incorrect to

> single out the notes as uniquely significant for copyright purposes and to proceed to deny copyright to the other elements that make some contribution to the sound of the music when performed, such as performing indications, tempo and performance practice indicators.[32]

Therefore, in the UK, the musical work is a broad and flexible concept.[33] In light of this, if there are challenges that arise from the application of copyright to folk music under UK law, it is unlikely that these difficulties arise due to copyright's definition of musical work.

The starting point of assessing such intellectual property concerns in the context of Irish folk music is to recognise that any work of music, regardless of genre, can be viewed as either in copyright or in the public domain. Determining whether a particular piece is in copyright requires first taking account of the fact that copyright arises automatically on the creation and

[24] Copyright Act 1911, www.opsi.gov.uk/RevisedStatutes/Acts/ukpga/1911/cukpga_19110046_en_1.

[25] Copyright Act 1956, www.opsi.gov.uk/acts/acts1956/pdf/ukpga_19560074_en.pdf.

[26] CDPA 1988, s 3(1). For Ireland, see the Copyright and Related Rights Act (CRRA), 2000, which follows the language of the CDPA closely. There is a lack of Irish case law exploring music cases, so UK case law is of key importance.

[27] CL Saw, 'Protecting the Sound of Silence in 4'33" – A Timely Revisit of Basic Principles in Copyright Law' (2005) 27 *European Intellectual Property Review* 467, 469; D Seymour, 'This Is the Piece that Everyone Here Has Come to Experience: The Challenges to Copyright of John Cage's 4'33"' (2013) 33 *Legal Studies* 532, 537–48.

[28] A Rahmatian, 'Music and Creativity as Perceived by Copyright Law' (2005) 3 *Intellectual Property Quarterly* 267, 268.

[29] *Sawkins v Hyperion Records Ltd* [2005] EWCA Civ 565, [2005] 1 WLR 3281.

[30] ibid para 53.

[31] ibid.

[32] ibid paras 55–56.

[33] *Coffey v Warner/Chappell Music* [2005] FSR (34) 747.

fixation of an original musical work – meaning that many new folk compositions are technically protected by copyright. For the public domain, the age of the musical piece matters, given that an existing work falls into the public domain when the copyright term expires, ie 70 years after the life of the author in the UK and Ireland. Yet, the boundaries of the copyright–public domain relationship can be uncertain. A musical work may actually contain a mixture of public domain material (stylistic conventions, basic patterns, etc) and original elements (new melodies, variations, arrangements of notes, etc).[34] For present purposes, I interpret the public domain concept as broadly as possible, to include musical works that have fallen out of copyright; ideas and non-original expressions, such as musical conventions and patterns; and the elements covered by the numerous copyright exceptions (fair dealing/fair use), which allow use of music without a licence in limited circumstances, eg quotation.

As discussed further below, complexities can arise in relation to cases involving the distinction between two different types of musical work – the 'composition' and the 'arrangement' – as well as the twin notions of authorship and joint authorship.

VI. Musical Works – Compositions and Arrangements

Of particular importance to discussions of folk music and copyright is the distinction between the copyright in the musical composition and the copyright in a subsequent 'arrangement' of that composition. Under UK (and Irish) law, a separate copyright can subsist in an arrangement of a composition as long as the arrangement is sufficiently original[35] and the requisite originality comes from the arranger.[36] The owner of the original copyright in the composition is not the owner of the new arrangement copyright, which vests in the arranger.[37] In other words, copyright can recognise rights in multiple, original arrangements of the same composition.

Although the Berne Convention does not expressly state that there is a requirement of originality, there is 'a clear indication' that the notion of intellectual creation is 'implicit in the conception of a literary or artistic work'.[38] The same logic applies to a musical work. Crucially, whether one considers the former UK standard of 'skill, labour and judgement' or the Court of Justice of the European Union standard of 'intellectual creation', it is clear that the threshold is not a burdensome one in the musical context: music performance and composition are inherently creative and thus have little problem satisfying this test.[39] Virtually any creative contribution to an existing tune or song will be sufficient for the arrangement to be protected. However, the effective use of this new arrangement copyright would be subject to licensing requirements because

[34] P Johnson, '"Dedicating" Copyright to The Public Domain' [2008] *MLR* 587.

[35] *Austin v Columbia* [1917–1923] MacG CC 398. See also *Roberton v Lewis* [1976] RPC 169; *Lover v Davidson* (1856) 1 CBNS 182, which involved accompaniment to an old air; *Wood v Boosey* (1868) LR 3 QB 223, which involved an operatic pianoforte score.

[36] *Redwood Music Ltd v Chappell & Co Ltd* [1982] RPC 109 (QBD). However, a straightforward 'cover' of a work may lack sufficient originality – see *Aston Barrett v Universal Island Rec. Ltd* [2006] EWHC 1009 (Ch). See also CRRA 2000.

[37] This would usually be the case unless an alternative has been agreed between the two parties.

[38] Berne Convention, Art 2(5). See also S Ricketson and J Ginsburg, *International Copyright and Neighbouring Rights – The Berne Convention and Beyond* (Oxford University Press, 2006) 402–03, noting that the preparatory documents for the Brussels Revision Conference show that the expression 'literary and artistic works' included an idea of intellectual creativity.

[39] Case C-5/08 *Infopaq International A/S v Danske Dagblades Forening* [2009] ECR I-6569 (ECJ (4th Chamber)), [2009] ECDR 16 259; *Newspaper Licensing Agency v Meltwater* [2010] EWHC 3099 (Ch); *SAS Institute Inc v World Programming Ltd* [2013] EWHC 69 (Ch), [2013] RPC 17. See also L McDonagh, 'Headlines and Hyperlinks: UK Copyright Law Post-*Infopaq*' (2011) 1 *Queen Mary Journal of Intellectual Property* 184.

the copyright in the new arrangement does not replace or nullify the copyright in the underlying work. This means that an arranger of a copyright work must obtain a licence from the owner of the underlying copyright work in order to release the new arrangement because the right to make 'adaptations' is one of the rights of the copyright owner.[40] The only exception to this is if the new arrangement is based on a public domain work; if this is the case, then the arranger will own the copyright in the arrangement, with no requirement to obtain a licence (though copyright only covers the original elements of the new arrangement – the underlying work remains in the public domain).

The conflict between these rights – the right of adaptation and the automatic protection of new original arrangements – has long been acknowledged. At the time of Berne, 'musical arrangements' were not protected as original works; they were merely viewed as potentially 'unauthorised indirect appropriations of works', ie as examples of infringement.[41] However, following the Berlin Revision of the Berne Convention, arrangements were given protection under Article 2(3) as original works, 'without prejudice to the copyright in the original work'.[42] This debate over the terms of Berne underlines the fact that a new arrangement of a copyright composition can simultaneously be an 'original' work in its own right and an 'infringing' work with respect to the underlying copyright in the composition (unless it is properly licensed).

VII. Authorship and Joint Authorship

As noted earlier, an arranger of a folk tune can be the author of, and thus can own copyright in, an original arrangement of a public domain work, though not the underlying piece itself, which remains in the public domain. In theory, the arrangement copyright includes the right to object to 'sound-a-like' records which mimic the arrangement. However, such cases can be difficult to prove.[43]

There have been several UK music copyright cases where a particular arrangement of a composition has been the subject of a legal dispute. Courts have sometimes found it difficult to clarify the distinction between the underlying work and a later arrangement, especially in joint authorship cases involving music. The nature of music performance as a group activity can lead to confusion over who is an author, and thus a copyright owner, and who is a mere performer, and thus not entitled to copyright protection.

Thankfully, the 2007 case of *Fisher v Brooker* clarified how to assess musical arrangements in the context of joint authorship. In *Fisher*, authorship of the famous 1960s song 'A Whiter Shade of Pale' was disputed. Gary Brooker had always been credited with the copyright in the musical work because he wrote the chords and melody of the song. According to Brooker, he recorded this as a bare 'demo', and presented it in the studio to the other band members, who then performed on the final recorded and released work – 'A Whiter Shade of Pale'. The song is famous for its organ instrumental sections, which were not part of the song at the time the demo was recorded but were instead improvised by band member Matthew Fisher during the performance and recording process. Therefore, the instrumental sections in question were created by a band member (Fisher)

[40] CDPA, s 21.

[41] Ricketson and Ginsburg (n 38) 435.

[42] Berne Convention, Art 2(3).

[43] *Roberton v Lewis* (n 35). See also *CBS Records Australia Ltd v Gross* (1989) 15 IPR 385, 393; *ZYX Music GmbH v King* [1997] 2 All ER 129.

in response and counterpoint to a chord structure devised by the main songwriter of the group (Brooker).[44]

Unfortunately, in its analysis, the High Court in *Fisher* did not properly disentangle the composition, as represented by the demo, from the arrangement, as represented by the final recorded work. Fortunately, this was rectified by the Court of Appeal in 2008, which maintained a clear distinction between the demo and the final arrangement, and ultimately upheld the claim of Fisher that he ought to be viewed as a joint author and owner of the eventual recorded and arranged work known as 'A Whiter Shade of Pale'.[45]

VIII. Irish Folk Music and Copyright Law

What cases such as *Sawkins* and *Fisher* demonstrate is that: (i) the definitions of music and musical work under the CDPA are broad and encompassing; (ii) arrangements, including of folk tunes, can be protected as separate musical works to the underlying works; and (iii) the low threshold of originality will often be satisfied by the improvisory, creative act of the musical performer, including in circumstances of joint authorship. These three points give credence to the argument that there is nothing about Irish folk music of itself that makes it unprotectable under copyright law.

At the same time, we must recall that a large proportion, though certainly not all, of the body of Irish folk tunes are in the public domain. Similarly, the musical stylistic conventions of Irish traditional music, such as motifs, reside in the public domain. These stylistic conventions can be used freely by all composers and arrangers in the creation of new works. Yet, there are many examples of compositions by living or recently deceased composers which are accepted as part of the living tradition. As noted earlier, these works are technically under copyright, as protection arises automatically upon the creation of an original composition that is fixed in some way. Given that most, if not all, new compositions are likely to be sufficiently creative (original) and will be fixed in some form – even if just in the notation shared via thesession.org – such new compositions in the traditional style can be said to be in copyright. In addition to new compositions, copyright may arise in new arrangements, eg where a musician takes an existing public domain tune and adds sufficient originality in the form of musical variations/additions. Such original arrangements of works of folk music – whether public domain works or those in copyright – would clearly be protected by copyright.

This has consequences: where there are multiple arrangements of an original tune/song which is still under copyright, the law says that licences are required from the copyright owner of that original tune/song. Furthermore, if a later folk music arrangement featured original elements of an earlier arrangement, a licence would need to be granted by the earlier arranger. Given how important arrangements of songs/tunes are to the practices of traditional music in a wide range of contexts – including US blues[46] and jazz,[47] North American fiddle music[48] and Irish folk music – this issue of licensing cannot be ignored. If all arrangers of traditional music attempted to enforce

[44] *Fisher v Brooker* [2007] EMLR 9 at para 36. See also *Godfrey v Lees* [1995] EMLR 307 (Ch D); *Beckingham v Hodgens* [2002] EWHC 2143 (Ch), [2002] EMLR 45.

[45] *Fisher v Brooker* [2008] Bus LR 1123, para 34 (Mummery LJ).

[46] CG Hines, 'Black Musical Traditions and Copyright Law: Historical Tensions' (2004) 10 *Michigan Journal of Race & Law* 463, 463–75. See generally G Oakley, *The Devil's Music: A History of the Blues* (BBC Books, 1976).

[47] PF Berliner, *Thinking in Jazz: The Infinite Art of Improvisation* (University of Chicago Press, 2009) 61–85. See generally I Monson, *Saying Something: Jazz Improvisation and Interaction* (University of Chicago Press, 2009).

[48] E Spielman, 'The Fiddling Traditions of Cape Breton and Texas: A Study in Parallels and Contrasts' (1972) 8 *Anuario Interamericano de Investigacion Musical* 39, 41–48.

their arrangements of folk songs and tunes against others, it would severely affect the traditional processes of the music, which rely on free sharing of tunes, variations and, effectively, arrangements.[49]

I discussed this quandary in a prior publication: the fact that Irish traditional musicians *can* claim copyright on their original arrangements, as such adaptations are invariably creative and thus sufficiently original under copyright law, leaves open the possibility of disruption of the folk tradition.[50]

Nonetheless, although it is sometimes said that authorship/ownership of new arrangements of public domain works threatens to put up property barriers over material that is often assumed to be in the public domain, this fear tends to be overstated.[51] Authors only have copyright protection in relation to the originality that they have added to the work, not any underlying public domain material. In other words, the protection only covers each specific arrangement. The underlying tune remains in the public domain.

An empirical study I carried out with Irish traditional musicians during 2007–11 demonstrates that one of the reasons why Irish folk music continues to thrive is the existence of social norms of sharing, attribution and reciprocity.[52] These norms are valued highly. At the same time, many Irish folk musicians do record albums and perform in commercial settings, so some knowledge of copyright is necessary. The empirical data I gathered from 2007 to 2011 show that although musicians might seek to enforce their rights over, for example, a composition or arrangement if used in a film or TV programme, they rarely do so when their compositions/arrangements are recorded on albums, or are performed at gigs/festivals, by their fellow musicians.[53] Research by Toynbee and Okpaluba (as well as by Enrico Bonadio and Bryan Khan for this volume) shows that similar traits can be observed in other musical contexts, including Jamaican reggae.[54]

Even if, ultimately, it is the norms that are paramount in the context of Irish folk music, given that the musician's compositions and arrangements can be protected by copyright law, it is worth asking: is there anything further that the law can offer to allow musicians working in a folk idiom to balance their rights with those of the wider community or network? One plausible way in which composers and arrangers could try to ensure the traditional modes of sharing and reciprocity continue to thrive in the modern world would be to license their works openly using an alternative licensing system such as Creative Commons.[55] However, this idea must be treated cautiously as it would have the effect of formalising the informal norms that have served Irish folk music well over the past centuries. There is no urgent reason why a formal licensing system ought to be imposed on a lifeworld of shared common practices that continue to work effectively at facilitating a thriving music scene.

[49] See generally M McCarthy, *Passing It On: The Transmission of Music in Irish Culture* (Cork University Press, 1999).

[50] L McDonagh, 'Protecting Traditional Music under Copyright (and Choosing not to Enforce It)' in E Bonadio and N Lucchi (eds), *Non-conventional Copyright – Do New and Atypical Works Deserve Copyright Protection?* (Edward Elgar, 2018) 151–73.

[51] *Sawkins v Hyperion Records* [2005] EWCA Civ 565, [2005] 1 WLR 3281, [2005] EMLR 688.

[52] McDonagh, 'Protecting Traditional Music' (n 50) 151–73.

[53] L McDonagh, 'Does the Law of Copyright in the UK and Ireland Conflict with the Practices of Irish Traditional Musicians? A Study of the Impact of Law on a Traditional Music Network' (PhD thesis, Queen Mary University of London, 2011).

[54] J Toynbee, 'Reggae Open Source: How the Absence of Copyright Enabled the Emergence of Popular Music in Jamaica' in L Bently, J Davis and J Ginsburg (eds), *Copyright and Piracy* (Cambridge University Press, 2010) 357–73; J Okpaluba, 'Free-Riding on the Riddim'? Open Source, Copyright Law and Reggae Music in Jamaica' in Bently et al (ibid) 375–86.

[55] There is the possibility, since 2014, under UK law of arguing for a fair dealing defence based on quotation within CDPA, s 30. However, no such musical case has yet arisen in UK law and a full theoretical analysis of that possibility is beyond the scope of this chapter.

IX. Conclusion

My research demonstrates that where conflicts exist between notions of copyright and the creative practices of Irish folk musicians, these are typically resolved via social norms rather than, for example, via legal decisions. Irish folk musicians may be willing to enforce their rights under copyright law if their compositions/arrangements are used on a film/TV soundtrack or in *Riverdance*; but at the local level, musicians tend not to enforce their copyrights against their fellow players.[56] There are several reasons for this – for one, the market is relatively small when compared with pop music, and there would be little monetary incentive to do so. But a more significant fact is that the norms of reciprocity, sharing and acknowledgement are key to the way the Irish traditional music community regulates itself.[57] The network of Irish traditional musicians is flexible enough to accommodate some forms of individual authorship and ownership through attribution; meanwhile, at the professional edges, copyright only comes into play with respect to commercial recordings, musicals and soundtracks. Overall, the 'commons' of Irish traditional dance music persists as a site of shared ownership, with copyright law having a minimal impact on the practices of musicians.

[56] L McDonagh, 'Exploring "Ownership"' (n 15).
[57] L McDonagh, 'Protecting Traditional Music' (n 50) 151–73.

18

Hungarian Musical Heritage Goes Viral – Hungarian Folk Music from a Copyright Perspective

PÉTER MEZEI AND GERGELY BÉKÉS*

I. Introduction

The contours of 'folklore' have always been hard to draw.[1] International sources, from the 1967 amendment of the Berne Convention, to the reports and guidelines of the World Intellectual Property Organization's (WIPO's) Intergovernmental Committee on Intellectual Property and Genetic Resources, Traditional Knowledge and Folklore (IGC)[2] and scholarly papers, struggle to offer a stable definition of this word.

In this chapter, we follow Kanwal Puri's concept, according to which folklore is

> a living phenomenon which evolves over time. It is a basic element of our culture which reflects the human spirit. Folklore is thus a window to a community's cultural and social identity, its standards, and values. Folklore is usually transmitted orally, by imitation or by other means. Its forms include language, literature, music, dance, games, mythology, rituals, customs, handicrafts, and other arts. Folklore comprises a great many manifestations which are both extremely various and constantly evolving. Because it is group-oriented and tradition-based, it is sometimes described as traditional and popular folk culture.[3]

We further follow Sam Ricketson's view, according to whom the basic traits of folklore are that

> (i) it is passed from generation to generation by unfixed forms; (ii) it is a community-oriented creation in that its expression is dictated by local standards and traditions; (iii) its creations generally are not attributable to individual authors; and (iv) it is being continually utilized and developed by the society in which it lives.[4]

* The authors are grateful to Miklós Both and Mátyás Bolya for their comments on the historic part of Hungarian musical folklore. We also express our gratitude to Enrico Bonadio, Tim Dornis and Chen Zhu for commenting on our paper, as well as Anushka Tanwar for her excellent research assistantship.

[1] MC Sims and M Stephens, *Living Folklore: An Introduction to the Study of People and their Traditions* (Utah State University Press, 2005) 1.

[2] On these international sources, see s IIIA.

[3] K Puri, 'Copyright Protection of Folklore: A New Zealand Perspective' (1988) 22 *Copyright Bulletin* 3, 19. See further Barbro Klein's short definition: '"Folklore" … denotes oral narration, rituals, crafts, and other forms of vernacular expressive culture.' See B Klein, 'Folklore' in J Wright (ed), *International Encyclopedia of the Social and Behavioral Sciences*, vol 8 (Elsevier, 2001) 5711.

[4] Cited by CA Berryman, 'Toward More Universal Protection of Intangible Cultural Property' (1994) 1 *Journal of Intellectual Property Law* 293, 311.

For the purposes of our chapter, we can conclude that it is a commonly accepted opinion that various forms of musical expressions are part of folklore, and hence there is a necessary overlap of folklore and copyright subject matter.[5]

No doubt, the term 'folklore' does not equal 'old' or 'outdated'.[6] Still, we can claim that from a purely quantitative point of view, a substantial part of folk materials has its own patina; in Dorothy Noyes's words, 'folklore therefore typically evokes both repudiation and nostalgia'.[7] It is also undoubted, as Dan Ben-Amos stated, that in most cases the subject of folklore is an *artistic* communication, which could be copyrighted.[8] At the same time, it is one of the strongest principles of copyright that the term of protection is limited by time; therefore, one could think that the positions of folklore and of copyright protection cannot cross each other. On the contrary, this study proves that the use of folklore often poses copyright questions.

The thousand years long history of Hungary has a rich and diverse corpus of expressions of folklore, including mythology and the origin story (eg the myth of *csodaszarvas*[9] or the story of Hunor and Magor), dances (eg *csárdás* or *verbunkos*), handicrafts (eg pottery or 'Szekler gates', which are folk-patterned and carved wooden entrance gates), motifs, language (dialects and local terminology) or dresses (eg *matyó* dresses or *cifraszűr*).[10]

Musical folklore (folk songs, rhymes, lullabies) is another extremely rich field of traditional knowledge in Hungary. Indeed, Hungarian musical folklore has two equally important subcategories: traditional folk music (as collected and recorded on wax-coated cylinders and later vinyl discs by notable Hungarian musicians, like Zoltán Kodály and Béla Bartók) and authentic Gypsy (Romani) music. This chapter does not cover all legal aspects of Hungarian folklore, but rather looks at the copyright aspects of Hungarian musical folklore. As we will show, the lack of direct copyright protection for folk music does not exclude the incentives for the use of Hungarian musical folklore both for preservation purposes and for the creation of new musical expressions.

This chapter is structured as follows. First, we provide a deeper insight into the two main branches (or sub-genres) of Hungarian folk music: traditional folk music (generally originating from the Hungarian peasant communities) and the authentic Gypsy music (which mainly served as 'entertainment' music in earlier ages, but has now become more like a way of living). Second, we will take a closer look at the relevant international and Hungarian copyright norms related to folklore. Third, we will introduce two case studies that show the practical aspects of the commercial use and cultural preservation of folk music in Hungary.

II. The Definition of Folk Music and a Short History of Hungarian Musical Folklore

The pure legal definition of folk music is unclear, although there have been encouraging attempts to resolve this issue in the last couple of years. According to Mátyás Bolya, folk music is the genre

[5] MJ Andersen, 'Claiming the Glass Slipper: The Protection of Folklore as Traditional Knowledge' [2010] *Case Western Reserve Journal of Law, Technology & the Internet* 151.

[6] Indeed, as the Hungarian musical scientist Lajos Vargyas noted: the mere fact that a folk song is recorded/noted means that such expression has existed at the time of recording/noting, but such existence tells nothing upon the exact date of the said song's coming into existence. *Cf* K Paksa, *Magyar Népzenetörténet*, 5th edn (Balassi, 2019) 39.

[7] D Noyes, 'Folklore' in A Kuper and J Kuper (eds), *The Social Science Encyclopedia*, 3rd edn (Routledge, 2004) 375.

[8] D Ben-Amos, 'Toward a Definition of Folklore in Context' (1971) 84 *Journal of American Folklore* 13.

[9] 'Miraculous Deer'.

[10] On the rich corpus of Hungarian folklore expressions, see especially Á Szemerkényi, *Magyar Népművészet* (Holnap, 2017).

of relatively small and closed communities, created as a kind of cultural self-sustaining activity, and mainly used for the amusement of the members of the community.[11] Mátyás Bolya claims that one cannot interpret the term 'authorship' in the context of folk music, since the folk songs were created by the community as a whole rather than by individuals.[12] At the same time, folk performers have continuously and unconsciously recreated the songs. It is therefore impossible to sharply split the conventional phases of creation (by authors) and interpretation (by performers), as is traditionally the case with classical music. Due to the lack of written forms of this tradition and because of the oral way of knowledge transfer, folk songs have always been available in different versions simultaneously.[13] Moreover, the layers and versions of consecutive generations jointly form the living material of folk music. As Pál Richter emphasised,[14] the central element of the concept of folk music is not the (mainly unknown) person, who created a particular song, but the facts that (i) the song was regularly used (performed) for a longer period within a closed community and (ii) during this period the song was shaped by the music and general cultural tradition of that community.

Although the first written traits of folk music in Hungary stem from the late Middle Ages,[15] Hungarian musical folklore well precedes the period of the conquest of the Carpathian Basin at the turn of the ninth and tenth centuries.[16] This is especially true for lullabies, which can be traced back to as early as the Finno-Ugric period of Hungarian history (ending *c*3500–3000 BCE).[17] However, the deeper we dig into the past centuries, the fewer resources we find on Hungarian folk music. One of the earliest written sources of Hungarian musical folklore is contained in the Latin language 'broader legend of Saint Gerard, Bishop of Csanád' from the fifteenth century. This legend included a travelogue according to which the pitch of the melodist songs of the female miller of the host of Saint Gerard 'necessitated the Bishop to stop reading'.[18]

It is widely disputed by the ethnographers and musicologists whether the term 'folk music' should be limited to the cultural activity of peasants (focusing on vocal folk songs) or should also cover all other groups of the society, especially urban people and Gypsy communities (covering mainly instrumental performances).[19] This discussion of the vocal and instrumental heritage of folk music is clearly present in Hungarian musical science.[20] Gypsies have been present in Hungary since the early 1400s.[21] A significant number of Gypsies settled (in the Roma language, *romungro* people), but other groups stuck to their unsettled (nomadic) life. Romungros had no vocal musical heritage, but picked up and adapted traditional folk songs to instrumental performances. In contrast, unsettled Gypsy communities had a significant vocal musical heritage, but they played no role in the history of instrumental music; indeed, the two groups of Gypsies did not even understand each other's language.[22] Overall, professional

[11] M Bolya, *Információelmélet és népzenekutatás* (MTA BTK Zenetudományi Intézet – L'Harmattan Kiadó, 2019) 31.

[12] ibid 31.

[13] ibid 32. See further J Bereczky, *A magyar népdal új stílusa* (Akadémiai Kiadó, 2013) 400.

[14] P Richter, 'Templomi gyakorlat vagy szájhagyomány? Adalék a népénekgyűjtések módszertanához' (2010) 18 *Magyar Egyházzene* 397.

[15] Paksa (n 6) 139–57.

[16] ibid 47–138.

[17] ibid 65–66.

[18] I Pávai, 'The History of Hungarian Folk Music Research' (*Folklife*), http://folklife.hu/roots-to-revival/traditional-culture/music-and-dance/the-history-of-hungarian-folk-music-research/.

[19] Bolya (n 11) 35–37. See further in detail in L Dobszay, 'Bevezetés' in L Dobszay and J Szendrey (eds), *A magyar népdaltípusok katalógusa stílusok szerint rendezve I* (Magyar Tudományos Akadémia Zenetudományi Intézet, 1988) 5–43.

[20] B Sárosi, *Dudások, cigányzenészek – A hangszeres magyar népzenei hagyomány*, 3rd edn (Nap, 2019) 9.

[21] B Sárosi, *Cigányzene …* (Gondolat, 1971) 11.

[22] ibid 21.

romungro musicians played an active role in the organic development of Hungarian musical folklore.[23] Nevertheless, unsettled Gypsy communities' vocal heritage has also been a part of Hungarian musical folklore.

The role of Gypsy musicians led to the centuries-old confusing equalisation of Hungarian folk music with Gypsy music. The organic coexistence of the two branches of Hungarian musical folklore confused even notable musicians, eg Ferenc Liszt (he is known as Franz von Liszt outside of Hungary). Liszt called the Hungarian musicians of the thirteenth century Gypsies, even though the earliest Gypsy communities did not move to the country until two centuries later.[24] Bálint Sárosi noted that Gypsies had no exclusivity in performing music for long. Indeed, we know about more non-Gypsy musicians until around the eighteenth century.[25]

As seen, rural and urban folk music should have been a part of Hungarian culture for centuries, but the preservation of this heritage started late, only in the nineteenth century – in particular, during the so-called Reform Age (the historical period, starting from the Diet of Hungary of 1825, that preceded the Revolution of 1848–49).[26] The work of the early folklorists, like Gábor Mátray, István Bartalus and Áron Kiss, should be hailed here. The latter was the first to publish a collection of children's game songs; a book that Béla Bartók later called the greatest publication of the nineteenth century.[27]

At the turn of the twentieth century, scientists like Béla Vikár, István Kereszty and János Seprődi started to use modern machine recording equipment (phonographs) to save audio recordings of vocal folk songs.[28] Their legacy was continued by two of the greatest Hungarian musicians of the twentieth century, Béla Bartók[29] and Zoltán Kodály,[30] who recorded mainly vocal folk performances (the lead melodies), and later annotated and published them in sheet-music books. They also published numerous scholarly publications on folk music.[31] Sometime thereafter, gramophones replaced phonographs, and offered an even higher quality of recording and dissemination of folk music in Hungary. This also made it possible for the next group of folklorists, led by László Lajtha, to record instrumental folk music as well.[32] The now huge collection of Hungary's folk music heritage has continuously been published in the 'Magyar Népzene Tára'. The collection was initiated by Bartók and Kodály as early as 1913, but its publication only started after the Second World War. The 12 volumes of the series were edited by the leading folklorists of Hungary.[33]

[23] A Kingsford-Smith, 'Kálmán Balogh: Hungarian Folk and Gypsy Music' (Culture Trip, 6 December 2016) https://theculturetrip.com/europe/hungary/articles/hungarian-folk-and-gypsy-music-an-interview-with-k-lm-n-balogh/. Some publications from the early 1800s indicated that the famous 'verbunkos' dances (of Hussars to recruit (*verbuvál*) future soldiers) were backed by the music played by gypsies from the Galánta region. See Paksa (n 6) 187.

[24] Pávai (n 18); Sárosi, *Cigányzene* ... (n 21) 40.

[25] ibid 40–59.

[26] Paksa (n 6) 12.

[27] Pávai (n 18); Paksa (n 6) 14–24.

[28] Paksa (n 6) 25–26.

[29] The digital version of the *Complete Collection of the Hungarian Folk Songs* by Béla Bartók is published by the Institute for Musicology of the Hungarian Academy of Sciences, http://systems.zti.hu/br/en.

[30] For some parts of the collection of Zoltán Kodály, see https://zti.hungaricana.hu/en/search/results/?list=eyJxdWVyeSI6ICJrb2RcdTAwZTFseS1yZW5kIn0.

[31] B Bartók, 'A magyar népdal' in B Bartók (ed), *Összegyűjtött írásai* (Zeneműkiadó Vállalat, 1966) 101–350; Z Kodály, *A magyar népzene* (Királyi Magyar Egyetemi Nyomda, 1937). On Kodály's and Bartók's folklorist research, as well as a collection of their publications on folk music, see especially J Baló, *Bartók és a népzene* (Doktori értekezés, 1948), https://core.ac.uk/download/pdf/19658904.pdf; S Becze, *Bartók, Kodály, Dohnányi* (Holnap, 2019) 39–51 and 73–85.

[32] Pávai (n 18).

[33] For the digital version of the more than 14,000 pages, see https://adt.arcanum.com/hu/collection/MagyarNepzeneTara/.

III. Musical Folklore and Copyright Law

International proposals to protect expressions of cultural heritage in general and folklore in specific, as well as academic literature in this field, are both manifold and unsuccessful. The list of proposed international solutions is longer than the number of countries that have effectively introduced any meaningful form of intellectual property rights (IP) (especially copyright) protection for folklore. Hungary's copyright history is not an exception to this. In this section, we first address the international background of protection of folklore and then introduce the Hungarian legislative environment or, more precisely, the absence of any IP-based protection for the 'author' of folk songs. As we will show, the lack of formal copyright protection of folklore has little negative effect on the creation and use (especially archiving and dissemination) of folklore-based expressions.

A. International Background

The international normative basis for the protection of folklore dates back to the 1960s, when a significant number of countries in Africa and Asia gained their independence. As a part of that, they joined both the leading international treaty on copyright law, the Berne Convention, and the United Nations. The latter is relevant for two reasons. First, WIPO (transformed from the United International Bureaux for the Protection of Intellectual Property in 1967[34]), an intergovernmental organisation dealing with global IP law, became a specialised agency of the United Nations in 1974; second, the United Nations Educational, Scientific and Cultural Organization (UNESCO) has paid close attention to the protection of cultural interests of (developing) countries. Both the Berne Convention and WIPO/UNESCO documents have proposed various solutions for the protection of folklore.

Article 15(4)(a) was inserted into the Berne Convention at the Diplomatic Conference of Stockholm in 1967.[35] According to it:

> In the case of unpublished works where the identity of the author is unknown, but where there is every ground to presume that he is a national of a country of the Union, it shall be a matter for legislation in that country to designate the competent authority who shall represent the author and shall be entitled to protect and enforce his rights in the countries of the Union.

The accepted provision skips any reference to folklore. Indeed, 'it is only the legislative history of the provision that indicates that folklore was (also) intended to be covered'.[36]

The 1976 Tunis Model Law on Copyright for Developing Countries declared all literary, artistic and scientific works to be eligible to become part of the folklore of a given nation.[37]

WIPO and UNESCO's 1982 Model Provisions Against Illicit Exploitation and Other Prejudicial Actions changed the tone of the definition of folklore by treating such contents as

[34] Entered into force in 1970.

[35] The proposal of the Working Group was adopted unanimously, with six abstentions. See 'Model Provisions for National Laws on the Protection of Expression of Folklore against Illicit Exploitation and Other Prejudicial Actions' (UNESCO-WIPO, 1985) UNESCO/WIPO/FOLK/ASIA/2, 5.

[36] ibid.

[37] Tunis Model Law on Copyright for Developing Countries, s 18(iv), www.wipo.int/publications/en/details.jsp?id=3177&plang=FR.

'expressions' or 'productions' instead of 'works'. Under the Model Provisions, such contents might include verbal expressions (eg folk talks or folk poetry), musical expressions (eg folk songs or instrumental music) and expressions by action (eg folk dances or rituals).

The 1989 UNESCO Recommendation on the Safeguarding of Traditional Culture and Folklore has provided for a broad system to identify, conserve, preserve and disseminate folklore on the national and international levels. It defined folklore in the broadest sense:

> Folklore (or traditional and popular culture) is the totality of tradition-based creations of a cultural community, expressed by a group or individuals and recognized as reflecting the expectations of a community in so far as they reflect its cultural and social identity; its standards and values are transmitted orally, by imitation or by other means. Its forms are, among others, language, literature, music, dance, games, mythology, rituals, customs, handicrafts, architecture and other arts.[38]

Nevertheless, it ignored the intellectual property aspects of the protection of expressions of folklore and focused on the protection of further relevant rights from the perspective of folklore documentation centres and archives, eg privacy, confidentiality or protection against misuse.[39]

WIPO has continued to work on the protection of folklore from the 1990s. The IGC has emphasised three main themes in this field: (i) genetic resources; (ii) traditional knowledge; and (iii) expressions of folklore.[40] For the purposes of this chapter, the last category deserves special attention. The IGC differentiated between three separate categories of folklore: registered, unregistered and secret cultural expressions.[41]

Although the Rome Convention on Neighbouring Rights was mainly silent on folklore, WIPO's Phonograms and Performances Treaty (WPPT) of 1996 has the utmost importance for the protection of folklore, at least for performers. According to Article 2(a), the protection of performers (including actors, singers, musicians and dancers) shall extend to any form of interpretation of literary or artistic works or expressions of folklore. This definition reflects the Rome Convention's definition of 'performers', but with two main differences. Both of these changes were inserted into the WPPT upon the proposal of the Argentine delegation; and one of these proposals was the inclusion of 'expressions of folklore' in Article 2(a).[42] Furthermore, under the agreed statement attached to Article 15 of the WPPT, 'It is understood that Article 15 does not prevent the granting of the right conferred by this Article to performers of folklore and producers of phonograms recording folklore where such phonograms have not been published for commercial gain'. These rules expressly allow for the neighbouring rights-based protection of folklore performers (or copyright-based protection, where performers are granted copyright, rather than neighbouring rights). The definition of phonogram producers is neutral in this respect, and tends to allow for the inclusion of folklore recordings.[43]

Finally, we mention UNESCO's Convention on the Protection and Promotion of the Diversity of Cultural Expressions, which 'Recognis[ed] that the diversity of cultural expressions, including

[38] 1989 UNESCO Recommendation on the Safeguarding of Traditional Culture and Folklore, Art A.

[39] ibid Art F.

[40] S Collins, 'Traditional Knowledge: Protecting the Intangible and Tracing the Development of International Protection of Folklore' in AEL Brown and C Waelde (eds), *Research Handbook on Intellectual Property and Creative Industries* (Edward Elgar, 2018) 217.

[41] ibid 156.

[42] *Records of the Diplomatic Conference on Certain Copyright and Neighboring Rights Questions* (WIPO, 1999) 244. See further J Reinbothe and S von Lewinski, *The WIPO Treaties on Copyright – A Commentary on WCT, the WPPT, and the BTAP* (Oxford University Press, 2015) 263.

[43] WPPT, Art 2(b), in line with Art 3(b) of the Rome Convention and Art 1(a) of the WIPO Convention for the Protection of Producers of Phonograms against Unauthorized Duplication of Their Phonograms.

traditional cultural expressions, is an important factor that allows individuals and peoples to express and to share with others their ideas and values'. It furthermore called for:

> Taking into account the importance of the vitality of cultures, including for persons belonging to minorities and indigenous peoples, as manifested in their freedom to create, disseminate and distribute their traditional cultural expressions and to have access thereto, so as to benefit them for their own development.

B. The Hungarian Approach

Even though Hungary is traditionally an early adopter of the international copyright treaties, the legislator was (and still is) somehow reluctant to follow the path that the international community suggested regarding the possible protection of folklore. The reason for the reluctance is that the international community has never reached a consensus on a possible treaty,[44] while the model provisions and recommendations of WIPO remained in the territory of soft law. Furthermore, it seems that the legal protection of folklore was important for the developing countries, mainly because the richer countries were able to develop other solutions for the preservation and promotion of folklore.[45]

As folklore expressions are not *expressis verbis* excluded from the scope of copyright or neighbouring rights protection, countries might be able to apply various alternatives in granting protection to folklore. These options range from economic to moral rights, unfair competition rules, public domain and *domaine public payant* protection.[46] Although these ideas seem to be rich, their relevance and effectiveness are far from realistic considering the basic features of folklore.

The Hungarian legislation has always been sceptical on this matter, too. A court decision[47] with historic relevance (decided under the 1969 Copyright Act, rather than the current Copyright Act of 1999) concluded that the tales of János Tombácz, the famous folk tale teller[48] from Szeged, are excluded from copyright protection. The opinion of the court was backed by a folklorist expert, who claimed that if a folk tale is adapted into an original piece of work, that transformation, by definition, excludes the tale from the scope of folklore. The experts also stated that the definitions of 'originality' and 'author' have special meanings within the folklore, since folklore is a living and mostly oral tradition of generations, so it is impossible to identify one single version of a tale as the original one. On the other hand, the Council of the Copyright Experts[49] said that there was no legal reason to exclude a tale from copyright protection simply because it had folklore roots but was transformed into an original work. However, the Supreme Court of Hungary followed the way of the folklorists and ruled against the tale teller. While the mentioned decision of the court deeply affected the legal practice in Hungary, the text of the Hungarian Copyright Act remained the same until 1999.

[44] Note that the aim of UNESCO's Convention is to promote cultural diversity.

[45] Maybe the first Hungarian piece of law for the protection of folklore was Decree No 79 of the Council of Ministers in 1951 on the foundation of the Állami Népi Együttes (Hungarian State Folk Ensemble). The primary aim of the Ensemble was promotion and presentation of Hungarian folklore (see Art 1(1)).

[46] Berryman (n 4) 312–18.

[47] BH1978, 471, https://library.hungaricana.hu/hu/view/DTT_DONT_OGYK000076273_08/?pg=35&layout=s.

[48] *Tombácz János meséi*, Új Magyar Népköltési Gyűjtemény (Akadémiai Kiadó, 1975).

[49] The Council was originally founded in 1884 within the Hungarian Patent Office, and it still plays an active role within the framework of the Hungarian Intellectual Property Office. The Council has always provided expert opinions, mostly in judicial procedures on issues of copyright law.

The current Hungarian Copyright Act[50] is the first legislative instrument in Hungary that explicitly excludes the expression of folklore from copyright protection. Article 1(7) of the Hungarian Copyright Act states that 'the expressions of folklore may not enjoy copyright protection. However, this may not prejudice copyright protection due to the author of a folk-art-inspired work of individual and original nature.' It seems that the codifiers of the Act tried to create a well-balanced situation, in which the pure expressions of folklore are clearly excluded from the protection while the adaptations of folklore are still covered. The main reason for the exclusion was the fact that the authors of folklore work are unidentifiable by principle.

Since there is no definition of the term 'folklore' either in the Hungarian Copyright Act or in any other piece of law in Hungary, there is a relatively wide terrain for questions in practice. Some legal practitioners tend to deem all music with folkloric roots as an expression of folklore, including mild adaptations of folk music. We feel this assumption is too wide, though, clearly, a well-founded classification is impossible without the expertise of ethnographers. We believe that the aim of the legislator was to exclude only the expression of the folklore in its original form,[51] while, at the same time, ensuring a high level of protection for the adaptation of folk music. This narrower interpretation could foster the reutilisation of folk music in a way that links the common tradition of Hungary to new audiences. However, as we will demonstrate in the case studies of section IV of this chapter, even the broader limitation of the copyright protection has no chilling effect.

From the angle of neighbouring right holders, one could argue that the situation is perfectly clear. Indeed, the Hungarian Copyright Act remains totally silent regarding the performances and sound recordings of folklore, which results in wide protection for the neighbouring right holders. On the other hand, one could also argue that the lack of definition of the protected performances and sound recordings in the Hungarian Copyright Act opens questions for debate.

Hungary has signed all the major international neighbouring right treaties, including the Rome Convention, the WPPT and WIPO's Beijing Treaty on Audiovisual Performances (although this last is less relevant regarding the copyright protection of folk music). At the same time, none of the definitions of the mentioned treaties have been reproduced by the Hungarian legislators. Therefore, competing terms are available in parallel in the legislation. This could indeed be confusing, mainly concerning the definition of performing artists, since the definition one should apply, for example, to the secondary use of sound recordings (Rome Convention, Article 12) differs from the one, for example, making available the same recording (WPPT, Article 10). However, the Hungarian legal practice and the court decisions mostly hide these discrepancies and apply the wider definition of the WPPT for all uses, including those that are covered by the thinner scope of protection of the Rome Convention.

The users of folk performances often claim that the fixations they use are not protected performances, but pure results of scientific fieldwork of ethnography. Therefore, they claim, the singers and instrumentalists are not performers, but simply the so-called informant or 'human object' of the collection. Without judging how unacceptable such objectification is in general, we will limit our analysis to the question of copyright.

Hungarian case law clearly shows that copyright protection extends to uneducated (but trained) performers, whose performances are sometimes not purposeful or unintentional either. One of the expert opinions of the Council of the Copyright Experts stated that the mere fact that the fixation took place during a scientific event (eg during a collection of folk songs) does not

[50] Act LXXVI of 1999 on Copyright.

[51] The Croatia Copyright Act, Art 8(3) applies exactly this approach.

exclude the performance itself from the neighbouring right protection.[52] The Copyright Experts also claimed that, in most cases, the performers of folk songs are identifiable; furthermore, the performances have a unique nature, which reflects the personalities of the performers. For the most part, we agree with this reasoning. We believe that the protection should be genre-blind; therefore, if the general conditions of neighbouring right protection are fulfilled, the performance should enjoy the same level of protection, irrespective of whether the recording session took place in a rural part of the country or in a highly equipped studio in the capital city.

Regarding the definition of the protected sound recording, the situation is perfectly clear, mainly because the relevant definitions of the international treaties are identical. The codifiers of the Rome Convention and the WPPT copied the text of Article 1(1) of the Convention for the Protection of Producers of Phonograms Against Unauthorized Duplication of Their Phonograms, which says that 'phonogram' means 'any exclusively aural fixation of sounds of a performance or of other sounds'. Although the definition itself was not reproduced in the Hungarian Copyright Act, there are no competing versions of the definition. To the best of our knowledge, there have been no relevant court cases regarding the rights of the producers of the fixations of folk songs.

IV. Case Studies

A. Deep Forest's *Boheme*: The Use of Traditional Folk and Gypsy Music

One of the most popular traditional Hungarian folk songs published on a commercial phonogram was released by the French pop group Deep Forest. More than four million copies of their 1995 album *Boheme* were sold over the years. In the track 'Freedom Cry', Deep Forest sampled the performance of Károly Rostás (also known as Huttyán) without any authorisation.[53]

Huttyán lived in a small, rural Gypsy settlement near Öcsöd, in Hungary. He was an instinctive, talented folk singer and dancer, and he knew many different traditional Gypsy themes by heart. When Claude Flagel, a French composer, visited Öcsöd in 1977, he archived performances of the local Gypsy community members, amongst them being performances by Huttyán. Just like in many other cases of the Socialist era of Hungary,[54] no written contract was signed by the parties. Some of these recordings were released in 1993, on Claude Flagel's album *Rom sam ame!*[55] – nine years after Huttyán died. Deep Forest licensed the use of Flagel's album,[56] but failed to authorise the use of Huttyán's performance.

The story of this track is well archived by the Hungarian court decisions,[57] expert opinions,[58] academic review,[59] news reports[60] and an award-winning documentary[61] released in 1996.

[52] SZJSZT 1/2015, www.sztnh.gov.hu/sites/default/files/SZJSZT_szakvelemenyek_pdf/szjszt_szakvelemeny_1_2015.pdf.

[53] Interestingly enough, Deep Forest's 1992 album sampled – in a similarly controversial way – from African folk music. See H Zemp, 'The/An Ethnomusicologist and the Record Business' (1966) 28 *Yearbook for Traditional Music* 44.

[54] BR Lange, 'Folk Music and Commercialization in *Danubian Trances* and *Boheme*' (2015) 7 *Dancecult* 102.

[55] For the recording, see www.discogs.com/Various-Rom-Sam-Ame-Traditions-Tsiganes-En-Hongrie/release/6562552. The album's cover also features Huttyán on the right-hand side of the image.

[56] Lange (n 54) 102.

[57] Legfelsőbb Bíróság Pfv 20.568/2009/6, www.sztnh.gov.hu/sites/default/files/SZJSZT_szakvelemenyek_birosagi_pdf/03-2004_fb_fi_itelet.pdf.

[58] SZJSZT 42/2000, www.sztnh.gov.hu/sites/default/files/SZJSZT_szakvelemenyek_pdf/szjszt_szakv_2000_042.pd.

[59] Lange (n 54) 101–04.

[60] Most recently, see T Borzák, 'Méltatlan helyzet – családi kálvária' (*Szabad Föld Online*, 5 February 2021), https://szabadfold.hu/csalad-otthon/meltatlan-helyzet-csaladi-kalvaria-286144/.

[61] *Huttyán* (directed by András Salamon, produced by MTV, 1996) https://nfi.hu/hu/film/huttyan.

The core facts of the case were undoubted and well founded. The record label has never challenged the fact that its phonogram contained samples of Huttyán's performance. It is also well known that the heirs of Huttyán brought court cases against the record label, and that they lost all cases mainly for procedural reasons, which are beyond the scope of this study.

In substance, the plaintiff claimed that the rights of Huttyán as a performing artist had been injured, as neither Claude Flagel nor the record label had an authorisation for the reproduction and distribution of his performance. On the other hand, the respondent claimed that Huttyán was not a performing artist, because he sang folk songs that were not protected by copyright in Hungary.

As a side note, we should mention here that Hungary joined the Rome Convention in 1994 (shortly before Deep Forest's album was released) and implemented the rules of the Convention in such a way as to cover not only the performances of literary or artistic works, but the expressions of folklore, too. It was evident that Huttyán had performed a traditional folk song, and according to the court decision his performance was protected by Hungarian law.

Due to procedural reasons, however, there was no room for the courts to focus on the copyright merits of the case, namely, whether the use of the performance was authorised or Huttyán's moral rights were affected by Deep Forest's sampling. Deep Forest changed the context of the traditional folk song to a pop track, and the original lyrics were cut into pieces to better fit with the rhythm and groove of the song.

Importantly enough, another track on the same album, 'Marta's Song', sampled an acapella performance of Márta Sebestyén, founding member of the world-famous folk ensemble Muzsikás. In an interview, Márta Sebestyén said[62] that Deep Forest did not ask for any authorisation in advance. Later, however, she and Deep Forest worked together, so we can assume that they agreed to the conditions, at least after the album was released.

From a copyright perspective, the author of Deep Forest adapted a traditional folk song. If the expressions of folk are excluded from the copyright protection in Hungary, their use needs no authorisation for the purpose of adaptation. At the same time, the result of the adaptation, namely the derivative work itself, is protected.

From a neighbouring rights perspective, Huttyán's performance was mixed with the performance of the musicians of Deep Forest. It is evident that the record label reproduced the track of Huttyán when they sampled his performance, and later they successfully distributed the album and sold millions of copies of it. The legislation of Hungary is fully compatible with the Rome Convention of WIPO, therefore performers have the exclusive right to authorise the reproduction and distribution of their performance,[63] even in the case where the performance itself is an expression of folklore. This right was clearly injured. Moral rights are excluded from the scope of the Rome Convention and are regulated by the WPPT. Nevertheless, at least since the WPPT's incorporation, a performer enjoys the right of attribution and the right of integrity. One could argue that the moral rights of a performer are injured when a performance of a folk song is sampled in a distinct genre where the lyrics are also substantially modified.

This case is often presented by journalists as the fight of a modern 'David' against 'Goliath', but we believe that this is rather a prototype of the legal wars a desperate heir can launch against a multinational record label full of resources. It shows how complex, fatiguing and fruitless a civil litigation could be if the plaintiff loses their focus in procedural questions.

[62] A Kalmár, 'Maradtam az a Márti, aki voltam' (*Szimpatika*, 31 January 2021), https://szimpatika.hu/cikkek/10240/maradtam-az-a-marti-aki-voltam.

[63] Rome Convention, Art 7(1c).

B. The Polyphony Project

The Polyphony Project is a perfect case study on how to collect non-protected folk songs into a database, which is protected by *sui generis* rights under the Database Directive of the EU.[64] The mission of the project was to record the oral tradition of Ukraine using audio and audio-visual equipment in order to preserve and present this unique cultural heritage of Ukraine for the future.[65] The project was initiated and led by the Hungarian ethnographer Miklós Both.

As a first step, ethnographers visited distant villages in Ukraine to find peasants for whom folk was a living material and not an archived culture. All fixations were made by multitrack and high-resolution recording devices to preserve every single motion, movement and note performed by the authentic performers.

During the post-production phase, all materials were processed by ethnographers, who analysed and categorised the songs and performances, wrote down all the lyrics and loaded them into a database. One can search by genre, the location of the recordings, the name of the performers, the themes and even the variations of the same song. Naturally, all recordings were mixed and mastered by professionals. As a result, the largest Ukraine online archive of musical folklore was created, which makes it possible to learn how to play a specific folk song in an authentic way.

As a novelty, the application makes it possible to pick up a single or multiple tracks or tessituras and listen to only a part of the performance instead of the whole. Multitrack recording has a history of over 50 years in the music industry; however, members of the public cannot regularly access other than the mixed and mastered version of the track. Therefore, this feature may affect the integrity of the performance,[66] mainly because a song is usually arranged in a way that the tessituras respond to each other, and if you highlight only one, this cooperation of the performers quickly evaporates.

Without doubt, all songs fixed for this project were expressions of folk, which are excluded from copyright protection both in Hungary and in Ukraine. At the same time, the scientific results of the project were loaded into a database in one of the Member States of the EU, namely Hungary.

According to Article 7 of the Database Directive, Member States shall provide for a right for the maker of a database which shows that there has been qualitatively and/or quantitatively a substantial investment in either obtaining verification or presentation of the contents. Recital 19 of the Database Directive makes it clear that the compilation of several recordings of musical performances on a CD does not come within the scope of the Directive, because it does not represent a substantial enough investment to be eligible under the *sui generis* right. The Court of Justice of the European Union (CJEU) analysed this recital in its *British Horseracing* decision, and found that

> the resources used for the creation as such of works or materials included in the database … cannot be deemed equivalent to investment in the obtaining of the contents of that database and cannot, therefore, be taken into account in assessing whether the investment in the creation of the database was substantial.[67]

[64] Directive 96/9/EC of the European Parliament and of the Council of 11 March 1996 on the legal protection of databases.

[65] www.polyphonyproject.com/en.

[66] WIPO WPPT, Art 5(1).

[67] Case C-203/02 *The British Horseracing Board Ltd and Others v William Hill Organization Ltd* ECLI:EU:C:2004:695, para 33.

At the same time – besides the sound and audiovisual recordings fixed specifically for this project – the database covers tones of other data obtained and verified by ethnographers and presented by the IT team of the project. The next question one should examine regarding the legal status of the database is whether its maker invested a substantial number of resources to obtain verification or presentation of the contents. We should consider the fact that, according to the *Directmedia* decision of CJEU,[68] a relatively small amount of money shall be deemed substantial. We can assume that the maker of the Polyphony Project database has invested substantial resources to verify the content and present it in a totally new way.

The maker of the database made the whole database available for free on the Internet. Nevertheless, the database maker still has a *sui generis* right to prevent extraction or reutilisation of the whole or of a substantial part of the database. According to the decision of CJEU, the fact that the database is accessible to the public

> does not relieve the national court of an obligation [], in assessing whether there has been extraction and/or re-utilisation of a substantial part of the contents of that database, to verify whether the materials allegedly extracted and/or re-utilised from that database constitute a substantial part, evaluated quantitatively, of its contents or, as the case may be, whether they constitute a substantial part, evaluated qualitatively, of the database inasmuch as they represent, in terms of the obtaining, verification and presentation thereof, a substantial human, technical or financial investment.[69]

V. Conclusion

We sum up our findings and arguments related to the treatment of Hungarian musical heritage under copyright law as follows.

First, Hungarian folklorists and musicologists define musical folklore generally the same way as international researchers. As seen above, Pál Richter only referred to two major features of folk music, namely: (i) the regular use (performance) of folk songs for a long period within a closed community; and (ii) during this period, the song was shaped by the music and general cultural tradition of that community. Richter's definition is substantially in line with Ricketson's approach (which lists four unique features of folklore). Some may note that while Richter is an ethnographer, Ricketson is a copyright professional, so the differences may have originated from the different approaches of the two disciplines. Viewed from this perspective, there are at least two factors that make the copyright-relevant outlines of folklore blurred to some extent. On the one hand, it is quite challenging to distinguish the original expression of folklore from the (vocal or instrumental) adaptation of folk music or works of individual authors. On the other hand, folklore is an oral, and therefore unfixed, knowledge of a community. No matter how many different versions the ethnographers can collect, the corpus will always be incomplete and fragmented. At the same time, without a reproducible reference point, the borders of folklore will always be debatable.

Second, these complications have limited relevance for the copyright treatment of folklore expressions. The features generally necessitate that the author-centric copyright protection is unavailable for folk music, which is historically unfixed, communitarian, orally transferred, adapted through improvisation and recorded mainly by scientists (rather than by the members of the community). All of these factors speak against the need for and the possibility of any

[68] Case C-304/07 *Directmedia Publishing GmbH v Albert-Ludwigs-Universität Freiburg* ECLI:EU:C:2008:552, para 24.
[69] Case C-545/07 *Apis-Hristovich EOOD v Lakorda AD* ECLI:EU:C:2009:132, para 74.

copyright (more precisely, author's rights) protection. However, if only the ethnographers have the privilege of reliably identifying the expression of folklore, and differentiate them from works of individual authors, the limitation of copyright protection could be questionable.

Third, the lack of individualistic/author-centric copyright protection does not exclude, on the one hand, the protection of performances and recordings of folk music by neighbouring rights; and, on the other hand, the preservation and dissemination of Hungarian musical folklore through public laws that reflect the social/cultural importance of musical folklore. Indeed, the two case studies provide perfect evidence that the enforcement of neighbouring rights is theoretically possible (Huttyán's case was mainly dismissed on procedural grounds), and that vivid projects of preservation and dissemination have existed in Hungary since the end of the nineteenth century.

In sum, the question of borrowing of musical folklore might be viewed from two perspectives. On the one hand, folk music has been 'internally' and organically developed for centuries. Like other fields of folklore, musical folklore is largely built on the intellectual roots of the community. It is therefore regularly repeated, and reflects the common elements of musical tradition, which is a clear form of adaptive borrowing. Consequently, due to this cultural embeddedness of folk music, the use of elements of musical folklore generally falls outside the scope of copyright law. On the other hand, viewed from an 'external' perspective, folk music has traditionally formed the basis of new musical expressions that might fit into the concept of 'work'. Even more importantly, the neighbouring rights system of Hungary allows for a broad protection of the performances and recordings of music containing folk elements.

19

Flamenco Music, Borrowing Practices and the Limits of Copyright

ANTONI RUBÍ-PUIG

I. Staging the Debate: Rosalía and Flamenco's Purity

Any approach to flamenco as a genre cannot evade the many tensions and frictions that baffle its cultural norms of production.[1] For sure, cultural norms of production in other genres might also be uncertain and infused by many tensions. Yet, in flamenco, these frictions and ambiguities are seminal: they define the genre's evolution and boundaries, and shape borrowing practices. The significance that is given to oral transmission, external influences or ethnicity impinges on how flamenco is apprehended and charted.

A recent controversy involving borrowing practices, amid accusations of cultural appropriation, may well illustrate some of the tensions inherent to flamenco as a music genre.[2] In 2018, Catalan-born artist Rosalía released her album *El Mal Querer*, which became an absolute hit and brought her international attention. The album is an innovative work which merges flamenco, trap and other pop music. In the video for the hit song 'Malamente', Rosalía appeared as she were a ghetto-girl Gypsy. The album and the video provoked a passionate polemic in Spain about whether Rosalía could be considered a flamenco artist; whether a hybrid work such as *El Mal Querer* could be labelled as flamenco and counted within the genre's boundaries; whether her borrowing from traditional flamenco sources was legitimate; and whether, due to her social economic status, she was unduly appropriating cultural values associated with flamenco and the Spanish Gypsy community.[3] Some of the criticisms underlined that her vocal flamenco techniques and skills were rather poor; that she cannot pass as a flamenco artist as she has not been trained in the traditional form; or that her characterisation as a low-class Gypsy girl was offensive

[1] As explained throughout this volume, the very notion of genre is problematic, but arguably it can still play a role in identifying patterns and practices within a particular cultural art form. When applied to flamenco, the notion of genre may, however, prove unworkable as flamenco embraces different art forms which are produced through different cultural norms. Some scholars and artists have indeed questioned that the same genre may comprise both traditional flamenco and new flamenco (*Nuevo Flamenco*), which appeared during the 1960s. In this contribution, flamenco is approached as a unitary genre. It is my view that the cultural norms of production in flamenco have been inherently ambiguous and still are; and that their understanding is conditioned by some ex post narratives in which some traits are exaggerated. See s IIB below.

[2] For a comprehensive discussion of the polemic, see P Manuel, 'The Rosalía Polemic: Defining Genre Boundaries and Legitimacy in Flamenco' (2021) 65 *Ethnomusicology* 32.

[3] ibid 41–48.

and could be deemed minstrelsy.[4] Many of the angry comments against the artist pointed out that flamenco has its own rules and norms, and that practices such as Rosalía's endanger its authenticity, genuineness and purity.

According to one commentator, this polemic is sustained on three myths, which are questionable, if not false.[5] First, criticism against Rosalía follows a narrative that exaggeratedly underscores the purity of traditional flamenco, which would have been alien to external influences.[6] Second, many of the arguments by critics overstress the links of flamenco with *gitanos* (Spanish Gypsies or Roma) and their ethnic persecution. Third, the criticism against the artist also overplays the importance of oral tradition as a pattern for education and transmission. Although these three tenets are not solid, they sustain a mainstream dogmatic narrative around flamenco which is very influential in defining the genre's boundaries and in assigning credentials and legitimacy to artists. Ethnicity and intragroup transmission and evolution – or, rather, the narrative built around them – still play an essential role in understanding flamenco. The significance given to these factors is conducive to widening or narrowing the genre.

This chapter aims to show that this mainstream narrative is improper and incomplete, but it also explores how it is still very powerful in policing borrowing practices in flamenco and marking the genre's boundaries. This contribution also examines the ways in which this traditional narrative has historically interacted with how copyright law and institutions have approached flamenco music over time.

II. Flamenco and Its Inherent Tensions

A. Basics of Flamenco Music

Definitions of flamenco are elusive.[7] As a cultural expression, it is mostly associated with a music genre that has been cultivated in some areas of Andalusia (Southern Spain), especially by Roma people or *gitanos*, for centuries. Some examples can also be found in other regions of Spain and abroad.[8] Historical sources about the origins and influences of flamenco are limited.[9] It is assumed that many features that are associated with traditional flamenco were established during the nineteenth century, although some traits have older origins.

Flamenco involves different art forms: *cante* (flamenco singing), *baile* (flamenco dancing) and *toque* (flamenco guitar).[10] Identification of some formal patterns in flamenco music is helpful to unveil some of the cultural norms that govern their production and use.

[4] ibid 48–54.

[5] PG Romero, 'No tocarla, la Rosalía es así' in J Carrión (ed), *La Rosalía. Ensayos sobre el buen querer* (Errata Naturae, 2021).

[6] In the same vein, A Fernández Mallo, 'Rosalía, Rito Sacrificial' in J Carrión (ed), *La Rosalía. Ensayos sobre el buen querer* (Errata Naturae, 2021) esp 155–56.

[7] See, eg N Márquez, 'Y Para Rematar: Contemplations on a Movement in Transition' in KM Goldberg et al (eds), *Flamenco on the Global Stage: Historical, Critical and Theoretical Perspectives* (McFarland, 2015) 260–61.

[8] This contribution is focused on Spain and Spanish copyright law. Examples from other countries such as France are mentioned incidentally. Some strong communities of flamenco artists and aficionados can be found in Latin American, eg in Chile, and especially in Japan.

[9] The last two decades have, however, witnessed some important advances in historiographical research. See J Vergillos, *Nueva Historia del Flamenco* (Almuzara, 2021) 22–23.

[10] This contribution focuses on *cante*; the rest of the art forms are just occasionally mentioned.

Several song types, which are known as *cantes* or *palos*, can be found in flamenco music.[11] There are a dozen basic and familiar *palos* and two dozen variants or less common types.[12] Each of them has some distinctive elements, such as vocal melodies, poetic form, metrical scheme or *compás*, and accompanying patterns.[13] Particular *cantes* are linked to different vocal techniques.[14] In many customary *cantes*, flamenco tends to combine short notes (syllabic parts) with longer ones.[15] Long notes are often melismatic and consist of groups of three, five or seven notes. The duration and number of notes in a melisma depend on the *cantaor*'s abilities and skills.[16]

The number of *palos* illustrates the high stylistic and melodic variety that can be found in flamenco. Some *cantes*, such as *fandangos*, *tangos* and *tanguillos*, are more festive and hummable. As they are less melismatic, they are more apt for collective performance. Because of that, they tend to be those more emulated or borrowed from by outsiders, especially in flamencoesque music (*música aflamencada*). In contrast, other *palos* are more serious and profound. This is the case, for instance, for *soleares*, *tientos* or *seguiriyas*, which tend to be perceived as more genuine and authentic. The latter are generally associated with *cante jondo* (or deep singing), which is considered as the essence of genuine flamenco. These styles are less hummable and generally are not to be sung in unison.[17]

Palos are sometimes linked with geographical locations. For instance, *granaínas* have their origin in the city of Granada and *malagueñas* are associated with the city of Málaga. It is assumed that some of the more traditional *palos* (*tonás*, *seguiriyas*, *romances*, *livianas*) existed before the nineteenth century in some areas in Andalusia.[18] In any case, the core group of *palos* was highly standardised at the beginning of the twentieth century.[19] *Palos* are generally the result of collective practices. However, some individuals have contributed to the diffusion and consolidation of some of them. That is the case, for instance, of Antonio Chacón (1869–1929), who popularised a type known as *tarantas*. Also, some individuals have intended to create new *palos*, such as *canasteras*, which were conceived by Camarón de la Isla (1950–92) and Paco de Lucía (1947–2014). Yet these patterns were not afterwards used or borrowed by other artists.

Palos work as general moulds which accommodate to more specific tunes known as *estilos* or *subcantes*, which consist of particular or distinctive melodies.[20] Hundreds of different *estilos* have been identified and mapped. They have been standardised to some extent and have entered the traditional repertoire within a particular *cante* or *palo*. *Estilos* work as stock that can be freely borrowed by flamenco artists outside of a particular family group or community.[21]

In traditional flamenco, there is nothing such as formal composition of a song as a definite work. Flamenco has more to do with a performative activity during which different music

[11] See P Manuel, 'Composition, Authorship and Ownership in Flamenco, Past and Present' (2010) 54 *Ethnomusicology* 106. In Spanish, two relevant references are JL Ropero Núñez and M Navarro Garcia, *Historia del flamenco* (Tartessos, 1995); JM Gamboa, *Una historia del flamenco* (Espasa-Calpe, 2005).

[12] Different complex graphics and maps cataloguing *cantes* can be found in the literature. See, eg N Kroher et al, 'Corpus COFLA: A Research Corpus for the Computational Study of Flamenco Music' (2016) 9 *Journal on Computing and Cultural Heritage* 1, 5.

[13] Manuel, 'Composition, Authorship and Ownership' (n 11) 107.

[14] For a comprehensive discussion, see R Márquez Limón, 'La técnica vocal en el flamenco: fisionomía y tipologías' (PhD thesis, Universidad de Sevilla, 2017) https://idus.us.es/handle/11441/63972.

[15] Kroher et al (n 12) 2–3.

[16] ibid 2–3.

[17] A Grimaldos, *Historia social del flamenco* (Península, 2010) 20.

[18] ibid 57.

[19] Manuel, 'Composition, Authorship and Ownership' (n 11) 110.

[20] ibid 107.

[21] ibid 112.

elements are mixed and merged.[22] In a typical flamenco rendition, a performer (*cantaor*) may borrow and use several *estilos* within a particular *palo*, for instance by singing three (*un tercrio*) or five *coplas* or groups of verses in different *estilos*, punctuated by guitar interludes (*falsetas*).[23] Verses are not necessarily connected from a conceptual or ideological standpoint; but lyrics associated with pain and suffering (persecution, working conditions, underclasses) are usual in more serious flamenco. Renditions are thus not unique or integrated and are far from the more common unitary structure of songs in popular music.[24] In a sort of collage, the artist decides how many verses to sing and the unrelated themes that he will tackle. Despite this openness, there are certain conventions as to the sequence to follow.[25] Besides, a familiar lyric or *copla* is usually associated with a particular *estilo*, but a *cantaor* may use other *estilos* in his rendition.

Estilos can be linked to certain areas or locations. Some artists have developed *estilos* that are recognisable by others. In this sense, some form of attribution or moral rights is present. However, this is linked to artists and not composers. One example of that is *soleá de Alcalá*: if a *cantaor* announces that he is going to sing 'por soleares de Alcalá', flamenco connoisseurs would know that his rendition in the form of a *soleá* would follow the *estilo* developed in the village of Alcalá de Guadaria by *cantaor* Joaquín el de La Paula (1875–1933).

Flamenco has been cultivated in different types of settings. The traditional narrative stresses the role of private gatherings in which families or groups of relatives sing and transmit their repertoire from generation to generation. Another setting involves *juergas de señoritos*, parties commissioned by rich owners or aristocrats. Some argue that authentic or genuine flamenco was not performed in such venues. Likewise, any commercial exploitations –for instance, in special clubs (*cafés cantantes*) or shows (*óperas flamencas*) – would not offer audiences the alleged pure and genuine flamenco, which would be reserved for the private home.

B. Inherent Tensions

As explained, flamenco would follow some general patterns or norms of production and exchange: it would have been mostly developed by *gitanos* within small family groups; it would have been orally transmitted and communicated within the group and to the extended flamenco community; it would not have been subjected to external influences, and innovations would come within the common stock by borrowing and reusing during renditions *estilos* and lyrics that were created by others or that belonged to the folk.

History shows, however, that these cultural norms of production are not that rigid and that they have probably never been so. They are the product of various tenets that are used to sustain a quasi-mythical narrative about flamenco as a pure music exclusively linked with *gitano* oral tradition when tensions about them are integral to the genre. Contrary to the orthodox narrative, flamenco's norms of production and exchange are indeed somewhat ambiguous.

[22] See J Heredia-Carroza, L Palma Martos and LF Aguado, 'Song, Performance and Authorship. The Case of Flamenco in Spain' (2019) 23 *Trames. A Journal of the Humanities and Social Sciences* 3, 4–5.

[23] Manuel, 'Composition, Authorship and Ownership' (n 11) 108–09.

[24] Grimaldos (n 17) 19.

[25] Manuel, 'Composition, Authorship and Ownership' (n 11) 108.

(i) Orality and Other Forms of Transmission and Diffusion

An important focal point in the construction of flamenco as a genre has been the *hogar*, the family home where a private reunion is held and music and dance are performed. It epitomises the setting where lyrics, melodies, styles and other elements are orally transmitted within the family from generation to generation. Actually, this independent intra-group transmission explains to some extent the variety of different *cantes* or styles[26] and the importance of flamenco families or sagas, such as Amaya, Carmona, Losada, Vargas, Pavón, Flores or Habichuela.

Obviously, flamenco transcends privacy, and has also been performed and taught outside of this very narrow setting. As previously mentioned, *juergas de señorito* – private parties organised by wealthy landowners and aristocrats in which flamenco singers, guitarists and dancers gathered and rendered their performances – served as an important locus for the communication of this genre. Also, flamenco was absorbed into commercial music, a phenomenon which is not exclusive to flamenco but affected much ethnic and folk music during the late nineteenth and the beginning of the twentieth century. Flamenco was thus performed in different venues, such as singing clubs (*cafés cantantes*) and arranged shows (*óperas flamencas*). Those settings led to the diffusion and transmission of flamenco outside of the family sphere, as well as to its intermingling with other music genres. What is important is that many forms of diffusion other than intra-family transmission were already in place when cultural norms of production began to take off during the nineteenth century.

Besides, there is another phenomenon that relativises the role of orality as the basic and exclusive culture norm of transmission: at least, since the last part of the nineteenth century, oral practices became broadly codified. Although transmission via orality is paramount, codification has contributed to the diffusion of flamenco beyond small local groups. Codification and standardisation of flamenco has developed in different waves. Several historical phenomena can be highlighted which have contributed to make oral tradition less important. The first examples of codification can be traced back to the late nineteenth century and include the writings by Antonio Machado y Álvarez (pen name 'Demófilo') (1848–93). In 1881, he published *Colección de cantes flamencos*, by which he intended to catalogue all the different *palos*.[27] Also in the late nineteenth century, the first recordings appeared and contributed to some alternative diffusion.[28] Technological improvements during the twentieth century just expanded this phenomenon, although many traditional flamenco artists were reluctant to be recorded.

During the twentieth century, other important codification efforts took place. *Cantaor* Antonio Mairena (1909–83) was worried about flamenco's purity and considered that serious *cante jondo* was neglected in favour of lighter styles. He was also fearful of commercial pressures and the impact they might have on traditional flamenco. In his view, a distinction should be made between 'cante Gitano-andaluz', which he deemed authentic *cante jondo* associated with private performance by Gypsy families, and adulterated 'flamenco', which was commercially performed initially in *cafés cantantes* in combination with Andalusian folk music.[29] He collaborated with Ricardo Molina (1917–68) and both published this vision in *Mundo y formas del cante flamenco* (1963), a work that has been later criticised for ossifying cultural practices in flamenco. Mairena's vision, or a particular reading of it, has, however, become the ideological basis of the conventional

[26] Grimaldos (n 17) 15–16.

[27] ibid 57–58.

[28] This phenomenon is not exclusive of flamenco music. Technologies such as shellac and slate discs led to consolidation and codification of many genres worldwide. See M Denning, *Noise Uprising. The Audiopolitics of a World Musical Revolution* (Verso, 2015).

[29] Grimaldos (n 17) 117–18.

flamenco narrative and has led to an aesthetic position labelled as 'mairenismo'. New forms of flamenco music that appeared during the 1960s and 1970s are reactions against this orthodox view of the genre.

Finally, other forms of codification emanate from the interest of some Spanish ethnomusicologists, who commercialised some influential albums on the traditional flamenco repertoire during the 1970s and made the genre more accessible to broader audiences.[30]

In sum, the role of intra-family upbringing and transmission is exaggerated. A flamenco artist may achieve an education outside of this environment and through tangible codified items. In other words, there has always been use and exchange outside of the home and beyond orality.

(ii) Authenticity, Purity and External Influences

Another important tenet in the mainstream narrative highlights the purity of genuine and authentic flamenco. *Cante jondo*, with its seriousness and hermetism, is generally considered the real flamenco and is used as the example of essence and purity in the genre as opposed to other, more commercial forms. The tenet also works as a hierarchical classification system: *cante jondo* is superior, while other flamenco or flamencoesque art forms are less pure or even degenerated.[31] The delegitimisation of the more commercial forms of flamenco has been a constant in traditional literature, at least since the last decades of the nineteenth century.[32] Also, some international scholars, such as Donn Pohren, have embraced this view, which disparages more commercial forms of flamenco and 'música aflamencada'.[33] One of the most famous episodes that helped build this narrative was the flamenco contest organised by Federico García Lorca (1898–1936) and Manuel de Falla (1876–1946) in Granada in 1922. According to García Lorca, the goal was to 'gain respect for *cante jondo* as an art; preserve it from musical adulteration and from the threat of *cafés cantantes* and *flamenco óperas*'.[34]

Traditional genuine flamenco would have been refractory to external influences as it would have been developed from within the genre in accordance with a series of conventions and cultural norms of production and use. However, many scholars have questioned this conviction and have discussed several music influences. For instance, according to some authors, Muslim calls for prayer and romances would have influenced some traditional *cantes*, such as *soleares* and *seguiriyas*.[35] Other scholars have highlighted Sephardi Jewish and Indian influences as historical precedents.[36] The influence of Andalusian folk music cannot be overlooked. Also, other, more distant influences have made their contributions to the development of flamenco. For instance, Caribbean music was used as a source of inspiration to *cantaor* Pepe Marchena (1903–76) to develop *colombianas*, a new type of *cante* around 1930. Since then, *colombianas* have become a

[30] J Bellido, 'Flamenco Music in Copyright Historiography' in K Bowrey and M Handler (eds), *Law and Creativity in the Age of the Entertainment Franchise* (Cambridge University Press, 2014) 188–89.

[31] This classification system is also accompanied by a terminological apparatus used to make distinctions: for instance, in genuine flamenco, a performer is a *cantaor* and not a *cantante* as in flamencoesque music, or a dancer is a *bailaor* and not a *bailarín*. Also, genuine flamenco is sometimes called 'flamenco por derecho' ('flamenco by the law'). See Manuel, 'The Rosalía Polemic' (n 2) 42.

[32] Grimaldos (n 17) 57–58; M Madridejos, 'El flamenco, entre la tradición y la traición' in JL Ortiz Nuevo, *Alegato contra la pureza* (Malpaso, 2020) esp 11–13.

[33] See D Pohren, *The Art of Flamenco* (Jerez Industrial, 1962); D Pohren, *Lives and Legends of Flamenco* (Society of Spanish Studies, 1964); D Pohren, *A Way of Life* (Bold Strummer, 1980).

[34] Lecture given on 2 February 1922 in 'Centro Artístico' of Granada under the title 'Importancia histórica y artística del primitivo canto andaluz llamado cante jondo'.

[35] P Lefranc, *El Cante Jondo. Del territorio a los repertorios: tonás, siguiriyas, soleares* (Universidad de Sevilla, 2000).

[36] Ortiz Nuevo (n 32) 188–89.

canonical *palo* and entered the traditional repertoire. A similar example includes *guajiras*, which are also based on Latin American music.

Some instruments were also initially unwelcomed by flamenco purists: this is the case of *cajón*, which was presumably developed by African slaves in the eighteenth-century colonial period, was popularised by Paco de Lucía and is now canonical in the genre.[37]

Popular music has been another important source of influence that has inescapably permeated traditional flamenco. As flamenco entered the commercial arena during the nineteenth century, it was sung in *cafés cantantes*, along with other types of music. Flamenco artists were also responsible for performing other genres at those venues; hence, it is natural to assume that this infused traditional flamenco. Likewise, during the twentieth century, *operas flamencas* developed as a show that included both flamenco renditions and other genres and styles. *Cuplé* and traditional Andalusian songs or *coplas* intermingled there with traditional flamenco. It is worth mentioning that some famed artists at that time were criticised with the same line of arguments and ferocity as those now addressed against Rosalía.[38]

During the last 50 years, flamenco has witnessed an expansion and has been subjected to many external influences. Especially during the 1960s and 1970s, important developments which are known as *nuevo flamenco* ('new flamenco') emerged. Qualifying this flamenco as 'new' is somewhat misleading, since the fusions with other genres and styles made by those artists were not novel but have been present in how flamenco has evolved from the beginning. For some scholars, flamenco has never been pure, but is inherently transgressive and hybrid.[39] As famous *cantaor* Enrique Morente (1942–2010) put it: 'this music has been in constant change since its origins'.[40]

(iii) Identity and Socioeconomic Embedding: The Role of Gitanos *in Flamenco Music*

Associating flamenco with low-class Andalusian Roma people (*gitanos*) stands out as the most conspicuous narrative in flamenco.[41] This link has been stressed since the nineteenth century and it is also plain in the works and writings of Demófilo, Federico García Lorca and Antonio Mairena.[42] Flamenco music has also been associated with the recounting of the historical persecution of Gypsies at the hands of *gachós* (non-Gypsies).

Roma people or *gitanos* have been living on the Iberian Peninsula for more than six centuries, and have historically formed the most important minority there. They have been persecuted and oppressed since they first entered Iberian territories. For instance, in 1499, a *Pragmática de los*

[37] MH Hayes, 'Choreographing Contemporaneity: Cultural Legacy and Experimental Imperative' in Goldberg et al (n 7) 282.

[38] This is the case, for instance, of artist Lola Cabello (1905–42). See Madridejos (n 32) 17–18.

[39] G Steingress, 'La hibridación transcultural como clave de la formación del Nuevo Flamenco' (2004) 8 *TRANS – Revista Transcultural de Música* 1. See in general Ortiz Nuevo (n 32).

[40] As quoted by Grimaldos (n 17) 23.

[41] However, there are other attributions which are highly influential. One of those is the important link between flamenco and Andalusia, which was stressed by, among others, Andalusian nationalist Blas Infante (1885–1936). See B Infante, *Orígenes de lo flamenco y secreto del cante jondo* (Junta de Andalucía, 1980). For some voices, flamenco represents the Andalusian folk music that was mostly appropriated by Gypsies during the 19th century. See Ortiz Nuevo (n 32) 64. This conception has made its way into the regional Constitution of Andalusia (Estatuto de Autonomía), Art 68.1 of which deems flamenco 'a singular element of Andalusian cultural heritage'.

[42] According to some scholars, Antonio Mairena exaggerated the role of *gitanos* in the development of flamenco music. See Manuel, 'Composition, Authorship and Ownership' (n 11) 112; see also M Bohórquez, 'Lo que la verdad esconde' (2018) www.expoflamenco.com/blog-archivo/lo-que-la-verdad-esconde.

Reyes Católicos ordered Roma people to leave the peninsula or to find a master to serve. Gypsies have generally been mistreated for centuries and many of their underprivileged socioeconomic circumstances persist nowadays. Those that entered the labour market suffered very adverse working conditions, especially in mining activities, and many traditional lyrics in flamenco narrate these poor living standards. A general perception of Gypsies as outcasts and pariahs has also been common.[43] Some scholars have defended the strong links between flamenco and political resistance against oppression and abuse.[44]

During the nineteenth century, a new romanticised bohemian image of *gitanos* emerged and contributed to strengthen the links between this group and flamenco. *Cafés cantantes* promoted a particular construction and taste that could appeal to most audiences. When foreign travellers began to explore these venues, a vision of Gypsies as exotic and adventurous developed. This colourful view sponsored by international travellers such as European writers of the Romantic period has also strengthened the main narrative in the genre.

Despite the strong relations between flamenco music and *gitanos*, the genre cannot be exclusively appropriated by this historically marginalised social group. There are other forces that have impacted on the construction and development of flamenco, and other traditional narratives link the genre not only to this ethnic minority, but also to regional (Andalusian) or social groups or classes (low-class labourers and miners). For instance, Washabaugh identifies four different distinct narratives or stories about the origins of flamenco, which are labelled 'gitano', 'Andalusian', 'populist' and 'sociological'.[45] Contributions of non-Gypsies (also referred as *payos*) to flamenco cannot be ignored:[46] some very famous artists such as Paco de Lucía or Pepe Marchena did not belong to the Roma minority.[47] Links with the Andalusian musical folk are also very robust.

The narrative about oppression and marginalisation has some shortcomings as well. Besides the opportunities provided by the commercial construction of the genre, flamenco has been institutionalised and entered the mainstream. Several forces of institutionalisation can be highlighted. To begin with, as flamenco was gaining commercial value, copyrightability of most expressions and management by collecting societies became ordinary.[48] Moreover, flamenco has been recognised in several laws and regulations, the most important of which is Andalusia's regional constitution (*Estatuto de Autonomía*). Public grants and funds are thus generally available for artists and promoters. Education programmes such as a PhD in Flamenco Studies are also available.[49] In 2010, flamenco as an art form was inscribed in the UNESCO List of Intangible Cultural Heritage of Humanity. Flamenco has not only been institutionalised, but has also gained prestige, and nowadays it is performed in the most serious and notable theatres in Spain.[50]

[43] In fact, this perception may have nourished 'antiflamenquismo', a movement against traditional music in Southern Spain. Flamenco and other folk music were perceived as going against social and economic progress, and generating a bad reputation for Spain at the international level.

[44] J López-Peláez Casellas, 'The Politics of Flamenco: La leyenda del tiempo and Ideology' (2017) 36 *Popular Music* 196, 198.

[45] W Washabaugh, *Flamenco. Passion, Politics and Popular Culture* (Routledge, 1996) 32–39.

[46] During the 19th century, Italian-Spaniard Silverio Franconetti Aguilar (1831–89) was perhaps one of the most relevant non-Gypsy flamenco artists.

[47] Famous *bailaora* Carmen Amaya (1918–63) said of Pepe Marchena that, as a master of *cante*, he deserved to be a Gypsy.

[48] See s IV below.

[49] An important milestone was the creation of the first flamencology chair (Cátedra de Flamencología) in Jerez de la Frontera in 1958.

[50] Paco de Lucía's performance at Madrid's Royal Theatre in 1975 was probably the first flamenco performance in one of those prestigious venues.

III. Borrowing Practices in Flamenco

The conventional narrative about flamenco also shapes the types of borrowing practices that are considered acceptable in the genre. However, since the cultural norms of production and use within flamenco are not completely rigid, new borrowing phenomena may end up being admissible. This genre's flexibility and openness have proved seminal to flamenco's evolution and global success.

For sure, music borrowings can take many different forms and involve different impacts.[51] A plethora of different borrowing practices can be mapped in flamenco, and copyright law does not always fit well with all those practices.[52] Despite the risk of oversimplification, a taxonomy of borrowing in flamenco is now proposed in four different categories:

1. An insider to flamenco approaches the genre and borrows from within (traditional borrowing).
2. An insider to flamenco approaches the genre and borrows from outside (exploration of new forms).
3. An outsider to flamenco approaches the genre and borrows from within the tradition (flamenco by non-Gypsies).
4. An outsider to flamenco borrows some elements from within the tradition and adds them to a different art form (flamenco and outsiders).

This classification presupposes that flamenco as a genre is alive and evolving, and not completely exhausted and fossilised. This classification also illustrates how the above-described tensions operate in practice.

A. Traditional Borrowing

The first category represents the orthodox way in which creativity has traditionally evolved in flamenco. Oral tradition and genuine practice within the private home contributed to produce distinct patterns (*cantes*, *palos*), which can be freely borrowed and used to develop a personal style in performing or to merge with new lyrics.[53] Learning the rules and following the conventions on borrowing become the standard praxis, albeit some external influences, even if minimal, permeate creativity, perhaps in an involuntary or unconscious manner. The mythical narrative pervades any debates on borrowing practices in this area, but traditional flamenco has been receptive to some innovations and appropriations, such as some influences from Arabic, Afro-American or Latin American music.[54]

The artistic agenda of some *cantaores* has been explicit in preserving traditional *cantes* while at the same time creating new lyrics to merge with them. This has been the case, for instance, of the highly acclaimed *cantaor* Fosforito (Antonio Fernández Díaz, born in Córdoba in 1932). As we have seen, some attribution rights are recognised for *cantaores* who have developed a personal style in singing or who have contributed to bolstering a particular *palo*.

[51] JP Burkholder, 'Borrowing' in S Sadie (ed), *The New Grove Dictionary of Music and Musicians* (Macmillan, 2001).

[52] As happens in other genres as well. See, eg OB Arewa, 'From JC Bach to Hip Hop: Musical Borrowing, Copyright and Cultural Context' (2006) 84 *North Carolina Law Review* 547.

[53] See s IIA above.

[54] See s IIA(ii) above.

Neo-traditional flamenco as played nowadays re-elaborates the catalogue of *palos*. New lyrics are being created, but the repertoire remains almost the same as it was during the first half of the twentieth century.[55]

B. Exploration of New Forms

The second category is especially exemplified by new flamenco (*nuevo flamenco*). During the 1960s and 1970s, some flamenco artists began to explore different genres and expressly borrowed elements from other traditions, such as Arabic, Maghrebi and Andalusi-Arabic music. New flamenco also brought about fusions with other modern popular music, like rock or blues. For instance, flamenco and rock were melded by bands like SMASH, whereas Veneno and Pata Negra, bands established by brothers Raimundo and Rafael Amador, famously fused flamenco and blues music. Although these borrowing practices were initially rejected, they were finally incorporated into the genre's repertoire.

To a great extent, new flamenco was a reaction to orthodoxy or 'marienismo', which was deemed to petrify the genre, and to the political situation.[56] In this regard, new flamenco was mainly developed during the last decade of General Franco's dictatorship, at a time when the political regime was presumably more open to external influences. Nonetheless, the influence of jazz and blues music has sometimes also been explained as a will to express shared experiences of mistreatment with black minorities.

For some authors, this new flamenco resorts to hybridisation, that is, a new, third music form or style in which different genres are coalesced.[57] This goes beyond other borrowing practices, such as mix or mélange, pastiche or imitation, or improvisation or bricolage.[58] Cultural norms of production in new flamenco are closer to modern practices in popular music. In this regard, the idea of song as something unitary becomes relevant, in contrast to traditional flamenco renditions.[59] Also, the idea of composition turns out to be more individualistically oriented. For these reasons, new flamenco is easier to be accommodated by the formal categories of copyright law.[60]

New flamenco was highly criticised by purists, and was often excluded from some important venues and diffusion settings, like some festivals, concerts or flamenco clubs (*peñas flamencas*). However, with time, many of these new styles were finally accepted and integrated into the genre. Several factors contributed to the acceptance of these new forms in flamenco. First, new flamenco artists tended to be insiders, in the sense that they were educated in the tradition, and they were mostly Gypsy, and therefore not perceived as outsiders. Some of the more famous examples include Camarón de la Isla, Juan Peña El Lebrijano (1941–2016) and Lole y Manuel.[61] This generation clearly sowed the seeds for other hybrid forms that appeared in the decades that followed. Second, new flamenco artists were also proficient in traditional

[55] Manuel, 'Composition, Authorship and Ownership' (n 11) 113.

[56] ibid 116.

[57] Steingress (n 39).

[58] ibid.

[59] During the same period, there was an important explosion of creativity, especially in works such as *rumbas* or *bulerías*, which are more unitary and homogeneous than traditional flamenco.

[60] See s IV below.

[61] Lole y Manuel was the usual name of the musical duo formed by Dolores Montoya Rodríguez (1954–) and Manuel Molina Jiménez (1948–2015).

or orthodox flamenco and used their own skills and knowledge in the task of exploring new forms of creativity. And third, commercial recordings that were released during that period usually included traditional flamenco pieces alongside the new flamenco compositions.

Another type of borrowing phenomenon in this category involves the incursions in other genres that are somehow ancillary to flamenco. Many flamenco artists became famous performers of genres such as *cuplé* and *copla*. Lola Flores (1923–95) is perhaps one of the most conspicuous examples. To what extent a particular rendition could be qualified as flamenco would depend on whether the flamenco input was secondary vis-à-vis the external element from a quantitative or qualitative standpoint. In many examples, denying that a particular item is flamenco is truly challenging.

All in all, if we assume that flamenco has historically been subjected to many influences from other cultures and genres and that new flamenco has simply boosted this phenomenon, this second category of borrowing turns out to be an essential source of evolving creativity in the field, if not the most significant one.

C. Flamenco by Non-Gypsies

The third category aptly illustrates one of the tensions discussed in this chapter. It enquires to what extent *payos* or non-Gypsies may be considered flamenco artists. A related question asks whether non-Andalusian or even non-Spanish can legitimately pass as flamenco artists.[62] The gist of the question depends on one's views on the role of *gitanos* in flamenco.[63]

As explained, contributions to flamenco come not only from Roma artists: traditional *cantaores* such as Tía Anica la Piriñaca (1899–1987) or Pepe Marchena and more innovative artists such as Paco de Lucía or Enrique Morente are among some of the most well-reputed names in the genre. There are a few factors that explain their accommodation within the flamenco family. First, for example, they extensively collaborated with Gypsy musicians and other artists. Second, they were trained within traditional flamenco and were highly skilled in the genre. Hence, sometimes these artists are called *gitanos blancos* (white Gypsies) and are not perceived as complete outsiders.[64]

D. Flamenco and Outsiders

The fourth category is reserved for those outsider artists that borrow from traditional flamenco to create new works or to render their performances. Distinct practices can be identified and include, among others, imitation of vocal techniques, use of traditional flamenco instruments and adaptation of melodic elements.[65] Borrowing practices are very heterogeneous, so cannot be approached in a unitary way. Some of them can be understood as reactions or oppositions to flamenco (countercultural views, appropriation and resignification).[66] Other practices use,

[62] For instance, some Catalan flamenco artists have been questioned in the past, but are generally not considered complete outsiders, and *cantaores* such as Maite Martín and Miguel Poveda have a good standing in neo-traditional flamenco.

[63] See s IIB(iii).

[64] A discussion of this issue can be found in Manuel, 'Composition, Authorship and Ownership' (n 11) 118–19.

[65] On adaptations and derivative works of flamenco, see the Court of Appeals of Cadiz's judgment of 22 November 1996, www.cerlalc.org/derechoenlinea/dar/index.php?mode=archivo&id=104.

[66] See P Ordóñez Eslava, 'Elogio de la apropiación. Prácticas impuras, flamenco y creación contemporánea' (2019) 32 *Cuadernos de Música Iberoamericana* 95, 102.

for instance, just allusions to traditional flamenco, or include samples or remixes of previous recordings.[67]

One important example of imitation of vocal techniques is flamencoesque music, which is popularly known as 'música aflamencada', or is even given the more disparaging label of 'flamenquito'. This often includes traditional instruments used in flamenco (guitar, *cajón*, castanets). Such creativity tends not to be qualified as flamenco. However, the lines between admitted flamenco styles and other forms are not always clear, especially when performed by Gypsy artists, who are part of the flamenco community. One example would be Ketama, who fused rumba and salsa. The difficulties increase, however, with the many recent forms, such as chill flamenco, experimental flamenco, electronic flamenco and punk flamenco. To what extent this is flamenco exploring new forms or other genres' creativity with some flamenco influences is debatable.

There are other practices that, in contrast, would clearly not be considered in the flamenco repertoire. For instance, jazz artists and composers have borrowed some melodic elements for their works. Relevant examples include *Flamenco Sketches* (1959) by Miles Davis and Gil Evans, or *Olé* (1961) by John Coltrane. Also, a musical quotation or allusion using a traditional flamenco instrument would not be deemed to belong to the genre. Generally, these practices would not prompt many criticisms. In fact, not all forms of cultural appropriation are perceived as reproachable, and some can be tolerated or embraced in ethical terms.[68]

Also in this category are some examples of outsiders who have formal training in flamenco and have mixed flamenco elements with other genres, traditions or components (for instance, Rosalía or Niño de Elche). Other popular artists with no formal traditional training in flamenco, such as C Tangana, have also incorporated some flamenco elements into their compositions. As indicated, the credentials of these as flamenco artists are controversial.

IV. Flamenco Meets Copyright: Resistance and Accommodation

The ways in which flamenco and copyright law and institutions have interacted unveil the influence of the traditional narrative, but also its neglect. On the one hand, traditional flamenco's links with oral tradition, folklore and ethnic expression of the Spanish Roma minority have been used both as tools of resistance to institutionalisation and as arguments against copyright protection.[69] On the other hand, as commercial pressures grew, the narrative was eroded and flamenco could be mostly accommodated into institutional copyright. The transformations brought by neo-traditional flamenco and new flamenco facilitated copyright accommodation.[70]

Traditional flamenco and their cultural norms of production escaped some of the concepts that are key to mainstream copyright law.[71] Notions such as authorship and work are mostly alien to traditional flamenco. First, production does not rely on an individual romantic genius, but collective efforts are embraced. In this regard, composers or other authors have not been

[67] The different borrowing practices – and the aesthetic motivations that underlie them – resemble the usual distinction within copyright law between target and weapon parodies.

[68] M Siems, 'The Law and Ethics of "Cultural Appropriation"' (2019) 15 *International Journal of Law in Context* 408.

[69] See Bellido (n 30) 178–81.

[70] In fact, current conditions in the production of flamenco music make most productions apt for copyright categories and norms. See in general M Castilla Barea (ed), *El flamenco y los derechos de autor* (Reus, 2010).

[71] Manuel, 'Composition, Authorship and Ownership' (n 11) 121.

customarily acknowledged and pre-eminence has generally been given to artists and performers who were able to make their renditions by resorting to common stock tunes. Lyrics, *cantes* and *estilos* were borrowed from the community creativity, which was diffused by oral transmission and which was generally perceived as freely reusable. Some of those elements, such as *palos*, would have not been copyrightable; others would definitely be in the public domain.[72] Nonetheless, even if some of those elements were protectable, their reuse during a performance was generally not thwarted.

Second, the concept of work as something unitary is also alien to traditional flamenco.[73] In this regard, traditional flamenco avoids using the term 'song' (*canción*). Instead, typical narratives refer to the singing action and a particular *cante* or *palo*. For instance, someone may say 'cantar por seguiriyas', which can be translated as the artist is going to sing a few *coplas* in different *estilos* in *seguiriyas*.[74] It is during a rendition where some creativity emerges: the *cantaor* may improvise some lyrics or melodies, or may merge some distinct elements. In those cases, the division between performance and creation is not straightforward. For this reason, individual performers have been recognised with some attribution rights in traditional flamenco.

Third, the understanding of ownership and appropriation differs from the romantic notions underlying copyright norms. Economic rights were generally not expected, and only some norms of attribution seem to have been in place.[75] Most rents have traditionally derived from performances and not from commercial recordings. In fact, many traditional artists were reluctant to record their renditions until they perceived them as a new source of revenue. These factors contributed to the irrelevance of rights allocation and the lack of subsequent controversies. All in all, very little litigation can be found in traditional flamenco.[76] This could be the product of several socioeconomic reasons, and in particular the strong distrust of the Spanish Roma minority towards courts and public authorities. Gypsies may resort to other forms of adjudication and settle any disputes on attribution or appropriation on their own.[77]

Historically, these factors contributed to situate flamenco outside of the institutional copyright system. Initially, collective management organisations such as the Sociedad de Autores Españoles (SAE)[78] perceived flamenco music as folklore music or in the public domain that could not be registered.[79] Hence, flamenco authors or other related individuals could not receive any royalties from public performances of their works or from mechanical uses. However, during the 1930s, the SAE began to demand that organisers of some flamenco performances pay fees for the use of registered music.[80] In those cases, the collective management organisation (CMO) used a dual system in which music was grossly classified into two big categories: high and low music, the latter including folk art forms and labelled 'música popular'.[81] Flamenco venues intended

[72] On flamenco and the public domain, see I Espín Alba, 'Flamenco, Folclore y dominio público' in Castilla Barea (n 70).

[73] Manuel, 'Composition, Authorship and Ownership' (n 11) 117. See s II1.

[74] ibid 109.

[75] See s IIA.

[76] Litigated cases concern instances of fusion flamenco and other similar genres, but do not affect traditional flamenco. One example of this is a dispute about the authorship and rights ownership on some albums of so-called 'chill flamenco' performed by the band Chambao (see Judgment of Commercial Court No 1 of Málaga of 31 July 2014, ECLI:ES:JMMA:2014:185).

[77] This phenomenon has also been described in the IP negative space's literature. See, eg A Perzanowski, 'Tattoos & IP Norms' (2013) 98 *Minnesota Law Review* 511.

[78] Now operating under the name Sociedad General de Autores y Editores (SGAE).

[79] Bellido (n 30) 174.

[80] ibid 177.

[81] ibid 180–81. See also Manuel, 'Composition, Authorship and Ownership' (n 11) 121–22.

to avoid payment by arguing that such music should be in the public domain.[82] Also, flamenco artists and promoters used other strategies and subterfuges to escape control and payment, for instance, by becoming invisible and operating fly-by-night venues, or by not offering transparency and alleging that the repertoire could not be anticipated as it was highly improvised in each party or *juerga*.

Especially from the 1950s, flamenco has been increasingly accommodated within the SAE's operations. As flamenco broadly entered the professional commercial sphere, copyrightability became unproblematic. Many flamenco artists had already found alternative ways to register some works in the SAE's repertoire and receive some royalties.[83] Besides, interest in flamenco at Madrid's Royal Conservatory of Music provided the genre with a seal of respectability.[84] As José Bellido shows, institutionalisation and the role of CMOs and musical studies ended up accommodating flamenco into the copyright regime and defining the notions of work and authorship that best fitted the genre.[85]

V. Performer as Author

As discussed in this chapter, composition has been secondary in traditional flamenco, which has mostly relied on improvisation and variation by repetition during performance. It was not until the 1960s and 1970s that an understanding of song composition closer to popular music practices began to emerge. This new paradigm generated some controversies about the allocation of rights.

The most famous of those disputes involved the famous guitar player Paco de Lucía and the heirs of *cantaor* Camarón de la Isla.[86] During almost three decades, Camarón and de Lucía produced several successful LPs in which de Lucía's father and brothers were also involved.[87] Besides including renditions of the more traditional repertoire, they recorded some of the most famous songs in new flamenco. One month before dying of lung cancer, Camarón gave a television interview in which he criticised the de Lucía's family and informed that, of the 164 songs that he had recorded, he was only credited as a coauthor of six of them.[88] After his death, his widow hired a team of lawyers to claim joint authorship of the other works. The matter did not reach the courts, but Paco de Lucía and his relatives voluntarily surrendered some of their rights. However, it is doubtful that Camarón could claim authorial rights on the musical compositions, lyrics or other works: in most of the pieces, his role was just that of a performer and his performer's related rights were already recognised.[89]

This polemic brings about questions about the limits of copyright as applied to flamenco renditions and improvisations. Abilities of flamenco performers are highly valued by experts and

[82] This type of argument is still used when the SGAE or other CMOs demand the payment of fees for the use of their repertoires during live performances at *juergas* and other events. The argument is generally dismissed by courts. See Espín Alba (n 72) 40, 71–72. Some recent examples include the use of music recordings in a flamenco dance school (Judgment of the Court of Appeals of Alicante of 13 September 2018, ECLI:ES:APA:2018:1803) and in a flamenco club (Judgment of the Court of Appeals of Zaragoza of 17 June 2019, ECLI:ES:APZ:2019:1536).

[83] Bellido (n 30) 181–82.

[84] ibid 183–84.

[85] ibid 192.

[86] See Manuel, 'Composition, Authorship and Ownership' (n 11) 125–30; J Heredia-Carroza, L Palma Martos and LF Aguado, 'Flamenco y derechos de autor. El caso de Camarón de la Isla' (2019) 195 *ARBOR, Ciencia, Pensamiento y Cultura* 791.

[87] Manuel, 'Composition, Authorship and Ownership' (n 11) 125.

[88] ibid 126.

[89] ibid 127–30.

audiences.[90] Hence, they tend to have better standing and esteem than composers in the flamenco world. However, to what extent a particular improvisation may meet the originality requirements to merit copyright protection or only amount to a highly skilled performance is a controversial issue.[91] It is also disputable whether such improvisation may generate a work of joint authorship. On the other hand, Spanish copyright law has not generally required fixation and some authorial works may be generated during improvisations.[92]

VI. Conclusion

Flamenco is visibly infused by a narrative that has exaggerated some of its traits and has quasi-mythologised its norms of production and use. Following this narrative, the gist of the genre has been associated with traditional music and other art forms developed by small Gypsy communities in Southern Spain which recount their historical persecution and are orally transmitted from generation to generation, whereas commercial and external diffusion is perceived as degrading genuine and pure flamenco. This narrative has been powerful in policing the limits of the genre and the acceptability of some borrowing practices in flamenco. It also explains the ambivalent interrelations between flamenco and copyright law.

This narrative lies, however, in exaggeration, and fails to recognise that flamenco music has been open to external influences. It also disregards that forms of diffusion other than oral transmission within small private groups have been prevalent since the nineteenth century. Commercial opportunities for *cantaores* and other artists prompted new developments and the reception of elements from other music genres. Explicit resistance against the traditional narrative led to an explosion of creativity which began in the 1960s and has embraced many types of borrowing practices. Contemporary flamenco provides a very rich example of a creative space in which a plentiful variety of styles coexist, ranging from neo-traditional renditions to experimental forms. Flamenco has also influenced outsider musicians, who have approached the genre from many distinct aesthetic and political agendas.

Borrowing practices in flamenco can take many and diverse forms, including the use and adaptation of different stock elements that are taken from the traditional repertoire or the fusion and hybridisation with other genres and styles. The initial or subsequent acceptance or rejection of any of these borrowing practices and their eventual incorporation into the norms of use and production in flamenco music is highly dependent on their relational aspects. In this regard, borrowing practices in flamenco can be deemed relational in three different ways. First, borrowers can be situated within a specific community or outside of it. Second, in their musical explorations, borrowers can look inwards or outwards. And third, borrowers also proceed in accordance with their relation with the mainstream traditional narrative, an account that they may adhere to or that they may reject and, indeed, contest.

[90] Heredia-Carroza et al, 'Song, Performance and Authorship' (n 22) 9.

[91] R de Román Pérez, 'La protección del cantaor y el bailaor: derechos de los artistas, intérpretes y ejecutantes. Los productores de fonogramas' in Castilla Barea (n 70) 186–88.

[92] See also in French law a dispute concerning rights on music improvisation by guitar player *tocaor* Manitas de Plata (*Live Improvisations (Manitas de Plata)* case: Cour de Cassation, Chambre civile 1, du 1 juillet 1970, 68-14.189).

20

Canzone napoletana, *Chanson française* and Southern Italian Folk Music: Who Took from Whom?

GIOVANNI MARIA RICCIO

I. Piedigrotta and the Birth of the Neapolitan Song

Neapolitan music does not exist as such. Or rather, considering a different perspective, Neapolitan music is not a single, unified, discrete phenomenon. Naples is a city that has always had a very strong artistic and musical tradition, which distinguishes it from the rest of Italy. However, the artistic expressions through which this tradition is manifested are heterogeneous.

A fundamental distinction can be drawn between art music, including opera, and a huge corpus of folk music. Naples developed a significant repertoire of popular song which had its inception at the end of the nineteenth century and reached its peak in the following decades, becoming world famous. This distinction between art and folk music is not a sharp one. These genres often interacted and sometimes even overlapped, but, for classification purposes, I will adopt this distinction, mainly analysing from a copyright perspective, on the one hand, the Neapolitan songs which still enjoy the greatest diffusion at an international level and their connection with art music, and, on the other, folk music.

Canzone napoletana and Neapolitan traditional folk music do not share the same background. Neapolitan song is the product of a middle-class revolution and of the advent of an entertainment industry, while the local folk music fulfils not a commercial function, but often a religious and ritual one.[1] For the purpose of this chapter, it is necessary to point out that the Neapolitan song does not have the same peculiar style, particularly when combined with dance, that is present in traditional folk music.

The birth of Neapolitan song is conventionally traced back to 1839, the year when the first Piedigrotta song festival was supposed to have taken place. The Piedigrotta festival is symbolic of the relationship between paganism and Christian religiosity, and between folk music, conceived mainly for religious purposes, and a flourishing music industry, which would benefit from a pre-existing tradition to turn it to its aims.

[1] This approach follows the seminal work of research by M Stazio, *Osolemio. La canzone napoletana 1880–1914* (Bulzoni, 1991).

Since the first century BCE, around Piedigrotta, in front of the Postillion hill (excavated by the Romans to connect the two sides of the city), rites in the form of bacchanalia were celebrated in honour of the god Priapus, to propitiate fertility and fecundity. In Christian times, the location became the centre of the cult of the Holy Virgin Mary. With the construction of a chapel in 1207, the area became a popular destination for local fishermen to manifest their devotion to the Virgin. In the mid-eighteenth century, in the same area of Piedigrotta, King Charles III decided to establish a military parade, and later transferred Carnival celebrations there.

Music has always had an important role in the Piedigrotta area. The Roman historian Suetonius claims that the Roman emperor Nero performed there.[2] In general, music had a ritual function in the age of the first Piedigrotta fest, and through the centuries became an important cultural tradition in the area, especially after the festival was 'institutionalised' during the Bourbon reign.[3] No wonder that Piedigrotta was chosen as the venue for the Neapolitan Song Festival, inaugurated on 8 September 1839. At that very first festival, a song that would come to acquire great popularity over time won the competition: 'Te voglio bene assaje', with text by the poet Raffaele Sacco and music by Filippo Campanella.[4]

The story of Piedigrotta is emblematic, because it highlights two aspects that are characteristic of Neapolitan culture and contributes to an understanding of the Neapolitan musical phenomenon. There is a similarity between a pagan festival, supplanted by the advent of Christianity, refusing to transfer its symbolic meaning to the Virgin Mary, who performs a function which was once allotted to Isis, Demeter and Venus, and the folk tradition that influenced the first Neapolitan songs. However, the folk tradition survived mostly in a marginal role: a sort of reference to a naive and picturesque population which had to be 'educated' to be useful for the middle-class hegemonic project. In this process, the advent of music publishing and the birth of an entertainment industry that would support the musical phenomenon was crucial. The common element, with respect to both the ritual festivities and the music, is the relationship between the ruling and the subordinate classes. A popular rite is transformed into a national festival, purified of pagan elements, which survive only in clandestine form, and made attractive to the whole population. This was true even of the bourgeoisie, who became the dominant social class in this period, while at the same time driving the new publishing and music industry.

In contrast, we see the abandonment of music as part of a rite and its replacement with a 'song form'. Thus, music shifts from being functional for both pagan and, later, Christian rituals to a commodity.

To properly understand this process, it is necessary to briefly analyse the political, economic and cultural context in which *Canzone napoletana* was born.

II. A Music for the Bourgeois Social Class?

Neapolitan song emerged with the unification of Italy in 1861 at the end of the Regno delle Due Sicilie (the 'Kingdom of the Two Sicilies'). As in many other areas of Europe, the first half of the nineteenth century marked the rise of the bourgeoisie, the social class responsible for the commodification of literary and musical works. It also saw the birth of the publishing market,

[2] JE Reed and A Thomson (eds), *Suetonius: The Lives of the Twelve Caesars; An English Translation* (Gebbie & Co, 1889) www.perseus.tufts.edu/hopper/text?doc=Perseus%3Atext%3A1999.02.0132%3Alife%3Dnero.

[3] For further information, see F Mancini and P Gargano, *Nel segno della tradizione: Piedigrotta. I luoghi, le feste, le canzoni* (Guida Napoli, 1991).

[4] P Scialò, *Storia della canzone napoletana. 1824–1931*, vol I (Neri Pozza, 2017).

which prospered thanks to the diffusion of Neapolitan music outside the Kingdom of the Two Sicilies. While the existing literature on *Canzone napoletana* has focused on an alleged connection to the folk music in the area surrounding Naples, this link appears ephemeral and overestimated. Indeed, some scholars have correctly pointed out that the rise of *Canzone napoletana* is closely linked to the economic interests of music publishers, who eventually contributed significantly to the creation of a relevant market. *Canzone napoletana* adopted the song form and was built around repeated sections (verses and chorus/refrain) typical of the French and German music traditions.

A song by the Neapolitan songwriter Salvatore Di Giacomo opens with the following lyrics: 'Ogne canzone tene 'o riturnello/ca è comme fosse 'o pierno 'e ogne canzone/e, ca pe tanto è cchiù azzeccuso e bello/pe quanto cchiù se 'ntreccia 'e 'spressione' ('Every song has a refrain/which is as if it were the pivot of every song/and is therefore more sticky and beautiful/the more it is intertwined with an expression').[5] It is thus the lyrics themselves which reveal the 'secret' of a successful song: the refrain which 'sticks' in the mind of the listener. Di Giacomo well understood the meaning of the 'song form'[6] – as a commercial product in addition to an artistic manifestation.[7]

As mentioned, *Canzone napoletana* is different from local folk music and responds to different needs. Folk music is a part of a ritual, and it fulfils a function within this ritual. Neapolitan song, however, lives a life of its own, and addresses other needs.[8] The primary purpose is pure entertainment and the aspiration of becoming an internationally recognised artistic form.

Not surprisingly, within the shift from folk music to Neapolitan songs, the themes addressed also changed. In addition to 'Je te voglio bene assaje', 'Funiculì Funiculà', written in 1880 by the journalist Giuseppe Turco with music by Luigi Denza, was performed at the first Piedigrotta festival and is also sometimes referenced at the beginning of Neapolitan songs.[9] The text of the song celebrates the inauguration of the first funicular railway, which took place in 1879, and which allowed people to climb up to Vesuvius, the Neapolitan volcano.

Why is this song so meaningful? There are at least two reasons. Both the text and the language are related to the stylistic features of chamber music, and the text is also related to some poetic forms typical of the period. The text highlights modernity, the new line of transport starting from the *villanelle* and leading both Neapolitans and tourists to the slopes of Vesuvius. This is distinct from the expressions of rural and popular themes within the folk tradition. It is not by chance that the song was presented again a few years later, also in Italian, nor that it is one of the Neapolitan songs that has witnessed the greatest popularity abroad.[10]

The text is not based on the real life of the local people, but is a sort of postcard for foreign countries, a vehicle for the diffusion of Neapolitan culture and, at the same time, an advertisement for the natural beauties of the place.

Both 'Te voglio bene assaje' and 'Funiculì Funiculà' were written at a time when music was not spread by record, but by the sale of music scores containing the lyrics by street vendors (as explained further). Thus, *Canzone napoletana* from its beginnings represented a new Naples, which, due to the representative intentions of the emerging middle class, was not directly connected to the rural, provincial world.

[5] See G Vacca, *Gli spazi della canzone. Luoghi e forme della canzone napoletana* (Libreria musicale italiana, 2013) 89.

[6] With the expression 'song form', reference is made to the structure of the song built around verses and chorus.

[7] I do not want to deny here that Di Giacomo intended to create an artistic product, but it was probably already conceived from a commercial perspective.

[8] At least in its genesis, it subsequently became an interclass art form.

[9] The song was a huge commercial success and its publisher (Ricordi) sold over 1 million copies in one year, see *Canzoni Italiane*, vol I (Fabbri editori, 1994) 21.

[10] The song was also turned into orchestral form by Nikolaj Rimskij-Korsakov in 1907 with the title 'Canzone napoletana' (Op 63) and incorporated into the final movement of Richard Strauss's symphonic poem *From Italy*.

Guillaume Cottrau is crucial to understanding the genesis of the Neapolitan song. In 1824, Cottrau, who moved to Naples in his childhood and belonged to an Alsatian family, published a book entitled *Passatempi musicali* (*Musical Pastimes*). The book was a combination of popular traditional pieces transcribed and arranged by musicians with an academic education and original folk-style compositions. 'Folk-style' achieved great popularity following the book's publication, giving birth to a new editorial genre.[11]

Other collections were published, including *L'eco di Napoli* (*The Echo of Naples*), edited by Vincenzo De Meglio and published by the famous publisher Ricordi.[12] Ricordi had far-reaching distribution capabilities, extending to the northern regions of Italy. These publications were designed for the city bourgeoisie and the music has a strictly entertainment function, creating a parallel repertoire to that of the arias of classical composers such as Donizetti and Bellini.

These pieces were written anonymously, but authorship was often 'plundered' by arrangers who claimed to be their creators. The authorship of these songs is a complicated issue. They were folk songs, almost always written by an unknown author or created by multiple people, over time, adding sections to the modular structure of the piece of music.

After the inauguration of the Piedigrotta festival, the 'copielle', which were an evolution of the 'fogli volanti',[13] became very popular. The *copielle* were illustrated sheets on which the lyrics of the songs and the sheet music, normally tablature for the mandolin, were printed to facilitate the dispersion even among those who could not read music. *Copielle* were sold for a few pennies and were often given as gifts.

The Piedigrotta festival attracted not only citizens from the city, but also many tourists. The *copielle*, therefore, served as an instrument for the dissemination of *Canzone napoletana* amongst the bourgeois class, not only in Naples, but nationally and internationally.[14] The dissemination of the Neapolitan song is a peculiar phenomenon because it initially took place in an era in which the discography was not yet widespread and, therefore, relied mainly on printed sheet music. Sheet music is a selective medium, because to access it one needs to be literate, and the general population at the time was not. Unmistakably, the synergies between the different elements of cultural production and distribution were designed in such a way as to insure a circulation of the musical works well beyond the original geographical context.[15]

In the following decades, additional reasons spurred the spread of Neapolitan song throughout the world.

At the beginning of the century, Naples, and southern Italy in general, were experiencing high levels of emigration, especially to North America. Many neighbourhoods called *Little Italy* were formed in the USA, including in New York, Boston (North End), Baltimore, Chicago and Philadelphia, and on the west coast in San Diego and San Francisco; in Australia (mainly Melbourne); and in Canada (Montréal and Toronto). These immigrants, to maintain a link with their homeland, found a foothold in the ancient and deep-rooted Neapolitan traditions, including music (opera), theatre and the figurative arts. Thereafter, not only did Neapolitans recognise

[11] Scialò, n 4.

[12] V De Meglio, *L'eco di Napoli* (Ricordi, 1877).

[13] The *fogli volanti* (literally, flying sheets or broadsides) were publications sold on the streets that took up the lyrics and music of popular songs. The flying sheets are important because they represented a tool to affirm the Neapolitan song within the bourgeois salons, paving the way to the affirmation of music publishing, first Neapolitan and then coming from the regions of northern Italy. See R Del Prete, 'La canzone del loisir. Il sistema produttivo dello spettacolo dal vivo a Napoli tra '800 e '900' in A Pesce and M Stazio (eds), *La canzone napoletana. Tra memoria e innovazione* (CNR. Istituto di Studi sulle Società del Mediterraneo, 2013) 147.

[14] ibid 161.

[15] M Stazio, 'I motivi di un progetto' in Pesce and Stazio (n 13) 17.

themselves in Neapolitan song, but so did all Italian immigrants – or, at least, all those coming from the southern regions of Italy.

From the end of the nineteenth century to the beginning of the twentieth century, at the historical period when Neapolitan songs were at the height of their popularity, about four million Italians landed in North America, 70 per cent of whom came from the southern regions.

Neapolitan music was an element of identity for the communities that were created in the USA. Neapolitan songs became, in fact, a means to remain Italian for those who were now permanently linked to their status as immigrants and who tried to export some aspects of their cultural roots. It is no coincidence, therefore, that in New York at the beginning of the twentieth century, an American Piedigrotta festival was organised. This festival certainly furthered the reputation of the Neapolitan song, even among Americans.

Enrico Caruso, the famous tenor who revived some Neapolitan songs, giving them popularity and success also in the American territory, played a very important role, along with other artists. Caruso also embodied a 'good' Italian stereotype, as opposed to the narrative of the Italian 'mafioso', and for this reason, he was widely supported not only by his fellow countrymen abroad, but also back at home.

The popularity of *Canzone napoletana* was cemented when Elvis Presley translated the iconic Neapolitan song 'O sole mio' into his 'It's Now or Never', which made its way to number one in the music charts in the USA, the UK and many other countries around the world.[16]

III. The Italian Legal Framework During the Rise of the *Canzone napoletana*

The rise of the *Canzone napoletana* was closely related to certain cultural phenomena, including industrialisation and urbanisation. In 1861, by Law No 4671 of the Kingdom of Sardinia, the Kingdom of Italy was established. The political unification also annexed the Kingdom of the two Sicilies, thus removing from Naples its previous role as its capital city.

The unification of Italy fed the rise of the bourgeoisie and the decline of the old aristocracy. Neapolitan songs became a way to convey a positive image of the city, far from the Lazzaresque representation of the Bourbonic era. In these songs, Naples became not only an expression of modernity, but also a bearer of universal values, disconnected from its rural past and overcoming geographical limits. In this sense, the choice of texts with broad themes (albeit resorting to the use of the dialect), the 'song form', including the musical instruments used, and finally the harmonic solutions (more like the Italian and French romance and song than the folk tradition) illustrate the choice to create a commercially attractive product, intended for the upper social classes rather than for the populace.

Canzone napoletana followed a path analogous to the contemporary legal framework on copyright in both the Kingdom of the Two Sicilies and the Kingdom of Italy.

In 1840, all Italian states had adhered to the Austro-Sardinian Convention of 1840, except for the Kingdom of the Two Sicilies, which joined the Convention following the unification of Italy in 1861.

At that time, the Kingdom of the Two Sicilies was provided with three legislative texts: the first one on patents (1810), the second on theatrical performances and music (1811) and the third on

[16] Elvis Presley also frequently performed another famous Neapolitan song, 'Torna a Surriento', under the title 'Surrender'.

literary and artistic property (1828). This third text granted the author a right on the reproduction of the works for the duration of his life and, to his heirs, for 30 years after his death.

The Neapolitan copyright law was clearly inspired by French law on the topic, although it had some distinctive elements. The 1828 decree granted literary and artistic property to the author during his lifetime and to his heirs for the subsequent 30 years, thus extending the duration of inheritance rights.

After the unification of the Reign of Italy, the first law of the kingdom on copyright, Law No 2337, was issued on 25 June 1865.

The legislative process that led to the approval of the final text was strongly influenced by Antonio Scialoja, a Neapolitan lawyer, judge and, later, member of the commission that adopted the Italian Copyright Law of 1865.[17] Scialoja's fundamental thesis represents a balance between the utilitarian vision, typical of common law legal systems, and the personalistic vision, typical of civil law legal systems, according to which a balance had to be found between the interests of the community and those of the authors, preferring, however, the utility of the good to its materiality.

The draft law for the new state was presented on 18 October 1864. The project was strongly opposed within the parliament because it was believed (by many sides) that an extension of the Austro-Sardinian Convention of 1840 would be sufficient. Scialoja, however, was left out of the discussion between copyright and literary property and focused mainly on recognising the author's right to reproduce their works. In Scialoja's opinion, this was the sole way to guarantee the independence of the author and to ensure that they were not subject to the publishers: by guaranteeing the author a remuneration from the sale of his work and preventing the possibility of the work itself being copied by others.

The debate on the new law focused mainly on the duration of the rights granted to authors. Scialoja, in fact, presented a mechanism according to which a duration of 80 years from the first publication would be recognised, 40 of which were the exclusive right of the author(s) and the remaining 40 of the heirs or other assignees. This approach was highly criticised by the most famous writers of the time, such as Alessandro Manzoni, who was worried that his early works would remain unprotected by law.[18] In letters written by Manzoni, including to the previous Minister of Justice Giuseppe Pisanelli, he attempted to appear, not as the defender of a personal privilege, but as speaking on behalf of the entire category of authors, who, in his opinion, would be damaged by the new law. Manzoni therefore proposed, like other juridical systems of the time, that protection should be associated with the life of the author and not with the publication of the work, a solution which came to characterise subsequent legislation.

Moreover, not surprisingly, Scialoja's ideas, matured both as a researcher and as a lawyer, did not touch the traditional cultural heritage from which the literary and musical works of the time took so much. In this historical era, the Neapolitan lower classes were often seen with benevolence, and to make it acceptable to the bourgeois class, their heritage was deprived of all the characteristics of the rural, peasant and, above all, magical-ritual context. Folklore, as the heritage of the past or a representation of a mythical and stereotyped present, was far from being considered 'an integral part of the current life of a community, of which it represents and interprets some salient and characteristic aspects'.[19]

[17] See L Moscati, 'Tra le carte di Antonio Scialoja. Avvocato e legislatore dei diritti sulle opera dell'ingegno' (2014) 3–4 *Rassegna forense* 1031.

[18] C De Vecchis and P Traniello, *La proprietà del pensiero. Il diritto d'autore dal Settecento a oggi* (Carocci editore, 2012) 89.

[19] L Mansani, *La tutela delle espressioni del folklore* (AIDA, 2005) 335.

Indeed, the concept of population (*popolo*) would be elaborated by Antonio Gramsci decades later with the idea of *nazional-popolare*. In the eighteenth and nineteenth centuries, the *popolo* – that is, the people living in a nation as a coherent and cohesive whole, tied together by common values and by a common culture produced by the language, the institution and the media – was not seen from a sociological perspective, but from a sentimental one, emphasising an abstract link of the common people to the nation and its identity, beginning from its geographical frontiers. Whereas, in the modern world, the bourgeoisie was supposed to be at the forefront, charged with the mission of carrying forward the empowerment of the lower classes, the Neapolitan bourgeoisie was in no such position. Not only did it not share its traditions (as sometimes happened with the old aristocracy), but it often repudiated them, steeped as they were in magic and ritual.

In this mindset, also demonstrated by those who drafted the copyright law, the artistic expressions of the lower classes were not only dismissed, but distorted, being described as homogeneous by the ruling classes.

Neapolitan songs, as mentioned above, are the ideological translation of this approach: according to a late-Romantic perspective, the lower classes are happy, naive people who live in an enchanted landscape. Naples itself is a postcard, as shown in the landscapes of the School of Posillipo, a successful congregation of painters during the nineteenth century.

In this way, a commercial 'product' was created that could be sold outside the narrow geographical boundaries of Naples. A product that became one of the reasons for the success of Neapolitan songs.

Bringing the discussion up to date, Italian law does not pay much attention to traditional works, limiting itself to the application of the Berne Convention and, in particular, Article 15.4.b), which states:

> In the case of unpublished works of which the identity of the author is unknown but which may be presumed to belong to a country of the Union, the legislation of that country shall have the power to designate the authority competent to represent the author and empowered to safeguard and enforce his rights in the countries of the Union.

However, Italy has never indicated what this competent authority should be, leaving the provision in question inapplicable.[20]

As a Neapolitan song is set in a 'song form', it does not have any eccentricity when compared to other forms of arts, such asPortuguese *fado*, *chanson française* etc. Even from a harmonic point of view, as suggested by some recent studies, the influences seem to be found mainly within the 'song form', as in the French *chanson* or in the German *Lieder*. Likewise, except for the recurring use of the mandolin, the musical instruments are quite common when compared to other national traditions.[21]

In comparison, more irregularities can be found in Neapolitan traditional folk music and, in particular, *tammurriate* (for the peasants who perform them, 'songs on the drum'). The characteristics of the *tammurriata*, beyond the purely musical aspect, are completely different from those of the song.

The *tammurriata* is performed exclusively at celebrations in honour of the Holy Virgin, a cult that has taken over the pagan cults honouring Demeter, the goddess of fertility. In fact, all the 'Madonnas' worshipped in the Campania area are portrayed sitting, including Demeter. Even Christian iconography incorporates pagan aspects, with the depiction of the Virgin accompanied

[20] ibid 335, 337.
[21] See specifically Vacca (n 5).

by ears of wheat, pigs or hens, and torches. All of these are symbols of the cults of death and rebirth, combined with the harvest of wheat and, in general, the harvest.

Similarly, in Campania, the tradition of the seven sisters, which later become the seven Madonnas, is still alive. It is a cult inspired by the seven Sibyls – the priestesses consecrated to the cult of Apollo. According to the tradition, one is ugly, black and associated with the mountains, where she is celebrated. She symbolises winter or the period of death that precedes the rebirth of the land and crops.

Tammurriata is a ritual within the rural and peasant world. The musical instruments used are also different: the tambourine is often used in the Neapolitan song, but it is different from the *tammorra*, a big drum made with an animal skin, usually goat or sheep, with tin rattles set in the frame of the drum.

Often in the *tammurriate* other percussion instruments are also used which are not present in the Neapolitan song: *tricheballacche*, *scetavajasse*, *putipù*, castanets (used by dancers). Furthermore, the *tammurriata* exists only if combined with a traditional dance, in which the movements of the dancers are full of symbolic meanings connected to sexuality and fertility. This is a fundamental aspect of the ritual function of the music. Thus, such movements are an expression of a strong sexuality following the model of the Dionysian tradition. The dance involves two dancers, who can be of the same sex, and summarises, from a symbolic point of view, sexual coupling, with movements of approaching and distancing between the dancers involved.

The sexual act and the act of religious devotion merge, in a syncretism that has nothing blasphemous, but depicts the relationship of populations with the earth, which, like the sexual act, generates life.

From a strict musical perspective, the rhythm section of the *tammurriate* is generally the same, but with some slight variations.

The *tammurriata* is an expression of the rural and peasant world, while the Neapolitan song is an expression of the world of the city and the urban environment. These worlds do not communicate with each other, because they respond to different parameters and needs.

The song has an author and an interpreter, and therefore fits comfortably within the rules of copyright. The *tammurriata*, however, like many other musical expressions and dances of southern Europe, has a non-commercial, ritual function and is collective, both in terms of authorship and in terms of execution.

It is not surprising, therefore, that the peasant world, and its music as well as its dances, has remained completely outside the rules of copyright.

IV. Borrowing and Appropriation of the Works

A peculiar case is that of the appropriation of traditional Neapolitan music[22] by the authors and the publishers of the *Canzone napoletana*. These songs (texts or music) are in the public domain, as generally composed in the seventeenth century, and the phenomenon mainly embraces works which originally belonged to the folk music (ie with an anonymous author) but was then taken and slightly modified by other authors.

There are several examples of this process, which began in the nineteenth century, associated with the industrial production of the works. Some themes of traditional folk music were

[22] It is uncertain whether the plagiarism of the works exclusively involved the lyrics or also the musical part of the compositions, considering that recordings of the original works are not available.

incorporated into newer songs, then credited to specific authors, without paying any reference to the fact that they were works excerpted from the traditional repertoire.

It is interesting that collectors and publishers of these songs reused certain aspects of traditional songs, purifying folkloric materials and making them attractive for an upper-class audience, both Neapolitan and international.

An interesting case is that of the song 'Michelemmà', a song published for the first time in 1824 with the subtitle 'Canzona di pescatore' ('Song of a Sailorman') by Guglielmo Cottrau. In reality, the musical piece utilises a text that is certainly of earlier composition, as there are traces of it in two late works of the seventeenth century.

This text is somewhat cryptic and has given rise to several interpretations, referring to the birth of an endive in the middle of the sea, or that the Turks are playing 'tressette' (a card game): it is therefore conceivable, as some have posited, that the references are of the mythical–religious origin. In any case, the lyrics of the song, or parts of it, have been found within the catalogue of Italian peasant music, not only Neapolitan, but from various other regions, including Sicily, Basilicata and Calabria.[23]

It is highly probable that the text was taken up by Cottrau in various areas in southern Italy due to his employment as Marine Commissioner, which found him often travelling in the various southern regions. In other words, Cottrau collected and transcribed a version of the piece, later claiming authorship himself. From a musical point of view, however, in the absence of recordings, it is impossible to determine whether there was an original contribution from Cottrau. What is certain is that the piece escapes the 'song form', being devoid of refrain and moving on an essentially strophic structure.

'Michellemmà' is another example of the misappropriation of the paternity of a work by other musicians. In fact, in the SIAE repertoires,[24] it is possible to find 22 works entitled 'Michelemmà'.[25] Some are original works, others simply take up both the music and the text of Cottrau's version. The most famous examples are the versions from Osanna, a musical group during the 1970s, who published their version in 2015; Roberto Murolo, a legendary singer within Neapolitan music; and another singer, Fausto Cigliano.

In all these cases, the authorship of both the music and the text are attributed to the registrant, without reference to the fact that it is a folk song in the public domain and without attributing the paternity to Cottrau. This is not an isolated case, but is in fact quite recurrent.

[23] See R Di Mauro, '"È nata mmiezo mare …" tra stroppole e intercalare. Forme e matrici in due celebri canzoni napoletane di primo Ottocento, Michelemmà e Io te voglio bene assaje' in E Careri and G Ruberti (eds), *Le forme della canzone* (Lim, 2014) 93.

[24] According to the Italian law, the deposition of the work is not a prerequisite for granting the rights to the authors.

[25] The SIAE (Società degli autori e degli editori) is the oldest Italian copyright collecting society, founded in 1881. Art 180 of the Italian Copyright Law granted an exclusive right to the SIAE in the sense that the SIAE was the only entity entitled to collectively manage copyright. The Italian legislator amended Art 180 through Art 19 of Decree-Law No 148/2017 (as amended by Law No 172 of 4 December 2017), which holds: 'The intermediation activity – however implemented, be it any direct or indirect form of intervention, mediation, mandate, representation or even transfer for the exercise of the rights of representation, performance, acting, broadcasting (including satellite communication to the public) and mechanical and cinematic reproduction of protected works – is reserved exclusively to SIAE and to other collective management organisations referred to in Legislative Decree No 35 of 15 March 2017.' Furthermore, Art 19(3) of Decree-Law No 148/2017, amending Art 20(2) of the Decree No 35/2017, has removed the reference to CMOs established in other Member States: 'The collection of rights revenue on the national territory by independent management entities established abroad is regulated by representation agreements, as referred to in this section'; therefore, the current wording of the provision explicitly provides that IMEs established in another Member State (but not CMOs, given that the specific reference has been removed) can collect rights in Italy exclusively through a representation agreement with an Italian CMO. Likewise, the wording of Art 42(2) of the Decree assumes the possibility for CMOs established in other Member States to directly intermediate in Italy solely in relation to the rights related to copyright.

The piece recorded by Osanna was a reworking of the original song, and the musical portion is unique. It is thus a derivative work, in which the creative effort is certainly present and, therefore, worthy of protection. This is different from the cases of Murolo and Cigliano, who recorded the pieces in their own name without contributing, in terms of originality, any significant artistic input.

A similar case is that of another famous song, 'O Guarracino'. As with 'Michelemmà', 'O Guarracino' has entire lines of folk songs. According to some scholars, 'O Guarracino' may even have originally been conceived as a popular nursery rhyme, with the music being added later, precisely to transform it into a song for the enjoyment of the bourgeois public.[26] In fact, the lyrics suggest that the song could have belonged to the street jester theatre and that it was performed mainly with percussion instruments. Even in the absence of recordings documenting the evolution of the musical piece, it is possible to hypothesise that the music was added later.

This is not to say that there are not authors with great intellectual honesty, who have filed pieces with the SIAE that were original works.

Artists like Gabriella Rinaldi, Massimo Carola and the band called Osanna, belonging to the Neapolitan new wave scene of the 1980s, adapted traditional text and came up with their own musical compositions. All this is faithfully reflected in the SIAE repertoires, which show that the songs were deposited, reporting the author of the upstream work as anonymous.[27]

In certain instances, even the musical part of 'Michelemmà' has been deposited with the SIAE as traditional and in the public domain, with the applicant claiming ownership only as an adapter of that work. The lyrics of the song are generally attributed to Guglielmo Cottrau, who made his version in 1829. However, there are countless other versions of the text, which belongs to the traditional music of the southern Italy, with some lyrics that are different from Cottrau's original ones.[28]

Roberto De Simone, probably the most prominent figure in the research and rediscovery of Campanian folk music, registered the track with the SIAE, acknowledging his authorship of both the music and the lyrics. However, in the album liner notes, the song itself is described as traditional, with De Simone's reworking.

Roberto De Simone is a fundamental figure in the evolution of Neapolitan music. He was a piano graduate, composer and former director of the San Carlo Theatre in Naples. At the end of the 1960s, he met some youths who formed the Nuova Compagnia di Canto Popolare, a musical band interested in the traditional repertoire of Campania. De Simone led these young people on a philological and ethnomusicological recovery of the tradition and cultural heritage of Campania, which embraced not only music, but also theatre performances and, in general, the entire vast folk repertoire of this geographical area.

De Simone, while respecting the tradition in his scholarly research, progressively elaborated it in his operas. With him, rigorous research – involving the musical instruments used, the gestures and the intonations of the singing – is accompanied by the need to make this music usable, without giving in to commercial exploitation. In 1976, De Simone, together with the Nuova Compagnia di Canto Popolare, created a historic opera of fundamental importance, with

[26] Vacca (n 5) 87.

[27] The registration is not reported with an ISWC (International Standard Musical Work Code) number in the SIAE's repertoire.

[28] The recording of the song made in the SIAE's repertoire by the actor Riccardo Pazzaglia, who translated the text into Italian (and therefore should be credited as a composer under Art 4 of the Italian Copyright Law), is peculiar, except that he also acknowledges the authorship of the music which, at least in the recorded version, does not differ from the original composition.

the purpose of understanding the melange in Neapolitan culture, entitled *La Gatta Cenerentola* (*Cinderella the Cat*).

Indeed, the composer reworked the eponymous fairy tale, contained in *Lo Cunto de li Cunti*, by Giambattista Basile, mixing it with other versions of the same fairy tale. From a musical point of view, *La Gatta Cenerentola* is also a work of undoubted interest, combining traditional Neapolitan music (*tammurriate, villanelle, moresche*) with an 'art music' repertoire. On closer inspection, the echoes of Pergolesi and other classical musicians are stronger than those of the traditional music (and, in general, also of the popular textual repertoire) that the composer makes full use of.

It is interesting to note that the songs from the theatre play in the SIAE registers are all attributed to De Simone. Is this an appropriation of the work? Or does folklore constitute an important influence, a starting point to produce new creative work? In other words, is it possible to grant protection only to folk and tradition influence (as in the construction of the story, which, although modified, follows that of Basile), or should the dominant aspect be the content of composer's subsequent interventions?

This point is also interesting because De Simone undoubtedly showed a great respect for the traditional and rural world, which, as a composer, he studied analytically by investigating its cultural and social roots from an innovative perspective. De Simone does not belong to, and further stands in contrast to, the stereotyped reconstruction of Naples and its tradition, nor does he draw on the popular repertoire to exploit it, economically or otherwise. But the dilemma remains, especially when observed through the prism of a strict copyright regime: is De Simone an author or an 'appropriator'?

Regardless of whether these are cases of appropriation of traditional textual or musical works or of works in the public domain, registering them with the SIAE grants the registrants the copyright, in addition to neighbouring rights which are due to them as performers. The main issue is that the SIAE does not control the filed works beyond formal checks; consequently, royalties are granted to the registrants by the collecting society even though the works are in the public domain.[29]

In conclusion, these cases show some lack of originality on the part of the registrants. The works were in the public domain but were appropriated by the artists, who affixed 'copyright symbols'[30] without being entitled to them, by registering these works as their own original compositions.

There is another form of appropriation worth noting. During the first phase of the *Canzone napoletana* (and then during the second half of the nineteenth century), in addition to the *fogli volanti* and the *copielle*, the so-called 'posteggiatori' also took centre stage. These were street musicians who used to play for restaurant clients, and they are still quite popular in Naples: their role is still to entertain customers and enrich the cultural environment.

Publishers often tried to assess the public's interest in new musical works by testing the new songs through the *posteggiatori*, who performed often simplified versions of these compositions (apart from rare exceptions, the *posteggiatori* were unable to read music) to decide, based on the public's requests, which songs to publish and which to discard. This is similar to the present-day mechanism of radios leading to the rejection or modification of new songs.

[29] Furthermore, since these are works that have fallen into the public domain, there are no heirs who can oppose the registration of the works. However, moral rights relating to the authorship of the works could be claimed by the heirs, even if there are no cases where the owners of the moral rights took legal actions in order to claim the authorship of the works of their ancestors.

[30] PJ Heald, 'Reviving the Rhetoric of the Public Interest: Choir Directors, Copy Machines and New Arrangements of Public Domain Music' (1996) 46 *Duke Law Journal* 241, 244.

A noteworthy copyright case is the song 'O Marinariello' (literally, 'The Little Sailor'). The first version was entitled 'O mare 'e ba'[31] and the text was authored by Diodato Del Gaizo. Del Gaizo was a peculiar character, a wandering monk and friend of street musicians, who set his poems to music. Being illiterate, he used a scribe and made a living going around the alleys of Naples, performing his songs accompanied by a mechanical rolling piano and selling sheets with the verses and music.

The song was published by the editor Bideri, who was accused of 'plagiarism' by Del Gaizo for modifying the words of the song. However, there are no official documents confirming any judicial proceeding. It is likely that the dispute was settled, considering Del Gaizo's low patrimonial capacity and the unfounded accusations made against the publisher, who had only replaced the original text with another text.

Del Gaizo's story also highlights an interesting comparison. On the one hand, we have the advent of the publishing sector, where music loses its magical and ritual function and becomes commodified, especially for the upper classes. It becomes music for export that, despite the language barriers, can be appreciated even outside the Neapolitan area. On the other hand, copyright is presented as an instrument of the ruling classes, creating proprietary barriers that oppose the transmission of knowledge. As a matter of fact, copyright overlaps anonymous works with those that are the result of collective creativity, which is typical of folk music. In this manner, those who want to take possession of folk songs have a free pass, caging the music within proprietary schemes that grant rights only to some, to the exclusion of others.[32]

The *Canzone napolitana*, as the Del Gazio case shows, represents an example of how the mechanics of appropriation of popular creativity by the ruling classes works to the detriment of the subordinate classes. Songs such as 'Michelemmà' and 'O Guarracino' are 'cleaned up', for presentation to the general public, by means of style. In fact, the folkloric material is translated into musical styles, accessible to the middle class, that are deprived of the characters associated with ritual (it is not a coincidence that the diffusion of the refrain replaces a modal structure) and, in the legal field, the copyright works as a mechanism to deprive the people, the collective authors of the different and traditional versions of the songs, of the rights on their original creations.

From the outset, the Neapolitan song was used as an export item to identify the entire city with its music. From a stylistic point of view, as will be explained, the 'song form' was soon adopted, with strophes and refrain (ie verses and chorus), on the model of the French song. Similarly, as far as harmony was concerned, operatic styles were mostly taken up, adapted to the 'song form'. Its usability and ability to express a universal language, then, contributed to the rapid spread of the Neapolitan song, supported, as has been said, by a very lively music publishing industry.

V. Is There a Neapolitan Style? (The Linguistic Element)

What are the common aspects of Neapolitan music? Upon close inspection, the only common element is the language.

[31] The title cannot be translated. In fact 'o mare' means the sea, while 'e ba' is a phoneme used by the traditional folk music in order to keep the metrics of the lyrics.

[32] D Carpitella, 'Folklore e diritto d'autore' [2003] *EM Rivista degli archivi di etnomusicologia* 92 (the original article was published in 1978) pointed out that copyright law regulations are based on the logic of profit resulting from an individualistic aesthetic, which is the opposite of popular artistic creativity.

It should be remembered that Italian is both an ancient and a modern language. In classical times, there was a split between literary Latin and vulgar Latin: the former was used in official documents, while the latter was spoken by the people. Gradually, dialectal blends developed, which are collectively referred to in southern Italy as the Neapolitan language, different from the Neapolitan dialect.[33]

At an administrative level, Neapolitan replaced Latin in 1442, by decree of King Alfonso I. Neapolitan was spoken not only by the people, but also in schools, as well as in royal audiences and by diplomats. From the beginning of the sixteenth century, Neapolitan was substituted as an administrative language by Castilian, by order of the Spanish king Ferdinand the Catholic.

In that same period, however, the practice of using the vulgar Tuscan language, another Romance language, became widespread. This practice became more widespread from 1554 on and developed further during the seventeenth century.

In Naples, the debate about language was quite vibrant. Naples, in fact, boasted a long linguistic tradition, rooted in famous authors such as Giambattista Basile and Andrea Perrucci. However, the language they used was not an archaic language, but a language invented, or at least 'retouched', in a cultured environment. In other words, it was not the language spoken on the streets, but a cultured language, like the Tuscan introduced as an official language.

At the beginning of the twentieth century, even in the lyrics of Neapolitan songs there was a dispute between two factions, animated by two renowned poets and songwriters: Salvatore Di Giacomo and Ferdinando Russo. The language of the latter is more raw, more faithful to the spoken language of the working class. Salvatore Di Giacomo's language is refined, not only from a semantic point of view, but also regarding the topics chosen for the lyrics of the songs, which are cleaned of their popular backgrounds and adapted to the taste of a middle-class audience.[34]

Once again, the works were created for a commercial purpose, detached from any magical-ritual reference and readapted to the needs of the new dominant class – the one driving the cultural market.

The themes are therefore often refined, moving from the eroticism typical of popular songs to romantic settings and feelings, in which it is not the body that pushes creativity, but the heart. Similarly, in Di Giacomo's work, landscape descriptions are frequent; the creation of a city that is stuck in its stereotypes, in its natural beauty. This is something that, as mentioned above, Di Giacomo shares with his contemporary, which portrays a postcard version of Naples, a Naples seen from the Posillipo hill.[35]

It should not be forgotten that Di Giacomo was supported by Benedetto Croce, a Neapolitan thinker and philosopher who, for decades, was considered to be at the centre of the entire national cultural scene. Croce therefore legitimised Di Giacomo, elevating him to a benchmark for subsequent generations.

This process led to two results. First, there was an absence of social conflicts, which had begun to appear in a reality where urbanisation became overbearing, within the lyrics of the songs. Instead, Di Giacomo's image of 'Neapolitan-ness' was based on the abstract – even those problems that sometimes emerge are related to the bourgeois class. The songs were no longer about young damsels looking for husbands or asking their spouses to accompany them to folk festivals;

[33] The Neapolitan language is the set of southern dialects, ie the dialects spoken in Campania, in Basilicata, in most of Abruzzo, in Molise, in Puglia excluding Salento, in northern Calabria, in southern Marche and in southern Lazio. According to Ethnologue, it is classified as an Indo-European and Romance language. Recently, UNESCO has recognised Neapolitan as a language instead of a dialect (see www.ethnologue.com/language/nap).

[34] See Vacca (n 5) 95.

[35] ibid 96.

on the contrary, the conflicts that exist in couples – even romantic ones – emerged, especially in upper social classes.

Second, Di Giacomo's iconography, his ability to cleanse the lyrics of their typically popular, overtly Neapolitan themes (especially with reference to popular contexts), was a vehicle for the dissemination of an art form – the Neapolitan song – which would be viewed by the Neapolitans themselves as a source of pride. The aesthetic was reassuring, but at the same time it created an identity platform on which everyone could recognise themselves, even outside their own geographical borders.

Indeed, the Neapolitan language is only apparently a common element, since Neapolitan is not a unique language, and it changes according to the specific contexts in which it is used. What do we mean by Neapolitan language? Is it the artificial language used by Basile in *Lo cunto de li Cunti*? Is it that of the *villanelle*? Or, as it appears, does the language undergo transformations and even 'artistic' adaptations, to be made more usable, more comprehensible? Is it Salvatore di Giacomo's language, which breaks away from popular themes to deal with universal aspects, that makes the songs a common heritage worldwide, precisely because themes that belong to everyone are dealt with? Or is Russo's the more realistic one? Once again, we are faced with a cul-de-sac.

VI. Is There a Neapolitan Music Style?

As previously highlighted, a Neapolitan song does not have its own style, but is influenced by both French and German songs (*chansons* and *Lieder*), as well as by the Italian operatic and romantic traditions. Often, to analyse the 'Neapolitan' character in music, reference is made to the use of the so-called Neapolitan minor scale, a harmonic minor scale with the second degree lowered by a semitone. Similarly, the Neapolitan scale is a major scale with the fourth degree raised by a semitone.

The Neapolitan scales have been widely used in the *Canzone napoletana* (such as in the famous song entitled 'Indifferentemente'), as well as in several Italian pop songs, often with the purpose of recalling a Neapolitan 'sound'.[36]

The Neapolitan scale, however, is not a prerogative of Neapolitan music – especially not of the *Canzone napoletana*. Beethoven, among others, also used it in the main themes of string quartets (Op 59, No 2 in E minor and Op 95 in F minor).[37] The Neapolitan scales, even if they cannot be considered as a proper style of Neapolitan music, are nevertheless used as a musical cliché, and could be considered a form of borrowing of a musical tradition, in the sense that the recurring intervals of these scales determine that the sonority produced is perceived by the listener as a 'Neapolitan' composition.[38]

In contrast, there are well-defined styles in the traditional music from Campania, as in the case of *tammurriata*.[39] During the 1970s in particular, the different rhythms that characterise the rites and festivals held in the Campania region in honour of the Virgin were documented.[40]

[36] See, eg the song 'Don Raffaè' by Fabrizio De Andrè, which is about the story of a famous exponent of the Neapolitan mafia. The author of the song uses the Neapolitan minor scale in order to recreate a Neapolitan pattern.

[37] As noted by A Schoenberg, *Theory of Harmony* (University of California Press, 1978) 28.

[38] Vacca (n 5) 86.

[39] See the rhythmical examples mentioned in R De Simone, *Canti e tradizioni popolari in Campania* (Lato Side, 1975) 24.

[40] ibid 23, 26.

Recordings made by ethnomusicologists have allowed us to highlight large rhythmic differences that are often difficult to decipher with an inexperienced ear. Yet, in the following decades, the participation in celebrations and rites of the new generation belonging to the rural social classes would become more episodic and discontinuous due to urbanisation. These events also began to attract young people from the cities, culturally extraneous to the events themselves.

This phenomenon has resulted in the levelling of the different rhythms and consequently a diminished sense of cultural diversity. In fact, except for ethnomusicologists, many people from urban areas, including the musicians who borrowed the rhythms of the *tammurriata*, approached folk music (and generally the folklore) in a non-philological way, taking up the basic rhythm and, consequently, dismissing the slight rhythmic variances between the different local expressions of the *tammurriata*.[41]

The discussion on the musical style of the *Canzone napoletana* and of the traditional Neapolitan folk music is interesting, considering that the Italian copyright law does not grant any copyright protection to style or to traditional musical expressions.[42]

Italian doctrinal jurisprudence generally denies any form of protection of styles, with the Italian Court of Cassation ruling on several occasions that copyright law does not protect the idea per se, but exclusively its representation, thus protecting exclusively the creative act, even if there is only minimal, and not absolute, originality. In other words, a level of creativity exists in the presence of a 'personal and individual expression of objectivity'.[43]

Therefore, according to Italian case law, the appropriation of the creative elements of a copyrighted work does not occur when an idea is copied, only when the expression of the idea is appropriated to exploit specific and identifiable forms expressed by other authors.[44] Any small differences among different works are irrelevant 'since plagiarism remains even when it is disguised (or masked) by only apparent variants'.[45]

In the musical field, the appropriation of the melodic line is generally considered necessary, 'as it is not sufficient that there is appropriation of a common and recurrent melodic scheme so as to constitute the use of acquired stylistic features or formulas by composers'.[46] More specifically, to ascertain the plagiarism, the courts generally examine first the melody, then the harmony and rhythm.[47]

Italian copyright law does not grant any protection to folk musical works. The lack of attention to folklore in the Italian copyright law should not be surprising. The law was enacted in 1941, during the fascist regime, and is inevitably reflective of its values. During this period, folklore and folkloric studies had been reduced to mere political propaganda and all expressions that did not promote the power of Italy had been silenced.

Likewise, the fascist regime opposed the Neapolitan dialect, as well as all other dialects, considering them to be potential centrifugal forces opposed to the central power.[48] Yet, the aversion to

[41] On this aspect in general, see C Geertz, *Local Knowledge: Further Essays in Interpretive Anthropology* (Basic Books, 1983).

[42] A Musso, 'Del diritto di autore sulle opere dell'ingegno letterarie e artistiche. Artt 2575–2583 cc' in F Galgano (ed), *Commentario al Codice civile* (Zanichelli, 2008) 27.

[43] See, eg Court of Cassation, 29 May 2020, No 10300.

[44] Court of Cassation, 14 July 2017, No 2039.

[45] See, eg Court of Cassation, 15 June 2012, No 9854; Court of Cassation, 28 November 2011, No 25173; Court of Cassation, 15 June 2012, No 9854.

[46] Court of Bologna, 9 May 1997, AIDA, 932 (1997). This outcome is generally shared by Italian legal scholars: see V De Santis, *La protezione delle opere dell'ingegno*, vol II (Giuffrè, 2004) 380; ZO Algardi, *Il plagio letterario e il carattere creativo dell'opera* (Giuffrè, 1966) 478.

[47] Court of Rome, 11 May 1999, Temi Romana, 1999, 644.

[48] A Simonini, *Il linguaggio di Mussolini* (Bompiani, 1978) 201.

dialects did not affect the *Canzone napoletana*. The law on copyright responded to a productivist ideology and, as mentioned, the Neapolitan song was conceived from a commercial perspective, as a product of the industrial society.

The Italian Code of Cultural Heritage (Legislative Decree No 42, 22 January 2004) originally did not grant protection to the products of folklore either. The Code only included in the definition of cultural heritage goods that have an ethno-anthropological interest (Article 10). Then Article 7-*bis* was added to the Code, following Italy's joining of the UNESCO Conventions for the Safeguarding of the Intangible Cultural Heritage (2003) and for the Protection and Promotion of Cultural Diversity (2005). This provision states that

> The expressions of collective cultural identity contemplated by the UNESCO Conventions for the safeguarding of the intangible cultural heritage and for the protection and promotion of cultural diversity … are subject to the provisions of this code if they are represented by material evidence.[49]

The approach of the UNESCO Conventions has certainly been innovative. It shifted the focus from a scenario where legal rights are granted to specific entities (the state or other public administrations; non-profit organisations; private citizens or companies) without providing any rights for the communities towards a different legal landscape where the importance of the communities is recognised as a central aspect. The Convention for the Safeguarding of the Intangible Cultural Heritage of 2003 is relevant here, with its notion of intangible cultural heritage, including 'the practices, representations, expressions, knowledge, skills – as well as the instruments, objects, artefacts and cultural spaces associated therewith – that communities, groups and, in some cases, individuals recognize as part of their cultural heritage' (Article 2).

In any case, neither Italian copyright law nor cultural heritage legislation (including the above-mentioned UNESCO Convention of 2003) grants any form of judicial protection to the style of the works (also intended as a manifestation of a cultural diversity) and against its appropriation, modification or disfigurement. Local communities do not hold any specific right and their empowerment has never been included in the legislative agenda.

VII. Fixation of the Work

Italian copyright law does not require the work to be fixed to be protected (Article 2576 of the Italian Civil Code). Thus, the works of the popular tradition, although not necessarily fixed in a specific medium (eg written, phonogram), are protected starting from their original manifestation, even if performed only in oral form. In fact, Article 14 of the Italian Copyright Law allows the author to fix their work in writing or reproduce it in another material form, as well as to protect the work irrespective of the way it is expressed.

The protection of orality also implies that both incomplete versions of works and variations of works are independently protected, however generally, as derivative works. The idea itself is obviously not protected, and the protection does not cover works that do not reach a sufficient degree of creative completeness.

The main issue, as already noted, is that the repertoires of traditional folk songs, as well as traditional folk dances, cannot be attributed to a specific author, since they are collective works

[49] See GL Bravo and R Tucci, *I beni culturali demoetnoantropologici* (Carocci, 2006).

whose lyrics are generally constructed according to a modular scheme, with additions from individual singers.[50]

Thus, folkloric creations generally remain outside the spectrum of the legislative copyright protection. In comparison, the law generally protects the works of the *Canzone napoletana*, which follow the usual rules of music under copyright without significant discrepancies, because even though appropriation exists, the creator is always identifiable.

Although the issue of fixation does not exist in Italy, the international legislation that deals with cultural traditions refers to recordings or testimonies that are not ephemeral, at least regarding the proof that the author must provide to obtain protection. For years, ethnomusicologists have highlighted that those recordings or transcriptions are useful, even if they are the mere representation of a precise moment, whereas these works should be analysed in a dynamic rather than a static perspective, to also examine the musical and textual evolution.

Once again, the copyright perspective does not fit with these forms of artistic representation. Moreover, an aspect that is in any case unsolvable is that of the recognition of royalties to a single author, since Italian copyright law does not provide for forms of attribution of rights to communities or to subjects who collectively represent them.[51]

VIII. Conclusion

Is there a Neapolitan style of music, or is it a prism with faces that often talk to each other on an empathetic and superficial level, without really distinguishing one from the other? As discussed in this chapter, the latter is the case. The Neapolitan song is often considered by assimilation to be Neapolitan music, although this is not the case.

As said, the only style that can be recognised as individualised is that of the Neapolitan folk and rural music. Even if these works are not celebrated worldwide like the *Canzone napoletana*, they still represent long-standing forms of musical expression in the region. Neapolitan song, even if presenting some specific aspects, is strongly aligned with the French and German musical traditions on the one side and the operatic tradition on the other.

The *Canzone napoletana* was influenced by the traditional Neapolitan folk music, especially in its early days. However, it was mostly a phenomenon of music borrowing of stylistic features and suggestions, considering the above-mentioned influences of the French *chanson*. Many of these Neapolitan songs belonging in the public domain have been appropriated by contemporary artists. This is because of the poor control of the SIAE registries, and is perpetuated further by the absence of copyright holders claiming rights.

[50] C Zuddas, 'Espressioni culturali tradizionali e opere orfane nell'era della rete: spunti dalla direttiva 28/2021/UE, I battelli del Reno' [2013] *Rivista on-line di diritto ed economia dell'impresa* 9 notes that cultural expressions traditionally are not protected by the Italian legislation on copyright because there is no identified author, as well as due to the nature of oral transmission of these expressions.

[51] This possibility is criticised by some Italian legal scholars who, with a short-sighted approach, argue on the possibility that more local communities may claim rights on the same work or on the general difficulty in finding which local community should be entitled to claim for copyright protection: see F De Propris, 'La tutela delle opere folkloriche' [2003] *EM Rivista degli archivi di etnomusicologia* 118. But see Mansani (n 19) 340.

21

Greek Traditional Music: Creativity, Copyright and the Commons

STAVROULA KARAPAPA

I. Introduction

Greek traditional music (in Greek: *Δημοτικό* or *Παραδοσιακό Τραγούδι)* is a literary and music genre that draws its material from oral literary tradition. It includes all the traditional songs and rhythms of the Greek regions, including mainland Greece and the islands, which – with the intense urbanisation of the last century – became a representative part of Greek folklore. Although the terms 'traditional music' and 'folk music' are often used interchangeably, the passage from traditional to folk music took place during the post-war decades of urbanisation, when 'authentic' music was transformed into folklore.[1] Having originally evolved in the various regions of Greece as part of local tradition and customs, traditional music, songs and dances are organically linked to the space, time, people and conditions of their creation,[2] and are in fact often directly associated with local customs, rituals and historical events. With the passage of time, it has become a code of expression and communication, a symbol of identity and a vessel of collective memory.

This chapter is concerned with the relationship of Greek traditional music with copyright. The creative process in traditional music differs from that in other music genres. Defining factors in shaping the character of traditional music are the reuse of known melodies, the evolution of lyrics as they are sung, and the capture of the ethos and culture of whole generations within songs. 'Borrowing' is essential in the composition of songs – 'for the craftsman, borrowing is one of the tools of his originality', as Greek poet Kostis Palamas has observed.[3] In addition, traditional songs are compositions of unknown – often more than one – creators and the result of additions, adaptations, but also modifications, over the years. As a result, each traditional song is the

[1] L Liavas, 'From the River of Tradition to Folklore' ('Από το ποτάμι της παράδοσης στο φολκλόρ') *To Vima* (17 August 2013) www.tovima.gr/2013/08/17/opinions/apo-to-potami-tis-paradosis-sto-folklor/. It should be noted here that the post-war decades of intense urbanisation had an impact on 'authentic' musical raw material as it transformed it into folklore. Traditional, self-taught 'folk' performers prevented the disappearance of traditional music, which continues and is regenerated, particularly in regions such as Crete, Epirus and Macedonia. Thus, with urbanisation, the traditional song is cut off from place and time and is performed in different conditions and places, usually in the form of 'revival' through local festivities and events, music and dance performances as well as sound recordings. In this sense, folklore represents an imprint of the traditional--isolated from the social--context in which it was initially created.

[2] ibid; see in general M Dragoumis, *Our Traditional Music* (*Η παραδοσιακή μας μουσική*), vol 1 (Centre of Minor Asian Studies, 2003).

[3] K Palamas, *The Twelve Lays of the Gipsy* (*O dodekalogos toy gyftou*) (Lawrence & Wishart, 1969).

result of the collective creativity of a people, embedding layers of history that can be found in fragments in the musical composition or the lyrics that accompany the song, with their roots in the Byzantine period, but also in antiquity. This form of creativity, which has resulted in a rich, diverse music genre, does not seem to align with copyright's concepts of originality and authorship, and puts into question the theoretical underpinnings of copyright law, according to which creativity and innovation are the result of incentives or reward. That is one aspect that is explored in this chapter; in particular, the chapter is concerned with how creativity of traditional composers has been spurred on and thrived outside the principles, concepts and narratives of copyright protection. An important component of the discussion is hence the kind of creativity involved in the composition of traditional music and an illustration of how this creativity tends to fall outside the framework of copyright. Indeed, Article 2 of the Greek Copyright Act[4] does not offer protection to expressions of popular culture, although the adaptation of such expressions is expressly included in the illustrative list of protected subject matter.

The formulation of the Act inevitably raises the reverse question – namely, how did the protection of copyright impact on folk creativity and therefore on the evolution of traditional music as a genre itself? This is a second aspect discussed in this chapter and one that is particularly important because, as will be explained below, many artists have retained some proprietary entitlements over traditional music by recording adaptations; indeed, there have been cases where collecting societies have requested licence fees from traditional singers to lawfully perform traditional music – not the protected adaptation – in public. This has resulted in controversy as traditional music is expressly outside the scope of copyright, whilst adaptations, arrangements and other alterations of expressions of folklore and popular culture can attract copyright. Despite the controversy, the relevant case law and the requests to amend the scope of Article 2,[5] the relationship of Greek traditional music with copyright law remains underexplored; the very few academic studies on the legal protection of folklore[6] discuss music peripherally without focusing on specific issues that emerge from the encounter of traditional music with copyright doctrine. In addition, they do not discuss how the particularities of this literary and music genre – for instance, in relation to creativity and authorship – relate to copyright law, theory and doctrine.

This chapter therefore attempts to address two issues: how did folk creativity emerge outside copyright principles, and how did copyright impact on folk creativity and possibly on the evolution of Greek traditional music as a genre? To address these issues, the chapter adopts a socio-legal approach. Its outline is as follows: it starts with an exposé of the historical evolution and characteristics of Greek traditional music; it moves on to explore the particular way in which this literary and music genre has developed and the unique creative processes that are involved in its production; it then identifies key areas of creativity that do not align with central copyright concepts – notably originality and authorship – and explains that Greek copyright does not

[4] Law 2121/1993. For the full text of this Act in English, see www.opi.gr/en/library/law-2121-1993.

[5] For instance, the Pampontian Federation of Greece has reportedly sought the revision of Art 2 before the Minister of Culture. See V Kariofillidis, 'The Music Committee of the Pampontian Federation of Greece on the Intellectual Property Rights of Traditional Songs from Pontos' ('Η Επιτροπή Μουσικής της ΠΟΕ στο Υπουργείο Πολιτισμού για τα Πνευματικά Δικαιώματα των Παραδοσιακών Ποντιακών Τραγουδιών' *Pontos News* (3 April 2017) www.pontosnews.gr/384542/pontos/i-epitropi-mousikis-tis-poe-sto-ypourg/; for a letter of the Pampontian Federation of Greece urging for the revision of Art 2 in Greek, see www.pontosnews.gr/files/2017/04/pneymatika-dikaiomata-sto-horo-tis-paradosiakis-moysikis.pdf. The key proposal made is that, with regard to traditional music, the law should expressly state that traditional music can neither be the object of copyright as such nor its adaptation (Art 2 of Law 2121/1993), nor can it be the subject of authorship (Art 6 of Law 2121/1993), as collective authorship could have only applied to traditional music that is created by the people. See www.avgi.gr/tehnes/236536_pneymatika-dikaiomata-kai-paradosiaki-moysiki.

[6] eg C Kotzaoglou, 'Problematic Issues about the Protection of Expressions of Popular Tradition and Folklore: Gaps in the Institutional Protection Framework and Cultural Policy Proposals' (Aristotelian University of Thessaloniki, 2014).

specifically protect folklore; finally, it sheds light on the legal protection of expressions of popular culture in Greece, with a particular focus on traditional music, with attention on the controversy that has emerged due to the copyright protection offered to adaptations and alterations of traditional music.

II. The Historical Evolution of Greek Traditional Music: Common Features

Greek traditional music includes all the songs and rhythms of the Greek regions, including mainland Greece and the islands.[7] The creators of these compositions are mostly unknown and the songs date from more than a century ago, while the roots of some of them go back to the Byzantine period and antiquity.

Greek traditional music spans more than one genre, often bearing the characteristics of the area in which it is performed or from which it originates. Apart from the regions, traditional music can be classified based on its content (eg love, marriage, death, diaspora, sea) and the occasion on which it is performed (eg weddings, festivals; in Greek, πανηγύρι), or their musical, rhythmic and structural characteristics (strophic, seven-syllable etc) and tempos (Syrtos, Kalamatianos, Tsamiko, Sousta, Ballos etc). Besides feasting and entertainment, traditional music had a useful, liturgical and ritual character. It spread to all aspects of social life, was associated with worship and preserved historical memory.

The oldest traditional songs on which we have information recording their origin are the Acritic songs of the ninth to eleventh centuries. A continuation of Byzantine music, traditional music traces its roots back to ancient Greece and demonstrates other influences (Arabic–Persian, etc). The sliding dances (συρτός) are mentioned in an inscription of the sixth century BCE. Many have their roots in the Byzantine period, but most were created during the years of Ottoman rule and the revolution of 1821. In Greek antiquity and during the Byzantine years, the production of traditional songs was usually a combination of music and dance. The traditional songs that have survived from these times are rare, usually preserved in fragments and often included as quotations in literary texts. The interest in traditional music and its systematic recording began with the development of the science of folklore. Many of the traditional songs created in the Byzantine period have survived to the present day through oral tradition and with adaptations that were created during the last century following the style of the older ones. The music is mainly vocal, but there are also polyphonic songs, mostly in Epirus, on pentatonic scales. Most songs are dance songs, although some songs follow a slow rhythm (*της τάβλας*).

A comparison of the older samples of traditional songs with the newer ones indicates that they follow certain basic rules and share common characteristics, such as the anonymity of the creator(s); a lack of information on the exact place and period of origin; the use of popular expressions through local idioms, simple and dense speech; a representation of the psyche and ethos of the people; the observed existence of variations, most of which are an indication of how acclaimed a song is; and the characteristic measure, often the iambic 15-syllable,[8] which is deemed evidence of links with ancient Greek music. These characteristics are unique to this

[7] For an overview, see S Baud-Bovy, *Essay for the Greek Popular Song* (*Δοκίμιο για το Ελληνικό Δημοτικό Τραγούδι*) (Peloponnisiako Laografiko Idryma, 1996).

[8] K Valai, 'View on the Greek Traditional Music' (Charles University, 2011–12).

musical genre and afford it authenticity.[9] Other characteristics include the principle of isometry, according to which each metric section contains a complete meaning; the use of pointless questions; the principle of the improbability;[10] and the use of personifications, whereby animate or inanimate objects can speak and take part in the action.

In terms of content, Greek traditional music is divided into the following main categories (among others):

1. Paraloges (*Παραλογές*), namely multi-line narrative songs on dramatic adventures of life, real or imaginary. The older ones have a great resemblance to the Acritic songs. They were widespread in the Balkans and present analogies with traditions, myths, tales and songs of the people of Central and Northern Europe.
2. Acritic songs, the development of which is thought to have started during the tenth century. They have survived through oral tradition and have, of course, undergone alterations. They are the most widespread in all of Hellenism: they spread from Pontus and Cappadocia to as far as Epirus, the Ionian Islands, Crete and Cyprus.
3. Songs of the underworld (*του Χάροντα*) are often mourning songs, associated with the pain associated with death and the loss of loved ones.
4. Historic songs narrate specific events, national or social, and are often emotionally charged. Almost in their entirety, they were created after the Fall of Constantinople or the revolution of 1821.
5. Kleftika (*κλέφτικα*) are one of the richest categories of traditional songs and were developed during the Ottoman rule as evidence for the constant resistance of the Greek nation against the Ottomans. They have a prominent place in the edifice of Greek folklore.

Further categories are developed based on the geographical origin of the songs: Steriana (Epirotika, Moraitika, Roumeliotika, Thracian, Makedonitika), songs from the islands, Asia Minor (Smyrna, Politika), Pontian, Eastern Romulia etc.[11]

It is estimated that there are over 20,000 traditional songs in Greece.[12] Even though traditional songs are still sung in many parts of Greece, nevertheless their production has declined, because the expressive needs of people are nowadays fulfilled through personal creativity.

III. The Genesis of the Traditional Song: Creativity and the Commons

The Greek traditional song is a product of the oral tradition and collective creation of unknown authors. In most cases, the reasons that led to the creation of songs, as a form of impersonal poetic and musical composition, go back to historical events or purely societal structures. In time, the name of the original creator is forgotten, it is blended with the contributions of unknown authors, and the song is transformed into an intellectual product of the community and a facet of tradition.

[9] See JP Burkholder, 'A Brief History and Typology of Musical Borrowing and Reworking' ch 2 of this volume.

[10] This is a technique according to which a song refers to situations that are excessive or impossible to occur in order to emphasise that the opposite or something else is happening.

[11] See in general L Liavas, *The Greek Song: From 1821 to the 1950* (*Το ελληνικό τραγούδι: Από το 1821 έως τη δεκαετία του 1950*) (Commercial Bank of Greece, 2009).

[12] K Panagopoulos, 'The Traditional, Popular Song' ('Το παραδοσιακό, δημοτικό τραγούδι') *MusicHeaven* (6 June 2013) www.musicheaven.gr/html/modules.php?name=News&file=article&id=3929.

Tradition in Greek (παράδοση < παραδίδωμι) is literally the energy of 'surrender', that is, the act of trusting and transferring – here, intangible heritage. In this sense, the traditional song becomes a chain that connects generations, shapes the sense of history, and forms an integral part of the collective identity and memory. Authorship has a unique character and is a collective process.

Context is also an important constituent of the authorial process as the song is built in historical layers. Songs undergo a lot of alterations, being reshaped and renewed in light of historical events, social changes and evolving traditions. They are passed down from generation to generation, shaped, modified or adapted, and transformed into a synthetic work of entire generations. With the passage of time and oral transportation to farther places, many songs observe radical alterations. This is a natural evolution when songs are transferred by word of mouth as they are often adapted to the phonology of the new place. Social reality reshapes and adapts tradition, as does anyone who sings the song and changes it, either due to insufficient recollection or with the purpose of enriching it with their own sentiment. This explains why a plethora of local variations of songs are preserved. Often, the melody remains unaltered, and it is just the lyrics that change – something that in music borrowing is referred to as 'contrafactum'. Well-known melodies have, in some cases, remained unchanged for centuries, with some having ancient origins. Just as the Greek language has moved from one generation to the next, constantly evolving, traditional music too has an uninterrupted continuity with music that was developed centuries ago. A key element of traditional songs is the close relationship between speech (lyrics) and music, which are born at the same time and subject to constant evolution, with contrafactum often being observed: the lyrics are made by being 'sung'. The use of ancient metric patterns, for instance, demonstrates such a continuity. The ancient roots are also traced in the very word 'song': in Greek τραγούδι, which originates from the word tragedy (τραγῳδία < ᾠδὴ τῶν τράγων, ie choral song of the satyrs).

The originality of a traditional song is closely aligned with its authenticity. In fact, originality is developed through appropriation and creative transformation of existing musical elements. As Emerson notes about originality, 'the legend is tossed from believer to poet, from poet to believer, everybody adding a grace or dropping a fault or rounding the form, until it gets an ideal truth'.[13] This is how traditional music is produced – by being shared, by appropriating known elements and constantly evolving. Appropriation defines the way in which traditional musicians embed their creativity in new music.[14] Creativity is linked to the commons, not only in the sense of collective authorship, but also in the sense of appropriation of elements that pertain to traditional music: it necessitates borrowing from pre-existing expression. Borrowing here is understood as creative 'loan', recitation or quote, and results in the authenticity of the output. Each new song is a recomposition of well-known traditional elements, which the anonymous creators adapt and enrich. This kind of creativity falls beyond copyright norms and doctrine and notions of property more broadly, including theoretical narratives that view incentives or reward as a direct corollary to creativity.

Menousis, a well-known Greek traditional song, offers an example of this kind of musical borrowing and cultural narratives emerging from a different time. Narrating a bitter story of

[13] RW Emerson, *The Complete Works of Ralph Waldo Emerson, Vol 8. Letters and Social Aims (1803–1882)* (University of Michigan Library, 2006) [6], https://quod.lib.umich.edu/cgi/t/text/text-idx?c=emerson;cc=emerson;view=toc;idno=4957107.0008.001.

[14] Having said that, it is very difficult to reconcile this kind of creativity with any notion of 'property'. In this regard, see V Stoichiţă, '"Intelligent Thieves": Ethics of Creativity among Professional Gypsy Musicians in Romania' ('Les "voleurs intelligents" ou l'éthique de la créativité selon les musiciens professionnels tsiganes de Roumanie') (2010) 12 *Gradhiva* 80, https://doi.org/10.4000/gradhiva.1856 (French version).

jealousy that resulted in a hateful crime of passion, the song captures concisely the transition from a conservative society of the past to a society of modernity.[15] Allegedly based on a true story, the song is alive in folk tradition and still survives in its many variations: the melody and main story remain the same, but there are several versions in which names and lyrics change. The roots of the song can be traced back to the Acritic songs of the Greek Middle Ages, and the song that we know today has evolved over time and through creative interventions of many unknown authors in various places around Greece.[16] Reflective of the ethos of another era, the song has been taught more recently in schools,[17] has inspired various non-traditional music composers, such as George Katsaros and Vangelis Papathanassiou, has become the central topic of a book[18] and was even adapted into a film (*O Menousis*, directed by Vassilis Kontaxis in 1969).

Transmitted orally from generation to generation, Greek traditional music was often not recorded in any form of writing. In that regard, two observations can be made. One is that traditional songs were not fixed in a tangible form before they were recorded in a studio; and secondly, they took their final form only when recorded. Even though there are some manuscripts surviving on Mount Athos that demonstrate the origins of some of the songs, most of the songs were preserved for centuries solely through oral tradition; they thrived and survived as living creations that were shaped through the use and experiences of the people, receiving new meanings or form every time they reached an audience. The spread of the traditional songs took place in parallel with church music and they were influenced by the Byzantine music tradition. Traditional music was fermented with Greek history, especially during the long period of Ottoman rule and the revolution of 1821, and as such they keep Greece's national memory and consciousness alive. In Greek traditional music, creativity is linked to the commons, not only in the sense of collective authorship, but also in the sense of appropriation and borrowing; originality can involve creative transformation of existing musical elements. What is more, the evolution of Greek traditional music resists fixation as a key requirement for copyright protection in most legal regimes. Greek traditional music lives and evolves representing a unique form of collective creativity that challenges theoretical underpinnings of copyright such as incentives or reward. What is then the threshold of legal protection afforded to traditional music in Greece?

IV. The Legal Protection of Traditional Music in Greece: Intangible Cultural Heritage and Copyright

The Constitution of Greece does not explicitly mention the protection of the expressions of popular culture, but there is an indirect relevance in the right of Greek citizens to maintain their identity by virtue of the following fundamental principles: the respect of personality,

[15] See E Liata, *Menousis: History and Tradition* (*Μενούσης: Ιστορία και παράδοση*) (National Research Foundation, Institute of Modern Greek Studies, 2011).

[16] L Kouzeli, '"Menousis": A Song with History' ('«Ο Μενούσης»: Ενα τραγούδι με ιστορία') *To Vima* (8 July 2011) www.tovima.gr/2011/07/08/culture/o-menoysis-ena-tragoydi-me-istoria/.

[17] For instance, it is part of the national curriculum in Cyprus, where it has been taught as a theatre workshop since 2012. See https://logom.schools.ac.cy/index.php/el/yliko/chrisimo-yliko and https://archeia.moec.gov.cy/sm/283/menousis_theatriko_ergastiri.pdf. It is also performed in school festivals, eg it was reportedly performed in 2013 in a primary school in Crete. See E Tsaousaki and St. Vedouras, 'Summer Festival in the 1st Primary School of Rethymnon' ('Καλοκαιρινή γιορτή στο 1ο Δημοτικό Σχολείο Ρεθύμνου') *Rethemniotika Nea* (20 June 2014) https://rethnea.gr/καλοκαιρινή-γιορτή-στο-1ο-δημοτικό-σχο/.

[18] ibid.

freedom of expression and the principle of environmental protection.[19] Traditional music and aspects of it receive protection under Law 3028/2002 on the protection of antiquities and cultural heritage in general[20] and Law 2121/1993 on intellectual property.

As early as 2002, the Greek state adopted the term 'intangible cultural property' to establish a legal framework towards the preservation of cultural heritage that until then had received protection as 'traditional and modern popular culture'. The law on the protection of antiquities and cultural heritage defines intangible cultural goods as expressions, activities, knowledge and information, such as myths, customs, oral traditions, dances, events, music, songs, skills or techniques that are testimonies of traditional, popular and learned culture. Traditional music falls under this definition. About a year after the Greek law was enacted, UNESCO adopted the Convention for the Safeguarding of the Intangible Cultural Heritage.[21] The Convention goes one step further than the Greek law, as it gives priority to the bearers of the elements of intangible cultural heritage, namely the various communities. According to Article 2(3) of the Convention, 'safeguarding' covers measures aimed at ensuring the viability of the intangible cultural heritage, including the identification, documentation, research, preservation, protection, promotion, enhancement, transmission, particularly through formal and non-formal education, and revitalisation of the various aspects of such heritage. Article 2 of the Convention has been interpreted to propose the development of a *sui generis* form of intellectual property protection for intangible cultural heritage,[22] and even though some countries have offered such protection, others – including Greece – have not[23] despite the fact that the Convention was ratified via Law 3521/2006.

In addition, as illustrated earlier, the kind of creativity that is part of the genesis of traditional music in Greece cannot be captured by, or align with, copyright doctrine. Concepts of collective authorship of unknown creators over the course of centuries and originality that relies on borrowing and cultural exchange fall outside the scope of copyright norms. Offer of copyright protection on this kind of music creativity would *have* to fall under some *sui generis* form of protection. However, this is not the case and, in fact, no *sui generis* and/or copyright protection is offered to traditional music, which remains a public good for people to enjoy.

Article 2(2) of the Greek Copyright Law (2121/93), which introduces additional subject matter to what can be protectable as 'work',[24] offers protection to:

> [T]ranslations, adaptations, arrangements and other alterations of works or of expressions of folklore, as well as collections of works or collections of expressions of folklore or of simple facts and data, such as encyclopaedias and anthologies, provided the selection or the arrangement of their contents is original. Protection afforded to the works listed in this paragraph shall in no way prejudice rights in the pre-existing works, which were used as the object of the alterations or the collections.

[19] For the full text of the Greek Constitution, see www.hellenicparliament.gr/UserFiles/f3c70a23-7696–49db-9148-f24dce6a27c8/001-156%20aggliko.pdf.

[20] Government Gazette 153/A/28.6.2002.

[21] For the full text of the Convention, see https://ich.unesco.org/en/convention.

[22] H Deacon and R Smeets, 'Intangible Heritage Safeguarding and Intellectual Property Protection in the Context of Implementing UNESCO ICH Convention' in N Akagawa and L Smith, *Safeguarding Intangible Heritage: Practices and Policies* (Routledge, 2018) 36, 39.

[23] A Korka, *Intangible Cultural Heritage: Comparative Study of Laws* (*Άυλη πολιτιστική κληρονομιά: συγκριτική μελέτη δικαίων*) (Ant, N Sakkoulas, 2020) 112.

[24] Art 2(1) defines work as 'any original intellectual literary, artistic or scientific creation, expressed in any form, notably written or oral texts, musical compositions with or without words, theatrical works accompanied or unaccompanied by music, choreographies and pantomimes, audiovisual works, works of fine art, including drawings, works of painting and sculpture, engravings and lithographs, works of architecture and photographs, works of applied art, illustrations, maps and three-dimensional works relative to geography, topography, architecture or science'.

The law affords protection to adaptations or other alterations of expressions of folklore, but not to folklore and expressions of folklore as such. Indeed, according to Article 2(5), expressions of popular culture are expressly excluded:

> The protection afforded under this Law shall not apply to official texts expressive of the authority of the State, notably to legislative, administrative or judicial texts, nor shall it apply to expressions of folklore, news information or simple facts and data.

Although rich in cultural value and historical significance, Greek traditional music receives protection as a form of intangible cultural heritage but not under copyright law. In this regard, the law ensures that it is a common good, in recognition of its inherent purpose: a music genre that is created by the people and being available to the people to use, re-use and re-invent. In copyright vernacular, it is part of the public domain.

It is for this reason that some narrow interpretations of Article 2 of Law 2121/93 have been unfortunate and resulted in controversy and conflict. In particular, the formulation of Article 2 has proven to be problematic in that it is possible for an adaptation of a traditional song to attract protection, whereas the song as such cannot be subject to copyright. Although this is legally sound, adaptations of traditional music have had the effect of leading to the propertisation of aspects of traditional music which are meant to remain free for all to use by escaping copyright protection. In fact, Article 2(2) has resulted in controversy many times, as owners of protected adaptations have brought forward claims relating to the use of the underlying music as such.

Indicative of this controversy is a judgment of December 2009 by the three-member court of first instance of Kozani, which held that expressions of popular music do not qualify as original copyright works of specific creators, even where an adaptation of a relevant song may have been recorded and published by a particular artist. In this case, a popular Pontian performer was accused of singing a song from the area of Pontos ('αητέντς επαραπέτανεν') in a Pontian centre without the permission of its author (aka the performer who first recorded the adaptation of the song), who allegedly had established rights on the song since 1980. The defendant artist claimed that the song in question is a traditional Pontian song, which has been mentioned in books since the nineteenth century and was recorded on a 45 rpm disc in 1950.[25] Through its lawyer, AEPI, a Greek collecting society, claimed that 'the song may be 200–300 years old, but Ms Lizeta Nikolaou adapted it as an original, since the Pontian people rendered it as a poem, orally, without music and orchestra'. Among the many supporting documents, the defence produced a score of the song, dating back to 1917. The issue took on great proportions and many members of Pontian unions participated to support the artist either morally or by offering evidence. The great response and solidarity lied in the fact that if the judgment had been in favour of AEPI, it would have created case law for further lawsuits to other traditional artists and associations. The performer was acquitted because, according to the court, the expressions of popular tradition cannot be characterised as original intellectual creations of specific creators and be the subject of property rights; these are the creations of anonymous traditional artists and, as such, part of the heritage of all people. The judgment was upheld on appeal by the appellate Court of Thessaloniki.

The judgment does not come as a complete surprise, as the performer in question would perform the traditional song, which is part of the public domain, instead of the copyright-protected adaptation. Adaptations can, and should, attract copyright in their own right[26] to the level that

[25] C Kotzaoglou, 'Reflections on the Protection of traditional Cultural Expressions and Folklore. Gaps in the institutional Framework for the Protection and Recommendations of Cultural Policy' ('Προβληματική γύρω από την προστασία των εκφράσεων λαϊκής παράδοσης και του folklore. Κενά στο θεσμικό πλαίσιο προστασίας και προτάσεις πολιτιστικής πολιτικής') (Aristotelian University of Thessaloniki, 2014) 57.

[26] Court of First Instance of Athens (ΜΠρΑθ), 4348/1998.

there is an original contribution and insofar as they do not involve mere copying or just follow instructions.[27] With regard to derivative musical works, they can be original when the alteration to the pre-existing work is deemed to be statistically unique, taking into consideration various elements such as the orchestration. An example of original adaptation is, for instance, 'Nisiotikos choros' by Nikos Skalkotas, which is based on the traditional song 'Mia Mylopotamitissa' and is integrated within the personal musical idiom of the composer.[28] Another example is 'Kleftikos choros' by the same composer, which encapsulates and reimagines elements of various kleftika songs and develops an iconic musical composition. It would be overarching to accept that copyright protection of the adaptation extends to an underlying song, melody and lyrics, which is part of popular culture and should remain free for the people to use and reuse,[29] especially where the underlying song has been preserved in some recorded form, eg where there is a record of the musical notation. However, expansive interpretations of the scope of protected adaptations – ie as new works that bear proprietary entitlements on the underlying song and not only the original contribution resting in the derivative work – have been put forward by collective licensing organisations, such as AEPI. The latter has reportedly stated, through its director, that 'many of the songs that people deem traditional are not. Remembrance (of a song) alone is not sufficient evidence. When someone performs or adapts a song, then this song is represented. This is often the case with traditional songs.'[30]

Indeed, there have been several cases where expansive interpretations of the legal protection pertaining to an adaptation of traditional music have emerged over the last couple of decades. The main allegation was that there was no payment of the licence fee for public performances of traditional music. Incidentally, all the reported cases were initiated by AEPI, a collective management organisation that ceased to operate in 2018 following an official investigation on its finances by Greece's Organization of Intellectual Property.[31] In some instances, AEPI was sending letters seeking licence fees from performers of traditional songs in live performances within Greece,

[27] G Koumantos, *Intellectual Property* (*Πνευματική Ιδιοκτησία*) (Sakkoulas, 2002) 138; L Kotsiris, *The Law of Intellectual Property* (*Δίκαιο Πνευματικής Ιδιοκτησίας*) (Sakkoulas, 2005) 83–84.

[28] In this regard, see H Vrontos, *About Nikos Skalkotas* (*Για τον Νίκο Σκαλκώτα*) (Ekdoseis Nefeli, 1999) 17 et seq.

[29] An interesting analysis is made by Dimitris Piperidis in his article in T Kotsidis, 'Intellectual Property Rights on Pontian Songs' *iNews* (19 November 2010) www.inewsgr.com/96/pnevmatika-dikaiomata-gia-ta-pontiaka-tragoudia.htm.

[30] See the statement by Giorgos Mizalis, Director of the AEPI records, in G Lialios, 'They Request Intellectual Property Rights from a Collective Group' ('Ζητούν από σύλλογο πνευματικά δικαιώματα') *Kathimerini* (23 October 2015) www.kathimerini.gr/society/835962/zitoyn-apo-syllogo-pneymatika-dikaiomata/.

[31] It should be noted that AEPI used to be an independent collective management organisation, being created in 1930, when music started being sound recorded in Greece. It used to operate on the basis of Art 50 of Law 4481/2017 (for full text, see www.opi.gr/en/library/law-4481-2017). There used to be complaints on its operation and on the excessive zeal it demonstrated towards the collection of licence fees, with the result that the Legal Council of the State ruled that it would be necessary for an authorised civil servant to be present during the imposition of a fine, with a view to certify any violations: 'The Legal Council of the State "Empties" the Fines of AEPI ('Το Νομικό Σύμβούλιο του Κράτους «αδειάζει» τα πρόστιμα της ΑΕΠΙ') *Radiofono* (25 February 2016) www.radiofoNogr/node/25618. As noted by the Greek Ministry of Culture and Sports, due to improper administration and management, it was led 'to a complete financial impasse, with many collected yet non-assigned rights to its beneficiaries–members, with debts to its beneficiaries–members from previous distribution periods, to third parties, to its employees and to the Greek State': Ministry of Culture and Sports, 'Final Withdrawal of AEPI's Operating License', 15 May 2018, www.culture.gov.gr/el/Information/SitePages/view.aspx?nID=2227; Also affirmed by the Misdemeanor Court of Athens, 391/2020. Following an inspection on AEPI's finance from the Organization of Intellectual Property of Greece, AEPI had reportedly not distributed collected levies in the region of €42 million to the relevant authors for the financial period between 2011 and 2014. N Lygerou et al, 'Scandal of a Century in AEPI: "Hole" of 50 Million euros in 4 Years' ('Σκάνδαλο ενός αιώνα στην ΑΕΠΙ: «Τρύπα» 50 εκατ. ευρώ μόνο σε 4 χρόνια') *Proto Thema* (21 February 2017) www.protothema.gr/greece/article/656117/skandalo-enos-aiona-stin-aepi-trupa-50-ekat-euro-mono-se-4-hronia/. AEPI was hence shut down in 2018 and a Special Service for Emergency Rights Management was put in place. See 'The Ministry of Culture Shuts AEPI Down' ('Το υπουργείο Πολιτισμού κλείνει οριστικά την ΑΕΠΙ') *iEfimerida* (15 May 2018).

eg performers of Pontian songs at the Eighth Pampontian Festival on 13 October 2012,[32] or outside Greece, eg the Pontian group The Argonauts in Waiblingen in Germany playing traditional music during the group's parties, via the German collecting society GEMA.[33] In other instances, the collecting society initiated judicial proceedings.[34] The three-member Court of Appeal of Thessaloniki in 2010 also acquitted the President of the Panhellenic Federation of Pontian Associations because the Federation's radio station broadcast Pontian songs without authorisation. After the judgment was issued, the President of the Federation remarked:

> I consider AEPI's claim that the alleged adaptations presented in Pontian songs with a change of some words in the lyrics are an adaptation in the sense of the law … If copyright belongs to some, this should be the Pontian unions and federations.[35]

Although to some this is a comment that aligns with a common sentiment of justice, it should be remarked that a central reason why expressions of popular culture are excluded from copyright protection emerges from the desire to keep this rich heritage free for all to use without restraints emerging from copyright norms. A way to ensure that adaptations of traditional songs can be shared in ways that conform with the cultural heritage objectives underpinning the very existence of traditional music would be to enable the use of such music in events promoting cultural heritage without the need for copyright licences. Indeed, there is a copyright exception available under Article 27(1) of the Greek Copyright Law that permits the public performance or presentation of a work without the consent of the author and without payment when this happens 'at official ceremonies, to the extent compatible with the nature of the ceremonies'. Case law from the Supreme Court of Greece indicates that not-for-profit musical and cultural events that do not result in personal benefit of the host legal entity are included within the meaning of 'official ceremony' according to Article 27.[36] The case in question concerned unauthorised public performances of musical compositions and songs, and making them available to a wider audience, by members of a cultural institution operated by the Municipality of Athens. The relevant works were subject to exclusive protection in Greece by the Hellenic Society for the Protection of Intellectual Property. The Supreme Court's approach towards the meaning of official ceremonies in Article 27 to include events held by cultural institutions is a positive development. Indeed, such an interpretation, which takes into consideration broader cultural heritage objectives, could empower cultural institutions and community groups to make culture accessible and could also encourage the spur of new creativity – given that this has traditionally been the generative force underpinning popular culture. It can enable expressive diversity and uninterrupted creative processes that align with the very nature of traditional creativity and can also incentivise

[32] Full text of letter: 'AEPI is asking Pontian performers to apologise' ('Η ΑΕΠΙ καλεί σε απολογία τους τραγουδιστές του Πόντου!') http://aepi-free.blogspot.com/2012/11/blog-post.html.

[33] G Lialios, 'They Request Intellectual Property Rights from a Collective Group' ('Ζητούν από σύλλογο πνευματικά δικαιώματα') *Kathimerini* (23 October 2015) www.kathimerini.gr/society/835962/zitoyn-apo-syllogo-pneymatika-dikaiomata/.

[34] One such case was brought against the Club of Friends of Music 'Arion', which was, however, acquitted by a court in Edessa for refusing to pay a licence fee to AEPI during the Estudiana music concert in Aridea. 'AEPI Lost Trial on Intellectual Property of Traditional Songs' ('«Έχασε» η ΑΕΠΙ δίκη για τα πνευματικά δικαιώματα παραδοσιακών τραγουδιών') *Radiofono* (15 October 2010) www.radiofoNogr/node/2355 (in Greek).

[35] Eleftherotypia, 13 October 2010, republished in: 'What Happened at the Courts when IP Sought Intellectual Property Rights on Traditional Songs?' ('Τι συνέβη στα δικαστήρια όταν η ΑΕΠΙ ζήτησε πνευματικά δικαιώματα για παραδοσιακά τραγούδια') *AthensMagazine* (27 January 2014) www.athensmagazine.gr/article/news/77064-ti-synebh-sta-diaksthria-otan-h-aepi-zhthse-pneymatika-dikaiwmata-gia-paradosiaka-tragoydia.

[36] Supreme Court (ΑΠ), 1525/2008.

contemporary artists to continue engaging creatively with cultural heritage both within and outside Greece, as international cultural exchange initiatives indicate.[37]

V. Conclusion

Traditional music in Greece is a code of expression and communication, a symbol of identity and a vessel of collective memory, dating back to the Byzantine years and antiquity. Creative processes in this music genre are authentic in that authorship tends to be collective and originality is built based on appropriation and borrowing. Greek traditional songs are hence the result of various historical layers and unknown individual contributions. Originality is developed through appropriation and creative transformation of existing musical elements. Traditional music in Greece receives protection as intangible cultural heritage under the law on the protection of antiquities and cultural heritage, yet it is excluded from copyright protection, together with all expressions of popular culture. Being outside of copyright, traditional music – a genre that was developed by the people of Greece over the course of centuries – is free to enjoy without the need to clear copyright. It is a common good. Contemporary artists can receive copyright over adaptations of traditional music, to the level that these are deemed to be original. The formulation of copyright law and the interpretations it has received by copyright owners and collecting societies in Greece has resulted in controversy, however. There have been claims that an adaptation of traditional music can put a hold on live performances of the underlying song unless a licence is cleared. It is submitted that adaptations ought to receive protection over the original elements that their author has contributed but they should not result in proprietary entitlements of the underpinning traditional song that are preserved in written records. In addition, the copyright exception allowing public performance of works in official ceremonies could be understood to include events held by cultural institutions, as has been affirmed by the Supreme Court of Greece. This can result in expressive diversity and uninterrupted creative processes that align with the very nature of traditional creativity. It can incentivise contemporary artists to continue engaging creatively with cultural heritage and even expand the international breadth of Greek traditional music.

[37] The international breadth of Greek traditional music can be demonstrated in works such as those of the Japanese music band Pyramidos, which regularly adapts traditional Greek songs.

Section D: Africa and Middle East

22

Israeli Music Genres: Appropriation and Borrowing as a Tool for National and Cultural Emergence and Structuring

OMRI RACHUM-TWAIG*

I. Introduction

This chapter will discuss the development of certain Israeli music genres during the formative years of the State of Israel (late 1940s until 1980s) and the effects of appropriation and borrowing on their emergence and design. To that end, I will attempt to portray the relevant background to the development of these musical genres, including both the national and cultural emergence of Israel and the legal norms existing at the time. I will argue that a combination of a rather relaxed copyright regime at the time, a strong demand for agile cultural development and the fact that Israel was, at its outset, largely an import country with a comparably small market allowed for appropriation and borrowing to be a significant tool in its folk and pop musical development. I will first discuss the background of the establishment of Israel, from both national and cultural perspectives. Then, I will discuss the legal background and the applicable copyright regime at the time. Next, I will focus on three main folk/pop musical genres developed in Israel largely based on borrowing and appropriation, and will finally suggest the key factors that supported such development.

A. The Establishment of Israel: A National and Cultural Emergence

Today, Israel is commonly referred to as the start-up nation, mainly due to the very high ratio of start-up companies per capita.[1] But Israel was a 'start-up' nation long before the technological context of the term emerged. Israel was established in 1948, ending the British mandate over the land of Palestine, after decades of promoting the new Israeli nationalism through the Zionist movement and from the shadows of World War II and the atrocities of the Holocaust. Alongside the national emergence that was the main catalyst of the establishment of Israel, a cultural and social emergence was required. In this sense, the establishment of Israel was a start-up enterprise – it required the agile and very quick establishment of cultural and social anchors between Jewish

* I wish to thank my friend and colleague Asaf Wiener for his invaluable comments on earlier drafts of this chapter.

[1] D Senor and S Singer, *Start-Up Nation: The Story of Israel's Economic Miracle* (Grand Central Publishing, 2009).

population coming from the entire diaspora, ranging from Arab countries such as Iran, Iraq, Syria and Egypt, through the Maghreb countries of North Africa to Eastern, Central and Western European countries, as of the very first years of the new state. This was obviously a material social challenge, since even though the strong nationalistic atmosphere among many Jews around the globe was a unifying force, the day-to-day living in the new and undeveloped State of Israel required a bigger social effort to reconcile.

In this context, the new enterprise of the State of Israel required cultural agility as well. Given that every ethnic group of Jews immigrating to the new state had its own original cultural grounds, a new, collective, Israeli culture was much needed. And while there were various cultural endeavours among Jewish residents of Palestine prior to the establishment of Israel, these were not necessarily known to the newcomers of the various waves of immigration in the early years of the state and could not serve as a central pillar for this cultural enterprise. As I will argue in this chapter, one main solution for the demand for agile development of a common Israeli culture in the field of music was based on appropriation[2] and borrowing, starting from the very early days of Israel with the development of Israeli folk music (Shirei Eretz Israel), borrowing mainly from Eastern European and Russian folk songs; and through later developments of genres such as Mediterranean/Eastern music (borrowing from Greek, Turkish and Arab music) and even contemporary pop music (borrowing from its global counterparts). This appropriation and borrowing relied largely on the folk culture of the origins of certain ethnic groups immigrating to Israel, most likely because these were readily available for certain authors and immediately accepted within big enough social groups.

B. Israeli Copyright Law

Much like other aspects of its establishment, Israel's legal regime was largely borrowed from the preceding British and even Ottoman legal regimes prevailing over the land of Israel. In 1948, Israel adopted the Governance and Law Arrangements Ordinance, 1948, under which, according to section 11, all laws existing in the land of Israel prior to 15 May 1948 would remain in force unless otherwise explicitly stated. One of these laws, the Copyright Law of 1911 (hereinafter the Old Copyright Law), which was a replica of the British Copyright Act 1911, remained in force in Israel until its replacement by the current Israeli Copyright Law of 2007.[3]

The Old Copyright Law provided for various accounts of modern copyright law, such as the types of protected works, the scope of protection, the originality requirement (which was not explicitly stated but stemmed from the original English version of the law) and certain provisions for permitted uses. For current purposes, it is sufficient to say that the Old Copyright Law protected musical works (both lyrics and composition). However, the Old Copyright Law provided for a rather limited scope of protection compared to modern formulations. In fact, section 1(2) of the Old Copyright Law provided that the exclusive bundle of rights for a copyright

[2] It should be noted that I use the term 'appropriation' in a very specific context. I do not necessarily refer to appropriation in the negative context commonly attributed to the term in property law or in cultural disputes, rather simply to denote that certain cultural aspects were taken from a culture external to Israel, sometime by individuals originating in that culture, and infused into the Israeli culture. It is also important to note that I do not assume that each and every appropriation and borrowing is conscious or intended. It may well be that some are simply a by-product of an unconscious creative process. See O Rachum-Twaig, 'Recreating Copyright: The Cognitive Process of Creation and Copyright Law' (2017) 27 *Fordham Intellectual Property, Media & Entertainment Law Journal* 287.

[3] For an impressive discussion of the copyright regime during the British mandate over Palestine, see MD Birnhack, *Colonial Copyright: Intellectual Property in Mandate Palestine* (Oxford University Press, 2012).

holder were to stage, publicly perform or reproduce the work or any substantial part thereof. While the Old Copyright Law did not explicitly provide for an adaptation or derivative work right to the copyright holder, it did explicitly determine that transforming a dramatic work to a non-dramatic work, and vice versa, as well as translating a work, would constitute copyright infringement.

The lack of a stand-alone adaptation right left the reproduction right as the focal point for discussing borrowing and appropriation used for the creation of new original works.[4] In fact, this would have required an argument according to which the new original work infringes the previous work borrowed from due to the existence of a substantially similar portion from the previous work in the new work, thus constituting infringement of the reproduction right.

As a final relevant note, the State of Israel implemented the Berne Convention effective as of 24 March 1950 by the Copyright Order (Berne Convention), 1953, thus granting the protections of the Old Copyright Law to foreign works created in member states or by authors who are nationals of members states of the Berne Convention.

With this background in mind, I will proceed to portray the development of three main Israeli music genres, which, to a certain extent, relied on appropriation and borrowing.

II. Appropriation and Borrowing in Milestone Israeli Music Genres

With the background discussion in mind, I will now review several Israeli music genres and analyse the effects of appropriation and borrowing thereon. I have chosen three distinct genres for discussion, which are both distinct chronologically and similar in their importance and impact on the musical development of the Israeli culture. I will first discuss the genre of Shirei Eretz Israel (SLI), which is attributed to the folk-like music widely performed and acknowledged in the few decades preceding and following the establishment of Israel, what may be described as the first Israeli music genre. I will then turn to discuss another significant music genre, which began its development in the 1960s and gained popularity and importance in the following decades (and even today), both in its popular acceptance and in its social and cultural effects on marginalised ethnic groups in developing Israel – the Eastern/Mediterranean music genre. Finally, I will discuss contemporary Israeli pop music as an independently developed rather than simply imported genre, reflecting the developed status of Israel as a country and the globalised nature of its economy and culture.

A. Israeli 'Folk' Music (Shirei Eretz Israel)

As previously discussed, the establishment of Israel – as a sovereign county and as a cultural nation – was an agile enterprise in all aspects. It thus also required agile development of common 'national cultural goods', which was not necessarily an organic process.[5] Shirei Eretz Israel, loosely translated as 'songs of the land of Israel', or SLI, is the common term for the music genre meeting

[4] For a discussion on the interrelations between the reproduction and derivative works rights, see O Rachum-Twaig, *Copyright Law and Derivative Works: Regulating Creativity* (Routledge, 2019) 131–45.

[5] Some have referred to this genre as an 'invented tradition'. See J Hirshberg, *Music in the Jewish Community of Palestine* (Oxford University Press, 1995) ch 9.

such need. Many scholars and art critics have struggled over the years to define what SLI actually are, but there seems to be a consensus that this genre refers to songs composed, performed and accepted in the land of Israel prior to the establishment of the State of Israel and in the few decades thereafter, the main purpose of which was to create a common national culture for establishing Israel.[6]

For current purposes, it is important to note that many contemporary definitions focused on the appropriative nature of this genre. Motti Regev, for example, characterised the genre as originating in 'Russian ballads and East-European rhythms brought to Israel by the founders of Israeli society in the first half of this century' and whose lyrics 'generally deal with national themes and agricultural topics'.[7] Motti Regen and Edwin Seroussi characterised the classic age of SLI as consisting of 'folk songs from the first and second aliyot (1880–1917), many of which were adaptations of Diaspora songs or Hebrew texts set to Russian melodies, and, more rarely, Arabic tunes'.[8] This is not surprising. Given that the population in the establishing State of Israel were of different ethnical origins,[9] without common cultural ground but with a strong need to establish unique national cultural elements, using 'shortcuts' to produce such new culture was almost inevitable. From a musical perspective, such shortcuts were readily available in folk songs of various origins imported to Israel by the respective immigrant communities.

In fact, borrowing and appropriation was so well grounded in the musical development of this genre and time that two monumental songs in the young Israeli heritage – the formal national anthem 'HaTikvah' and the informal national song 'Jerusalem of Gold' – both heavily appropriated folk songs of other origins.

'HaTikvah' is based on a poem with a similar name originally written by Naphtali Herz Imber in 1877–78 and later first published in Jerusalem in 1884 under the title 'Tikvatenu'.[10] The melody was set to the text by Samuel Cohen, most likely in 1887, and was based on, as the composer personally attested, a Moldavian–Romanian 'folk' song titled 'Carul cu Boi'. In fact, 'Carul cu Boi' was not an old song; rather, it was more or less contemporary at the time.[11] The melody of both 'Hatikvah' and 'Carul cu Boi' reappears in other works of the same era, the most famous of which is Bedřich Smetana's 'Vltava' ('The Moldau') in his work *Má Vlast*, dated 1874–79.[12] 'Jerusalem of Gold' is a song written and composed in 1967 by Neomi Shemer, one of the most prominent songwriters of early Israeli music and a significant figure in the genre of SLI. The song was commissioned by Teddy Kolek, the mayor of Jerusalem, for the May 1967 Israeli Song Festival, and shortly thereafter, due to the uniting of the city of Jerusalem in the Six-Day War, was celebrated by Israelis from various perspectives. In fact, 'Jerusalem of Gold' was so popular and widely accepted in Israeli culture of the time that some referred to it as the unofficial anthem of Israel.[13] For current purposes, it is noteworthy that, as later acknowledged by Shemer herself, the

[6] See M Regev and E Seroussi, *Popular Music and National Culture in Israel* (University of California Press, 2004) 52–55.

[7] M Regev, 'The Field of Popular Music in Israel' in S Firth (ed), *World Music, Politics and Social Change* (1989) 145–55.

[8] Regev and Seroussi (n 6) 9.

[9] It should be noted that the population in Israel, immediately upon its incorporation in 1948, was much more homogeneous than discussed here, and it was only in the year 1950 that significant waves of immigration from Arab and north African countries arrived in the very young Israel. However, even among the relatively homogeneous Jewish population arriving from Europe and Russia, cultural differences were still apparent.

[10] E Seroussi, 'Hatikvah: Conceptions, Receptions and Reflections' (2015) 9 *Yuval* 2, 2–3.

[11] ibid 10–11. For a recording of 'Carul cu Boi', see www.youtube.com/watch?v=adTjy-TIW_Q. It should be noted that, at least from a cultural standpoint, if Herz Imber were himself exposed to the folk tunes underlying 'Carul cu Boi', this should be probably not be seen as an appropriation with a negative normative connotation.

[12] ibid 25. For a recording of Smetana's 'Vltava' in *Má Vlast*, see www.youtube.com/watch?v=3G4NKzmfC-Q.

[13] D Gavrieli-Nuri, 'The Social Construction of 'Jerusalem of Gold' as Israel's Unofficial National Anthem' (2007) 12(2) *Israel Studies* 104.

melody of the song was borrowed from a Basque folk song.[14] While the foregoing is not a full account of the musicological characteristics of the genre of SLI, it is clear that appropriation and borrowing were a quintessential part of the development of the genre and landmark exemplars thereof. The function of the appropriation and borrowing here is likely to be understood in the context of the need for an agile development of a new national culture in the establishing State of Israel. I will later discuss the factors that, I suggest, allowed for such appropriation and borrowing in this specific genre.

B. Mediterranean/Eastern Music

Musica Mizrahit, loosely translated as 'eastern music', is a prominent Israeli pop/folk music genre established in the 1970s as a cultural voice of Israeli Jews of Arab descent (eg Morocco, Yemen, Egypt), as an alternative to the prevailing genres of SLI and Israeli rock, which were associated with Ashkenazi middle/upper-class Jews.[15] It is characterised by Arab/Mediterranean melodies and rhythms incorporated into Westernised forms of pop/folk songs and, not surprisingly, was first created and acknowledged by lower-class Jewish immigrants of Arab/Mediterranean descent. Musica Mizrahit was not acknowledged as a respectable musical genre by prevailing musical institutions until the mid-1980s, and was often perceived as inferior due to its foreign origins and its method of transmission, which focused on karaoke, weddings and other non- or semi-professional performances.[16]

Musica Mizrahit obtained its cultural status from the 1990s onwards, to become a widely accepted Israeli pop genre, both by important musical institutions and also by the public, including those of the Mizrahi Jewish population, who were often ashamed to acknowledge that they listened to such genre, producing a sequence of star singers such as Zohar Argov, Ofra Haza and later, through the early 2000s, Sarit Hadad, Eyal Golan and Omer Adam. This development of the genre of Musica Mizrahit attracted much scholarly attention due not only to its cultural effects, but also to its sociological effects, reflecting much of the sociological turmoil of developing/developed Israel in the respective years, mainly in the context of the tension between Mizrahi and Ashkenazi Jewish Israelis.[17] Indeed, the development of the genre, and mainly its popular acceptance, were not without a struggle, and to a great extent were part of what is referred to as the Mizrahi revolution.

In the context of this discussion, it is noteworthy that Musica Mizrahit – like SLI – was also characterised as having a high degree of borrowing and appropriation. For example, one of the reasons it was first rejected by institutionalised music in Israel was because this genre was perceived as a 'low culture' consisting of 'predictability through the use of musical cliches and outright copying … in contrast to most types of Western popular music which emphasise originality'.[18] While the latter part of the foregoing conclusion is highly debatable, it seems widely

[14] ibid 105; T Segev, 'Naomi Shemer Lifted "Jerusalem of Gold" Melody from Basque Folk Song' *HaAretz* (5 May 2005) www.haaretz.com/1.4853519. Shemer herself explained that she may have heard the underlying Basque lullaby years before.

[15] Regev and Seroussi (n 6) 1.

[16] ibid 191–92. Regev and Seroussi mention that this genre was also referred to as 'cassette music' because it was mainly distributed on cheaply copied tape cassettes sold from open stands in the central bus station of Tel Aviv.

[17] For elaboration on the development of Musica Mizrahit and its sociological role, see ibid ch 10; J Halper, E Seroussi and P Squires-Kidron, 'Musica Mizrakhit: Ethnicity and Class Culture in Israel' (1989) 8(2) *Popular Music* 131.

[18] ibid 140.

accepted that Musica Mizrahit was indeed characterised by certain amounts of musical borrowings. For example, Edwin Seroussi explained that:

> In its initial stages musiqa mizrahit was not specifically Israeli, but mainly Israeli covers of imported Greek, Arabic or Turkish popular music adapted from records, cassettes or radio performances and 'made' Israeli by substituting Hebrew lyrics for the original ones. Prominent among these imported musical styles were the songs performed by Greek singers who appeared or established themselves in Israel, such as Aris San, or mellow Mediterranean ballads in the style of the Sanremo festival in Italy.[19]

Indeed, cases of alleged appropriation of songs in the genre of Musica Mizrahit were occasionally brought up in the mass media.[20] The nature and function of appropriation and borrowing in Musica Mizrahit are quite different from those suggested with respect to SLI, as I will discuss further later in this chapter. For now, it is sufficient to mention that such appropriation and borrowing have a dual function both in the realm of genres and cultural development, but also in the realm of sociology and social status in the corresponding era in the development of the Israeli society.

C. Contemporary Pop Music

The last genre to be discussed here is the genre of contemporary Israeli pop music, which is, to a certain extent, a direct continuance of previous contemporary music genres in Israel, such as Israeli rock and even SLI.

There is no significant musicological literature on today's contemporary pop music in Israel. Therefore, much of the description in this section will be based on my personal knowledge, media coverage and some inferences from the musicological literature on the ancestral genre of Israeli popular rock music that prevailed from the 1980s to the 1990s. Israeli rock was characterised by musicologists as an effort to rebel and create an alternative to the then prevailing SLI using methods and aesthetics from the Anglo-American rock genre, while infusing it with Israeli culture together with 'Israeliness'.[21] I argue that the Israeli contemporary pop genre, traceable to the late 1990s and mainly during the first two decades of the 2000s, is characterised by the exact opposite.

The recent decades in Israeli culture and society are characterised by a significant globalisation effort. Israeli start-up companies aim to sell their products, and later the entire enterprise, to the global marketplace and mainly the USA. The Israeli film and television industry is thriving

[19] E Seroussi, '"Mediterraneanism" in Israeli Music: An Idea and Its Permutations' (2002) 7 *Music & Anthropology*. For a performance of a prominent song of San – 'Boom Pam' – see www.youtube.com/watch?v=zpMqxP7PX8c.

[20] Zohar Argov's famous 'Elinor' was allegedly composed based on Stelios Kazantzidis's 'Ypárcho'. See A Friedman, 'From "Elinor" to "King of the World": Israeli Songs that Made Alyiah' *Ynet* (28 January 2017) www.ynet.co.il/articles/0,7340,L-4909262,00.html (in Hebrew). For Argov's 'Elinor', see www.youtube.com/watch?v=R1yPjpKJmso. For Kazantzidis's 'Ypárcho', see www.youtube.com/watch?v=bU_3yoFrmw0. Egyptian singer Amro Mustafa alleged that Lior Narkis appropriated one of his songs in 'Giving You Years'. See R Nahmias and A Yagil, 'Egyptian Star: "Israeli Steal Our Songs"' *Ynet* (28 December 2010) www.ynet.co.il/articles/0,7340,L-4005733,00.html (Hebrew). Eyal Golan was accused of appropriating from Lebanese singer Wael Kfoury in his 'Shadows of Her Figure'. See 'Judge on Your Own: Eyal Golan Copied a Song from a Lebanese Singer?' (*Channel 2 News*, 12 February 2014) www.mako.co.il/news-israel/entertainment/Art-845d1394b072441004.htm (in Hebrew). Dudu Aharon allegedly copied from a Greek composer, Pantazis Konstantinos, in his hit song 'Tell Her'. See L Penn and J Khouri, 'Composers: Dudu Aharon and Saranga Stole from Our Songs' *Haaretz* (10 November 2010) www.haaretz.co.il/gallery/1.3297511 (in Hebrew).

[21] M Regev, 'To Have a Culture of Our Own: On Israeliness and Its Variants' (2000) 23 *Ethnic and Racial Studies* 223, 233–34; M Regev, 'Musica Mizrakhit, Israeli Rock and National Culture in Israel' (1996) 15 *Popular Music* 275, 279–80; Regev and Seroussi (n 6) 8.

mainly based on success stories of script deals with and remakes of local programmes by leading global studios and streaming services.[22] Likewise, Israeli pop music is aiming for global recognition, and local songwriters and performers look to extend their success abroad. In fact, whereas Israeli rock was characterised by importing global features of the genre fused with Israeliness, contemporary pop looks to export local music to the global market despite its Israeliness. Local versions of leading television-based song contests offer the winners recording deals with global labels or representation of Israel in the Eurovision contest. Israeli pop stars often leave Israel (mainly for the USA and the UK) in an attempt to gain global recognition.[23] It is noticeable that contemporary Israeli pop relies strongly on styles, harmonic sequences and, often, actual melodies from hit songs in global markets such as those of the USA or the UK. Popular singers and producers attempt to assimilate the prevailing global style, and whereas prior appropriations attempted to distinguish the local works from their foreign counterparts by including lyrics with local or national connotation, contemporary authors commonly attempt to mimic global style both in music and lyrics for the purpose of creating a locally produced 'international' experience.[24] It is thus not surprising that appropriation and borrowing are witnessed in the formation of contemporary pop in Israel. In some cases, the appropriation is subtle and not overly distinct, for example by borrowing certain bass lines, limited melodies, short harmony sequences or unique rhythm.[25] In other cases, appropriation in contemporary Israeli pop is more conspicuous, and is even the subject of legal disputes. For example, Neta Barzilay's hit 'Toy', which won the Eurovision contest in 2019, allegedly copied a whole bass line from the White Stripes' 'Seven Nation Army', leading to a lawsuit filed by the latter.[26] As I will later suggest, the function of appropriation and borrowing in the Israeli contemporary pop genre is quite different from those of the previous genres discussed. Given the different market for this genre and other factors

[22] See, eg G Gilbert, 'Prisoners of War: The Israeli Inspiration for Homeland' *The Independent* (8 May 2012) www.independent.co.uk/arts-entertainment/tv/features/prisoners-war-israeli-inspiration-homeland-7720560.html (discussing the remake leading to famous TV series Homeland); A Hennigan, 'The Decade Israeli TV Captured the World's Imagination. Will It Last' *Haaretz* (25 December 2019) www.haaretz.com/israel-news/2010-2019-decade-in-review/.premium.MAGAZINE-the-decade-israeli-tv-captured-the-world-s-imagination-1.8317364; J Steinberg, 'Uma Thurman Will Star in Remake of Israeli Drama "False Flag"' *The Times of Israel* (12 March 2020) www.timesofisrael.com/uma-thurman-will-star-in-remake-of-israeli-drama-false-flag; M Saval, 'Holy Land Meets Hollywood with "When Heroes Fly", "Shtisel" Stars on the Rise' *Variety* (10 June 2019) https://variety.com/2019/tv/features/holy-land-meets-hollywood-with-when-heroes-fly-shtisel-stars-on-the-rise-1203235299.

[23] See, eg B Shalev, 'Ninet: No Longer Israel's Musical Sweetheart' *Haaretz* (22 March 2017) www.haaretz.com/israel-news/culture/.premium-ninet-no-longer-israel-s-musical-sweetheart-1.5452146; S Halperin, 'Israeli Singer Asaf Avidan on His Accidental Hit: 'Reckoning Song' Remix 'Changed Everything' (Q&A)' *The Holywood Reporter* (24 January 2014) www.hollywoodreporter.com/news/general-news/israeli-singer-asaf-avidan-his-673660; J Pareles, 'Asaf Avidan, Folk-Rock and Pithy Poetry' *The New York Magazine* (6 May 2016) www.nytimes.com/2016/04/10/arts/music/asaf-avidan-folk-rock-and-pithy-poetry.html; S Halperin, 'Israeli Pop Star Noa Kirel Sets Her Sights on the US with Sassy English Single, "Please Don't Suck"' *Variety* (14 July 2021) https://variety.com/2021/music/news/noa-kirel-please-dont-suck-israeli-pop-star-interview-english-1235019434; TOI Staff, 'Pop Duo Static & Ben El Sign with Major US Record Label' *Time of Israel* (14 March 2018) www.timesofisrael.com/pop-duo-static-ben-el-sign-with-major-us-record-label; S Ghermezian, 'Israeli Singer Noga Erez Makes US TV Debut Performing on "Jimmy Kimmel Live"' *The Algemeiner* (13 April 2021) www.algemeiner.com/2021/04/13/israeli-singer-noga-erez-makes-us-tv-debut-performing-on-jimmy-kimmel-live.

[24] This is also evident in the marketing efforts of local singers and artists. Previous Eurovision contest winner, Dana International, added 'International' to her stage name for a reason. This was also the case with pop singer Roni Duani, who broke through in the early 2000s under the stage name 'Roni Superstar'. In today's pop scene, star performers such as Noa Kirel (sometimes going by the stage name 'Noa Killer') and Static & Ben-El include international and global terms and identifiers in their stage names, performances and lyrics.

[25] See B Shalev, 'What Stands Behind the Storm of Israeli Hits Which Are Too Similar to Famous Foreign Songs' *Haaretz* (30 May 2019), www.haaretz.co.il/gallery/music/selective-hearing/1.7303114 (Hebrew).

[26] According to media coverage, the lawsuit was settled with Barzilay agreeing to share half of Toy's royalties with the White Stripes. See A Marshall, 'Jack White Wins Wurovision. Kind Of' *New York Times* (7 February 2019) www.nytimes.com/2019/02/07/arts/music/jack-white-eurovision-toy-netta.html.

to be discussed, it should not be a surprise that such appropriation and borrowing have led to legal scrutiny and even disputes.

I will now turn to discuss the various factors that I consider facilitate and allow for such appropriation and borrowing, from legal, cultural and market perspectives.

III. How Was This (Legally) Possible?

In this section, I will dive more deeply into the underlying factors facilitating and explaining why and to what extent appropriation and borrowing are a dominant part of the development of the Israeli music genres discussed above. As I will suggest, the legal copyright framework in Israel over the years has been one supporting factor, but it alone cannot explain the entire phenomenon. I argue that, together with relaxed legal concepts, the need for national cultural assets resulted in cultural anchoring achieved by certain appropriation and borrowing in music genres, supported by the market status of Israel at the time, it being a small, remote and import-based market. I will begin by portraying a general framework to discuss the role of copyright in the development of genres, will then discuss the actual copyright law framework prevailing in Israel and will finally discuss the external cultural and market factors and their effect on appropriation and borrowing.

A. A Genre Theory of Copyright

I have argued elsewhere that one could learn about the normative bases of copyright law and its compatibility with the creative world from certain conclusions of the scholarship of genre theory. In what I framed as the 'genre theory of copyright', I suggested that genre theory, despite the diverse approaches in the literature, recognises a central pillar at the core of how genres are generated and develop – common building blocks.[27] Common building blocks have two distinct, but equally important, functions in the creation and development of genres.

The first function is as a working tool to enable authors to create within and engage with existing genres. This is identified throughout an array of different theoretical approached to genres. Alastair Fowler, for example, argued that a proper understanding of genre identifies it as a tool that facilitates creative expression, and that the relationship between texts and their genres is not one of passive participation but rather one of active change.[28] He also explained that certain authors need rules and conventions to create, while others need a framework for creativity and a reminder to evaluate their work in light of these rules.[29] Tzvetan Todorov also expressed this dynamic approach to genre, which emphasises the significance of common building blocks as a constitutive tool that facilitates creativity and the development of genres. One of his most important arguments in this context was his answer to where genres come from. Todorov answered: 'Quite simply from other genres. A new genre is always the transformation of an earlier one, or of several: by inversion, by displacement, by combination.'[30] Another commentator who focused on the constitutive aspect of the common building blocks is David Fishelov. Fishelov suggested

[27] O Rachum-Twaig, 'A Genre Theory of Copyright' (2016) 33 *Santa Clara High Technical Law Journal* 1, 31–45. See also Rachum-Twaig, at *Copyright Law and Derivative Works* (n 4) 731.

[28] A Fowler, *Kinds of Literature* (Oxford University Press, 1982) 20.

[29] ibid 28.

[30] T Todorov, *Genres in Discourse* (C Porter trans, Cambridge University Press, 1990) 15.

that genre is a set of rules that are enabling in their nature more than they are regulatory or restraining, in the sense that they do not refer to a pre-existing action but enable a new one.[31] To demonstrate how this approach to genre takes place, he reviewed different metaphors for genre used in literature. One important metaphor that I discussed elsewhere is the biological species metaphor.[32] Fishelov offered a Darwinian evolutionary approach to genre, according to which organisms are analogous to texts, biological species are metaphors for genres and the natural environment is a metaphor for the 'cultural environment'. He also stressed that the evolutionary survival of a genre depends not on the continuity of a 'correct' interpretation of it, but on its continuous productivity.

Generic productivity, according to Fishelov, is divided into two stages: the primary stage and the secondary stage. The primary stage of productivity happens when works that constitute a genre influence and encourage the creation of new works that are perceived as part of the same genre by both authors and readers. The secondary stage happens when new texts are produced considering a generic formula. Fishelov gave examples of secondary productivity, including translation, parody, imitation (preserving the form but changing the content) and adaptation (preserving the content but changing the form or the medium).[33]

The second function of common building blocks discussed in genre literature is as a meaning-making tool. The common building blocks have a significant impact on another part of the creative field – the audience. They affect the way the audience gives meaning to works of authorship.

Todorov argued that the historical existence of genre has two sides. The first side is the author who creates texts as a function of the existing generic system (even if not in accordance with it). The second side is the reader who understands texts as a function of the same generic system, even if sometimes unconsciously.[34] Similarly, John Frow argued that genres do not function only as a classificatory mechanism; instead, they mainly function as representative frameworks that play a crucial part in the everyday meaning-making process.[35] Fowler explained the common building blocks' contribution to the meaning-making of artistic texts through a comparison to communication theory. According to him, non-artistic interpersonal communication preserves messages in a manner that allows their reception and understanding, even though the redundancy of information they contain causes uncertainty. This occurs through the situational context in which the communication occurs. Fowler argued that artistic texts have no real situational context, and they should therefore carry a substitute that will allow the same meaning-making process.[36] Fowler added that the artistic coding 'validates' the work itself and the message it contains, in the sense that credibility and the possibility to enjoy are communicative expressions. Thus, a reader's attention is more easily captured by conventional and known properties of texts (generic characters, for example), and every convention used by the author influences the

[31] D Fishelov, *Metaphors of Genre* (Penn State University Press, 1993) 14.

[32] ibid 18.

[33] ibid 35–39. It is important to note that the derivative work right in copyright law is often referred to as the 'adaptation' right. Despite the resemblance between adaptation in Fishelov's terms and the right to make derivative works, there is no full overlap between the two. Maintaining the content of a text while changing its medium or form is just one type of action that could result in a derivative work. Aside from that, a derivative work could be made by what Fishelov defined as 'imitation', which means maintaining the form while changing the content.

[34] Todorov (n 30) 18–19.

[35] J Frow, *Genre* (2006) 19. For another modern approach to genre that views it more as a 'source of meaning' than a 'set of rules', see S Wang, 'Text Types and Dynamism of Genres' in J Renkema (ed), *Discourse, of Course: An Overview of Research in Discourse Studies* (2009) 81, 83; J Swales, 'On Models of Applied Discourse Analysis' in CN Candlin (ed), *Research and Practice in Professional Discourse* (2002) 61.

[36] Fowler (n 28) 46.

meaning of text. This description led Fowler to state that the most important code in the artistic *langue* is genre and that it is used as a meaning-making tool: 'It is an instrument not of classification or prescription, but of meaning.'[37] This approach holds that genre is a heuristic tool that serves the reader-interpreter or, as Adena Rosmarin put it:

> The genre is the critic's heuristic tool, his chosen or defined way of persuading his audience to see the literary text in all its previously inexplicable and 'literary' fullness and then to relate this text to those that are similar or, more precisely, to those that may be similarly explained.[38]

With the dual function of building blocks in the development of genres in mind, I argue that this could be used to reflect on existing copyright law doctrines and their consistency with genre theory's understanding of how realms of works of authorship are established. To be clear, while genre theories generally focus on literary works as their subject matter, the concepts discussed above apply equally to other works as well. As Frow stated in the beginning of his book titled *Genre*, genre theory deals with

> kinds or genres of speech, writing, images, and organised sound: forms of talk and writing, of drawing and painting and sculpting, of architecture, of music, and mixed forms like film, television, opera, and drama. It is a book about how genres organise verbal and non-verbal discourse, together with the actions that accompany them, and how they contribute to the social structuring of meaning.[39]

Moreover, the spectrum of possible kinds of common building blocks is relatively wide. It begins with high levels of abstraction, such as artistic styles, general themes, conceptual structure of works (such as verse/chorus, rondo, etc) and what is referred to in the copyright discourse as 'ideas'. Additionally, common building blocks may be found in much lower and more particular levels of abstraction. Thus, a certain text (or melody, character, painting, etc) may constitute a building block for the development of other text in the same creative environment. In the musical context, these could be certain rhythmic patterns, harmonic sequences, modulations, melody 'hooks' and other, more particular, segments of a work which copyright law commonly refers to as 'expressions'. I further argued that copyright law is aware, even if intuitively, of the common building blocks' importance to the creative world, and copyright law reflects their importance to a great extent. It does so in two main doctrines: the idea/expression dichotomy (and the *scènes à faire* doctrine that derives from it) and the fair use doctrine.

At the heart of copyright law stands a basic principle: the idea that a work of authorship is based on is not protected by copyright; such protection is provided only to the author's expression of the idea – the original expression only.[40] Courts and authors employ this distinction to determine whether a certain work or parts thereof are copyrightable and whether their use by another is infringing the author's rights.[41] In fact, the idea–expression dichotomy is based on the notion that prohibiting the free use of ideas will impede two of the main goals of copyright law: the encouragement of creativity and the preservation of an adequate public domain.[42] The *scènes à*

[37] ibid.

[38] A Rosmarin, *The Power of Genre* (University of Minnesota Press, 1986) 25.

[39] Frow (n 35) 1.

[40] See 17 USC § 102(b) ('In no case does copyright protection for an original work of authorship extend to any idea, procedure, process, system, method of operation, concept, principle, or discovery, regardless of the form in which it is described, explained, illustrated, or embodied in such work').

[41] See, eg *Whelan Assocs, Inc v Jaslow Dental Lab, Inc* 797 F.2d 1222, 1234 (3d Cir 1986); *Dunlap v G&L Holding Group, Inc* 381 F.3d 1285, 1296 (11th Cir 2004).

[42] Nimmer explained that this principle is based, among other things, on the constitutional right to freedom of speech and that this doctrine affects preliminary copyright protection very little; it is mainly used in infringement actions, particularly for determining whether a disputed use is substantial enough to constitute infringement. See MB Nimmer and D Nimmer, *Nimmer on Copyright* (2014 edn) vol 1, § 2.03[D].

faire doctrine, which derives partially from the idea–expression dichotomy, refers to instances in which a certain idea or work requires the use of specific expressions.[43] Common examples of such instances are the use of a sheriff character and a shooting duel in a Western film and the appearance of a car chase in a police thriller.[44] In contrast to the idea–expression dichotomy, which does not provide copyright protection to ideas, the *scènes à faire* doctrine does not concern the copyrightability of such scenes; rather, it serves as a tool for determining whether a second work is infringing on the copyright of the first work by only using such scenes.[45] However, I argue, the significant match between genre theory's understanding of the common building blocks' importance to the promotion of creativity and of copyright law is not complete. The mismatch is most evident regarding derivative works. The right to make derivative works allows the owner of a work of authorship to forbid the making of works that are substantially based on the underlying work. Thus, the first author has a de facto right to bar the use of the common building blocks that his work is based on in the making of new works, a constraint that naturally limits the ability of the audience to identify these common building blocks in future (derivative) works.

In the context of the discussion on appropriation and borrowing in the development of music genres in Israel, and from a legal perspective, it is clear that certain basic doctrines in local copyright could potentially support this cultural phenomenon. However, given the mismatch between the functions of common building blocks in the development of genres and the derivative works right in copyright law, it may be worthwhile focusing on this legal framework and its applicability in Israeli law at the relevant time periods.

B. Adaptation and Derivative Works in Israeli Copyright Law

As previously explained, until 2008, Israeli copyright law was a colonial version of the English Copyright Act of 1911. The Old Copyright Law had a very limited concept of a derivative work or adaptation right granted to authors of first works as an exclusive right. In fact, the adaptation right was limited to cross-medium transfers (dramatic to non-dramatic and vice versa) and to translation of works.[46] This may have been a supportive factor to the types of borrowing and appropriation found in both SLI and Musica Mizrahit, which, as discussed above, borrowed melodies and sometimes entire compositions from Eastern European and Greek/Arab music, respectively, attaching them to new, Israeli and local lyrics, thus not infringing the exclusive translation right.

As I explained elsewhere, however, the lack of an explicit adaptation or derivative works right does not necessarily portray the complete picture. The basic reproduction right in copyright law gradually extended over the nineteenth century to also cover reproduction of portions of existing works in a manner that creates substantial similarity.[47] And, as explained, the Old Copyright Law did provide the author with an exclusive right to reproduce the work or any substantial part thereof.[48] However, it was only in 1970 that the Israeli Supreme Court contextualised this

[43] The exact translation of the term from French is 'scenes that must occur', and this is the normative basis for the legal doctrine. ibid § 13.03[B][4].

[44] For the application of the doctrine in case law, see, eg *Atari Inc v North American Philips Consumer Electrics Cor* 672 F.2d 607, 616 (7th Cir 1982); *Reyher v Children's Television Workshop* 533 F.2d 87, 87 (2d Cir 1975); *Hoehling v Universal City Studios Inc* 618 F.2d 972 (2d Cir 1980).

[45] *Nimmer on Copyright* (n 42) § 13.03[B].

[46] Copyright Law, 1911, s 1(2).

[47] See Rachum-Twaig, *Copyright Law and Derivative Works* (n 4) 4.

[48] Copyright Law, 1911, s 1(2).

provision and set certain ground interpretation rules to determine when the similarity or resemblance between works constitutes copyright infringement.[49] This may be another supportive factor to appropriation and borrowing associated with SLI, prevailing in the several decades before the establishment of Israel and until the late 1960s. However, if Israeli copyright law in the 1970s and onwards provided for certain exclusive rights that could prevent appropriation and borrowing in musical genres, other supporting factors should be suggested to explain the dominance of this feature in later genres such as Musica Mizrahit and contemporary pop music.

To complete the picture, Israel's new Copyright Law of 2007 includes an independent broad derivative works right prohibiting the making of a work substantially based on pre-existing works without the first author's consent.[50] Together with the already existing relatively broad reproduction right prevailing since the 1970s, it appears that appropriation and borrowing in later genres, and specifically in contemporary pop, are potentially subject to judicial scrutiny, and thus other, perhaps non-legal, factors should be identified to explain this phenomenon. In the next two subsections, I will suggest certain factors which, I believe, had a role in facilitating appropriation and borrowing in the genres discussed in this chapter, despite potential legal challenges.

C. Cultural Anchoring

As previously discussed, the development of music genres in Israel, and specifically SLI and Musica Mizrahit, was tied to the general national and cultural development of the State of Israel. SLI were composed, sung and promoted as a new Israeli musical heritage mainly due to the need to promote the agile development of an Israeli culture in the early days of the state, especially given the fact that the Israeli population was composed of an aggregate of Jews of various geographical and national origins. Appropriation and borrowing were key tools to enable both the agile production of such cultural products and facilitate their reception within the local audience. In similar vein, albeit with some distinct differences, Musica Mizrahit served as a cultural backdrop to a social movement attempting to stop the marginalisation of Jews of Arab descent (Mizrahi Jews) in the early Israeli existence. This, too, required cultural products that such group could call their own, and here, too, appropriation and borrowing played a key role in allowing such genre development both from the authors' side and the audience side.

I suggest that these phenomena could be viewed as cultural anchoring, in the sense that certain appropriation and borrowing, and even copying, could create an anchoring effect that assists in fixating consumption habits and facilitating the acceptance of certain works or types of works by the audience. This follows Raustiala and Sprigman's seminal approach of the 'piracy paradox', in which they suggested an analysis of the fashion products market, challenging the basic underlying assumption of copyright law according to which copyright protection promotes creativity and is justified. The authors focused on the fashion market as a case study for a prosperous market of innovation and creativity characterised by the lack of intellectual property protection and by repeated copying and design piracy.[51] The authors showed that the fashion market is not adversely affected by copying of design; rather, it prospers because of it. They called this anomaly the 'piracy paradox', and explained it with two models that characterised the fashion market – induced obsolescence and anchoring.

[49] See CivApp 559/69 *Almagor v Godick* PD 24 825 (1970).

[50] Israeli Copyright Law, 2008, ss 11(6) and 16.

[51] K Raustiala and C Sprigman, 'The Piracy and Paradox: Innovation and Intellectual Property in Fashion Design' (2006) 92 *Virginia Law Review* 1687, 1689.

They used the first model (induced obsolescence) because fashion items express social status. They become desirable when a certain audience uses them, but they become less luxurious when more and more people own them. Thus, the more copies a status-based product has, the less it is worth, so those clients wishing to preserve their social status purchase new designs – eventually promoting innovation and creativity in the market.[52] The second model (anchoring) is about the anchoring of the demand for a certain design in the market. This model complements the first. The authors argued that to preserve the circle of induced obsolescence, designers must signal to their audience when a new design would enter the market. For this, they must establish a trend. The authors argued that disseminating the new design by allowing copies to circulate helps the originators convey the message and signals to their consumers when fashion changes, what defines the new fashion and when to purchase it to stay on the status wheel.[53] The anchoring model suggested by Raustiala and Sprigman could serve a similar but different purpose for the current discussion. As opposed to the function of anchoring coupled with induced obsolescence to allow authors to capitalise on their work in fashion and trend-related industries, anchoring could play an important role in the collective effort to create a new genre and have it accepted by the public. In this sense, continuous acts of appropriation and borrowing by SLI authors, mainly form Eastern European genres and styles, assisted in anchoring this musical genre as an Israeli folk music genre with unique national characters mainly found in the lyrics of the songs, while preserving a familiar style of music for the local population to accept. In a slightly different way, the ongoing appropriation and borrowing by Musica Mizrahit authors, both from external genres and styles (such as Greek and Arab music) but also between local authors, assisted in anchoring this style and genre among the target social group of Mizrahi Jews in Israel, both as an empowering act for an otherwise marginalised social group and also for the purpose of reclaiming their ethnic identity within the national culture development based mainly on European styles and musical standards.[54] While the anchoring effect may explain the strong motivation for appropriation and borrowing in the development of the various music genres discussed, it cannot, alone, explain why this was possible despite certain legal challenges and exposure, or why such legal concerns did not, in most cases, materialise. In the next sub-section, I will try to explain the role that another non-legal factor played facilitating this phenomenon, which is closely tied to the characteristics of the Israeli market in its early years and up to the turn of the millennium.

D. Market Factors

The final factor that must be discussed to portray the entire picture of why appropriation and borrowing were dominant and possible (without legal obstacles) in the development of the music genres discussed is the market factor. In this regard, I argue that the music genres that developed in the formative years of the State of Israel, while it was characterised as a small, non-global and import-based market, enjoyed certain leeway in appropriating and borrowing from external sources, given the relative lack of interest in the local cultural consumption habits at the time. This contrasts with later periods, mainly the late 1990s onwards, in which Israeli contemporary pop developed, when Israel went through a certain amount of market transformation, situating

[52] ibid 1718–21.

[53] ibid 1728–29.

[54] For elaboration on the function of Musica Mizrahit as part of the social movement of Mizrahi Jews, see A Nock, 'Israel and the Emergence of Mediterranean Identity: Expressions of Locality in Music and Literature' (2006) 11 *Israel Studies* 143, 153–55; A Horowitz, 'Dueling Nativities: Zehava Ben Sings Umm Kultum' in RL Stein and T Swedenburg (eds), *Palestine, Israel and the Politics of Popular Culture* (2005) 202–06.

it as a global player with an export-dependent market and growing consumption power. I argue that these developments explain why appropriation and borrowing characterising SLI and Musica Mizrahit were under the foreign authors' radar, and why, in contrast, appropriation and borrowing in Israeli contemporary pop attracts legal attention and, at times, actual legal challenges.

According to statistics provided by the World Trade Organization, in 1948, the export of merchandise from Israel constituted approximately 5 per cent of the respective import. This ratio increased to 33 per cent in 1958, 48 per cent in 1968, 53 per cent in 1978, 78 per cent in 1998 and 94 per cent in 2008.[55] It is thus clear that in its first few decades, Israel relied heavily on imports, which constituted more than double its exports. While this characterised the import/export ratio of merchandise, it may well be that in terms of cultural foreign trade, although no formal data exists, the ratio was dramatically higher in favour of the importation of cultural goods. This could also be viewed from a perspective of population numbers in Israel along the years. In 1960, Israel had a population of 2,150,400, constituting 1.2 per cent of the then US population and 0.45 per cent of the European Union's population. In 2000, Israel's population was 6,289,200, constituting 2.2 per cent of the US population and 1.3 per cent of the EU population.[56] Compared to the population growth of the USA, Israel doubled its population over these four decades, and tripled its population in comparison to the EU.

Given these market and demographic data, it is no surprise that the Israeli market was not considered a high-profile market in its formative years in the context of sale of goods and services, and most likely not in the market for enforcement of copyright in musical works. This should be added to the fact that the scarcity of global communication channels and the then existing technology made it extremely difficult to identify copyright infringement generally, and more specifically in a distant, rather 'closed' jurisdiction. This may explain why, even though some of the appropriation and borrowing practices in the early days of Israel, as part of the SLI and Musica Mizrahit genres, were potentially infringing copyrights of foreign authors and composers, no legal challenges were observed. The incentive to enforce such rights in a small, developing market, with a very limited prospect of damages being obtained, was apparently very low. This is coupled with language and access obstacles, as well as technological difficulties, with respect to both the identification of any infringements and the legal system itself.

These factors led to the following effective result – no actual or potential sanctions were imposed on appropriation and borrowing from external sources and cultures in the early development of genres in Israel. Whether the appropriation and borrowing were conscious or not, the actors in these genres developed and acted in a cultural environment where such appropriation and borrowing were not considered wrong, were not sanctioned and became culturally accepted.

But with the globalisation of the Israeli market, its increasing consumption power and the growth in export of musical goods (and artists) and their integration in the global market for musical works, this seems to have changed, as is evident in the development of the Israeli contemporary pop genre. Given the similar nature and characteristics of works associated with the genre and parallel genres in other jurisdictions, mainly the USA and UK, the incentive to scrutinise potential appropriation and borrowing constituting copyright infringement increases, as evident in the 'Toy' case discussed above. The success of the song in the Eurovision contest and beyond was clearly a catalyst for the legal proceedings initiated and the proprietary outcome of the dispute. This may mean that while the legal and market factors have changed over the course of time, actors in the contemporary genre in Israel are still embedded in the previous conception regarding the freedom to appropriate and borrow, which, in turn, leads to potential legal scrutiny and disputes.

[55] World Trade Organization data, https://data.wto.org/.

[56] OECD.stat, demography and population, historical population data, https://stats.oecd.org/.

IV. Conclusion

This chapter discussed three main genres in Israeli music and their reliance on appropriation and borrowing. I explained that the development of such genres was closely tied with parallel national and social developments, the agile nature of the establishment and development of the State of Israel and the need to create, almost from scratch, common national and cultural perceptions.

Although Israel, from its outset, has globally acceptable copyright principles and afforded copyright protection to musical work, I showed that the then existing copyright framework did not provide an explicit robust protection against adaptations and derivative works which are key products of appropriation and borrowing in music genres. However, I showed that Israeli law, over the course of the discussed decades, did provide legal bases to challenge such appropriation and borrowing, which begged the question: why were these so apparent and remained unchallenged?

As I suggested, the prevailing legal regime itself could not account for the entire phenomenon; rather, other factors most likely played key roles in enabling and facilitating it. One key factor discussed was cultural anchoring and the need to rely on appropriation and borrowing from external sources to create common cultural ground and have the audience accept them quickly. Another key factor discussed was the market characteristics of Israel during the various decades, starting as a small, import-based market with relatively low consumption abilities, thus rendering it uninteresting for foreign copyright challenges. Together with language and technological barriers, appropriation and borrowing, even if potentially infringing copyright, went unnoticed and without sanction. These circumstances, however, no longer apply to the more contemporary genres of music, which are of a global nature, such as contemporary Israeli pop, and while actors in this contemporary genre may have absorbed the previously prevailing conception that appropriation and borrowing are widely accepted and could be freely engaged in, this may now attract legal scrutiny and cause disputes which may, in the coming years, affect the manner in which the genre continues to develop.

23

Feel the Benga Beat: Music Borrowing and Copyright Law in Kenya

MARISELLA N OUMA

I. Introduction

Music in Africa has developed over the years with influence from its own rich, diverse tradition, as well as Western and Latin American influences. Culture, including popular culture at the global level, also plays a significant role in defining the music of a particular community or country. Like other aspects of culture, music from the continent has influenced music from other regions, and has likewise been influenced by music from other cultures around the world. For instance, Afrobeat music in Ghana and Nigeria is influenced by West African music, jazz and calypso, as well as some elements of Western pop music. It is notable that there are different instruments that have evolved from the traditional instruments and music techniques. Examples of the latter include guitar playing, rhythms, harmony and style, which have also borrowed from each other.

Other genres have developed in different parts of Africa, including *taarab* in Tanzania, *chimurenga* and *kanindo* in Zimbabwe, *mbalax* in Senegal, *makossa* in Cameroon, *benga* in Kenya, *rumba* and *soukous* in the Democratic Republic of Congo (DRC, formerly Zaire) and *kwaito* in South Africa. These genres have developed over the last 60 years, and even where they have borrowed from other genres, they have distinct sounds and are to a certain extent also influenced by traditional music within the local community.

Recently, there have been developments of new genres such as *Afrobeats*, mainly from Nigeria, with artists such as Burna Boy and Wizkid taking centre stage in the global arena.[1] Others include *amapiano*, which was originally from South Africa but has been adopted by artists across the continent, especially East and Southern Africa;[2] and *bongo* from Tanzania, which features artists such as Diamond Platinumz, RayC, Harmonize and Venessa Mdee.

[1] Burna Boy's album *Twice as Tall* won the 2021 Best Global Music Album at the Grammy Awards in 2021. Afrobeats builds upon previous music such as Afrobeat and may be described as the sound of Lagos, Nigeria. 'It is high energy autotune-heavy with a constant percussive beat of elector-hip-hop sound and a technological revolution transforming pop music around the world. It is the story of Africa's cultural influence and its music industry on the rise. It is the story of how one country's music went global. Afrobeats is not Afrobeat. Afrobeats is electronic, catchy; the sound of urban millennial Africa': G Osiebe, 'Methods in Performing Fela in Contemporary Afrobeats 2009–2019' (2020) 79(1) *African Studies* 88.

[2] Amampiano borrows from other genres in South Africa such as kwaito, jazz lounge and house to create the distinct sound that draws heavily from the synthesizer.

Benga in Kenya, which is said to have developed in the western part of Kenya on the shores of Lake Victoria among the Luo community from the 1970s, has to a large extent influenced music that is found in other parts of Kenya. Given the influence that it has had on music within the country, it is important to provide a quick overview of the theoretical perspectives and then the history and development of benga from the 1940s to the present day.

On the other hand, copyright law was introduced in Kenya during the colonial period, but it has taken a while to get entrenched in the music industry. It is notable that at the time benga was created and continued to develop, the application of copyright law was restricted to the British publishers who were domiciled in the then colony. The music genre developed outside the parameters of copyright law, but this changed in the 2001, when the Copyright Act No 12 of 2001 was passed. This not only provided the legal framework, but also put in place the regulatory as well as administrative framework for an effective management of copyright and related rights in Kenya. This will be discussed further below under the section on the legal jurisdiction(s) associated with benga.

II. Theoretical Perspectives

Africa, with more than 700 ethnic communities, has a diverse and rich culture that has developed over the years and is part of the cultural identity of the different communities in the continent. The United Nations Educational, Scientific and Cultural Organization (UNESCO) defines culture as a 'complex whole which includes knowledge, beliefs, arts, morals, laws, customs, and any other capabilities and habits acquired by [a human] as a member of society'. The cultural diversity is also evident at the country and community levels, and this holds together the authentic social fabric of traditional practices, including music.[3]

African music, like other forms of culture, can be seen as both a musical and a social phenomenon.[4] Undoubtedly, music in the different ethnic communities is influenced by internal factors such as culture. It is also influenced by external factors, such as music from other cultures within the country as well as outside the country. Western and Arab influences include instruments such as the guitar and melodies including taarab, from the East Coast of Africa.[5] Creativity builds upon creativity, and music is no exception. *Benga* music, without doubt, has borrowed from other forms of music, such as the music from the Luo community, as well as the Western instruments that were introduced during the colonial times, and the music has evolved over time. It is thus a product of social as well as historical processes in Kenya. The nyatiti, a string instrument from the Luo community in the western part of Kenya, has to a certain extent contributed to the growth and development of benga music, as will be discussed later in the chapter.

According to Emielu, given that music is a social phenomenon, 'social reconstruction' is based on the perception that historical processes influence the creation of African popular music as it is a social concept. The social reconstruction theory as it applies to music posits 'a socially constructed [musical] phenomenon' and 'can be socially deconstructed and socially reconstructed contingent upon prevailing socio-musical processes and socio-historical processes'.[6] Emielu identifies three processes in the social reconstruction theory.

[3] www.africanunion-un.org/post/african-culture-versatile-approach-to-realize-the-africa-we-want.

[4] K Nketia, *The Music of Africa* (WW Norton, 1975).

[5] See A Emielu, 'Some Theoretical Perspectives on African Popular Music' (2011) 30 *Popular Music* 371, 388.

[6] ibid. The social reconstruction theory posits that 'a socially construed phenomenon can be socially deconstructed and socially reconstructed contingent upon socio-historical processes'.

The first is the social construction phase. This phase is characterised by the creative combination of the available resources to produce the creative content and subsequent interaction with third parties, such as the audience. In the case of benga, this could be traced to the origins of the music within the Luo traditional music and particularly instruments such as the nyatiti, an eight-stringed traditional lyre, and the *ohangla* drums. The former was seen to influence how the acoustic guitar that forms the core of benga was played.[7] Furthermore, the music was played in a band to an audience, which is basically the social process that shaped the music.

The second phase, social deconstruction, is seen as the stage where the musical style begins to lose its absolute advantages as emergent social and historical forces influence the music. This may be a result of individual, group or generational dynamics, as well as new socio-technological and economic demands.[8] By the 1970s, benga was no longer the preserve of the Luo community, but had spread to other parts of western Kenya, as well as to central and eastern Kenya and the Rift Valley region. Initially, benga was dismissed as music for the lower class, but it grew to become a distinctive Kenyan style and the audience had also changed to include the growing middle class. This also saw the incorporation of elements from the *lingala* music from the DRC.

The third stage, the reconstruction stage, is characterised by multiple modes of expressions, which may to a certain extent directly draw from the original form of the musical style or may be completely different. The 1980s saw the emergence of a new crop of artists who either built upon the existing sound or came up with new music based on the original sound.[9]

III. Historical Background of Benga Music in Kenya

Kenya is a country located in the eastern part of Africa. The current population estimate is 56 million, with more than 43 ethnic groups and a diverse cultural heritage. It has a vibrant music industry, with different genres of music, such as taarab, which has a strong Arab influence, rumba, ohangla, *mwomboko*, gospel, urban expressions (jazz and Afro-fusion) hip hop (*genge* and *kapuka*) and benga.

A. Origins of Benga

From a simple traditional, village entertainment to a national and regional music genre, the origins of benga music can be traced to the shores of Lake Victoria in the western part of Kenya. It has a distinct sound characterised by a

> combination of a sharp lead guitar overriding the rhythm and bass. Together with the arrangement and sectioning, the pace of the guitars, with their steady rise to a climax or crescendo and an equally quick refrain, clearly set benga apart from other forms of music.[10]

It has a fast-paced tempo and a staccato technique of playing the lead guitar. The guitar is a quintessential instrument that follows the vocals. The main instruments used in this genre of music are the lead (solo) guitar, rhythm guitar, bass guitar and drum kit.

[7] The technique used for playing the acoustic guitar was similar to how the nyatiti was played, that is, the single note picking as opposed to strumming.

[8] Emielu (n 5).

[9] GF Barz, 'Meaning in Benga Music of Western Kenya' (2001) 10 *British Journal of Ethnomusicology* 102.

[10] Ketabul Music, *Shades of Benga: The Story of Popular Music in Kenya: 1946–2016* (Ketabul Music, 2017) 65.

The original benga sound can be traced back to the late 1940s to the early 1960s, and is rooted in the traditional Luo music and in particular the instruments, namely the eight-stringed nyatiti and the one-stringed fiddle known as the *orutu*.[11] The technique used to play the nyatiti influenced the way that benga musicians played the acoustic guitar. A nyatiti performance was usually a solo performance, in which the musician plays the nyatiti and sings accompanied by the *gara*, which are leg rattles tied to the leg as well as a metal toe ring, the *nyaduong*.[12] The performance was usually for entertainment at social functions and the musician would compose the lyrics depending on the occasion.

According to Barz,[13] the nyatiti defines the characteristics of benga; the distinct and playful interaction between the bass and lead guitars in benga is like the interdependence of the bass and treble lines found in the nyatiti sound. There is also a similarity between the benga drumbeats and the use of gara leg rattles. Finally, the praise singing that was a central feature in the nyatiti performance is common to benga.[14] The orutu also contributed to the sound of benga, which is characterised by the high-pitched electric lead and bass guitars of the 1970s, the Golden Era of benga. The most distinctive link between benga and the traditional Luo nyatiti music is the tempo. In this aspect, benga has taken after the nyatiti, with its fast pace, which is moderated by the drum, that is like the nyaduong on the toe of the nyatiti player.[15]

B. Development of Benga

Music, like other aspects of culture, is also influenced by external factors such as wars, travel and interaction with other cultures. There are several people from the Luo community and other communities in Kenya who were enlisted by the colonial government to serve in the Second World War. Some were already musicians, while others learnt how to play instruments while in the army. When they returned to the country after the war, they brought back new skills and musical instruments, including the accordion and guitar. The former was used a lot in central Kenya and influenced what became known as mwomboko music and dance. The guitar, on the other hand, took root in western Kenya and became an integral part of the music that developed there, such as benga among the Luo and *omutibo* among the Luhya.

The distinct guitar style may also be attributed to a group of Luo men, who, after the Second World War, left for the DRC in search of work and learnt the finger-style guitar-playing technique. Olima Anditi was deemed to be one of the greatest guitarists between the 1950s and 1960s, and popularised the finger-picking style on the guitar.[16] The period also saw an influx of musicians from the DRC touring and visiting the country, and they also used the finger-picking style for solo guitars. Of note were renowned guitarists Mwenda Jean Bosco, Eduardo Masengo and Losta Abelo. However, this was in the early 1950s, and by that time the finger-picking style of guitar playing had already become part of the developing benga music in western Kenya.

[11] ibid.

[12] It is important to note that nyatiti was made popular by musicians such as Otuoma Ogola, who also popularised the acoustic guitar technique used by the benga musicians.

[13] Barz (n 9).

[14] ibid.

[15] J Muleka, 'Pioneering a Pop Musical Idiom: Fifty Years of the Benga Lyrics in Kenya' (2018) 7 *Journal of Arts and Humanities* 61.

[16] I Eagleson, 'Continuities and Innovation in Luo Song Style: Creating the Benga Beat in Kenya 1960 to 1995' (2014) 9 *African Music* 97.

The influence of the nyatiti would be seen in the way the musicians played the guitar. Benga was also played in the Luyha community, also in western Kenya, though their sound had a stronger influence from the traditional *isukuti* music. Other musicians from central, other parts of western as well as the eastern parts of Kenya used the same techniques for their music.

In the 1960s, benga musicians stopped using acoustic guitars and replaced them with electric ones. The period between 1970 and 1980 was known as the 'Golden Era of benga'. This was attributed to the emerging urban middle class, who preferred Western music to traditional music. Nairobi, a well-established regional and international commerce hub, with investment capital from major record labels such as Phonogram as well as local music producers such as AIT, Chandarana and Melodica, was fertile ground for the growth of the music industry. The local music producers recorded and marketed electric guitar band music, including benga. This also saw the proliferation of large bands, which would brand themselves as orchestras or jazz bands. Bands such as the Victoria Kings dominated the airwaves. The radio play would be followed by tours in the region both by local bands as well as foreign bands. At that point, there was a significant Congolese influence on benga music.

There are several musicians of note who contributed to the development of benga over the years. One of them was John Ogara Odondi. The practice of using several acoustic guitars is attributed to him. Other prominent benga artists include DO Misiani, Gabriel Omolo, Juma Odundo and Jose Kokeyo. Benga continued to develop, and by the late 1980s there were several additions, such as the solo mode of singing, which was popularised by Okatch Biggy and is believed to have been borrowed from other genres, namely lingala from the DRC and *kiswahili dansi* from the Kenyan coastal region.[17] In the early 1990s, the second rhythm guitar was dropped and replaced by the 'double string', which led to what came to be known as 'benga international', which had a significant Congolese music influence but still has some elements of the original benga music.

IV. Relation with Other Genres

Benga music is closely associated with rumba music from the DRC. As mentioned in the preceding section, the 1970s saw the emergence of bands both in Kenya and the DRC. Victoria Kings was one of the first big benga bands in Kenya. It was the brainchild of Phares Oluoch Kanindo, who had one of the largest production outfits in Kenya. He introduced the Congolese influence and encouraged the bands under his production house to imitate the Congolese bands. Being a large music producer, he exported benga to other countries, including Zimbabwe, where benga came to be known as kanindo.

This was an era that saw substantive borrowing across the genres, giving both genres of music a rich and distinct sound. For instance, the fusion of benga guitars with rumba resulted in a very distinct sound that was a crowd puller. The two-part sequence of the music is also found in other genres both within and outside the country. Many musicians in Kenya were influenced to a certain extent by the musicians from the DRC in the 1960s and 1970s. During this time, there was an influx of musicians from the DRC who visited Kenya or even set up their base there. The jury is still out as to who influenced the other, but one thing that is clear is that there are elements of the two genres of music that are similar.

Over the years, benga has become a 'pop beat' for Kenyan music. Benga boasts several renowned musicians, such as Fanuel Amimo, Sukuma bin Ongaro and Christopher Monyoncho

[17] ibid.

from the Luhya and Kisii communities in the western part of Kenya; the Kalenjin sisters, from the Rift Valley; DK Mwai and Joseph Kamaru, of central Kenya; and the Kalambya sisters and Kakai Kilonzo from eastern Kenya. These artists defined early benga music in Kenya and influenced the current crop of benga artists, such as Eric Wainaina, Suzzana Owiyo and Idi Achieng, who have created new genres by fusing benga with other modern styles.

V. Music Creativity Perceived by benga

Music, like language, is a human universal, involving perceptually discrete elements organised into hierarchically structured sequences.[18] Creativity may be seen as a product or process, and is often given value by the author in terms of rendition and how it is perceived by the audience. In different genres, the creative element may be perceived from the types of instrument used, how they are used and the structure of the music, as well as the melody and the vocals.

The guitar and the technique used to play the instrument defines the music style and is the essence of benga music. The lead guitar is a quintessential part of the genre, and the lead guitar usually complements the voice. It is also common for the guitar to fill in where there are no vocals.[19]

In the case of benga, the rhythm identifies the style and instrumentation, even in the absence of lyrics. The style and instrumentation are derived from the traditional music of the community where the musician(s) come from. For benga music, this can be traced back to the traditional Luo music and in particular the employment of two distinctive but mutually inclusive elements, namely the high-pitched voice that renders the lyrics, and the accompaniments, namely three or four guitars, a drum set and other percussion instruments, such as rattles and bottles rubbed with a metallic object.[20] In some instances, the style and instrumentation may be borrowed from the neighbouring community.[21]

During the 'Golden Era' of benga music, there were significant additions to the benga ensemble, including the 'first rhythm' guitar. The regular, recurrent pulse is anchored in the high-energy bass, which interwines with the guitar and the accompanying lyrics.[22] The song is usually divided into two parts. The first, which is usually slower, has the vocals and narration of the lyrics. The second part usually has a fast-paced tempo and is mainly instrumental and danceable, making it the climax of the song. A benga song lasts for at least five minutes, although some in the 1980s would last 10 minutes, which was similar to rumba from the DRC. The music composed under this latter genre would be similar in sound, save for the lyrics and language.

VI. Norms Regarding Music Borrowing

Music borrowing can occur in different forms, and there is no exception in the case of benga. Some scholars note that borrowing is part and parcel of the creative aspect of music. In many cases, a musical composition is likely to have borrowed from an existing one. Burkholder, in his analysis, notes that in classical music there are different types of borrowing which encompass

[18] A Patel, 'Language, Music, Syntax, and the Brain' (2003) 6 *Nature Neuroscience* 674.
[19] Muleka (n 15).
[20] ibid.
[21] ibid.
[22] ibid.

modelling, variations, paraphrasing, arranging, setting, *cantus firmus* stylistic allusion, culminative setting, pragmatic quotation, collage, patchwork and extended paraphrase.[23] Borrowing may be in the form of influencing or inspiration, variation of an existing work, sampling or outright copyright of an existing work, whether contemporary or traditional. This may bring into question the issues of authenticity, originality or creativity.

Copyright law, as discussed below, allows, to a certain extent, borrowing of a portion of a work for the creation of a new work. This is either under the authority of the rights holder for a consideration or under the exceptions and limitations as set out under the Kenyan Copyright Act. The latter does not provide for satire and parody as one of the exceptions and limitations to copyright.

According to Carroll, borrowing for the purpose of creating new works is an accepted norm in Western musical practice. This is anchored in the copyright laws of various countries.[24] Musical borrowing may broadly be defined as 'taking something from an existing piece of music and using it as a new piece'.[25] It could be the melody, arrangement or structural plan, but must have an identity, as coming from a particular work. Music borrowing can be looked at in terms of rhythm, performance, harmony, notational systems and the medium.[26]

In the case of benga music, borrowing can be seen from the structure, where elements of the traditional Luo music have been incorporated. The basic structure of benga, as discussed above, is comprised of a lead guitar and two or three other guitars, with other accompaniments such as the drum and the other percussion instruments. This can be said to have been borrowed from the nyatiti performance and could thus be seen to be a modification, in terms of instruments, to create the benga music. When one listens to this music, one can immediately identify the defining characteristics of benga. This is what has allowed the spread of benga to other communities across Kenya.

VII. Legal Jurisdiction(s) Associated with Benga

Copyright law in Kenya is a relatively recent development, as the first national law was the Copyright Act of 1966. However, its history can be traced back to 1897, when, under the colonial regime, the application of UK law – the English common law, doctrines of equity and the statutes of general application – was extended to the then Protectorate. This was through the reception clause of the English East African Order in Council. This, in effect, extended the application of the English Copyright Act of 1842, the International Copyright Act of 1844, the Fine Arts Copyright Act of 1862 and the Copyright (Musical Compositions) Act of 1888.[27] The reception clause subsequently allowed for the application of subsequent UK copyright laws, such as the English Copyright Act of 1911.

It is notable that during the formative years of benga, in the 1940s, copyright law in Kenya was mainly to protect the copyright of British publishers in Kenya by restricting the growth of publications that were deemed by the colonial government to be seditious, blasphemous, repugnant

[23] F Bimbot, E Deruty, G Sargent and E Vincent, 'Music Perception' [2016] *An Interdisciplinary Journal* 631.

[24] CM Carroll, 'Musical Borrowing – Grand Larceny of Great Art' (1978) 18 *College Music Symposium* 12.

[25] JP Burkholder, 'The Uses of Existing Music: Musical Borrowing as a Field' (1994) 50 *Quarterly Journal of the Music Library Association* 863.

[26] DO Ondieki, SO Ogama and EA Akuno, '"Zilizopendwa": The Ramifications for Development and Revival' (2014) 3 *The World of Music* 47.

[27] GM Sikoyo, E Nyukuri and JW Wakhungu, 'Intellectual Property Protection in Africa: Status of Laws, Research and Policy Analysis in Ghana, Kenya, Nigeria, South Africa and Uganda' (Report Centre for Technology Studies, 2016) 17.

to morality or against government policy. This, in effect, created a sense of superiority for the colonial government as the local population was not subject to these laws.

The development of benga was not affected by the norms and rules of copyright protection during the colonial period. This was good for the growth of the music as 'borrowing' was not prohibited under the existing copyright law. There was substantial borrowing in terms of rhythm, harmonisation and the medium, hence the similarity in the songs that were produced during that period and beyond.

The Copyright Act Chapter 130 of the Laws of Kenya was enacted in 1966. It borrowed heavily from the 1956 UK Copyright Act and was subsequently amended several times. The 1966 Act extended the protection of copyright to nationals of countries who were party to the Universal Copyright Convention (UCC). The copyright protection granted to the artists in the music industry, including benga artists, would apply to other artists from other countries that were members of the UCC. However, given that there was significant borrowing between the musicians in Kenya and the DRC, the law was not an impediment to the growth of benga music as it was hardly enforced, and the DRC was not party to the UCC. There were no cases that were brought to court on infringement of copyright regarding this genre of music.

The 1966 Copyright Act provides for protection of different categories of works such as literary, artistic, and musical works. Section 2 of the Act defines musical works as works consisting of music, exclusive of the lyrics or performance meant to accompany the music. The lyrics are protected as literary works, while the performances are protected as separate works.

Sound recordings are also protected under the 1966 Copyright Act.[28] Producers of sound recordings enjoy the exclusive rights to control the direct or indirect reproduction of a sound recording in any manner or form, distribution, importation into the country and communication to the public, as well as broadcasting of the works. The 1960s and 1970s, as discussed in the section above on the development of benga, were a great time for the music industry, and record companies such as AIT, Chandarana and Melodica gave a boost to benga. The local producer Oluoch Kanindo was also instrumental in the spread and popularisation of benga beyond the Kenyan borders, to countries such as Zimbabwe.

The Act also provides for protection of the rights of performers of sound recordings. During this period, there was a proliferation of live bands, which were known as 'jazz' bands and 'orchestras'. This was influenced by the rumba bands from the DRC, giving rise to benga bands such as Victoria Jazz, Continental Kilo Jazz and Shirati Jazz.

In 1982, the Act was amended to introduce the traditional reliefs to copyright infringement, such as injunctions, damages and enhanced criminal sanctions. This came at a time when the fortunes of the musicians in Kenya were dwindling owing to the global recession and increased unauthorised copying of music across the genres. The major record labels withdrew from the market, creating a vacuum that was taken up by local artists, especially benga musicians. This also saw the spread of benga to other parts of the country and in different languages.[29] It was exacerbated by the fact that there was limited enforcement of copyright and related rights in the music industry and there were hardly any cases of music copyright infringement brought before the courts.

In 2000, the Attorney General, by Regulations, extended copyright protection to authors of copyright-protected works in Berne Convention member states.[30] Copyright protection is

[28] Copyright Act of 2001, s 28 (ch 130 of the Laws of Kenya).

[29] I Eagleson, 'Continuities and Innovation in Luo Song Style: Creating the Benga Beat in Kenya 1960 to 1995' (2014) 9 *African Music* 109.

[30] The Copyright (Amendment) Regulations, 2000, LN 125/2000. Kenya acceded to the 1971 Paris Act of the Berne Convention on 11 June 1993.

territorial, and this amendment was significant in that the law recognised the works of artists from outside the country and protected them as such. Then the enactment of the Copyright Act of 2001 brought about several changes. This Act was passed mainly to comply with the Trade Related Aspects of Intellectual Property Rights (TRIPS) Agreement, as Kenya was a member of the World Trade Organization, as well as to incorporate the latest developments in copyright law at the international level.[31] It also created the institutional framework for administration and enforcement of copyright and related rights, which included the establishment of the Kenya Copyright Board (KECOBO), as well as the regulation of collective management organisations. These changes to the copyright law are important to the music industry as they made provisions that would facilitate the effective management of copyright in Kenya. In 2019, the Act was amended to include the latest developments in the digital environment.[32] The most recent changes were in 2022, and they introduced a formula for the sharing of royalties, as well as registration of copyright and related rights in a national registry.[33]

Although Kenya had a copyright regime since 1966, enforcement of copyright laws did not materialise until the 2000s, with the formation of KECOBO. KECOBO is mandated under the law to administer and enforce copyright in Kenya. Prior to that, copyright only existed on paper. The Act provides for the protection of literary, artistic and musical works, and grants exclusive rights to the author/owner of the works, which include the rights to reproduction, public performance, communication to the public, adaptation and translation, as well as broadcasting rights, subject to the exceptions and limitations.[34]

It is notable that a work shall still be eligible for copyright protection even if it has used another work without the authority of the rights holder. The rights holder may, however, sue the owner of the work for copyright infringement. This brings to the fore the issue of originality. A work is deemed to be original when there is sufficient skill and effort to give it an original character. This is irrespective of the quality of the music or even the similarity in music, as discussed in the case of benga. The melodies, arrangements and structural plans in this genre of music are quite similar.

More copyright infringement cases have been instituted and determined recently. This may be attributed to the administrative structures that have been put in place since the 2001 Copyright Act and the inclusion of the protection of copyright and other intellectual property rights in the Constitution of Kenya.[35] However, these cases are mainly on literal or outright infringement, where one uses a song without the authority of the rights holder.[36]

The use of existing music for new compositions is not new in the music industry, and has occurred over the years in Kenya, within and across genres. It may be structural, a simple variation of existing music, its arrangement, setting or even the stylistic allusion, pragmatic quotation or collage.[37] It is evident from the foregoing discussions that there was a lot of 'borrowing' in the production of benga in terms of the above.

There is a dearth of case law in Kenya in the music sector and in relation to benga music. In 2018, two Kenyan artists, Willy Paul and Kaligraph Jones, were accused of plagiarising a song

[31] See I Rutenberg, M Ouma and P Munyi, *Intellectual Property Law in Kenya* (Wolters Kluwer, 2019) 37.

[32] These included the provisions for the safe harbours for internet service providers under s 35B.

[33] Copyright (Amendment) Act No 14 of 2022.

[34] Copyright Act of 2001 as amended in 2019, s 26.

[35] The Constitution of Kenya 2010, Art 40(5) provides that the state shall promote and protect intellectual property rights of the people of Kenya. This makes protection of copyright a constitutional right as copyright is protected like any other property in Kenya.

[36] *John Boniface Maina v Safaricom Limited* [2013] eKLR.

[37] This was common in classical music. See Burkholder (n 25).

by the Kenyan rappers Gorilla and Saddat. The later claimed that the 'hook' used by the former in their song titled 'Bora Uhai' was like that in their song. The matter, however, did not proceed to court.

The question is whether music borrowing is allowed under the law and, if so, under what circumstances. From a broad perspective, copyright is conferred on the creation of a new work using an existing work; the Kenyan Copyright Act provides that such work shall not be ineligible for copyright protection, as stated above. It does, however, prohibit literal and non-literal infringement of existing works. The structure of all benga music, as discussed in the section above on music creativity, is similar, thus one may not be in breach of copyright law for merely borrowing the structure. This brings about the issue of originality. This is based on various tests, primarily the 'sweat of the brow', or use of skill and judgement. One can argue that there is sufficient skill and judgement in the creation of music within the genre even though benga music seems to be based on the same structure, melody, and arrangement.

VIII. Conclusion

This chapter has explored the concept of music borrowing with regard to benga music in Kenya. Although it has not yet gained international fame, the genre has to some extent influenced contemporary music found in Africa in countries such as Kenya, Tanzania and Zimbabwe. The use of a lead guitar with up to three other guitars is a creative and distinctive feature of this genre which can be said to have been borrowed from the traditional Luo music and the nyatiti performance, both in structure and form. The interaction between the benga artists in Kenya and other artists, especially from the DRC, led to a certain level of borrowing on both sides which enriched the music and endeared it to more audiences across the borders. The new generation of artists, such as Eric Wainaina, Ida Achieng and Suzzana Owiyo, continue to keep the genre alive.

Copyright law has, until recently, played a minimal role, and artists over the years have managed to 'borrow' from existing music to create new genres and even modify the existing ones. The courts are yet to pronounce themselves specifically on the issue of music borrowing, as has happened in other parts of the world. Music borrowing is fundamental to the growth and development of music if it is not against the existing legal norms, such as copyright and related rights.

24

The Many Facets of Borrowing and Creativity in South African Music

TOBIAS SCHONWETTER AND BRAM VAN WIELE*

I. Introduction

South Africa is home to one of the richest and most diverse musical traditions in the world. Local genres and styles include, but are not limited to, *gqom*, *kwela*, *marabi*, *mbaqanga*, *kwaito*, *amapiano*, Afrikaner folk songs and South African jazz. This mix of different and overlapping genres and styles reflects South Africa's history and tremendous social and cultural diversity. Music, song and dance have and continue to play an important part in life, culture and traditional practices by the people and the various tribes of South Africa. Often, music is a form of celebration or of resistance, and it encapsulates identities and cultures.

That said, it is difficult, if not impossible, to delineate what 'South African music' is or even define what 'African' means in the context of South African music. As numerous foreign influences have contributed to the development of music in the country, one can also ask when can music truly be considered 'South African'? Consider the famous song 'The Lion Sleeps Tonight', which will be discussed in more detail in this chapter. While the song has South African origins, it does not include the complex drumming rhythms one might expect from 'African' music.[1]

It is beyond the purview of this chapter to provide a comprehensive overview of 'South African music' and its history; this has been done elsewhere.[2] Instead, against the backdrop of South Africa's history, this chapter canvasses the development of some of the most well-known genres and styles.[3] It then looks at how issues linked to music borrowing and copyright protection came to the fore in the context of some of South Africa's most famous songs and records. In discussing these cases, the chapter considers key aspects of musical borrowing, such as attribution, recognition and collaboration, as well as various ways of reworking existing music.

The first piece of South African music discussed in this chapter is South Africa's national anthem. This anthem is unique in that it combines two pre-existing anthems: 'Nkosi Sikelel' iAfrika', which had been the official anthem of the African National Congress (ANC) since 1925,

* The authors would like to thank Charlise Finch, Kyle Janse and Takura Takavarasha for excellent research assistance.

[1] CA Muller, *Focus: Music of South Africa*, 2nd edn (Routledge, 2008) 7.

[2] For an in-depth analysis of South African music, see ibid. See also S Dlamini, C Ballantine and N Ramanna, 'South Africa' in *Continuum Encyclopedia of Popular Music of the World*, vol 6 (2005) 100.

[3] For a detailed timeline, see 'The Development of Music in South Africa Timeline 1600–2004' (South African History Online) www.sahistory.org.za/article/development-music-south-africa-timeline-1600-2004.

and 'Die Stem van Suid-Afrika', which was the official national anthem of South Africa during the apartheid period. The current national anthem uses five different languages to reflect South Africa's multiracial status and provides an interesting example of the influence of political and historical factors on music borrowing.

The chapter then introduces the song 'The Lion Sleeps Tonight'. This internationally renowned song is known in many languages, but its South African origins are rarely recognised. This part of the chapter will discuss the development and South African elements of the original song 'Mbube', how it was reworked and the legal battle that ensued. Linking the song to the music style it defined, we will discuss how the South African music styles of *isicathamiya* and mbaqanga gained further global attention and recognition.

Thereafter, the chapter looks at the (at the time controversial) 1986 album *Graceland* by Paul Simon. This album was a collaborative recording, including a host of South African artists. It was recorded during some of the most oppressive years of apartheid. While recognising the album's wide-ranging impact, including on music and politics, this chapter focuses on the role of collaboration, attribution, assimilation and appropriation.

II. A Broad Overview of the Development of Music in South Africa

Around 1000 BCE, the region now known as South Africa was first settled by the Khoi, and several hundred years later by Bantu-speaking farmers.[4] The Khoisan, a group comprising the Khoi and the related San peoples, sang wordless polyphonic chants and yodelled a cappella with bird and other animal sounds.[5] Bantu-speaking peoples include the Zulu, Xhosa and Pedi, and currently make up the majority of black South Africans.[6] Traditional Zulu music has influenced and dominated many genres and styles in South Africa, including *mbube* and isicathamiya, which are discussed in more detail later in this chapter.

In the seventeenth century, the region was colonised by the Dutch. In terms of music, the arrival of European missionaries led to the introduction of Western Christian religion and musical styles like choral singing.[7] This Christian influence can, for instance, be seen in the famous Xhosa hymn 'Nkosi Sikelel' iAfrika'.[8] The development of South African music was also influenced by musical practices of slaves brought from Madagascar, the East Indies and elsewhere.[9] Slaves, but also indigenous tribes, adopted Western instruments and ideas. The Khoi, for instance, developed the ramkie, a three- or four-string guitar, which they used to mix Khoi and Western folk songs.[10]

Following British occupation in the 1800s, Western instrumentation was also used to adapt rural songs, which contributed to a new, hybrid style of creating music.[11] The movement of black workers to the mining areas of South Africa during this period meant that different types of

[4] RM Byrnes (ed), *South Africa: A Country Study*, 3rd edn (Federal Research Division, Library of Congress, 1996).

[5] AA Agordoh, *African Music: Traditional and Contemporary* (Nova Science Publishers, 2005) 10.

[6] Government Communications, 'Official Guide to South Africa 2018/2019' (GCIS, 2019) 12, 15, www.gcis.gov.za/official-guide-south-africa-201819.

[7] 'Xhosa' (South African History Online) www.sahistory.org.za/article/development-music-south-africa-timeline-1600-2004.

[8] ibid.

[9] Dlamini et al (n 2) 100–01.

[10] 'The Development of Music' (n 3).

[11] ibid.

traditional regional folk music started to blend, including those with Western influences.[12] In the mid-1800s, minstrel troupes also began to tour the country.[13] These minstrels influenced the emergence of a new culture of choirs and choir competitions. The emergence of isicathamiya, for instance, can be traced back to when South Africans started to perform their adaptations of the repertoires of these visiting minstrel troupes.[14]

By the turn of the twentieth century, various pre-apartheid policies were adopted, followed by the enactment of various laws that further restricted the rights of the black majority.[15] During the period known as 'apartheid' from the late 1940s to the early 1990s, the South African government put in place and enforced laws and policies of racial segregation that entrenched whites in a position of privilege and curtailed the rights and privileges of non-whites.[16] The Population Registration Act of 1950, for instance, required every South African to be classified and registered as one of a distinct racial group: Bantu (Black), Coloured or White. A fourth category, Asian (Indian and Pakistani), was later added. The Group Areas Act of 1950 divided the country into residential areas based on racial classifications, and non-white South Africans were moved to settlements outside of the major urban centres, called townships. Although the Group Areas Act was repealed in 1991, townships still exist today – the largest one being Soweto, near Johannesburg. It was often in these townships that numerous African musical sounds and styles further blended with Western influences like choral music and jazz.

One of the styles that evolved in townships during the 1950s is the popular music style kwela. The primary instrument of kwela is the penny whistle. The style was influenced by the pan-city music style of marabi, which was developed in the late 1920s and was rooted in American jazz mixed with sounds of African rhythm.[17] Kwela is also the predecessor of mbaqanga, which is discussed in more detail later in this chapter. Like contemporary township styles such as African jazz, vocal jive and sax jive, kwela is characterised by a swing beat. This is different from related styles such as marabi and mbaqanga, which have a driving straight beat.[18]

Over the years, resistance against apartheid grew and included protests, demonstrations, strikes and ultimately armed opposition, led by the ANC and others. Numerous resistance leaders were arrested and sentenced to long prison sentences (or execution), including Nelson Mandela, who was released from prison in 1990 and would later become South Africa's first democratically elected president. As various boycotts and sanctions were imposed on South Africa by the international community from the late 1960s, the country became increasingly isolated. This isolation influenced the development of music in South Africa and arguably contributed to the emergence of distinctly South African styles and genres. Local musicians faced considerable challenges. For instance, repressive laws restricted movements, and thus performances, of black musicians as well as the opportunity of collaboration between artists from different ethnicities. Strikes would often take the form of the masses dancing and singing what would come to be known as *igwijo*, or *freedom* songs. Resistance would also take the form of published works by musicians such as

[12] ibid.

[13] The *Encyclopedia Britannica* defines minstrelsy as 'an American theatrical form, popular from the early 19th to the early 20th century, that was founded on the comic enactment of racial stereotypes': 'minstrel show' (*Encyclopedia Britannica*) www.britannica.com/art/minstrel-show.

[14] S Dlamini, 'Isicathamiya' in *Bloomsbury Encyclopedia of Popular Music of the World*, vol 7 (2019) 296, 299.

[15] For a chronological overview, see YG-M Lulat, *United States Relations with South Africa: A Critical Overview from the Colonial Period to the Present* (Peter Lang, 2008) liii–liv.

[16] See Prohibition of Mixed Marriages Act 1949; Population Registration Act 1950; Group Areas Act 1950; Pass Laws Act of 1952.

[17] C Lottering, 'Lively African Jazz' (South Africa Online) https://southafrica.co.za/marabi.html.

[18] Dlamini (n 14) 359.

Miriam Makeba and Hugh Masekela. However, many of these icons had to flee South Africa and perform their music abroad due to the repressive laws and fear of reprisal. South Africa's history of racial and socioeconomic segregation has profoundly impacted musical traditions and production. Music by black artists, for instance, was hardly recognised and developed largely parallel to its European counterpart.

South Africa's Interim Constitution (1993) and current Constitution (1996), as well as the country's first democratic elections in 1994, marked the end of apartheid. Currently, democratic South Africa recognises 11 official languages,[19] of which the most common ones are isiXhosa, isiZulu, Sesotho, Afrikaans and English. One of the most important musical developments in the post-apartheid era is kwaito.[20] This genre drew from, among others, rap, hip-hop, disco, ragga and house music, but it is its use of these genres that is particularly distinctive.[21] Indeed, kwaito has in some ways revolutionised the South African music industry and continues to develop in remarkable ways. As Ballantine comments:

> The resulting hybrids are complex and diverse; they involve fusions with, for example, precolonial idioms, 'neo-traditional' styles, local popular music of the 1950s, protest music of the apartheid era, Western popular music, gospel, jazz, classical music and ethnically marked music from other parts of the globe.[22]

Kwaito has subsequently influenced other genres and resulted in the birth of genres such as gqom and amapiano.

III. The National Anthem of South Africa

The official end of apartheid and the beginning of a new constitutional dispensation came with a new national anthem for the country. In 1994, a proclamation issued by President Nelson Mandela stated that the national anthem of South Africa would comprise a combination of two pre-existing anthems: 'Nkosi Sikelel' iAfrika' ('God Bless Africa') and 'Die Stem van Suid-Afrika' ('The Voice of South Africa').[23]

'Nkosi Sikelel' iAfrika' was composed in 1897 by Enoch M Sontonga, who was a teacher at a Methodist mission school. He wrote the opening stanza and chorus in isiXhosa, and, by some accounts, later also composed the music.[24] Sontonga died in 1905. Some commentators suggest that the melody was based on 'Aberystwyth', a Welsh hymn composed by Joseph Parry in 1876, and travelled to Africa through Welsh missionaries.[25] Parry died in 1903. The song displays patterns

[19] See South African Constitution, s 6(1).

[20] See, eg M Bradshaw, 'How Kwaito Became a Global Force' *The Guardian* (London, 11 August 2011) www.theguardian.com/music/2011/aug/11/kwaito-south-africa-house.

[21] C Ballantine, 'Kwaito' in *Bloomsbury Encyclopedia of Popular Music of the World*, vol 7 (2019) 348–49.

[22] ibid 351.

[23] E Bornman, 'Post-apartheid South Africa: A United or a Divided Nation?' in SL Moeschberger and RA Phillips DeZalia (eds), *Symbols That Bind, Symbols That Divide: The Semiotics of Peace and Conflict* (Springer, 2014) 185.

[24] DB Coplan and B Jules-Rosette, 'Nkosi Sikelel' iAfrica and the Liberation of the Spirit of South Africa' (2005) 64 *African Studies* 287.

[25] See J Mclaren, 'Joseph Parry's Te Deum: Premiere for Lost Composition' (*BBC News*, 14 July 2012) www.bbc.com/news/uk-wales-18770309; O Dean, 'An Anthem to Ignorance: South Africa's Case of Nkosi Sikelel' iAfrika' (Intellectual Property Watch, 20 June 2012) www.ip-watch.org/2012/06/20/an-anthem-to-ignorance-south-africas-case-of-nkosi-sikelel-iafrika. However, it remains difficult to find the original source for this claim.

of Methodist hymn singing and composition, as well as African praise singing.[26] In 1927, seven additional isiXhosa stanzas were added by the poet Samuel EK Mqhayi. Mqhayi died in 1945. The Sesotho version called 'Morena Boloka' was first recorded in 1929.[27] This version was not derived from Sontonga's version and comprises different lyrics and a slightly different melody.[28] Research by Siemon Allen shows that the composer remains uncredited on this recording as well as many of the following recordings.[29] Despite this uncertainty regarding the composer, the Sesotho version is often attributed to Moses Mphahlele.

'Nkosi Sikelel' iAfrika' was later adopted as a Pan-African liberation song and was sung during the anti-colonial movements throughout Southern Africa. Variations of the hymn were adopted as national anthems by five African countries after independence, namely Tanzania (1961), Zambia (1964), Zimbabwe (1980), Namibia (1990) and South Africa (1994). The Swahili version of the song is currently still the national anthem of Tanzania. In South Africa, the ANC adopted the hymn in 1925 as its official anthem to be sung at the closing of all its meetings. The hymn was also sung at various rallies and protests. In the 1970s and 80s, the hymn gained international recognition as a symbol of the anti-apartheid movement.

In May 1957, the white minority government adopted 'Die Stem van Suid-Afrika' as the official national anthem of South Africa.[30] The hymn is considered to be closely tied to the apartheid regime. The lyrics were written as a poem by Cornelis Jakob Langenhoven (1873–1932) in May 1918, and ultimately set to music composed by Marthinus Lourens de Villiers (1885–1977) in 1920.[31] De Villiers later assigned the copyright in the musical work to Langenhoven. After Langenhoven died in 1932, his heirs and the administrator of his estate assigned the copyright in both the literary work and the musical composition to the South African government. This transfer of ownership took place in 1957, the same year that the song was adopted as the official national anthem of South Africa, and was later confirmed by the Stem van Suid-Afrika Act of 1959.[32] That same year, an English version was also adopted for official use, and used together with the Afrikaans version.[33] While the direct translation of 'Die Stem van Suid-Afrika' is 'The Voice of South Africa', the official English version is known as 'The Call of South Africa'. This version is the result of the combination of various translations and initially had only one stanza. It was revised slightly in 1959.

After the end of apartheid, the combination of 'Nkosi Sikelel' iAfrika' and 'Die Stem van Suid-Afrika' was adopted as a double anthem, but it was extremely long. The Anthem Committee was established by the Minister of Arts, Culture, Science and Technology at the request of President Nelson Mandela's cabinet, to create a choral and instrumental shortened version of the anthem. The Anthem Committee made various proposals to the cabinet, including new words for the

[26] Coplan and Jules-Rosette (n 24) 288–89.

[27] The song was published by Wilberforce Institute Singers on 22 June 1930.

[28] DB Coplan, *In Township Tonight! – Three Centuries of South African Black City Music & Theatre*, 2nd edn (University of Chicago Press, 2008) 62.

[29] S Allen, 'The South African National Anthem: A History on Record' (Flatinternational – South African Audio Archive, 15 October 2013) https://flatint.blogspot.com/2013/10/the-south-african-national-anthem.html.

[30] Between 1938 and 1957, *Die Stem van Suid-Afrika* was accepted as the co-national anthem, together with 'God Save The King'/'God Save The Queen'.

[31] According to some commentators, music composed by Langenhoven was not well received, and a competition was organised in 1919 to compose the music. Although the composition is often dated as 1921, Marthinus Lourens de Villiers completed the work on 31 May 1920.

[32] Die Stem Van Suid-Afrika Act No 2 of 1959.

[33] The English version was first published in 1952. It was adopted for official use on 29 November 1957.

English stanza.[34] The new national anthem was officially adopted in 1997 and is essentially an adaptation of 'Nkosi Sikelel' iAfrika' and 'Die Stem van Suid-Afrika', comprising parts and translations of both songs, as well as some lyrical changes.[35] The first stanza starts with two lines, sung in isiXhosa and isiZulu, respectively. The second stanza continues in Sesotho. The third stanza is sung in Afrikaans and consist of a section of 'Die Stem van Suid-Afrika', the national anthem of South Africa during the apartheid era. The fourth and final stanza is a modified version of the English version of 'Die Stem van Suid-Afrika': 'The Call of South Africa'.

It is generally accepted that Jeanne Zaidel-Rudolph composed the orchestral setting and additional English words of the new anthem.[36] The two pre-existing anthems were maintained and coupled by adding a modulation chord. This resulted in the new anthem beginning and ending in a different key. The English lines that comprise the fourth stanza do not appear directly in the official English version of 'Die Stem van Suid-Afrika'. Instead, they are a condensed and modified version of the last three lines of the first verse of the original English version. Some themes and words were maintained.

Because the anthem comprises both literary and musical works, as well numerous adaptations and translations of these works, it has proved difficult to determine copyright ownership in the anthem. Under current South African copyright law, the duration of copyright protection in literary and musical works is 50 years from the end of the year in which the author dies. Hence, the copyright in the literary and musical work 'Nkosi Sikelel' iAfrika' have expired – under both current and previous copyright statutes – and the song has thus passed into the public domain. The literary work 'Die Stem van Suid-Afrika', created by Langenhoven, has been out of copyright since 1982.[37] However, the musical composition created by de Villiers, as well as the English words and their new composition, are still under copyright.

Following queries from the public regarding copyright ownership in the new national anthem, the South African Musical Rights Organization (SAMRO) published a commissioned legal analysis on their official website.[38] According to this analysis, as the rights to 'Die Stem van Suid-Afrika' were assigned to the South African government, the work is 'effectively in the public domain',[39] even though copyright protection continues to exist in some elements of it. However, as correctly pointed out by Dean, a reversionary right still applies to the assignment of the rights as far as the musical composition is concerned. While the current Copyright Act from 1978 does not contain reversionary right provisions, previous copyright legislation, which still applies in this context to works created between 1916 and 1966, stipulates that the copyright in a work assigned during the author's lifetime reverts to the executor of the author's estate 25 years after the author's death.[40] More specifically, this means that the copyright in the musical work 'Die Stem van Suid-Afrika' would have reverted to the executor of de Villiers's estate 25 years after de Villier's death, and the South African government would in fact be the copyright owner of the work.[41]

[34] MS Levy, 'The National Anthem Is Owned by Everyone' (SAMRO, 17 June 2012) www.samro.org.za/news/articles/national-anthem-owned-everyone.

[35] Proc 68 in Government Gazette 18341 of 10 October 1997.

[36] 'Compositions', http://jeannezaidel-rudolph.com/Compositions.

[37] Copyright Act, s 3(2).

[38] Levy (n 34).

[39] ibid.

[40] See South Africa's Patents, Trade Marks, Designs and Copyright Act 9 of 1916, s 5(2).

[41] This reversionary right is discussed in more detail later in this chapter as part of the story of 'The Lion Sleeps Tonight'.

IV. 'Mbube'/'The Lion Sleeps Tonight'

Most people are familiar with the song 'The Lion Sleeps Tonight' and its central vocal melody.[42] This melody has its origins in the ethnic song 'Mbube' – isiZulu for 'lion', composed in 1939 by Solomon Linda, a Zulu-speaking South African. Over numerous years, this song was reworked into the hit song 'The Lion Sleeps Tonight', which was later included in Disney's film *The Lion King*.[43] Despite his key role in creating this central piece to the world-famous song, Linda died a poor man, and the benefits his family initially received from his work can be considered inadequate and unjust. During the 1990s, when *The Lion King* was popular, his heirs allegedly received around 17,000 USD in royalties. Moreover, one of his daughters died of HIV/AIDS in 2001, unable to afford the antiretroviral drugs that could have prolonged her life. To many, the South African origins of the song are unknown. However, in the late 1990s, the Executor of Linda's estate brought a copyright infringement action against Disney in South Africa. This legal action, described in more detail below, concluded in a legal settlement that awarded Linda's heirs a stake in the proceeds from the song and its adaptations. Furthermore, it established Linda's role in creating the song and the song's South African heritage. In recent year, this case and the song's history has regained media attention by its coverage in the 2019 Netflix music documentary series *ReMastered*.[44]

A. From 'Mbube' to 'The Lion Sleeps Tonight'

Solomon Linda was born in 1909 near Pomeroy in the labour reserve of Msinga.[45] He performed and competed in choral competitions with a local group of close-harmony singers, The Evening Birds. Solomon Linda also started working as a packer in a storeroom at Gallo Records, South Africa's oldest record company.[46] Linda attracted the attention of Gallo's talent scout Griffiths Motsieloa. During a recording session of the song 'Mbube' by The Evening Birds in 1939, Linda improvised a melody over the top of a low male voice chant by the group. It is this melody and the pulsing chant that create the unique identity of this song.

The subsequent release of the record led to high sales numbers in Southern Africa.[47] Copyright subsisted in the song by virtue of the South African Patents, Designs, Trade Marks and Copyright Act 1916. While 'Mbube' evidences clear African musical traits, such as call and response and a cyclical structure, it does not include drums, which are often associated with African music. Instead, it uses the power of the human voice. The deep and strong vocal sounds present in 'Mbube' are in fact a particular feature of much of the music originating from South Africa. As pointed out by Muller, the song particularly exhibits other Southern African elements: the phrases in the call and response

[42] A detailed discussion of this case can be found in O Dean, 'Stalking the Sleeping Lion' [2006] *De Rebus* 15; O Dean, *Awakening the Lion – The Case of the Lion Sleeps Tonight* (Tafelberg, 2013).

[43] The film *Lion King* was released in 1994 (and again in 2019), followed by the stage show in 1997.

[44] The case was covered in the episode 'The Lion's Share', directed by Sam Cullman.

[45] V Erlmann, 'Fantasies of Home – The Antinomies of Modernity and the Music of Ladysmith Black Mambazo' in S Frith (ed), *Popular Music: Critical Concepts in Media and Cultural Studies* (Routledge, 2004) 271.

[46] Gallo Records was founded in 1926 by Eric Gallo. In 1932, Gallo established the first professional recording studio in South Africa, which was also the first and only studio in sub-Saharan Africa.

[47] Mbube became the first South African record to surpass 100,000 sales.

format overlap, and it is performed in four-part harmony.[48] The song's chord progression references the harmonic cycle of marabi, a pan-ethnic music style developed in the townships.[49]

In the early 1950s, and together with other records from Gallo, recordings of 'Mbube' made their way to Decca Records in the USA. Decca was not interested, but through US ethnomusicologist Alan Lomax, who was at that time director for folk music at Decca, the record was introduced to famous folk singer Pete Seeger of the folk group The Weavers.[50] Seeger created his own version of the song. Because no sheet music (including lyrics) was available to perform the song, Seeger transcribed the song by ear. This process worked well for the music, but resulted in the inaccurate transcription of 'uyimbube', isiZulu for 'you are a lion', as 'ah-wimoweh'. In 1952, The Weavers released the song in the USA with its new name 'Wimoweh', and it made it into the American pop charts. The melody composed by Linda was repeated throughout the song. While Seeger publicly acknowledged Linda's contribution and allegedly gave instructions to forward his royalty payments for 'Wimoweh' to Linda, it appears that not all these royalties arrived as intended.[51]

It is noteworthy that at that time, copyright registration was still a prerequisite for copyright protection in the USA.[52] In its copyright registration in 1951, 'Wimoweh' was credited to the pseudonym Paul Campbell.[53] This pseudonym was used by The Weavers between 1948 and 1953 to claim copyright in the arrangement of old folk songs – which some claimed 'Mbube' was.[54] At the time, it was common practice in the USA for folk artists to combine traditional lines or stanzas of songs with their own compositions, and to register copyright for those derivative compositions.[55] While these arrangements include previously composed works that are in the public domain, they are original works in their own right, and hold a separate copyright. At this time, the copyright in 'Mbube' had not yet been registered in the USA. 'Wimoweh' was subsequently reworked and recorded by numerous artists, including Jimmy Dorsey, Yma Sumac, Bill Hayes and Karl Denver. One of the few times Linda was credited for 'Wimoweh' was by The Kingston Trio, who covered the song in 1959 and attributed the song writing credits to 'Campbell–Linda'.

In January 1952, following the assignment of the copyright in 'Wimoweh' by Campbell, the US music publisher Folkways registered a claim to copyright in the song with the US Copyright Office. A few months later, Gallo Records acquired from Linda the rights in 'Mbube' in exchange for 10 shillings and registered a claim to 'Mbube' in the USA.[56] This led to various agreements between Gallo and Folkways in which they determined their respective rights in the two songs. According to Dean, who later acted at the lawyer for Linda's estate, these arrangements essentially bestowed ownership of the copyright in both 'Mbube' and 'Wimoweh' in the USA upon Folkways, whereas Gallo held these rights in South Africa and some other African territories.[57] Among

[48] Muller (n 1) 7.

[49] C Ballantine, 'Marabi' in *Bloomsbury Encyclopedia of Popular Music of the World*, vol 7 (2019) 387–88.

[50] R Malan, 'In the Jungle: Inside the Long, Hidden Genealogy of "The Lion Sleeps Tonight"' *Rolling Stone* (New York, 25 May 2000) www.rollingstone.com/feature/in-the-jungle-inside-the-long-hidden-genealogy-of-the-lion-sleeps-tonight-108274.

[51] ibid.

[52] The US acceded to the Berne convention on 16 November 1988.

[53] The Weavers (eds), *The Weavers' Song Book*, arranged by Robert De Cornier (Harper & brothers, 1960).

[54] The argument that Mbube was not an original song was raised by various artists as well as by Disney during the legal proceedings in 2004.

[55] R Springer, 'Folklore, Commercialism and Exploitation: Copyright in the Blues' (2007) 26 *Popular Music* 33, 35–38; GT Meade, 'Copyright: A Tool for Commercial Rural Music Research' (1971) 30 *Western Folklore* 206, 207.

[56] US Copyright Office registration number EU0000281531.

[57] Dean, 'Stalking the Sleeping Lion' (n 42); Dean, *Awakening the Lion* (n 42) 5.

other things, various cross licences ensured, to some extent, mutual benefit in the worldwide exploitation of these two songs.[58]

In the 1960s, songwriter George David Weiss, hired by producers Hugo Peretti and Luigi Creatore, wrote a new version of the song with English lyrics. The song was not attributed to either Linda or Paul Campbell. This version, titled 'The Lion Sleeps Tonight', was performed by the doo-wop group The Tokens. This song comprised the low male voice chant found in 'Wimoweh' and 'Mbube', but moved Linda's melody to the centre of the song as the tune of the song itself. 'The Lion Sleeps Tonight' was published by Token Music Publishing Company. This version would be rearranged and covered numerous times, and was used in Disney's *The Lion King*, including the film (and its later remake) and the stage show, as well as sequels and spin-offs.

In 1980, the copyright in 'Mbube' in the USA came up for renewal.[59] This right to renew vested in the author or their heirs.[60] Folkways thus entered into an assignment agreement with Linda's wife Regina, as his sole heir, relating to all the rights she had in the song. The consideration given for this assignment was one dollar. Folkways subsequently registered the renewal term in their own name.[61] By that time, Folkways had already acquired the rights in 'Wimoweh' after it had been renewed in Campbell's name in 1979.[62] Shortly after Regina's death in 1990, Folkways secured further assignment from Regina's four daughters for all rights they might hold in 'Mbube', then or in the future.[63] It should be noted that at that time there was a legal dispute between Folkways, which owned the rights in 'Wimoweh' and 'Mbube' in the USA, and Abilene music, which had in the meantime acquired the rights in 'The Lion Sleeps Tonight'.[64] The arbitration, which was confirmed in the subsequent litigation, resulted in ownership in 'The Lion Sleeps Tonight', as far as the USA was concerned, resting with Abilene.[65]

B. Legal Battle

Linda died impoverished in 1962, leaving behind his wife and four children. An exposé published in 2000 on the story of Solomon Linda and 'Mbube' caused significant uproar in South Africa and started a process to reclaim royalties in the song to the benefit of the heirs and to recognise its origins.[66] With initial support from Gallo Records, and later the South African government, proceedings were initiated in South Africa in the name of the executor of Linda's estate against Disney and certain (sub-)licencees of Abilene. While there were disputes regarding the various versions, the court case related to the copyright in 'Mbube'. The main argument was that under the Imperial Copyright Act of 1911,[67] which applied to all the so-called 'British Reversionary

[58] Dean, 'Stalking the Sleeping Lion' (n 42) 17; Dean, *Awakening the Lion* (n 42) 5.

[59] Works created before 1 January 1978 were subject to renewal registration in their 28th year. The renewal term for Mbube was 67 years. 17 USC § 304(a)(1)(A). US Copyright Office registration number RE0000066071.

[60] 17 USC § 304(a)(1)(C).

[61] US Copyright Office document number V1972P298.

[62] US Copyright Office registration number RE0000038975.

[63] Dean, 'Stalking the Sleeping Lion' (n 42) 17.

[64] See *Folkways Music Publishers, Inc v George David Weiss, June Peretti, Luigi Creatore and Abilene music Cor* 989 F.2d 108 (2d Cir 1993).

[65] Interestingly, the arbitrators added a provisio that a small portion (allegedly 10%) of the performing rights should be sent to the heirs of Linda. Whether such an amount ever reached the Linda family remains unclear.

[66] Malan (n 50).

[67] Copyright Act 1911.

Territories', including South Africa, the rights assigned by Linda should have reverted to the executor of his estate 25 years after Linda's death.[68] Section 5(2) of the 1911 Act states:

> [W]here the author of a work is the first owner of the copyright therein, no assignment of the copyright, and no grant of any interest therein, made by him (otherwise than by will) after the passing of this Act, shall be operative to vest in the assignee or grantee any rights with respect to the copyright in the work beyond the expiration of twenty-five years from the death of the author, and the reversionary interest in the copyright expectant on the termination of that period shall, on the death of the author, notwithstanding any agreement to the contrary, devolve on his legal personal representatives as part of his estate, and any agreement entered into by him as to the disposition of such reversionary interest shall be null and void, but nothing in this proviso shall be construed as applying to the assignment of the copyright in a collective work or a licence to publish a work or part of a work as part of a collective work.[69]

When the former Territories later adopted their own copyright laws, such reversionary rights were removed from the newer statutes; yet, they could still apply to grants made on or before the commencement of the newer laws. More specifically, in South Africa, the reversionary right after 25 years continued to apply to assignments and grants made by the author on or before 10 September 1965.[70] In this case, the executor of Linda's estate argued that, accordingly, all copyright in 'Mbube' for South Africa and the former British Reversionary Territories would have reverted to him in 1987, and not the heirs. This, in turn, would mean that the assignment by Regina to Folkways would be without force or effect beyond 1987, as would the subsequent assignment by Linda's daughters. In other words, from 1987, the copyright in 'Mbube' vested in the executor of the estate, and until he assigned these rights, Disney and other licencees of Abilene would have been infringing the executor's copyright in the song.

In 2006, before the case went to trial, the parties and Abilene music reached a settlement. Although Abilene was not a party in the case, it became involved in the settlement negotiations as the licensor of 'The Lion Sleeps Tonight'. It had licensed the song to all defendants and had granted an indemnity to Disney in relation to this licence, which Disney called upon. The settlement operated worldwide and comprised compensation in the form of a lump sum payment[71] to the estate for the past infringements as well as an undertaking to pay royalties for future uses of the song worldwide for a period of 10 years.[72] A trust would be established to administer the funds for the benefit of the heirs.[73] It would also be publicly recognised that 'The Lion Sleeps Tonight' was derived from 'Mbube', and Linda would be named co-composer of the song, effectively reconfirming that the song is part of South African culture. In return, the executor of Linda's estate would withdraw the litigation and waive all further claims against Abilene and its licencees.

As far as the economic rights are concerned, 'Mbube' entered the public domain in South Africa in 2013.[74] Accordingly, at least in South Africa, the settlement gave the estate of Linda royalties beyond the expiry of the copyright. In some other common law countries where the estate also owns the copyright in 'Mbube', such as the UK and Australia, the song is still protected, and legal action is theoretically still possible. Although copyright still subsists in the USA, the estate does not own any rights in the USA.[75]

[68] The British Imperial Copyright Act was effectively enacted in South Africa as the Third Schedule to the Patents, Designs, Trade Marks and Copyright Act No 9 of 1916.

[69] Copyright Act 1911, s 5(2).

[70] South Africa became a republic in 1961 and adopted its own copyright law in 1965. The 1911 Act was replaced in 1978, and that Act, as amended and pending the enactments of the new Copyright Act, still remains in force.

[71] The amount was not disclosed.

[72] Dean, 'Stalking the Sleeping Lion' (n 42) 21; Dean, *Awakening the Lion* (n 42) 43.

[73] Dean, 'Stalking the Sleeping Lion' (n 42) 21; Dean, *Awakening the Lion* (n 42) 43.

[74] Copyright Act 1978, s 3(2)(a).

[75] As a result of the 1976 Copyright Act and the 1998 Copyright Term Extension Act, the copyright in 'Mbube' in the USA expires in 2047.

C. 'Mbube' as a Style and Isicathamiya

'Mbube' came to characterise the popular a cappella choral style of isicathamiya. This style was named after the isiZulu term 'cathama', meaning 'walk[ing] softly like a cat on tiptoe in a stalking manner'.[76] The style was developed by Zulu migrant communities and is a mix of Christian gospel music, blackface minstrelsy and South African folk traditions. It is performed in call and response fashion by black male choirs that vary in size from four to over 20 performers. These groups are arranged around four vocal ranges – soprano, alto, tenor and bass – and they sing in a four-part harmony.[77] Isicathamiya performances are associated with choreography and the choirs typically adhere to a strict dress code of uniforms or matching formal wear, often including ties or bowties, caps or hats and linen gloves.

Its precursor style, which emerged in the 1930s, was later named after Linda's famous song. The major impact of this song, together with Linda's influence on the style, led to the word 'Mbube' becoming a synonym for the genre.[78] But its roots can be traced back further, to the popularisation of blackface minstrelsy in the 1890s, and particularly the visit to South Africa of the African-American musicians Orpheus M McAdoo and the Virginia Jubilee Singers.[79]

The style has evolved with the transformation of preindustrial Zulu society and has existed in various manifestations.[80] From mbube, it shifted to a more boisterous 'bombing' sound in the 1940 called *ibombing*, followed by softer and more 'refined' manifestations in the 1960s and 1970s. Various stylistic developments and innovations to the style have been attributed to Solomon Linda and the Evening Birds. For instance, they abandoned the *isikhunzi* principle of one singer per voice part and strengthened the bass section with multiple singers, introduced the falsetto main voice and redefined the relationship among the various voice parts.[81]

The inclusion of mbube and its successor isicathamiya in popular music caused this style of music to become popular outside of Africa and marked the start of a global opening of doors to South African music and musicians. Isicathamiya was made world famous by South African choral group Ladysmith Black Mambazo and other South African artists' contributions on the 1986 album *Graceland*, to which we turn now.

V. *Graceland*

A. Collaboration and Borrowing

The 1986 *Graceland* album is a collaboration between Paul Simon and host of other artists, including a large group of mostly black South African artists.[82] It comprises a mixture of US and South African music styles. Together with some musicians flown in from the USA, Simon recorded most of the South African parts of the album in Johannesburg. Here, he collaborated with a number of

[76] S Dlamini, 'Isicathamiya', *Bloomsbury Encyclopedia of Popular Music of the World*, vol 7 (2019) 296.

[77] ibid 296.

[78] S Frith, *Popular Music and Identity* (Psychology Press, 2004) 271.

[79] See V Erlman, 'Migration and Performance: Zulu Migrant Workers' Isicathamiya Performance in South Africa, 1890–1950' (1990) 34 *Ethnomusicology* 199, 203–04.

[80] V Erlman, '"Singing Brings Joy to the Distressed": Race, Class, Social Control and Resistance in Zulu Migrant Workers' Choral Competitions' (History Workshop, Johannesburg, 1987) https://wiredspace.wits.ac.za/handle/10539/7795?show=full.

[81] Erlmann, 'Fantasies of Home' (n 45) 271.

[82] The album also included collaborations with a number of US artists.

South African artists, including Tao Ea Matsekha, General MD Shirinda, Morris Goldberg, Lulu Masilela, the Boyoyo Boys and Joseph Shabalala and his isicathamiya group Ladysmith Black Mambazo. The South African recordings were mostly melodies and jam sessions, which would later be worked into the final album.[83]

Other parts of songs were recorded in different locations, including Los Angeles; Lafayette, LA; London; and New York. Some of the South African artists joined Simon in the USA for the final stages of recording and mixing, as well as several promotional performances. The final album features a mix of genres, including the South African genres of isicathamiya and mbaqanga. In fact, the inspiration or motivation for Paul Simon to visit Johannesburg and record this album was the 'township jive' style of mbaqanga. Simon was introduced to the style by one of his friends, who handed him a bootlegged cassette. Mbaqanga as a genre is difficult to describe. The term has been used to refer to a range of musical styles, from African jazz in the late 1940s and 1950s, to jive in the 1950s and 1960s, and other styles of mbaqanga in the following years.[84] Key features of mbaqanga relate to the interconnection between vocal and instrumental parts. As Meintjes explains, 'the instrumental lines are often translations of vocal lines and that the instrumental tracks are foregrounded in the mix along with the vocals'.[85]

The album is a great example of both artistic and stylistic collaboration, including musical and linguistic styles. The songs on *Graceland* were composed with various levels of input from Simon and the other artists, and represent and reference a broad range of musical styles.

The most collaborative and South African track is arguably the eighth track on the album, called 'Homeless'.[86] This song, a collaboration between Ladysmith Black Mambazo and Simon, includes Zulu sound and language, a traditional African call and response structure, as well as various elements of isicathamiya.[87] Interestingly, in the album's liner notes, Simon describes in detail the song's collaborative process. He describes how the lyrics and melody were composed, how musical and linguistic changes were suggested, and the integration of Zulu and English in the lyrics. This explicit description in the liner notes can be considered an indication of the significance of the collaborative process – at least as far as the album's public image is concerned.

B. Controversies

Some commentators have questioned whether the album is the result of true, arm's-length collaboration, pointing to the power differential between Simon and the other musicians, and features of appropriation, exploitation and domination.[88]

While collaboration on the album was typically recognised through co-writing and arrangement credits, this was not applied consistently throughout the album. It appears that many contributors were not properly credited for their creative contributions. One example is the lack of credits for musicians who were paid to play backups as a studio band but who provided a clear and distinctive contribution to the compositional process.[89] As Feld notes:

[83] See D Collier, *Media Primitivism: Technological Art in Africa* (Duke University Press, 2020) 69.
[84] L Dalamba, 'Mbaqanga' in *Bloomsbury Encyclopedia of Popular Music of the World*, vol 7 (2019) 418–24.
[85] L Meintjes, 'Paul Simon's Graceland, South Africa, and the Mediation of Musical Meaning' (1990) 34 *Ethnomusicology* 37, 44.
[86] S Feld, 'Notes on World Beat' (1988) 1 *Public Culture Bulletin* 31, 33.
[87] Muller (n 1) 61–63.
[88] See Meintjes (n 85) 47–48.
[89] ibid 41.

> All of the performance styles (the grooves, beats, sounds, genres) are South African in makeup (whatever influences they synthesize and incorporate). While the contribution of Simon's lyrics is clear and important, the contribution of the music, its unique and distinct and formative influence on the quality and particularity of the record, is clearly downplayed.[90]

Apart from acknowledging (at least some of) the contributors, Simon recognises the influence of earlier works of other South African musicians in the album's 'special thanks' liner notes.

While there have been accusations of Simon unfairly profiting from South Africa's traditional Zulu music, he also provided international exposure for the music as well as South Africa's local musicians.[91] According to some, many of the musicians on the album have benefited financially from the collaboration, pointing to the fact that Simon paid his musicians triple the union wages and to the profits gained by Lady Black Mambazo because of their subsequent international success.[92]

Furthermore, controversy arose over Simon's disregard of the international cultural boycott against South Africa at that time. The recording of *Graceland* came at a crucial point in South African political history. As resistance against apartheid was growing, the mid-1980s were likely the most repressive years in apartheid history – with the South African government expelling journalists and declaring numerous states of emergency. Parallel to these developments, there was an increasing international public awareness as well as a growing resistance to apartheid, including an international call for a cultural boycott by South Africans in exile. This said, cultural boycotts against South Africa had already been part of the fight against segregation for a long time.[93] Under the academic and cultural boycott, supported by the United Nations (UN) and the ANC, artists were prohibited from participating in any activities or collaborations of any kind in South Africa because of its segregations policies. In 1968, the UN General Assembly requested all states and organisations 'to suspend cultural, educational, sporting and other exchanges with the racist regime and with organisations or institutions in South Africa which practice apartheid'.[94] Later, in the 1980s, the UN started creating a blacklist of performers who travelled to South Africa.[95] When Simon ignored the cultural boycott and travelled there in 1985, some of those familiar with the struggles of black South Africans under the apartheid regime expressed concern that this could weaken the fight against apartheid. However, those in support of Simon's project have pointed out it significantly increased international exposure for South African artists, whose styles, including Soweto township jive, mbaqanga and kwela, provided the foundations for much of the album's distinct sound.[96] Notably, after the boycott was lifted in 1991, Simon was invited by Nelson Mandela to play five shows in South Africa. During the subsequent African tour, Simon was joined by some of the performers on the album, as well as exiled South African musicians Miriam Makeba and Hugh Masekela.

[90] Feld (n 86) 34.

[91] SA Pager, 'Traditional Knowledge Rights and Wrongs' (2016) 20 *Virginia Journal or Law & Technology* 82, 151.

[92] C Hamm, *Putting Popular Music in Its Place* (Cambridge University Press, 1995) 337.

[93] For an overview, see 'South Africa's Academic and Cultural Boycott – Timeline' (South African History Online) www.sahistory.org.za/article/south-africas-academic-and-cultural-boycott-timeline.

[94] UNGA Res 2396 (1968).

[95] Apart from music performers, the list also included other actors, including sports men, novelists and film directors.

[96] eg Hugh Masakela and Miriam Makeba went on to produce a record for Ladysmith Black Mambazo on Paul Simon's record label. Feld (n 86) 32–33.

VI. Conclusion

Borrowing has been central to the creation of music in South Africa. This chapter has shown the broad spectrum of borrowing that has been happening in South Africa, from colonial influences and the copying of foreign sounds to indigenising borrowed structures.[97] Mbube and kwaito are but a two examples of how foreign sounds have been borrowed and transformed into unique genres. But South African music is also a valuable resource, with foreign artists reworking South African songs, collaborating with local musicians and incorporating elements of South African styles and genres. Frequently, borrowing has been a two-way process – a process of 're-borrowing' – where the South African genres and styles that are used in foreign music are themselves a product of foreign input and influence.

Another, very recent example of borrowing South African music in the broader sense occurred during the early stages of the COVID pandemic. At that time, various initiatives on social media sought to boost morale and create a sense of community. One of the most popular initiatives was the 'Jerusalema Challenge', where groups of staff at businesses, hospitals, police forces and other workplaces collectively danced to the song 'Jerusalema' and posted their recordings online in 2020. The challenge went viral, gaining popularity around the world. The song was created by South African artist Master KG and featured vocalist Nomcembo Zikode. The song is perhaps best described as a house song with gospel influences. The lyrics are sung in isiZulu. In early 2021, however, it was reported that Warner Music Group, which owns the exclusive rights, started to demand licence fees from several organisations in Germany for the use of the song.[98] This led to considerable social media backlash, and was publicly perceived as a money-making scheme, resulting in some organisations deleting their videos of the challenge.[99]

The examples of South African music discussed in this chapter have highlighted the general importance of borrowing and transformative appropriation for promoting creativity in this field. Often, existing works are reused and become a key ingredient for new creations, or even new styles and genres. New, digitally enabled remixing and sampling capabilities at the hands of professionals and amateurs alike have amplified this trend.

Against this backdrop, it becomes a major concern when overzealous copyright frameworks curtail such creativity and, as a result, stifle domestic innovation in the music sector. This often happens in a misguided attempt to foreground the rewarding of those who have already created copyrighted works but without due consideration of the downsides for future creators and the innovation ecosystem. The current South African copyright regime protects, among others, musical works, sound recordings and literary works,[100] and contains several aspects which potentially impede borrowing in the context of music. For example, the threshold for one of the key requirements for obtaining copyright protection – originality – is now much lower than in other parts of the world. This is because, unlike other jurisdictions, South Africa essentially still applies the 'sweat of the brow' doctrine to determine whether a work fulfils the originality requirement,[101]

[97] Muller (n 1) 265.

[98] T Landsberg, 'Warner Demands Licence Fees for "Jerusalema" Videos' (*DW*, 17 February 2021) www.dw.com/en/warner-demands-licence-fees-for-jerusalema-videos/a-56594810.

[99] AFP, 'Warner Music Demands German Police Pay Up for "Jerusalema" Videos' (*eNCA*, 16 February 2021) www.enca.com/news/warner-music-demands-german-police-pay-jerusalema-videos.

[100] Performers are protected by the Performers' Protection Act 11 of 1967.

[101] This view was confirmed in *Haupt t/a Softcopy v Brewers Marketing Intelligence (Pty) Ltd* 2006 (4) SA 458 (SCA); however, *Moneyweb (Pty) Ltd v Media 24 Ltd and Another* 2016 (4) SA 591 (GJ) may indicate a departure from this doctrine.

and by doing so, many works which are not protected elsewhere due to a lack of originality enjoy copyright protection in South Africa. This, in turn, makes it more complicated to legally borrow from such works. This situation is aggravated by the fact that the adaptation right is inadequately defined in the Copyright Act,[102] and to the extent that the term is defined, the definition appears (too) wide. Moreover, South Africa's Copyright Act has long been criticised as outdated in several respects, and that, too, appears to impede follow-up creativity through borrowing. More specifically, the copyright exceptions and limitations contained in the Act, ie the provisions which would allow the permission-free use of prior works, seem too narrow and too focused on analogue technology to meaningfully support modern modes of music borrowing. And while fair use-type provisions appear to aid creativity and transformative reuse in the music sector in other parts of the world, no such provision yet exists in South African copyright law, even though a Copyright Bill proposes to introduce a fair use regime in South Africa.

Yet, despite what appears to be a sub-optimal domestic copyright framework for music borrowing, the cases in this chapter demonstrated that such borrowing has nevertheless taken place and continues to occur. It is argued here that copyright enforcement is presently not strong enough to fully prevent such borrowing. As a result, a lack of relevant case law is characteristic of the subject of music-related copyright infringement. But, as observed by one of the authors of this chapter in a different context: 'when copyright enforcement begins in earnest, then, without mechanisms in place to secure non-infringing channels of access [musicians, and especially those making use of prior works from others] will be in a precarious position.'[103]

[102] See Copyright Act, s 1(1) definition of 'adaptation'.

[103] C Armstrong, J de Beer, D Kawooya, A Prabhala and T Schonwetter, 'Summary and Conclusions' in C Armstrong, J de Beer, D Kawooya, A Prabhala and T Schonwetter (eds), *Access to Knowledge in Africa: The Role of Copyright* (UCT Press, 2014) 341.

Section E: Asia and Oceania

25

History, Functionality and Dignity: Traditional Chinese Music Borrowing and Copyright Protection in China

TIANXIANG HE AND JING LI

I. The Definition of Traditional Music in the Chinese Context

This chapter focuses on the music genre known as traditional Chinese music and the copyright issues of music borrowing related to it. Traditional music is known as the art of music which has been created, preserved and transmitted within a national community, and it is mostly handed down from generation to generation, with specific genre characteristics, aesthetic features and cultural connotations. Carugno argues that, in general, traditional music has four main features: it is (i) inherited from the past; (ii) orally transferred; (iii) survives mainly through practice; and (iv) functions as a marker of the community's identity.[1]

The term 'Chinese traditional music' is often used interchangeably with other terms such as 'national music' and 'folk music' in China, which can be confusing.[2] Since China is a big country with thousands of years of history and officially has 56 nationalities living inside its territory, the term 'national music' (*guo yue*) should cover both 'ancient music' (*gu yue*) and 'folk music' (*min yue*). Another related term is 'the music of the Chinese nationality' (*Zhonghua minzu*), which is a term that 'covers all fifty-six nationalities living within the territorial borders of the People's Republic of China (PRC)'.[3] Furthermore, the widely referred term 'music of local regions' (*difang yinyue*) means traditional music of the Han people, while the term 'music of the national minority' (*shaoshu minzu yinyue*) refers to the music of the national minorities. However, it is believed that this distinction has artificially created 'false distinctions between genres, categories, aesthetics, and people'.[4]

With the above overlapping terms in mind, it is important to mention that the seminal textbook entitled *The Introduction of National Music*, published in China in 1964, introduced a

[1] G Carugno, 'How to Protect Traditional Folk Music? Some Reflections upon Traditional Knowledge and Copyright Law' (2018) 31 *International Journal for the Semiotics of Law* 263.

[2] H Liu, 'National Music, Folk Music and Chinese Traditional Music: Analysis beyond the Historical Transition' (2019) No 1 *Music Research* 5–17 (刘红：《' 国乐' ' 民族音乐' 与' 中国传统音乐' –并非作' 历史变迁' 理解的现象观察与思考》，《音乐研究》2019年第1期).

[3] S Tuohy, 'The Social Life of Genre: The Dynamics of Folksong in China' (1999) 30 *Asian Music* 54.

[4] F Lau, '"Center or Periphery?": Regional Music in Contemporary China' (2015) 2 *International Communication of Chinese Culture* 35.

five-genre system and listed them in separate chapters: folk song (*min ge*), national music instrument (*minzu qiyue*), sing and dance music (*minjian gewu yinyue*), narrative songs (*shuochang yinyue*) and operatic music (*xiqu yinyue*).[5] After several decades of development, the term 'national music' has now been incorporated into the expression 'traditional music' in formal musical education, which focuses on the 'cultural factors' of China rather than the identity of the authors.[6] Genre classification is a complicated issue,[7] and there can be no correct answer to it. For the purpose of this chapter, the concept 'traditional music' as a genre in China today generally refers to national music, which includes ancient music and folk music.

Against this background, this chapter analyses to what extent Chinese traditional music is borrowed and developed by contemporary musicians, and how legal norms of copyright law affect that practice. In general terms, music borrowing refers to taking elements out of an existing piece of music and putting it in a new piece.[8] The importance of borrowing was overshadowed by a romantic conception of music composition, which was embedded in the copyright law. It was observed that the biggest hurdle for music borrowing is the copyright requirement of 'originality'.[9] Today, due to the availability of social media platforms and accessible tools for the creation and distribution of music, musical works can be created and spread quickly and easily. The practice of music borrowing is so common today that it is necessary to consider more carefully the extent to which copy and borrowing traditional music has been and could be a great source of innovation in music, as borrowing is inevitable even in most 'original' works.[10] The difference is one of degree rather than kind. Thus, establishing a legal boundary between lawful borrowing and copyright infringement in the context of Chinese traditional music is very important.

II. The History of Chinese Traditional Music and Music Borrowing

A brief history of Chinese traditional music and music borrowing will help better understand this music genre. Chinese traditional music stretches back to ancient *Shijing*, the *Classic of Poetry* said to have been compiled by Confucius.[11] It is regarded as the oldest collection of poems and songs. The chapter entitled 'Guo Feng' includes the earliest compilation of folk songs.[12] It is believed that the Chinese folklore reflects the culture and identity of China and is a symbol of national pride.[13] However, it was pointed out that folk music was largely neglected in China until the advent of Communism since 'elite Confucian theory dominat[ed] official sources through imperial times'.[14] To better reflect the contemporary issue of music borrowing, this chapter only focuses on the evolution of Chinese traditional music in post-imperial China since 1912.

[5] Research Institute of Music of the Chinese Academy of Arts, *The Introduction of National Music* (People's Music Publishing House, 1964) (中国艺术研究院音乐研究所, 民族音乐概论, 人民音乐出版社, 1964).

[6] Liu, 'National Music' (n 2) 5–17.

[7] Tuohy (n 3) 51–58.

[8] JP Burkholder, 'The Uses of Existing Music: Musical Borrowing as a Field' (1994) 50(3) *Notes* 863.

[9] OB Arewa, 'From JC Bach to Hip Hop: Musical Borrowing, Copyright and Cultural Context' (2006) 84 *North Carolina Law Review* 547.

[10] ibid 582.

[11] *The Book of Songs: The Ancient Chinese Classic of Poetry* (Grove Press, 1996).

[12] Tuohy (n 3).

[13] D Liu, 'Can Copyright Lend Its Cinderellaic Magic to Chinese Folklore' (2006) 5 *John Marshall Review of Intellectual Property Law* 203.

[14] S Jones, 'Reading between the Lines: Reflections on the Massive "Anthology of Folk Music of the Chinese Peoples"' (2003) 47 *Ethnomusicology* 290.

The imperial Qing Dynasty was replaced by the Republic of China (ROC) in 1912 and later the PRC in 1949. As evident in the case of China, different social structures lead to different understandings of music genres and styles. Music has been highly politicised throughout Chinese history. In the traditional Chinese culture, the music was 'meant not to please but rather to educate',[15] and music was considered 'one of four basic social elements, along with morals, laws and politics'.[16] The educational nature of music in China is important as it relates to the development of the genres that contributed to the development of Chinese traditional music after 1912. These include songs from Chinese folklore, opera, ancient music and new influences from Western classical music.

For example, after the establishment of the ROC, many Chinese students chose to study in Japan and Europe. As a result, the Chinese intelligentsia built a close relationship with the European and Japanese cultures, and once back home, they were eager to hear the music from these foreign countries on their own soil. Accordingly, Chinese music began to mix with Western styles, especially in the 1920s and 1930s. In the meantime, *Guo Feng*, during the last century, continued to draw the attention of scholars and officials, who called for the creation of a new 'Air of the States' (*Xin guo feng*) in order to restore 'a national poetry' style from the 1920s onwards.[17] The term *Feng* continues to be used today, examples including the term *caifeng*, which literally means 'collect the wind' and refers to folk music investigation in the field.[18] It is believed that Chinese ethnomusicologists have been collecting 'the music of the people' in the field since the 1940s.[19] In the 1930s, the National Conservatory of Music published *Zhong Guo Min Ge Xuan Ji* (Chinese Folk Song Anthology). 'Kang Ding Qing Ge' (Kang Ding Love Song), 'Zai Na Yao Yuan De Di Fang' (In That Distant Place) and 'Xiu He Bao' (Sewing the Brocade Purse) – some of the representative folk songs of that period.[20] The use of folk tunes and the rewriting of lyrics demonstrated the government's 'careful attempt to exploit the deeply rooted folk tradition for its political purpose'.[21]

After the establishment of the PRC in 1949, the influence of the Soviet Union dominated Chinese folk music scholarship for some time.[22] Music and the other arts at that period of time were required 'to serve the interests of workers, peasants and soldiers' and 'to convey the messages of China's Communist government'.[23] During this period, revolutionary songs were often used to 'educate the masses and to promote political campaigns and socialist ideologies and values'.[24] Chairman Mao Zedong insisted that writers and artists should study different social classes in society, their mutual relations and their respective conditions in order to produce literature and art that is 'rich in content and correct in orientation'.[25] In addition, Chairman Mao urged artists

[15] W-W Law and W-C Ho, 'Music Education in China: In Search of Social Harmony and Chinese Nationalism' (2011) 28 *British Journal of Music Education* 374.

[16] ibid.

[17] Tuohy (n 3) 50.

[18] ibid.

[19] S Jones, 'Source and Stream: Early Music and Living Traditions in China' (1996) 24 *Early Music* 378.

[20] XC Hallis, 'Chinese Art Song from 1912 to 1949' (DMA thesis, University of Texas at Austin, 1995) 14.

[21] C Hung, 'The Politics of Songs: Myths and Symbols in the Chinese Communist War Music, 1937–1949' (1996) 30 *Modern Asian Studies* 910.

[22] Tuohy (n 3) 49.

[23] W-C Ho and W-W Law, 'Values, Music and Education in China' (2004) 6 *Music Education Research* 152.

[24] S Li and F Yan, 'Searching for Red Songs: The Politics of Revolutionary Nostalgia in Contemporary China' (2019) 242 *China Quarterly* 509.

[25] Z Mao, 'Talks at the Yenan Forum on Literature and Art' (1942) www.commonprogram.science/documents/TALKS%20AT%20THE%20YENAN%20FORUM%20ON%20LITERATURE%20AND%20ART.pdf.

to use the artistic legacy of China and the international art form to promote the socialist regime. A large-scale campaign was launched to educate the largely illiterate rural population by setting revolutionary lyrics to existing folk tunes, which were often referred to as *hong ge* (red songs),[26] and it aimed to 'turn indifferent peasants into ardent participants in a revolution directed by the Party'.[27] As Lee indicates, many contemporary folk songs have borrowed ethnic folk song (*min ge*) styles, and they often use lyrics that contain implicit political messages.[28]

Songs during the Cultural Revolution (1966–76) were, in general, borrowed from traditional music and rearranged. Although traditional Peking opera was banned, Mao recognised its popularity in China and reformed the genre to suit his goals.[29] Music borrowing led to the development of the eight-model revolutionary Peking operas (*ba da ge ming yang ban xi*), which reformed traditional Peking opera by 'borrowing modern staged drama, adopting realistic settings, props and costumes, and using symphonic orchestras in place of traditional musical instruments'.[30] However, traditional Chinese music was reviewed negatively in general due to its feudal nature during the Cultural Revolution. For example, songs like 'The Red Lantern' and 'Azalea Mountain' were found to have borrowed the melody from the socialist anthem 'L'Internationale' rather than traditional Chinese music.[31]

Due to the cultural revolution and other social movements, China's music industry did not really develop until the late 1970s, when extensive economic reform was introduced. In the late 1980s, popular music was formally recognised by the mainstream music industry.[32] Following the Reform and Opening-up period, China's music sector grew rapidly in the 1990s, resulting in a wide variety of music styles and genres. As Wong puts it, 'Within the space of generations, institutions, customs and social relationships were changed or refashioned, with traditional music first being ignored and then reshaped to meet the western challenge'.[33] Interestingly, pre-1949 revolutionary or patriotic songs (*hong ge*), as already discussed, were revived and popularised in the 1990s due to the 'Patriotic Education Campaign'.[34] The patriotic songs were renewed so as to 'unite China's people under the concept of "one China" and to recover their national pride after the humiliation of so much foreign aggression'.[35]

When traditional music becomes popular, music borrowing also becomes evident. For much of the second half of the twentieth century, mainland China, Hong Kong and Taiwan were 'partners' in terms of a music piracy economy.[36] With the legitimate and underground circulation of popular music from Hong Kong and Taiwan, the mainland market thrives and elements of traditional music in mainland China have been frequently borrowed in popular music composed and sung by

[26] B Li, 'Folk Songs and Popular Music in China: An Examination of Min'ge and Its Significance within Nationalist Frameworks' (2016) Pomona Senior Theses, Paper 162, http://scholarship.claremont.edu/pomona_theses/162.

[27] Hung (n 21) 926.

[28] G Lee, 'The "East Is Red" Goes Pop: Commodification, Hybridity and Nationalism in Chinese Popular Song and Its Televisual Performance' (1995) 14 *Popular Music* 99.

[29] M Galikowski, *Art and Politics in China, 1949–1984* (Chinese University Press, 1998) 201.

[30] Zhang Xueying, 'Changes in Nightlife' (*China Today*, 2009) www.chinatoday.com.cn/ctenglish/se/txt/2009-08/20/content_212816.htm.

[31] Y Ludden, 'China's Musical Revolution: From Beijing Opera to Yangbanxi' (2013) Theses and Dissertations – Music 19, 141, https://uknowledge.uky.edu/music_etds/19.

[32] J Street et al, 'Copyright and Music Policy in China: A Literature Review' (August 2015) CREATe Working Paper 2015/06, 6.

[33] IKF Wong, 'From Reaction to Synthesis: Chinese Musicology in the Twentieth Century' in B Nettl and P Bohlman (eds), *Comparative Musicology and Anthropology of Music: Essays on the History of Ethnomusicology* (University of Chicago Press, 1991) 37.

[34] W-C Ho, 'Social Change and Nationalism in China's Popular Songs' (2006) 31 *Social History* 447.

[35] ibid.

[36] Street et al (n 32) 7.

musicians from Taiwan and Hong Kong, such as Jay Chou, who started the 'New Chinese Popular Music Style',[37] and even sampled by famous rappers like Gunna from the USA.[38] However, it is possible that some types of unauthorised borrowing will inevitably trigger copyright issues.

As history shows, music borrowing was never a problem in China when it was in a state of 'legal and moral flux'.[39] It was the rapid development of the market economy and the advent of the Copyright Law of China (CLC) in 1991 that changed everything. Interestingly, music borrowing practice was not a problem in the USA for a long time when 'the emphasis on productivity and professional skill overshadowed the importance of the originality of a musical work'.[40] In musical copyright infringement analysis, the three most basic elements of a musical piece that can render originality are melody, harmony and rhythm.[41] However, it is also believed that the art of arranging music involves more than decorative works since the arranger also contributes 'a great deal of original composing when engaging in arrangements'.[42] When a musical piece borrows and rearranges elements from traditional music, copyright issues may arise. The following section thus examines the issue of traditional music borrowing under the CLC.

III. Borrowing of Traditional Chinese Music under the Chinese Copyright Law

The existing rules of the CLC that concern copyright infringement are, in general, no different from other jurisdictions: once a copyrighted work or a substantial part of it is used without authorisation and without any justification, such as fair use, it is a copyright infringement.[43] However, the core issue related to traditional music borrowing in China is not so much concerned about whether the borrowed parts are substantial or not as whether we can protect traditional music using copyright, as nearly all such music is deemed out of copyright protection.

As discussed in the first section of this chapter, 'traditional music' in China as a genre includes both ancient music and folk music. There are no special rules concerning the protection of ancient music. If the author can be identified and the duration of the copyright protection (50 years post mortem) is passed, then the musical work is already in the public domain. For example, pop singer Leehom Wong was praised for his incorporation of the music of ethnic minorities from China, as well as the traditional Beijing opera and Kunqu.[44] Seemingly no copyright issues will arise if the borrowing is focusing on the traditional music, which is a public domain work, rather than a derivative work of it that is still under copyright

[37] S-T (Stone) Han, 'Jay Chou's Kuso Music: Cultural Fusion in the Age of the Internet' (2021) CMC Senior Theses 2611, 7.

[38] M Gilberg, 'Gunna Cashes Out on Highly Anticipated Debut Album "Drip or Drown 2"' (*Bark*, 2019) https://redwoodbark.org/52128/reviews/gunna-cashes-out-on-highly-anticipated-debut-album-drip-or-drown-2/.

[39] H Rees, 'The Age of Consent: Traditional Music, Intellectual Property and Changing Attitudes in the People's Republic of China' (2003) 12 *British Journal of Ethnomusicology* 138.

[40] MV Francis, 'Musical Copyright Infringement: The Replacement of Arnstein v Porter – A More Comprehensive Use of Expert Testimony and the Implementation of an "Actual Audience" Test' (1990) 17 *Pepperdine Law Review* 493.

[41] ibid 498.

[42] JL Friedman, 'Copyright and the Musical Arrangement: An Analysis of the Law and Problems Pertaining to This Specialized Form of Derivative Work' (1980) 7 *Pepperdine Law Review* 126.

[43] CLC, Arts 52 and 53.

[44] G Wang, 'The ABCs of Chinese Pop: Wang Leehom and the Marketing of a Global Chinese Celebrity' (2012) 4(1) *Journal of Transnational American Studies*, http://dx.doi.org/10.5070/T841012820.

protection. For the folk music, Article 6 of the CLC provides that 'Regulations for the protection of copyright in expressions of folklore shall be separately established by the State Council'. However, besides a draft entitled Regulations on the Protection of Copyright in Folk Literary and Artistic Works published by the National Copyright Administration (NCA) in 2014, which was hidden shortly after publication as it stirred up a huge amount of controversy at the time,[45] there is no established rule regarding the protection of traditional Chinese music, which is clearly covered by the concept of 'expressions of folklore'.[46]

The difficulties lie in the definition of traditional Chinese music: if it should be 'inherited from the past', then it must be old enough to be out of copyright protection. Otherwise, there is no need to discuss the special way to protect it, as the CLC can provide adequate protection via the normal route. The next issue concerns the lack of evidence regarding the first original version and whether it is published officially, as in general it was 'orally transferred' and 'survived mainly through practice'. Moreover, if traditional Chinese music is regarded as 'a marker of the community's identity', then who can be the owner of the related rights, if any? The next section explores the existing judicial practices in China, as the above issues have been considered by several Chinese courts.

IV. The Cases Concerning Borrowing of Traditional Music in China

There have been a number of copyright disputes in China regarding 'music arrangement (*bian qu*) as well as adaptation of traditional musical works. To better illustrate the situation in China, three landmark music copyright disputes that concern the borrowing of traditional Chinese music have been picked as examples.

A. The 'Long Song' Case[47]

Zhu Zhengben was the composer of the popular revolutionary song 'Seeing off the Red Army for Ten Times' ('Shi Song Hong Jun', hereinafter 'Seeing Off'), which described in a musical way the scene where the main force of Communist Party members Zhu De and Mao Zedong's Red Army left the Jinggang Mountains in early 1929.[48] Based on the folk song 'Long Song' ('chang ge') from the Gannan District of Jiangxi Province, Zhu Zhengben employed creative techniques to rearrange the song 'Seeing Off' and added some new content to it, and the lyrics were written by

[45] NCA, 'National Copyright Administration on "Regulations on the Protection of Copyright in Folk Literary and Artistic Works (Draft for Comments)" Notice of Public Consultation' (NCA, 2 September 2014) www.ncac.gov.cn/china-copyright/contents/12228/346301.shtml.

[46] Y Huang, *Legal Protection for Folk Literature and Art* (Intellectual Property Publishing House, 2008) 46 (黄玉烨：《民间文学艺术的法律保护》，知识产权出版社，2008年版，第 46页); WIPO Intergovernmental Committee on Intellectual Property and Genetic Resources, Traditional Knowledge and Folklore, 'Glossary of Key Terms Related to Intellectual Property and Genetic Resources, Traditional Knowledge and Traditional Cultural Expressions' (2019) WIPO/GRTKF/IC/40/INF/7, 19.

[47] *Wang Yong v Zhu Zhengben, CCTV and Wang Yunzhi* [2003] Beijing Haidian District People's Court, HMC No 19213, [2005] Beijing No 1 Intermediate People's Court, YMZ No 3447.

[48] S Wei, 'Study on the Historical Truth of Saying Goodbye to Red Army' (2012) No 2 *Journal of Gannan Normal University* 35 (孙伟：《十送红军的历史真相研究》，《赣南师范学院学报》2012年第2期).

Zhang Shixie. 'Seeing Off' was later picked as the theme song of the TV series *The Long March*. Wang Yunzhi, who was the former head of the General Administration Symphony Orchestra of China, adapted the score of 'Seeing Off'. The new composition was attributed to Wang Yunzhi at the end of each episode without mentioning Zhu Zhengben. Zhu Zhengben disagreed with this practice and sent a letter to China Central Television (CCTV) and the production team of *The Long March* requesting remuneration. As a result, when the rest of the *The Long March* was finally broadcast, Zhu was listed as one of the authors of the theme song 'Seeing Off' along with Zhang Shixie, and CCTV paid them accordingly.

The story did not end there. On 11 November 2003, Wang Yong sued Zhu Zhengben, Wang Yunzhi and CCTV before the Haidian District Court of Beijing and claimed that 'Seeing Off' copied part of his song 'Sending Comrades to Beijing' (hereinafter 'Sending'), created in 1959, and therefore constituted copyright infringement. Wang Yong asked the District Court to confirm that 'Sending' is a derivative work of the Jiangxi folk song 'Long Song', which enjoys independent copyright protection, and to order the defendants to stop infringing his copyright and apologise. On 16 November 2004, the court first confirmed that 'Sending' was an adaptation of the 'Long Song', and that Wang Yong owned the copyright over 'Sending'. The rationale behind this conclusion is straightforward: although 'Sending' had some similarities to 'Long Song' in terms of beat, melody, tone and style, etc, there were many differences in theme, expression and song combination that make it distinct from 'Long Song'. Because of these differences, the court held that 'Seeing Off' is an adaptation of the traditional Chinese music 'Long Song' and can enjoy its own independent copyright protection. It also indicated that it is crucial to consider that folk songs usually have a long history and are the result of efforts by generations of people that have helped to pass them down, and have transformed and promoted them. Therefore, it is in the public interest that no one can monopolise them. The adapters can only enjoy the exclusive right to their original contribution to the traditional music, but not to the parts borrowed from folk music. In addition, folk music is characterised by improvisation and variation. In the transmission of folk songs from generation to generation, singers in different regions often improvise the words or the tunes of the songs according to their needs. Accordingly, many different versions of a folk song – such as the 'Long Song' of this case – may exist. These treasures of folk art provide an inexhaustible source of inspiration for various creators. As a result, even though the court recognised that prior access was presumed in the case of 'Sending' and 'Seeing Off', and that Zhu may have borrowed some elements from 'Sending', the borrowing was not substantive, so the plaintiff's claim of copyright infringement was not supported.[49] Wang Yong then appealed to Beijing No 1 Intermediate People's Court.

On 29 June 2005, the Intermediate People's Court confirmed that Zhu Zhengben accessed the song 'Sending' before he created the song 'Seeing Off'. As to the issue of whether 'Seeing Off' was adapted from 'Sending', the court held that 'Sending' is a derivative work of 'Long Song', and in determining whether a derivative work is infringed, the key is to identify whether the allegedly infringing work used the original part of the derivative work and whether substantial similarity can be found.[50] The court opined that although prior access could be established and four bars in 'Seeing Off' and 'Sending' were found to be similar, the four bars were not consecutive bars and could not form a complete sentence. The two songs 'Seeing Off' and 'Sending' were therefore not substantially similar; accordingly, Zhu Zhengben did not infringe the copyright of Wang Yong's work.[51]

[49] *Wang Yong v Zhu Zhengben, CCTV and Wang Yunzhi*, No 19213.
[50] *Wang Yong v Zhu Zhengben, CCTV and Wang Yunzhi*, No 3447.
[51] ibid.

This case shows that the court managed to compare two derivative musical works of the traditional Chinese music 'Long Song' in a professional way: to comprehensively and scientifically analyse the relationship between the songs, the court used various methods such as comparison of the scores alone, comparison of the scores with lyrics and comparison of the whole recording. At the same time, it listened carefully to the opinions of the parties, general witnesses provided by the parties and expert witnesses, and sought to make a comprehensive judgment from the perspective of professionals and ordinary audiences. The court first pointed out that since both 'Seeing Off' and 'Sending' were derived from the 'Long Song', they cannot claim copyright over the main melody. Accordingly, no copyright infringement can be found between 'Seeing Off' and 'Sending'. As to the issue of whether 'Sending' is an adaption of 'Long Song', the court indicated that, when comparing different musical works, the focus should be on the differences in melody, structure, creative techniques, themes and feelings of the works. While melody and structure are certainly the main factors to be examined, the more important objects to be examined are the style, theme and feelings expressed in the music. After comparison, the court concluded that the differences in theme, expression and style between 'Sending' and 'Long Song' are obvious. The court further opined that the popularity of 'Sending' is partly due to its similarity with the 'Long Song', but the differences in lyrics are also important: 'Sending' is about the story of model workers from the Jinggang Mountains sending gifts to Chairman Mao. It is the chemistry of the combination of the score and lyrics that made it distinct and original. More importantly, in these two instances, the courts all confirmed that folk songs, including the 'Long Song' and its derivative works, tend to change over time and develop into many variations. If the derivative work contains recognisable new expressions, it should be deemed original and enjoy independent copyright protection.

B. The Wang Luobing Case

Controversy surrounds the late Chinese composer and folk song collector Wang Luobin (1913–96). Wang collected many melodious folk songs in the Xinjiang Uyghur Autonomous Region for three decades before he passed away. It was reported that he wrote down Uyghur folk songs such as 'Raise Your Cover Head', and went to the Kazakh people in Minle County, where he recorded the wanderer song 'Wait For You To Dawn' and other folk songs. He also adapted the folk song 'In That Distant Place', based on local Uyghur folk songs.[52]

The controversy focused on 'problems of ownership and authenticity, in particular legal issues of copyright (who has the right to profit) and moral authority (who has the right to represent)' when folk music is borrowed and sold as a tangible commodity.[53] In 1993, the well-known singer Luo Dayou covered and published some of Wang's Uyghur folk songs. Luo refused to pay the licence fee and argued that these songs belonged to the Uyghur people. With his statement, Luo Dayou made the point that the owner of folk music should not be a specific composer but all the members of a specific community. Here a controversy crops up: who should be the rightful owner? For folk songs, it is often very hard to identify a single author, and it is more like 'the result of cumulative creation by an ethnic group or region'.[54] Things became more complicated

[52] L Cui, 'Wang Luobin and His Songs' (*Beijing Review*, 19 May 2009) www.bjreview.com.cn/special/2009-05/19/content_196462.htm.

[53] R Harris, 'Wang Luobin: Folk Song King of the Northwest or Song Thief?' (2005) 31 *Modern China* 382.

[54] Liu, 'Can Copyright Lend' (n 13) 205.

when Wang Luobin licensed the copyright of 10 songs to Ling Feng in 1993, with a remuneration of 20,000 Yuan RMB.[55] This was criticised by the public, especially music experts and local people in Xinjiang Uyghur Autonomous Region. During 1994 and 1995, two leading Chinese music journals, *Zhongguo yinyue* (*Chinese music*) and *Renmin yinyue* (*People's music*), published many articles that discussed the Wang Luobin case.[56] Some Uyghur commentators accused Wang of stealing the Xinjiang folk songs, which 'implies a sense of collective ownership of a musical tradition by a defined minority nationality'.[57]

The focus is on the legal nature of music borrowing: if the new arrangement of a folk song contains no creative effort and is merely a transcription, then the transcriber cannot claim copyright over the song, according to the CLC.[58] However, Article 13 of the CLC also provides:

> Where a work is created by adaptation, translation, annotation or arrangement of a pre-existing work, the copyright in the work thus created shall be enjoyed by the adapter, translator, annotator or arranger, provided that the copyright in the original work is not infringed upon.

This means that the adaptor could enjoy independent copyright protection over the original expressions they added to the folk song. In the case of Wang Luobin, it is clear that his songs 'owe their origins in whole or in part to legally recognised ethnic minorities',[59] but seemingly his contributions to many of the songs he collected are more than trivial and can earn independent copyright protection.[60]

According to Article 3 of the CLC, the work must be able to be presented in a certain form. But as discussed above, most folklore is communicated orally from generation to generation, and often no tangible form can be found.[61] It was Wang Luobin who took notes, recorded the oral folk songs and rearranged the songs according to his understanding. The musical works were thus fixed and became well known by the Chinese audience. It is obvious that Wang Luobin played a crucial role in promoting the folk songs that he collected, and Wang may qualify as the author of the derivative work of those folk songs if his contribution can be deemed original, according to the 'Long Song' case. But since the Uyghur community was unhappy, the focus shifted to the issues of ownership and attribution, for which there is no clear answer.

C. The 'Wusuli Boat Song' Case[62]

This case is of great significance regarding the legal status of folk songs that came from a minority group. Guo Song was the composer of the famous song 'Wusuli Boat Song' ('Wusuli Chuan Ge'), which is an adaptation of a folk song of the Hezhe ethnic group living in Hei Long Jiang Province. On 12 November 1999, during the gala show for the Nanning International Folk Song Art Festival, the host from CCTV emphasised that the 'Wusuli Boat Song' was composed by Guo

[55] J Chen, 'Wang Luobin, a Beijing Cultural Figure with a Strong Iron Backbone' (Chnmusic, 2016) www.chnmusic.cn/yydj/2016/1003/3605.html.

[56] Rees (n 39) 151.

[57] Harris (n 53) 389.

[58] For a detailed account of the originality standard in China, see T He, 'The Sentimental Fools and the Fictitious Authors: Rethinking the Copyright Issues of AI-Generated Contents in China' (2019) 27 *Asia Pacific Law Review* 218.

[59] Rees (n 39) 156.

[60] Harris (n 53) 396.

[61] CH Farley, 'Protecting Folklore of Indigenous Peoples: Is Intellectual Property the Answer?' (1997) 30 *Connecticut Law Review* 31.

[62] *Government of Sipai Hezhe Ethnic Village of Raohe County v Guo Song and CCTV* [2001] Beijing No 2 Intermediate People's Court, RZZC No 223, [2003] Beijing Higher People's Court, GMZ No 246.

Song and was not a folk song of the Hezhe ethnic group.[63] The gala show was later made into VCDs for distribution across the country, and Guo Song was listed as the author of the song. As a result, the Hezhe ethnic group refused to accept the above statement that the 'Wusuli Boat Song' had no connection with the Hezhe minority group. Later, the local government of Sipai Hezhe Ethnic Village, Raohe County, filed a lawsuit at Beijing No 2 Intermediate People's Court against Guo Song and CCTV.

The plaintiff claimed that the 'Wusuli Boat Song' was based on folk songs of the Hezhe ethnic group, such as 'Thinking of the Man I Love' ('Xiang Qing Lang') and 'Return of the Hunting Brother' ('Shou Lie De Gege Hui Lai Le'), which are protected as an expression of folklore under Article 6 of the CLC, so the Hezhe people were entitled to the moral and economic rights associated with the song.[64] The defendant Guo Song argued that there were three Hezhe ethnic villages in China, and the plaintiff was just one of them and therefore unqualified to file a lawsuit on behalf of the whole Hezhe ethical group.[65] Guo further argued that the traditional folk tunes of the Hezhe ethnic group, as typified by 'Thinking of the Man I Love', was just a four-line melody without lyrics, while the 'Wusuli Boat Song' had both newly composed tunes and lyrics and was composed in collaboration with several songwriters using Western musical techniques.[66]

The court of first instance first recognised that the local government was entitled to sue as it is the political representative of a Hezhe ethnic group and the representative of the common interests of that group.[67] The court further confirmed that the traditional folk tune of the Hezhe ethnic group was protected as an expression of folklore under the CLC.[68] The court opined that 'under the premise of prohibiting distortion and commercial abuse … reasonable development and utilisation of folklore is encouraged so that it can be promoted and continuously developed'.[69] The court further argued that the use of folklore works in recreations required adherence to the principle of fairness, as stipulated in Article 4 of the General Principles of Civil Law. Therefore, the source of the 'Wusuli Boat Song' should be stated.[70] Moreover, Article 12 of the 1991 CLC also provided that:

> Where a work is created by adaptation, translation, annotation or arrangement of a pre-existing work, the copyright in the work thus created shall be enjoyed by the adaptor, translator or arranger, provided that the exercise of such copyright shall not prejudice the copyright in the original work.

Accordingly, since the 'Wusuli Boat Song' is an adaptation of the traditional folk tunes of the Hezhe ethnic group, as exemplified in the songs 'Thinking of the Man I Love' and 'Return of the Hunting Brother',[71] the court concluded that any future use of the 'Wusuli Boat Song' shall clearly indicate that the song is an adaptation of the folk tune of the Hezhe ethnic group. The second instance upheld the ruling of the Beijing No 2 Intermediate People's Court.[72]

The 'Wusuli Boat Song' case is a good example of the willingness of the courts to protect traditional Chinese folk songs. As indicated above, Article 6 of the CLC states that the measures for

[63] F Song, 'Wusuli Boat Song Case Concluded, Media Calls for Protection of Folklore Works' (*Chinanews*, 29 December 2002) www.chinanews.com.cn/2002-12-29/26/258358.html.
[64] *Government of Sipai Hezhe Ethnic Village of Raohe County v Guo Song and CCTV*, No 223.
[65] ibid.
[66] ibid.
[67] ibid.
[68] ibid.
[69] ibid.
[70] ibid.
[71] ibid.
[72] *Raohe County v Guo Song and CCTV*, No 246 (n 62).

the protection of copyright in expressions of folklore shall be formulated separately by the State Council. But no such regulations have ever been enacted, other the hidden draft bill mentioned above. It is obvious that the court managed to protect a traditional Chinese folk song even when there was no specific rule provided. In this case, because it is difficult to identify the original creator of the folk song, the court went on to rule that the local government should hold the copyright on behalf of the minority groups. As observed, when the court believes it is impractical to establish ownership, the rights rest with the state.[73] However, no monetary damages were awarded in this case besides the 'reasonable expenses related to the litigation'.[74] This shows that the court is prudent in providing protection for folk songs when no specific legal rules are provided.

V. Conclusion

It is obvious from the discussion above that music borrowing concerning traditional Chinese music or folk songs is a complicated issue. First, considering the cases discussed in this chapter, it could be argued that adaptations of traditional Chinese folk songs can be protected under the CLC as long as the author has made an original contribution to the traditional music. Accordingly, the person who adapted the song enjoys independent copyright protection, and the enforcement of copyright is feasible if the traditional music borrowed is either out of copyright protection or is without an identifiable author. Then, if two songs have borrowed elements from the same traditional music and one raised a copyright infringement claim, it is crucial for the court to first exclude the common parts that came from the source, then to identify and compare their respective original contributions. Furthermore, determining the correct method to compare the songs concerned is highly controversial, as judges are often not suitable referees for such a technical question. Solutions might either be to use an expert witness, which was the case in the above-mentioned 'Long Song' case, or suitable technology, as forensic experts in China have employed algorithms or have developed software systems to check music plagiarism.[75] No doubt, the technical solutions are helpful for the court to decide music borrowing cases based on a practical and stable criterion. When comparing the derivative works, 'originality' plays a crucial role in determining whether the similar parts are protected or not. In terms of copyright infringement determination, Chinese courts are no different than courts of other countries in finding prior access and substantial similarity. Finally, it is clear from the 'Wusuli Boat Song' case that if a specific ethical group can be identified, their collective wisdom should be respected by the author disclosing the original source of the tune.

It is this latter issue that is most challenging: can we really establish a justifiable regime to protect those traditional Chinese music pieces? The cases discussed above show that the balance between protecting tradition and promoting innovation is often sensitive and vulnerable, as it is also a fact that many musicians in China are motivated by or inspired by traditional music,

[73] Q Lin and Z Lian, 'On Protection of Intangible Cultural Heritage in China from the Intellectual Property Rights Perspective' (2018) 10(12) *Sustainability* 16.

[74] *Raohe County v Guo Song and CCTV*, No 246 (n 62).

[75] Y Yuan et al, 'Perceptual vs Automated Judgments of Music Copyright Infringement' (2020) PsyArXiv, July 10, doi:10.31234/osf.io/tq7v5; see also J Huijun, X Wei and X Jing, 'Objective Evaluation of Music Plagiarism' (2021) 60 *Journal of Fudan University (Natural Science)* 375 (蒋慧军，徐 伟，肖京:《音乐抄袭的客观评价》，《复旦学报（自然科学版）》2021年第3期.); T He et al, 'Music Plagiarism Detection via Bipartite Graph Matching' (2021) arXiv:2107.09889.

which breathes new life into their own music, and this can also keep the traditional music alive. The decision by the court to use the general principles of civil law to protect traditional Chinese music in the 'Wusuli Boat Song' case is certainly a plausible one, but there are also Chinese court rulings with similar facts that do not support the idea of using general principles of civil law to protect traditional Chinese music, and they have even denied the request for copyright protection of traditional music based on the simple fact that no specific regulation has ever been promulgated.[76] One should be aware that China is a civil law country. Without *stare decisis*, any judgments that aim to create new laws will not have a general impact until the rules created are transformed into law.[77]

On 30 November 2020, President Xi Jinping stressed that it was necessary to 'promptly study and develop methods for the protection of traditional culture, traditional knowledge and other areas' during the twenty-fifth collective study of the Political Bureau of the Central Committee of the Communist Party of China.[78] Based on Article 6 of the CLC, it is likely that China will come up with a more detailed regulation to protect folklore, including traditional Chinese music. However, a delicate balance must be struck between the protection and the promotion of traditional Chinese music so that it can be preserved and utilised. Eventually, this will promote the world's cultural diversity, sustainable cultural development and cultural security, and will help develop cultural industries related to folklore and artworks.[79] It seems that China still has a long way to go to reach the goal of passing a law to cover all expressions of folklore rather than musical works alone, and the existing proposals are not satisfactory either because they are theoretically flawed or because they may not actually benefit the ethnic group, as providing copyright protection to folk songs will not 'slow down or stop the disintegration of the collective innovation mechanism of traditional culture',[80] which is an irreversible result of globalisation. In the future, it would be better to move the protection of traditional Chinese music out of the CLC due to the incompatibilities identified,[81] and to use other mechanisms, such as the Intangible Cultural Heritage Law,[82] to provide suitable protection.

[76] Chixi Village Group, Tushi Village, Ganzhu Town, Guangchang County v Yeguo Wei [2018] Fuzhou Intermediate People's Court of Jiangxi Province, G10MC No 97.

[77] T He, 'Transplanting Fair Use in China? History, Impediments and The Future' (2020) 2020 *University of Illinois Journal of Law, Technology & Policy* 391.

[78] L Qiu, 'Xi Jinping Stressed during the 25th Collective Study of the Central Political Bureau to Comprehensively Strengthen the Protection of Intellectual Property Rights, Stimulate Innovation and Promote the Construction of a New Development Pattern' (2020) www.xinhuanet.com/politics/leaders/2020-12/01/c_1126808128.htm.

[79] K Hu, 'The Construction of Copyright Protection Theory of Folk Literature and Art Works with Chinese Characteristics' (2022) 44 *Chinese Journal of Law* 133 (胡开忠:《中国特色民间文学艺术作品著作权保护理论的构建》，《法学研究》2022年第2期. 第133页).

[80] G Cui, 'Abandoning the Notion of Collective AuthorshipThe End of the Problem of Folk Literature Copyright' (2005) No 5 *Law and Social Development* 72 (崔国斌:《否弃集体作者观 – – 民间文艺版权难题的终结》，《法制与社会发展》2005年第5期. 第72页).

[81] Liu, 'Can Copyright Lend' (n 13) 205–08.

[82] The Intangible Cultural Heritage Law of China (2011).

26

Music Borrowing in the History of Japanese Music

RYU KOJIMA*

I. Introduction

This chapter attempts to analyse the issue of 'music borrowing' in the history of Japanese music to explore its implications for copyright law.

After the Meiji Restoration in 1868, Japan tried to establish a nation state and introduced various 'Western' and 'modern' legal concepts, including copyright. The first copyright act was enacted in 1899, the same year Japan entered the Berne Union.[1] However, like other parts of the world, cultural expressions had been created, imitated, disseminated and transformed, and a certain social order existed in such cultural activities long before a formal copyright system was established. By analysing various social norms and perceptions among relevant actors in multiple Japanese cultural activities, including those of a pre-modern era, we may be able to find some implications and develop a better understating of the circumstances in which copyright law could function in our contemporary society.[2]

The chapter proceeds as follows. First, I will briefly examine various dimensions of 'music' in Japanese history. Second, I will analyse the technique of 'secondary creation' in Japanese 31-syllable poems (*waka*) in the pre-modern era (the so-called *honka-dori*). Third, I will look at the imitation, dissemination and adaptation of Japanese folk music (*minyo*) after the Meiji Restoration (ie in Japan's post-1868 period, when modernisation started). Next, I will draw some implications for music borrowing and copyright law from a Japanese perspective. Finally, I will conclude with an analysis of the function of customary norms in traditional Japanese culture.

* This chapter is based on my presentation at the Doshisha University Intellectual Property Law Forum (*Doshisha Daigaku Chitekizaisan-ho Kenkyu-kai*) on 26 June 2021. I would like to express my sincere gratitude to the participants for their valuable comments. Any remaining errors should be attributed to the author.

[1] The excerpt of the Old Copyright Act is the website of the Copyright Research and Information Center (www.cric.or.jp/english/clj/clold.html). Prior to the Old Copyright Act, the Publication Ordinance was enacted in 1869 (one year after the Meiji Restoration), although the main purpose of the ordinance was to regulate speech rather than to protect authors and/or copyright holders.

[2] The recent debates on 'IP's Negative Space' reflects an awareness of this problem. See EL Rosenblatt, 'A Theory of IP's Negative Space' (2011) 34 *Columbia Journal of Law & the Arts* 319.

II. Various Dimensions of 'Music' in Japanese History

A. The Positioning of Syllable Poems (*Waka* and *Haiku*) in Japanese Music

Historically, the term 'music' (*ongaku*) is said to have been first used in the official historical record, *Shoku Nihongi*, published in 797 AD, in the beginning of the Heian period.[3] It is important to highlight that the original meaning of the word *ongaku* referred to the activities of playing musical instruments by the aristocratic class.[4] In this respect, *ongaku* has sometimes been understood as Japanese Imperial Court music and dance (*gagaku*).[5]

However, a question immediately arises: are Japanese syllable poems included within this category of 'music'? We have two kinds of syllable poems in Japan. The first type is 31-syllable poems (*waka*), which consist of 31 syllables in five lines of 5, 7, 5, 7 and 7 syllables each,[6] and the other is 17-syllable poems (*haiku*), which consist three lines of 5, 7 and 5 syllables each.[7]

When we look at the description of *waka* in Chinese characters, it contains the letter 'song', therefore, it is not incorrect to include *waka* within the category of music. *Waka* has been 'sung' on ceremonial occasions such as *utakai* (poetry reading).[8]

It is interesting to note that several representative textbooks and encyclopaedias on the history of Japanese music do not include *waka* amongst their items.[9] Based on this understanding, *waka* may have been conceptualised as a form of poetry and categorised as literature.

According to one textbook on Japanese music, however, Japanese music has two categories, namely, 'music to intonate/cantillate' (*utau ongaku*) and 'music to narrate' (*kataru ongaku*). An explanation of *waka* is also included in the part of music to intonate/cantillate.[10]

Further evidence that syllable poems were counted in the category of music can be found in one of the famous anthologies, *Wakan Roei Shu* (Anthology of Japanese and Chinese Poems to Sing), which was edited by Kinto Fujiwara (966–1041), an aristocrat and a master of Chinese and Japanese classical literature.[11] The title of the anthology contains the word 'sing', which evidences that *waka* was sung at ceremonies and parties among aristocrats.

The other form of Japanese syllable poem, *haiku* (which comprises 17 syllables), has a close relationship with *waka*. In Japan, a genre called *renga* has existed since ancient times. The form of *renga* began as the composition of a single *waka* in which two or more poets supplied alternating sections of a poem.[12] *Renga* became extremely popular in the medieval period and the style was well established by the fourteenth century. The standard length of a *renga* was 100 verses.[13]

[3] The Heian Period started in 794 when the capital was moved from Nara to Kyoto. For details of 'Shoku Nihongi', see https://jhti.berkeley.edu/Shoku%20Nihongi.html.

[4] O Yamaguchi, 'Ongaku' in *Nihon Dai Hyakka Zensho* (*The Japan Comprehensive Encyclopedia*) (Shogakkan, 1994). The author relied on the online database of the Japan Knowledge version.

[5] For details of *gagaku*, see www.kunaicho.go.jp/e-culture/gagaku.html.

[6] See 'waka' in *Encyclopedia Britannica*, www.britannica.com/art/waka-Japanese-poetry.

[7] See 'haiku' in *Encyclopedia Britannica*, www.britannica.com/art/haiku.

[8] The typical ceremonial event of *utakai* is *Utakai Hajime* (the Imperial New Year's Poetry Reading), which is an ongoing occasion held at the Imperial Palace at the beginning of the New Year (www.kunaicho.go.jp/e-culture/utakai.html).

[9] H Yoshida, *Nihon Ongaku no Rekishi* (*The History of Japanese Music*) (Sogensha, 1965); K Hirano, Y Kamisango and S Gamo (eds), *Nihon Ongaku Daijiten* (*Encyclopedia on Japanese Music*) (Heibonsha, 1989).

[10] M Takeuchi, *Nihon Ongaku no Naze?* (*Whys in Japanese Music*) (Sayusha, 2017) 68.

[11] JT Rimer and J Chaves (eds), *Japanese and Chinese Poems to Sing: The Wakan Rōei Shū* (Columbia University Press, 1997).

[12] See 'renga' in *Encyclopedia Britannica*, www.britannica.com/art/renga.

[13] ibid.

Although the popularity of *renga* declined at the end of the Sengoku period (the age of provincial wars between 1467 and 1600), the tradition of *renga* was transformed into *haiku* during the seventeenth century (the Edo period). The term *haiku* is derived from the first element of the word *haikai* (a humorous form of *renga*) and the second element of the word *hokku* (the initial stanza of a *renga*).[14] It is said that Basho Matsuo (1644–94), regarded as one of the greatest *haiku* masters and the author of *Oku no Hosomichi* (The Narrow Road to the Deep North), elevated the level of *haiku* to artistic excellency.[15]

Considering all these historical elements, *waka* and *haiku* can be discussed within the category of 'music' in Japanese music history.

B. The Tradition of 'Music to Narrate' in the History of Japanese Music

In Japanese history, one of the representative examples of 'music to narrate' was *heikyoku*, where players of the Japanese lute (*biwa*) narrated parts of *The Tale of Heike* (*Heike Monogatari*). *The Tale of Heike* is a war chronicle that depicts the rise and fall of the Taira clan[16] during the twelfth century. In the second half of the twelfth century, two major *samurai* clans, namely Genji (Minamoto clan) and Heike (Taira clan), had a severe battle to attain hegemony. Eventually, Genji destroyed Heike in 1185 at the Battle of Dan-noura (current Shimonoseki City in Yamaguchi Prefecture) and established the first *samurai* government (*Kamakura Bakufu*) in Japanese history.

As one of the characteristics of *heikyoku*, it was mainly performed by visually impaired people who played Japanese lutes and narrated the story. During the medieval period, there existed a guild called Todoza among the players that monopolised the narratives of *The Tale of Heike*. Todoza was established in the beginning of the fourteenth century and enjoyed the privilege under the protection of the Muromachi shogunate.[17]

The narrators of *The Tale of Heike*, known as *biwa hoshi* ('lute priests'), were dressed like monks and formally belonged to one of the Buddhism schools (Tiantai or Tendaishu), who entertained people by playing Japanese lutes and narrating stories. At that time, *biwa hoshi* were considered to be somewhere between sacredness and secularity, and served as a 'medium' between those two different worlds.[18]

In the early modern era, Todoza continuously enjoyed a certain privilege under the reign of the Tokugawa shogunate (1603–1867) and expanded its influence in broader areas of Japan, including Kyushu Island (in the south-west part of Japan). Todoza consisted of a strict hierarchy of 73 ranks. It conducted acupuncture practices, provided financial services, and had some autonomous jurisdiction to solve civil and criminal cases.[19] Todoza also assumed the role of providing 'social security' among the visually impaired players.

[14] See 'haiku' (n 7).
[15] See 'Basho Matsuo' in *Encyclopedia Britannica*, www.britannica.com/biography/Basho-Japanese-poet.
[16] Japan Search, 'Heike Monogatari' ('The Tale of Heike') https://jpsearch.go.jp/en/gallery/ndl-BnGj90W3KP2.
[17] H Kato, *Media no Hassei: Sei to Zoku wo Musubu Mono* (*The Emergence of Media: Connecting the Sacredness and Worldliness*) (Chuokoron-shinsha, 2009) 329. The Muromachi era was between 1338 and 1573.
[18] ibid 348.
[19] ibid 343.

The 'music to narrate' has also had an influence on modern and contemporary Japanese music. In *heikyoku*, particularly inventively composed parts are referred to as *fushi*. The expression *fushi* can be found in modern and contemporary Japanese folk songs/folklores, including *rokyoku* (*Naniwa-bushi*). *Rokyoku* is 'a genre of Japanese musical storytelling which enjoyed its greatest popularity from the late nineteenth to the mid-twentieth century'.[20]

One of the earliest and most famous copyright infringement cases in Japan concerned the unauthorised reproduction and dissemination of recordings of *rokyoku*. At that time, Kumoemon Tochuken (1873–1916), a famous performer of *rokyoku*, acquired nationwide popularity, although the 'performer's right' was not protected under the old Copyright Act, which was enacted in 1899. The Supreme Court mentioned that *rokyoku* was 'low taste' music and did not fall within the definition of copyrighted works. Therefore, the Supreme Court interpreted the legal concept of 'infringement of right' in tort liability (Article 709 of the Japanese Civil Code) narrowly,[21] and concluded that unauthorised reproduction and distribution of records did not constitute tort liability.

Since Kumoemon's performance of singing *rokyoku* was said to be full of improvisation, we may well acknowledge copyrightability in his performance from a contemporary perspective. Partly because this case was brought as an incidental private action together with a criminal case, the Japanese Supreme Court may have narrowly construed the various relevant legal concepts upon the requirement of strict interpretation from the perspective of criminal law.[22] Following this Supreme Court judgment, the 'performer's right' was protected under the old Copyright Act of 1920 mainly because at that time the concept of 'neighbouring right' had not been fully developed both domestically and internationally. When the current Copyright Act was enacted in 1970, performer's rights finally attracted protection.[23]

Together with 'music to narrate' such as *rokyoku*, Japanese traditional folk songs (*minyo*) have also had a great impact on modern Japanese popular songs.[24] Although *minyo* is generally defined as 'songs that were born in everyday life among common people and inherited through generations',[25] the current usage dates to the 1890s, when the German term 'Volkslied' was first introduced into Japan.[26]

Debates arose regarding several *minyo*, such as 'Oiwake-bushi', 'Haiya-bushi', 'Okesa-bushi' and 'Tanko-bushi', over ascertaining the place of origin and the dissemination to various geographical areas,[27] which is analysed here also from the perspective of 'music borrowing'.

Based on the above, the rest of this chapter focuses on: (i) *honka-dori* borrowing practice in *waka*; (ii) the dissemination and imitation of Japanese folk songs (*minyo*); and (iii) the function of customary norms in the *haiku* community.

[20] M Waseda, 'Naniwa-bushi in Hawai'i: The Rise and Fall of a Japanese Narrative Art in Diaspora' (2020) 52 *Yearbook for Traditional Music* 93.

[21] The Judgement of the Supreme Court (The Third Criminal Division) on 4 July 1914, *Keiroku*, vol 20, p 1360. The Japanese Civil Code was enacted in 1896.

[22] Y Nomi, 'Tochuken Kumoemon Jiken to Meiji Taisho no Fuho Koi Riron' ('The Case of Kumoemon Tochuken and the Theory of Tort Liability in Meiji and Taisho Era') (2009) 44 *Gakushuin Hogakkai Zasshi* 217.

[23] Japanese Copyright Act, Art 89. For a translation of the Japanese Copyright Act, see www.japaneselawtranslation.go.jp/en/laws/view/4001.

[24] Kato (n 17) 391.

[25] R Tai, 'Minyo' in *Nihon Dai Hyakka Zensho* (*The Japan Comprehensive Encyclopedia*) (Shogakkan, 1994). The author relied on the online database of the Japan Knowledge version.

[26] ibid.

[27] K Shimazoe, *Minyo to wa nani ka* (*What Are Folk Songs?*) (Ongaku no Tomo Sha, 2021) 88.

III. *Honka-dori* in *Waka*

In the world of *waka* (31-syllable poems), *honka-dori* 'is the practice of a poet borrowing the language or imagery of earlier well-known poems, and using it to compose contemporary, original poems of their own'.[28]

The literal translation of *honka-dori* is 'taking *honka*', where a borrowed poem is called a *honka*. The following is a typical example of *honka-dori* by the Japanese poet Sadaie Fujiwara (Teika Fujiwara) (1162–1241), who advocated the rule of *honka-dori* at the beginning of the thirteenth century. In the following example, the original poem (*honka*) was said to be created between the end of the seventh century and the beginning of the eighth century, and was recorded in one of the major anthologies of *waka*, *Man-yo-shu*.[29]

An example of the *honka-dori waka* and its *honka* is quoted below:

The ***honka-dori waka***:

Koma tome-te / Sode uchi-harau /Kage mo nashi / Sano no watari no / Yuki no yugure

(Teika Fujiwara)

（駒とめて　袖うちはらふ　かげもなし　佐野の渡りの　雪の夕暮）（藤原定家）

Translation: There is no shade to stop my horse and shake the snow from my sleeves, in the snowy evening at Sano crossing.

Its ***honka***:

Kurushiku-mo / Furi kuru ame ka / Miwa no saki / Sano no Watari ni / Ie mo ara-nakuni

(Okimaro Naga: this waka was in Man-yo shu – the oldest extant anthology, which was made in the late eighth century.)

（苦しくも　振りくる雨か　三輪の崎　佐野の渡りに　家もあらなくに）（長意吉麻呂）

Translation: I'm in trouble, not being able to take refuge from the rain at cape Miwa. I wish there were a house at Sano crossing.

Source: Kosuke Tsuchida, The Methodological Development of Honka-dori in Medieval Waka, and the Formation of a Quotation Database, Aesthetics No.15, p.64 (2011), available at http://www.bigakukai.jp/aesthetics_online/aesthetics_15/text15/text15_tsuchidakosuke.pdf (Last visited on April 15th, 2022).

Before Teika Fujiwara introduced the rule of *honka-dori*, it was said that one of the masters of *waka*, Kiyosuke Fujiwara (1104–77), tolerated the behaviour of 'stealing old poems'. 'Stealing old poems' meant secretly reshaping old poems, attempting not to be recognised by readers in doing so. In this regard, Teika wanted to depart from 'imitation' by explicitly addressing old poems in *honka-dori*.[30]

In one of the monographs written by Teika, he recommended to his pupils the following rules. First, not a single line should be taken from a work that was created in the last 70 or 80 years.

[28] B Grafström, *Teaching Haiku Composition to English Language Learners through Honka-dori* (Akita Daigaku Kyoyo Kiso Kyoiku Kenkyu Nenpo, 2017) 17.

[29] *Man-yo-shu* was published in the middle of the eighth century. See 'Man-yo-shu' in *Encyclopedia Britannica*, www.britannica.com/topic/Manyo-shu.

[30] Y Watanabe, *Waka to wa Nani ka* (*What Is Waka*) (Iwanami Shoten, 2009) 105.

Second, although older poems could be borrowed, there was a limit of three lines. Taking two lines plus three to four letters could be tolerated. Third, the freshness of the newly created poem would be lost if it chose the same topic as the *honka* (original poem). Authors would therefore be immune from criticism in situations where the given topic is altered.[31]

IV. Dissemination and Imitation of Japanese Folk Songs (*Minyo*)

Regarding Japanese folk songs (*minyo*), many 'original' versions were disseminated throughout Japan and transformed into derivative ones through in *honka-dori*. One of the typical examples is 'Tanko-bushi' (A Song about Coal Mining), a famous Bon festival dance song.[32]

There were many twists and turns in the development into 'Tanko-bushi'.[33] The origin of 'Tanko-bushi' is said to be 'Rappa-bushi',[34] which was first created and sung by a popular ballad singer, Azenbo Soeda (1872–1944). Interestingly, the melody of 'Rappa-bushi' can be traced back to a military song, 'Batto-tai no Uta' (The Song of Batto-tai), which was created in 1884. This military song was based on the Battle of Tabaru-zaka (in Kumamoto Prefecture) in 1877, one of the most intense battles during the Seinan Civil War[35] after the Meiji Restoration.[36]

'Rappa-bushi' spread throughout Japan, and from it the song 'Sentan-bushi' (A Song of Eliminating Coals) was created in the Chikuho area in Fukuoka Prefecture, where the economy was boosted by the proliferation of coal mines. 'Sentan-bushi' was introduced in the world of *geisha* (*karyu-kai*) in the city of Tagawa, where the Mitsui Tagawa coalmine was located.[37] It was developed as 'Tanko-bushi' sung by *geisha* with musical instruments such as strings (*shamisen*) and drums. 'Tanko-bushi' was transferred to the city of Fukuoka (the prefectural capital), where the newly rich coal industrialists went on an extravagant spree and danced to this song at parties.[38] In the 1920s, 'Tanko-bushi' spread throughout Japan as a Bon festival dance song.

Regarding 'Tanko-bushi', there was a dispute about its originator. As we have observed, 'Tanko-bushi' originated in the city of Tagawa in the Chikuho area. However, in August 1945, immediately after World War II, the Japan Broadcasting Corporation (NHK) started to broadcast a radio programme, *Tanko he okuru Yube* (The Evening to Be Sent to Coal Mines), to encourage the coal mines to enhance their production of coal.[39] In this framework, the programme featured American soldiers singing 'Tanko-bushi' in Miike coal mine. Miike coal mine was situated in the city of Omuta in the southern part of Fukuoka Prefecture, about 80 kilometres away from the city of Tagawa, where 'Tanko-bushi'was created. When 'Tanko-bushi' was sung in Miike by American

[31] ibid 120.

[32] According to the Encyclopedia Britannica, *Bon* or *Obon* is 'one of the most popular annual festivals in Japan, observed July 13–15 (August 13–15 in some places), honoring the spirits of deceased family ancestors and of the dead generally', www.britannica.com/topic/Bon-Japanese-festival.

[33] Shimazoe (n 27) 101.

[34] In Japanese, *Rappa* means trumpet.

[35] Seinan is the south-west part of Japan.

[36] For details of the Seinan Civil War, see T Saito, 'The Reconsideration of the Seinan War History: From the Results of Excavation' (2014) The National Institute for Defense Studies News No 191, www.nids.mod.go.jp/english/publication/briefing/pdf/2014/briefing_e191.pdf.

[37] The Mitsui Group is one of the largest conglomerates (*Zaibatsu*) in Japan.

[38] S Inoue, 'Kitakyushu Tanko-bushi' in K Asano (ed), *Nihon Minyo Daijiten* (*The Encyclopedia of Japanese Folk Music*) (Yuzankaku Shuppan, 1983) 158.

[39] ibid 158.

soldiers and broadcast via public radio, the phrase was changed from the original version as shown in Table 26.1.

Table 26.1 The difference between the two versions of 'Tanko-bushi' in Ita (Tagawa) and Miike

Version	Lyric
Ita (Tagawa) version	Over the vertical shaft of *Ita* has the moon come out
Miike version	Over *Miike* coal mine has the moon come out

After this event, most broadcasting and music records of 'Tanko-bushi' adopted the Miike version. In 1962, the mayors of the cities of Tagawa and Omuta met at a studio of the local broadcasting station in the city of Fukuoka, where a ceremony of 'reconciliation' was held to decide Tagawa (Ita) as a 'head family' and Miike as a 'branch family'.[40]

Coal mines also played an important role in the dissemination of 'Rappa-bushi' into the Amami and Okinawa regions.[41] In 1897, the people of Yoron Island, the southernmost island of Kagoshima Prefecture and one of the southwestern islands off Kyushu and in the Okinawan archipelago, moved to the town of Kuchinotsu in Nagasaki Prefecture (the present city of Minami-Shimabara) because of the turmoil caused by a typhoon and the following famine and epidemics. Kuchinotsu was a place to reload excavated coals from Miike coal mine.

After people returned to Yoron Island from Kuchinotsu, they brought back 'Rappa-bushi', as sung in the coal mines, which was transformed into 'Yoron Rappa-bushi'/'Yoron Kouta' and became popular on the island. Eventually, it was named 'Juku no Haru' (The Spring of the 19-Year-Old), which was sung in 1975 by Yoshio Tabata (1919–2013), a famous singer and guitarist, and became a blockbuster hit in mainland Japan. The above-mentioned stories of the dissemination and making of derivative works of Japanese folk songs are summarised in Table 26.2.

Table 26.2 When Japanese folk songs became popular

Period	Song	Sounds/lines
Around 1884	The Song of Batto-tai (military song)	7 sounds and 5 sounds × 10 lines
1886	The Song of the Normanton Sinking	7 sounds and 5 sounds × 4 lines
Around 1904	'Rappa-bushi' (popular song)	7 sounds and 5 sounds ×4 lines
The beginning of the Taisho era (the beginning of 1910s)	New 'Rappa-bushi' (popular song)	7 sounds and 5 sounds × 4 lines
Around 1910s	'Sentan-bushi' (work song)	7 sounds and 5 sounds × 4 lines
Around 1937	'Tanko-bushi' (Bon dance song)	7 sounds and 5 sounds × 4 lines
Between 1900s and 1920s	'Yoron Rappa-bushi'/'Yoron Kouta'	7 sounds and 5 sounds × 4 lines
1972	'Juku no Haru' (popular song)	7 sounds and 5 sounds × 4 lines

Table compiled by the author, based on K Shimazoe, *Minyo to wa Nani ka* (What Is Folk Songs?) (Ongaku no Tomo Sha, 2021) 113.

[40] T Takeuchi (ed), *Nihon Minyo Jiten III* (*Encyclopedia on Japanese Folk Songs III*) (Asakura Shoten, 2018) 618.
[41] Shimazoe (n 27) 104.

V. Some Implications of 'Music Borrowing'

A. Implications from *Honka-dori*

Honka-dori was a technique to end the stagnation of *waka* during the era of Teika Fujiwara in the twelfth century medieval Japan. When the *honka* (original poem) is taken in a sophisticated and subtle way and adapted in the *honka-dori*, it is rediscovered, regenerated and regains its attractiveness.[42]

As previously observed, the three rules of *honka-dori* have been clearly defined. Based on the first rule, the original poem (*honka*) should be deemed a 'classic', known to everybody at the time of creating the new poem with *honka-dori*. Second, the *honka-dori* part should not exceed more than half of the new poem, since *waka* consists of 31 syllables (5–7–5–7–7). Which part of the original poem should be taken is a critical issue here. Third, if the same settings as the original poem are used, the new poem is not regarded as original, ie a 'change of scenery' is expected in making a new poem based on an earlier one.

As *honka-dori* rules are strict, *waka* readers needed to be equipped with various elements, including the accumulation of cultural capital (notably a broader knowledge of previous poems), creativity and flexibility, to create new *honka-dori*. When new poems are created satisfying these conditions, the old poem (*honka*) is revitalised and reappraised. The practice of *honka-dori* clearly visualises the fact that the activities in the *waka* community are continuously inherited within a timeless tradition. From a contemporary perspective, the case of *honka-dori* exemplifies that a certain social order is maintained without relying on formal legal rules.[43]

B. Dissemination and Imitation in Japanese Folk Songs

The making and dissemination of derivative works in Japanese folk songs, including 'Rappa-bushi' and 'Tanko-bushi' happened because of various conditions in modern Japanese society. The rapid Industrial Revolution, the large-scale free movement of people and social groups, and the rapid development of various media, especially audio media and broadcasting, for example, all contributed to develop the phenomenon.

As folk songs come from people's everyday lives and are continuously sung from generation to generation,[44] composers and songwriters of derivative versions are not strictly specified. This being the case, it is difficult to ascertain the authors/creators in order to grant an exclusive right (namely, copyright or an author's right) to control the exploitation of such folk songs and their derivative works in the process of dissemination and imitation.

The dispute to determine the 'originator' of 'Tanko-bushi' and the settlement between the two mayors illustrates the 'civic pride' of the two coal mining regions. Because of the incidental broadcasting after World War II, the later Miike version of 'Tanko-bushi' gained nationwide popularity and the authority of the Bon dancing song throughout Japan: derivative works can thus acquire a broader social legitimacy and authenticity than original works.

[42] Watanabe (n 30) 125.

[43] RC Ellickson, *Order without Law: How Neighbors Settle Disputes* (Harvard University Press, 1994).

[44] Tai (n 25).

VI. The Function of Customary Norms in Traditional Japanese Music Culture

The chapter has brought the two examples of *honka-dori* and 'Tanko-bushi', which are different in nature, to illustrate the diversity of 'music borrowing' in Japanese music history. *Honka-dori* was established in the medieval period and is mainly related to the aristocratic culture of *waka*. Being equipped with such cultural capital must have been essential for aristocrats and higher-class *samurai* to survive and flourish in their respective communities. The trajectory of the birth of 'Tanko-bushi' can be evaluated as a product of modernisation where people acquired more freedom of movement than in the pre-modern era and were significantly affected by new media during industrialisation.

Regardless of such differences, certain social norms and customs sustained cultural activities and relevant actors in terms of creations, imitation/secondary creations and dissemination of cultural expressions. Some important social and customary norms, therefore, partially overlap with the function of contemporary copyright and other intellectual property rights, although such contemporary legal rules may not fit perfectly well with them.

Both the Japanese Civil Code and the Copyright Act deal with the relationship between these legal norms and the customary rules of creative communities. Article 92 of the Civil Code states that 'if a custom is inconsistent with the provisions of laws and regulations that are not related to public policy and it is found that the party to the juridical act has the intention to abide by that custom, that custom prevails'.[45] This provision is based on Article 90 of the Civil Code on public policy, prescribing that 'a juridical act that is against public policy is void'.[46]

An interesting Japanese case highlighting the conflict between copyright and customary norms involving *haiku*.[47] In this case, an author contributed a *haiku* poem to a magazine specialising in *haiku*. The editor then published the work after making certain alterations without getting the prior consent of the contributor. The contributor brought a lawsuit based on the author's moral right to maintain the integrity of the work. The Tokyo High Court noted that the custom of masters' correcting *haiku* dated to the era of Basho Matsuo[48] in the Edo Period and remained the same even in contemporary *haiku* (Judgment of the Tokyo High Court on 4 August 1998, *Hanrei Jiho* No 1667, 131). The contributor must have been aware that an alteration of *haiku* might occur. The court noted that many editors also corrected contributions in such magazine columns, and there had been no complaints – or very few – from readers or contributors regarding this practice. The court finally found that the author's right to maintain the integrity of the work should be understood as a default rule, namely, 'a provision in any law or regulation not related to public policy' under Article 92 of the Civil Code. The existing custom of correcting the *haiku* for publication was permissible at the time of the author's contribution. The contributor's manifested intention – which was contrary to the custom – could not be demonstrated in the case; therefore, the correction of the said *haiku* was found

[45] For a translation of the Japanese Civil Code, see www.japaneselawtranslation.go.jp/en/laws/view/3494.

[46] ibid.

[47] See R Kojima, 'Free and Open Source Software (FOSS) and Other Alternative License Models in Japan' in A Metzger (ed), *Free and Open Source Software (FOSS) and other Alternative License Models: A Comparative Analysis* (Springer, 2015) 287–88.

[48] As was previously mentioned, Basho Matsuo (1644–94) is deemed to be one of the greatest *haiku* poets. See above (n 15).

to be permissible in accordance with the traditional custom of the *haiku* community.[49] It can therefore be said that the *haiku* case exemplifies the issue of 'cultural conflict' in contemporary society.[50]

VII. Concluding Remarks

In this chapter, I observed and analysed several examples of 'music borrowing' in Japanese music culture. Examining various dimensions of 'music' in Japanese history, I concluded that Japanese syllable poems, namely *waka* (31-syllable poems) and *haiku* (17-syllable poems), can be conceptualised as falling within the category of 'music'. Since ancient times, *waka* has been 'sung' on ceremonial occasions, and *haiku* inherited the legacy of *renga*, which was developed from *waka*.

Based on this premise, the chapter closely analysed the technique of 'secondary creation' in *waka* in the pre-modern era (a technique known as *honka-dori*). It found that strict rules existed in adapting the original poems (*honka*) in newly created works of *honka-dori* to revitalise the spirit of the original poems.

The chapter has also analysed the dissemination and imitation of Japanese folk songs (*minyo*) in the modern period, taking 'Tanko-bushi' as an example. It has shown that the large-scale free movement of people and social groups and the rapid development of the broadcast media triggered by the Industrial Revolution contributed greatly to the development of these phenomena.

The above-mentioned two cases of *honka-dori* and *minyo* are closely associated with the social norms and customs that sustained cultural activities and relevant actors in terms of creation, imitation/secondary creation and dissemination of cultural expressions. The Tokyo High Court's judgment in the correction of *haiku* case indicated that these cultural norms could even override statutory norms, including copyright law.

Through this study, it is possible to identify the existence of social and customary norms in maintaining the social order of different categories of Japanese music in different periods. By observing and analysing both the contemporary and traditional cultural practices of 'music borrowing', we can acquire a better understanding of the conditions under which copyright law could function effectively in a Japanese context.

[49] In the first instance, the Tokyo District Court reached the same conclusion based on the same fact finding as the second instance and relied on the doctrine of 'implied consent' (Judgment of the Tokyo District Court on 29 August 1997, *Hanrei Jiho*, No 1616, 148).

[50] A Riles, 'Cultural Conflicts' (2008) 71 *Law & Contemporary Problems* 273; K Knop, R Michaels and A Riles, 'From Multiculturalism to Technique: Feminism, Culture, and the Conflict of Laws Style' (2012) 64 *Stanford Law Review* 589.

27

Creation and the Dreamtime: Indigenous Music in Australia

MICHAEL BLAKENEY

I. Introduction

Australian Aboriginal peoples have had the longest continuous existence on Earth. Carbon-dated human remains provide evidence of at least 65,000 years of the occupation of Australia.[1] Evidence of fires in South-West Victoria suggest a human presence in Australia 120,000 years ago.[2] Whatever the date of origin of Australian Aboriginal peoples, it is considerably greater than the longevity of copyright protection by a factor of 950, calling into question the suitability of copyright law to protect the Australian Aboriginal musical compositions, assuming that authors and copyright owners could be identified.[3]

When the first white settlers arrived in 1788, an estimated 300,000 to more than one million Aboriginal and Torres Strait Islander peoples inhabited the Australian continent.[4] Diseases introduced by European settlement, together with massacres and conflicts with settlers, resulted in severe depopulation, but by the 2016 population census persons identifying as Aboriginal numbered 727,485.[5] At the time of European settlement, Aboriginal society comprised in excess of 450 language groups of varying sizes.[6] Today this number has reduced to around 250 language groups.[7]

Given the antiquity of Australian Aboriginal peoples, it was assumed that their music was part of the public domain. This borrowing commenced at a time before the negative attributes

[1] C Clarkson et al, 'The Archaeology, Chronology and Stratigraphy of Madjedbebe (Malakunanja II): A Site in Northern Australia with Early Occupation' (2015) 83 *Journal of Human Evolution* 46; AH Lynch et al, 'Using the Paleorecord to Evaluate Climate and Fire Interactions in Australia' (2007) 35 *Annual Review of Earth and Planetary Sciences* 215; JM Bowler et al, 'New Ages for Human Occupation and Climatic Change at Lake Mungo, Australia' (2003) 421 *Nature* 837.

[2] SP Carey et al, 'The Moyil Site, South-west Victoria, Australia: Fire and Environment in a 120,000 Year Coastal Midden – Nature or People?' (2018) 130 *Proceedings of the Royal Society of Victoria* 71.

[3] See M Blakeney, 'Protecting Cultural Expressions of Indigenous Peoples: The Australian Perspective' (1999) 89 *Copyright World* 5.

[4] E Bourke, 'Australia's First Peoples: Identity and Population' in C Bourke, E Bourke and WH Edwards (eds), *Aboriginal Studies: An Introductory Reader in Aboriginal Studies*, 2nd edn (University of Queensland Press, 1998) 38.

[5] Australian Bureau of Statistics, 'Estimates of Aboriginal and Torres Strait Islander Australians' (31 August 2016) www.abs.gov.au/statistics/people/aboriginal-and-torres-strait-islander-peoples/estimates-aboriginal-and-torres-strait-islander-australians/latest-release.

[6] See RMW Dixon et al, *Australian Languages: Their Nature and Development* (Cambridge University Press, 2002).

[7] ibid.

of cultural appropriation had been developed in Australia. This chapter examines the potential impact of copyright law on the borrowing of Aboriginal music.

II. The Aboriginal Music Genre

As was mentioned above, there currently are around 250 Aboriginal language groups, each of which shares a common language, territory and cultural attributes. This has some relevance to the concept of Australian Aboriginal music as a genre. The size of the Australian continent is twice that of Europe and there is no suggestion that there is such a thing as a European music genre. Indeed, in this book, four separate music genres are identified as having a European origin, each based on a separate European language. By parity of reasoning, it could be argued that there are several hundred Australian Aboriginal music genres. However, this has never been suggested, and indeed it is possible to identify certain themes and instruments that feature in Aboriginal music creations across the language groups.

Aboriginal music can refer to a list of things: music and lyrics, instrumental pieces and rhythms and song cycles that are created primarily by Aboriginal peoples or based on the Aboriginal motifs. It is possible to divide the genre into traditional and contemporary categories. 'Traditional' refers to musical works that have drawn on material from the pre-existing Aboriginal cultural base. Contemporary aboriginal music draws on the full range of contemporary music styles and forms, including pop, hip-hop, country and western, jazz, disco, opera, rap, rhythm and blues, techno and garage.

Traditional music forms, such as Songlines, are associated with ceremonial observances which have developed across the millennia.[8] These traditional forms involve musical instruments, language and performance that are unique to particular Aboriginal peoples, but some elements have become common to Aboriginal groups through much of the Australian continent since the commencement of British colonisation in the eighteenth century. In addition to songs that are said to have come directly from ancestral beings, others are said to be 'dreamt' or 'caught' by singers via ancestral inspiration.[9]

Aboriginal Australian musicians and performers have adopted and interpreted many of the imported Western musical styles, and non-Aboriginal artists and performers have adapted, used and sampled Aboriginal musical styles and instruments in their works.[10]

Two instruments are characteristic of Aboriginal music across the continent: the didgeridoo and clapsticks. The didgeridoo consists of a long tube, without finger holes, through which the player blows with vibrating lips to produce a continuous drone while using a circular breathing technique in which air is taken *in* through the nose while simultaneously pushing air *out* through the mouth using air stored in the cheeks. Didgeridoos are traditionally made of eucalyptus wood, usually with a beeswax mouthpiece, but modern versions use contemporary materials. The use of the didgeridoo has been traced back 1500 years to Aboriginal groups in northern Australia,

[8] See J Isaacs, *Australian Aboriginal Music* (Aboriginal Artists Agency, 1979); M Breen, *Our Place, Our Music Aboriginal Music, Australian Popular Music in Perspective*, vol 2 (Aboriginal Studies Press, 1989).

[9] JJ Bradley, '"Singing through the Sea": Song, Sea and Emotion' in S Shaw and A Francis (eds), *Deep Blue: Critical Reflections on Nature, Religion and Water* (Routledge, 2014) 17–32.

[10] See P Dunbar-Hall and C Gibson, 'Singing about Nations within Nations: Geopolitics and Identity in Australian Indigenous Rock Music' (2000) 24 *Popular Music and Society* 45; P Dunbar-Hall and C Gibson, *Deadly Sounds, Deadly Places: Contemporary Aboriginal Music in Australia* (UNSW Press, 2004).

where it was played by initiated males in ceremonial situations.[11] Although today it is regarded as the national instrument of Australian Aborigines, many northern Aboriginal peoples object to its use by both uninitiated people of either gender and by non-Indigenous players.[12] The distinguished Australian composer, Peter Sculthorpe, has included the didgeridoo in a number of his chamber and orchestral works.[13]

A second musical instrument which characterises Aboriginal music are clapsticks, a type of drumstick which are struck together usually to maintain the beat to the didgeridoo and create a rhythm to accompany a song. Curved blades of paired boomerang clapsticks produce accompaniments in 'singles' or 'doubles', resulting from the simultaneous rapping or clattering together of the extremities of each blade; 'rattled' effects are produced by bringing extremities together in rapid alternation by rotary movements of the wrist.[14]

Another instrument which is mentioned in the context of Aboriginal music is the bullroarer. This consists of a weighted wooden stick attached to a length of cord which is swung in a circle to produce a vibrato sound, with modulations produced by variations in the swing. Bullroarers have been used in various sacred ceremonies by most Aboriginal groups in Australia. Their use is confined to initiated males, and in some clans breaches of the secrecy surrounding the instrument was punishable by death.[15] To take account of this sacred secret, the Australian band Midnight Oil used an imitation bullroarer in its song 'Bullroarer' on its *Diesel and Dust* album (1987).[16] However, a real bullroarer was used by John Antill in the orchestration of his ballet *Corroboree* and by Paul Hogan in his 1988 film *Crocodile Dundee II*. In any event, unlike the didgeridoo, the bullroarer has been a feature in several cultures throughout the world, including ancient Greece.[17] This is illustrated by the American composer Henry Cowell's *Adagio for Cello and Thunderstick* (bullroarer).[18]

III. Songlines

The central tenet of traditional Australian Aboriginal beliefs is the 'Dreamtime', described for the first time by anthropologists in the late nineteenth century to refer to their understanding of the Aboriginal explanation of the creation of the world by creator ancestors, who emerged at the dawn of creation from the earth and from spirit homes in the sky.[19] Each Aboriginal group has unique Dreamtime stories which explain the features of their land (or country). In the majority of these stories, the creator ancestors walked and sang across the originally featureless uninhabited land and as they sang geographical features, mountains, rocks, lakes and rivers were created, together with plants, animals and people.[20] The land became a record of the travels

[11] A Moyle, 'The Australian Didjeridu: A Late Musical Intrusion' (1981) 12 *World Archaeology* 321.

[12] See L Barwick, 'Gender "Taboos" and Didjeridus' in K Neuenfeldt (ed), *The Didjeridu: From Arnhem Land to Internet* (John Libbey, 1997) 89–98; F Magowan, 'Playing with Meaning: Perspectives on Culture, Commodification and Contestation around the Didjeridu' (2005) 37 *Yearbook for Traditional Music* 80.

[13] See P Sculthorpe, *Sun Music: Journey's and Reflections from a Composer's Life* (ABC Books, 1999).

[14] AM Moyle, *Aboriginal Sound Instruments* (Australian Institute of Aboriginal Studies, 1978) 8.

[15] J van Baal, 'The Cult of the Bull-Roarer in Australia and Southern New Guinea' (1963) 119 *Bijdragen tot de Taal-, Land- en Volkenkunde* 201.

[16] M Lawrence, *Midnight Oil* (Melbourne Books, 2016) 216.

[17] K-P Köpping, 'Bull-Roarers' (2005) 2 *Encyclopedia of Religion* 1320.

[18] Referred to at https://omeka-s.grinnell.edu/s/MusicalInstruments/item/7436.

[19] See P Wolfe, 'On Being Woken Up: The Dreamtime in Anthropology and in Australian Settler Culture' (1991) 32 *Comparative Studies in Society & History* 197; CW Parrinello, 'Aboriginal People' (2013) 29 *Faces* 32.

[20] Parrinello (n 19) 43.

of the creator ancestors.[21] The tracks of the creator ancestors were signposted in 'Songlines', which became a musical summary of the creation process,[22] described in Bruce Chatwin's 1987 book, *The Songlines*.[23] It has been stated that 'music is the central repository of Aboriginal knowledge'.[24] By learning Songlines, Aboriginal peoples become familiar with thousands of sites (dreaming places), even though they may have never visited them.[25] People knowledgeable in the Songlines can travel extensive distances across Australia's harsh desert interior, sometimes through the lands of a number of peoples, following the routes of the original spirit ancestors, which are signposted by 'stanzas in the song saga that link sources of water and food essential for survival'.[26] A Songline can span the lands of several different language groups, and different parts of the song can be in those different languages. However, the language of the song is not critical, as opposed to the melodic rhythm of the song, which describes the nature of the land over which the song passes. Listening to the song is the same as walking on the Songline and observing the land.

From a copyright perspective, the authorship of the Songlines is lost in the mists of antiquity.

The first material fixations of the songs, apart from the geographical features represented by them, occurred in the transcriptions of anthropologists. Aboriginal peoples consider that the songs must be continually sung to keep the land 'alive' and that the singing of stanzas in the wrong order can be regarded as sacrilegious. Preserving the sacred integrity of Songlines is probably beyond the scope of copyright law and, as discussed below, is more appropriate for *sui generis* protection of traditional cultural expressions. Songlines have also played an important part as evidence of land ownership in claims under the Australian native title system.[27]

IV. Ethnographic Recordings, Borrowing and Cultural Appropriation

A potential source of the misappropriation of Aboriginal songs and music are ethnographic recordings. The process of recording of Aboriginal songs and music commenced in 1890s and continued well into the twentieth century.[28] Peter Sculthorpe has acknowledged the borrowing of Aboriginal melodies from anthropological texts and recordings.[29] For example, the melodies for his 'Song of Tailitnama' (rock wallaby song) (1984) and 'Djilile' (1986) (whistling duck on a billabong) were derived from the recordings made in the late 1950s by the anthropologists AP Elkin and Trevor Jones. His 'Elcho Island Lament', which opens Sculthorpe's *Kakadu Songlines*

[21] G Koch, *We Have the Song, so We Have the Land. Song and Ceremony as Proof of Ownership in Aboriginal and Torres Strait Islander Land Claims* (AIATSIS Research Publications, 2013) AIATSIS Research Discussion Paper No 33, 32–33.

[22] See L Kelly and M Neale, *Songlines. Power and Promise* (Thames & Hudson, 2020).

[23] B Chatwin, *The Songlines* (Franklin Press, 1987).

[24] CJ Ellis, *Aboriginal Music* (University of Queensland Press, 1985) 83, quoted in N Higgins, 'Songlines and Land Claims; Space and Place' [2020] *International Journal of Semiotic Law*, www.researchgate.net/publication/342766831_Songlines_and_Land_Claims_Space_and_Place.

[25] R Tonkinson, *The Mardudjara Aborigines – Living the Dream in Australia's Desert* (Holt, Rinehart & Winston, 1978).

[26] D James, 'Signposted by Song: Cultural Routes of the Australian Desert' (2013) 25 *The Historic Environment* 30, 33.

[27] See Higgins (n 24); Koch (n 21); R Moyle, 'Songs, Ceremonies and Sites: The Agharringa Case' in N Peterson and M Langton (eds), *Aborigines, Land and Land Rights* (Australian Institute of Aboriginal Studies, 1983).

[28] JM Gibson, 'Ethnographic Sound Collections and Australian Aboriginal Heritage: Kaytetye Song Traditions Remembered' (2019) 25 *International Journal of Heritage Studies*, 537; T Jones, 'Australian Aboriginal Music: The Elkin Collection's Contribution toward an Overall Picture' in RM Berndt and CH Berndt (eds), *Aboriginal Man in Australia: Essays in Honour of Emeritus Professor AP Elkin* (Angus & Robertson, 1965) 285–374.

[29] See A Ford, 'As Simple As That: Peter Sculthorpe' in *Composer to Composer: Conversations about Contemporary Music* (Quarter Books, 1993) 36–44.

(1988), was said to be derived from his study of Northern Australian aboriginal music[30] and his use of the didgeridoo in his compositions have been characterised as an acknowledgement of his Australian origins.[31] According to its programme notes, *Nourlangie* (1989), for 'solo guitar, strings and percussion, with optional didjeridu', is inspired by the eponymous monolith in the Kakadu National Park.[32]

The borrowing of melodies from Aboriginal culture which has characterised Australian music from the mid-twentieth century was said to be associated with the 'Jindyworoback' movement in Australian literature,[33] described by the Australian musicologist Roger Covell as a movement which aimed 'to seek a closer identification with the Australian landscape through Aboriginal traditions and even through borrowings from the languages of the Aborigines'.[34] Manifestations of this movement in music were the use of an Aboriginal title or references to Aboriginal dreamings in programme notes, as seen with the Sculthorpe compositions mentioned above. This borrowing Covell attributes to 'a longed-for "short-cut" to cultural maturity and national identity'.[35] A more direct cultural borrowing was the use of Aboriginal melodies in the musical compositions of Australian composers John Antill, Clive Douglas, James Penberthy, Alfred Hill, Mirrie Hill and Margaret Sutherland.[36] These borrowings were not necessarily direct quotations. Paget refers to Gregg Howard's categorisation, which suggests that the uses of Indigenous melodies fall into one of the following three categories:

1. the derived material may be so abstracted from its original form as to lose its recognisable identity;
2. in an attempt to accommodate this fact, the composer may contrive the musical expression to the extent that the derived material is caricatured; and
3. the material may be allowed to retain its recognisable identity and is 'framed' by rather than integrated into the musical fabric.[37]

A negative aspect of this cultural homage to Aboriginal creation were the attempts by Australian composers to make Aboriginal music more accessible to the general public by rearranging it with European harmony and rhythm to accommodate Western aesthetic tastes.[38]

Paget notes, by way of example, Symons's observation that Mirrie Hill's quotations of Aboriginal melodies in her *Arnhem Land Symphony* were 'undeniably attractive but hardly Aboriginal in character'.[39]

In the contemporary era of sensitivity to cultural appropriation, this 'acknowledgement' has been criticised as the lifting of 'artefacts representing some generalized concept of Aboriginality, often in well-meaning ways, whilst of course continuing to perpetuate colonizing attitudes'.[40]

---

[30] F Richards (ed), *The Soundscapes of Australia: Music Place and Spirituality* (Ashgate Publishing, 2007) 22.

[31] See J Paget, 'Has Sculthorpe Misappropriated Indigenous Melodies?' (2013) 35 *Musicology Australia* 86.

[32] www.fabermusic.com/music/nourlangie-937.

[33] D Symons, 'The Jindyworobak Connection in Australian Music, c.1940–1960' (2002) 23 *Context* 33.

[34] R Covell, *Australia's Music: Themes of a New Society* (Sun Books, 1967) 64, referred to in Paget (n 31) 90.

[35] Covell (n 34) 65.

[36] See D Symons, 'The Jindyworobak Connection in Australian Music, c.1940–1960' (2002) 23 *Context*, 33.

[37] G Howard, 'Clive Douglas (1903–77)' in F Callaway and D Tunley (eds), *Australian Composition in the Twentieth Century* (Oxford University Press, 1978) 38; Paget (n 31) 91.

[38] D Crisp, 'The Influence of Australian Aboriginal Music on the Music of Contemporary Australian Composers' in J Isaacs (ed), *Australian Aboriginal Music* (Aboriginal Artists Agency, 1979) 50.

[39] Symons (n 33) 42–43; Paget (n 31) 91.

[40] L Lim, 'Crossing Cultural Boundaries and Ecstatic Transformation' (2006) 67 *Sounds Australian* 10. For a whimsical approach to Australian ethnomusicology, see E Mackinlay, 'Decolonising Australian Ethnomusicology through Autoethnography: A Retelling of Pandora's Story' (2012) 5 *Creative Approaches to Research* 3.

V. Borrowing within the Genre

It should be noted that the ethnographic music collections are a useful resource for current Aboriginal communities.[41] In Arnhem Land, in the Northern Territory of Australia, didjeridoo accompaniments are considered 'inalienable expressions of ancestral identity' and the songs and didjeridoo rhythms of tribal rituals cannot be sold, having been laid down in the ancestral past.[42] However, a number of successful musicians from Arnhem Land, such as the singers Mandawuy, Galarrwuy and Geoffrey Gurrumul Yunupingu and the music group Yothu Yindi, have made use of the didgeridoo in popularising the music of the Yolgnu people of Arnhem Land.[43] A distinction has been drawn between the rhythms of ritual performance which are restricted to players who are considered 'to know and be able to tell' the meanings of the songs and their rhythm and general melodic rhythms available to all. However, in the absence of a *sui generis* traditional cultural expressions law, confining the traditional rhythms to authorised players will be difficult.

In addition to Australian popular bands, the English funk and acid jazz band Jamiroquai featured the didgeridoo in its earlier records. The American composer and performer of ambient and electronic music, Steve Roach, has also used the didgeridoo, as did Kate Bush in her album *The Dreaming* (1982). Probably, the best known non-Aboriginal player of the didgeridoo is Charlie McMahon, who formed the Sydney band Gondwanaland. He also invented the didjeribone, a sliding didgeridoo made from two lengths of plastic tubing, played in the same way as a trombone.

The question has been raised whether it is acceptable to create new instruments based on the shape and form of the didjeridoo without this being regarded as 'cultural kleptomania'.[44] This is another matter that goes well beyond the claims of copyright law but is more appropriate to traditional cultural expression.

VI. Copyright Law as a Modality to Protect Aboriginal Music

A major problem that has been identified in envisaging the protection of traditional cultural expressions in conventional intellectual property terms is Erika-Irene Daes's observation that Indigenous peoples

> regard all products of the human mind and heart as interrelated, and as flowing from the same source: the relationships between the people and their land, their kinship with the other living creatures that share the land, and with the spirit world.[45]

[41] See M Thomas, 'Taking Them Back: Archival Media in Arnhem Land Today' (2007) 13 *Cultural Studies Review* 20.

[42] F Magowan, 'Playing with Meaning: Perspectives on Culture, Commodification and Contestation around the Didjeridu' (2005) 37 *Yearbook for Traditional Music* 84.

[43] F Magowan, 'The Land is Our (Märr). Essence; It Remains Forever: Yothu–Yindi Relationships as Yolngu Identity in Traditional and Popular Music' in M Stokes (ed), *Music, Identity and Ethnicity* (Berg, 1994) 32–53; P Hayward and K Neuenfeldt, 'One instrument, Many Voices' in Neuenfeldt, *The Didjeridu* (n 12) 1–10; D Hudson and F Tietjen, 'The didjeridu – a portal to culture' in Neuenfeldt, *The Didjeridu* (n 12) 31–38.

[44] K Neuenfeldt, 'The Essentialistic, the Exotic, the Equivocal and the Absurd: The Cultural Production and Use of the Didjeridu in World Music (1994) 2 *Perfect Beat* 88, 92.

[45] E Daes 'Discrimination Against Indigenous Peoples', UN doc, E/CN4/Sub.2/1993/28, 28 July 1993, [21].

Thus, she states that it is 'inappropriate to try to subdivide the heritage of indigenous peoples into separate legal categories such as "cultural", "artistic" or "intellectual", or into separate elements such as songs, stories, science or sacred sites', as this would imply giving different levels of protection to different elements of heritage.[46] Daes concludes that 'it is clear that existing forms of legal protection of cultural and intellectual property, such as copyright and patent, are not only inadequate for the protection of indigenous peoples' heritage but inherently unsuitable'.[47] Similarly, Rosemary Coombe[48] and Jessica Lai[49] question the applicability of private law concepts to indigenous cultural expressions.

Where Aboriginal music can satisfy the requirements of material fixation, identifiable authorship and creation within 70 years, the Australian Copyright Act 1968 provides an infringement remedy in relation to the unauthorised borrowing of the works owned or licensed by individual creators. The most recent decision of the Australian Federal Court in relation to copyright infringement resulting from borrowing is *Larrikin Music Publishing Pty Ltd v EMI Songs Australia Pty Ltd*,[50] which concerned the borrowing by the pop group Men at Work, in its 1981 recording of the song 'Down Under', five bars from the song 'Kookaburra', beginning with the lyrics 'Kookaburra sits in an old gumtree', which had been composed in 1934 by Miss Marion Sinclair. The borrowing from 'Kookaburra'was played in the opening flute riff of the 93-bar song in 'Down Under'. Colin Hay, author of the lyrics and chords of 'Down Under', accepted 'that the flute riff makes a reference to part of the melody of Kookaburra'.[51] Hay's attempt to,'inject some Australian flavour into the song' was held to be an infringement of 'Kookaburra'.[52]

Where copyright law might be applicable to Aboriginal music, it does not recognise the communal harm which may result from the unauthorised reproduction or performance of Aboriginal music. There have been several cases concerning Aboriginal art in which this issue has been raised, but to date there has been no Australian case concerning Aboriginal music in which copyright issues have been raised. However, the principles addressed in the art cases are equally applicable to music.

The claim of communal proprietorship in sacred Aboriginal images was rejected by the Federal Court in *Yumbulul v Reserve Bank of Australia*.[53] That case concerned an attempt by representatives of the Northern Territory Galpu clan to prevent the reproduction by the Reserve Bank of the design of a Morning Star Pole on a commemorative banknote. The Galpu asserted that the communal obligation of the artist was such that he owed an obligation to the clan to prevent the design of the pole from being used in any way which was culturally offensive. Although sympathetic to this argument, the trial judge considered that the artist who had created the pole had successfully disposed of his intellectual property rights in it through a legally binding agreement. He lamented that 'Australia's copyright law does not provide adequate recognition of

[46] ibid [31].

[47] ibid [32].

[48] R Coombe, *The Cultural Life of Intellectual Properties: Authorship, Appropriation and the Law* (Duke University Press, 1998); R Coombe, 'Critical Cultural Legal Studies' (1998) 10 *Yale Journal of Law & the Humanities* 463.

[49] JC Lai, *Indigenous Cultural Heritage and Intellectual Property Rights: Learning from the New Zealand Experience* (Springer, 2014) ch 3.

[50] [2010] FCAFC 47.

[51] ibid [21].

[52] ibid [98]. Discussed in W Potter and HA Forrest, 'Musicological and Legal Perspectives on Music Borrowing: Past, Present and Future' (2011) 22 *Australian Intellectual Property Journal* 137.

[53] (1991) 2 Intellectual Property Reports 481.

Aboriginal community claims to regulate the reproduction and use of works which are essentially communal in origin',[54] and concluded by recommending that 'the question of statutory recognition of Aboriginal communal interests in the reproduction of sacred objects is a matter for consideration by law reformers and legislators'.[55] Unfortunately, the Australian Parliament has not yet risen to this challenge.[56]

VII. Music Borrowing and Moral Rights[57]

Perceived inadequacies of Australian copyright law as a vehicle for the protection of the spiritual expressions of Aboriginal peoples have prompted several suggestions for the modification of that law.[58] In early 1996, the Aboriginal and Torres Strait Islander Commission established an Indigenous Reference Group to manage the consultations initiated by the Attorney General's Department to consider modifications to the copyright law. A report produced by consultants in June 1997 addressed methods for protecting indigenous knowledge under the patents and copyright systems.[59] In relation to copyright, the report recommended that the Copyright Act 1968 should be amended to recognise 'Indigenous cultural ownership in Indigenous … music, … and provide rights in that material which allow Indigenous people the rights of prior consent and to negotiate rights for suitable use'.[60]

In 2000, the Moral Rights Act had amended the Australian Copyright Act 1968 to include the protection of the moral rights of attribution and the right to not have a work treated in a derogatory manner. In 2001, the federal government, in its arts policy for the general election of that year, promised that amendments to this moral rights regime would 'give Indigenous communities a means to prevent unauthorized and derogatory treatment of works that embody community images or knowledge'.[61] On 23 July 2001, the government announced an independent inquiry (the 'Myer Review') into the contemporary visual arts and crafts sector to recommend actions for governments and the sector to enhance their future.[62] The inquiry found that the communal rights of Aboriginal peoples were ignored in the current moral rights law, that 'the right to

[54] ibid 490.

[55] ibid 492.

[56] See M Blakeney, 'Communal Intellectual Property Rights of Indigenous People in Cultural Expressions' (1998) 1 *Journal of World Intellectual Property* 985.

[57] This section reprises M Blakeney, 'Protecting the Spiritual Beliefs of Indigenous Peoples – Australian Case Studies' (2013) 22 *Pacific Rim Law & Policy Journal* 391.

[58] See K Wells, 'The Cosmic Irony of Intellectual Property and Indigenous Authenticity' (1996) 7 *Culture and Policy*, 45; M Mansell, 'Barricading Our Last Frontier – Aboriginal Cultural and Intellectual Property Rights' in G Yunupingu et al (eds), *Our Land Is Our Life: Land Rights – Past, Present and Future* (University of Queensland Press, 1997) 195–209; T Janke, *Our Culture: Our Future. Report on Australian Indigenous Cultural and Intellectual Property Rights* (Frankel & Co, 1998); T Janke and R Quiggin, *Background Paper on Indigenous Cultural and Intellectual Property and Customary Law* (WA Law Reform Commission, 2005); T Janke and P Dawson, 'New Tracks: Indigenous Knowledge and Cultural Expression and the Australian Intellectual Property System', submission to IP Australia, *Finding the Way. A Conversation with Aboriginal and Torres Strait Islander Peoples*, 31 May 2012; NP Stoianoff and A Roy, 'Indigenous Knowledge and Culture in Australia – The Case for Sui Generis Legislation' (2015) 41 *Monash Law Review* 746.

[59] T Janke, *Our Culture Our Future: Report on Indigenous Cultural and Intellectual Property Rights* (Michael Frankel/ Australia Council of the Arts, 1998).

[60] ibid para 9.2.

[61] Liberal Party of Australia, 'The Howard Government: Putting Australia's Interests First: Election 2001 – Arts for All 21' (Liberal Party, 2002).

[62] Contemporary Visual Arts and Craft Inquiry, *Report of the Commonwealth by the Contemporary Visual Arts and Craft Inquiry* (AGPS, 2002) 21.

integrity and prohibition of derogatory treatment of an artistic work embodying traditional ritual knowledge should be extended to include a treatment that causes cultural harm to the clan' and that there should be amending legislation.[63] In December 2003, a draft Copyright Amendment (Indigenous Communal Moral Rights) Bill 2003 was distributed for comment to a number of organisations.[64] The Bill was criticised for its complexity and the ambiguity of its language,[65] and in February 2006, it was announced that a revised version of the Bill would be made available later that year. But, this Bill languished, and in 2006, the 215-page Copyright Amendment Act 2006 was enacted to give effect to the copyright provisions of the Australia–United States Free Trade Agreement of 2004 without any reference to Indigenous rights.[66]

The recommendations of the Myer Review remain unimplemented and the energies of the Australian Government in this area have been devoted to the long-drawn-out negotiations in the Inter-Governmental Committee of the World Intellectual Property Organization (WIPO) for a treaty on traditional cultural expressions (TCEs).

VIII. Indigenous Cultural Protocols

In the absence of legislation, Aboriginal and Torres Strait Islander peoples have promulgated and commissioned a number of cultural protocols to prescribe appropriate dealings with their cultural expressions.[67] Although not legally binding, the protocols are important in raising the profile of Indigenous peoples' sacred beliefs in a cultural context.[68] Additionally, compliance with these protocols is made a precondition for university ethics clearance and for public funding.[69] In 2019, the Australian Council for the Arts published *Protocols for Using First Nations Cultural and Intellectual Property in the Arts*.[70] This was a revision of protocols published in 2002 and revised in 2007. These protocols were primarily to support activities funded by the Australian Council for the Arts that engage with Indigenous peoples, their communities and their cultural heritage, but were also intended to be a guide for anyone working with Indigenous artists.[71] The protocols enunciated the principles set out in the United Nations Declaration on the Rights of Indigenous People (UNDRIP), which is discussed below.

These principles are:

- respect – the rights of indigenous people and communities to own, protect, maintain, control and benefit from their cultural heritage;

[63] ibid 152.

[64] See J Anderson, 'Indigenous Communal Moral Rights: The Utility of an Ineffective Law' (2004) 30 *Indigenous Law Bulletin* 8; J Anderson, 'The Politics of Indigenous Knowledge: Australia's Proposed Communal Moral Rights Bill (2004) 27 *University of New South Wales Law Journal* 585.

[65] See C Sexton, 'In Conversation with the Honourable Justice Lindgren' (2004) *Intellectual Property Forum: Journal of the Intellectual Property Society of Australia and New Zealand* 8.

[66] See K Weatherall, 'Of Copyright Bureaucracies and Incoherence: Stepping Back from Australia's Recent Copyright Reforms' (2007) 31 *Melbourne University Law Review* 967.

[67] Listed in T Janke and R Quiggin, 'Indigenous Cultural and Intellectual Property and Customary Law' (Law Reform Commission of Western Australia, 2005) Background Paper 12, 484.

[68] See J Anderson, 'The Pragmatic Politics of Protocols' paper presented at *Sharing the Cultural and Theoretical Space*, AIATSIS Biannual Conference on Indigenous Studies (Canberra, 25 November 2004).

[69] See K Bowrey, 'Alternative Intellectual Property: Indigenous Protocols, Copyleft and New Juridifications of Customary Practice' (2006) 6 *Macquarie Law Journal* 65.

[70] Australian Council for the Arts, *Protocols for Using First Nations Cultural and Intellectual Property in the Arts* (Australia Council, 2019).

[71] ibid 3.

- self-determination – the right of indigenous people to be empowered in decisions that affect their arts and cultural affairs;
- consultation and consent – the right of indigenous people to be consulted and give their free prior informed consent for the use of their cultural heritage;
- interpretation – the right of indigenous peoples to be recognised and represented as the primary guardians and interpreters of their cultural heritage; cultural integrity and authenticity; secrecy and confidentiality;
- attribution – the right of indigenous peoples to be respectfully acknowledged and attributed as the traditional owners and custodians of their cultural heritage;
- benefit sharing – the right to benefit from their contribution and for the sharing of their cultural heritage, particularly if commercially applied;
- continuing cultures – recognition that indigenous cultures are dynamic and evolving, and the protocols within each group and community will also change; recognition and protection; indigenous people have the right to protection of their cultural heritage and intellectual property rights in that cultural heritage; laws, policies and contracts should be developed and implemented to respect these rights.[72]

The earlier 2007 Protocols for producing Indigenous Australian Music[73] provide several examples of the application of the principles listed above. An example of the principle of respect is the policy declared by the Musicological Society of Australia (MSA) in its *Guidelines for the Recognition of Indigenous Culture and Custodianship of Country at National MSA Public Events*, to 'recognise the Indigenous custodianship of country where MSA public events are held and acknowledge the continuing significance of Indigenous culture in Australia'.[74]

In relation to consent and empowerment, the 2007 protocols give the example of Yothu Yindi, which declares that 'all traditional songs that have been performed or released have been done so as a result of substantial consultation with clan leaders and traditional lawmakers.[75]

An example of the custodianship principle is reflected in the CD *Jurtbirrk Love Songs from North Western Arnhem Land*, which contains the statement:

> This music CD and booklet contain traditional knowledge of the Iwaidja people. They were created with the consent of the custodians. Dealing with any part of the music CD or the texts of the booklet for any purpose that has not been authorised by the custodians is a serious breach of the customary laws of the Iwaidja people and may also breach the Copyright Act 1968.[76]

An illustration of the cultural sensitivities involved in Aboriginal music production is the warning in the *Jurtbirrk Love Songs* CD that:

> This music CD and booklet contain voices and images of Iwaidja speakers from Minjilang in the Northern Territory of Australia. If someone shown in this booklet or playing or singing on the CD has passed away, hearing their name or voice may cause sadness or distress to some people' and that' before using this music CD and booklet, advice should be sought from Indigenous Australian Community members regarding the use of these materials in the classroom, community or public forum.[77]

[72] ibid.
[73] Australian Council for the Arts (n 70).
[74] E MacKinlay and S Wild, *MSA Guidelines for the Recognition of Indigenous Culture and Custodianship of Country at National MSA Public Events,* (Sydney, MSA, 1999).
[75] See Y Yindi, 'Our Homeland', www.yothuyindi.com/ourhome.html.
[76] Jurtbirrk, *Love Songs from North Western Arnhem Land*, inside sleeve (Batchelor Press, 2005).
[77] ibid.

IX. International Proposals for the Protection of Traditional Cultural Expressions

Agitation for an international instrument providing for the protection of the cultural and intellectual property rights of indigenous peoples had precipitated a joint UNESCO–WIPO World Forum on the Protection of Folklore, which was convened in Phuket, Thailand, in April 1997. At that meeting, the representatives of organisations of Indigenous and Aboriginal peoples called for the promulgation of an international convention to protect traditional creations. At the WIPO General Assembly in 2000, the member states agreed to the establishment of an Intergovernmental Committee on Intellectual Property and Genetic Resources, Traditional Knowledge and Folklore (IGC). Three interrelated themes were identified to inform the deliberations of the Committee: intellectual property issues that arise in the context of (i) access to genetic resources and benefit sharing; (ii) the protection of traditional knowledge, whether or not associated with those resources; and (iii) the protection of expressions of folklore.[78]

The protection of folklore was taken up at the fourth session of the IGC in 2002 and a paper prepared for that session pointed out that in discussions in various intergovernmental, regional and national and non-governmental fora, the meaning and scope of the term 'traditional cultural expressions' (TCEs) referred 'to more or less the same subject matter such as "expressions of folklore"'.[79] In analysing the nature of TCEs 'relevant to [the] question of IP protection', it was pointed out that expressions of traditional culture 'may be either intangible, tangible or a combination of the two', but that 'the underlying traditional culture or folkloric knowledge from which the expression is derived is generally intangible'.[80]

For the past 20 years, the IGC has attempted to formulate a treaty to protect TCEs.[81] Over that period, the WIPO member states have been unable to reach agreement on a treaty text. In its latest iteration, TCEs are defined in an article, yet to be agreed,

> as any forms in which traditional culture practices and knowledge are expressed, [appear or are manifested] [the result of intellectual activity, experiences, or insights] by indigenous [peoples], local communities and/or [other beneficiaries] in or from a traditional context, and may be dynamic and evolving and comprise … musical forms … tangible or intangible forms of expression, or combinations thereof.[82]

The square brackets enclose terms which are not yet agreed. Musical forms are defined in a footnote as '[Such as songs, rhythms, and instrumental music, the songs which are the expression of rituals]'.

Three alternative objectives of the law are listed in Article 2, ranging from the provision of protection against the misappropriation, misuse and unauthorised use of TCEs to preventing the erroneous grant or assertion of intellectual property (IP) rights over TCEs and promotion of the

[78] See WIPO, 'Matters Concerning Intellectual Property Genetic Resources Traditional Knowledge and Folklore', WIPO Doc, WO/GA/26/6, 25 August 2000.

[79] 'Preliminary Systematic Analysis of National Experiences with the Legal Protection of Expressions of Folklore', WIPO/GRTKF/IC/4/3, 20 October 2002, para 21.

[80] ibid.

[81] See M Blakeney, 'The Negotiations in WIPO for International Conventions on Traditional Knowledge and Traditional Cultural Expressions' in JC Lai and AM Dominicé (eds), *Intellectual Property and Access to Im/material Goods* (Edward Elgar, 2016) 227–56.

[82] Intergovernmental Committee on Intellectual Property and Genetic Resources, Traditional Knowledge and Folklore, 'The Protection of Traditional Cultural Expressions: Draft Articles', WIPO doc, WIPO/GRTKF/IC/40/, 9 April 2019.

'appropriate use of [TCEs] for sustainable, community-based development were so desired by indigenous peoples and local communities'.

Article 3 of the draft treaty provides two alternative criteria for protection of TCEs. The essence of these criteria is that they are maintained collectively by a community; that they are associated with the cultural and social identity and traditional heritage of the community; and that they are transmitted from generation to generation for a term to be agreed, currently ranging between not less than 50 years or five generations.

Article 4 contains three alternative definitions of the beneficiaries of protection. Agreement has not yet been reached on whether indigenous peoples are eligible beneficiaries.

Article 5 contains three options defining the scope of protection. One sticking point is defining the availability of TCEs to users which are in the public domain.

The administration of rights to TCEs is sought to be agreed in two options in Article 6, which envisages the identification of a competent authority.

Exceptions and limitations are set out in four alternative options for Article 7.

Three alternatives are provided in Article 8 for the term of protection of TCEs. These range between the length of time that a TCE remains a traditional expression for a community to a time limited by statute.

Article 9 contains two options which agree that TCEs should not require formalities for protection.

Article 10 contains four options for sanctions which generally leave it to countries to prescribe their own sanctions.

Of the balance of the provisions, Article 12 seeks to establish the relationship between the treaty and other international agreements. Yet to be agreed is the relationship with UNDRIP. One option is that in a situation of legal conflict, the rights conferred by UNDRIP should prevail.

Concern has periodically been expressed, particularly by developing countries, about the slow progress in WIPO of the formulation of an international instrument to deal with TCEs, as well as with traditional knowledge. The members of the African Regional Intellectual Property Organization (ARIPO) took the decision not to await the results of the international negotiations, but to promulgate their own Protocol on the Protection of Traditional Knowledge and Expressions of Folklore. (Swakopmund Protocol).[83] This initiative was followed by the Melanesian group of countries (Fiji, PNG, Solomon Islands and New Caledonia) adopting a Framework Treaty on the Protection of Traditional Knowledge and Expressions of Culture in September 2011.[84]

X. Australia and the Protection of TCEs

Australia has taken a generally conservative approach to proposals for the protection of TCEs. IP Australia, which is responsible for the protection of industrial property in Australia, is conducting a consultation into the areas of traditional knowledge and the protection of genetic resources, with a view to informing its participation in the IGC on these subjects,[85] but no

[83] Available at www.aripo.org/wp-content/uploads/2019/06/Swakopmund-Protocol-on-the-Protection-of-Traditional-Knowledge-and-Expressions-of-Folklore-2019.pdf.

[84] See M Blakeney, 'Protecting Traditional Knowledge and Expressions of Culture in the Pacific' (2011) 1 *Queen Mary Journal of Intellectual Property* 80.

[85] See www.ipaustralia.gov.au/about-us/public-consultations/indigenous-knowledgeconsultation/.

equivalent consultation is being conducted into TCEs by the Attorney General's Department, which is responsible for copyright and related laws.

TCEs are mentioned, directly and indirectly, in several international agreements and free trade agreements (FTAs) to which Australia is a party. The General Agreement on Tariffs and Trade 1994 in Article XX(f) excludes from the prohibition of discrimination in trade agreements restrictions that are 'imposed for the protection of national treasures of artistic, historic or archaeological value'. Article 19.1(3) of the Comprehensive and Progressive Agreement for Trans-Pacific Partnership (CPTPP), 2018, to which Australia is a party together with Canada, Japan, Mexico, New Zealand, Singapore and Vietnam, redefines Article XX(f) as applying to the support of 'creative arts of national value'. In a footnote to that provision, 'Creative arts' are defined to include 'the performing arts – including theatre, dance and music … indigenous traditional practice and contemporary cultural expression'.

This provision is also contained in chapter 15 of the ASEAN–Australia–New Zealand FTA, which entered into force for Australia in January 2010.

The CPTPP in Article 29.8 provides that 'Subject to each Party's international obligations, each Party may establish appropriate measures to respect, preserve and promote traditional knowledge and traditional cultural expressions'.

This same language is used in Article 8 of the ASEAN–Australia–New Zealand, Article 11.17 of the China–Australia FTA, which entered into force on 10 December 2015, and Article 17.18 of the Peru–Australia FTA, which entered into force on 11 February 2020.

The China–Australia FTA in Article 11.17(2) provides that the parties 'agree to further discuss relevant issues concerning … folklore, taking into account future developments in their respective laws and in multilateral agreements'. The Peru–Australia FTA contains similar language in Article 17.18(2), which affirms the parties' 'continuing commitment to working towards a multilateral outcome on intellectual property' through the WIPO IGC.

XI. Conclusion

It should be noted that from a musicological perspective, borrowing can take several different forms: 'self-borrowing, transformative imitation, quotation, allusion, homage, modelling, emulation, recomposition, influence, paraphrase and indebtedness'.[86] This diversity probably explains why music borrowing has been established as a subject of inquiry since the emergence of musicology as a separate field of study. JP Burkholder, the pioneer of this branch of musicology and a contributor to this volume, noted that:

> The use of existing music as a basis for new music is pervasive in all periods and traditions, parallel to and yet different from the practices of borrowing, reworking and allusion that contribute to the formation of traditions and the creation of meaning in literature, architecture, painting and sculpture.[87]

Of course, one person's borrowing might be regarded as another person's theft.[88] In the context of Aboriginal music, there is a colonial background of land expropriation and displacement,

[86] See H Brown, 'Emulation, Competition, and Homage: Imitation and Theories of Imitation in the Renaissance' (1982) 35 *Journal of the American Musicological Society* 1.

[87] JK Burkholder, *Borrowing: Types of Borrowing* (Grove Music Online, Oxford Music Online, 2007–11) [1]. See also O Arewa, 'From JC Bach to Hip Hop: Musical Borrowing, Copyright and Cultural Context' (2006) 84 *North Carolina Law Review* 547.

[88] See A Schultz, 'Other Places, Whose Music? Some Introductory Comments on Appropriation and Tradition' (1991) 30 *Sounds Australian* 8.

labour exploitation and general misappropriation. Anthony Seeger asserts that 'the exclusion of traditional knowledge and folklore from copyright legislation resembles colonial relationships established by military might in an earlier era.'[89] Terri Janke, the leading Australian Aboriginal spokesperson on the protection of traditional knowledge and traditional cultural expressions, criticises the unauthorised, unremunerated and unacknowledged borrowing of Indigenous music, referring to the release in 1992 of *Deep Forest*, an album by French recording artists Eric Mouquet and Michel Sanchez, which mixed New Age electronics with UNESCO field recordings of music from a number of Indigenous African peoples.[90] Similarly, the accusation of cross-cultural appropriation was made in relation to Paul Simon's collaboration with the African ensemble Ladysmith Black Mambazo to produce his very successful album *Graceland*.[91]

It has been observed that 'the cultures of many people have been fair game for artists in many disciplines, time out of mind', and that 'some people carry a burden of guilt that makes them virtually unable to enjoy ANY appropriation of black culture by white'.[92] The WIPO TCEs treaty is a positive step forward, albeit at a glacial pace.[93] In the absence of progress in the international sphere, it is worth endorsing Liza Lim's suggestion that:

> In thinking about better models for correct cultural exchange, at a minimum this would have to include payment for time and information, seeking permission to use any kind of cultural property, and ultimately, true collaboration where artists share equivalent financial and intellectual property rights.[94]

[89] A Seeger, 'Traditional Music Ownership in a Commodified World' in S Firth and L Marshall (eds), *Music and Copyright*, 2nd edn (Routledge, 2004) 160.

[90] T Janke, 'Deep Forest and the Commercial Exploitation of Indigenous Music' (1997) 3 *Music Forum: Journal of the Music Council of Australia* 27.

[91] V Erlmann, *Music, Modernity, and the Global Imagination* (New York, Oxford University Press, 1999) 169.

[92] N Currie, 'Issues in the Appropriation of Sources for Musical Composition' (1991) 30 *Sounds Australian*, 15, 17.

[93] See M Blakeney, 'Protecting the Knowledge and Cultural Expressions of Aboriginal Peoples' (2015) 39 *University of Western Australia Law Review* 180.

[94] L Lim, 'A "Hidden Centre": Crossing Cultural Boundaries and Ecstatic Transformation' in C Hope and J Marshall (eds), *Sound Scripts: Proceedings of the Inaugural Totally Huge New Music Festival Conference 2005*, vol 1 (Edith Cowan University, 2006) 12, quoted by Paget (n 31) 89.

28

E tū, Stand Up: Copyright and Māori Music

JONATHAN BARRETT*

I. Introduction

'The beginning of the singing of the Atua [gods] is with Te Pō (The Night)'. So begins the English translation of Matiaha Tiramōrehu's 1849 treatise on the traditions of Māori, the indigenous people of Aotearoa New Zealand.[1] The music of the Māori *atua*, this creation narrative tells us,[2] summonsed the universe into existence. According to Brian Flintoff, a master carver, who has contributed significantly to the revival of traditional Māori instruments:

> All the different types of Māori song stem from the emotions displayed by the gods during the creation aeons. There are songs of sorrow, anger and lament; of loneliness, desire and joy; of peace and love. The voices of the instruments and the movement or dance support and embellish the songs.[3]

Because each musical instrument is derived from a particular god, instruments have spiritual as well as entertainment value.[4] Furthermore, all tunes were traditionally 'intended to complement words: the instruments were not used just to make musical sounds'.[5] Not only, then, does music

* Associate Professor in Commercial Law and Taxation, Wellington School of Business and Government, University of Wellington Te Herenga Waka. I do not have Māori *whakapapa* (genealogy) and do not claim to speak for Māori or to directly interpret Māori culture. I recognise that *tauiwi* (non-Māori) research involving *te ao* Māori (the Māori world) may perpetuate colonial practices and exercise control over indigenous culture: see, generally, LT Smith, *Decolonizing Methodologies: Research and Indigenous Peoples*, 2nd edn (Zed Books, 2012). In conducting this research, I have sought to comply with Te Tiriti o Waitangi Statute of the Victoria University of Wellington Te Herenga Waka. Terence Hikawai (Ngāti Kahungungu ki Wairoa, Ngāti Pāhauwera) reviewed this chapter, but any errors are mine alone. The title of this chapter pays respect to the Upper Hutt Posse's 'E Tū, stand proud, kia kaha, say it loud!', New Zealand's first rap record. This composition was a call and a challenge (*wero*) to many young Māori to stand up and be noticed, including in the field of music. I record my *whakamā* (embarrassment) in not obtaining the posse members' approval to use this phrase in relation to Māori music, but wish to thank Terence for sharing his own experience of the influence of this seminal composition on him and a whole generation. He has gifted his *kōrero* (story) about *E Tū* to me and has permitted me to share that story with the readers of this chapter. I am deeply grateful for his guidance and generosity.

[1] M Tiramōrehu, *Te Waiatatanga mai o te Atua: South Island traditions* (M van Ballekom and R Harlow eds, University of Canterbury, 1987). See also M Reilly, 'Te Tīmatanga mai of te Ao: The Beginning of the World' in M Reilly, S Duncan, G Leoni et al (eds), *Te Kōparapara* (Auckland University Press, 2019) 12, 20; AC Clements, 'Māori Waiata (Music): Re-writing and Re-righting the Indigenous Experience' (2015) 1 *IK: Other Ways of Knowing* 132.

[2] For a discussion of Māori creation narratives, see Te Rangi Hīroa, *The Coming of the Māori* (Māori Purposes Fund, 1949) 433.

[3] B Flintoff, *Taonga Pūoro Singing Treasures: The Musical Instruments of the Māori* (Craig Potton Publishing, 2017, first published 2004) 12.

[4] ibid 14.

[5] ibid 16.

lie at the root of Māori creation narratives, it is a whole that does not easily lend itself to analysis of potentially separable elements, such as tune, rhythm or lyrics. 'Traditional music reflects natural sounds and, like the language, its intonation conveys a mood that is complemented by the words.'[6]

This chapter examines the fundamental importance of music and musicality to Māori culture; the obligations undertaken by the Crown to protect this cultural treasure; the Crown's failure to honour its duties; the inadequacies of British-heritage copyright laws in protecting Māori cultural treasures; and the potential for laws that synthesise different worldviews to protect indigenous culture, while upholding basic copyright principles.

From a European perspective, we might say Beethoven's *Ode to Joy* is a cultural treasure and, of course, it is.[7] The music was composed and continues to exist in a highly complex socio-political context, but the composition does not have a comparable cultural and existential quiddity to a *waiata* (sung poem) that may have been the principal record of *whakapapa* (genealogy) of a social group[8] and helps to embed its living members within their particular ecosystem, joins them with their ancestors, who are elements of that ecosystem, and connects to their group's arrival in Aotearoa and, ultimately, to creation narratives. According to Karaitiana Taiuru (Kāi Tahu, Ngāti Kahungunu and Ngāti Toa):

> Anything with whakapapa is a taonga [treasure]. Whakapapa in its simplest sense is genealogy, in a wider sense whakapapa attempts to impose a relationship between an iwi and the natural world. Moreover, whakapapa is a metaphysical framework constructed to place oneself within the world. Whakapapa is one of the most prized forms of knowledge and great efforts are made to preserve it.[9]

Aspects of Te Tiriti o Waitangi Treaty of Waitangi 1840 (the Treaty), the country's founding document, have lingering contentiousness,[10] but there can be no plausible doubt that the British Crown, succeeded by the New Zealand Crown, undertook to protect Māori *taonga*.[11] Since the concept of intellectual property was well established in Western law and philosophy at the time of the signing of the Treaty,[12] there is no reason to think the Crown understood 'properties' to exclusively refer to tangible things. In this regard, the Waitangi Tribunal[13] has observed:

> Though the term has a number of other more mundane meanings, successive carefully reasoned reports of the Tribunal over many years now have come to treat 'taonga', as used in the Treaty, as a tangible or intangible item or matter of special cultural significance.[14]

[6] ibid 23.

[7] See L Goehr, *Imaginary Museum of Musical Works: An Essay in the Philosophy of Music* (Oxford University Press, 1992) 214.

[8] Traditional social groups are *whānau* (family), *hapū* (clan) and *iwi* (tribe). The Māori nation is a modern political grouping. These groups are flexible and may serve different purposes.

[9] K Taiuru, 'Why Data Is a Taonga: A Customary Māori Perspective' (Taiuru.Māori, November 2018) www.taiuru.maori.nz/wp-content/uploads/Data-is-a-taonga.pdf.

[10] The consequences of the Treaty may be contentious, particularly in the political field, but it seems unlikely that any serious historian with a grasp of *te reo* (Māori language) believes that the *rangatira* (chiefs) who signed the Treaty intended to cede 'sovereignty' – an alien concept to them – to the Crown. See J Barrett and L Strongman, 'Sovereignty in Postcolonial Aotearoa New Zealand: Ambiguities, Paradoxes and Possibilities' (2013) 36 *PoLAR: Political and Legal Anthropology Review* 341.

[11] Art 2: The Crown 'confirms and guarantees … full exclusive and undisturbed possession of their Lands and Estates Forests Fisheries and *other properties*'. The Māori text uses '*taonga*' to correspond with 'properties'.

[12] See, eg A Moore and K Himma, 'Intellectual Property' in EN Zalta (ed), *The Stanford Encyclopedia of Philosophy* (Winter 2018 edn) https://plato.stanford.edu/archives/win2018/entries/intellectual-property/.

[13] The Treaty of Waitangi Act 1975 (NZ) established the Waitangi Tribunal as a permanent commission of inquiry to make recommendations on Māori claims relating to Crown actions in breach of the Treaty.

[14] Waitangi Tribunal, *The Petroleum Report* (WAI 796, 2003) 5.3, cited by Rt Hon Dame Helen Winkelmann, 'Interim Guidance – Wearing Taonga in all Courts' (Courts of New Zealand, 25 May 2021) www.courtsofnz.govt.nz/assets/media-releases/2021/20210525-CJ-Wearing-Taonga-in-Court.pdf.

The Waitangi Tribunal's landmark Wai 262 report demonstrates how the Crown has failed to protect Māori *taonga*.[15] Unlike, say, *toi* (visual art), *haka* (dance) and *ta moko* (tattoos), traditional music has not been subject to wide-scale appropriation and commercial exploitation; nor has it been protected or nurtured by the Crown. Christian missionaries, for example, were free to smother indigenous aural arts – to the extent they could.[16]

Recently, innovative legislation has been crafted that incorporates *te ao* (world, worldview) of Māori into a statutory form,[17] and the Haka Ka Mate Attribution Act 2014 provides minimalist, *sui generis* protections for 'Ka Mate', the famous *haka*, but, generally, the government has been slow to respond to Wai 262. More recently, greater commitment to its cultural obligations under the Treaty has become evident. Niue, an island that is part of the Realm of New Zealand, has introduced legislation that seeks to balance copyright and traditional knowledge. The Tāoga Niue Act 2012 provides an indication of what Wai 262-compliant legislation might look like in balancing traditional knowledge and copyright, including in the field of music.

II. Traditional Music and Hybridisation

This part of the chapter outlines key features of Māori music.

A. *Waiata* and *Mōteatea* (Sung Poems)

In the absence of writing,[18] oral communication, in oration or song, was and, despite literacy,[19] remains pre-eminent in Māori culture,[20] whether in the rhetoric of a speaker on the *marae ātea* (courtyard outside a meeting house) or in *mahi* (work), such as a team drawing a *waka* (boat) up onto a beach.[21] Gianna Leoni (Ngāi Takoto and Ngāti Kuri) and her coauthors advise that:

[15] Waitangi Tribunal, *Ko Aotearoa Tēnei: A Report into Claims Concerning New Zealand Law and Policy Affecting Māori Culture and Identity* (Wai 262) (2011) 41 https://forms.justice.govt.nz/search/Documents/WT/wt_DOC_68356416/KoAotearoaTeneiTT2Vol1W.pdf.

[16] See, eg M McLean, 'Towards a Typology of Musical Change: Missionaries and Adjustive Response in Oceania' (1986) 28 *World of Music* 29.

[17] Two statutory provisions indicate legislative boldness and the possibility of synthesising Māori beliefs with positive law. Te Urewera Act 2014 (NZ), s 11(1) provides: 'Te Urewera [a vast forest] is a legal entity, and has all the rights, powers, duties, and liabilities of a legal person'. Likewise, Te Awa Tupua (Whanganui River Claims Settlement) Act 2017 (NZ), s 14(1) makes a legal person of 'an indivisible and living whole, comprising the Whanganui River from the mountains to the sea, incorporating all its physical and metaphysical elements'.

[18] Writing is not, of course, the only graphical means of communication. Visual arts may transmit complex ideas between members of interpretive communities. *Ta Moko* (facial tattoos) are an example of communication through symbols. See SKJ Gallagher, '"A Curious Document' Ta Moko as Evidence of Pre-European Textual Culture in New Zealand' (2003) 27(3 & 4) *BSANZ Bulletin* 39.

[19] For example, Lachy Paterson observes 'Māori writers often tended to a more oral style, such as addressing the readers directly, incorporating *waiata*'. See L Paterson, 'Māori Literacy Practices in Colonial New Zealand' in T Ballantyne, L Paterson and A Wanhalla (eds), *Indigenous Textual Cultures: Reading and Writing in the Age of Global Empire* (Duke University Press, 2020) 90. Paterson also notes (91): 'Māori women in the Bay of Plenty dictating messages to scribes, including singing *waiata*, for their husbands who had been taken to Auckland as prisoners of war in the conflicts of the 1860s.'

[20] According to the Waitangi Tribunal, 'oral transmission is still an important mechanism for cultural retention. In oral cultures, little distinction is drawn between song, poem, and story, probably because stories can be more accurately remembered if they are arranged in poetic form, and the task of retention is easier if the poems are supplemented by rhythm and melody.' See Wai 262 (n 15) 41.

[21] M McLean, *Maori Music* (Auckland University Press, 1996) 98 refers to heaving songs (*rangi waka*, *tō waka* and *tōtō waka*).

> Before the arrival of Europeans, haka and different forms of waiata were used as a form of discipline, to recite whakapapa, to entertain, to pass on knowledge of historical events and to tell stories, and these were passed down through the generations.[22]

After the arrival of Europeans, it seems that *waiata* also performed the role of providing social commentary on encounters between *iwi* and *tauiwi* (outsiders).[23]

The Waitangi Tribunal reports:

> The term waiata is more generic than mōteatea, and has come to include some Māori songs with Pākehā melodies in the modern style. Mōteatea is now applied exclusively to waiata in the old style – what might be called classical Māori chants. In any event, 'mōteatea' is a more evocative term, since its root meaning is to grieve or lament.[24]

The composer and performer Te Ahukaramū Charles Royal (Ngāti Whanaunga and Ngāti Tamaterā) provides the following non-exhaustive list of types of *mōteatea*: *pātere* (songs composed by women as a reply to jealousies and/or slander); *apakura* (laments); *pao* (short chanting songs); *ruri* (songs of an amorous nature); *oriori* (lullabies); *matakite* (songs of visions); *mata* (prophetic songs); and *kaioraora* (cursing songs).[25]

'The most numerous of the *waiata* are laments (*waiata tangi*) and love songs (*waiata aroha* and *waiata whaiāipo*). Other qualifying terms can be so specific that hundreds of songs can be recorded without finding another the same.'[26] Songs specifically described as *waiata* include: *waiata tangi* (laments for the dead); *waiata aroha* (love songs); *waiata whaiāipo* (lovers' songs); *waiata whakaaraara pā* (sentinels' songs); and *waiata karakia* (ritualistic songs).[27] Royal further identifies: *waiata whakautu tono pākūwhā* (songs to answer marriage proposals); *waiata mō te moe punarua* (songs for marriage to two wives); *waiata nā te tūrehu* (songs from the 'fairy folk'); *waiata whakautu whakapae* (songs replying to statements made about a person); and *waiata wawata* (songs expressing a desire for another person).[28]

B. *Karakia* (Incantations)

Basil Keane (Ngā Puhi, Ngāti Kahungunu, Rangitāne) advises that 'The Māori natural world teemed with gods and unseen beings and required thoughtful navigation. Tohunga (priests) assisted people with special incantations and rites to appease the gods.'[29] According to Te Rangi Hīroa (Ngāti Mutunga):

> The priests established oral communication with their gods by means of karakia. A karakia may be defined as a formula of words which was chanted to obtain benefit or avert trouble. A vast number have been composed by all tribes to meet every possible contingency in human life and they cover a range

[22] G Leoni, M Wharerau and T White, 'He Tōtai Tuakiri: The "Imagined" Criteria of Māori Identity' in Reilly et al (n 1) 372, 387.

[23] M Reilly and E Olssen, 'Te Tūtakitanga o ngā Tāngata: The Meeting of Peoples' in Reilly et al (n 1) 158, 166.

[24] Wai 262 (n 15) 41.

[25] Te Ahukaramū C Royal, 'Mōteatea – Traditional Māori Song Poetry', paper presented at *Oceania Meets Asia: World Music Days 2009*, International Symposium and Festival Dialogue in Music conference, Beijing, 3 November 2009, 1–2 (cited in Wai 262 (n 15) 41). See also McLean (n 21) 110–11 for a taxonomy of *waiata*.

[26] ibid 110.

[27] Royal (n 25) 1–2.

[28] ibid.

[29] B Keane, 'Traditional Māori Religion – ngā karakia a te Māori' in *Te Ara – the Encyclopedia of New Zealand* (2011) www.TeAra.govt.nz/en/traditional-maori-religion-nga-karakia-a-te-maori/print.

> which exceeds the bounds of religion. It is therefore impossible for one English word to cover adequately all the meanings of karakia.[30]

Mākereti (Te Arawa),[31] an indigenous ethnologist who analysed the customs of her *iwi* from the viewpoint of a woman, quotes a *karakia* chanted during the planting of *kūmara* (sweet potato), but declines to translate it, arguing:

> It would be wrong for me to attempt to translate the karakia. I cannot do it, nor is it likely that anyone else alive to-day could give its real meaning. In the first place, the words of the different karakia are very ancient, and the words used are obsolete. In the second place, religious formulae depend for their meaning on a knowledge of the religious background and history of a people over a long period, and though some lines might be translated to give a certain meaning, it is more than likely that the translation would not give the true meaning known to the old Tohunga, for only the old Tohunga knew the inner meaning of the words. Therefore it would be sacrilege for me to attempt to translate these sacred karakia.[32]

Suffice to say, *karakia* are sacred compositions and *tauiwi* appropriation would be egregiously offensive.[33]

Mākereti issued a general caution about translating *te reo* Māori into English, saying the real meaning of a word 'is in the way it is spoken'.[34] According to Derek Schulz:

> Te reo didn't have a written script, but what it did have was a far more sophisticated musical use of sound than the clipped, corralling density characteristic of Ingarihi [English] … There was no way te reo could be translated under these circumstances, without seriously damaging it.[35]

C. *Haka*

The pre-eminent ethnomusicologist Mervyn McLean explains:

> The haka is a posture dance with shouted accompaniment. Most New Zealanders would consider themselves familiar with it, if only because of its customary use by the All Blacks and other football teams as a preliminary to the game. The famous 'ka mate' haka performed the All Blacks is also amongst the most commonly performed at Māori meetings.[36]

D. *Taonga Pūoro* (Musical Instruments)

According to McLean:

> Of the four customary classes of musical instruments, only idiophones and aerophones were common in New Zealand. Drums (membranophones) were absent. Stringed instruments (chordophones) are

[30] Hīroa (n 2) 489–90.

[31] Mākereti's birth name was Margaret Pattison Thom. See J Northcroft-Grant, 'Papakura, Mākereti' in *Dictionary of New Zealand Biography, Te Ara – the Encyclopedia of New Zealand* (1996) https://teara.govt.nz/en/biographies/3p5/papakura-makereti.

[32] Mākereti, *The Old-Time Maori* (Victor Gallancz, 1938) 186–87.

[33] Remarkably, NCT 127, a K-pop band, appropriated a *karakia*. See 'Māori karakia features in Korean pop song' (*RNZ*, 28 November 2018) www.rnz.co.nz/news/te-manu-korihi/377018/maori-karakia-features-in-korean-pop-song. While the band subsequently apologised, they did not remove the *karakia* from the song.

[34] Mākereti (n 32) 58.

[35] D Schulz, 'Letter to the Editor' *Dominion Post* (Wellington, 6 July 2021) 20.

[36] McLean (n 21) 44–45. Possibly, because of the popularity of 'Ka Mate' and its theatrical performance by the All Blacks, it is commonly assumed, albeit incorrectly, that the *haka* is exclusively a *peruperu* (war dance) and performed only by *tane* (men).

represented only by a single unconfirmed report from Canon Stack[37] of a presumed South Island instrument called the kū.[38]

The most significant idiophone was the *pahū* (wooden gong). Other idiophones include: *tō kere* (akin to castanets); *pakuru* (strips of resonant wood); and *rōria* (akin to a jaw harp), made from an elastic strip of *kareao* (supplejack – a native liana).[39]

The principal aerophonic instruments are typically likened to Western trumpets and flutes.[40] The four instruments usually described as trumpets are: *pū harakeke* or *tētere* (flax trumpet); *pūtātara* or *pū moana* (shell trumpet); *pūkāea* (wooden trumpet); and *pūtōrino* (bugle flute).[41] Flute-like instruments include *kōauau* (carved bone flute) and *nguru* (nose flute).[42] *Nguru* is unique to Aotearoa.

> It has an up-turned snout end, into which the player exhales through one nostril, and two perforated holes, or 'note-stops' (*wenewene*), along the length of the stem, which produce melodious, low-sobbing notes that invoke the voice of Hineraukatauri, the female ancestral spirit of Māori music. *Nguru* can be made of wood, stone, or whale ivory … and were often played at times of great sorrow, such as *tangihanga* (funerary events).[43]

Traditional musical instruments were and may continue to be used for specific purposes. (Cultural practices may vary significantly between different groups and places.) 'The sound of the *pūtātara* (shell trumpet) announces arrivals to a *marae* or the birth of a child. It is also used to summon people for formal learning or as a call to arms.'[44] 'The *pūkāea* (long trumpet) used to welcome people and announce events or occasions of importance and was also a war trumpet.'[45] The *karanga weka* mimicked the call of the *weka* (woodhen, a kind of rail).[46]

> The *pūtōrino* (bugle flute) is shaped like the cocoon of the case moth (*tūngou ngou*). It is said to possess both female and male 'voices'. Some instruments emit a third voice, said to be a *wairua* [spirit]. *Pūtōrino* are made from split and hollowed hardwood, sealed together with natural gums and bound by fine split vines.[47]

Other instruments include *kōauau* (flute) and *hue* (calabash).[48]

For much of the twentieth century, traditional instruments, which are often works of remarkable carving skill with compelling aesthetic appeal,[49] were treated as museum pieces and locked away in glass cases in museums. Along with the master carver, Flintoff, Hirini Melbourne (Ngāi Tūhoe, Ngāti Kahungunu), a composer and performer, and Richard Nunns, an ethnomusicologist and performer, are generally credited with reviving the use of traditional instruments.[50]

[37] See JW Stack *South Island Maoris: A Sketch of Their History and Legendary Lore* (Whitcombe & Tombs, 1898).

[38] McLean (n 21) 166.

[39] ibid 171–73.

[40] ibid 174–75. McLean also notes that *kōrotohū* (whizzers) and *pūrorohū* (bullroarers) were carvings swung on a chord to make aeolian sounds but were typically used as children's toys.

[41] ibid 176.

[42] ibid.

[43] 'Nguru (nose flute)', Museum of New Zealand Te Papa Tongawera https://collections.tepapa.govt.nz/object/591588.

[44] 'Māori Musical Instruments', Museum of New Zealand Te Papa Tongawera, www.tepapa.govt.nz/discover-collections/read-watch-play/maori/maori-musical-instruments.

[45] ibid.

[46] ibid.

[47] ibid.

[48] 'Māori musical instruments' (n 45). ibid.

[49] Ernst Gombrich observed: 'The Maoris of New Zealand … have learned to work veritable wonders in their wood carvings'. See EH Gombrich, *The Story of Art* (Phaidon, 2006) 22.

[50] See 'Remembering Richard Nunns' (*RNZ*, 7 June 2021) www.rnz.co.nz/concert/programmes/upbeat/audio/2018798809/remembering-richard-nunns.

Melbourne and Nunns composed and performed in a classical style, but contemporary musicians may incorporate traditional instruments into a musical 'boil up' of mixed ingredients of aural art.[51]

E. Hybridisation

In his history of popular music in Aotearoa New Zealand, Chris Bourke recounts the first musical encounter between *iwi* and *tauiwi* on 18 December 1642, 'when Dutch explorer Abel Tasman sailed into Golden Bay. Māori paddling waka greeted his two ships by blowing on a shell "which gave sound like the moors' Trumpets". The Dutch sailors responded with notes from the ships' baroque trumpets.'[52]

Like many colonised peoples, Māori were active adopters and adapters of those elements of European culture they found useful, including literacy and Christianity.[53] Hymns were an important feature of the missionary strategy of conversion. Mclean observes:

> Throughout Polynesia, one of the results of missionary intervention was the enforced abandonment of prohibited items, including song and dance. Another was the deliberate filling of the vacuum so created by substituting a repertoire of hymns whose texts, sentiments and tunes were of the missionaries own choosing.[54]

The ability of missionaries to establish European modes of worship may, however, be overstated.[55] Hone Kaa (Ngāti Porou and Ngāti Kahungunu) tells the story of a visit by William Williams, an Anglican bishop and scholar of the Māori language, to the Ngāti Porou *iwi* in 1837:

> [H]e held a service of worship. His attempt to lead the first hymn was met with a puzzling lack of response, so he stopped. One of the local kaiwhakaako [teachers] restarted the hymn in a style the iwi themselves had developed, utilising the same words but with a more indigenous approach that paralleled the chanting of mōteatea (traditional chants). Williams was taken aback by the power of the singing in the new style, but also by how fast the adaption had taken place in the absence of missionary control.[56]

In the Victorian era, brass and military bands became popular among Māori, as did waltzes; these and other features of European popular culture were incorporated into indigenous composition.[57] Michael Brown records:

> Sheet music of Māori *waiata* with piano accompaniment were a distinctive aspect of New Zealand music publishing in the early decades of the 1900s, an era when pianos were very popular. Many of these

[51] See M Sheehan, 'Contemporary Popular Waiata Provide a Place of Belonging' (2017) 6 *MAI Journal* 208, 209.

[52] C Bourke, 'Popular Music' in *Te Ara – the Encyclopedia of New Zealand* (2014) www.TeAra.govt.nz/en/popular-music/print. See also generally C Bourke, *Blue Smoke: The Lost Dawn of New Zealand Popular Music, 1918–1964* (Auckland University Press, 2001).

[53] See generally Paterson (n 19).

[54] McLean (n 21) 272.

[55] In the comparable context of 19th century South Africa, Jean and John Comaroff quote a British missionary who believed that through hymn singing 'the great truths of salvation would become imperceptibly written on the minds of the people'. However, through indigenous adoption and adaptation, hymn singing 'would be made to take on the pulse of indigenous self-assertion, to harmonize the aspirations of independent, black Salvation'. See J Comaroff and J Comaroff, *Of Revelation and Revolution: Christianity, Colonialism, and Consciousness in South Africa*, vol 1 (University of Chicago Press, 1991) 241.

[56] H Kaa, 'In Search of a Maori Hermeneutic' (Episcopal Divinity School, Cambridge, MA, 2000) 19, cited by H Kaa, *The Hāhi Mihinare: The Māori Anglican Church* (Bridget Williams Books, 2020) 154 fn 63.

[57] McLean (n 21) 274.

> waiata are still performed today … waiata usually featured Western-style melodies and were printed with English translations in addition to the Māori lyrics.[58]

Widely disseminated songs include: the lullaby 'Hine e hine', written by Te Rangi Pai (Fanny Rose Howie) around 1907; 'Hoea rā' by Paraire Tomoana (1917); and 'Pōkarekare ana', arranged by Tomoana (between 1914 and 1917). The lyrics to 'Pō atarau', also known as 'Now Is the Hour' and 'Haere rā', are attributed to Maewa Kaihau (1920) and set to the melody of 'Swiss Cradle Song' (1913) by Australian composer Clement Scott.[59]

Māori artists continue to adopt and adapt musical genres from outside, including reggae[60] and rap. The Patea Maori Club's infectious 'Poi E' (1984) is the most famous *te reo* song to top the New Zealand top 40 charts.[61] Today, Rob Ruha 'is part of a group of Māori artists including Maisey Rika, Ria Hall and Troy Kingi who come from a kapa-haka background and have a distinct Māori flair to their music'.[62]

In a twist worthy of Caliban's use of Prospero's language to curse him,[63] Alien Weaponry's *te reo* lyrics, set to thrash metal music, critique colonialism and its consequences.[64] They 'have found a way to explore their Māori identities in a manner that is comfortable for them, despite what the outside world thinks of their appearance and genre of music'.[65] According to Maree Sheehan (Ngāti Maniapoto-Waikato, Ngāti Tūwharetoa):

> Contemporary popular waiata offer a powerful expression of Māori identity and belonging. Contemporary waiata carry forward elements of traditional waiata on both the marae and the kapa haka stage through musical, melodic, rhythmic and harmonic motifs that are distinctively Māori. These elements, along with the use of te reo Māori and other cultural references, produce material representations of Māori cultural identity and the expression of a Māori worldview.[66]

Another common practice is to set *waiata* to Western tunes to teach *te reo* to children and other learners. Some tunes are Western in style, but others may use copyright-protected compositions.[67]

While Māori may have become bi-musical and hybridisers, there is nothing to suggest that Europeans adopted Māori music. Indeed,

> the central elements of the Māori and European music systems are incompatible and have remained mutually exclusive. The opposite is true of European traits which are non-central to the Māori system. These could and did intrude into traditional forms such as waiata and pao as well as poi and game songs, resulting in historically transitional songs with elements of both the European and Māori.[68]

[58] M Brown, 'Waiata Māori: the Sheet Music' (DigitalNZ) https://digitalnz.org/stories/5d66e5298a86ae05a1488019.

[59] Bourke (n 52). Bourke does not discuss whether the underpinning music was licensed or appropriated.

[60] Bob Marley's only visit to New Zealand had a seminal influence of the development of reggae in the country. See G Shute, 'How Bob Marley's 1979 Western Springs Concert Changed NZ Music' (*RNZ*, 16 April 2019) www.rnz.co.nz/national/programmes/nat-music/audio/2018690775/how-bob-marley-s-1979-western-springs-concert-changed-nz-music.

[61] See www.youtube.com/watch?v=DQLUygS0IAQ.

[62] J Boynton, 'Māori Music Making Its Mark' (*RNZ*, 30 November 2017) www.rnz.co.nz/news/te-manu-korihi/345065/maori-music-making-its-mark.

[63] See William Shakespeare, *The Tempest* (1610–11) act 1, scene 2.

[64] See SV O'Regan, 'Can a Thrash Metal Band Help Save the Maori Language?' *The Atlantic* (19 October 2017) www.theatlantic.com/entertainment/archive/2017/10/can-a-thrash-metal-band-help-save-the-maori-language/541593/.

[65] Leoni (n 22) 388.

[66] Sheehan (n 51) 209. Sheehan provides an illuminating analysis of the development of contemporary *waiata* (210–12).

[67] A government-owned company publishes the lyrics and scores for *waiata* to be used in schools. It is scrupulous in identifying Māori lyricists and composers, but seems cavalier when dealing with *tauiwi*.

[68] McLean (n 21) 275.

Today, composers are creating works that incorporate elements of classical music from both cultures.[69] These developments represent a 'third space' (after the autochthonous and colonial eras) that Georgina Tuari Stewart argues 'uses the productive tension of cultural contact and interaction to create new, unanticipated cultural forms and products'.[70]

III. Composition, Ownership and Cultural Appropriation

This part of the chapter considers the creation and control of Māori music.

A. Composition

Alan Merriam identifies three sources for the creation of music: 'the supernatural or superhuman, through individual composition, and by means of borrowing', with different cultures tending to emphasise one of these sources.[71]

(i) Individual Authorship

For Māori, 'pride of place is reserved for individual composition'.[72] This authorial identification is not, however, akin to, say, the Romantic conception of the creative genius.[73] According to Sir Hirini Moko Mead (Ngāti Awa, Ngāti Tūwharetoa, Tūhourangi), *pūmanawa* (creative talent) 'comes to the individual through the parents and down through one's ancestry … Whakapapa determines the distributions of talents'.[74] Furthermore, it is the named composer as a member of a particular social group that is the crucial consideration. McLean notes that

> importance is attached to knowing the name of the composer of a song and the circumstances of composition. It is by this means, along with the internal evidence of the text [eg, place names], that ownership of a song, and hence an individual's right to sing it, is established.[75]

Of course, *waiata* are invariably sung by choirs. The words of *waiata* can also be adduced to prove a group's right to land.[76]

---

[69] See, eg 'Matariki' (New Zealand Symphony Orchestra, 2021) www.nzso.co.nz/concerts-and-tickets/season-2021/matariki/. See also A Latham, 'A Gift Built from Familiar Materials' *Dominion Post* (Wellington, 24 July 2021) 13 on the ensemble Tararua. IA is a collective that 'mix taonga pūoro with electronic music' but has also created contemporary soul music that only uses traditional instruments. See 'Introducing: IA' (*RNZ*, 2022) www.rnz.co.nz/national/programmes/music101/audio/2018796445/introducing-ia.

[70] GT Stewart, *Māori Philosophy: Indigenous Thinking from Aotearoa* (Bloomsbury Academic, 2021) 26.

[71] AP Merriam, *The Anthropology of Music* (Northwestern University Press, 1964) 77.

[72] McLean (n 21) 211.

[73] See generally M Woodmansee, *The Author, Art, and the Market: Rereading the History of Aesthetics* (Columbia University Press, 1994).

[74] HM Mead, *Tikanga Māori: Living by Māori Values* (Huia, 2003) 254–55.

[75] McLean (n 21) 217.

[76] eg sch 48 of the Ngāi [Kāi] Tahu Claims Settlement Act 1998 (NZ) records: 'Ōkārito is well known as the place occupied by the kōtuku (white heron) and there are many Ngāi Tahu waiata (songs) that tell the tale of the kotuku.'

(ii) Group and Anonymous Compositions

Due to the social importance and complexity of some songs, principal composers are likely to have engaged others to help in the creation process.[77] McLean notes that one *oriori* 'is too complex to have been the product of one brain and is reputed to have taken 25 years to complete'.[78] And so, while the Ngāti Porou composer Edward Rangiuia is identified as the author of numerous compositions, his 'longer esoteric songs, especially, were group efforts' to which 'lesser tohunga' contributed.[79] This is not a matter of misrepresentation; rather, Rangiuia had great *mana* (prestige), and his own talent can be seen as a metonym for his tribe's accumulated knowledge and teaching.

Whereas group compositions may be attributed to a single composer, for some songs no author attribution is available. Given the age of the compositions, it is possible the names of their composers have simply been forgotten.[80] Otherwise, the length and complexity of the verse may indicate collective composition.[81] Another explanation lies with the nature of the songs. *Karakia*, *tauparapara* and *whakārāra pā* are the chants of particular communities that are central to the survival of those groups and may include secret and sacred genealogical information.[82] McLean reports that

> [t]he composers of karakia … according to Arapeta Awatere,[83] were the priests of the traditional schools of learning or where wānanga … The esoteric songs they composed were by their nature secret and on this account may have been kept anonymous by design.[84]

Protection of the sacred secret is problematic in a Western legal system set-up that only protects the intellectual property in qualifying works for a finite period.

(iii) Intra-cultural Borrowing

It seems that borrowing, adaptation and parody were also normal forms of composition and were considered perfectly legitimate by Māori. According to McLean, 'Borrowing is an overlapping category as the individual responsible for a reworked song would claim authorship'.[85] The anthropologist Elsdon Best reported:

> the finest specimens of native songs are all old compositions, and that modern songs are largely based on old ones. The writer once had an opportunity to observe the composition of a song by a man and wife who wished to lament the death of a neighbor's child. The task of composing a short song occupied them about three quarters of an hour, but an examination of it showed that it was largely the result of plagiarism.[86]

[77] McLean (n 21) 214.

[78] ibid.

[79] ibid.

[80] Compare with Mākereti (n 32).

[81] McLean (n 21) 215.

[82] *Whakapapa* literally means the laying of one thing down on another. Genealogy in this sense is not just a matter of constructing a family tree; rather, it can be seen as the framework for the Māori system of knowledge. See N Mahuika, 'A Brief History of Whakapapa: Māori Approaches to Genealogy' (2019) 3(2) *Genealogy* 32.

[83] On Awatere's achievements and eventful life, see HR Awatere, 'Awatere, Arapeta Marukitepua Pitapitanuiārangi' in *Te Ara – the Encyclopedia of New Zealand* (2000) https://teara.govt.nz/en/biographies/5a27/awatere-arapeta-marukitepua-pitapitanuiarangi.

[84] McLean (n 21) 215.

[85] ibid 213–14.

[86] E Best, *Games and Pastimes of the Maori* (Government Printer, 1977, first published 1925) 201–02.

McLean rejects the charge of plagiarism as 'an overstatement and an oversimplification'.[87] Indeed, doctrinaire approaches to plagiarism seem to be a particular concern of academics and copyright lawyers. Artists in the Western tradition, for example, have always copied, borrowed and adopted.[88] Rather than characterising borrowing in the creation of *waiata* as plagiarism, it may be more useful to compare the practice to postmodern concepts of bricolage and intertextuality.[89]

B. Ownership

With regard to ownership, it seems likely that group or anonymous composition of a song conferred ownership in the tribe. However,

> even when group composition was not involved, ownership would ultimately devolve to the tribe if the song became popular enough to enter the group repertoire … once composed, a song became part of the oral literature of the community and at this point no longer belonged to the composer but to the group.[90]

'Ownership' here does not imply Western property law, including rights to sell or otherwise alienate things; rather, 'indigenous peoples create and own or protect traditional knowledge collectively, and the responsibility for using and transferring knowledge is guided by traditional laws and customs'.[91]

C. Cultural Appropriation

'When two different cultures meet, there is a shock, a result of their reciprocal diversity.'[92] Umberto Eco identifies possible outcomes of this cultural clash, including conquest, exoticism, pillage and exchange. Each of those forms of cultural engagement is evident in *iwi-tauiwi* encounters, as is an attempt to suppress certain features of Māori culture. A commonly cited example is Māori children historically being punished for speaking *te reo* in school.[93] However, as Michel Foucault tells us, resistance and recalcitrance are always present when power is exerted.[94] We also need to be alert to presuming an absence of Māori agency. For example, it is plausible that post-1945, as Māori rapidly urbanised,

> te reo became the language of the past, of the old people, of the marae … growing up in the 1960s and 1970s [students] were busy following the high educational goals set by their parents. But doing well in school and university did not involve speaking Māori.[95]

[87] M McLean, 'Innovations in Waiata Style' (1977) 9 *Yearbook of the International Folk Music* 27, 30.
[88] See generally R Shore, *Beg, Steal & Borrow: Artists Against Originality* (Elephant Books, 2017).
[89] For a discussion of bricolage and intertextuality, see FJ D'Angelo, 'The Rhetoric of Intertextuality' (2009) 29(1) *Rhetoric Review* 31.
[90] McLean (n 21) 217.
[91] Wai 262 (n 15) 51.
[92] U Eco, *Serendipities: Language and Lunacy* (W Weaver trans, Columbia University Press, 1998) 52.
[93] See, eg M Neilson, 'Te Wiki o Te Reo Māori: Beaten for Speaking Their Native Tongue and the Generations That Suffered' *New Zealand Herald* (14 September 2020) www.nzherald.co.nz/nz/te-wiki-o-te-reo-maori-beaten-for-speaking-their-native-tongue-and-the-generations-that-suffered/F7G6XCM62QAHTYVSRVOCRKAUYI/.
[94] M Foucault, 'The Subject and Power' in J Faubion (ed), *Power* (R Hurley et al trans, The New Press, 2000) 326, 342.
[95] See TK Hoskins, K Tocker and A Jones, 'Discouraging Children from Speaking Te Reo in Schools as a Strategic Māori Initiative' (2020) 9 *MAI Journal* 143, 150.

The contemporary conception of cultural appropriation broadly corresponds with Eco's conception of pillage, and involves taking from another culture without permission.[96] As Silke von Lewinski observes, from a Western legal perspective, many such items may be in the public domain,[97] and therefore ripe for exploitation by anyone.[98]

The limitless choices that enable Europeans to mix and match features of their own and other cultures are not available to people deeply embedded in a particular culture. As Mead observes of *toi*:

> How can we then allow other people to meddle in the future of our symbolic system? In a real sense we own Māori art for we inherited by right of birth. It is our cultural and intellectual property. Māori art is us; and if it is alive and well, so are we.[99]

On occasion, Māori have successfully used moral suasion to protect misuse of their *taonga*. Examples include preventing use of a *haka* by the University of Arizona football team.[100] However, it seems that indigenous peoples must have access to laws that protect the fundamental elements of their cultures. This should not be a matter of seeking to preserve cultures, which are always dynamic, at a point in time, like an insect caught in amber, or to quarantine the presumptively authentic from the contaminating influence of the modern,[101] but rather to allow the recognised stewards of a particular culture to decide when the occluded core of their culture is out of bounds to outsiders.

According to Rangihiroa Panaho (Ngāpuhi, Ngāti Whātua), 'Te ao Māori – the Māori world – had always been in a state of flux; the boundaries between Māori and Pākehā art and culture have always been transmutable'.[102] Consequently, 'With an active history of cross-cultural intermixture of aesthetics, subject, technique and materials, neither Māori nor Pākehā artists can claim possession of an acculturated art tradition … These borrowings and appropriations have become part of our culture, our identity'.[103] Nevertheless, given the historical context of colonisation, 'it is now essential for Māori to resume control, re-establish boundaries for appropriation and move taha (things) Māori back to the centre'.[104]

IV. Copyright and Traditional Knowledge

New Zealand copyright law is informed by the British tradition[105] and, for current purposes, the basic relevant provisions of the Copyright Act 1994 (NZ) are substantively like the corresponding provisions of the Copyright, Designs and Patents Act 1988.[106] One key

[96] See, eg M Solomon, 'Protecting Maori Heritage in New Zealand' in BT Hoffman (ed), *Art and Cultural Heritage: Law, Policy and Practice* (Cambridge University Press, 2003) 352, 359.

[97] S von Lewinski, 'Introduction' in S von Lewinski (ed), *Indigenous Heritage and Intellectual Property: Genetic Resources, Traditional Knowledge and Folklore* (Kluwer Law International, 2008) 1, 1–2.

[98] See, eg RJ Coombe, 'The Properties of Culture and the Politics of Possessing Identity: Native Claims in the Cultural Appropriation Controversary' (1993) 6 *Canadian Journal of Law and Jurisprudence* 249.

[99] HM Read, 'Māori Art Restructured, Reorganised, Re-examined and Reclaimed' (1996) 2(1) *He Pukenga Kōrero Kōanga* 1.

[100] S Yeoman, 'Arizona Wildcats to Stop Pre-Game Haka' *New Zealand Herald* (2 October 2015) www.nzherald.co.nz/sport/news/article.cfm?c_id=4&objectid=11522837.

[101] See D Lowenthal, 'Authenticity? The Dogma of Self-Delusion' in M Jones (ed), *Why Fakes Matter: Essays on Problems of Authenticity* (British Museum Press, 1992) 184, 187.

[102] R Panoho, 'Māori: At the Centre, on the Margins' in M Barr (ed), *Headlands: Thinking through New Zealand Art* (Museum of Contemporary Art, 1992) 122, 124.

[103] ibid 123.

[104] ibid 124.

[105] G McLay, 'New Zealand and the Imperial Copyright Tradition' in U Suthersanen and Y Gendreau (eds), *A Shifting Empire: 110 Years if the Copyright Act 1911* (Edward Elgar, 2013) 30.

[106] Annotations to many provisions of the New Zealand Act specifically cross-refer to provisions of the United Kingdom Act.

difference lies with copyright protection in New Zealand generally lasting for 50 years after the death of the author.[107]

A. Wai 262

The Waitangi Tribunal considered, inter alia, whether New Zealand's intellectual property laws sufficiently protect Māori *mātauranga* (system of knowledge), *taonga* works and *taonga*-derived works.[108] The Tribunal recognised that

> IP laws are not designed to and therefore cannot be the sole means of protecting the relationship of kaitiaki with their *mātauranga* Māori and taonga works, protection that goes to the heart of the Treaty guarantee of *tino rangatiratanga* – authority and control – over taonga.[109]

Kaitiakatanga (stewardship) may cross over in certain respects with intellectual property law, such as preventing unauthorised copying, but the subject matter of guardianship is often a corporeal thing, whether it is an element of the natural environment or an artefact imbued with cultural and spiritual meaning.[110]

The Waitangi Tribunal recommended *sui generis* legal protections,[111] which would run parallel with intellectual property rights compliant with the Agreement on Trade-Related Aspects of Intellectual Property Rights.[112] Critically, the Tribunal did not contemplate a guardianship right trumping other rights; rather, 'all interests will be balanced in a principled, transparent way'.[113]

Since publication of Wai 262, the government's response has been cautious, if not prevaricating.[114] However, in late 2018, the relevant ministry announced that it would be reconsidering the report's recommendation in parallel with a review of copyright law.[115] In 2019, the Cabinet further agreed that the Minister for Māori Development should develop a draft all-of-government strategy to address the issues raised in the Wai 262. In 2020, a preliminary report was published.[116]

B. Ka Mate Haka Act

The Ka Mate Haka Act recognises *iwi* claims to communal and perpetual moral rights in 'Ka Mate'. The legislation, which was enacted following the Treaty settlement between the Crown

[107] Copyright Act 1994 (NZ), s 22(1). New Zealand is required to increase the copyright period to 70 years within 15 years of 31 May 2023, in accordance with the New Zealand–United Kingdom Free Trade Agreement.

[108] Wai 262 (n 15) 44–48.

[109] ibid 702–03.

[110] See ibid 115–18.

[111] ibid 702–03.

[112] TRIP Agreement, Annex 1C to the Agreement establishing the World Trade Organization.

[113] Wai 262 (n 15) 702–03.

[114] In 2015, the Ministry of Justice advised the United Nations: 'The New Zealand government response to WAI 262 is complex and involves a range of agencies. Policy development will continue, with reference to international instruments and best practice. Specific policy and timing decisions are yet to be made.' See Ministry of Justice, *New Zealand's Sixth Periodic Report under the International Covenant on Civil and Political Rights* (April 2015) 39 www.justice.govt.nz/assets/Documents/Publications/government-response-April-2015.pdf.

[115] Ministry of Business, Innovation and Employment, *Issues Paper: Review of the Copyright Act 1994* (November 2018) 109.

[116] Te Puni Kōkiri Ministry of Māori Affairs, *Wai 262 – Te Pae Tawhiti, Targeted Engagement Report, Preliminary Proposals for Crown Organization* (2020) www.tpk.govt.nz/en/a-matou-mohiotanga/crownmaori-relations/wai-262-te-pae-tawhiti-targeted-engagement-report.

and Ngati Toa Rangatira,[117] recognises the *iwi* as *kaitiaki* (guardians) of 'Ka Mate'. However, the only remedy specifically available under the Act is a declaratory order regarding attribution. There is no provision, say, for an injunction to prevent derogatory treatment.

Under copyright law, the chant that accompanies 'Ka Mate' would be classified as a 'musical work'.[118] The right of attribution is coterminous with copyright, so expires 50 years after the death of the author.[119] Since Te Rauparaha died in 1849, any copyright or moral right would have long expired.[120] In contrast, the attribution right under the Ka Mate Haka Act is granted in perpetuity. Ostensibly, Ngati Toa Rangatira, an *iwi*, may enforce this right despite not being a juristic person with an identifiable governing board.[121] The Act therefore confers some, albeit restricted, moral rights in a particular community. Symbolically, this is an important development because it chips away at one of the critical barriers to *iwi* control of their creative outputs: that is, the individualised and time-bound nature of intellectual property rights.

C. Niue

Niue is a micronation within the Realm of New Zealand.[122] Despite its small population,[123] *Vagahau Niue* (the Niue language) and Niue culture are distinct and different from those of its closest neighbour, the Cook Islands. Niue became a member of the World Intellectual Property Organization in 2015,[124] and acceded to the Berne Convention on 24 June 2016 (effective 24 September 2016).[125] These developments are noted because they demonstrate that Niue accepts copyright in principle.

The omnibus Niue Act 1966 establishes the extent to which New Zealand statutes apply in Niue: for example, the Copyright Act 1994 (NZ) applies in full.[126] Local statutes supplement this body of imported law. The Parliamentary Counsel Office (PCO), which has provided legislative services as part of New Zealand's aid to Niue,[127] drafted the Bill which was enacted as the Tāoga Niue Act 2012 (Niue).[128] The Tāoga Niue Act, which is consistent with Wai 262, overrides copyright law in certain regards and provides a high degree of protection for certain manifestations of Niue culture.

[117] Ngati Toa Rangatira and Trustee of the Toa Rangatira Trust and the Crown, 'Deed of Settlement of Historical Claims', www.ngatitoa.iwi.nz/sitecontent/images/Folders/General/Ngati-Toa-Rangatira-and-Toa-Rangatira-Trust-and-The-Crow.pdf.

[118] Copyright Act 1994 (NZ), s 2(1)(b).

[119] Copyright Act, s 22.

[120] Musical works were not protected in New Zealand before the introduction of the Copyright Act 1913 (NZ). Moral rights were introduced by the Copyright Act 1994 (NZ).

[121] In practice, Te Runanga O Toa Rangatira Inc, an incorporated society that manages the assets of the *iwi*, is likely to ensure compliance with the Ka Mate Haka Act. See Ministry of Business, Innovation & Employment Hīkina Whakatutuki, *Haka Ka Mate Attribution Act 2014 Guidelines*, www.mbie.govt.nz/assets/4066ff743b/haka-ka-mate-guidelines.pdf.

[122] See Interpretation Act 1999 (NZ), s 29, definition of 'New Zealand'.

[123] The population of Niue peaked at 5200 in 1966 but had reduced to an estimated 2000 in 2021, with most people having emigrated to New Zealand: see 'Niue' in *CIA World Factbook* (17 May 2021) www.cia.gov/the-world-factbook/countries/niue/.

[124] WIPO, 'Niue', www.wipo.int/members/en/details.jsp?country_id=246.

[125] WIPO, 'WIPO-Administered Treaties', www.wipo.int/treaties/en/ShowResults.jsp?treaty_id=15.

[126] See Niue Act, s 686.

[127] 'New Zealand Aid Programme: Strategic Plan 2015–2019' (MFAT, 2015) www.mfat.govt.nz/assets/Aid-Prog-docs/New-Zealand-Aid-Programme-Strategic-Plan-2015-19.pdf.

[128] See L Schmich, PV Peirce and M Allen, 'Parliamentary Counsel Office Legislative Drafting Assistance to Pacific Nations Evaluation Report' (MFAT, 2015) www.mfat.govt.nz/assets/Uploads/Parliamentary-Counsel-Office-Legislative-Drafting-Assistance-to-Pacific-Nations_Evaluation-Report.pdf.

The Tāoga Niue Act incorporates principles of regional and international agreements, notably, the Pacific Model Law[129] and UNDRIP.[130] Following the Pacific Model Law, 'expression of culture' means 'any way in which traditional knowledge appears or is manifested, irrespective of content, quality or purpose, whether tangible or intangible', and includes musical instruments. The term 'traditional knowledge' means any knowledge:

- created, acquired or inspired for traditional economic, spiritual, ritual, narrative, decorative or recreational purposes;
- transmitted from generation to generation;
- regarded as pertaining to a particular traditional group in Niue; and
- collectively originated and held.

Tāoga Niue includes both tangible and intangible things.

While New Zealand copyright law applies in Niue, schedule 3 to the Tāoga Niue Act, which covers consequential amendments to other legislation, provides that 'the courts of Niue must not protect a copyright … if it would be offensive to Niue culture to do so' or it 'affects traditional knowledge or expression of culture unless the requirements in relation to prior and informed consent under the Tāoga Niue Act 2012 are satisfied in relation to that traditional knowledge or expression of culture'.

D. Cook Islands

The Cook Islands were annexed by New Zealand in 1901, but became self-governing in 'free association' with New Zealand in 1965. The PCO also provides advice to the Cook Islands, and, it may be inferred, drafted changes to the country's copyright and cultural protection laws.

In 2013, the Cook Islands repealed the Copyright Act 1962 (NZ), which had applied in the islands by virtue of section 627 of the Cook Islands Act 1915 (NZ). Coterminous with the commencement of the Copyright Act 2013 (Cook Islands), the Traditional Knowledge Act 2013 (Cook Islands) came into effect. The Traditional Knowledge Act establishes a system of registration and protection of sacred traditional knowledge from intellectual property claims.

V. Conclusion

This chapter has examined the fundamental importance of music and musicality to Māori culture. *Waiata* (sung poems) have been woven into every area of life, and may include *whakapapa*, the arguably sacred genealogical information about families and larger social groups that

[129] In 2002, the Pacific Community agreed on Guidelines to the Model Law on Traditional Knowledge and Expressions of Culture. See *Regional Framework for the Protection of Traditional Knowledge and Expressions of Culture* (Secretariat of the Pacific Community, 2002), including the Model Law for the Protection of Traditional Knowledge and Expressions of Culture, www.forumsec.org/resources/uploads/attachments/documents/PacificModelLaw,ProtectionofTKandExprssnsofCulture20021.pdf.

[130] United Nations Declaration on the Rights of Indigenous Peoples (UNDRIP) GA Res 61/295, UN GAOR, 61st session, 107th plenary meeting, UN Doc A/RES/61/295 (13 September 2007). New Zealand originally opposed UNDRIP, but has since endorsed it. UNDRIP, Art 11 asserts the right of indigenous peoples 'to practise and revitalize their cultural traditions and customs', including maintaining, protecting and developing 'the past, present and future manifestations of their cultures', such as the performing arts. States have duties to protect these cultural rights (UNDRIP, Art 31).

establishes the framework of Māori knowledge systems. Nevertheless, intra-cultural borrowing was and remains a common practice. In exercises that may, from a Western perspective, present as plagiarism, members of one group might adopt and adapt a composition of another group. From the time of the first European settlement in the 1840s, Māori also engaged in inter-cultural borrowing; for example, adopting and adapting hymns, setting *te reo* Māori lyrics to Western tunes and forming brass bands. Today, the broadest range of musical genres incorporate indigenous lyrics.

In an encounter between two cultures, neither remains unaffected, and from the perspective of creativity that outcome may be desirable because creative practices which cross the borders of two cultures hold the potential for enriching both. But the typical context of cultural encounter has been colonialism, so that one culture has dominated, in various ways, the other. Europeans have not only imposed their culture on indigenous peoples, they have also extracted what they desire from those subjugated cultures, and continue to do so through cultural appropriation and commercial exploitation. Elements of Māori culture, such as tattoo patterns and *haka*, have been plundered by outsiders, but indigenous music was, perhaps, sufficiently idiomatic and alien to resist appropriation. Indeed, since encounter with outsiders, it has been Māori who have avidly adopted and adapted foreign music to suit their own tastes. Nevertheless, the Crown has a Treaty duty to protect Māori cultural treasures and has been particularly lax in preserving and promoting classical indigenous instruments and music.

In a seminal article, Sir Eddie Durie (Rangitāne, Ngāti Kauwhata, Ngāti Raukawa) asked:

> Was New Zealand settled, ceded, annexed or conquered? If it was settled are we to assume that Maori had no settled law? The debate on that matter is not helpful for it exists in a monocultural paradigm. I would rather ask whether the settlers will settle. Will we recognise the laws of England or the laws of New Zealand and if the latter, will we hone our jurisprudence to one that represents the circumstances of the country and shows that our law comes from two streams?[131]

In the Haka Act, Te Urewera Act and Te Awa Tupua (Whanganui River Claims Settlement) Act, the New Zealand Parliament has demonstrated an ability to craft specific legislation that synthesises the Māori worldview and positive law. New Zealand advisors have helped to draft legislation that delivers for the peoples of Niue, and the Cook Islands, the sorts of protections for their cultural treasures that the Waitangi Tribunal recommended for Māori in a context of intellectual property laws.

The Waitangi Tribunal demonstrated in Wai 262 how the balance in power between Māori and European cultures might be recalibrated in the field of copyright and traditional knowledge. Once the sacred has been secured from misappropriation, open engagement between cultures presents possibilities for equitable synthesis and true reciprocity. Darcy Nicholas (Te Āti Awa, Ngāi Te Rangi, Taranaki, Ngāti Ruanui, Ngāti Hauā) observes: 'Across the world of creative artists it is important that cultural knowledge is shared so we can better understand and learn from each other. The result is often creative art that embraces the universality of the human spirit.'[132]

[131] ET Durie, 'Will the Settlers Settle? Cultural Conciliation and Law' (1996) 8 *Otago Law Review* 449, 462.

[132] D Nicholas, 'Owen Mapp – a Māori Perspective' in O Mapp, *Dragons & Taniwha – 50 Years an Artist Carver* (Pātaka Art + Museum, 2018) 11.

INDEX